The New England Museum Guide

For Alexandra and David
on Valentine's day
with much love,
Margareth + co
- [illegible] -

Other Swordsmith Books

The Internet Guide for Seniors
The Adult Student's Guide
The Red Sox Fan Handbook
History of Windham County, Volume I
History of Windham County, Volume II

see your bookseller for more information or order from
www.swordsmith.com

The New England Museum Guide

Compiled by Leigh Grossman and Jamie Johnson

Swordsmith Books
Pomfret, Connecticut

A Swordsmith Book

Published by
Swordsmith Productions
PO Box 242
Pomfret, CT 06258
www.swordsmith.com

ISBN: 1-931013-06-3

Cover photos courtesy of Florence Griswold Museum (p. 24), Stepping Stones Museum for Children (p. 80), Tolland Jail and Museum (p. 84), Whitfield State Museum (p. 31), L. C. Bates Museum (p. 144), Maine Forest and Logging Museum (p. 146), Marshall Point Lighthouse Museum (p. 152), Fuller Museum of Art (p. 247), Barrett House (p. 340), Old Stone House Museum (p. 463), and Park-McCullough House (p. 464).

Swordsmith Books are distributed by
LPC Group
1436 West Randolph Street
Chicago, IL 60607
(800) 626-4330
www.coolbooks.com

Printed in the U.S.A.

10 9 8 7 6 5 4 3 2 1

CONTENTS

Acknowledgments

Many people contributed to the thousands of hours of work that went into the creation of this first edition of *The New England Museum Guide*. Editorial assistants Anne Bourgeois and Stacy Cortigiano made many of the initial calls to museums. The first drafts of many museum entries were drafted by Cris Cadiz, Stacy Cortigiano, Wendy Goldberg, Donna Ogle, Julie Woodland, and intern Shawn Munson. Lesley McBain did the bulk of the proofreading.

Special thanks go to Peggy Salvas and Judy Black at the Pomfret Post Office, who handled the thousands of letters and other mail generated in the course of creating this book. Thanks also to the hundreds of museum administrators who contributed time and energy to the book, sent us information and photographs, made suggestions for the final book, and shared their anecdotes and experiences.

—Leigh Grossman and Jamie Johnson

About the Entries

We developed the entries in this book by asking every museum in New England—about 1,500 in all—for information about themselves. Entries were written based on information provided by the museums; some museums just filled out our questionnaire, while others sent much more detailed information and pictures. Edited entries were indexed by state, town, subject, and by highway, to make them as easy as possible to find. A few museums asked not to be included, and not all of them responded to requests for information. Those who returned information were given detailed entries, while others who we didn't hear back from were listed by name, town, and phone number at the end of each state's section. We were unable to track down a few museums (either we couldn't find contact information, or the information we had was inaccurate), and we apologize to anyone we inadvertently excluded.

The information in this book is accurate to the best of our knowledge. Because of the nature of museums, many small details will have changed by the time you read this. Exhibitions will have been added or dropped; hours will have evolved slightly as administrators react to the needs of their members and visitors; fees may have changed slightly; some area codes and phone numbers may have changed. Please contact museums to double check details before you visit. If you know of any information that is inaccurate or out of date, please let us know by e-mailing us at information@swordsmith.com, or writing to Swordsmith Books, PO Box 242, Pomfret, CT 06258. Updates and corrections will be posted on Swordsmith's website at www.swordsmith.com.

INTRODUCTION

Why write a museum guide? For one thing, it's not always easy to find museums. Everybody can find the big ones, but what about the little treasures that are hidden away on back roads? Or the museum you drive by every day on the way to work that never seems to be open? We wanted to write a guide to all the museums in New England, large and small—how to find them, what to see, and when to go.

One of the first things we asked each museum was "What is it that's special about your collection?" We wanted to capture that specialness in our entries, to give a quick overview that would enable people to quickly spot the museums that were worth making a special trip for. But we didn't want to stop there. Some of the best museum experiences aren't the ones you make a special trip for—they're museums you stumble onto just because you happen to be in the area, sometimes museums that you would never have thought to visit. That's why we added indexes by town and by road, so you can quickly find something nearby no matter where you are in New England—whether you're out looking for an adventure or just have a few hours to kill in a strange town during a child's college interview, or a spouse's class reunion, while the friend you're visiting is at work, or while you're waiting for a ride somewhere.

The museums in this book run the gamut from huge to tiny, from city to country, from old to new. There are traditional art museums, historical buildings, and natural history museums, but there are also sports museums, automotive museums, living history museums, children's museums, nature preserves, toy and doll museums, battlefields, and everything in between. There are detailed descriptions of more than 600 buildings in the pages that follow, and contact information for more than 1,500 museums in all. No matter what your tastes are—or what your family's tastes are—you'll find museums that you enjoy here.

The museums are listed alphabetically within each state. Each listing gives you an overview, driving directions, cost and hours, what to see, and information about other attractions to visit nearby. At the end of each state are short listings for other museums in that state, containing name, town, and phone number. At the back of the book, the museums that have complete entries are listed by state, subject, and highway, to make the museum you want easy to find (the state index also has museums with two or more names listed under both). There is also an index by town that includes all 1,500 museums in the book.

If you've got a favorite museum that you'd like to tell us more about, please let us know. You can e-mail information@swordsmith.com, or write to Swordsmith Books, PO Box 242, Pomfret, CT 06258. Happy museuming!

—LEIGH GROSSMAN
JAMIE JOHNSON

June, 2001

CONNECTICUT

The Alexey von Schlippe Gallery of Art

University of Connecticut at Avery Point
1085 Schennecossett Road
Groton, CT 06340
(860) 405-9052
www.uconn.edu/vonschlp.html

Overview

The Alexey von Schlippe Gallery of Art highlights a broad range of regional as well as national and international artists who are producing innovative, original works in all media.

Directions and Hours

Take I-95 to exit 87. Take a right at the second set of lights. Take a left at the next set of lights. Go straight for approximately 3 miles to UCONN's entrance. Go straight on campus and take the last left. Follow signs to the gallery—a large stone Gothic mansion—it will be on the right.

The museum is open from March through December and is handicap accessible.

Hours: Wednesday through Sunday from 1:00-4:00 and Thursday 2:30-5:30.

Admission and Membership

$3 is the suggested donation. Membership information is available at the gallery and on the website. A student discount is available.

What to See

Alexey von Schlippe was a former UCONN professor and internationally known painter. The gallery includes some 500 of his works—the basis of the gallery's permanent collection. Schlippe's work is featured on an ongoing basis. Other exhibits rotate every six weeks. The Gothic architecture of the mansion and its grounds are also an attraction.

The gallery will be featuring regular programs, including artist lectures, jazz concerts, and poetry readings in the future. It is also forming liaisons with local and regional schools to develop workshops as well as educational tours.

There is no gift shop, but there are several fine local restaurants and others in nearby Groton.

While You're in the Area

There are many attractions in the Groton/New London area, including Mystic Seaport (p. 56), and Olde Mystick Village (p. 103), The Lyman Allyn Museum (p. 45), and the Garde Theatre.

American Clock and Watch Museum

100 Maple Street
Bristol, CT 06010
(860) 583-6070

Overview

The American Clock and Watch Museum is located on historic federal hill in Bristol, a town known as America's clock making town. The original building is an 1801 post-Revolutionary mansion. The 1955 Ebenezer Barnes wing was constructed using paneling and materials from Bristol's earliest residence (1728).

Directions and Hours

From I-84 east: Take exit 31 (Route 229). Go north 5.5 miles. Turn left onto Woodland Street at the Clock Museum sign and drive for one mile.

From I-84 west: Take exit 38 (Route 6). Go west for 9 miles to Bristol Commons shopping plaza. Turn left at the light after the railroad track onto Maple Street, then drive two blocks to the museum.

The museum is open seven days a week April 1 to November 30, and is 75% handicap accessible.

Hours: 10:00 A.M. to 5:00 P.M.

Admission and Membership

$5 for adults, $2 for children 8-15, and kids under 8 free. Children under 8 years of age must be accompanied by an adult. Senior, AAA, and group discounts are available. Membership is $20/year for individuals and $30/year for a family. A life membership is available for $750, a sustaining membership (15 years) for $200, and an active membership (5 years) for $75/individual, $115/family.

What to See

The museum has about 1,500 antique clocks and watches on display. The museum also has a research library located in the colonial style Miles Lewis House, the historic Ebenezer Barnes wing, and the modern Edward Ingraham wing. The grounds have an authentic early American sundial garden with period flowers and herbs.

There is a gift shop but the museum has no café. There are a number of restaurants and fast food establishments within one mile.

While You're in the Area

The New England Carousel Museum (p. 102), Lake Compounce, and ESPN (all located in Bristol), and the Lock Museum of America in Terryville (p. 43), are all located nearby.

The Avon Historical Society, Inc.

Box 448
Avon, CT 06001
(860) 678-1043
www.avonct.com

Overview

The Avon Historical Society maintains and operates four sites open to the public, which offer a variety of perspectives on Avon's history from the 1830s to the present day. The society also sponsors events and speakers.

Directions and Hours

The museums are convenient from I-84 or I-91, but are in different locations in Avon. Please call for directions.

The Derrin Farmhouse is open mid-May to September, Sunday from 2:00-4:00. The farmhouse is partially handicap accessible.

The Living Museum is open May through October, Sunday from 2:00-4:00, and it is handicap accessible.

The Avon Free Public Library History Room is open Tuesday, 2:00-4:00 and by appointment. It is handicap accessible.

The Pine Grove School is open June through October, Sunday from 2:00-4:00 and is partially handicap accessible.

Admission and Membership

Donations are accepted. Membership is $15/year for individuals, $25/year for families, and $10/year for senior citizens.

Groups receive a half-price discount with reservations, and the museum is free to members.

What to See

The Derrin Farmhouse, located at 249 West Avon Road, is an eighteenth-century farmhouse currently undergoing restoration. The Living Museum features an exhibit of Avon history at 8 East Main Street. The Pine Grove School, on West Avon Road at Route 167, is an 1865 schoolhouse.

The Avon Free Public Library historical archives are located in the Avon History Room. The Library's address is 281 Country Club Road. Researchers and interested residents may find information on the general history of the town, original old homes and buildings in Avon, and geneologies of original families. The collection includes photographs, postcards, scrapbooks, maps, deeds, and other pieces of memorabilia, along with the first library for the town of Avon is a "must see."

The society hosts an Annual Miniature and Dollhouse Show in February, with visitors from 43 Connecticut towns and several states. The show will be on February 3 in 2002.

Each location has a small gift area where visitors can purchase souvenirs.

While You're in the Area

Other nearby attractions are the Hill-Stead Museum (p. 33) in Farmington, the Wadsworth Athenaeum (p. 88), Mark Twain House (p. 48), and Harriet Beecher Stowe House (p. 28) in Hartford, and the Hublein Tower in Bloomfield.

Ballard Institute and Museum of Puppetry (BIMP)

University of Connecticut
6 Bourne Place U-212
School of Fine Arts, Depot Campus
Storrs, CT 06269-5212
(860) 486-4605
www.sp.uconn.edu/~wwwsfa/bimp

Overview

The Ballard Institute and Museum of Puppetry houses thousands of puppets, including hundreds which were stars in theatrical productions at the University of Connecticut. The museum began in 1987 in an effort to preserve the thousands of puppets created by Frank Ballard and his students in the 25 years of Puppetry at UCONN under Frank's direction. The puppets, photographs, stage sets, and paper archives now number well over 4,000 catalogued items. Rotating exhibits include the artistry of Frank Ballard, Sidney Chrysler, Rufus and Margo Rose, and other world-class puppeteers, as well as the works of current students and graduates of the UCONN Puppet Art Program (the only U.S. program to offer BA, MA, and MFA degrees in the art of puppetry).

Directions and Hours

From I-84: Take the UCONN exit (exit 68). Follow Route 32 south to the intersection with Route 44. Turn east onto Route 44. Pass two traffic lights, then watch carefully for Weaver Road. Turn right onto Weaver Road. You are

Marionettes used in Frank Ballard's production of Boris Gudunov. *Photo courtesy of Frank Ballard.*

now on the grounds of the old state Mansfield Training School. Follow the signs and the meandering road to Bourne Place (on the right). Turn into the little road and park along the circle. On weekends visitors may also park in the area below Bourne Place, which is the lot for the Small Business Institute. The Depot campus is also accessible from Route 195 and the main part of the UCONN campus.

The museum is open from late April through the first week in November, and is handicap accessible.

Hours: Friday, Saturday, and Sunday noon-5:00 P.M. Tours and other special arrangements may be made. Research using the archives can also be arranged.

Admission and Membership

While there is no admission, a donation of $2 per adult and $1 for children and seniors is requested. An annual donation of $35 gives "Friends of BIMP" status.

What to See

The museum has a wide variety of puppets from various eras and parts of the world, including "Scooter" from *The Muppet Show* and several pieces by Bil Baird, a fifteenth century Sicilian black knight, and several eighteenth century Asian shadow puppets.

The museum has a hands-on children's room, where kids (and adults) can play with the puppets and see occasional performances by area puppeteers.

The Institute sponsors annual workshops for adults in various elements of puppetry.

Programming varies throughout the year, so you should call ahead to see what is planned. Some upcoming programs are: Nancy Laverick's "World of Phantasmagoria" (April 29-July 29, 2001), Dedication of "Spring's Garden" (June 2, 2002), "Puppet Potpourri" (August 12-November 4, 2001), the work of Rufus and Margo Rose (April-November, 2002), and the miniature opera world of Sidney Chrysler (April-November, 2003).

Children's programming is available for children of varying ages.

The museum has a gift shop. The museum itself does not have food service, but there are many cafés and restaurants in the area, including the UCONN dairy bar and Jonathan's on the main campus of the university.

While You're in the Area

Interesting museums and attractions nearby include the William Benton Museum of Art (p. 95), the Natural History Museum (p. 101), the Atrium Gallery at the School of Fine Arts building (p. 100), the Babbidge Library, and the Dodd Center. UCONN's School of Agriculture offers tours of various animal facilities.

The Barker Character Comic and Cartoon Museum

1188 Highland Avenue (Route 10)
Cheshire, CT 06410
(203) 699-3822
www.barkeranimation.com

Overview

The Barkers have been collecting comic and cartoon related items for over 50 years. The Barker Character Comic and Cartoon Museum documents all segments of American film and popular culture with toys and memorabilia that date from "The Yellow Kid" in 1895 to the present.

Directions and Hours

From New Haven on I-91 north: Take exit 17 to exit 68 west to I-691. Get off at exit 3. At the end of the exit take a left onto Route 10 and proceed 1.7 miles. Look for the Barker Animation sign on the left.

From New Haven on the Merritt Parkway (Route 15): Proceed to the end of the Parkway North in Meriden. Take exit 68 west to I-691. Get off at exit 3 and follow the direction above.

From Hartford on I-91 south: Take exit 18 to

I-691. Get off at exit 3 and follow the directions above.

From Hartford on I-84 west: Take exit 27 to I-691. Get off at exit 3 and follow the above directions.

From Waterbury and Danbury on I-84 east: Take exit 27 and follow the above directions.

The museum is open year-round. It is handicap accessible.

Hours: Tuesday-Saturday 11:00 A.M. to 5:00 P.M.

Admission and Membership

There is no admission cost. Individuals and families are always welcome but groups and organizations must register two weeks prior to visiting.

What to See

The museum features more than 60,000 items, including turn of the twentieth century comic books, rare cartoons, the beginning of Disney with early Mickey Mouse items, a Little Orphan Annie decoder ring, Roy Rogers, Gene Autry and Tom Mix western memorabilia, 1930s and 40s Fisher Price Toys made out of wood, Tin Toy wind-ups, 350 lunchboxes hanging from the rafters, McDonald's Happy Meal toys, *Scooby Doo* Pez candy dispensers, *Toy Story I* and *II* toys, and more. There is also a 1930 big screen that shows original cartoons from the 1930s. Also on the grounds is the Barker Animation Art Gallery which sells original animation arts cels, drawings, and prints.

The museum has an extensive collection of original California Raisin animation sets, props, and artwork actually used in the filming of the award-winning commercials and TV specials. The museum also has all the original artwork used in the filming of the Gumby TV series and some of the original ViewMaster sets.

The museum does have a gift shop located in the Art Gallery. There is no café, but Route 10 has many restaurants for dining of all types.

While You're in the Area

Nearby attractions and museums include Kidcity (p. 41), the Barnes Museum (p. 5), the West Rock Nature Center (p. 94), the Peabody Museum (p. 69), and the Yale Center for British Art (p. 98).

Barnes Museum

85 North Main Street
Southington, CT 06489
(860) 628-5426

Overview

The Barnes Museum was the home of a prominent local family for three generations, and contains all their original furnishings.

Directions and Hours

From I-84: Take the Queen Street exit and go south on Route 10 for about 3 miles. The museum is on the left in the center of Southington, on Route 10.

The museum is open year round and the first floor is handicap accessible.

Hours: Winter: Monday, Tuesday, Wednesday, and Friday 1:00-5:00 P.M., Thursday 1:00-7:00 P.M., and the first and last Saturday of each month 1:00-5:00 P.M. Summer: Same as winter but closed on Saturdays.

Admission and Membership

Admission is $2 for adults, $1 for children. Free passes can be received from the Public Library. Membership friend levels are: $500, $250, $100/year, $25/year, and $25/year.

What to See

Original furnishings include an extensive glass collection, rugs, Victorian clothing, and toys.

A "What Is It?" program is presented in schools with similar programs presented in convalescent homes, senior living communities, and to various civic and fraternal organizations.

Events held annually include a Victorian

Party in June (on the first Sunday afternoon in June), a Christmas Open House (the first Friday evening and following Sunday in December), and an evening of reading in December, and High Teas at various times during the year.

In November the museum holds a Christmas Boutique, and in February and March a winter lecture series. Children's programming is available.

The museum does have a gift shop with Barnes Museum related items including T-shirts, magnets, and notes. There is not a café on the premises, but there are several restaurants within walking distance.

While You're in the Area

The Clock Museum in Bristol (p. 1), Lake Compounce, and the New England Carousal Museum (p. 102) are located nearby.

The Barnum Museum

820 Main Street
Bridgeport, CT 06604
(203) 339-1104
www.barnum-museum.org

A scene from a 3,600-piece scale model miniature circus, hand carved over 60 years by William Brinley of Meriden, Connecticut. Photo courtesy of The Barnum Museum.

Overview

The Barnum Museum, designed by P.T. Barnum and donated to his adopted city of Bridgeport, opened in 1893 and continues to tell the story of the great showman's life and times. Key among the museum's permanent collections are artifacts related to Barnum and many of his attractions, including the famed Fejee Mermaid; Pa-Ib, the 2,500-year-old Egyptian mummy donated by Barnum's widow; tiny General Tom Thumb's elegant street carriages, and the velvet court suit he wore in audiences with President Abraham Lincoln, England's Queen Victoria, and other crown heads of Europe; Jenny Lind memorabilia, and much more. Owned by the city of Bridgeport, the museum has been listed on the National Register of Historic Places since 1972.

Directions and Hours

Take Connecticut Turnpike (I-95), get off at exit 27 (Lafayette Boulevard), continue to the fourth light, turn right on to State Street, continue to the second traffic light, then turn right on to Main Street. The museum is on the left about 1½ blocks. Signs for the museum are posted.

The museum is also easily reached via the Merritt Parkway, Route 15/8 Connector, Metro North and Amtrak Railroads, Municipal Bus Terminal, and Bridgeport/Port Jefferson Ferry.

The museum is open year round, and is handicap accessible.

Hours: Tuesday to Saturday 10:00 A.M. to 4:30 P.M.; Sunday noon-4:30 P.M. Special guided tours are conducted Saturday and Sunday at 2 P.M. and are included with regular museum admission.

Admission and Membership

Admission is $5 for adults, $4 for senior citizens and college students, $3 for children aged 4-18, and free for museum members, Bridgeport senior citizens, and children under 4. Membership is $25/year for individuals, $45/year for families, $100 for Sustaining, $250 for Contributing, $500 for Patron's Circle, and $1,000 for Director's Circle.

What to See

In addition to its major focus on P.T. Barnum and his famous attractions, The Barnum Museum has an exhibition highlighting Bridgeport's contributions to the Industrial Revolution, a sprawling 3,000-piece hand-carved miniature circus, a children's activity area, a 7,500-square-foot special exhibitions wing, and a gift shop offering a wide assortment of books about Barnum, the circus, clowns, and Victorian-style toys and novelties. The museum also offers educational and entertainment programs for children and adults.

While You're in the Area

Nearby attractions and museums include Beardsley Park, the Maritime Aquarium at Norwalk (p. 46), Mathews Park, and the Lockwood-Mathews Mansion (p. 102).

The Bates-Scofield House Museum

Darien Historical Society
45 Old Kings Highway North
Darien, CT 06820
(203) 655-9233

Overview

The Bates-Scofield House is a circa 1736 New England saltbox house that interprets eighteenth century farm life in Middlesex Parish. The house is named for both the Bates family, who built the house, and the Scofields, who later lived in it. In 1964 the Darien Historical Society restored the old farmhouse.

Directions and Hours

Take I-95 to exit 13. Turn left onto Post Road. At the second light turn left onto Brookside Road. Bear right at the curve. The house and parking lot will be on the left.

House tour hours: Wednesday, Thursday, and Sunday 2:00-4:00 P.M. It is advisable to telephone ahead. Society and library hours: Tuesday and Friday 9:00 A.M. to 2:00 P.M. and Wednesday-Thursday 9:00 A.M. to 4:00 P.M. It is advisable to call ahead.

Admission and Membership

$2.50 for non-members, free for members and children. Group tours are by appointment. Please contact the Darien Historical Society for membership information.

What to See

Built around a central chimney with a big fireplace and beehive oven, the Bates-Scofield House contains eighteenth and early nineteenth century furniture from the region. The garden that is adjacent to the house is maintained by the Garden Club of Darien and harbors over 30 different varieties of herbs known to have been used in eighteenth century Connecticut. The house was recently repainted to match the colors and high-gloss glazes that the house originally had.

The Darien Historical Society collections incude local history archives, and a collection of quilts, costumes, and accessories. On exhibit at the society's headquarters (adjacent to the Bates-Scofield Hosue) are art and other objects from the society's collection.

While You're in the Area

Nearby attractions and museums include Boothe Memorial Park and Museum (p. 100), Charles Ives Birthplace (p. 100), Charter Oak Cultural Center (p. 100), the Danbury Museum and Historical Society (p. 101), the Danbury Railway Museum (p. 101), the Eliot Beardsley Homestead (p. 101), the Bruce Museum of Arts and Science (p. 11), the Fairfield Historical Society (p. 24), and the Ogden House & Gardens (p. 66).

Beinecke Rare Book and Manuscript Library

121 Wall Street
New Haven, CT 06520
(203) 432-2977
www.library.yale.edu/beinecke/

Overview

The Beinecke Rare Book and Manuscript Library is Yale University's principal repository for literary papers and for rare books and early manuscripts in the fields of literature, history, theology, and the natural sciences.

Directions and Hours

From the New Haven Green: On foot, take College Street north to Wall Street. Take a left on Wall Street. Enter the plaza on the right in the middle of the first block. The Beinecke Library is the large white marble building facing east.

From outside New Haven: Take I-95 (North or South) to I-91 North (toward Hartford). Take I-91 to exit 3, Trumbull Street. Follow the exit ramp directly onto Trumbull Street and continue to Prospect Street (the fourth traffic light). Turn left onto Prospect for one block. Make a right onto Grove Street. Park on Grove Street which is the just north of the Beinecke Plaza. The Library is surrounded by streets that are closed to traffic.

From outside Connecticut: New Haven is located on the shore of Long Island Sound. The city is served by Tweed-New Haven Airport, which offers connections through New York, Chicago, and other regional hubs. Currently the only jet service is through Chicago. The closest international airports are New York City's LaGuardia and Kennedy airports, Newark International Airport, and Hartford/Springfield's Bradley International. Bus service to New Haven is available at each of those airports. Amtrak has daily service to New Haven's Union Station from Boston and Washington, DC via New York's Penn Station. Metro North has hourly service from New York's Grand Central Station. New Haven provides bus service to the Green from the train station—buses J, U, and the SLE (Shore Line East) Commuter Connection all stop at several points on or near campus.

There is limited metered street parking (bring quarters) on Grove Street. There are two public parking lots in easy walking distance from the Beinecke, one on Grove and Church (two blocks east) and the other on Broadway opposite the Yale Bookstore (two blocks west).

The library is open year round and is handicap accessible.

Hours: Monday-Friday 8:30 A.M. to 5:00 P.M. and Saturday 10:00-5:00 except during Yale recesses. The recesses affect only the Saturday hours. The library is closed on major holidays and on Saturdays in August.

Admission and Membership

There is no charge for admission. There are no age restrictions on who can attend the library but it would not be very interesting to small children.

What to See

In addition to its general collection of rare books and manuscripts, the library houses the Yale Collection of American Literature, the Yale Collection of German Literature, the Yale Collection of Western Americana, and the Osborn Collection. The Beinecke collections afford opportunities for interdisciplinary research in such fields as medieval, Renaissance, and eighteenth-century studies, art history, photography, American studies, the history of printing, and modernism in art and literature. The library also has some displays including the Gutenberg Bible, some Audubon bird prints, and other changing exhibitions throughout the year. Outside the library there is a sculpture garden created by Isamu Noguchi.

The museum does not have a gift shop or a café but there are many excellent restaurants in downtown New Haven.

While You're in the Area

Also nearby are Yale University Art Gallery (p. 104), Yale Center for British Art (p. 98), and Peabody Museum of Natural History (p. 69).

Blue Slope Country Museum, Inc.

138 Blue Hill Road
Franklin, CT 06254
(860) 642-6413

Overview

The primary purpose of this working farm museum is to gather, demonstrate, and preserve the historical importance of farm tools and implements as they were developed over time. Educational programs and events perpetuate the spirit and value of our rural heritage.

Directions and Hours

The museum is located 35 miles southeast of Hartford at exit 23 on Route 1. Or 5 miles northwest of Norwich via Routes 2 and 32 (take exit 81 or 82 on Route 395).

Open by appointment other than summer and fall Open House events. The museum is partially handicap accessible.

Admission and Membership

Admission and membership fees have not yet been determined.

What to See

The museum exhibits agricultural tools and implements from the early 1700s to the mid-1950s with an emphasis on how these items progressed over time. There is also a library with bound volumes of agricultural publications from the 1700 and 1800s. Visitors may tour the working dairy farm on site and ride a sleigh or wagon pulled by draft horses.

Special programs run in the summer and fall.

There is no gift shop or café, but there are several food choices within five miles.

While You're in the Area

Historic Lebanon and Norwich Connecticut are nearby.

Brayton Grist Mill-Marcy Blacksmith Tool Museum

Pomfret Historical Society
PO Box 152
Pomfret Center, CT 06259-0152

Overview

This fine example of a one-man mill operation of the 1890s has original milling equipment. The tool exhibit represents the craft of three generations of blacksmiths.

Directions and Hours

The museum is located on Route 44 at the entrance of the Mashamoquet Brook State Park. From the north, take 395 to exit 97 (Route 44), then take 44 west about six miles to the museum. From the south, take 395 to exit 93 (Route 101). Take 101 east until it merges with Route 44, then follow 44 to the Park entrance.

Open May-September, Saturday and Sunday, 2:00-5:00. The first floor is handicap accessible.

Admission and Membership

Free, but donations are accepted.

What to See

The two lower floors and the first floor are dedicated to the grist mill. The Mashamoquet Brook is on the west side of the building. The upper floor includes exhibits about blacksmithing and wagon making.

Visitors can purchase maps and cards at the mill. Pete's, an outdoor hot dog and seafood restaurant, is nearby, and other restaurants are within easy driving distance.

While You're in the Area

The Putnam Antiques District is about five miles away on Route 44.

Brookfield Museum and Historical Society, Inc.

165 Whisconier Road
PO Box 5231
Brookfield, CT 06804
(203) 740-8140

Overview

The Brookfield Museum and Historical society has extensive files on local buildings and is devoted to local history, genealogy records, industry, photos, and schools. The museum works closely with school systems as an educational resource.

Directions and Hours

The museum is located near the intersection of Routes 25 and 133 in the center of Brookfield. Take exit 9 off I-84, and go north on Route 25.

The museum is open April through early December or by appointment. It is handicap accessible.

Hours: Saturdays noon-4:00 P.M., first Sunday of the month noon-4:00 P.M.

Admission and Membership

Admission is free. Annual memberships begin at $10.00.

What to See

The Brookfield Museum and Historical Society hosts changing exhibits of local interest. The museum also has an excellent computerized genealogical research facility. There is a colonial flower garden on site that is maintained by the Brookfield Garden Club.

The museum works with local grade schools to present a living one room schoolhouse program.

There is a gift shop featuring items of local interest such as pottery, books, and coverlets. The museum has no café, so visitors might want to bring a lunch or snack along.

While You're in the Area

Other places to visit while in the area include the Danbury Museum (p. 101), the Danbury Train Museum (p. 101), the New Milford Museum (p. 63), and the Brookfield Craft Center.

Walking Weekend

Visitors can set out on their own voyage of discovery on Columbus Day Weekend during the Annual Walking Weekend. Celebrating the rich cultural heritage and natural beauty of the Quinebaug and Shetucket Rivers Valley National Heritage Corridor, Walking Weekend offers more than 70 mostly free guided tours led by knowledgeable volunteers, with something for every age and fitness level. Visitors can saunter, stride, or hike through the brilliant autumn colors of northeastern Connecticut, through rolling meadows and along the streets of historic villages. Walks vary from traditional museums and nature sanctuaries to a nighttime walk through an eighteenth-century graveyard or a tour of Norwich's Victorian architecture.

The Heritage Corridor encompasses a total of 35 towns, 26 in Northeastern Connecticut and 9 in South Central Massachusetts. For visitors who want to make a weekend of it, there are dozens of B&Bs and country inns nearby. Walking Weekend is sponsored by Quinebaug-Shetucket Heritage Corridor, Inc. and organized by Northeast Connecticut Visitors District, the tourism office of Connecticut's Quiet Corner.

For information on the current Walking Weekend and a schedule of tours, contact Northeast Connecticut Visitors District at (888)628-1228 or www.CTquietcorner.org

Brooklyn Historical Society Museum and Daniel Putnam Tyler Law Office

25 Canterbury Road (Route 169)
Brooklyn, CT 06234
(860) 774-7728

Overview

The Brooklyn Historical Society Museum is a look at Brooklyn's history with an emphasis on the life of General Israel Putnam. There is a permanent exhibit dedicated to General Putnam, along with temporary exhibits showcasing other aspects of Brooklyn's history.

Directions and Hours

Take 395 to exit 91. The museum is located just south of the intersection of Route 6 and 169 in the center of town.

The museum is open from the Wednesday prior to Memorial Day through the Sunday of Labor Day weekend. It is handicap accessible.

Hours: Wednesday and Sunday 1:00-5:00.

Admission and Membership

Admission is free. Membership is $10/year for individuals and $20/year for families.

What to See

In addition to the tribute to Revolutionary War General Israel Putnam, visitors can also see the Daniel Putnam Tyler Law Office. Located behind the museum building, it shows the office of Israel Putnam's great-grandson as it appeared while he practiced law in Brooklyn from 1822 to his death in 1875.

In 2001 there will be a special exhibit titled "Civil War Diaries." It is a look at the history of the First South Carolina Volunteers through the words of Colonel Thomas Wentworth Higginson, Major Seth Rogers, and Captain James S. Rogers.

There is no gift shop, but visitors can eat at local sandwich shops,

While You're in the Area

The Prudence Crandall Museum (p. 72) and the New England Center for Contemporary Art (p. 102) are located nearby.

Bruce Museum of Arts and Science

1 Museum Drive
Greenwich, CT 06830
(203) 869-0376
www.brucemuseum.org

Overview

The Bruce Museum specializes in exhibitions that feature both arts and sciences in an interdisciplinary context. The museum presents over 15 changing exhibits annually. Its permanent exhibit, "Changes in Our Land," features a visual display of the environment and historical development of the Greenwich area.

Directions and Hours

Take I-95 south to exit 3. Go left on Arch Street, which becomes Museum Drive.

Or take I-95 north to exit 3. Go right on Arch Street, which becomes Museum Drive.

Or take the Merrit Parkway to the North Street exit. Follow signs to central Greenwich. At the end of North Street, bear left onto Maple Avenue. At the light, bear right onto Putnam Avenue. Take an immediate left onto Milbank Avenue. Follow Milbank to the end, bearing straight at rotaries and turning right onto Bruce Park Avenue. Take the next left onto Steamboat Road. At the light, go left onto Museum Drive.

Or from Highway 1/Post Road, turn left onto Greenwich Avenue, which becomes Steamboat Road. At the light, take a left onto Museum Drive.

The museum is open year round, and it is handicap accessible.

Hours: Tuesday to Saturday 10:00-5:00, Sunday 1:00-5:00, closed Mondays and major holidays. Open special school Monday holidays.

Admission and Membership

$4 for adults, $3 for seniors and students, children under 5 are free. Discounts are available for groups of 10 or more with advanced reservations. Everyone is free on Tuesdays. Members are free at all times. Memberships are $45/year for individuals, $30/year for seniors, and $45/year for senior couples.

What to See

In addition to its regular and rotating exhibits, the museum also includes a minerals gallery and a marine touch tank. The Bruce Museum's Education Workshop provides hands-on learning experiences for children of all ages. The museum also offers regular Family Days with activities related to featured exhibitions. One feature not to miss is sculpture installations on the museum grounds.

The museum sponsors an annual Spring Crafts Festival in May, one week prior to Memorial Day Weekend, and an annual Fall Arts Festival in October, held on Columbus Day weekend. Upcoming programs are "Empire of the Sultans," October 27, 2001-January 27 2002, and "The West," scheduled for February 9-June 2, 2002.

Children's programming includes an award-winning Neighborhood Collaborative after school program, the Brucemobile outreach program, and a hands-on science gallery associated with featured exhibits.

There is a gift shop open during museum hours. Although there is no café, visitors are welcome to picnic on the museum grounds. The museum is within walking distance of numerous shops, restaurants, and delicatessens.

While You're in the Area

The Bush Holley Historic Site (p. 12) is nearby in Cos Cob, Connecticut. The Greenwich chapter of the National Audubon Society is another local attraction.

The Antiquarian and Landmarks Society promotes interest in special places by preserving and interpreting properties and collection of importance to Connecticut's heritage. Founded in 1936, The Antiquarian and Landmarks Society is the oldest statewide preservation organization. Today the society owns 14 historic properties around the state, nine of which are open to the public as museum houses. These architecturally significant houses (11 are on the National Register of Historic Places) are located in 10 towns and trace the four centuries of Connecticut's history from seventeenth century settlement to twenty-first century living in rural and urban settings. In addition to guided tours, A&L offers diverse programming at the museum properties, its Harford headquarters, and other locations. Membership is open to all interested individuals who appreciate the storied and deep-rooted layers of history and accomplishment found in the state.

Contact the Society at 66 Forest, Hartford, CT 06105, (860)247-8996, www.hartnet.org/als.

Bush-Holley Historic Site

39 Strickland Road
Cos Cob, CT 06807
(203) 869-6899
www.hstg.org

Overview

The Bush-Holley Historic Site features the circa 1730 National Historic Landmark Bush-Holley House, the center of Connecticut's first art colony. From 1890 to 1920, over 200 art students studied at the Holley's boarding house with American Impressionists John Henry Twachtman, J. Alden Weir, Theodore Robinson, and Childe Hassam.

Directions and Hours

From the north: Take exit 4 off I-95 then make a right U-turn onto Sound Shore Drive and follow the signs for ½ mile.

From the south: Take exit 4 off I-95, then turn left over I-95 right onto South Shore Drive and follow signs for ½ mile.

From the Merritt Parkway north from New York City: Take North Street (exit 31). At the end of the ramp turn left and follow signs for the business district. Follow North Street approximately four miles to the end of the road. Turn left onto North Maple Avenue. At the traffic light, make a hard left onto East Putnam Avenue. Follow East Putnam Avenue approximately one mile to Strickland Road in Cos Cob and take a right. Follow Strickland Road and take a right at the stop sign to the I-95 overpass. The Bush-Holley House will be on the right. Park under I-95 overpass and walk up to Bush-Holley Historic Site visitor center (yellow building with front porch).

From the Merritt Parkway south from Stamford: Take North Street (exit 31). At the end of the ramp turn right and follow the directions above.

Free on-site parking is available. The site is three blocks from the Cos Cob Metro North Station and less than an hour's train ride from New York's Grand Central Station.

The visitors center is open year round. The house is open from April-December Wednesday through Sunday 12:00-4:00 and January to March Saturday 11:00 A.M. to 4:00 P.M. and Sunday 1:00 P.M. to 4:00 P.M. only. The museum is partly handicap accessible.

Hours: Visitors Center: Wednesday through Sunday from noon to 4:00 P.M.

Admission and Membership

Admission to the visitor center is free. Bush-Holley House Tours (last tour at 3:00 P.M.) is $6 for adults, $4 for senior citizens and students, and free for children 12 and under. Membership is $50/year for families and $35/year for individuals. Other memberships options are: $1,000 for a Benefactor, $500 for a Patron, $250 for a Donor, and $100 for a Sponsor.

What to See

Guided tours feature eighteenth and nineteenth century Connecticut furniture and Impressionist art. A visitor center houses changing exhibitions, a sound and light show, and a family hands-on history gallery.

The "Art Colony of the Bush-Holley Historic Site" exhibition opens in March 2001, the "Bush Family and the New Nations" exhibition opens in September 2001, and the "Ideal American Suburb" exhibition opens in April 2002. Children's programming is also available.

The museum does have a gift shop but does not have a café.

While You're in the Area

The Whitney Museum in Stamford (p. 104), the Putnam Cottage (p. 103), and the Maritime Center (p. 46) are nearby.

Butler-McCook Homestead and Gardens (Antiquarian and Landmarks Society)

Main Street History Center
394 Main Street
Hartford, CT 06103
(860) 522-1806 or (860) 247-8996
www.hartnet.org/als

Overview

Eliza Butler, her husband Reverend John McCook, and their seven children lived in the house built for her grandfather in 1782. The house stayed in the family until 1971. Family possessions accumulated over nearly 200 years make an unusual collection. Landscaped in 1865, the original garden design still remains, creating a restful place in the midst of urban Hartford. The Main Street History Center houses the exhibition "Witnesses on Main Street," chronicling the family and its Main Street neighborhood.

Directions and Hours

From I-91: Take the Capitol Area exit (#29A) then take the first exit, Columbus Blvd. Go straight at the stop light on Arch Street, then left on Main. The museum will be on the left, opposite Capitol Avenue.

From I-84: Take the Capitol Avenue/Asylum Street Exit (#48) then bear right toward the State Capitol. Turn left and follow Capitol Avenue to its end on Main Street. The museum is straight ahead.

The museum is open year round after fall 2001.

Hours: Wednesday-Saturday 10:00 A.M. to 4:00 P.M., and Sunday 1:00-4:00 P.M. The Main Street History Center and the first floor of the homestead are handicap accessible.

Admission and Membership

$5/ticket for both center and house. Group discounts are available.

What to See

The house collections include Japanese armor, American paintings, Victorian toys, Connecticut antique furniture, Lydia Rouse schoolgirl embroidery, a collection of family portraits, Egyptian figurines, and Victorian furniture.

Programs include Christmas on Main Street, guided walking tours, and an 1865 Jacob Weidenmann Garden, as well as children and family educational programs.

The Main Street History Center, located in an early twentieth century addition, will open in the late fall of 2001. The center will house the exhibition "Witnesses on Main Street," which reveals the history of the house and family in the context of their greater Main Street neighborhood. The interactive exhibit will be complemented with extensive programming. Afterschool and summer programs will also be developed as part of the Main Street History Center project.

There is a gift shop. There is no café, but several restaurants are located within walking distance of the Butler-McCook Homestead.

While You're in the Area

The Wadsworth Atheneum (p. 88) and the Old State House (p. 103) are located on Main Street, Hartford.

Canton Historical Museum

11 Front Street
Collinsville, CT 06019
(860) 693-2793

Overview

Housed in a former Collins Company building, the Canton Historical Museum has a vast Victorian collection representing all phases of life in the nineteenth century. The collection includes a large display of Collins Company tools.

Directions and Hours

From US 202 and 44: Take 179 South to Collinsville, then go one mile.

From I-84: Take the Farmington exit, Route 4 to 179 north to Collinsville.

From I-91: Take Route 44 west to Canton. Follow signs to Collinsville.

The museum is open year round, but from December to March on Weekends only. It is not handicap accessible.

Hours: Winter: Saturday and Sunday 1:00-4:00 P.M. Summer: Wednesday through Sunday 1:00-4:00 P.M.

Admission and Membership

Admission is $3 for adults, $2 for senior citizens, and $1 for children. Membership is $10/year for individuals, $15/year for families. Special discounts are available.

What to See

The museum houses a reconstructed nineteenth century general store, an original Canton post office, a barber shop, a children's room, a bride's parlor with wedding dresses from 1860-1896, and a railroad diorama circa 1900 of Collinsville and Hartford Railroad.

In November the museum holds a Christmas Boutique and in February and March a winter lecture series.

The museum does have a gift shop. There is no café, but LaSalle Market and ABC Pizza are located nearby.

While You're in the Area

Collinsville is a center for arts and antiques. Also located nearby is the Roaring Brook Nature Center (p. 73).

The Captain Nathaniel B. Palmer House

40 Palmer Street
Stonington, CT 06378
(860) 535-8445

Overview

The Captain Nathaniel B. Palmer House was the home of the Stonington native who discovered Antarctica in 1820. The house features a cupola from which views of Long Island Sound may be seen.

Directions and Hours

Take 95 to exit 91. Follow the signs, heading south, to Stonington Village. Turn left onto N. Main Street and turn right at the first traffic light onto Route 1. At the next traffic light turn left onto Route 1A, N. Water Street. Palmer Street is the first left after Lambert's Cove.

The house is open from May 1 to November 1, and is mostly handicap accessible.

Hours: Tuesday-Sunday 10:00-4:00; in the winter by appointment.

Admission and Membership

$4 for adults, $2 for children 6-12, children under six are free. Membership is $20/year for individuals, $30/year for families.

Admission to the Palmer House and the Old Lighthouse Museum is free with membership. Groups of ten or more are admitted for $3 per person. A combination ticket to the Palmer House and Lighthouse Museum is $6 for adults and $3 for children.

What to See

One room in the house is dedicated to exhibits on Captain Palmer's life and career. It relates the discovery of Antarctica with a scale model of his ship *Hero*. The exhibits also detail Palmer's involvement in the China trade and the clipper ships he designed.

Annually on the first week of December, the house holds "Christmas at the Palmer House: Teas and Trees," a Victorian-style tea. The house is also decorated with seven trees.

The second Saturday of December is "Children's Victorian Tea." There are also programs throughout the year for children.

There is a gift shop. There is no café, but there are restaurants a few blocks from the house.

While You're in the Area

The Old Lighthouse Museum (p. 103), Mystic Seaport Museum (p. 56), and Mystic Marine Life Aquarium (p. 54) are also in the area.

Children's Museum of Southeastern Connecticut

409 Main Street
Niantic, CT 06357
(860) 691-1111
http://childrensmuseumsect.org

Overview

The Children's Museum of Southeastern Connecticut is an interactive learning experience for children between the ages of 1 and 12. The museum has a kid-sized town for role play and a construction area with blocks and Brio Builder. There are also seasonal exhibits such as the Discovery Garden and a submarine exhibit.

Directions and Hours

From I-95 North: Take exit 72 (Rocky Neck State Park). Go left at the bottom of the ramp onto 156. The Museum is approximately 2½ miles on the left.

From I-95 South: Take exit 74. At the bottom of the ramp go right onto 161. Stay on 161 until it ends. Take a right onto 156 (Main Street). The museum is approximately ½ mile on the right.

The museum is open year round.

Hours: Tuesday-Saturday, 9:30 A.M. to 4:30 P.M., Fridays until 8:00 P.M., Sunday noon to 4:00 P.M. Closed Monday September through June. The museum is handicap accessible.

Admission and Membership

$4.00 per person age 2 and up. Group rate for 10 or more children is $3.00 per person with adults free. There is also a AAA discount. There is no restriction on who can attend the museum but older children may not be as challenged. Basic membership is $40/year for unlimited admission for one year for four people, $45/year for five people, $50/year for 6 people, and $55/year for 7 people.

What to See

The museum has live animals, including snakes, newts, and tarantulas. Collections of historic and natural history interest are rotated throughout the year. During the summer the discovery gardens include a climbing wall and a dinosaur dig.

Children's programming includes a Museum Without Walls program which travels to schools, libraries, and community centers, with a large array of science, art, and history programs.

The museum also does preschool programs and off-site programming.

There is a gift shop. There is no café but there are numerous restaurants within walking distance.

While You're in the Area

Nearby attractions and museums include the East Lyme Art League (p. 101), the Smith-Harris House (p. 103), and the Millstone Information and Science Center (p. 102).

Connecticut River Museum

67 Main Street
Essex, CT 06426
(860) 767-8269
www.ctrivermuseum.org

Overview

The Connecticut River Museum was formed in 1974 to collect, preserve, and interpret the rich material culture and natural history of the Connecticut River through exhibitions and educational programs. The museum is housed in an 1878 steamboat warehouse and adjacent boathouse, located on the banks of the Connecticut River in the historic village of Essex

Directions and Hours

From the South: Take I-95 to exit 69 to Route 9 north. Take exit 3 off Route 9 and follow the signs to the Connecticut River Museum

From the North: Take I-91 to exit 22S to Route 9 south. Take exit 3 off Route 9 and follow the signs to the Connecticut River Museum.

The museum is open year round.

Hours: Tuesday-Sunday from 10:00 A.M. to 5:00 P.M.

Admission and Membership

Admission is $4 for adults, $3 for students and seniors, and $2 for children 6-12. Children 6 and under are free. Group tours are available at the museum at a special rate. There are different levels of membership. Benefits include free admission to the museum and certain activities, a gift shop discount, a newsletter, and previews.

What to See

Waterfront activities and an in-the-water boat collection highlight summer programs on the dock. Displays of models, photographs, and artifacts tell the story of the river and the people who have lived in its valley. The museum's collections include a full-size replica of the *Turtle*, the first operating submarine built by David Bushnell during the Revolutionary War.

Educational programs are available on and off site. Lectures and other special programs take place throughout the year, including the Antique and Classic Boat Show, the Steam and Launch Show, Traditional Vessels Week, the Governor's Cup Regatta, and Trees in the Rigging.

The museum does have a gift shop.

While You're in the Area

Nearby attractions and museums include the Pratt House (p. 71), and the Essex Steam Train & Riverboat (p. 101).

Connecticut Trolley Museum

Connecticut Electric Railway Association, Inc.
58 North Road
East Windsor, CT 06088
(860) 627-6540
www.ceraonline.org

Overview

The Connecticut Electric Railway Association, Inc., includes a gallery and visitor's center with a locomotive and restored streetcars on display, and antique trolley cars that people can ride on. There is also a fire museum.

Directions and Hours

Take 91 to exit 45. Travel east on Route 140 for approximately 1½ miles.

The museum is open from April through Memorial Day and Labor Day through December, and is partially handicap accessible.

Hours: Saturday 10:00-5:00, Sunday noon-5:00; Memorial Day-Labor Day: Wednesday-Saturday 10:00-5:00, Sunday noon-5:00.

Admission and Membership

$6 for adults, $5 for seniors, $3 for children 5-12, $1 for children 3-4. Membership is $20/year for individuals, $15/year for junior individual, $0 for seniors, $35/year for families, and various levels of contributing memberships.

Groups of ten or more receive a discount rate of $5 for adults, $4 for seniors, and $2.50 for children 5-12.

What to See

The museum offers unlimited rides for a three-mile round trip on the antique trolley cars. There are also three cars in the visitor center.

Admission to the trolley museum also includes admission to the Fire Museum. There are antique fire engines on the property.

The museum holds a December "Winterfest," including nighttime trolley rides through a tunnel of Christmas lights.

There is a gift shop. There is no café, but there are a variety of sandwich shops and restaurants nearby.

While You're in the Area

Nearby attractions and museums include the Connecticut Fire Museum (p. 101), the New England Air Museum (p. 61), Bradley International Airport, the Windsor Locks Walter Fyler House (p. 101), and the Oliver Ellsworth Homestead (p. 103).

CRT's Craftery Gallery

1445 Main Street
Hartford, CT 06120
(860) 560-5315

Overview

CRT's Craftery Gallery is devoted to increasing the public's understanding and awareness of the visual fine arts and other cultural expressions of people of African descent and heritage in the Americas.

Directions and Hours

Take I-84 to the Capitol Avenue exit 48B. From the exit ramp, turn left onto Capitol Avenue. When Capitol ends, turn left onto Main Street.

Or, follow Route 4 (Farmington Avenue) until it joins Asylum Street. Follow Asylum as far as you can, then bear right on Ford Street (by Bushnell Park). Go one block and turn left on Pearl Street. Go four blocks and turn right on Main Street.

The museum is open year round and is handicap accessible.

Hours: Tuesday through Sunday 1:00-4:00.

Admission and Membership

Admission is free.

What to See

The gallery was established in 1972, and now serves as one of Connecticut's year-round creative environments for the fine arts that draws from the African American experience.

While You're in the Area

Interesting attractions and museums nearby include the Amistad Foundation at the Wadsworth Atheneum (p. 88), the Pump House Gallery (p. 103), the Old State House (p. 103), and the Artworks Gallery (p. 100).

The Cyrenius H. Booth Library

25 Main Street
Newtown, CT 06470
(203) 426-4533

Overview

In 1925, Miss Mary Elizabeth Hawley purchased the land and buildings of the old Newtown Inn on Main Street. The Inn had stood vacant for the previous three years and there was much speculation as to the fate of the property. It was not until her will was read that the town learned of her plans to build a state-of-the-art library to be named for her maternal grandfather, Dr. Cyrenius H. Booth. The Booth Library opened in 1932. Under Hawley's bequest, the library must maintain its collection of over 2,000 historical artifacts in a public display.

Directions and Hours

The library is located on Route 25, one mile from Route 84. The library is on Main Street near the flagpole in the center of the street.

The museum is open year round and is handicap accessible.

Hours: Monday-Thursday 10:00-8:00, Friday 12:00-5:00, Saturday 1:00-5:00, Sunday 1:00-5:00 from September-June and closed July and August.

Admission and Membership

Admission is free.

What to See

Exhibits from the Hawley family are on view, and 12 glass cases hold rotating special exhibits. Special collections include the Mary Elizabeth Hawley Historical Collection, featuring furniture, china, utensils, rugs, art and handiwork representing several periods of Newtown's history; the Julia Brush Genealogy Collection, a nationally recognized collection of over 900 volumes on the families and local history of neighboring Connecticut towns; the John Angel Collection comprised of books and sculpture; the Wasserman Lighting Collection of antique lighting fixtures; the Jacqueline Starr Smith collection of children's classics; and local history in print and microfilm.

The library has an active children's program and an adult series of lectures. Visitors can dine at the Inn at Newtown, just beyond the library.

While You're in the Area

Nearby attractions and museums include the

Matthew Curtiss House (p. 102), the Barnum Museum in Bridgeport (p. 6), Beardsley Park, the Maritime Aquarium at Norwalk (p. 46), Mathews Park, and the Lockwood-Mathews Mansion (p. 102).

Daniel Benton Homestead

Metcalf Road
Tolland, CT 06084
(860) 872-8673

Overview

The 1720 Daniel Benton Homestead is the oldest remaining house and the only Pilgrim Century house remaining in Tolland County. The Homestead was lived in by the Benton family until 1932 and retained many of its original features including feather grained raised paneling and two different sections of painted flooring. Hessian prisoners were quartered in this house during the Revolutionary War. When visitors are done viewing the house they can explore 20 acres of country walking trails.

Directions and Hours

Take Route 84 to exit 68 in Tolland (Route 195). Turn north on Route 195 toward Tolland. Then turn left onto Cider Mill Connecter, following the signs. Travel approximately 2 miles to Metcalf Road. The house is located approximately ¼ mile down Metcalf Road on the right side of the road, surrounded by a white fence. There is an OPEN sign in front of the house.

The homestead is open from mid-May to mid-October, Sunday 1:00-4:00 P.M. From mid-October to mid-December the homestead is open two Sundays per month—call ahead for an appointment and for special programs. The museum is partially handicap accessible.

Admission and Membership

Admission is a $2 donation. Seniors and groups get a 10 percent discount. Membership to the Tolland Historical Society is $7/individual.

What to See

The homestead has many interesting architectural details including original windows, two working bake ovens, two original 1720 walk-in cooking fireplaces, two graves on the property, a pig run, and a cellar that quartered Hessian prisoners. Programs are run that focus on eighteenth century life.

Children's programming includes school and youth group programs and workshops.

The museum does have a small gift shop and several restaurants are located within 10 miles.

While You're in the Area

Some attractions within the town of Tolland are the Tolland County Jail and Warden's Home (p. 84), the Tolland County Courthouse (p. 84), and the Hicks-Stearns Family Museum (p. 32).

Daniel Benton Homestead. Photo by Leigh Grossman.

Denison Pequotsepos Nature Center

109 Pequotsepos Road
PO Box 122
Mystic, CT 06355

Overview

The Nature Center's natural history museum features an introduction to the woodlands, meadows, and wetlands of Southeastern Connecticut's rich and diverse ecologies. Live owls, turtles, frogs, fish, and other animals delight visitors. Bird flight patterns, animal skeletons, and pelt identifications are also part of the exhibits.

The DPNC sanctuary includes over 300 acres of open space owned by the Denison Family Association and Avalonia Land Conservancy, with over seven miles of marked trails for birding, hiking, and animal watching.

Directions and Hours

Take I-95 to exit 90. Follow signs for Route 27 north. Travel less than a half mile, and take right on Jerry Browne Road. Travel one mile to three-way stop. Turn right onto Pequotsepos Road and travel ½ mile. DPNC on left side.

The Nature Center is open year round. Monday-Saturday, 9:00-5:00; Sunday 10:00-4:00. Wheelchair accessible.

Admission and Membership

$6 for adults, $4 for children under 13 and seniors 65 and older. Membership is $25 for individual, $35 for couples, $45 for families, and $20 for seniors.

What to See

In addition to live animals, the museum includes mounted beavers, otters, mallards, turkeys, bobcats, and more. Visitors can learn about owls, possums, lightning bugs, and other meadow animals in the *Night in the Meadow* theatre, which brings the hours after dark to life for children. Butterfly and nest collections are also fun to explore.

Throughout the year, the Nature Center offers environmental education programs for all ages. From babies to seniors, the Nature Center inspires its visitors with an appreciation for nature and teaches personal environmental ethics. During the week of Earth Day every April, DPNC offers activities for the whole family including live entertainment, puppeteers, craft making, food from around the world, and more. Weeklong summer camp programs for children ages 4-12 run throughout the summer months.

Nature Center trails are perfect for birding, hiking, and cross-country skiing. Visitors can circle ponds and pass vernal pools along the way, spying on a myriad of native animals during any time of the year.

The Nature Center gift shop offers handcrafted jewelry, birding books, natural home décor, bird feeders and seed, and plenty of games and puzzles for children. The Nature Center also provides picnic areas to visitors, and many restaurants are within a mile or two from the sanctuary.

While You're in the Area

The Mystic Aquarium (p. 54), Mystic Seaport (p. 56), Indian and Colonial Research Museum (p. 49), and plenty of shopping opportunities are within two miles of the Nature Center.

Dinosaur State Park

400 West Street
Rocky Hill, CT 06067
(860) 529-8423
www.dinosaurstatepark.org

Overview

Dinosaur State Park contains over 500 real Jurassic Period dinosaur tracks that are 200 million years old. Visitors can activate a sequence of lights to mark the paths of individual dinosaurs. These tracks are housed under a geodesic dome, making it the only protected dinosaur trackway in the world. An 80-foot-long diorama depicts the setting in which the park's tracks were made, and visitors can participate in interactive exhibits. A 30-foot "cut" through the East Berlin Foundation interprets local geology and highlights fossil tracks from the Connecticut Valley. Fossil fish and plants are displayed nearby. There is also a picnic area and 2½ miles of gravel-surfaced nature trails that wind through 50 acres of fields, forests, and wetlands. A 300-foot boardwalk takes visitors into the heart of a swamp.

Directions and Hours

From I-91: Take exit 23 (West Street) and travel one mile east.

The museum is open year round.

Hours: Tuesday-Sunday, 9:00 A.M. to 4:30 P.M. The park grounds are open daily from 9:00 A.M. to 4:30 P.M. The bookshop is open Tuesday-Sunday 9:30 to 4:00 P.M. Dinosaur State Park is handicap accessible.

Admission and Membership

$2 for adults, $1 for ages 6-17, children under 6 free. Membership is $15/year for individuals and $20/year for families. A supporting membership is $40/year, a Coelophysis is $75/year, a Dilophosaurus is $150/year, and corporate memberships are $250/year. Life membership is $400, and includes a spouse.

What to See

Dinosaur State Park has one of the largest enclosed dinosaur trackways in the world. Multimedia interactive displays include a life-size Triassic Diorama, a life-size Jurassic Diorama, reconstruction of a geologic formation, and highlights of the discovery of the tracks. The park also has a arboretum that contains hundreds of trees and shrugs belonging to plant families originating in the Age of the Dinosaurs. The Track Casting area is open May 1 to October 31 from 9:00 A.M. to 3:30 P.M. Visitors can bring casting materials and make their own cast from a real fossil track. Casting materials suggested are: 10 pounds of plaster of paris, ¼ cup vegetable oil, large plastic buckets, cloth rags, and paper towels. One cast per family is allowed.

Children's programming includes films during the weekend and daily in summer (except Mondays.) Auditorium and guided programs are available.

Dinosaur State Park Day is a celebration of the anniversary of discovery of the dinosaur tracks. Music, magicians, clowns, crafts, and activities for children along with games, face painting, and refreshments occur every August.

There is a small gift shop open Tuesday-Sunday 9:30 A.M.- 4:00 P.M. There is no café but there are many restaurants within a few miles.

While You're in the Area

Nearby attractions and museums include the Academy Hall Museum/Rocky Hill Historical Society (p. 100), the Museum on the Green (p. 53), the Welles Shipman Ward museum (p. 92),

Portion of dinosaur trackway and life-size early Jurassic diorama, located inside the exhibit center. Photo courtesy of Dinosaur State Park.

the Welles Chapman Tavern, and the Connecticut Audubon Center of Glastonbury (p. 100).

Dr. William Beaumont House

PO Box 151
Lebanon, CT 06249
(860) 642-6579
www.lebanonct.org

Overview

Dr. William Beaumont, considered the "Father of Gastric Physiology," published a book in 1830 describing digestion that is still used today. His birthplace is a tribute to early nineteenth century medicine with exhibits of period medical instruments and a recreated doctor's examining room.

Directions and Hours

From Hartford: Take I-84 east toward Boston. Take exit 59 toward Providence and merge onto I-384. I-384 will become Route 6 east. Stay straight and go onto CT 87. CT 87 will become the Jonathan Trumbull Highway. The museum is on the Lebanon town green.

From Boston: Take Interstate-91 north to the Route 3 north exit (number 25-26 toward Glastonbury/Old Wethersfield). Keep left at the fork in the ramp and merge onto Maple Street, which becomes Route 3 north. Take the Route 2 exit toward Norwich then take the Route 66 exit (number 13) towards Willimantic. Keep left at the fork in the ramp and turn left onto Route 66 then turn right onto Church Street and then left onto Lebanon Road. Lebanon Road will become Exeter Road. Turn right onto Route 87 (the Trumbull Highway). The museum is on the Lebanon town green.

The Dr. William Beaumont House is open from May 15-October 15 and is not handicap accessible.

Hours: Saturdays 1:00-5:00 P.M. and by appointment.

Admission and Membership

Admission is by donation. Membership in the Lebanon Historical Society is $7.50/year.

What to See

The Dr. William Beaumont House is an example of the restoration of a 1750 house. The house includes four rooms with furniture of the period: a kitchen with a large fireplace and oven, a buttery, a front parlor with a fireplace, a bedroom with a fireplace, and a small room recreated as a doctor's examination room. On exihibit are antique medical instruments typical of the period, donated by the Beaumont Club, Yale University.

Programs are planned by the Lebanon Historical Society each year and are of a historical nature that include a lecture series, monthly membership meetings, children's programs, guided tours, and group visits. Children's programming includes visits from area schools, special children's workshops, and history research.

There is a gift shop at the Lebanon Historical Society Museum. Nearby places to eat include Arch Pizza Restaurant, Uncle D's Restaurant, and the Lebanon Green store.

While You're in the Area

The house is within walking distance to other historic homes: the Governor Trumbull House (p. 26), the War Office (p. 103), the Trumbull Junior House (p. 38), and the Congregational church. Visitors can also visit Beaumont Park, the original site of the Beaumont House.

Eolia

Harkness Memorial State Park
275 Great Neck Road
Waterford, CT. 06385
(860) 443-5725 / (860) 437-1523
www.harkness.org
www.dep.state.ct.us/rec/parks/eolia.htm

Overview

The mansion Eolia, named for the island home of the Greek god of winds, was built in 1906 and purchased by Edward and Mary Harkness in 1907. The 200+ acres were a working farm and the Mansion was the Harkness's summer home. Currently, during the season, docents conduct tours which last approximately 20 minutes through the first two floors of the mansion; garden tours are also available.

The Roman Renaissance Revival-style mansion has 42 rooms and was designed by the architectural firm of Lord & Hewlett. Starting in 1909, architect James Gamble Rogers designed interior renovations (Classical Revival style), the pergola (tearoom) and carriage house (support complex). During this time, Rogers was also involved in the layout of the west garden with the firm of Brett & Hall.

From 1918 to 1929, Beatrix Jones Farrand (landscape designer, one of the founders of the American Society of Landscape Architects) redesigned the west garden and created and installed the East Garden, the Boxwood Parterre and the Alpine Rock Garden. The estate was left to the State of Connecticut in 1950. The mansion and gardens at the park have been restored to the conditions that existed in the early 1930s.

Directions and Hours

From Boston and Providence, take I-95 South to exit 81; end of exit ramp, turn left onto access road and proceed to stop light. At light, turn left onto Cross Road and continue to intersection with Route 1. Turn left onto Route 1 and continue to light at Avery Lane (Route 213). Turn right onto Avery Lane and follow to Park. Avery will become Great Neck Road. The park will be on your right.

From New York and New Haven, take I-95 North to exit 75; bear right, at end of exit, onto Route 1. Go 3 miles to Avery Lane and proceed as above.

From Hartford, take Route 91 South to Route 9 South, merging into I-95. Go Northbound and follow New York/New Haven directions above.

Harkness Memorial State Park is officially open to the public from Memorial Day weekend in May through Labor Day weekend in September. Please note that the mansion is closed on Mondays. The main floor of the mansion is handicap accessible, as are the gardens.

Everyone is welcome to Harkness Memorial State Park and Eolia; however, touring the second floor of the mansion does require negotiating a long staircase, which some seniors and very small children may find challenging.

During the summer season, the park closes each day at sunset.

Admission and Membership

Parking during the season is $4.00 per vehicle. There is no admission charge to tour the mansion; however, tour guide services and restoration projects, which are sponsored by Friends of Harkness Memorial State Park, Incorporated, depend upon donations from a generous public. Cost of membership is a minimum $10.00 per year contribution to Friends of Harkness, for which the member will receive the quarterly newsletter, *Eolian*.

What to See

Although the original furnishings of the mansion were dispersed years ago, Mrs. Harkness's bedroom has been furnished in period style; photographs throughout the mansion show the original decor. The unique gardens have been restored to their original plantings and are maintained by volunteers with the Friends of Harkness working in conjunction with park staff.

The property's spectacular, sweeping vistas remain the single most attractive element throughout the property, overlooking Long Island Sound.

Special arrangements can be made through the Supervisor's office for use of the mansion at other times of the year for meetings, weddings, celebrations, and such. The rental schedule and costs may be found at the DEP website.

While You're in the Area

Southeastern Connecticut is a treasure house of architectural gems in quaint village settings. However, visitors will not want to miss the world-class attractions of Mystic Seaport (p. 56), replicating the once-thriving whaling villages along the northeastern seaboard, and Mystic Aquarium (p. 54), both located a short drive across the Thames River off I-95.

Also nearby are the Florence Griswold Museum (p. 24), featuring works of the American Impressionists who lived and studied there, and the Lyman Allen Art Museum (p. 45).

Fairfield Historical Society

636 Old Post Road
Fairfield, CT 06430
(203) 259-1598
www.fairfieldhistoricalsociety.org

Overview

The Fairfield Historical Society is a museum and research library pertaining to Fairfield from its founding to the present day. Collections include Native American artifacts, fine and decorative arts, agricultural artifacts, costumes, and maritime artifacts. The library collections include books, manuscripts, maps, photographs, and diaries.

Directions and Hours

Take 95 south to exit 22 and turn left at the end of the ramp. Pass through two traffic lights and turn right at the stop sign onto Post Road. Turn right at the next stop sign.

Or, take 95 north to exit 22 and turn right at the end of the ramp. Pass through one traffic light and turn right at the stop sign onto Post Road.

The historical society is open year round, and is handicap accessible.

Hours: Tuesday-Saturday 10:00-4:30; Sunday 1:00-4:30.

Admission and Membership

$3 for adults, $1 for children. Membership is $25/year for individuals, $40/year for families, and various levels of contributing memberships.

What to See

The museum has permanent and changing exhibits, workshops, and seminars for adults and children. Included in these is a genealogy workshop. There are also school programs and preschool story and craft hours.

There is no gift shop. The museum has no café, but there are many restaurants in Fairfield and surrounding towns.

While You're in the Area

The Ogden House and Gardens (p. 66), Connecticut Audubon Society (p. 101), the Connecticut Birdcraft Museum (p. 100), the Discovery Museum (p. 101), and the Barnum Museum (p. 6) are in the area.

Florence Griswold Museum

96 Lyme Street
Old Lyme, CT 06371
(860) 434-5542
www.flogris.org

Overview

The Florence Griswold Museum is a National Historic Landmark located in the heart of the historic district of Old Lyme, Connecticut. It is home to the Lyme Art Colony, America's best-known center of Impressionist painting. This historic site offers 11 acres along the river, an education center, a restored artist studio, gardens, and the 1817 Griswold House and Museum. Family Explorer Guides help parents and children discover the museum together.

Directions and Hours

Traveling on I-95 South: Take exit 70; at bottom of exit ramp, turn right onto Lyme Street. The Museum is the second building on the left.

Traveling on I-95 North: Come over the bridge at the mouth of the Connecticut River. Stay in the right lane. Take exit 70; at the bottom of the exit ramp, turn left at light onto Route 156. Turn right at second traffic light onto Halls Road. Take Halls Road to the end. At the end, take a left at the light onto Lyme Street. The Museum is the second building on the left.

There are brown state highway signs marking the way.

When coming from Hartford, take I-91 south to Route 9 south. Follow Route 9 to the end and get on I-95 going north and follow the directions above.

Hours: January-March, Wednesday-Sunday 1:00 to 5:00; April-December, Tuesday-Saturday 10:00 to 5:00 and Sunday 1:00 to 5:00. The Museum is partially handicap accessible.

Admission and Membership

Admission is $5 for adults, $4 for seniors and students. Visitors under 12 are free. AAA members receive 2-for-1 admission. NEMA and AAM members receive free admission. Membership is $35 individual, $50 dual/family

What to See

The Florence Griswold Museum brings alive the work of the American Impressionists in the very place where they lived and painted. A visit to the museum, a National Historic Landmark, offers museumgoers a renowned collection of American art including over 400 paintings and 2,000 drawings and watercolors by approximately 135 artists associated with the Lyme Art Colony. Nothing so completely expresses the spirit of the colony as the 41 panels painted directly on the walls and doors of the house, especially in the famed dining room. Period rooms recreate aspects of the region's history and galleries offer changing art exhibitions.

The Museum's grounds invite exploration. Visitors may stroll on eleven acres of scenic beauty bounded by the picturesque Lieutenant River and walk through the "old-fashioned" historic gardens of Florence Griswold. On the edge of a meadow, the restored studio of the American Impressionist William Chadwick appears as if the artist has just stepped away. The lush surroundings continue to attract artists today, both professional and amateur, who discover for themselves the quality of light and the spirit of place found there.

Upcoming programs include "Home for the Holidays: A Festive Holiday Exhibition" in December 2001 and hands-on exhibitions for visitors of all ages such as "Joy in the Making" and "Impromptu Encounters with Art."

The museum's Hartman Education Center offers Sunday hands-on projects that relate to the

William Chadwick, "On the Porch." Photo courtesy of the Florence Griswold Museum.

current exhibitions, and is stocked with books, games, and puzzles. Throughout the fall, visitors can receive art materials and try their hand at painting "en plein air" along the Lieutenant River or in the gardens. The museum also offers all younger visitors a Family Explorer Guide which provides fun and informative activities they can enjoy as they tour the Museum.

There is a gift shop filled with unique items, children's items, etc. There are wonderful places to eat in Old Lyme and neighboring towns. The Museum is within walking distance of the Bee & Thistle Inn (www.beeandthistleinn.com) and The Old Lyme Inn (www.oldlymeinn.com) which provide both fine accommodations and fantastic food!

While You're in the Area

The Lyme Art Association (p. 45) is also in Old Lyme.

Fort Trumbull State Park Visitors Center

90 Walbach Street
New London, CT 06320
(860) 259-7110

Overview

The Fort Trumbull State Park Visitors Center plans to open in October 2001. It will feature military history from the Revolutionary War to the Cold War.

Directions and Hours

From I-95 Northbound: Take Exit #83 toward downtown New London. At the bottom of the exit ramp, go straight through the light onto Huntington Street. Go straight through the next three lights. At the stop sign go straight, continuing on Huntington Street. At next stop sign, take an extremely slight left onto Tilley Street. Take Tilley Street to the end and turn right onto Bank Street. New London Fire Department will be on the right. At the light, turn left onto Howard Street. Take the second left onto Walbach Street (through railroad underpass). Hughies Restaurant will be on your right. Take Walbach Street to the end and Fort Trumbull will be directly in front of you.

From I-95 Southbound: Take exit #84S-N-E to downtown New London. Get in the left lane and take the left hand exit #84S onto Eugene Street. Stay in the middle lane and go straight through the light. At the next light go straight (New London Police Department will be on your left). At the light go straight, continuing on Eugene Street and get into the left lane. At the light, turn left onto Tilley Street. At the light turn right onto Bank Street (New London Fire Department will be on your right.) At the light, turn left onto Howard Street. Take the second left onto Walbach Street (through railroad underpass). Take Walbach Street to the end; Fort Trumbull will be in front of you.

The visitors center will be open year round as of October 2001, and it is handicap accessible.

Hours: Park hours, daily 8:00 A.M. to sunset.

Admission and Membership

Please call for information after the museum has opened.

What to See

Please call for information after the museum has opened.

While You're in the Area

Fort Griswold, the U.S. Coast Guard Museum (p. 86), and the U.S.S. *Nautilus* (p. 34) are also in the area.

Governor Jonathan Trumbull House

169 West Town Street
Lebanon, CT 06249
(860) 642-7558
www.lebanonct.org

Overview

The Trumbull House was the home of Connecticut's Revolutionary War governor, the only Colonial governor to support the war for independence. Washington, Franklin, the Adamses, Rochambeau, and Lafayette came here for conferences. Built between 1735 and 1740, the house is furnished with period antiques including some of the Trumbull possessions.

Directions and Hours

From Hartford: Take Route 2 to Colchester, then Route 16 to Route 207 to Lebanon.

From Route 395: Take Route 32 to Route 87, which leads right to the center of Lebanon.

The museum is open May 15 to October 15, Tuesday-Saturday from 1:00-5:00 P.M.

Admission and Membership

$2 donation is requested for adults. Children under 12 are free with an adult. The home is administered by the Connecticut Daughters of the American Revolution.

What to See

In addition to its historical value, the museum contains nine rooms of colonial furniture.

There is a small gift shop but no café. There is a restaurant in town where visitors can eat.

While You're in the Area

The Lebanon Historical Museum and Visitors Center (p. 42) is also on the mile-long Town Green, which is an attraction in itself.

Guilford Handcraft Center

411 Church Street
Guilford, CT 06437
(203) 453-5947
www.handcraftcenter.org

Overview

The Guilford Handcraft Center is a nonprofit school, gallery, and shop devoted to art and fine craft. The Center's Mill Gallery presents a full schedule of regional and national exhibits highlighting the best in contemporary art and fine craft.

Directions and Hours

From I-95: Take exit 58 and go north for 1/8 of a mile on Route 77.

The center is open year-round and is handicap accessible.

Hours: Monday-Saturday 10:00 A.M. to 5:00 P.M., Sunday noon-4:00 P.M.

Admission and Membership

Admission is free. Membership is $30/year for individuals, $45/year for families.

What to See

The Guilford Handcraft Center's Mill Gallery hosts ongoing programs of regional, national, and international exhibits that feature both Fine Art and Fine Craft. Future exhibits include the Center's seventh North American Glass Biennial, a contemporary basket exhibit in 2002, "New Perspectives on Ancient Traditions," and an exhibit of functional, contemporary wood. All exhibits are presented with special events and programming including on-site demonstrations and workshops in the school building with special guest artists.

In mid-July the Center's annual Craft EXPO is held on the Guilford Green, which features over 100 craftspeople.

Photo courtesy of Guilford Handcraft Center.

Children's classes in art and craft are offered year round and the center also hosts a summer youth program of weeklong classes that are devoted to learning about and practicing the cultures and crafts of other countries.

There is a gift shop and there are many restaurants/eateries around the Guilford Green.

While You're in the Area

The Center is one mile north of the historic Guilford Green, which is a popular destination for shopping and eating. Local historical sites include the Henry Whitfield State Museum (p. 31), the Thomas Griswold House (p. 82), and the Dudley Farm (p. 101).

Harriet Beecher Stowe Center

77 Forest Street
Hartford, CT 06105
(860) 522-9258
www.hartnet.org/stowe

Overview

The Harriet Beecher Stowe Center is the home of the famous author, who wrote *Uncle Tom's Cabin*. It is also the site of the Stowe Center Research Library. Along with the neighbor Mark Twain Memorial, the center preserves the last corner of Nook Farm.

Directions and Hours

Take 84 to exit 46, and turn right onto Sisson Avenue. Take a right onto Farmington Avenue, then right onto Forest Street.

The museum is open year round, but is not handicap accessible.

Hours: Tuesday-Saturday 9:30-4:30; Sunday noon-4:30; Memorial Day-Columbus Day Monday 9:30-4:30, as well.

Admission and Membership

$6.50 for adults, $6 for seniors, $2.75 for children 6-16, free for children under 6 and Stowe Center members. Membership is $25/year for individuals, $45/year for families, $10/year for full-time students, and various levels of contributing membership.

What to See

The Stowe Center houses a research library and Victorian gardens.

There is a gift shop. There is no café, but there are neighborhood restaurants and coffee shops.

While You're in the Area

The Mark Twain House (p. 48) and the Connecticut Historical Society (p. 101) are also in the area.

Harry C. Barnes Memorial Nature Center

175 Shrub Road
Bristol, CT 06010
(860) 589-6082

Overview

The Harry C. Barnes Memorial Nature Center sits on 70 acres of varied habitat, from open meadow to forested woodland. Well-marked trails guide visitors through swamp and forest and along a trout stream. Visitors can explore trails, a small vernal pond home to a myriad of reptiles and amphibians, and an interpretive center. Inside, visitors can examine the collection of mounted animals common to the area and then visit downstairs in the newly renovated Live Animal Room, where indigenous reptiles and amphibians are housed.

Directions and Hours

From Hartford: Take I-84 to exit 38 (Bristol via Route 6 west). Follow Route 6 west into Bristol. Pass Bristol Plaza, and keep going straight until you see Friendly's Restaurant on the right. Turn right onto Jerome Avenue. Go 1.7 miles and turn left onto Shrub Road. Go another 1.7 miles and Barnes Nature Center is on the right.

From Waterbury: Take I-84 east to Bristol (exit 31). Turn left at the light onto Route 229 and follow to Route 6. Take the first right onto Jerome Avenue. Go 1.7 miles and turn left onto Shrub Road. Go another 1.7 miles and Barnes Nature Center is on the right.

From Terryville: Follow Route 6 into Bristol. Look for an Exxon gas station on the left. Turn left at the gas station onto Burlington Avenue (Route 69). Follow this road for 2.2 miles, turn right onto Shrub Road. Go .3 miles and Barnes Nature Center is on the left.

The nature center is open year round, and is handicap accessible.

Hours: Wednesday-Friday 3:00-5:00 P.M., Saturday 10:00 A.M. to 4:00 P.M., Sunday 12:00-4:00 P.M.

Admission and Membership

Admission is free. School field trip programs have a minimum fee of $60 per hour of instructional time. Prices for school field trips range from $4.50-$6.00 per student. Membership is $25/year for individuals, $50/year for families, $75/year for Sponsors, $100-$500/year for Patrons, and $500+ for Benefactors.

What to See

A new Raptor Program is scheduled to be running by the Summer of 2001. The Nature Center will be renovated to house unreleasable birds of prey which will be used in educational programs for visitors and schools.

Children's programming includes Sunday family programs, scout workshops, in-school presentations, and school field trips. School field trip topics include: Interesting Insects, Sensory Walk, Life in the Water, Wetland Ecology, Our Earth, Wildlife Along the Trails, Glacial Geology, and World of Birds. Some school presentations offered are Exploring the Animal Kingdom, Reptiles and Amphibians, Reptiles, Animal Tracking, Hibernation and Migration, Beautiful Birds, Amphibians, Map and Compass, and Skulls and Skeletons.

The nature center does have a gift shop. There are several restaurants on nearby Route 6.

While You're in the Area

Interesting attractions and museums in the area include the Bristol Carousel Museum (p. 102), the Bristol Clock and Watch Museum (p. 1), and Lake Compounce Amusement Park.

Hartford Police Museum

101 Pearl Street
Hartford, Connecticut
(860) 722-6152

Overview

The museum has an interesting collection of Hartford Police Department memorabilia, including a police cruiser and numerous pictures, patches, and badges.

Directions and Hours

Take Interstate 91 north or south to exit 29, the Capitol area exit in the center of Hartford. Follow the exit to the traffic circle at the end (Pulaski Circle). The first right off the traffic circle is Jewell Street. Follow Jewell to Trumbull Street, right onto Trumbull, right onto Pearl Street.

The Police Museum is open year round from 9:00-5:00, Monday-Friday. The museum is handicap accessible. Due to limited staff, the doors may be locked periodically throughout the day for short periods of time while staff members run errands.

Admission and Membership

Admission is free. There are no memberships.

What to See

Located in the heart of downtown Hartford, the Police Museum is a major repository for pieces of the Hartford Police Department's past history and equipment, and is staffed by knowledgeable volunteers.

There is no gift shop or café, but many dining opportunities are available within a short distance.

While You're in the Area

The Wadsworth Atheneum (p. 88), Bushnell Park Carousel, State Capitol (p. 103), Old State House (p. 103), Bushnell Memorial Hall, Hartford Stage Company, and the Riverfront area are all within easy walking distance.

Hatheway House (Antiquarian and Landmarks Society)

55 South Main Street
Suffield, CT 06078
(860) 668-0055 or (860) 247-8996
www.hartnet.org/als

Overview

The Hatheway House tour showcases life in Connecticut before the Revolutionary War (with the Burbank family) and after (with the Phelps family.) The center chimney main block (1761) was expanded by the second owner in 1794 following the latest fashions. A flower garden can be also be viewed.

Directions and Hours

From I-91 take Route 20 West to Bradley Airport. Follow Route 75 north about 5 miles to the center of Suffield.

The museum is open from mid-May to mid-October.

Hours: Wednesday, Saturday, Sunday 1:00-4:00 P.M. In July and August the house is also open on Thursdays and Fridays. The house is handicap accessible on the first floor only.

Admission and Membership

$4 for adults, $1 for students. Group discounts are available. Membership is $35/year for individuals and $50/year for a family.

What to See

The house has a large assemblage of in-situ eighteenth century wallpaper located on the second floor. It also houses the first documented work by Asher Benjamin, who is considered to be America's first architect. The house itself is an early example of neo-classical architecture in the Connecticut River Valley. Signed and dated woodwork from 1794 is also present.

There is no gift shop but the museum sells postcards and publications. There are several pizza places and small coffee-shops within a two mile drive.

While You're in the Area

The King House Museum (Suffield Historical Society) (p. 102), Old Newgate Prison in East Granby (p. 67), and the New England Air Museum in Windsor Locks (p. 61) are nearby.

The Hempsted (Hempstead) Houses (Antiquarian and Landmarks Society)

11 Hempstead Street
New London, CT 06320
(860) 433-7949 or (860) 247-8996
www.hartnet.org/als

Overview

Two important survivals of colonial New England are located together in downtown New London: the Joshua and Nathaniel Hempsted Houses. The Joshua House dates from 1678, one of the oldest documented frame houses in the state and a recognized stop on the Underground Railroad in the nineteenth century. The Nathaniel Hempsted House (also known as "Huguenot House") is an unusual stone house dating from 1758-59, built by a fifth generation Hempstead possibly using Acadian refugee labor. Ten generations of the same farming/seafaring family lived at the Hempsted Houses site. The houses are filled with authentic period furnishings, some original to the family.

Directions and Hours

The Hempsted Houses are located at the corner of Hempstead, Jay, and Truman Streets. From I-95 take exit 83/84-S to Huntington Street. Turn right to the corner of Jay and Hempstead Street. Watch for signs.

The museum is open from mid-May to Mid-October.

Hours: Thursdays-Sundays, noon-4:00 P.M. The houses are not handicap accessible.

Admission and Membership

$4/adults, $1/children. There is a 10% discount to qualified groups. There are no age restrictions on who can attend the museum, but strollers are not permitted.

What to See

Thanks to nearly 50 years of diary writing by third-generation American colonist Joshua Hempsted (1678-1758), these museum houses document the everyday lives of ordinary New Englanders from colonial times. Later generations of the family became deeply involved in Abolition and the Underground Railroad. The houses were restored with care and authenticity, furnished with local and family pieces.

A special exhibit, "Trash to Treasures," uses archaeological finds to document the story of the Stone House and the many immigrant groups that have helped build this port city. Hands-on group and school programs are offered.

There is a small gift shop. There is no café but there are many good local eating spots.

While You're in the Area

Other New London attractions include Fort Trumbull State Park Visitors Center (p. 26), the Lyman Allyn Art Museum (p. 45), the Old Town Mill (p. 68), the U.S. Coast Guard Museum (p. 86), and the U.S. Custom House Museum (p. 86).

Henry Whitfield State Museum

PO Box 210
248 Old Whitfield Street
Guilford, CT 06437
(203) 453-2457
www.hbgraphics.com/whitfieldmuseum

Overview

Built in 1639 as the home of Reverend Henry Whitfield, a founder of Guilford and the town's first minister, this granite house also originally served as a fort for the community. Today, the "Old Stone House" is Connecticut's oldest house, New England's oldest stone house, and a National Historic Landmark.

Directions and Hours

Take I-95 to exit 58. Take Route 77 South to Guilford Green. Turn right onto Broad Street and take an immediate left onto Whitfield Street. After one mile, bear left at the fork in the road and take the first left onto Stone House Lane. Turn into the first driveway on the left

Henry Whitfield State Museum. Photo courtesy of Thomas P. Benincas Jr., and the Henry Whitfield State Museum.

Hick-Stearns Museum. Photo by Leigh Grossman.

The museum is open year round, but is not handicap accessible.

Hours: February 1-December 14: Wednesday-Sunday, 10:00 A.M. to 4:30 P.M. December 15-January 31: Monday-Friday by appointment. The museum is closed New Year's Day, Thanksgiving Day, and Christmas Day.

Admission and Membership

$3.50 for adults 18-59, $2 for children 6-17, $2.50 for students with ID and seniors over 59, and children under six are free. If you visit the Henry Whitfield State Museum, the Prudence Crandall Museum, Old New-Gate Prison and Copper Mine, or the Sloane-Stanley Museum, the admission ticket is good for half-price admission on your next visit to any of the four state museums.

What to See

The Whitfield Museum features three floors filled with seventeenth to nineteenth century furnishings, with a strong emphasis on furniture from the 1600s. A museum since 1899, the house was restored by noted architects Norman Isham and J. Frederick Kelly in the early 1900s, and is an example of Colonial Revival restoration work. Also on the property is the Visitor's Center, which houses two changing exhibit galleries, travel information, a gift shop, a research library, and rest rooms.

Children can do a scavenger hunt as they tour the building.

There is a gift shop featuring museum and Guilford souvenirs, a selection of books, children's toys and games, and historic reproductions. The museum has no café but Guilford features a wide assortment of eating establishments located at the town harbor, around the Guilford Green, or along the Boston Post Road (Route 1).

While You're in the Area

Thomas Griswold House Museum (p. 82), Hyland House (p. 37), and Dudley Farm Museum (p. 101), are located in Guilford.

Hicks-Stearns Museum

42 Tolland Green
PO Box 278
Tolland, CT 06084-0278
(860) 875-7552

Overview

The Hick-Stearns Museum was a family home since 1845 and includes their furnishings and accessories. Family members have endowed school buildings and scholarships. The most visible endowment is the Ratcliffe-Hicks School of Agriculture at the University of Connecticut in Storrs.

Directions and Hours

From I-84 east, take exit 68 and take a left. From I-84 west, take a right off the exit. At stoplight at the beginning of Tolland Green, take a right and then an immediate left onto Tolland Green Road. The museum is on the right. It is a three story, three color Victorian house.

The museum is open from April through mid-December by appointment only and is not handicap accessible.

Admission and Membership

Admission fees vary. Please contact the museum for more information. All children must be accompanied by an adult.

What to See

The Hicks-Stearns House features interactive and themed tours with costumed guides. Some of the themes have included: "Packing for the *Titanic*," "1880s Christmas," and "Life in a Victorian Family." There are many events throughout the year such as summer lawn concerts, a Victorian Lantern Light Tour in mid-October, and a Victorian Christmas Open House in early December. The museum portrays a more formal aspect of Victorian living yet includes generous helpings of the wit and wisdom of the times in all tours.

The house is a unique and inviting location for small businesses, adult, school, youth, and senior group meetings. Craft classes are also held.

There is a gift shop and while there is no café, there are family restaurants nearby including a quaint eatery in an historic building.

While You're in the Area

There are a variety of interesting attractions in the area including the 1720 Daniel Benton Homestead (p. 19), the 1856 Warden's Home and Jail Museum (p. 84), and Tolland County Courthouse which is listed on the National Historic Register. Visitors can also enjoy the many antique shops around as well as the local apple orchards.

Hill-Stead Museum

35 Mountain Road
Farmington, CT 06032
(860) 677-4787
www.hillstead.org

Overview

The Hill-Stead Museum is a 1901 Colonial Revival mansion designed by the sixth registered female architect in Connecticut. It houses Impressionist masterpieces such as paintings by Monet, Degas, Whistler, and Cassatt. Original furnishing are still present in the mansion. There are also extensive trails throughout the 152-acre scenic property as well as a sunken garden. During the summer there is a poetry festival featuring acclaimed writers and musicians.

Directions and Hours

The Hill-Stead Museum is approximately two hours from New York City and Boston, and ten minutes from Hartford.

From I-84 east or west: Take exit 39 and follow Route 4 west. Turn left onto Route 10 south. At the first light turn left onto Mountain Road. The museum entrance is ¼ of a mile up the hill on the left.

The museum is open year round and is handicap accessible on the first floor where 90% of the collection resides.

Hours: May-October 10:00 A.M. to 5:00 P.M.; November-April 11:00 A.M. to 4:00 P.M. The grounds are open daily free of charge 7:00 A.M. to dusk. Closed Mondays.

Admission and Membership

$7 for adults, $6 for students and seniors, and $4 for children ages 6-12. Membership is $30/year for an individual and $50/year for a family. Benefits include free admission to the museum, a subscription to the museum newsletter, program discounts, a 10% discount in the museum shop, and an invitation to the annual members' party.

What to See

This 33,000 square foot 1901 country home with a Mount Vernon veranda boasts 36 rooms, 19 of which are open for public tours. The museum has the only surviving and intact Impressionist painting collection amassed by an

American patron. A sunken garden occupies nearly an acre and has high stone walls, brick walkways, hedges, and nearly 100 varieties of perennials.

The museum holds a Sunken Garden Poetry Festival, which has become a nationally acclaimed summer event that brings renowned poets and musicians together with more than 10,000 visitors. Performances are held on alternate Wednesday nights June through August. Musical performances begin at 6:30 P.M. and poetry at 7:30. Admission is free.

There are several family festivals each year: Hay Day in Autumn, the Winter Carnival, the May Market Plant and Craft Sale, a Monet in May annual dinner auction, and various lectures, seminars, children's programming, and special tours are offered throughout the year.

The museum does have a gift shop. There is no café but there are numerous restaurants in Farmington: The Grist Mill, Apricots, The Silo, Piccolo Arancio, and convenience food too.

While You're in the Area

Nearby museums include the Stanley-Whitman House (p. 79), the Day-Lewis Museum (p. 101), the Old Stone Schoolhouse (p. 103), and the Farmington Historical Society's Day-Lewis Museum (p. 102). Visitors can also fly fish on the Farmington River.

Historic Ship *Nautilus*/ Submarine Force Museum

Naval Submarine Base New London
Groton, CT 06349-5571
(860) 694-3558
www.submarinemuseum.com

Overview

The Historic Ship *Nautilus*/Submarine Force Museum gives visitors a glimpse into the lives of the men who served on submarines. Guests learn about the evolution of the "silent service" from Bushnell's *Turtle*, used in the Revolutionary War, to the modern Los Angeles, Ohio, and Seawolf class submarines. Visitors can walk the decks that made Naval history: the world's first nuclear powered vessel, the first ship to the North Pole, and the first submarine to journey "20,000 leagues under the sea."

Directions and Hours

Take exit 86 off I-95. Follow the signs to the *Nautilus*/Sub Museum, approximately 1½ miles from the exit.

The museum is open year round and is handicap accessible

Hours: Summer: May 15-October 31, Wednesday-Monday 9:00-5:00, except Tuesdays 1:00-5:00. Winter: November 1-May 15, Wednesday-Monday, closed on Tuesdays.

Admission and Membership

Admission to the museum is free. Membership in the Submarine Force Library and Museum Association is $20/year for individuals, $100 for life/individual.

What to See

In addition to the *Nautilus*, the museum has a permanent collection of battle flags, scale models, and submarine related artifacts.

There is a museum store, but the museum has no café. There are several fast food and family style restaurants within a couple of miles of the facility.

While You're in the Area

The Alexey von Schlippe Gallery of Art (p. 1) is also in Groton.

Holley-Williams House and Cannon Museums

Junction Routes 41 and 44,
Lakeville, CT 06039
(860) 435-2878
www.salisburyassociation.org/hhm

Overview

The Holley-Williams House is the center of a complex of family museums located in Lakeville's National Historic District. The original ironmaster's 1768 dwelling is connected to the early nineteenth century classical-revival home of the Holley family, whose members include a governor of Connecticut, educators, and prominent inventors. Allied buildings: a seven-hole outhouse, ice house, heritage gardens, and the Cannon Museum—a favorite with children—whose hands-on exhibits highlight the critical role played by the Salisbury Furnace in making cannon for the rebel forces in America's Revolutionary War.

Photo courtesy of Hopkins Vineyard.

Directions and Hours

From New York's Route 22, take Route 44 at Millerton, go 8 miles east. From Connecticut's Route 7, take 44 west at Canaan, 10 miles. From Great Barrington, Massachusetts, take Route 41 south 12 miles to the junction of Route 44.

The museums are open Fridays through Sundays, 12:00-5:00 P.M. all summer, and at other times by appointment.

Admission and Membership

$3 per person, $5 per family. Special rates available for groups of 10 or more. Annual individual and family memberships, $25-$100.

What to See

Tour the mansion with Maria Holley Williams, in the year 1876, a living-history presentation emphasizing the roles of women in society. Special exhibits include Holley Pocket Knives, period dress, toys, seven generations of schoolbooks, a hands-on nineteenth century kitchen, and portraits by Erastus Salisbury Field and other folk artists.

While You're in the Area

The museums are within walking distance of a number of good restaurants, and of Lake Wononscopomuc, which has picnic groves, playgrounds, and rowboats for day visitors. Nearby are the Sharon Audubon Reserve; entrances (with parking) to the Appalachian Trail, suitable for short hikes; old inns, taverns, and public golf courses.

Hopkins Vineyard

19 Hopkins Road
New Preston, CT 06777
(860) 868-7954
www.hopkinsvineyard.com

Overview

The Hopkins Vineyard has a winery available to tour as well as a nineteenth-century barn. The vineyards are located on slopes overlooking Lake Waramaug and have lovely panoramic vistas.

Directions and Hours

From New York City: Saw Mill or Hutch to 684

north to I-84 east to 7 north to 202 east to 45 north (New Preston).

From Boston: 93 to the Mass Pike west to I-84 west to Hartford.

From Hartford: I-84 west to 4 west (Farmington) to 118 west to 202 west to 45 north. From New Preston: 45 north to North Shore Road (on left) to Hopkins road (second right).

The vineyard is open May-December, Monday-Saturday 10:00-5:00, Sunday 11:00-5:00. In January-February, the vineyard is only open on Friday-Sunday; March and April, Wednesday-Sunday. The vineyard is closed Thanksgiving and Christmas. Handicap accessible with assistance.

Admission and Membership

Admission is free.

What to See

Tours of the winery are available by request, and vineyard tours are self-guided. On the third weekend in May, the vineyard hosts an annual "Barrel Tasting" and in the third week in September, there is an annual "Harvest Party." Special tours relating to chemistry or the culinary arts are available for children.

Visitors can purchase a wide selection of wine-related items in the gift shop. There is also a wine bar where wine by the glass, cheese, a paté platter, and tea are served. Next door, visitors can dine at the Hopkins Inn and Restaurant.

While You're in the Area

There are numerous other sites in the area including the Institute for American Indian Studies (p. 102), the Sloane-Stanley Museum (p. 77), and the Lake Waramaug State Park and Campground.

Historic Guilford

Experience four centuries of history by visiting all four of Historic Guilford's museums—the Henry Whitfield State Museum (1639, p. 31), the Hyland House (ca. 1690-1710, p. 37), the Thomas Griswold House Museum (ca. 1774, p. 82), and the Dudley Farm Museum (ca. 1910, p. 101). While each museum is operated by individual organizations, all four are working together to increase awareness of Guilford's historic treasures and to promote Historic Guilford as a travel destination. For further information, visit the museums online at www.guilfordct.org, or contact the individual museums.

The Huntington Homestead Museum

36 Huntington Rd. (Route 14)
PO Box 231
Scotland, CT 06264
(860) 456-8381
www.huntingtonhomestead.org

Overview

Samuel Huntington's birthplace is today the Huntington Homestead Museum. The Homestead is one of the three surviving houses associated with Connecticut's four signers of the Declaration of Independence and the only one open to the public. Besides being a signer, Huntington was President of the Continental Congress, President of the United States under the ratified Articles of Confederation, and 10-term Governor of the State of Connecticut. The Homestead has been designated a National Historic Landmark since 1972.

Directions and Hours

From north of Plainfield, CT: Take Route 395 south to exit 88. Take a right onto Route 14A. Go through the traffic signal and continue on route 14A for approximately 1¼ miles until you hit a stop sign. Then turn right onto Route 14 and continue on through Plainfield, into

Canterbury and then Scotland. The Homestead is ¼ mile west of the town center on the right.

From south of Norwich, CT: Take Route 395 north to exit 83. Take a left onto Route 97 and pass through the villages of Occum and Baltic. Continue on Route 97 to the town of Scotland. At the intersection of Route 14, go left onto Route 14 (Huntington Road) for ¼ mile. The Homestead is on your right, approximately 13 miles from 395.

The museum is open from May through October, and is not handicap accessible.

Hours: First and third Saturdays from 11:00 A.M. to 3:00 P.M. Also open by appointment any time.

Admission and Membership

The museum is free, but donations are accepted. Membership is free; see the website for further information.

What to See

The Homestead is a well-preserved, unrestored rarity still in a rural setting. The structure recently has been stabilized and is the site of revolutionary war era encampments and an annual "Voices from the Past" program in the fall. The museum has quality copies of manuscripts from Huntington to such dignitaries as Benjamin Franklin, at the time when he was President of the Continental Congress, discussing topics ranging from dealing with the treachery of Benedict Arnold to treaty negotiations during the time of conflict.

The Homestead Museum plans on building a replica of the original one room over one room house using traditional methods and tools which will be open to anyone wishing to learn these methods.

There is a small gift shop. The nearest restaurant is a 10 minute drive away, but the Scotland General Store serves grinders and is right in the town center.

While You're in the Area

The museum is is in the heart of the Quinebaug Shetucket River Valley National Heritage Corner and is within easy driving distance of the Windham Textile Museum (p. 97) and the Lebanon Historical Society Museum (p. 42).

Hyland House

85 Boston St
Guilford, CT 06437
(203) 453-9477
www.hylandhouse.com

Overview

The Hyland House, a museum of early colonial life and architecture, was built circa 1690-1710. Scheduled for demolition in 1916, it was purchased and restored by the Dorothy Whitfield Historic Society. It has been open to the public as a living historical environment since 1918.

Directions and Hours

Take exit 58 off I-95. Turn toward Guilford Green. At the bottom (south end) of the Green turn left on Boston Street. The house is 200 yards away on the left.

Hyland House is open June through Labor Day, 10:00-4:30 every day except Monday. Groups are welcome by appointment. The museum is partially handicap accessible.

Admission and Membership

$2 for adults, children and members free. Group rates may be available. Annual membership is $10/single, $15/family, $30/contributing, $100/sustaining membership, $250/life.

What to See

Hyland House is the second-oldest museum in Guilford, and one of the earliest Colonial houses in New England. There is a walk-in fireplace in the lean-to kitchen, an herb garden that highlights plants that the colonists used for medicines, dyes, and cooking, and a collection of seventeenth and eighteenth century artifacts including cooking utensils and quilts displayed in the house.

Annual programs include Twilight Tours, Archaeology programs from recent digs, and a Ghost Story Tour. There are also several outreach programs with the Guilford School System in which over 500 children visit the House for "Early Guilford Days" and Scavenger Hunts.

There is no gift shop or café, but the house is within walking distance of The Green where several restaurants are located.

While You're in the Area

The Whitfield House (p. 31) and the Griswold House (p. 82) are within half a mile.

Isham-Terry House (Antiquarian and Landmarks Society)

211 High Street
Hartford, CT 06105
(860) 522-1984 or (860) 247-8996
www.hartnet.org/als

Overview

The Isham-Terry House is an example of the Italianate-style home so popular in the mid-nineteenth century. It remains unchanged and its interior records life a hundred years old.

Directions and Hours

From I-91: Take the Trumbull Street exit from I-91. Continue straight paralleling I-84 (the street changes names three times). The museum is at the corner of Walnut and High Street. Parking is accessed from Walnut Street.

From I-84 East: Take the High/Ann Street exit. Turn left on Ann Street then take a left onto Chapel Street (which turns into Walnut Street).

The museum is open from April to December.

Hours: Sunday, 1:00-4:00 P.M. The house is not handicap accessible.

Admission and Membership

$4 for adults, $1 for students. Group discounts are available. Membership is $35/year for individuals and $50/year for a family.

What to See

The furnishings are all original to the house, presenting a preserved time capsule. Visitors are particularly intrigued by the kitchen and bathroom.

There is no gift shop. Since the museum is located in Hartford, there are many places to eat: food courts, the Hartford Civic Center, and downtown Hartford.

While You're in the Area

The Wadsworth Atheneum (p. 88), the Mark Twain House (p. 48), the Old State House (p. 103), the Butler-McCook Homestead (p. 13), and the Harriet Beecher Stowe House (p. 28) are located nearby.

Jonathan Trumbull Jr. House Museum

780 Trumbull Highway (Rt. 87)
Lebanon, CT 06249
(860) 642-7987
www.lebanonct.org

Overview

The Jonathan Trumbull Jr. House Museum, located in the Lebanon Green National Register District, is owned and maintained by the town of Lebanon. Built in 1769, this Georgian style house was the home of Jonathan Trumbull Jr., secretary to General George Washington during the Revolution and later a United States representative and senator and governor of Connecticut from 1797 to 1809. Local history declares that Washington stayed at the house March 4, 1781. Master joiner Isaac Fitch carved woodwork and a cherry balustrade in the house. Six corner fireplaces, a century-old ginkgo tree, and period gardens also enhance the setting.

Directions and Hours

The house is located on Route 87, half a mile north of the junction of Route 87 and Route 207 (in the center of Lebanon) and half a mile south of the junction of Routes 87 and 289 (at the north end of the town green).

The Jonathan Trumbull Jr. House is open from mid-May to mid-October on Saturdays from 1:00-5:00 P.M. or by appointment.

The museum is partially handicap accessible.

Admission and Membership

$2 for adults, children and students of all ages are free.

What to See

The house was restored in 1977-78 to the period of its most prominent owner, Jonathan Trumbull Jr., who lived there from 1769 to 1809. Modern amenities were removed and the house was furnished with period reproductions, all usable by the public. A complete photographic record of the restoration, including before and after photos, is on view for study. Also available is an architectural and social history of the house, detailing the changes made to it by various owners over 200-year history. An exhibition of conjectural architectural drawings and old photographs illustrates many of these changes. A video interview with the restoration carpenter, Craig Rowley, filmed in the house can also be viewed.

There is no gift shop or café, but the house offers books on local history and souvenirs for sale. There are several dining opportunities within a short driving distance.

While You're in the Area

The Lebanon Green, 27 open acres in the center of town, is the most distinctive feature of the area. It is the largest green in Connecticut and one of the largest in New England, and it is the only one still in agricultural use. A walking path around the Green allows visitors to view a number of eighteenth and nineteenth-century houses. During the American Revolution, the Lebanon Green was the focal point of Connecticut's contribution to the patriot cause.

One-half mile south of the Jonathan Trumbull Jr. House is a cluster of historic building museums, including the Governor Jonathan Trumbull Sr. house (p. 26), home of the Revolutionary War governor; the War Office (p. 103), where the governor conducted daily operations of the war effort; the Wadsworth Stable, a high-style outbuilding; and the Beaumont Homestead (p. 22), birthplace of Dr. William Beaumont, America's pioneer medical researcher. Nearby is the First Congregational Church (ca. 1804-07), designed by John Trumbull, the great artist of the Revolution.

Also nearby is the modern Lebanon Historical Society Museum and Visitors Center (p. 42), featuring exhibitions on local history and information on all the historic sites around the green. East of Town Hall is the home of William Williams, signer of the Declaration of Independence, and the birthplace of William Buckingham, governor during the Civil War. West of Town Hall is Redwood), designed and built by master joiner Isaac Fitch in 1778-79, and the headquarters of the Duc de Launzun during the encampment of the French Hussars in Lebanon, November 1780-June 1781.

Keeler Tavern Museum

132 Main Street
Ridgefield, CT 06877
(203) 435-5485

Overview

The Keeler Tavern Museum, built around 1713 by Benjamin Hoyt, has been a farmhouse, tavern, and stagecoach stop, a hotel, and the home of noted architect Cass Gilbert. It is furnished with eighteenth and nineteenth century pieces, some of which belonged to the Keeler family.

Directions and Hours

From I-95: Take exit 15 to Route 7 north. Get on Route 33 and follow it to Route 35 (at the fountain). The museum is located 25 feet from the fountain on the right.

From the Merritt Parkway: Take exit 39 to Route 7 north. Get on Route 33 and follow it to Route 35 (at the fountain). The museum is located 25 feet from the fountain on the right.

From I-84: Take exit 3. Get on Route 7 south and follow to Route 35 south. Travel on Route 35 South through the town of Ridgefield. The museum is located on the left, about 25 feet from a fountain.

The museum is open from February 1 to December 31, and is closed in January. Its hours of operation are: Wednesday, Saturday, and Sunday 1:00-4:00 P.M.

The museum is handicap accessible.

Admission and Membership

Admission is $4 for adults, $2 for seniors and students, and $1 for children under 12. Membership levels are: $1,000 for life, $150/year for a patron or business, $75/year for a contributor, $35/year for a family, $20/year for an individual, and $15/year for students or seniors.

What to See

Tours of the house are given by costumed guides. A ca. 1915 Garden House, which was designed for entertaining, overlooks a brick-walled garden. Today it is used for concerts, lectures, special events, and may be rented for weddings or other social occasions. The garden is open for public viewing.

Educational programs and museum tours are held for Ridgefield schools. "Camp Keeler" is held on July 11-12 and 17-19.

The museum has a gift shop.

While You're in the Area

Also in the area is the Aldrich Museum of Contemporary Art (p. 100).

Keeney School House Museum

106 Hartford Road
Manchester, CT 06040
(860) 647-9983
www.manchesterhistory.org

Overview

The Keeney School House is located in a one-room school built in 1751. The museum is interpreted as a schoolhouse from the period when Washington was president.

Directions and Hours

From the west: From I-384 take exit 3. Go north on Main Street and take a left at the first traffic light onto Hartford Road. Then take a right at the second intersection onto Pine Street and then a left at the first intersection onto Cooper Hill Street. The museum is on the next corner on the right.

From the east: From I-384 take exit 3. Take a left at the end of the ramp onto Charter Oak Street. Go through the light to Hartford Road and follow the direction above.

The museum is open from April-October.

Hours: Monday 9:00 A.M. to noon and Sunday 1:00-4:00 P.M. Closed major holidays.

Admission and Membership

$2 per person, children 16 and under free when accompanied by an adult. Membership is $15/year for an individual and $20/year for a family. Includes admission to the Old Manchester Museum (p. 67).

What to See

The schoolhouse contains wooden desks and benches, horn books and a period outhouse, as well as other displays to give visitors the feel of a late eighteenth-century one-room school.

The museum does have a gift shop (at the Old Manchester Museum). Several restaurants are located within a half mile.

While You're in the Area

The Manchester Historical Society also operates

the Old Manchester Museum (p. 67). Other museums and attractions in the area include the Connecticut Fireman's Historical Society Museum (p. 101) and the Lutz Children's Museum (p. 102).

Kidcity

119 Washington Street
Middletown, CT 06457
(860) 347-0495
www.kidcitymuseum.com

Overview

Kidcity is a hands-on educational playground for kids 6 months to 10 years and their accompanying adults. The museum is located in the 1835 Camp-Sterns House, which served as the convent for St. Sebastian's Church for 70 years. The house was relocated in 1997—moving 400 feet down Washington Street—and has been renovated and filled with exhibits.

Directions and Hours

From Hartford: Take I-91 south to exit 22 South. Go 6+ miles on Route 9. At exit 15, go right. Kidcity is 1½ blocks up on the left, at #119 Washington Street.

From West Hartford: Take Route 9 south. At exit 15, go right. Kidcity is 1½ blocks on your left, at #119 Washington Street.

From Old Saybrook: Take Route 9 north. At exit 15, go left. Kidcity is 1½ blocks on your left.

From New Haven/Meriden: Take I-91 north to exit 18. Follow Route 691 (which becomes Rt. 66/Washington Exit) for 6.5 miles. #119 Washington Street is on the right.

From Waterbury: Take Route 84 to exit 27. Follow Route 691 for 14+ miles (becomes Washington Street/Route 66). Kidcity is on the right.

From Eastern Connecticut: Take Route 66 West over Portland Bridge into Middletown. Rt. 66 turns right onto Washington Street. Kidcity is the 3rd building on the left at #119.

From Fairfield: Take Merritt Parkway to exit 68. Follow signs for Route 66 East/Middletown. Follow Route 66 East for 6.5 miles. Look for #119 on the right.

The museum is open year round, and is handicap accessible first floor only.

Hours: Sunday, Monday, and Tuesday 11:00 A.M. to 5:00 P.M. Wednesday, Thursday, Friday, and Saturday 9:00 A.M. to 5:00 P.M. Please call to reserve a time for group visits.

Admission and Membership

$2 for adults, $5 for children, and babies under one free. Membership is $25/year for one child, $50/year for two children, and $55/year for three or more children. Please call for other membership options. The museum requests at least one adult per four children.

What to See

Exhibits include a clipper ship, a musical planet video theater, a farm room for babies and toddlers, an interactive main street for preschoolers, a global music exhibit, the Borrower's Library, an Invention Station for kids over five, and a Community Room for birthday parties, book clubs, presentations, and Sunday afternoons of game playing.

Kidcity's Party Room is available for birthdays for children turning eight or younger. During a two-hour party visitors celebrate in the party room and then explore the museum.

There is no gift shop but t-shirts are sold. The museum has no café but there are many restaurants in town.

While You're in the Area

Butternut Hollow, Daniel's Raymond Farm, Long Hill Estate, Wadsworth State Park, the Middletown Riverfront, and Wesleyan University are all nearby.

Lebanon Historical Museum and Visitors Center

856 Trumbull Highway
PO Box 151
Lebanon, CT 06249
(860) 642-6579
www.lebanonct.org

Overview

Visitors can explore Lebanon's rich and diverse history at this new, fully accessible, museum and visitors center which is located on the historic Lebanon Green. The complex includes the interactive museum exhibition, "Turning The Soil: The Land and People of Lebanon," changing exhibitions, an historical and genealogical research center, and a 24-hour Visitor Information Center. Public programs are also offered on a regular basis.

Directions and Hours

The LHS Museum is located on Trumbull Highway (Route 87), on the Historic Lebanon Green, 33 miles from Hartford (exit 18 off of Route 2) and 33 miles from Mystic (exit 81W or 82 off I-395). There is parking at the Museum.

Take I-84 east to exit 55 for Route 2 (Norwich/New London). Proceed on Route 2 to exit 13 (Marlborough). Turn left onto Route 66 east. Follow Route 66 east to intersection with Route 87 at stoplight in Colombia. Turn right onto Route 87 south and proceed seven miles to the north end of the Lebanon Green. Continue on Route 87. The Lebanon Green will be on your right. (Route 87 is also Trumbull Highway). The Museum (cream colored cape with stone wall in front) is located on your left, at 856 Trumbull Highway, just north of the intersection of Routes 87 and 207.

Merritt Parkway/Wilbur Cross Parkway: Take exit at Meriden to I-691 (also Route 66). Head east on Route 66 to Middletown. Continue on Route 66 to the intersection of Route 87 at stoplight in Colombia. Turn right onto Route 87 south. Proceed seven miles to stop sign at north end of the Lebanon Green. Continue on Route 87; the Lebanon Green will be on your right. (Route 87 is also the Trumbull Highway).

The Museum (cream colored cape with stone wall in front) is located on your left, at 856 Trumbull Highway, just north of the intersection or Routes 87 and 207.

Lebanon Historical Museum and Visitors Center. Photo by Leigh Grossman.

From Rhode Island and Eastern Connecticut: Take Route 6 to Route 395 south or follow Route 95 to Route 395 north.

Take exit 81 west from 395 north (exit 82 from 395 South). Follow Route 32 north. Take a left onto Route 87 north, and follow it until you reach the intersection of Routes 87 and 207. Continue on Route 87 (Trumbull Highway). The Museum is the second building on the right, just north of the intersections of Routes 87 and 207, at 856 Trumbull

Highway (cream colored cape with stone wall in front).

From Massachusetts: Take I-84 west to exit 70 (Route 32). Follow Route 32 south to Willimantic. In Willimantic at stop light by Dunkin Donuts, turn right onto Route 32 south. Follow sign and turn left to stay on Route 32 and head to Route 289. At next stop sign, you will see sign for Route 289; turn right on to Route 289 (Mountain Street—a large yellow victorian house will be on your left). Follow Route 289 about five miles to the intersection of Route 87. Veer left onto Route 87 south. The Lebanon Green will be on your right (Route 87 is also the Trumbull Highway). The Museum (cream colored cape with stone wall in front) is located on your left, at 856 Trumbull Highway, just north of the intersection of Routes 87 and 207.

The museum is open every Wednesday from 9:00-1:00 and every Saturday from 1:00-5:00, year-round, and by appointment. Group visits are welcome by appointment. The museum is fully handicap accessible.

Admission and Membership

$2 donation requested. Memberships are available.

What to See

"Turning the Soil: The Land and people of Lebanon" is an interactive exhibition exploring how people have used Lebanon's land from the time of the Paleo-Indians to the present. Visitors will see projectile points, maps, historic documents, tavern artifacts, school furnishings, farm tools and a century of photographs. People can hear the voices of Lebanon residents in three audio areas, and enjoy activity stations where they can test "egg knowledge," handle reproductions of eighteenth century items, or compare Native American and English concepts of property.

"The Grant Huntington Retrospective" honors the life and work of talented photographer Grant Barnes Huntington (1955-1997) and showcases examples of his Lebanon and California work. Huntington visited Lebanon in 1996 and 1997. Photographs taken during his visits were published by the Town of Lebanon in the book, *Around The Lebanon Green.*

The Lebanon Historical Society's Annual Antique Show on the Lebanon Green is held on the last Saturday in September

The museum offeres regular "Hands on History Workshops for Young People." School and youth group visits are welcome

There is a gift shop, but no café. Visitors can eat at the Lebanon Green Store (sandwiches and a full deli); nearby Arch Pizza, on Beaumont Highway (pizza and Italian fare); and Uncle D's Log Cabin, on Trumbull Highway (a varied menu). Many additional restaurants are located in the neighboring towns of Norwich, Windham, and Colchester.

While You're in the Area

The LHS Museum is located on the beautiful and historic mile-long Lebanon Green where the Hussars—the Duc de Lauzun's legion of foreign soldiers—drilled during the winter of 1780-1781, before marching on to Yorktown. A walking path enables visitors to stroll the Green and visit six historic sites of national significance which are open to the public, The Governor Jonathan Trumbull House (p. 26), the War Office, the Wadsworth Stable, the Dr. William Beaumont House (p. 22), the Jonathan Trumbull Jr. House Museum (p. 38), and the First Congregational Church, the only surviving architectural work of Lebanon's John Trumbull, painter of the American Revolution.

Lock Museum of America, Inc.

230 Main Street (Route 6)
Terryville, CT 06786-0104
(860) 589-6359
www.lockmuseum.com

Photo courtesy of the Lock Museum of America.

Overview

The Lock Museum of America has a large collection of 22,000 locks, keys, and ornate hardware that traces the history of the American lock industry.

Directions and Hours

From Interstate 84: Take exit 38. The museum is on Route 6.

The museum is open from May 1-October 31 and is handicap accessible.

Hours: Tuesday-Sunday, 1:30-4:30 P.M.

Admission and Membership

Adults $3, seniors $2.50, children 4-12 free. Membership is $20/year for a single person, $25/year for a family, and $100/year for a company. Please contact the museum for other membership options.

What to See

The museum has eight display rooms, the newest of which displays an extensive lock collection that includes a Cannon Ball Safe, 30 early era time locks, Safe Escutcheon Plates, and a number of British safe locks, door locks, padlocks, handcuffs, and keys. There is another room, known as the Eagle Lock Company Room, that houses over 1,000 locks and keys manufactured from 1854 to 1954. Also displayed are bank locks, vault locks, safe lock, time locks, ornate hardware (several pieces of which are gold plated and enameled), a display of how a pin tumbler lock works, a display of mounted door knobs and escutcheons made during the Victorian era, colonial locks and ornate European locks dating form the 1500s, locks manufactured from 1860 to 1950, an original patent model of the Mortise Cylinder Pin Tumbler lock designed by Linus Yale Jr. in 1865 and considered the greatest invention in the history of lockmaking, and a 4,000 year old Egyptian-made pin tumbler lock.

The museum offers several books for sale.

While You're in the Area

Other museums nearby include: the American Clock and Watch Museum (p. 1) and the Carousel Museum of New England (p. 102).

Lourdes in Litchfield

PO Box 667
83 Montfort Road
Litchfield, CT 06759
(860) 567-1041

Overview

Lourdes in Litchfield is a place of pilgrimage located in the northwest corner of Connecticut. The shrine is a place of peace and tranquility where people can commune with God and experience healing.

Directions and Hours

Take exit 42 off Route 8 to Route 118. Go west off Route 118 toward the town of Litchfield. The Lourdes of Litchfield is ¼ mile east of the town green. Make a right onto Montford Road from Route 118.

The grounds are open year round from dawn

to dusk. From May to October there is a daily mass at 11:30, except for Mondays. The shrine is handicap accessible.

Admission and Membership

There is no cost to enter the grounds. The grounds are Roman Catholic but anyone who desires a place of quiet and reflection is welcome.

What to See

In addition to the shrine and peaceful grounds the Lourdes of Litchfield offers a series of programs that are offered year round.

There is a gift shop. The museum has a café that is open from May to October.

While You're in the Area

Other places to visit in the town of Litchfield include the Tappin Reeve House (p. 104) and the White Memorial Foundation (p. 104).

Lyman Allyn Art Museum

625 Williams Street
New London, CT 06320
(860) 443-2545

Overview

The Lyman Allyn Art Museum at Connecticut College is the principal comprehensive art museum serving southeastern Connecticut. It houses a collection of more than 15,000 objects.

Directions and Hours

Take 95 north or south to exit 83 and follow the brown "cultural attraction" signs. The museum is about a mile from the exit.

The museum is open year round, but is not handicap accessible.

Museum hours: Tuesday-Saturday 10:00-5:00; Sunday 1:00-5:00.

Admission and Membership

$4 for adults, $3 for seniors and students, and children under six are free.

What to See

The museum's collection includes contemporary, modern, and early American fine arts, American impressionist paintings, and the Fortune Galleries at the Deshon-Allyn Mansion. There are temporary exhibitions of American art from public and private collections.

There are also changing children's programs.

The museum has a gift shop and a café.

While You're in the Area

The Science Center of Eastern Connecticut (p. 103) is about a mile away, while the Children's Museum of Southeast Connecticut (p. 15) is eight miles away. The Florence Griswold Museum (p. 24) is at exit 70 on I-95.

Lyme Art Association

90 Lyme Street
Old Lyme, CT 06443
(860) 434-7802

Overview

The Lyme Art Association is the oldest summer art colony in the country, beginning in 1902. The art association continues its long tradition of exhibiting art by living American painters and hosts a diverse schedule of art shows that range from members' works to children's works. Exhibitions of the founding artists are held periodically and are taken from the Association's archives.

Directions and Hours

From Route 95: Take exit 70. Follow the well-marked signs to the front door.

The art association is open year-round and is handicap accessible.

Hours: Tuesday-Saturday 12:00-4:30 P.M., Sunday 1:00-4:30 P.M.

Admission and Membership

$4 per person. Discounts are given to students. Membership starts at $30 and up.

What to See

The Lyme Art Association has eight major shows a year and many special events. The exhibition gallery was designed by Charles A. Pratt, designer of the Freer Gallery in Washington, D.C.

The association offers an active fine arts education program for 7-12 year olds.

The Lyme Art Association does not have a gift shop or a café but visitors can eat at the Old Lyme Inn, directly across the street and Bee and at Thistle Inn, two doors down.

While You're in the Area

Other museums nearby include: the Florence Griswold Museum (p. 24) and the Lyme Academy of Fine Art (p. 102).

Mansfield Historical Society Museum

954 Storrs Road (Route 195)
PO Box 145
Storrs, CT 06268
(860) 429-6575
www.mansfield-history.org

Overview

The museum is located in the former town office building and the original Town Hall, built in 1842, which is Mansfield's oldest remaining public building. The museum features changing exhibits relating to local history. The society also has an extensive research library and archives.

Directions and Hours

From I-84, take exit 68. Travel east on Route 195 past the University of Connecticut. The museum is on the left, approximately two miles from the campus.

Open from June to September, Thursday and Sunday from 1:30-4:30, and year-round by appointment. The Old Town Hall is handicap accessible, but the lower level of the main building is not accessible. Photographs of that display area are available.

Admission and Membership

Admission is $2, free to members and children under 12. Membership: $10/individual, $15/family, $25/sustaining, $35/corporate, $50/contributing, and $150/patron.

What to See

The museum has extensive collections of photographs, furnishings, costumes, and artifacts relating to local history. Exhibits change regularly. Long-term exhibits chronicle the early silk industry in Mansfield and the founding and early years of the Storrs Agricultural School, now the University of Connecticut. Two more long-term exhibits on agriculture and town government are planned for the 2002 season. The museum also features recreations of a country store and two kitchens from 1800 and 1900. Mansfield will be celebrating its 300th anniversary in 2002-2003; there will be special exhibits, programs, and events to celebrate this event.

School tours, museum loan kits, and in-class programs are offered.

There is no museum shop, but publications, maps, postcards, and the like are sold. The museum does not have a café, but there are many restaurants and sandwich shops nearby.

While You're in the Area

Area sites of interest include the Gurleyville Gristmill, the Connecticut Museum of Natural History (p. 101), the William Benton Museum of Art (p. 95), and the Ballard Institute and Museum of Puppetry (p. 3). Also nearby are the University of Connecticut's Dairy Bar and agricultural barns.

The Maritime Aquarium at Norwalk

10 North Water Street
Norwalk, CT 06854
(203) 852-0700
www.maritimeaquarium.org

Overview

The Maritime Aquarium focuses solely on one body of water: Long Island Sound. The Aquarium features more than 1,000 marine animals native to the Sound and its watershed. Tanks portray successive levels of life in the Sound, from shallow tidal areas filled with oysters, sea horses, lobsters and small fish to the 110,000-gallon Open Ocean tank with nine-foot sharks, bluefish, striped bass, rays, and other creatures found in the Sound and the ocean beyond.

Directions and Hours

From I-95 north: Get off exit 14. At the stop sign at the end of the exit ramp, go straight. At the next stop sign, go straight again and down the hill. At the light, turn right onto West Avenue. At the third light, turn left onto North Main Street. At the first light, turn left onto Ann Street. Go under the railroad overpass to a stop sign. Turn right onto North Water Street and then right into the parking lot. The aquarium's main entrance is across the street.

From I-95 south: Take exit 15. The exit ramp splits. Stay to the right, following overhead sign that say "South Norwalk/Maritime Aquarium." At the light at the end of the exit ramp, turn left onto West Avenue. At the fifth light, turn left onto North Main Street. At the first light, turn left onto Ann Street. Go under the railroad overpass to a stop sign. Turn right onto North Water Street and then right into the parking lot. The aquarium's main entrance is across the street.

From the Merritt Parkway north: Take exit 39A and merge south onto Route 7. Take Route 7 to its end, staying in the middle lane (watch for overhead signs saying "South Norwalk/Maritime Aquarium." At the stop sign at the end of the exit ramp, turn right onto West Avenue. At the fourth light, turn left onto North Main Street. At the first light, turn left onto Ann Street. Go under the railroad overpass to a stop sign. Turn right onto North Water Street and then right into the parking lot. The aquarium's main entrance is across the street.

From the Merritt Parkway south: Take exit 40A. Turn right at the light onto main Avenue. Take Main Avenue for 1.1 miles. Turn right onto Route 123 North, following signs for I-95. Cross the railroad tracks, go under the overpass and turn left onto Route 7 southbound. Take Route 7 to its end, staying in the middle lane (watch for overhead signs saying "South Norwalk/Maritime Aquarium." At the stop sign at the end of the exit ramp, turn right onto West Avenue. At the fourth light, turn left onto North Main Street. At the first light, turn left onto Ann Street. Go under the railroad overpass to a stop sign. Turn right onto North Water Street and then right into the parking lot. The aquarium's main entrance is across the street.

The Maritime Aquarium is open on every day of the year from 10:00-5:00 except Thanksgiving Day and Christmas Day. It is handicap accessible.

Admission and Membership

General admission is $8.75 for adults, $8.00 for seniors over 62, and $7.25 for children ages 2-12. Children under two are free.

IMAX Theater admission (not including "All Access"): $6.75 for adults, $5.75 for seniors, and $5.00 for children.

Combination (General admission + IMAX): $13.50 for adults, $11.50 for seniors, and $10.00 for children.

What to See

Maritime Aquarium visitors encounter many marine species that are native to the Long Island Sound. In addition, historic vessels and interactive nautical displays offer a sampling of Long Island Sound's maritime heritage. New exhibits are always opening in both the main exhibit area and the gallery.

In Falconer Hall, harbor seals cavort in a special indoor-outdoor tank. Visitors can watch the seals being fed at 11:45 A.M., 1:45 P.M., and 3:45

P.M. daily. The newest additions to the Aquarium are two playful river otters named Bell and Sprite. "Jellyfish Encounter" is a permanent exhibit area that offers a sting-free way to discover these primitive but amazing creatures.

The aquarium offers special exhibitions, which are included with the price of admission. "Sounds of the Sea" and "The A-Mazing Sea" are two recent exhibitions.

The Maritime Aquarium's Boat Shop offers weekend and evening courses about the art of wooden boatbuilding.

The IMAX movie theater has an eight-by-six-story screen and six-channel surround sound.

Kids especially enjoy the supervised Touch Tank, where they can safely interact with live sea stars, crabs, whelks, and other tidal creatures. The Ray Touch Pool lets youngsters go home bragging that they petted a live ray. Special children's programs include summer camp and vacation "adventures" over Christmas break, winter and spring vacations, and select school holidays.

There is a gift shop and a cafe.

While You're in the Area

The Maritime Aquarium is in the heart of the historic waterfront neighborhood of South Norwalk (SoNo). The town constantly bustles, and has many types of restaurants, shops and attractions. In the first weekend in August, the SoNo Arts Celebration takes place. SoNo's working maritime heritage lives on at Tallmadge Brothers Co., one of the East Coast's largest oystering companies.

Harbor seal and girl at The Maritime Aquarium. Photo by Jim Herity.

The Mark Twain House National Historic Landmark

351 Farmington Avenue
Hartford, CT 06105
(860) 247-0998
www.MarkTwainHouse.org

Overview

The Mark Twain House is the three-story Gothic mansion where the author lived, wrote, and raised his family between 1874 and 1891. The 19-room home was decorated by Louis Comfort Tiffany and is one of only two of Tiffany's domestic interiors open to the public.

Directions and Hours

Take I-84 to exit 46 and turn right onto Sisson Avenue. Turn right onto Farmington Avenue.

The museum is open from May through October, and December. Only the first floor is handicap accessible.

Museum hours are Monday-Saturday 9:30-4:00; Sunday noon-4:00.

Admission and Membership

$9 for adults, $8 for seniors, $7 for children 13-18, $5 for children 6-12. Membership is $35/year for individuals, $50/year for families, and various levels of contributing membership.

There is a discount for groups of ten or more if

the reservation is made at least two weeks in advance.

What to See

The museum's 50,000-piece collection includes many person possessions of Mark Twain and his family. These include heirloom furnishings and original art. The highlight of the tour is the third floor billiard/study where Twain did most of his writing.

Twain did most of his writing and much of his entertaining in his billiard room/study on the third floor of Hartford's Mark Twain House. Courtesy of The Mark Twain House.

A new Education and Visitors Center will feature exhibit galleries and a theater. It will open in the summer or fall of 2003.

There is a full calendar of children's programs based on Victorian holiday celebrations.

There is a gift shop. The museum has no café, but there are numerous places to eat in West Hartford and Hartford.

While You're in the Area

The Mark Twain House is located next door to the Harriet Beecher Stowe House (p. 28).

Mashantucket Pequot Museum and Research Center

110 Pequot Trail
PO Box 3180
Mashantucket, CT 06339-3180
(800) 411-9671
www.mashantucket.com

Overview

The Mashantucket Pequot Museum, comparable in size to the Air and Space Museum in Washington, is a large museum that includes history, science, nature, art, realistic dioramas and immersion environments, state of the art computers, videos, and films, all of which combine to follow the cultural heritage and history of the Pequots from the last Ice Age to the present day.

Directions and Hours

Follow signs from I-95, exit 92, or I-395, exit 79A to the Mashantucket Pequot Reservation which is located off Route 2. It is only seven miles from Mystic and 1½ miles from Foxwoods Resort Casino. Free parking is available.

The museum is open year-round but closed on Thanksgiving, Christmas, and New Year's Day. It is handicap accessible.

Hours: Summer: (from Memorial Day Weekend through Labor Day) open seven days a week 10:00 A.M. to 7:00 P.M. (last admission at 6:00 P.M.). Winter: open six days a week 10:00 A.M. to 6:00 P.M., closed Tuesdays.

Admission and Membership

Adults $12, seniors $10, children ages 6-15 $8, and children under 6 free. With advance reservations, groups of 10 or more can receive group discounts. One chaperone is required for every 10 students. For information please call Group Services at (860) 396-6839. Research facilities are available at no charge to the general public. Call 1-800-411-9671 for library hours. Membership is $35 for an individual, $55 for a family or dual membership, $250 for a contributing member, $500 for a supporting member, and $1,000 for a Patron.

What to See

Permanent exhibits range in time from the last Ice age to the present and include a caribou kill in the 9000 B.C., collections of historical and contemporary Eastern woodlands Native art and artifacts, a portrait gallery of contemporary Pequots, a film called *The Witness*, which focuses on the seventeenth century massacre at Mystic, videos and films showing life on the reservation, and a recreation of a sixteenth century Pequot coastal village.

Lectures, workshops, and film series are ongoing. For eight weeks every summer the land near the Mashantucket Pequot Reservation serves as a classroom for college students who look for clues into the past.

The Information Resources Department (which includes the Research Library, the Children's Research Library, and Archives & Special Collections) preserves and reclaims the cultural heritage of the Mashantucket Pequot Tribal Nation, as well as the histories of other Native North Americans. The Research Library currently has over 40,000 titles. The children's research library serves students through eighth grade, introducing them to indigenous people through programs and collections.

Children's programming includes museum tours, which can be tailored to almost any age group. Tours focus on some of the following topics: Through the Eyes of a Pequot Child (contemporary to sixteenth century village kids), the Animals of Mashantucket, Gifts of the Land, Mashantucket's Natural History, and Life on the Reservation: 1667 to Present. Classroom Programs include Archaeology's Window to the Past: Interpreting Refuse Piles—Can You Dig It?, Life Without a Supermarket: a Sixteenth Century Native Coastal Community, and Special Topic for Teens: Debating the Pequot War.

The museum has a gift shop and a restaurant.

While You're in the Area

An attraction near the museum is Foxwoods Resort Casino.

Mattatuck Museum

144 West Main Street
Waterbury, CT 06702
(203) 753-0381
www.mattatuckmuseum.org

Overview

The Mattatuck Museum, located on the Green in downtown Waterbury, is a treasure house of collections focusing on over three centuries of the heritage of the region and the master artists of Connecticut. The museum houses a 300-seat performing arts center, an art studio classroom, and a research library.

Directions and Hours

From the east (Hartford): Take I-84 to exit 21 (Meadow Street). Straight off ramp bearing right onto Meadow St. Right at third light (West Main Street). Shell gas station is on the right. *Follow general directions below.

From the south (Bridgeport): Take Route 8 to exit 32. Straight ahead past Freight Street. Take a right onto West Main Street (second light). *Follow general directions below.

From the west (Danbury): Take I-84 to exit 21 (Meadow Street). Take right at the end of ramp (at light) and then a right at fourth light (West Main Street). Shell gas station is on the right. *Follow general directions below.

From the north (Torrington): Take Route 8 to West Main Street. Exit left at light onto West

Main Street. *Follow general directions below.

General Directions: As you continue on West Main Street approaching the Green, get in the middle lane facing the red light. On the left is the museum with its copper-clad entrance tower. Proceed around the statue to the left (north) side of the Green. Turn left at once onto Park Place; parking is available behind the museum.

Public parking lots are located on Park Place, the one-way street intersection West Main Street between the museum and the YMCA, just past the staff parking lots. Parking tokens for the lot are available at the museum (.50 per hour).

Hours: open year-round, Tuesday-Saturday 10:00-5:00, Sundays 12:00-5:00. The museum is closed Sundays in July and August.

Admission and Membership

Admission is $4 for adults 16 and over. Free for members and children. Membership rates start at $25 for seniors, $40 for individuals. The museum is handicap accessible.

What to See

The Mattatuck Museum's history collection is featured in the "Brass Roots" exhibit, displaying a variety of decorative arts objects and items related to Waterbury's industrial history. Highlights include Woodbury furniture, Waterbury clocks, novelty watches, brass buttons, early cameras, Art Deco tablewares, and Charles Goodyear's rubber desk.

The fine art collection focuses on work by American masters who have been associated with the state of Connecticut. Artists include John Trumbull, Erastus Salisbury Field, Frederic Church, John F. Kensett, George Inness, Worthington Whittredge, Maurice Prendergast, Everett Shinn, Alexander Calder, Josef Albers, Milton Avery, Yves Tanguy, Kay Sage, and Arshile Gorky. The art galleries also feature new computer kiosks allowing visitors access to images and information about the entire fine art collection.

The Mattatuck Museum is especially active in community programming including a wide range of lectures, guided tours, performances, and other events. Approximately four to six exhibits change annually. In the fall of 2001, the museum will feature an important exhibit of the Luminist paintings of John Frederick Kensett. The museum hosts its annual Festival of the Trees fundraiser after Thanksgiving. A Mardi Gras fundraiser is usually held in February. A Calendar of Events can be found on the museum's website.

Children's programming includes summer science and art camps and afterschool programs during the school year.

An acclaimed café, coffee bar, and store offer services to visitors year round.

While You're in the Area

In Waterbury, visitors can go to the Timexpo Museum (soon to open, p. 104) and in Middlebury, there is the Quassy Amusement Park (seasonal). The Mattatuck Museum is also located approximately 40 minutes from Hartford and New Haven, 90 minutes from New York City.

Photo courtesy of the Mattatuck Museum.

Menczer Museum of Medicine and Dentistry

230 Scarborough Street
Hartford, CT 06105
(860) 236-5613
http://library.uchc.edu/hms

Overview

The Menczer Museum of Medicine and Dentistry grew from the possessions and collections of Connecticut physicians. The museum has instruments, furnishings, portraits, medicines, and a library dating back to 1846 with books from 1702. Also displayed are dental instruments including tooth keys, water turbine drills, and a full setup of 1920s dental equipment.

Directions and Hours

From I-84 west take exit 46 (Sisson Avenue). Go through the light at the end of the ramp and to the next overhead light. Turn right on to Whitney Street and proceed north until North Whitney reaches Asylum Avenue. The street becomes Scarborough Street. The museum is in the Hartford Medical Society building, the last red brick building on the right. There is plenty of free parking space.

The museum is open year round, but is not handicap accessible.

Hours: Weekdays 10:00 A.M. to 4:30 P.M.

Admission and Membership

The museum is $2.00 for adults and $1.00 for students and seniors. Scouts can make a contribution.

What to See

The museum wants visitors to know that more than one man was responsible for the development of anesthesia. A Connecticut dentist named Horace Wells tried nitrous oxide on himself in 1844 to have a tooth pulled. He felt no pain and went on to teach everyone in Hartford about anesthesia—doctors and dentists alike. The museum displays several medical devices first made in Connecticut: Perkins tractors, surgical adjustors, and a blood cupping set. The museum is one of a few museums that features both dental and medical displays, and is supported by both the dental and medical societies.

Special tours depending on age are available.

There is a small gift shop. The museum has a kitchen for catering and a dining room where groups can eat. The museum is also close to Elizabeth Park, where visitors can picnic and feed the ducks.

While You're in the Area

The museum is within one mile of the Elizabeth Park and the Connecticut Historical Society (p. 101) and within three miles of the Museum of American Political Life at the University of Hartford (p. 102), the Mark Twain House (p. 48), the Wadsworth Athenaeum (p. 88), and the state capitol and library (p. 103).

Milford Historical Society

34 High Street
Milford, CT 06460
(203) 874-2664
http://sites.netscape.net/milfordhistoric/index.html

Overview

The museum includes three historic buildings. The Eells-Stow House (ca. 1700) is the oldest house in Milford. The Clark-Stockade House was built ca. 1770 and was the first Milford house built outside of the stockade. The Bryan-Downs House was built ca. 1780.

Directions and Hours

From I-95 heading north, take exit 37 (High Street). Take a right. Go one mile to the Milford Green. Continue two blocks. The museum is on the right.

From I-95 heading south, take exit 36 (Plains Road). Go left to the traffic light. Take a left onto Route 1. At the second light, take a right

(High Street). Go ¾ mile to Milford Green. Continue two blocks to the Museum on the right.

The museum is open Memorial Day weekend to Columbus Day weekend, Sundays from 1:00-4:00 P.M. and by appointment. It is not handicap accessible.

Admission and Membership

$2 for adults, $1 for children. Group rates are available. Membership is $10/year.

What to See

The museum consists of three historic houses, furnished with seventeenth and eighteenth century furniture. The Bryan-Downs House has the Claude Coffin Indian Collection and a changing Summer Exhibit. A colonial herb garden features over 40 herbs. Special colonial craft demonstrations are held periodically.

Upcoming events include the Yankee Peddler Fair (September 2001 and September 2001) and a Christmas Candlelight Tour in December 2002.

Children's tours are conducted by docents in period costumes, by arrangement.

There is a gift shop, but no café. Visitors can eat at one of many cafes on the Milford Green, one block away.

While You're in the Area

A submarine built by Simon Lake in 1934 is one block away. Also nearby are a Memorial Bridge and Tower built in 1889, the second longest Green in New England, the Milford Landing Marina, and many antique shops.

Monument House Museum

Fort Griswold State Park
57 Fort Street
Groton, CT 06340
(860) 445-1729

Overview

The Monument House Museum was started by the Anna Warner Bailey chapter of the Daughters of the American Revolution. It features displays on life in early Groton and on Fort Griswold, which was attacked by the British on September 6, 1781.

Directions and Hours

On I-95 take exit 97 and follow signs.

The museum is open 10:00-5:00 daily from Memorial Day through Labor Day and on weekends from Labor Day to Columbus Day. It is handicap accessible

Admission and Membership

Admission is free.

What to See

The museum features Revolutionary War period displays and Daughters of the American Revolution displays.

The museum has no café but they sell limited souvenirs and books.

While You're in the Area

Fort Trumbull in New London (p. 26), the U.S.S. *Nautilus* and the Sub Force Museum (p. 34) are other attractions nearby.

Museum on the Green

1944 Main Street
PO Box 46
Glastonbury, CT 06033
(860) 633-6890

Overview

The Museum on the Green is dedicated to educating and promoting community activity and interest in Glastonbury's heritage through publications, exhibits, and special programs. Themes covered by the museum include American Studies, Anthropology, Archaeology, Art, Historic Persons, Maritime, Native American

Studies, Numismatics, Photography, Social History, Technology, Victoriana, and Women's Studies.

Directions and Hours

Take I-91 to exit 25. Then follow Route 3 to Route 2 east and get off exit 7. Get on Route 17 south and take the Hubbard Street exit.

The Museum is open year round on Mondays and Thursdays from 10:00-4:00, or by appointment. It is not handicap accessible.

Admission and Membership

Admission is free. Call for membership information.

What to See

In addition to tours of the museum grounds, library, and cemetery, a few programs are offered. Special walking tours are given to groups of schoolchildren, Cub Scouts, Brownies, and seniors. Children's programming is available, with lectures and interpretations offered on request.

Every year there is an antique show on the first Saturday in August. A farm festival is held each year, and other events include an annual antique festival, antique auctions, and house tours.

There is a small gift shop.

While You're in the Area

Other Historical Society of Glastonbury properties include the Welles Shipman Ward museum (p. 92) and the Welles Chapman Tavern.

Mystic Aquarium

55 Coogan Boulevard
Mystic, CT 06355-1997
(860) 572-5955
www.mysticaquarium.org

Overview

Mystic Aquarium is the home for over 3,500 specimens, 200 species, and 34 exhibits. Some of the featured specimens include an Australian mudskipper, a giant Pacific octopus, a sea nettle jellyfish, a moon jellyfish, and a leopard shark. The major focus of most of the exhibits is to let visitors experience the ocean planet's most beautiful and productive ecosystems and how they work. Mystic Aquarium also has treated and released 66 stranded marine mammals, including dolphins and whales.

Directions and Hours

From I-95: Take exit 90. Free parking for cars, buses, and RV's.

The museum is open year round and is handicap accessible. Closed Thanksgiving, Christmas, and New Year's Day.

Hours: Doors open: 9:00 A.M. daily. Doors close: 5:00 P.M. September-June, 6:00 P.M. July-Labor Day.

Admission and Membership

Admission is $16 for adults, $15 for seniors, $11 for children 3-12; aquarium members and children age 2 and under are free. Group rates for 10 people or more are available with advance reservation. Membership is $100/year for a family, $65/year for a couple, $45/year for an individual, $65/year for a senior couple, and $40/year for a senior individual. Special renewal rates are offered.

What to See

Mystic Aquarium has many exhibits that teach visitors about marine animals. These exhibits include: "Where Rivers Meet the Sea," featuring life in coastal waters, "Coral Reefs: Oases of Life in a Blue Desert," a gallery devoted to life in a coral reef, "Conserving Our Ocean," an interpretive display on fisheries conservation, and "Upwelling Zones," which focuses on how nutrients from the deep feed life at the surface.

In Spring 2001 a new California sea lion show will begin, focusing on the ability of sea lions to help humans in search and recovery. In 1999 a one-acre beluga whale exhibit was added, where visitors can view a coastal Alaskan shoreline and view beluga whales and harbor seals through a series of 20-foot-long windows, and can also see informal marine mammal demonstrations throughout the day.

The advanced technology used in ocean exploration today can be discovered in "The Challenge of the Deep," an exhibit center conceived of by the discoverer of the *RMS Titanic,* Dr. Robert D. Ballard. Indoor exhibits include the Sunlit Seas building, which features 40 new fish and invertebrate exhibits. A 30,000-gallon Coral Reef exhibit is full of rays and other fish. The Pribilof Islands is an outdoor complex that has northern fur seals and Steller sea lions. The Roger Tory Peterson Penguin Exhibit allows guests to view African blackfooted penguins both in and out of the water.

Mystic Aquarium has an Aquatic Animal Study Center, a research and animal-care facility allowing veterinarians and staff to provide care for marine animals.

Mystic Aquarium offers education programs that are both formal and informal and also offers academic credit through local universities, including the University of Connecticut. On-site education programs teach scientific skills through hand-on learning, through theatre, puppetry, labs, and lectures. Aquarium teachers also travel to schools within a 75-mile radius.

There is a gift shop and a café.

While You're in the Area

The Clock Museum in Bristol (p. 1), Lake Compounce, and the New England Carousal Museum (p. 102) are located nearby.

The Mystic Art Association

9 Water Street
Mystic, CT 06355
(860) 536-7601
www.mystic-art.org

Overview

Located in the heart of historic downtown Mystic, The Mystic Art Colony was formed by Charles H. Davis in 1914. Davis, a painter who studied Impressionist techniques in Paris and the Barbizon area of France, returned to the United States and chose Mystic as a summer retreat to paint and still be within a day's travel of Boston and New York. He was joined by other artists and formed the Society of Mystic Artists and later the Mystic Art Association. The MAA continues today as a community-based organization, providing 5,000 square feet of exhibition space for regional artists and invitational exhibits as well as an extensive selection of classes for adults and children throughout the year.

Directions and Hours

Take Route 95 to exit 89 (the Allyn Street exit). If heading north on 95, turn right at the end of the exit, if heading south turn left. Continue straight on Allyn Street to the traffic light (intersection of Route 1). Go left at the light and continue on Route 1 down the hill. At the bottom of the hill, turn right on to Route 215 and continue straight for one block, look to the left for Mystic Art Association sign at entrance to public parking lot, turn left into the lot; MAA is straight ahead.

The Mystic Art Association is open seven days a week from 11:00-5:00. The building and all the galleries are handicap accessible.

Admission and Membership

A $2 donation is requested for adults. Membership for an individual is $25; a family is $35. MAA members are admitted free and receive a monthly newsletter with information about upcoming shows, trips, lectures, and classes.

What to See

The Mystic Art Association is located in downtown Mystic and is part of a special consortium of family-focused attractions in the region called the Family Fun Trail.

Exhibitions at the MAA change approximately every five weeks and include juried fine art shows as well as an annual photography, furniture invitational, children's, and holiday shows. Pieces of the permanent collection are on display throughout the year.

While You're in the Area

The grounds of the Mystic Art Association border the Mystic River and offer a wonderful spot for a picnic. Close proximity to historic downtown Mystic also makes it possible to walk to local restaurants and unique shops.

Mystic Seaport®

PO Box 6000
75 Greenmanville Avenue
Mystic, CT 06355-0990
(860) 572-0711
www.mysticseaport.org

Overview

Mystic has a long history of being the center of maritime activity as a shipbuilding town, constructing more than 600 vessels between 1784 and 1919. Today Mystic Seaport® is a 37-acre living history museum, portraying nineteenth century New England coastal life. Visitors can explore the village and historic ship area as well as the Preservation Shipyard and Exhibit Galleries that portray Mystic's longtime relationship with the sea.

Directions and Hours

Mystic Seaport® is 10 miles east of New London in Southeastern Connecticut. The museum is located on Route 27 about one mile south of Interstate 95 exit 90. Free parking is available. Amtrak trains also serve Mystic from New York and Boston on a limited schedule. Dockage is available at the museum for visiting yachts, but advance reservations are recommended.

The museum is open daily year-round daily except on Christmas Day. Handicap access is limited due to the historic ships, buildings, gravel roads, and stone sidewalks. The staff works hard, however, to provide easy access wherever possible and to modify presentations to the special needs of guests. An interpreter for the hearing impaired is available every third Saturday of the month and a Guide to Access and a Braille information guide are available at the Visitor Reception Center.

Hours: Ships and exhibits are open from 10:00 A.M. to 4:00 P.M. The museum grounds are open from 9:00 A.M. to 5:00 P.M.

Admission and Membership

$16 per adult, $8 per youth (ages 6-12), and 5 and under always free. The second consecutive day you visit Mystic Seaport is free. Group rates are available for parties of 15 or more. Adult group rates are $12 per person with advance reservations. Call (860) 572-5331 for more information. School, youth, and special needs groups are $7 per person for groups of 10 or more. Adult chaperones $7. Advance reservations are required. Please call (860) 572-5322 for more information. Membership is $35/year for individuals, $45/year for a dual membership, $55/year for a family, $100/year for Participating, $175/year for Sustaining, $250/year for Associate, $500/year for Benefactor, and $3,000 (single payment) for a Life Membership.

What to See

The museum has many historic vessels located in a restored shipyard and a staff that helps visitors to interpret numerous exhibits. Mystic also houses a maritime research library and manuscript collection, offers a youth sailing program to encourage maritime skills, has a planetarium that is designed to promote navigation skills, and also offers academic programs on the graduate and undergraduate level.

There is a gift store that is located near the south entrance to Mystic Seaport. The hours are: 10:00 A.M. to 5:30 P.M., seven days a week. The store is also on the web. Mystic Seaport® has a variety of food facilities for all ages and preferences.

While You're in the Area

Mystic Aquarium (p. 54) is located about a mile away. Also in the area is Olde Mistick Village (p. 103), the Mystic Factory Outlet Stores, and Foxwoods Resort and Casino.

Nathan Hale Homestead (Antiquarian and Landmarks Society)

2299 South Street
Coventry, CT 06238
(860) 742-6917 or (860) 247-8996
www.hartnet.org/als

Overview

"I only regret that I have but one life to lose for my country," are the legendary, last words of the 21-year-old Captain Nathan Hale, Connecticut State Hero, before the British hanged him as a spy in 1776. The Hale family farm, built the same year, offers a glimpse into life during the Revolutionary War era. The period rooms contain many items of the Hale family memorabilia, including Nathan's army trunk. Nathan's fowling gun and bible are among the remaining family artifacts. The homestead is located in a peaceful country setting that has not changed since Nathan and his brother marched off to war in 1775.

Directions and Hours

From the west: Take I-84 to I-384 to Route 6. Take a left at South Street to Hale Homestead.

From the east: Take I-84 to Coventry (exit 67) and follow Route 31 south. Turn left at the junction with Route 44 and take a right on Silver Street. At the end of Silver Street turn left onto South Street and continue to the homestead, which will be on the right.

The homestead is open from mid-May to mid-October. Some areas of the Nathan Hale Homestead are handicap accessible.

Hours: Wednesday-Sunday 1:00-4:00 P.M.

Admission and Membership

Adults $4, children $1. Membership is $35/year for an individual and $50/year for a family.

What to See

Revolutionary War hero Nathan Hale was born on this site in 1755. Surrounded by over 500 acres of forest and picturesque rural landscape, the present structure was built in 1776 by Nathan's family and reflects then-new American ideas in refined country living. The simple, elegant lines of the house follow the Georgian style of architecture, and the house's center-hall plan is thought to be the first of its kind in the area. A lengthy ell projecting from the rear of this building is believed to incorporate portions of the original farmhouse in which Nathan grew up. Construction and furnishings of the homestead tell the story of the transition of American life from the colonial era to the early days of the Republic, as experienced by the Hale family. There are also several artifacts belonging to Nathan Hale, among them a much-prized silhouette of Nathan, sketched on an upper-floor door. Hale Homestead was restored by George Dudley Seymour, founder and trustee of the Antiquarian & Landmarks society.

In addition to house tours, the site hosts Colonial Lifeways programs and Colonial Camp for children, an Evening at Hale in June (Nathan Hale's birthday celebration), a fall Lantern Tour in October, colonial-themed birthday parties, and open hearth cooking programs. An heirloom vegetable and herb garden add to the visitor's experience.

Children's programming includes a Colonial Lifeways Program for school and scout groups.

The homestead does have a gift shop. Several places to eat are located on Route 31 (Main Street in town).

While You're in the Area

Located nearby is the Capriland Herb Farm, the Strong Porter House (p. 81), Nathan Hale Cemetery, and Nutmeg Vineyard.

Nellie McKnight Museum

70 Main Street
Ellington CT 06029
(860) 875-7160

Overview

The Nellie McKnight Museum was bequeathed to the Ellington Historical Society by Nellie McKnight, a teacher, librarian, and town historian. The museum was her home for 61 years and includes displays of Indian artifacts, old photographs, antique toys, clothes, furniture, and household items pertaining to the history of Ellington.

Directions and Hours

The museum is open May-October by appointment only, and is not handicap accessible.

From west: Take Route 84 east through Hartford to exits 64-65 (Route 30 and 83). Bear left at the exit for 83 north; go right on 83 north approximately seven miles to Route 286. Left on Route 286 ½ mile to the center of Ellington. The museum is on the left.

The Nellie McKnight Museum. Photo courtesy of the Ellington Historical Society.

From east: Take Route 84 west to exit 67 (Route 31). Turn right on Route 31 north to Rockville. Proceed about one mile to Route 74 west. Left on Route 74 west through Rockville; right on Route 83 north for three miles. Left on Route 286 one-half mile to the center of Ellington. The museum is on the left.

From north: From Route 91 take Route 190 to Somers. Right on Route 83 to Route 286. Turn right on Route 286, and go ½ mile to the center of Ellington. The museum is on the left.

Admission and Membership

Donations are accepted for admission. Membership is $8/year for individuals, $15/year for families, $5/year for seniors, $100 lifetime family membership.

What to See

The museum contains a 1950 Venetian Glass Collection, original stenciling in the kitchen and living room, a working loom and samples of Nellie McKnight's weaving, old spinning wheels, and a 1910 German doll and clothing.

The museum has an Open House in the spring during "The Fair on the Green" as well as tours at Christmas to view holiday decorations. There is a weaving demonstration on Nellie McKnight's loom at each of these events. Each spring there are school tours for the third grade classes in town.

The museum does not have a gift shop or cafe. There are many restaurants in the area.

While You're in the Area

Nearby attractions and museums include the Vernon Historical Society Museum and Library (p. 104), the New England Civil War Museum (p. 103), the Connecticut Fire Museum (p. 101), Fyler House (p. 101), the Maple Sugar House and Tobacco Cultural Museum (p. 102), the Tolland Jail and Museum/Tolland County Courthouse (p. 84), and the Daniel Benton Homestead (p. 19).

New Britain Industrial Museum

185 Main Street
New Britain, CT 06051
(860) 832-8654
www.nbim.org

Overview

The New Britain Industrial Museum houses a collection of products produced in the "Hardware City of the World" over the last 200 years.

Directions and Hours

From I-84: Take exit 35 onto Route 72. Follow the signs to New Britain. Take the Main Street exit. At the exit light turn right, then right again at the next light and right onto Main Street.

From Route 9 south: Take left exit 27. Turn right at the exit light. Turn right at the 3rd light onto Main Street. The museum is on the right.

From Route 9 north: Take exit 26. At the exit light go 300 feet to the Chestnut Street light. Take a left at the light. At the second light turn right onto Main Street.

The museum is open year round. It is handicap accessible.

Hours: Monday through Friday 2:00-5:00 P.M., noon-5:00 P.M. on Wednesdays.

Admission and Membership

Admission is free. Membership is $20/year for individuals and $25/year for families.

What to See

The museum's collection of products include those made by The Stanley Works, Landers, Frary & Clark, Fafnir Bearing, American Hardware, North & Judd, Corbin, and others over the last 200 years. Products of the future are also on display.

There is a gift shop, and visitors can eat at restaurants nearby.

While You're in the Area

The New Britain Museum of American Art (p. 102), the New Britain Youth Museum (p. 59), and the New Britain Youth Museum at Hungerford Park (p. 60) are located nearby.

New Britain Youth Museum

30 High St.
New Britain, CT 06051
(860) 225-3020
www.newbritainyouthmuseum.org

Overview

Founded in 1956, the New Britain Youth Museum encourages children and families to explore the history and cultures of Connecticut and the world.

Directions and Hours

Take I-84 east or west to exit 35 (Route 72). From Route 72 take the Columbus Boulevard exit. Go straight through the light at the end of the exit. At the next light turn right. Go past the YWCA on the right and turn into the driveway past the Y. The museum is in the back.

The museum is open year-round. Hours are Tuesday-Friday 1:00-5:00. In the winter, the museum is also open on Saturday from 10:00-4:00. It is handicap accessible.

Admission and Membership

Admission is free but donations are accepted. Membership: $25/individual, $40/family, $50/supporting, $100/sustaining, and $250/patron.

What to See

The museum displays changing exhibits of cultural and historical artifacts, childhood memorabilia, and original illustrations from children's books. There is also a puppet theater for visitors to put on their own performances, and a changing children's activities area with construction toys and games. Recently, the museum has received a $20,000 grant to redesign the exhibit space "Journey through Time."

The museum has many programs for children. Noon on Saturdays, the museum features a free movie, and a craft or art-related activity at 2:00. Movies are free and there is a .50 materials fee per child to participate in the craft classes. All ages are invited to attend, but young children will need adult supervision and assistance. Story time is held twice daily, Tuesday-Friday. There are also preschool programs throughout the year ($20 members, $24 nonmembers) and the Family Cultural Celebration Series where musicians and storytellers entertain and educate. The museum also hosts outreach programs. Call ahead for information about current special programming.

The New Britain Youth Museum offers group programs on a wide variety of subjects from cultures around the world to American Indians, Ancient Egypt, Art of the Eskimo, Optical Toys, Early Schoolroom, Early Settler Children, Dinosaurs, and Immigration, to name a few. Guided tours of exhibits and special craft classes are also available. Group programs must be booked ahead of time.

Individuals can book a unique birthday party for their children at the museum. There are a wide variety of themes to choose from or that can be specially requested. Parties are held on Fridays only.

The museum has a gift shop and a picnic area available for small groups.

While You're in the Area

There are many interesting sites in the area including the New Britain Industrial Museum (p. 59), the New Britain Museum of American Art (p. 102), and the New Britain Public Library History Room.

New Britain Youth Museum at Hungerford Park

191 Farmington Ave.
Kensington, CT 06037
(860) 827-9024
www.newbritainyouthmuseum.org

Overview

The New Britain Youth Museum at Hungerford Park appeals to children, youth, and adults. This family nature center provides a unique opportunity to explore the world around us.

Directions and Hours

From I-84, take Route 72 east (Exit #35—New Britain). Take the Corbin Avenue exit (first exit off 72). Take right at end of exit. At the fifth light (about one mile) take a right. At the next light, take a left (Farmington Ave.). Hungerford is the third building on the left.

From Hartford-W. Hartford: Take I-84 west, exit 35 to Route 72 (left exit) toward Middletown. Then take the first exit off Route 72 (Corbin Ave. #372). Continue with above directions.

From I-91 and Route 9: Take 9 north toward New Britain. Route 9 becomes Route 72. Turn left onto Farmington Ave. Hungerford is the third building on the left.

The museum is open year-round. Winter hours are Tuesday-Friday 1:00-5:00, Saturday from 10:00-5:00. Summer hours are Tuesday-Friday 11:00 to 5:00, Saturday 10:00 to 5:00. Handicap accessible.

Admission and Membership

Admission is $2/adults, $1.50/seniors, $1/children, and children under two are free. Membership: $25/individual, $40/family, $50/supporting, $100/sustaining, and $250/patron.

What to See

The family nature center provides a unique opportunity for children and families to discover the natural world. Hungerford offers a pond observation station, weather station, pleasant forest trails, wildflower meadow, international vegetable garden, and xeri-scape garden. There are also farm yard animals, indoor exhibition area, exotic animals, reptiles, and wildlife rehabilitation center. The center has recently acquired two magnificent birds: a male red-tailed hawk and female great horned owl.

The nature center has many programs for children of all ages. Hoppers, the ongoing program for 3-to-5-year-olds gives children the opportunity for discovery in a familiar setting (class size is limited to 10 and pre-registration is required). There are also special preschool programs with weekly classes, designed for the young preschooler with an accompanying adult. This program encourages exploration, thinking, and social skills. Parts of some classes will be held outdoors. Class size is limited to eight adult/child pairs and pre-registration is required.

After school programs for elementary students are designed for active outdoor exploration of seasonal changes, nature, and animals. Crafts and cooperative games add to the fun. For those children who will be experiencing the Scientific Method at school, the center presents Nature Investigators. The areas under investigation include animals (wild and tame), weather, platns (wild and cultivated), and basic chemistry. This program will run throughout the school year. All programs have fees and pre-registration; please call or write for more information.

The center also has vacation programs for children as well as activities for the whole family. Please call for current programming.

The museum has a gift shop and a picnic area available for small groups.

While You're in the Area

There are many interesting sites in the area including the New Britain Industrial Museum (p. 59), the New Britain Museum of American Art (p. 102), and the New Britain Public Library History Room.

New England Air Museum

Bradley International Airport
Windsor Locks, CT 06096
(860) 623-3305
www.neam.org

Overview

The New England Air Museum is the largest museum in the Northeastern United States, featuring many one of a kind artifacts. Helicopters, amphibians, modern jets, racers, and airplanes that served in World War II are on display. Visitors can even monitor the Bradley International Airport control tower.

Directions and Hours

The museum is located midway between Hartford, Connecticut, and Springfield, Massachusetts, off I-91. Take I-91 north or south to exit 40 (Route 20). Take the second right off Route 20 to Route 25 north and follow the signs.

The museum is open year round, and is handicap accessible.

Hours: 10:00 A.M. to 5:00 P.M. every day.

Admission and Membership

Admission is free for children under 6, $3.50 for children ages 6-11, $7 for age 12 and up, and $6 for seniors. Group and other special discounts are available. Membership is $40/year for individuals and $50/year for families.

What to See

There are 134 aircraft in the collection, 172 engines, and many other artifacts including instruments, aircraft parts, uniforms, and personal memorabilia. The Museum's library is one of the nation's largest aviation research libraries and consists of 65,000 periodicals, 18,000 books, and 3,000 tech manuals along with hundreds of films, thousands of photographs and more. The aircraft collections includes historical items such as the oldest aircraft in the United States (the Silas Brooks Balloon Basket), a famous racing airplane (the Laird Solution), the VS-44 Flying Boat, which is the last of the four-engine American flying boats, and other artifacts such as the original page from Amelia Earhart's log mailed to her husband partway through her world flight. Newly installed exhibits on the

57th Fighter Group and Kaman Corporation have been added.

There is a wide variety of children's educational programming which includes Storybook Aviation Adventures, a program for preschoolers that ties a story with one of the museum's exhibits, Adventure in Flight, a one day program exploring the principles of flight, Sunday Soaring, an introduction to aero modeling where children build and fly a rubber band propelled delta model, and Workshop in Flight, a half-day program designed to meet the requirements for the Boy and Girl Scout Merit Badge. Capturing a Moment in Time is a aviation camp for adults, which includes a weeklong program of tours, lectures, and demonstrations on a wide variety of topics.

There is a gift shop called Wings 'N Things, and there is a café.

While You're in the Area

Old New-Gate Prison (p. 67), Connecticut Trolley Museum (p. 17), and the Basketball Hall of Fame (p. 288) are located nearby.

New Haven Colony Historical Society

114 Whitney Avenue
New Haven, CT 06510
(230) 562-4183

Overview

Established in 1862 and housed in a 1929 Georgian Revival building, the New Haven Colony Historical Society collects, preserves, and interprets the history of New Haven. Museum exhibitions and public programs explore the city's diverse and remarkable history from the colonial to the contemporary. Library collections will expand visitors' historical and genealogical interests.

Directions and Hours

Take I-95 to Route 91, then take exit 3 to Trumbull Street. At the end of the ramp go straight through the first traffic light. At the next traffic light turn right onto Whitney Avenue. The Historical Society is 100 yards on the left. Parking is in the rear of the building.

The museum is open year-round and is handicap accessible.

Hours: Tuesday-Friday 10:00 A.M.-5:00 P.M. Weekends 2:00-5:00 P.M. Library: Tuesday-Friday 1:00-5:00 P.M. Closed Mondays and most major holidays.

Admission and Membership

Admission to the museum is $2 for adults and $1.50 for seniors and students. Membership is $35/year for individuals and $50/year for families. Special member programs are offered year round.

What to See

The museum offers a wide array of paintings and objects documenting New Haven's fascinating past. From the colonial to the contemporary, local history is presented in special and permanent exhibitions all year long. Works by local and nationally acclaimed artists are on display, as well as the results of local invention. The original model of Eli Whitney's cotton gin, Charles Goodyear's rubber inkwell, A.C. Gilbert's Erector set, and much more from industrials who shaped the world are on display. Research facilities in the library include 30,000 printed items, over 250 manuscript collections, and extensive genealogical and architectural records.

There is a gift shop, and sandwich shops and restaurants are a short walk from the Historical Society.

While You're in the Area

The Yale Center for British Art (p. 98), the Eli Whitney Museum (p. 101), and the New Haven Green are all within walking distance of the Historical Society.

New Milford Historical Society and Museum

6 Aspetuck Avenue
PO Box 359
New Milford, CT 06776
(860) 354-3609
www.nmhistorical.org

Overview

Historical buildings such as the donated Knapp House (ca. 1800), and the relocated Boarman Store (ca. 1790 and now an air-conditioned exhibit hall) display Victorian furnishings and workmanship. The museum galleries house paintings by Ralph Earl, Richard Jennys, and William Jewett.

Directions and Hours

Traveling west on I-84 take exit 15 (Route 67). Take Route 67 north to New Milford (about 20 miles).

Traveling east on I-84 take exit 7 (Route 7). Follow Route 7 north to New Milford (about 15 miles)

Aspetuck Avenue is situated at the north end of the Village Green.

The museum is open Memorial Day through October and is not handicap accessible.

Hours: Thursday, Friday, and Sunday 1:00-4:00 or by appointment.

Admission and Membership

$3 for adults, $1.50 for students and seniors. Members are admitted for free.

What to See

The period buildings portray New Milford's bygone industries such as Merwin-Wilson pewter, silver, tobacco, lime, and woodfinishing. Also on display are textiles, toys, and records about New Milford forefathers.

There is a one-room schoolhouse summer camp program for children.

There is a gift shop at the museum, and within walking distance are several dining establishments.

While You're in the Area

The Institute of the American Indian (p. 102) in Washington, Connecticut (on Route 199) is approximately 10 miles away.

Noah Webster House

227 South Main Street
West Hartford, CT 06107
(860) 541-5362
www.ctstateu.edu/~noahweb/noahwebster.html

Overview

The Noah Webster House is the birthplace of Noah Webster and, inspired by his spirit of discovery, is dedicated to helping adults and children learn about the importance of history by having access to historical materials and rewarding experiences.

Directions and Hours

From I-84: Take exit 41 (South Main Street). Go north on South Main Street. The museum is about a mile up the street on the left.

The museum is open year round but its hours change by time of year. The museum is open from September through June Thursday-Monday 1:00-4:00 P.M., and July through August Thursday, Friday, and Monday 11:00 A.M. to 4:00 P.M., Saturday and Sunday 1:00-4:00 P.M. The museum is handicap accessible except for upstairs rooms.

Admission and Membership

$5 for adults; AAA, senior, and group discounts are available. Membership prices range from $10-$75.

What to See

The museum promotes and cultivates an interest in history by telling stories of West Hartford and its residents' history. Through exhibitions, special events, lectures, tours, and school programs, the Noah Webster House interprets not only the life of the American lexicographer but also the time and place where he lived. The museum offers guided tours of the 1748 house as well as exhibitions and programs pertaining to the history of West Hartford.

Children's programs serve as many as 10,000 children each year.

There is a gift shop. The museum has no café, but there are two restaurants located in nearby Canterbury.

While You're in the Area

Other museums in West Hartford include the Science Center of Connecticut (p. 76) and the Museum of American Political Life (p. 102) at the University of Hartford.

Noank History Society, Inc.

17 Sylvan Street
Noank, CT 06340
(860) 536-7026 or (860) 536-3021

Overview

The Noank History Society, Inc. focuses on Noank's history of shipbuilding, its fisheries, and its artist colony, as well as family research.

Directions and Hours

I-95 to exit 117, Route 1 North (left) to Route 215. Right off Route 215 on to Mosher Avenue; right on Ward Avenue, across Main Street to Sylvan Street.

The museum is open year from July 4-October 12.

Hours: Wednesday, Saturday, and Sunday 2:00-4:00 P.M. or by appointment.

Admission and Membership

Admission is free. Membership cost is $5/year for an individual and $8/year for a family.

What to See

The Noank History Society, Inc. hosts an artist's show every summer at the Lathan/Chester Store Museum on Main Street in Noank.

Children's programming is sometimes available.

The museum does not have a gift shop or a café but visitors can eat at local restaurants.

While You're in the Area

Nearby attractions and museums include Mystic Seaport (p. 56), Mystic Aquarium (p. 54), Denison Homestead (p. 101), and the U.S.S. *Nautilus* Memorial and Museum (p. 34).

Northeast States Civilian Conservation Corps Museum

166 Chestnut Hill Road
Stafford Springs, CT 06076
(860) 684-3013

Overview

The Northeast States Civilian Conservation Corps Museum is housed in an original Civilian Conservation Corps (CCC) camp building.

Directions and Hours

From I-91: Take exit 47E (Stafford Springs exit, Route 190). Stay on Route 190 east to Somers Center. At the intersection of Route 83 and Route 190 stay on 190. The museum is 3.2 miles ahead. Look for a sign with a shield that says MUSEUM.

The museum is open Memorial Day through Labor Day and is handicap accessible.

Hours: 12:00-4:00 P.M. 7 days a week and by appointment in Winter.

Admission and Membership

Admission is by donation. Membership is $5/year to join the local chapter of the National Association of CCC Alumni.

What to See

The museum has a large archive of original photographs, honorable discharge papers, and camp newsletters. Memorabilia highlights CCC camps that were in Connecticut, but the museum has a room containing memorabilia from all over the country.

Children touring the museum can participate in a scavenger hunt and discover hands-on activities. Prizes are given for completion of the hunt.

The museum periodically holds a public education program entitled "CCC Days: A Living History of the United States Civilian Conservation Corps (1933-1942)." The program features CCC camp foods, a saw cutting demonstration, movies documenting the CCC, and more.

There is a gift shop. Visitors can eat at Baker's Fare, Munn's Pub, and other eateries in downtown Stafford Springs.

While You're in the Area

Interesting attractions to visit while you are in the area include the Shenipsit State Forest (the museum is within the forest), Stafford Speedway, and Soapstone Mountain (with hiking trails, picknicking and an outdoor tower).

Photo courtesy of the Northeast States Civilian Conservation Corps Museum.

Northrop House Museum

Sherman Historical Society, Inc.
10 Route 37 Center
Sherman, CT 06784
(860) 354-3083
www.shermanhistorical.org

Overview

The Northrop House Museum is a local history museum with three buildings on two separate properties located in Sherman Center, the town's historic district. The David Northrop House is the headquarters and museum for teaching local history through collections of furniture, domestics, architecture, family traditions, photographs, and research.

Directions and Hours

Sherman Center is located at the intersection of Routes 37 east/west and 39 north. From Interstate 84, Danbury, travel north on Route 7 through New Milford to the light at Route 37 and head west. Or from exit 5, head north on Route 37 or 39. From New York State, take Route 22 to Route 55 to Route 39, south.

The museum is open weekend afternoons from May to October. It is open during December and other times by appointment. Call to verify hours.

The Old Store is open from April to December, Wednesday-Sunday, 12:00-4:00. Call 860/350-3475.

Admission and Membership

There is no admission to the museum. A family membership is $25.

What to See

The Northrop House is furnished with local artifacts and used for receptions, workshops, open-hearth cooking, school tours, and educational activities. Volunteers, along with professional restoration contractors, have preserved this 1829 home of David Northrop, landholder, cattle dealer, and storekeeper. His son David Ward Northrop was educated at Wesleyan University and was in law practice in Middletown. He was a Secretary of State, Postmaster of Middletown, and a Wesleyan Trustee.

The homestead was part of a working farm in Sherman and the Historical Society maintains the old cow barn, which will soon display early farm tools and a carriage in the collection. It is used for the annual Barn Sale—a fund-raising activity—an annual Ice Cream Social, and storage.

The Old Store is a Sherman landmark built about 1810 by the Northrop family and has served the town for 200 years. The Society purchased it, preserved it, and gave it a new use as an Old Store Museum and Museum Gift Shop. Run entirely by volunteers, it serves the town once again as its only gift shop. In this building is a second floor gallery of local history with changing exhibits, a reference room, and an art gallery space for photographers and artists to display local work.

In addition to the seasonal exhibits in each building, visitors can also observe the grounds, the kitchen herb garden, the town circle including the Library and the Market Green, and take a walking tour of the Mallory Trail over a bog swamp.

While You're in the Area

Visitors may wish to visit the Sloane-Stanley Museum of Antique Machinery (p. 77) on Route 7 north in Kent, The New Milford Museum and Historical Society (p. 63), the Danbury Railroad Museum (p. 101) and The Sherman Players in season.

Ogden House & Gardens

1520 Bronson Road
Fairfield, CT 06430
(203) 259-6356
www.fairfieldhistoricalsociety.org

Overview

The Ogden House and Gardens is an eighteenth-century authentically furnished saltbox house. The house depicts the life of its first owner, David Ogden.

Directions and Hours

Take I-95 south to exit 20. Take a right turn onto Bronson Road.

Or, take I-95 north to exit 21. Take a left onto Mill Plain Road, and bear left onto Sturges Road. Then turn right at the stop sign onto Bronson Road.

From the Merritt Parkway north, take exit 44 and turn left at the end of the ramp onto Congress Street. Then turn left onto Hillside Road and bear left at the stop sign onto Bronson Road.

Or, take the Merritt Parkway south to exit 44. Turn left at the light, then take a left at the next light onto Route 58. Then turn right onto Congress Street, continue as above.

The museum is open mid-May to mid-October, but is not handicap accessible.

Hours: Saturday-Sunday 1:00-4:30.

Admission and Membership

$2 for adults, $1 for children. Membership is $25/year for individuals, $40/year for families, and various levels of contributing membership.

What to See

In addition to the house and gardens, the Ogden House and Gardens offers weeklong summer history camps for children ages 8-11. There is also an annual outdoor Fall Festival.

There is a gift shop. The museum has no café, but there are many restaurants in Fairfield and surrounding towns.

While You're in the Area

The Fairfield Historical Society (p. 24), Connecticut Audubon Society (p. 100), the Connecticut Audubon Birdcraft Museum (p. 100), the Discovery Museum (p. 101), and the Barnum Museum (p. 6) are also in the area.

Old Manchester Museum

126 Cedar Street
Manchester, CT 06040
(860) 647-9983
www.manchesterhistory.org

Overview

The Old Manchester Museum is located in an 1859 two-room school house built by the Cheney family for their children. The museum features local history that reflects the diversity of Manchester, focusing on its widespread commerce and industry utilizing waterpower.

Directions and Hours

From the west: From I-384 take exit 3. Go north on Main Street and take a left at the first traffic light onto Hartford Road. Then take a right at the second intersection onto Pine Street and then a left at the first intersection onto Cooper Hill Street. The museum is on the next corner on the right.

From the east: From I-384 take exit 3. Take a left at the end of the ramp onto Charter Oak Street. Go through the light to Hartford Road and follow the direction above.

The museum is open year-round and is handicap accessible.

Hours: Monday 9:00 A.M. to 12:00 P.M. and Sunday 1:00-4:00 P.M. Closed major holidays.

Admission and Membership

$2 per person, children 16 and under free when accompanied by an adult. Membership is $15/year for an individual and $20/year for a family. Includes admission to the Keeney School House Museum (p. 40).

What to See

Besides exhibits on the Cheney family, visitors can see mid-1800s dresses and furniture, "School House" corner, "Country Store" corner, silverware and china, a pharmacy and medicine exhibit, a Cheney Brothers Silk exhibit, and a military exhibit. The museum also features an exhbit of Spencer Rifles—the first successful repeating rifle, used in the civil war. The museum also houses the Manchester Sports Hall of Fame.

In May the museum gives tours to third graders.

The museum does have a gift shop. Several restaurants are located within a half mile.

While You're in the Area

The Manchester Historical Society also operates the Keeney School House Museum (p. 40). Other museums and attractions in the area include the Connecticut Fireman's Historical Society Museum (p. 101) and the Lutz Children's Museum (p. 102).

Old New-Gate Prison and Copper Mine

Newgate Road
East Granby, CT 06026
(860) 653-3563 or (860) 566-3005

Overview

Mining operations began at the Old New-Gate location in 1707. However, mining was not profitable, and in 1733 the Colony of Connecticut purchased the caverns and made them into a prison. It was used to house prisoners during the American Revolution, and in 1790 became the state prison. Closed as a prison in 1827, New-Gate has primarily been used as a tourist attraction since the 1860s.

Directions and Hours

Old New-Gate Prison is located on Newgate Road, one mile north of Route 20 in East Granby, Connecticut. Newgate Road is about ½ mile from the intersection of Routes 187 and 20 in East Granby. From I-91 take exit 40 and follow the signs on Route 20 to New-Gate.

The museum is open from mid-May through October. Above ground is handicap accessible, but the mine is not wheelchair accessible.

Hours: Wednesday through Sunday from 10:00 A.M. to 4:30 P.M.

Admission and Membership

Admission is $4 for adults, $3 for senior citizens 60 and over, and $2 for children 6-17. Children under 6 are free. With advance reservations school groups are free and other groups of ten or more half price; half price admission can also be obtained with special ticket from other Connecticut Historical Commission Museums. For membership information please write to: Friends of New-Gate, Inc., PO Box 3, Granby, CT 06035.

What to See

Visitors are able to walk through the underground caverns and learn about the mining operations and how prisoners were maintained there. The aboveground buildings are interpreted by signage. The one original building still standing is the Guardhouse, where several cells exist and exhibits are shown. A spectacular view of western Connecticut and Massachusetts can be seen from the grounds. Next to the parking lot is a short hiking trail.

The museum does have a gift shop. There is no café but there are picnic tables.

While You're in the Area

Nearby attractions include The Connecticut Fire Museum on Route 140 (p. 101), the East Windsor Connecticut Trolley Museum on Route 140 (p. 17), East Windsor New England Air Museum on Route 75 (p. 61), Windsor Locks Walter Fyler House on 96 Palisado Avenue, Windsor (p. 101).

Old Town Mill

8 Mill Street
New London, CT 06320
(860) 443-6375

Overview

The Old Town Mill, originally built in 1650 by John Winthrop, Jr.—the founder of New London—sits on one of the oldest industrial sites in Connecticut. The mill was burned in 1781 by traitor General Benedict Arnold, during his raid on the Port of New London. The mill was rebuilt soon after and to this day still shows the ingenuity and hand-hewn beam construction of that era.

Directions and Hours

From Providence, proceed south on I-95; take exit 84N to Williams Street. Make a left on State Pier Road. Go under overpass, and make a left onto Mill Street.

From New Haven, proceed north on I-95 and take exit 83. Turn left on Williams Street and then right on State Pier Road. Go under overpass, and make a left onto Mill Street.

The museum grounds are open year round until sunset. The grinding room is open by appointment; please call ahead. The museum is handicap accessible.

Admission and Membership

Admission is free.

What to See

The Old Town Mill is currently at the preliminary stages of restoration. The mill ground corn, wheat, and other grains for the early colonists. The flume, the water wheel, and grinding stones are some mechanisms of the mill that visitors can observe.

Student tours can be arranged.

The museum does not have a gift shop or café, but New London has several restaurants.

While You're in the Area

Visitors may also want to see the nearby Lyman

Allyn Art Museum (p. 45), the U.S. Custom House Museum (p. 86), and the Coast Guard Academy Museum (p. 86).

Osborne Homestead Museum

500 Hawthorne Avenue
Derby, CT 06418
(203) 992-7832
www.dep.state.ct/educ/kellogg.htm

Overview

The Osborne Homestead Museum highlights the life and times of a woman (Francis Osborne Kellogg) who was a leader in business conservation in the first half of the twentieth century.

Directions and Hours

From Route 8 or the Merritt Parkway take the exit for Route 34 (West Derby). Travel on 34 West for 1.5 miles. Then turn right onto Lakeview Terrace and left onto Hawthorne Avenue.

The museum is open from mid-April to mid-December, although you can call for group tours year round. It is not handicap accessible.

Hours: Thursday and Friday 10:00 A.M.-3:00 P.M., Saturday 10:00 A.M.-4:00 P.M., Sunday 12:00-4:00 P.M.

Admission and Membership

Admission to the museum is free, but a donation is encouraged.

What to See

This fully furnished Colonial Revival home houses a collection of nineteenth century silver, eighteenth and nineteenth century Delftware, eighteenth and nineteenth century furniture, as well as ceramics and textiles. The 12 room home is on the National Register of Historic Sites and also includes a rose garden, a butterfly garden, and a rock garden.

Special decorations and festivities occur for a few weeks after each Thanksgiving. Children's programming includes storytelling, making Victorian crafts, and special museum tours.

There is a gift shop, buy there is no café, so visitors can eat in downtown Derby.

While You're in the Area

On the estate there is an environmental center, and adjacent to the property is a 400 acre state park with trails and diverse habitats.

Peabody Museum of Natural History, Yale University

170 Whitney Avenue
PO Box 208118
New Haven, CT 06520-8118
(203) 432-5050
www.peabody.yale.edu

Interior view of the Great Hall of Dinosaurs, Peabody Museum of Natural History, Yale University. Photo by William K. Sacco.

Overview

The Peabody Museum of Natural History was founded in 1866 and contains one of the great scientific collections in North America. The collections include more than 11 million objects representing specimens and artifacts in biology, paleontology, botany, geology, anthropology, and historic scientific instruments. Featured exhibits include dinosaurs, Mesoamerica, Native Americans of North America, mammals, insects, meteorites, Ancient Egypt, minerals, dioramas, and a discovery room for children.

Directions and Hours

Take I-91 to exit 3 (Trumbull Street). At the bottom of the exit ramp go through the light to the second light and then turn right onto Whitney Avenue. The museum is located one block north on Whitney Avenue. Continue past the museum for one block then turn left into Yale Lot 22. Follow the signs to the Peabody Visitors Parking. On weekends parking is available in all designated Yale parking lots.

The museum is open year round, and is handicap accessible.

Hours: Monday-Saturday 10:00 A.M. to 5:00 P.M., Sunday noon-5:00 P.M. The museum is closed January 1, Easter Sunday, Independence Day, Labor Day, Thanksgiving Day, Christmas Eve and Day, and New Year's Eve.

Admission and Membership

Admission to the museum is $5 for adults and $3 for children 3-15 and senior citizens 65 and older. Membership is $40/year for individuals, $60/year for a household of two adults with children, $15/year for students, and $50/year for a dual membership. The admission price is reduced for groups of 20 or more.

What to See

The Peabody Museum houses the only collection of dinosaur fossils in Connecticut. The fossils include Brontosaurus and Stegosaurus and the giant turtle, Archelon. On view in the Great Hall, these dramatic skeletal fossils are displayed against the backdrop of the Pulitzer-award winning mural, "The Age of Reptile" by artist Rudolph Zallinger. Throughout the museum are exhibits that provide insights into the cultures, world views, and daily lives of people from around the world. The exhibit Daily Life in Ancient Egypt showcases a dramatic look inside a seventh century B.C. tomb, a unique view of desert burial, and world-renowned objects that reveal the everyday life of a long-lived civilization that never ceases to fascinate.

Upcoming exhibits include: The African Roots of the Amistad Rebellion: Masks of the Sacred Bush (closing December 2001); The Search for Human Origins (tentative opening November 2001); Peru: From Village to Empire (September 21, 2001-January 3, 2002); Machu Piccu: A Royal Estate in the Clouds (tentatively spring 2002). Programs for families and children are held throughout the year. Programs and special events are listed on the museum's website. For monthly information call the infotape at 203-432-5050.

There is a gift shop, and visitors can get information about restaurants within walking distance of the museum at the Admissions Desk located in the lobby of the museum.

While You're in the Area

There are two other Yale University Museums nearby: The Yale University Art Gallery (p. 104) and the Yale Center for British Art (p. 98) Other museums in the area include the New Haven Colony Historical Society (p. 62) and the Shoreline Trolley Museum (p. 103).

Plainville Historic Center

29 Pierce Street
Plainville, CT 06062
(860) 747-6577

Overview

The Plainville Historic Center features town history, natural history in the region, and the history of the Farmington Canal, Connecticut's longest canal. The papers of Governor John Harper Trumbull are also displayed along with costumes, a Tunxis Indian exhibit, a children of yesteryear room, farming equipment, tools, and many other artifacts and documents.

Directions and Hours

From I-84 take exit 34 (Route 72). Take exit 1 off of Route 72 and turn left on North Washington Street. Turn left on West Main Street and right Pierce Street.

The museum is opened from May 1 through mid-December and is handicap accessible.

Hours: Wednesday and Saturday 12:00-3:00. Store, office, and research open Wednesday and Thursday 9:15-2:15 (call to check).

Admission and Membership

Donation $1. Memberships start at $10.

What to See

The Plainville Historic Center's displays include a Victorian parlor, the Alfred Hepworth Art Collection, the Farmington Canal Room, the Children of Yesteryear Room, a country kitchen, the Nature Room's Birdarama (containing a beautifully mounted and displayed bird of prey exhibit), a barn and tool collection, a study area with research files, and the Governor John H. Trumbull files.

Four additional collections are housed in the library, which was built in 1931 of Weymouth granite and designed by Walter P. Crabtree of Hartford, was given to the town by a citizens' committee. These collections—a rock and mineral collection, a shell collection, Governor Trumbull's collection of bird eggs and Indian artifacts, and the Henry Castle collection of scrapbooks—are available for viewing during library hours (Monday and Saturday 10:00-5:00, Tuesdar, Wednesday, and Thursday 10:00-9:00).

In Norton Park 700 feet of the old Farmington Canal have been restored.

Children's programs are offered on request.

There is a gift shop, and there are many restaurants to choose from, nearby.

While You're in the Area

There are museums in all of the surrounding towns.

Pratt House

19 West Avenue
Essex, CT 06426
(860) 767-0681

Overview

The Pratt House is a 1732 house that reflects through architectural changes the growth of Essex.

Directions and Hours

Take Route 91 to 9 south and then take exit 3. From Route 95, take 9 north to exit 3. Follow signs to Essex village. The Pratt House will be on the left.

The house is open June through August, Saturday and Sunday from 1:00-4:00. The house is not handicap accessible.

Admission and Membership

Admission is free.

What to See

The Pratt House is furnished with antiques from the eighteenth and nineteenth centuries.

While You're in the Area

The Connecticut River Museum (p. 16), Florence Griswold House (p. 24), and Ivorytown Playhouse are nearby, and in Old Saybrook, visitors can see the General William Hart House (p. 101).

Prudence Crandall Museum

PO Box 58
Junction of routes 14 and 169
Canterbury, CT 06331
(860) 546-9916

Overview

Prudence Crandall opened the first academy for young black women in New England, from 1833-34. The museum is located in her original home and schoolhouse, and contains exhibitions, period furniture, and pictures and documents related to Crandall's life and work—including her correspondence with Mark Twain and William Lloyd Garrison.

Connecticut Historical Commission

The Historical Commission operates four museums throughout the state: the Henry Whitfield Museum in Guilford (p. 31), the Prudence Crandall Museum in Canterbury (p. 72), Old New-Gate Prison and Copper Mine in East Granby (p. 67), and the Sloane-Stanley Museum in Kent (p. 77). Admission tickets at these four state museums are good for half-price admission to any of the four state museums, regardless of where or when the ticket was purchased. The commission also plays a role in selecting sites for the Connecticut Freedom Trail Auto Tour (currently 69 sites in 30 towns, with a book and tape available; see http://amistad.mysticseaport.org/forum/links/others/conn.hist.comm.html for more information). Contact the Connecticut Historical Commission at:

Connecticut Historical Commission
59 South Prospect Street
Hartford, CT 06106
(860) 566-3005
Fax (860) 566-5078
www.cthistorical.com

Directions and Hours

From Norwich area: Take 395 to to exit 88. Stay on 14A until the inersection of Routes 14A and 169. The museum will be on your left.

From Willimantic area: Take Route 14 toward Canterbury until you see 169. The museum will be on your right.

From Brooklyn area: Take Route 169 toward Canterbury until you see the intersection of 169 and 14. The museum will be in front of you.

The museum is open Wednesday-Sunday 10:00-4:30 from February 1 through December 15, and is partially handicap accessible. There is a small museum book and gift shop.

Admission and Membership

$2.50 for adults, $1.50 for children and seniors 60+. Group discounts are available by appointment. AAA members get a 2 for 1 discount.

What to See

The museum consists of three period rooms furnished according to the time period during which the academy was functioning as a boarding school for black girls. A small research library is available by appointment. Exhibits and interpretation discuss the events surrounding the academy's 16 months of operation—the social and legal aspects surrounding the controversial school, the role of racism and women in society during that time, as well as local and black history. Local reaction eventually made Crandall close the school, for the safety of her students.

Children's programming is seasonal. (For example, there is a tree trimming party on the first Saturday in December.)

The museum has no café, but there are two restaurants located in nearby Canterbury.

While You're in the Area

The museum is close to the Lebanon Historical Society Museum (p. 42), Brooklyn Historical Society Museum (p. 11), and Windham Textile and History Museum (p. 97). Route 169 is a National Scenic Highway.

Putnam Elms

191 Church Street
Brooklyn, CT 06234
(860) 774-1567

Overview

Putnam Elms is the home of the Colonel Daniel Putnam Association. It is an interesting farm house built in 1782 with beautiful grounds with special trees and bushes.

Directions and Hours

Take Church Street off Route 6. Putnam Elms is about ¼ mile north on the left. Church Street is between Brooklyn Center and Danielson.

The museum is open from Memorial Day through Columbus Day, but is not handicap accessible.

Hours: Wednesday and Sunday 1:00-4:00.

Admission and Membership

Admission to the museum is free. Membership information is available upon request at the museum.

What to See

Putnam Elms has started some old fashioned gardens which they hope to enlarge. There is no gift shop or café but Hank's Restaurant is nearby on Route 6 with excellent food.

While You're in the Area

Old Trinity Church, the oldest Episcopal Church building still standing in the Connecticut Episcopal Diocese, is located nearby.

Roaring Brook Nature Center

70 Gracey Road
Canton, CT 06019
(860) 693-0263
www.sciencecenterct.org (click on RBNC link)

Overview

The Roaring Brook Nature Center offers visitors an opportunity to enjoy the natural beauty of Connecticut's countryside, while learning about local flora and fauna. Five miles of trails meander through a variety of habitats—home to an extraordinary number of wildlife species, including over 150 species of birds.

Directions and Hours

The center is located 1½ miles off Route 44 in Canton.

The center is open year round, and is handicap accessible.

Hours: Tuesday-Saturday 10:00-5:00; Sunday 1:00-5:00; Monday 10:00-5:00 in July and August.

Admission and Membership

$3 for adults, $2 for children and seniors. Membership is $55/year for families. Other levels of membership are available.

What to See

The center houses both permanent and seasonal displays. There is also a replica of an Eastern Woodland and an Indian longhouse. The nature center has a wildlife attraction area and a collection of live animals, including two bald eagles.

The center sponsors children's afterschool classes, vacation programs, and special concerts.

There is a gift shop. There is no café, but there is a picnic area and nearby restaurants.

While You're in the Area

The Science Center of Connecticut (p. 76) is about 20 minutes away by car.

Roseland Cottage/Bowen House (SPNEA)

556 Route 169
Woodstock, CT 02681
(860) 928-4074
www.spnea.org

Overview

Roseland Cottage was the summer home of a prominent family, and hosted many of the great political figures of the late nineteenth century. "The Pink House"—still famous locally for its unusual color—was built in 1846 and is one of the finest examples of Gothic Revival architecture. The house still contains the original family furnishings, and the entire complex—including outbuildings, a formal garden, an icehouse, and a carriage barn—has been restored. One of the outbuildings houses the oldest surviving indoor bowling alley in the country.

Directions and Hours

Take 84 east to exit 69, then take a right onto Route 74. Turn left onto Route 44 to Pomfret, then follow Route 169 north.

Or, take Route 395 to exit 97 in Putnam to Route 44 west. Take a right turn onto Route 171 and follow it to Route 169 north.

The museum is open from June 1-October 15, but is not handicap accessible.

Hours: Wednesday-Sunday 11:00-5:00. Also open for the Fourth of July and Columbus Day.

Admission and Membership

$5 for adults, $4 for seniors, $2.50 for children under 12. Membership is $35/year for individuals, $45/year for families.

SPNEA members and children under five are admitted for free. Discount rates are available for group tours.

What to See

Roseland Cottage was the site of lavish Fourth of July parties. Guests have included four U.S. presidents and famous writers such as Oliver Wendell Homes and Harriet Beecher Stowe. The original carriage these prominent guests arrived in is still on the property.

A gallery has been created in the Carriage Barn. The 2001 season will feature the "Lost Gardens of New England" exhibit. This space will feature a new SPNEA traveling exhibit each year.

There are museum visits and outreach programs for school groups. The museum also provides children's educational public programs.

There is a gift shop. There is no café, but there are sandwich shops and restaurants nearby.

Bowen House/Roseland Cottage. Photo by Leigh Grossman

While You're in the Area

While in the area, people can visit the Palmer Arboretum (p. 103), in addition to numerous shops and studios. The museum is on a national scenic road and in the middle of a historic district.

Salmon Brook Settlement and Historical Society

208 Salmon Brook Street
Granby, CT 06035
(860) 653-9713
www.salmonbrookhistorical.org

Overview

The Salmon Brook Settlement consists of four structures: the 1732 Abijah Rowe House, the 1790 Weed-Enders House, the 1780 Cooley School, and a 1914 tobacco barn chock full of exhibits.

Directions and Hours

Take Route 91 to exit 40. Follow Route 20 west to Granby center. Turn left at the traffic light onto Routes 10 and 202 south. The Salmon Brook Historical Society is approximately one-half mile on the left.

The entire exhibit is open from June through September. The Abijah Rowe House and the Weed-Enders House are also open year round on Thursday from 9:00-12:00, except for the two weeks following Christmas. The museum is not handicap accessible.

Hours: Sunday 2:00-4:00 and Thursday 9:00-12:00.

Admission and Membership

$2 per person. Membership is $10/year for individuals and $15/year for families.

What to See

The Abijah Rowe House features a collection of schoolgirl art and quilts, some of which can be shown upon request. The Weed-Enders House has a parlor decorated in the Victorian style and houses a gift shop and a genealogical research library, which is available with the assistance of the archivist/genealogist. The Cooley School is a one-room schoolhouse and is set up much as it was originally in 1870. The spacious tobacco barn includes various exhibits, featuring general store-, church-, and farm-related displays and even a horse-drawn hearse.

Society for the Preservation of New England Antiquities

Founded in 1910 to protect New England's cultural and architectural heritage, SPNEA is internationally known as a museum and national leader in preservation, research, and innovative programming. Its mission is to preserve, interpret, and collect buildings, landscapes, and objects reflecting New England's daily life between the mid-seventeenth century and the present.

SPNEA owns and operates 35 historic properties throughout New England. Guides place the houses, along with their landscapes, former occupants, and furnishings, into a social and historical context to create an engaging view of history.

SPNEA's vast collection of furniture, paintings, decorative arts, and household objects—many on view in their original locations at the historic houses—documents 350 years of domestic life in New England. SPNEA's holdings in its Library and Archives, housed at the Harrison Gray Otis House in Boston, are equally rich, with over a million historic images and other primary materials pertaining to New England's cultural history.

Public programs include changing exhibits in SPNEA's gallery in downtown Boston at One Bowdoin Square, walking tours, courses on architecture and decorative arts, crafts, and horticultural workshops, symposia, concerts, tours of historic areas, and festivals. Each year over 200 public programs are offered at SPNEA properties, along with innovative school and youth programs.

Members are admitted free to all SPNEA properties. For more information on SPNEA or membership call 617-227-3956 or visit SPNEA's website at www.spnea.org

In December 2001 the Salmon Brook Settlement will sponsor a Granby house tour, showcasing a variety of old and new homes decorated for the holidays. An upcoming exhibit will feature a collection of vintage clothing, and the museum organizes a biannual flea market, held in May and October.

While You're in the Area

The Old Newgate Prison & Copper Mine in East Granby (p. 67), the New England Air Museum in Windsor Locks (p. 61), and the Phelps Homestead in Simsbury (p. 103) are also in the area.

Science Center of Connecticut

950 Trout Brook Drive
West Hartford, CT 06119
(860) 231-2824
www.ScienceCenterCT.org

Overview

The Science Center of Connecticut's attractions include a planetarium, live animals, and traveling exhibits.

Directions and Hours

Eastern Connecticut (east of Hartford and the Connecticut River): Take I-84 west to exit 43 (the exit ramp is on the right side of the interstate) and then at the end of the ramp take a right onto Park Road. Take a left at your 1st intersection (Trout Brook Drive). The Science Center is ¾ of a mile on your right.

Western and Southwestern Connecticut: I-84 east to exit 43 (the exit ramp is on the left side of the interstate), then follow the directions above from the end of the ramp.

Southeastern Connecticut: Take Route 2 to Hartford then pick up I-84 west to exit 43 (exit ramp on right of interstate) and follow the directions from the end of the ramp for Eastern Connecticut.

South-Central Connecticut: Take Route 9 North to I-84 east to exit 43 (exit ramp on left side) and follow direction from the end of the ramp for Eastern Connecticut.

Directly north (Massachusetts) or directly south (New Haven): Take I-91 to Hartford and connect to I-84 West to exit 43 (exit on right side) then follow the directions from the end of the ramp for Eastern Connecticut.

Northwestern Connecticut: Take Route 44 over Avon Mountain and through Bishops Center (a major intersection). At the next major intersection (second light), turn right onto Trout Brook Drive. The museum is 2-3 miles down the road, on the left, just after the intersection with Farmington Avenue (the fourth light).

The museum is open year round.

Hours: Tuesday, Wednesday, Friday and Saturday 10:00 A.M. to 5:00 P.M., Thursday 10:00 A.M. to 8:00 P.M., and Sunday 12:00 to 5:00 P.M. Closed Mondays.

Admission and Membership

Admission to the museum is $6 for adults and $5 for seniors and children. Membership is $40/year for individuals, $55/year for families, $35/year for seniors/students, and $100/year for family plus/grandparents.

What to See

In addition to the exhibits, the Science Center of Connecticut has a planetarium that offers astronomy and laser shows, a wildlife sanctuary featuring live animals, and science demonstrations. All programs are geared toward children of all ages. The exhibits and special programs change often so please call or visit the museum's website for up to date information.

There is a gift shop called the Explore Store. Visitors can eat at many nearby restaurants.

While You're in the Area

Roaring Brook Nature Center (p. 73) and the Noah Webster House (p. 63) are nearby.

Shaw-Perkins Mansion

The New London Historical Society, Inc.
11 Blinman St.
New London, CT 06320
(860) 443-1209

Overview

The Shaw-Perkins mansion is a historic site that was the naval headquarters during the Revolutionary War. It survived the burning of New London, September 6, 1781. The Shaw-Perkins family owned the mansion until 1907 when the New London Historical Society purchased the property.

Directions and Hours

From I-95 North, take exit 83 Downtown onto Eugene O'Neill Drive. Take a left on Tilley, a right on Bank, and then a right on Blinman St.

From the north, take I-395 to Route 32. Follow signs to Downtown New London. Turn onto Eugene O'Neill Drive, left onto Tilley, right on Bank, and then a right onto Blinman.

From the Northwest, take Route 11 to Route 85 into New London. Stay on Broad Street. Take a left onto Huntington. Continue straight onto Tilley, right on Bank, and then a right onto Blinman.

The house is open year-round, Wednesday-Friday from 1:00-4:00 and Saturday from 10:00-4:00. Closed major holidays. The first floor is handicap accessible.

Admission and Membership

Admission is $5/adults, $4/seniors, and $2/students. Annual membership is $20 for individuals. Members can tour the house for free. There are special rates for seniors and families. There is a $15 fee for using the library. Patrons should call to make an appointment.

What to See

The Shaw-Perkins mansion features eighteenth-century portraits of the Shaw family painted by Ralph Earl and contains examples of the family furniture. There is also a nineteenth-century whaling collection. Visitors can see the extensive eighteenth to twentieth century New London genealogical reference library. The library's historical manuscript collection dates from the eighteenth to nineteenth centuries. This collection includes letters from George Washington, John Hancock, Esek Hopkins, Nathaniel Greene, and Benedict Arnold.

Guided tours are available when the house is open, and visitors are free to enjoy the perennial gardens and grounds that surround the mansion.

The Society's publications may be purchased at the small bookshop. There is no café although there are coffee shops, pizza places, a lobster house, and grinder shops within walking distance.

While You're in the Area

Visitors can visit the Hempstead Houses (p.30) only three blocks west of the Shaw-Perkins Mansion. The U.S. Customs House (p.86) is on upper Bank Street. Other sites in New London include the Monte Cristo Cottage, Eugene O'Neill's boyhood home (p. 102) and the Nathan Hale Schoolhouse (seasonal) (p. 102). Fort Trumbull (p. 26) is only ½ mile to the south.

Sloane-Stanley Museum and Kent Iron Furnace

Route 7
Kent, CT 06757
(860) 927-3849

Overview

The land and building of the Sloane-Stanley Museum were donated to the State of Connecticut by The Stanley Works to commemorate its 125th anniversary of manufacturing quality tools for the American craftsman. Eric Sloane (1905-1985), a noted Connecticut artist, writer, and tool collector, donated the fine early American tools on exhibit in the museum. The site of this museum was once alive with the activity of the Kent Iron Furnace. The furnace began productions of pig iron in 1826 and continued for almost 70 years. The ruins of the furnace with its granite blocks and Gothic arch can be seen just below the museum. The museum also features a recreation of Sloane's Warren, Connecticut, studio.

Directions and Hours

The museum is located on Route 7 in Kent, one mile north of the intersection of Route 341 and Route 7.

The museum is open from mid-May through October, but is not handicap accessible.

Hours: Wednesday through Sunday from 10:00 A.M. to 4:30 P.M.

Admission and Membership

Admission is $3.50 for adults, $2 for senior citizens 60 and over, and $2.50 for children 6-17. Children under 6 are free. With advance reservations school groups are free and other groups of 10 or more half price; half price admission can also be obtained with special ticket from other Connecticut Historical Commission Museums.

What to See

One of the many books that Mr. Sloane wrote, *The Diary of an Early American Boy*, is represented at the museum with a small wood-backed, leather bound 1805 diary purported to be written by Noah Blake, who had received the diary for his fifteenth birthday. Using the notations in the diary, Mr. Sloane built a small cabin next to the museum in 1974. In the lobby of the museum is a diorama of the Kent Iron Furnace as it appeared in the late nineteenth century. Also included are photographs depicting the operation of the blast furnace during the period of operation.

In late September the museum will hold a Connecticut Antique Machinery Fall Event.

The museum does have a gift shop. There is no café but there are picnic tables.

While You're in the Area

Nearby attractions include Kent Falls State Park and the Connecticut Antique Machinery Association (p. 100).

Solomon Rockwell House. Courtesy of the Winchester Historical Society

Solomon Rockwell House

Winchester Historical Society
225 Prospect Street
PO Box 206
Winsted, CT 06098-0206
(860) 379-8433

Overview

The Solomon Rockwell House was constructed in 1813 for Solomon Rockwell and his wife Sarah. Built in the Greek Revival Style, the house features eight Ionic columns. The house is furnished with many pieces from the Rockwell family. In addition a fine art collection is on display of local families done by Erastus Salisbury Field and John Broadbent. A military room has an excellent collection of Civil War memorabilia.

Directions and Hours

The Solomon Rockwell House is located one

block off Route 44 on Route 263 (Lake Street) in Winsted.

From Route 8: Take Route 44 west approximately 1½ miles to Route 263.

The house is open from mid-May through mid-October and by appointment at other times. The house is not handicap accessible.

Hours: Sunday 2:00 to 4:00 P.M.

Photo courtesy of the Stanley-Whitman House. Photographer Linda Klusek.

Admission and Membership

Admission is free although donations are always appreciated. Membership is $10/year for an individual and $18/year for a family.

What to See

The Solomon Rockwell House's local family portraits by well-known artists have been on national tour. The military room has a collection of Civil War memorabilia including rifles, swords, and uniforms of local veterans. The children's toy room houses a 1900 Victorian, 11-room dollhouse and a rocking horse that is covered in real horse hair. Gowns and clothing are also displayed on mannequins in several rooms. The Winsted Fire Museum is housed in the carriage house.

The museum does not have a gift shop or café but there are several restaurants in the area.

While You're in the Area

Nearby attractions and museums include the Hitchcock Museum and Chair Factory (p. 101) and the Hill-Stead Museum (p. 33).

Stanley-Whitman House

37 High Street
Farmington, CT 06032
(860) 677-9222
www.stanleywhitman.org

Overview

The Stanley-Whitman House was built in 1720 and represents one of the best known examples of early New England architecture. The house embodies the style of the eighteenth century and interprets the history and culture of eighteenth-century Farmington.

Directions and Hours

Take I-84 to exit 39. Proceed straight on Route 4 west for 0.8 miles to a light at the intersection of Routes 4 and 10. Turn left at the light (Route 10 or Main Street) and proceed 0.2 miles to the next light. Turn left on Mountain Road. Head east for 0.2 miles and take a left onto High Street. Go 0.1 mile; look for a museum sign on the right. The house is a brown saltbox on the right.

Or, take Route 32 to Route 66. Once you are on Main Street in Willimantic the museum is located across the street from the granite mills.

The museum is open May to October. It is

partially handicap accessible.

Summer hours (May-October): Thursday-Sunday 1 P.M. to 4:30 P.M..

Winter hours (November-April): Friday-Sunday 1 P.M. to 4 P.M.

Admission and Membership

$5 for adults, $2 for children, $4 for seniors or AAA members. Group tours are $3 per person. Various levels of membership are available.

What to See

The Stanley-Whitman House features fine seventeenth- and eighteenth-century furniture and decorative arts. The museum offers Living History programs and Interactive programs for school groups. In addition, there is a "Please Touch!" tour that allows children to learn about colonial life from a child's point of view and from a hands-on approach.

The museum has a gift shop but no café. There are many restaurants along Route 4.

While You're in the Area

Visitors may also want to see the Hill-Stead Museum, also in Farmington (p. 33).

Photo courtesy of Stepping Stones Museum for Children.

Stepping Stones Museum for Children

Mathews Park
303 West Avenue
Norwalk, CT 06850
(203) 899-0606
www.steppingstones.museum.org

Overview

Stepping Stones is an interactive learning environment for children between the ages of 1 and 10, featuring hands-on exhibit areas and educational programs that explore the themes of science and technology, the arts, and culture and heritage.

Directions and Hours

Take I-95 exit 14N and 15S.

Admission and Membership

$6 per person, children under 1 free. Group discounts are available for schools and other child-serving organizations. There are no age restrictions on who can attend the museum, but the exhibits are geared toward ages 1-10 as well as parents and caregivers. There are three levels of membership: Explorer $60, Discoverer $100, and Trailblazer $150. Benefits vary for each level.

What to See

Color Coaster, the museum's only permanent exhibit, is a 27-foot tall audio-kinetic sculpture designed for Stepping Stones by artist George Rhoads. Toddler Terrain is a gallery featuring activities geared specifically for children ages 3 and older. Other children's exhibit areas include: Waterscape, Express Yourself!, I Spy Connecticut, and In the

Works. The museum also has a Performance Gallery and Resource Center for parents, teachers, and caregivers with information on museum-related activates and educational practices.

The museum's programming changes frequently, so please call for up-to-date information.

The museum has a vending/snack area, and there are many restaurants in the SoNo district, just a short distance from the museum.

While You're in the Area

Nearby attractions and museums include Boothe Memorial Park and Museum (p. 100), Charles Ives Birthplace (p. 100), the Charter Oak Cultural Center (p. 100), the Danbury Museum and Historical Society (p. 101), the Danbury Railway Museum (p. 101), the Eliot Beardsley Homestead (p. 101), Darien Historical Society (p. 7), the Bruce Museum of Arts and Science (p. 11), Fairfield Historical Society (p. 24), and Ogden House & Gardens (p. 66).

The Stevens-Frisbie House

Cromwell Historical Society
PO Box 146
395 Main Street
Cromwell, CT
(860) 635-0501

Overview

The Stevens-Frisbie House is filled with antique furniture. It is also a repository for anything of age pertaining to the town of Cromwell, such as town records, bank records, business records, items manufactured in town, personal effects, and genealogies, among other items.

Directions and Hours

Take Route 9 to exit 19. Turn east onto West Street. After about one mile, turn left onto New Lane. The historical society is at the end on the right.

The museum is open the first Sunday of each month from 2:00-4:00. It is not currently handicap accessible.

Admission and Membership

Donations are accepted. An individual membership is $20/year.

What to See

The Stevens-Frisbie House is a Victorian filled with period furniture, rugs, and paintings, giving visitors a glimpse of Victorian life. Artifacts include a collection of hand-painted china, children's games, mechanical banks, books, sewing items, clothing, hats, a Mira music box, and a Victrola.

Children's programming is available upon request. The museum has a gift shop but no café.

While You're in the Area

The Middlesex County Historical Society (p. 102) in Middletown and the New Britain Museum of American Art (p. 102) are nearby.

Strong Porter Museum

Coventry Historical Society
2382 South Street
Coventry, CT 06238
http://geocities.com/coventrycthistory

Overview

Down the road from the Nathan Hale Homestead is a charming 1800 century saltbox house built circa 1730 and expanded in 1758 by the Porter family. It now includes local artifacts and memorabilia of Coventry, a carpenter's shop, carriage sheds, and a barn with exhibits. Also on exhibit is a newly restored and relocated privy.

Directions and Hours

Follow signs for the Nathan Hale Museum. The museum is accessible from I-84, Route 6, and Route 44.

From the west: Take I-84 to I-384 to Route 6. Take a left at South Street.

Thomas Griswold House. Photo courtesy of Alan P. Haesche.

While You're in the Area

Other nearby attractions worth seeing include the Nathan Hale Homestead (p. 57), the Brick Schoolhouse (by appointment only), The famed Caprilands Herb Gardens, the Ballard Institute and Museum of Puppetry (p. 3), and the Connecticut State Museum of Natural History at the University of Connecticut (p. 101).

From the east: Take I-84 to Coventry (exit 67) and follow Route 31 south. Turn left at the junction with Route 44 and take a right on Silver Street. At the end of Silver Street turn left onto South Street and continue to the museum, which will be on the left.

The museum is open May-October on the first and third weekends from 1:00-4:00. It is not handicap accessible.

Admission and Membership

Admission is free. Membership is available through the Coventry Historical Society website.

What to See

The Society maintains an exhibit of historical Coventry Flasks and antique farm tools as well as seasonal exhibits.

During the year special society activities may include Lantern Tours in the fall and Christmas House Tours. (The Brick Schoolhouse, also owned by the Society, is staffed by a local Girl Scout troop, dressed in period costumes, on selected weekends.)

There is no gift shop or café, but there are many restaurants in the area to choose from.

Thomas Griswold House Museum

171 Boston Street
PO Box 636
Guilford, CT 06437
(203) 453-3176
www.ThomasGriswoldHouse.com

Overview

The Thomas Griswold House is a classic New England saltbox dwelling that stands on a commanding knoll on the old Post Road (now designated as a state scenic road) in Guilford, Connecticut. Thomas Griswold III built this house for his two sons on land that had been in the Griswold family since 1695. The house is styled in the early nineteenth century style. An upstairs room is dedicated to temporary exhibits of items from the Guilford Keeping Society's collection, primarily nineteenth century clothing and Guilford photographs. There are several outbuildings on the property—a large barn, a blacksmith shop from Rhode Island, two corn cribs, and a Victorian privy. The gardens, which contain only plants available before 1820, are maintained by the Guilford Garden club.

Directions and Hours

From I-95: Take exit 59. Turn right at the end of the exit ramp onto Goose Lane. Cross Route 1 at the traffic light and then at the end of one block at the blinking light and the stop sign turn right onto scenic Route 146. The Thomas Griswold House Museum is .7 miles on the left side.

The museum is open from June-September, Tuesday-Sunday 11:00-4:00 and in October Saturday-Sunday 11:00-4:00. In November the house is open only by appointment. The museum is not handicap accessible.

Admission and Membership

$2 adults, $1 students and seniors. Children under 12 are admitted free of charge. Discount rates for groups are available by reservation. Membership is $8/year for individuals and $15/year for families. Members attend free.

What to See

The Guilford Keeping Society has a document collection, which includes some Guilford town records, collections of family papers, and records of old Guilford businesses. They also have a collection of Guilford photographs that reside in the Guilford Room of the Guilford Free Library, which are available for use all year round.

The Keeping Society sponsors periodic archeological explorations each year. Classes are held for 3 days at the Thomas Griswold House Museum from 9:00 A.M. to 12:00 P.M. Adults and high school students may sign up for one or more of the days at a cost of $40 per person per day or $120 for the entire dig project. Skills and techniques taught include site preparation, sonages (test holes), uses of digging tools, record keeping, and specimen preservation. Basket-making classes and hearth cooking classes are also held at the museum.

There is a gift shop.

While You're in the Area

Other interesting places to visit while you are in the area are: the Henry Whitfield State Museum (p. 31), the Hyland House (p. 37), and the Dudley Farm Museum (p. 101).

Thompson Historical Society

Larned Memorial Library and the Old Town Hall
Thompson Common
PO Box 47
Thompson, CT 06277
(860) 923-3200
www.thompsonhistorical.org

Overview

Thompson's original library and town hall sit on a picturesque town common.

Directions and Hours

From Route 395: Take Route 200 (exit 99) to Thompson Hill.

The museum shop is open the first Saturday of every month March-December 10:00 A.M. to 2:00 P.M. It is handicap accessible. Call for an appointment to visit the archives.

Admission and Membership

Admission is free, but donations are accepted. Membership is $1/year for a junior (high school senior or under), $5/year for an individual, and $10/year for a family (entire household). A sustaining membership is $25/year.

What to See

Displayed in the Old Town Hall are many artifacts related to Thompson's past, including an antique fire pumper that belonged to the Thompson Fire Engine, a Vernon Stiles Inn sign, and an early map of Thompson.

There is a museum shop that features goods from local artists and artisans. The White Horse Inn is across the common.

While You're in the Area

An interesting attraction to visit while you are in the area is the Putnam Antiques District.

Tolland Jail and Museum/Tolland County Courthouse

52 Tolland Green
PO Box 107
Tolland, CT 06084
(860) 870-9599

Overview

This Tolland Jail served all of Tolland County from 1856-1968. It housed up to 32 prisoners and includes an attached warden's home which features six rooms furnished with items used by Tolland families in the nineteenth and early twentieth century. There are also displays of Tolland's early businesses. Across the street from the museum is the restored Tolland County Court House, also operated by the Tolland Historical Society.

Directions and Hours

The museum is located at the junction of Routes 195 and 74. From I-84, take exit 68 and go north on Route 195 for about half a mile.

The museum is open from May through October or by special appointment at any time for groups. It is handicap accessible.

Hours: Wednesday 9:00 A.M.-noon, Sundays 1:00-4:00 P.M.

Admission and Membership

Admission to the museum is $2/adult. Children under 12 and scouts are free. Bus tours $1/adult. Membership is $7/year for individuals and $15/year for families.

What to See

The 1856 jail is unique and of special interest to children who are free to enter the cells and experience the daily life of the "jail birds." The former Warden's Home built in 1893 is Victorian in style. The parlor, dining room, bedroom, children's room, and kitchen are furnished with items donated by Tolland families, and show how people lived during the nineteenth century in Tolland.

In 2001 there will be a special exhibit titled "Yesterday's Child Exhibit" and in 2002 an exhibit called "From Top to Bottom" (consisting of hats, shoes, and parasols) which will run from May to October. Programs for school groups, scouts, and home schoolers are available.

There is a gift shop, and there are several places to eat close by.

Tolland Jail and Museum. Photo by Leigh Grossman.

While You're in the Area

The Daniel Benton Homestead (p. 19) which is also operated by the Tolland Historical Society, is nearby as are the Hicks-Stearns family museum (p. 32) and the Art of Tolland Center. All are located on or near the green.

Torrington Historical Society

192 Main Street
Torrington, CT 06790
(860) 482-8260

Overview

The Torrington Historical Society operates the Hotchkiss-Fyler House Museum and the adjacent history museum. The Hotchkiss-Fyler house museum was built as a private residence in 1900 and was occupied by two generations of the family. The house is noteworthy as an excellent example of Victorian architecture and craftsmanship. Adding to the museum's appeal is the fact that the house is completely furnished and decorated as it was when lived in by Mrs. Gertrude (Fyler) Hotchkiss in the mid-twentieth century. The history museum (opening September 2001) features an exhibit of Torrington's history, showcasing unique objects and photographs from the permanent collection. An industrial history exhibit in the carriage house includes a functional machine shop powered by overhead pulleys and leather belts.

Directions and Hours

Torrington is north of Waterbury on route 8. From Hartford Routes 4 and 202 pass through the city. Follow Route 202 to the center of Torrington. Proceed north on Main Street. The museum is on the east side of the street, adjacent to Saint Francis Church.

The museum is open from April 15-October 31 and from mid-December through December 30 for a Victorian Christmas at the house museum. The John H. Thompson Library is open to researchers year round Tuesday through Friday 1:00-4:00.

The history museum and the carriage house are handicap accessible.

Hours: Tuesday- Friday 10:00-4:00, Saturday and Sunday noon-4:00.

Admission and Membership

$4 for adults, members and children under 12 are free. Membership is $20/year for individuals,

Museums of Tolland Annual Lantern Tour

The museums on the Green in Tolland have presented a lantern tour each October since 1996. Each year, directors from each of the museums write and produce a script, based on a local event found in newspapers of the late Victorian era, 1880s to 1900. The audience is part of the performance, meeting "real" people of the era (as well as some rather eccentric fictional characters) as they move with lantern-carrying guides between scenes set in the courtroom, the jailer's parlor and behind bars in the county jail, and at the Hicks home and the town hall. A fictional subplot is added by the writers to spice up the scenes of small-town life, and the plot is interwoven with references to broader events of the times, such as inventions, music, politics, and fashion.

The play is presented on two consecutive weekends, both Friday and Saturday nights, with six performances each night. For further information, dates, and times of performances, call the Hicks-Stearns Museum (860-875-7552) or the Old Jail and Museum (860-870-9599). Other participating museums are the Arts Center in the old town hall and the Old Tolland County Courthouse.

Old Tolland County Courthouse. Photo by Leigh Grossman.

$30/year for families, and $15/year for seniors.

Discounts are available for members of NEMA, AAM, and AASLH.

What to See

Mrs. Hotchkiss amassed an interesting collection of furniture and decorative arts for her home on Main Street. The original contents of the house include French style furniture, oriental carpets, and an extensive collection of glass and porcelain. Also included are oil paintings by Connecticut artists Ammi Phillips, Winfield Scott Clime, and George Lawrence Nelson. Five different species of wood are used in the interior trim, mahogany, birch, ash, oak, and maple. Interior decorative treatments include murals, elaborate stenciling and ornamental plaster.

The museum's exhibit of Torrington's history includes many industrial products which were made in Torrington. The nineteenth century is represented by brass kettles, a parlor guitar, wooden clocks, and papier-mache products. Twentieth century products include an Eagle bicycle, Union Hardware ice skates, and brass goods. The exhibit also includes information about Native Americans, immigration, community life, and John Brown, the abolitionist, who was born in Torrington.

While You're in the Area

Downtown Torrington Historic District, John Brown's Birthplace (Connecticut Freedom Trail site on John Brown Road), Burr Pond State Park, and John Minetto State Park are also located nearby in Torrington.

The U.S. Coast Guard Museum

U.S. Coast Guard Academy
15 Mohegan Avenue
New London, CT 06320
(860) 444-8511
www.uscg.mil

Overview

This is the museum for the Unites States Coast Guard, the branch of the military responsible for rescuing mariners, interdicting smugglers, and providing lighthouses and other aids to navigation.

Directions and Hours

The museum is located directly off I-95, between New York City and Boston. Follow signs to the Coast Guard Academy.

The museum is open year round and is handicap accessible.

Hours: Monday-Friday 9:00-5:00, Saturday 10:00-5:00, and Sunday 12:00-5:00.

Admission and Membership

The museum is free.

What to See

Visitors can walk the decks of the barque *Eagle* in season, tour the campus of the U.S. Coast Guard Academy, and watch the Friday afternoon parade review of the Corps of Cadets (also seasonal). Children's programming is available by appointment.

The Academy has a gift shop and a café.

While You're in the Area

There are many local sites of interest in New London, including Mystic Seaport (p. 56), Mystic Aquarium (p. 54), and the Mashantucket Pequot Museum (p. 49), in addition to smaller art museums, historic houses, and historic natural sites.

The U.S. Custom House Museum and New London Maritime Society

150 Bank Street
New London, CT 06320
(860) 447-2501
www.MarkTwainHouse.org

Overview

The U.S. Custom House, built in 1833, was designed by Robert Mills, the nation's first federal architect, to be "New London's ornament on the water." It is the oldest continuously operating custom house in the United States. This Greek revival structure has stood witness to decades of locally and nationally significant events. It was here that the slave ship *Amistad*'s African crew took their first step to freedom.

Directions and Hours

Take the downtown New London exit off I-95. Continue on Eugene O'Neill Drive until it ends at a light. Turn left onto Green Street. At the next light, turn left onto Bank Street. The Custom House is a square, granite building with a portico on the right side of the street.

The Custom House is open year round, but is not handicap accessible.

Hours: May-October, Wednesday and Saturday, 1:00-4:00; November-April by appointment.

Admission and Membership

$5 for adults, $2 for seniors, students, and children. New London Maritime Society members are admitted free. Membership is $25/year for individuals and $35/year for families.

What to See

In addition to the historical significance and architecturally interesting features of the building itself, visitors to the Custom House can view exhibits featuring aspects of the region's maritime history. This includes the Fresnel Lens from New London Ledge Lighthouse and materials from early America's Cup Races as well as the ill-fated *Polaris* expedition.

The Custom House Museum also holds the Frank McGuire Maritime Library, a collection that includes the personal correspondence of Ingolsby B. Crawford, New London's first customs collector.

The New London Maritime Society sponsors monthly lectures featuring local authors and historians.

There is no gift shop or café, but there are numerous places to eat within walking distance on Bank Street.

While You're in the Area

The museum is within walking distance and/or a short drive from the Shaw-Perkins Mansion (p. 77), the Hempstead Houses (p. 30), Monte Cristo Cottage (p. 102), the Lyman Allyn Art Museum (p. 45), and the Hygienic Art Gallery (p. 102).

Vintage Radio & Communications Museum of Connecticut

711 Main Street
East Hartford, CT 06108
860-673-0518
Web address
Members.aol.com/radioclctr

Overview

Run by an organization dedicated to the preservation of old time electronic communication history, the museum's display includes radio, TV, motion picture equipment, telegraph, telephone, teletype, victrolas, lime lighting, and Tesla equipment.

Directions and Hours

From I-84 east or west, take exit 56 (Governor Street) Turn right onto Governor St. At the end of Governor Street, turn right onto Main Street (Route 5 South). The museum is the last driveway on the right before the I-84 overpass. 711 Main is in the rear behind the IHC (Industrial Health Care).

The museum is open year round, Thursday and Friday 10:00-2:00, Saturday 11:00-4:00, Sunday 1:00-4:00, and is handicap accessible

Admission and Membership

$4 Adults, $2 Senior citizens, $1.50 students, kids 12 and under free. Large groups of kids are $1 per person. Annual memberships are $20 individual, $30 family, $15 senior citizen.

What to See

The museum features an extensive research library, a video library, and a viewing room. Interactive displays encourage visitors to touch, and personal guided tours are given by volunteers who know the history behind each piece. among the exhibits are industrial displays of telephone central switching equipment, a display showing how communications crystals were made from raw quartz, a standard cell display from Eppley Labs in Newport, RI, and many exhibits of Connecticut history,

Crystal radio building classes are offered for all ages. A radio history and repair class running for five sessions is offered each summer in conjunction with Manchester Community College. Four swap meets are held each year, two indoors in the winter and two outdoors in the summer.

The museum has has a gift shop. There is no café, but several nice restaurants are nearby in the East Hartford area.

While You're in the Area

Among the many Hartford-area museums are the Mark Twain House (p. 48), the Harriet Beecher Stowe Center (p. 28), and the Wadsworth Atheneum (p. 88)

Wadsworth Atheneum Museum of Art

600 Main Street
Hartford, CT 06103-2990
(860) 278-2670
www.wadsworthatheneum.org

Overview

The Wadsworth Atheneum Museum of Art is named for its founder, the arts patron and philanthropist Daniel Wadsworth (1771-1848). Established in 1842, the Wadsworth Atheneum is America's oldest public art museum, and the second-largest in New England. It was the first American museum to acquire works by Caravaggio, Frederic Church, Salvador Dali, Joan Miro, Alexander Calder, Piet Mondrian, Joseph Cornell, and Max Ernst. The museum collects works by contemporary artists in a variety of media.

Directions and Hours

The Wadsworth is located in downtown Hartford, approximately 100 miles from Boston, Providence, and New York City, and minutes from I-91 and I-84. From Springfield and points north, or New Haven and points south: Take I-91 to the Capitol Area exit 29A. Take the second exit from the ramp, marked Prospect Street. Turn right onto Prospect. The rear of the museum is on the left, one block up.

From New York and points west: Take I-84 eastbound to the Capitol Avenue exit 48B. From the exit ramp, turn left on Capitol Avenue. When Capitol ends, turn left on Main Street. The museum is on the right, two blocks up.

From Boston and points east: Take I-84 westbound to the Downtown Hartford exit 54 (this is a left exit). Immediately after crossing the Founders Bridge, turn left on Columbus Boulevard. Turn right on Arch Street. Turn right on Prospect Street. The rear of the museum is on the left, one block up.

From Route 4 and northwestern CT: Follow Route 4 (Farmington Avenue) until it joins Asylum Street. Follow Asylum as far as you can, then bear right on Ford Street (by Bushnell Park). Go one block and turn left on Pearl Street. Go four blocks and turn right on Main Street. The museum is on the left, one block up.

From Route 2 and southeastern CT: Take the Downtown Hartford exit. Follow directions from I-84 westbound above.

Metered street parking and commercial garages and lots are located within walking distance. On Saturdays and Sundays only, visitors may park for free in Travelers lot #7 on Prospect Street behind the museum.

The museum is open year round. The museum is fully handicap accessible and the theater is equipped with infrared assistive-listening devices for the hearing impaired.

Hours: Tuesday-Sunday 11 A.M. to 5:00 P.M. Open until 8:00 P.M. on the first Thursday of most months. Closed Mondays, New Years Day, July 4, Thanksgiving Day, and Christmas Day.

Admission and Membership

Admission is $7 for adults, $5 for senior citizens 60+ and college students, $3 for youths ages 6-17; children under 6 are free. Discounted rates, generally of $1 off per person, are available to groups of 10 or more with advance reservations. The museum is free all day Thursdays and before noon on Saturdays. Selected special exhibitions require an additional fee of $5-$10. Membership is $40/year for an individual or $55/year for a household, and includes unlimited free general admission to the museum, a subscription to the bimonthly newsletter, discounts in The Museum Shop and The Museum Café and on films, parties, and other programs.

What to See

The Wadsworth Atheneum's world-renowned collections comprise nearly 50,000 objects and include Hudson River School landscapes, Renaissance and Baroque paintings, modernist pieces, French and American Impressionist paintings, Meissen and Sevres porcelains, costumes and textiles, American furniture and decorative arts of the Pilgrim Century through the Gilded Age, and cutting-edge contemporary art. The Atheneum also presents more than fifteen special shows and installations each year. Many are inspired by masterworks in the museum's holdings, while others are solo shows of contemporary artists.

Major upcoming special exhibitions include: Picasso: The Artist's Studio (June 8-September 23, 2001), Images from the World Between: The Circus in Twentieth-Century American Art (September 22, 2001-January 6, 2002), and Michiel Sweerts 1618-1664 (September 21-December 1, 2002).

The Martin Office of Museum Education offers classes and workshops for children, as well as the Family Sundaes series of theater performances and hands-on activities. In addition, "treasure hunt cards" for self-guided exploration of the museum are available free of charge.

The Museum Shop is open during all public hours and offers a wide range of books, cards, posters, toys, jewelry, and other gifts. The Museum Café is open 11:30 A.M.-2:30 P.M. Tuesday-Sunday. For reservations call (860) 728-5989.

While You're in the Area

Nearby attractions include the Old State House (p. 103), Bushnell Park, Riverfront Plaza, the Bushnell performing arts center, the Hartford Stage, and the State Capitol. All are within walking distance. Nearby art and historical attractions include the Mark Twain House (p. 48) in Hartford, the Hill-Stead Museum in Farmington (p. 33), and the New Britain Museum of American Art (p. 102).

The Wadsworth Atheneum. Photo by Lynton Gardiner.

Waterford Historical Society, Inc.

PO Box 117
Waterford, CT 06385-0117
(860) 442-2707
www.hstg.org

Overview

Waterford Historical Society offers several properties that depict life in the 1700s and 1800s. These properties include: the Jordan Park House (Waterford's first library), the Beebe-Phillips House (built in 1838), the Terry Wilmot Garden (located in front of the Beebe-Phillips House and upkept by the Thames Garden Club), the 1740 Jordan Schoolhouse (the oldest surviving public building in Waterford), the Margaret W. Stacy Memorial Barn/Museum (with an extensive collection of farm implements, equipment, and other Waterford artifcts, a blacksmith shop, equipped with a working forge and numbers tools), and the J. Morgan Miner, Jr. Education Center (used for seminars, educational meetings, and pre-approved events).

Directions and Hours

From I-95 north: Take exit 75. After the fourth traffic light turn right onto Avery Lane then turn left at the last driveway on the left.

From I-95 south: Take exit 81 and turn left at the traffic light. Take another left on Cross Road and proceed to Boston Post Road. Turn left and then after one traffic light turn right onto Avery Lane and proceed to the last driveway on the left.

The Waterford Historical Society is open from June 30-September 30 and by appointment. It is not handicap accessible.

Hours: Wednesday-Friday 1:00-4:00 P.M. There are no winter hours but the society is available for research upon request.

Admission and Membership

Admission by donation. Children must be accompanied by an adult. Membership is $10/year for an individual, $16/year for a family, and $200 for a life membership.

What to See

Of special interest is the museum's collection of antique tools, farm equipment, and horse drawn vehicles.

Every May a program called "Sheep to Shawl" is conducted by fifth grade children for a one day display of shearing sheep to carding, dyeing, and weaving the wool, as well as demonstrations of the arts, crafts, and artifacts of the colonial period.The museum does not have a gift shop or a café but a few restaurants are located nearby.

While You're in the Area

Nearby attractions include Mystic Seaport (p. 56), Mystic Aquarium (p. 54), and the New London County Historical Society at the Shaw Mansion (p. 77).

The Webb-Deane-Stevens Museum

211 Main Street
Wethersfield, CT 06109
(860) 529-0612
www.webb-deane-stevens.org

Overview

These three historic houses (including two National Historic Landmarks) exhibit architecture, economics, decorative arts, and stories from American history. There are also cultural exhibits from the War of Independence to the Industrial Revolution to the Colonial Revival.

Directions and Hours

Take I-91 to exit 26 and follow the signs.

The museum is open year round, but is not handicap accessible.

Hours: May-October, Wednesday-Monday 10:00-4:00; November-April, Saturday-Sunday 10:00-4:00.

Admission and Membership

$8 for adults, $7 for seniors, $4 for students, and

free for members. Membership is $15/year for individuals.

Group tours are $6 per person. AAA members are $7 per person.

Photo courtesy of The Webb-Deane-Stevens Museum.

What to See

Murals in the Webb House depict the five days George Washington visited there in May of 1781. The original wallpaper is still in the chamber where it is believed Washington slept. Murals also depict the planning that led to the Revolutionary War victory at Yorktown.

There are seasonal changing exhibits in each house. "Discovery Days" is a summer program for children from kindergarten to grade six. There are also Christmas exhibits in each house.

There is a gift shop. The museum has no café, but restaurants are nearby.

While You're in the Area

The Wadsworth Atheneum (p. 88), the Mark Twain House (p. 48), the Harriet Beecher Stowe House (p. 28), and the Hurlbut-Dunham House (p. 102) are also in the area.

Weir Farm National Historic Site

735 Nod Hill Road
Wilton, CT 06897
(203) 834-1896
www.nps.gov/wefu

Overview

Weir Farm National Historic Site is the only National Park Service site in Connecticut, and the only Park Service site dedicated to an American painter. The site preserves the summer home and workplace of J. Alden Weir (1852-1919), a leading figure in American art and in the development of American Impressionism. The house, studios, farm buildings, and landscape integral to Weir's artistic vision survive largely intact, making it the finest remaining landscape of American Impressionism. The eighteenth century farm has been used continuously by artists since 1882. Ranger-led tours include Weir's studio and sculptor Mahonri Young's 1930s studio where Young worked on the *This Is the Place Monument* and the *Brigham Young* statue now in the United States Capitol in Washington, D.C.

Directions and Hours

Take Route 7 to Route 102 west in the Branchville section of Ridgefield. From 102, take the second left onto Old Branchville Road and continue to the first stop sign. At the stop sign turn left onto Nod Hill Road and go approximately ¾ mile. Visitor Center is on the right and parking lot on the left.

Grounds are open dawn to dusk, year round.

The Visitor Center is open Wednesday-Sunday, 8:30 A.M.-5:00 P.M.

Studio Tours: Wednesday-Saturday, 11:00, 1:00, and 3:00. Sunday, 1:00 and 3:00.

Stonewalls Walking Tour: Every Sunday at 11:00.

Accessibility is limited. Guided tours are approximately one hour and involve standing and walking around a gently sloping landscape

Local artist Jen Shelley paints the Weir Farm landscape. Photo courtesy of National Park Service, Weir Farm NHS

with uneven terrain and protruding tree roots and rocky outcroppings. One historic studio requires going up two uneven steps. Please call ahead for details.

Admission and Membership

Admission and guided tours are free. The Weir Farm Trust, private partner of NPS, offers membership for $35 per individual and $50 per family. Benefits include discounts at the gift shop and at Trust programs/events.

What to See

In addition to ranger-led studio tours, visitors can explore visitor center exhibits and view the site video or a computerized slide loop of artwork. A $2 Painting Sites Trail brochure can be purchased in the gift shop that locates spots in the landscape where Weir painted. Hiking trails are open to the public on park property, as well as in the adjoining 110-acre Weir Preserve maintained by the Nature Conservancy.

Spring and summer children's art classes are offered by the Weir Farm Trust.

A small gift shop located in the visitor center. There is no café, but there are restaurants nearby in Ridgefield and Wilton.

While You're in the Area

There are many nearby attractions. In Ridgefield, visitors can see the Keeler Tavern Museum (p. 39) or the Aldrich Museum of Contemporary Art (p. 100); in Wilton, the Wilton Historical Society and Heritage Museum (p. 96) or the Woodcock Nature Center (p. 104); in Danbury, the Charles Ives Center for the Arts (p. 100), the Danbury Railway Museum (p. 101), the Danbury Museum and Historical Society (p. 100), or the Military Museum of Southern New England (p. 102); and in Norwalk, the Lockwood-Mathews Mansion Museum (p. 102), the Maritime Aquarium at Norwalk (p. 46), or the Stepping Stones Museum for Children (p. 80).

Welles Shipman Ward House

PO Box 46
972 Main Street
Glastonbury, CT 06033
(860) 633-6890

Overview

The Historical Society of Glastonbury operates the Welles Shipman Ward House. The 1755 house is furnished in the eighteenth-century style and includes outdoor exhibits.

Directions and Hours

Take I-91 to exit 25. Follow route 3 to route 2 east. Take exit 7 onto route 17 south. Go through two lights; the house is on the left.

The museum is open every third Sunday from April through November, and is not handicap accessible.

Hours: 2:00-4.00 PM.

Admission and Membership

$2 per person, children under 12 are free. Memberships are available.

What to See

The Welles Shipman Ward House features period eighteenth-century furniture and other collections from the 1790 through the 1830s. The property also includes three barns, a horse-drawn vehicle collection, and a house garden.

A small gift shop is on the premises, and there are many nearby eating establishments.

While You're in the Area

Nearby attractions and museums include the Museum on the Green (p. 53), the Connecticut Audubon Center of Glastonbury (p. 100), the Welles Shipman Ward museum (p. 92), and the Welles Chapman Tavern.

Westport Historical Society

25 Avery Place
Westport, CT 06880
(203) 222-1424

Overview

Listed in the National Register of Historic Places, the Wheeler House is a Victorian Italianate house with bulls-eye windows, decorative brackets, and a gracious front verandah. The grounds include the Bradley-Wheeler Cobblestone Barn, with the only octagonal roof barn in Connecticut.

Directions and Hours

From I-95 take exit 17, go left to Route 33 to Route 1. Turn right on Route 1, then left on Main Street, and right onto Avery place.

From the Merritt Parkway take exit 41, go south on Route 33 to Route 1. Turn left on Route 1, left again on Main Street, and right onto Avery Place.

The Impressionist Art Trail

Not far from New York and easily reached by good rail service, Connecticut was an ideal place for scores of American Impressionists to paint. These artists brought with them world-class training, extraordinary talent, and a rare appreciation for the gentle countryside, old New England villages, and picturesque shoreline that are Connecticut's alone. Some stayed and some did not, but the very best helped to create on canvas with brilliant colors and broken brushwork what has become known around the world as American Impressionism.

Now American Impressionism can be seen on the Connecticut Impressionist Art Trail (www.arttrail.org), a guided visit to 10 museums boasting some of the finest American Impressionist paintings in the world. Visitors can discover where artists lived and created their images, along with a countryside whose beauty still inspires and a country life that still renews.

Visitors can start the Art Trail at any point they like, and visit as few or as many of the museums as they wish. Along the way, there are attractive hotels, country inns, B&Bs, and many fine restaurants.

Members include the Bruce Museum (p. 11) in Greenwich, the Lyman Allyn Art Museum (p. 45) in New London, the Bush-Holley Historic Site (p. 12) in Cos Cob, the New Britain Museum of American Art (p. 102) in New Britain, the Florence Griswold Museum (p. 24) in Old Lyme, the Wadsworth Atheneum (p. 88) and the Hartford Steam Boiler Inspection and Insurance Company (p. 101) in Hartford, the Weir Farm National Historic Site (p. 91) in Wilton, the Hill-Stead Museum (p. 33) in Farmington, and the Yale University Art Gallery (p. 104) in New Haven.

The house is open year-round, Monday-Friday 10:00-4:00 and Saturday 12:00-3:00. Visitors are encouraged to call first.

Admission and Membership

Admission is free. Membership levels are $20 students/senior citizens, $25 individual, $50 family, $100 Patron, $100 business, $250 Benefactor, and $1,000 Angel.

What to See

The Wheeler House has period rooms including a parlor, kitchen, and bedroom that have been restored to their Victorian elegance. The Museum of Westport History is in the Bradley-Wheeler Barn. The Westport Historical Society also has an extensive costume collection from the nineteenth century, archives, and a library as well as changing exhibits.

In the Summer of 2001, there will be a special program about costumes and in the Fall of 2001, the society will feature a photography exhibit. There is also programming for children.

The Wheeler House has a gift shop. There is no café but there are eating establishments on Main Street.

While You're in the Area

There are many sites in the area including the Maritime Aquarium (p. 46), the Lockwood Mathews Mansion (p. 102), the Barnum Museum (p. 6), the Quick Center, and the Stepping Stones Museum for Children (p. 80).

West Rock Nature Center

1020 Wintergreen Avenue
Hamden, CT 06514
(203) 946-8016

Overview

The West Rock Nature Center features 40 acres of woodlands and trails near West Rock Ridge State Park. Nature Center program's focus on Connecticut wildlife.

Directions and Hours

Take exit 59 off of Route 15. Go right at the end of the exit onto Whalley Avenue. Follow about two miles. Turn left on Blake Street. The fourth left onto Springside Avenue. Follow one mile to a stop sign. Turn left onto Wintergreen Avenue. West Rock Nature Center is ½ mile on the right.

The center is open year round, but is not handicap accessible.

Hours: Monday-Friday 10:00-4:00; from April through October, Saturday 11:00-3:00 .

Admission and Membership

Admission is free. Certain programs have age restrictions; please call ahead.

What to See

The Visitors Center features five interactive nature displays as well as posters, charts, and program information. There is a reptile display in the Nature House. Visitors may also tour the wildlife garden, use the picnic area, or walk on 4 main trails.

Programs include Landscaping Your Yard for Wildlife, bird walks, slide shows, nature walks, turtle and snake programs, candle making, animal tracking, Talking to Turkeys, fall hawk migration, bird house building and hiking. New programs are scheduled each year and are listed in the Nature Center's newsletter.

In addition to programs, the Nature Center hosts an annual Fall Festival held on the second Saturday in October. There is also year-round children's programming.

There is no gift shop or café, but there are restaurants along Whalley Avenue, on the way to the Center.

While You're in the Area

The Peabody Museum in New Haven (p. 24) and Beardsley Park in Bridgeport are other area attractions.

Wethersfield Nature Center

30 Greenfield Street
Wethersfield, CT 06109
(860) 721-2956

Overview

The Wethersfield Nature Center has programming for all ages, featuring live animals and hiking trails.

Directions and Hours

North on I-91: Take exit 24. At the end of the ramp go right (north) onto Silas Deane Highway (Route 99). At the eleventh stop light, approximately two miles (after the Food Bag Convenience Store on the right), take a left onto Nott Street. After the stop sign, take the second right onto Folly Brook Boulevard. Then take the first right onto Greenfield Street.

South on I-91: Take exit 28 for Route 5/15 (Berlin Turnpike-Wethersfield-Newington). Take the next exit 85 (99 south-Wethersfield-Rocky Hill). At the third traffic light, go right onto Nott Street. After the stop sign, take the second right onto Folly Brook Boulevard. Take the first right onto Greenfield Street.

North on Route 5/15 Wilbur Cross Highway (toward Hartford): Take the exit indicating "Wethersfield 99 South". At the third traffic light, take a right onto Nott Street. After the stop sign, take the second right onto Folly Brook Boulevard. Then take the first right onto Greenfield Street.

West from Putnam Bridge: Stay on Route 3 to Route 99 (Silas Deane Highway). Turn right onto Silas Deane Highway (Route 99). At the fourth stop light, take a left onto Nott Street. After the stop sign, take the second right onto Folly Brook Boulevard. Take the first right onto Greenfield Street.

Hours: Fall, Winter, and Spring: Monday 9:00 A.M.-1:00 P.M., Wednesday 10:00 A.M.-2:00 P.M., Friday 9:00 A.M. to 1 P.M., Saturday 10:00 A.M. to 1:00 P.M. Summer: Monday-Friday 8:00 A.M. to 4:30 P.M., Saturday 10:00 A.M. to 1:00 P.M. The nature center is handicap accessible.

Admission and Membership

Admission to the museum is free, although donations are appreciated. Membership is $15/year for individuals, $12/year for individual seniors (age 65 and over), $25/year for families, and $50+/year for group/corporate.

What to See

The Nature Center's pride is its animal habitats. The center is very serious about the animals' care and diet. The animals are friendly and enjoy human contact. The Nature Center also has several collections available for public viewing, including fossils, Native American artifacts, and taxidermy pieces.

During the summer the nature center offers an eight-week "Adventures In Summer" program for children K-6, where children can learn about the natural world by exploring and having fun. Activities include hands-on science, live animals, arts and crafts, and outdoor activities such as hiking and swimming. Children's programming is offered at all times and for all ages.

There is a gift shop. Visitors can eat at restaurants on Route 99 (Silas Deane Highway), which is a major business thoroughfare.

While You're in the Area

The Wadsworth Athenaeum (p. 88), the Lutz Children's Museum (p. 102), the Connecticut Audobon Society at Glastonbury (p. 100), Northwest Park, the Hungerford Outlook Environment Center, the Connecticut Science Museum (p. 76), Westmore Park, the Roaring Brook Nature Center (p. 73), and the Somers Indian Museum (p. 103) are located nearby.

William Benton Museum of Art

University of Connecticut campus
245 Glenbrook Road
Storrs, CT 06269
(860) 486-4520
www.Benton.Uconn.edu

Overview

The William Benton Museum is the state's art museum and one of its best-kept secrets, located at the heart of the University of Connecticut campus at Storrs. Each year a dozen changing exhibitions are presented. The collection numbers more than 4,000 works of art from the sixteenth century to the present.

Directions and Hours

From Hartford: Take I-84 east to exit 68, Route 195. Take Route 195 south for 6.5 miles.

From Norwich and New London: Take Route 32 north to Willimantic, then Route 195 north to Storrs.

The museum is open year round, and is handicap accessible.

Hours: Tuesday-Friday 10:00-4:30; Saturday and Sunday 1:00-4:30.

Admission and Membership

Admission is free. Members receive many benefits including information about Museum activities, invitations to special events and opening receptions, travel opportunities, "Looking Around" (a quarterly arts calendar), and a discount in the Museum Shop. Membership Categories are Student, $10; Single, $20; Double, $30; Supporting, $60; Contributing, $125; Sustaining, $250; Patron, $500; Donor, $1,000 or more. Each level of membership offers a special range of additional benefits.

What to See

Special pieces in the collection include works by Mary Cassatt, Thomas Hart Benton, Rembrandt Peale, George Braque, and Reginald Marsh. (Note that some of these works are not always available for viewing.)

Ongoing education programs are offered for children and adults.

The Museum Shop offers a unique selection of gifts for adults and children including jewelry, books, stationery, sculptures. and art items. There is no café, but there are numerous restaurants on campus including Jonathan's and the Nutmeg Grills in the Student Union.

While You're in the Area

Other nearby museums include the Natural History Museum (p. 101) on the Storrs campus and the Ballard Puppetry Museum (p. 3) on the Mansfield campus.

Wilton Historical Society

224 Danbury Road
Wilton, CT 06897
(203) 762-7257

Overview

The Wilton Historical Society offers two eighteenth century houses with 11 period rooms that show the evolution of style from 1740 to the 1900s. Several special collections, a nineteenth century barn that displays woodworking tools and farm implements, and a working blacksmith shop can also be explored.

Directions and Hours

From the Merritt Parkway: Take exit 39B. The historical society is 5 miles north.

From I-84: Take exit 3. The historical society will be 12 miles south.

From I-95: Take exit 15. The historical society will be 8 miles north.

The museum is open year round Monday-Thursday 10:00-4:00; Sunday 1:00-4:00 when special exhibits are running.

Admission and Membership

$4. for adults. No restrictions for admission. Group discounts are available.

What to See

The museum consists of two eighteenth century houses that house collections of dolls, toys, and dollhouses. There is also a large collection of costumes and textiles as well as a ceramics collection with an emphasis on Norwalk Redware and

Stoneware. The period rooms are historically accurate—the original paint colors have been replicated, period wallpaper designs reproduced, and the rooms decorated with period appropriate accessories.

From December to February each year collectors loan dolls, toys, and dollhouses to the historical society along with an electric train. Special exhibits are planned; please call for details.

Children's programming is done in conjunction with local schools.

The houses have no café, but Orem's Diner is located nearby, as well as the Wilton Center, which provides visitors with numerous dining options.

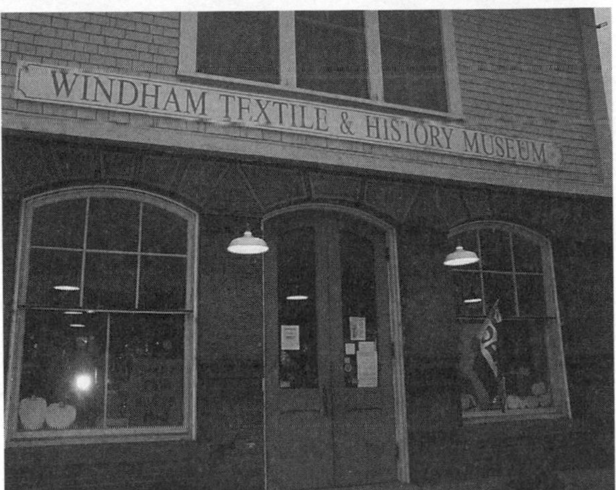

Windham Textile and History Museum. Photo by Leigh Grossman.

While You're in the Area

Nearby attractions and museums include the Weir Farm National Historic Site (p. 91), the Keeler Tavern Museum (p. 39), the Aldrich Museum of Contemporary Art (p. 100), the Wilton Historical Society and Heritage Museum (p. 96), the Woodcock Nature Center (p. 104), the Charles Ives Center for the Arts (p. 100), the Danbury Railway Museum (p. 101), the Danbury Museum and Historical Society (p. 101), the Military Museum of Southern New England (p. 102), the Lockwood-Mathews Mansion Museum (p. 102), the Maritime Aquarium at Norwalk (p. 46), and the Stepping Stones Museum for Children (p. 80).

Windham Textile and History Museum—"The Mill Museum"

157 Union and Main Street
Willimantic, CT 06226
(860) 456-2178

Overview

The Windham Textile and History Museum is located in an architecturally distinct mill building, and across the street from a restored mill complex. Visitors learn about New England's waterpowered textile industry in one of the state's most impressive industrial sites.

Directions and Hours

From Hartford: Take 84 east to 384. Get off at the Route 6 exit and follow Route 6 to route 66. This will lead you to Main Street in Willimantic.

From South/North: Take Route 32 to Willimantic to Route 66. Once you are on Main Street in Willimantic the museum is located across the street from the granite mills.

The museum is open year round, and is handicap accessible. There is a small gift shop.

Summer hours (May through October): Thursday-Sunday 1 P.M. to 4:30 P.M..

Winter hours (November through April): Friday-Sunday 1 P.M. to 4 P.M.

Admission and Membership

$4 for adults, Students/seniors $2. Membership is $15/year for individuals, $25/year for families. Group discounts are available.

What to See

The Windham Textile and History Museum includes the Dunham Hall Library which was built by the thread mill for the benefit of its immigrant workforce and the community at large. There is a large collection of antique sewing machines, including many rare and specialized models. There are also rotating exhibits on local history and industry in the main hall.

The museum has regular children's programming which includes crafts, reenactments, summer activities, and holiday events.

The museum has a gift shop, which sells books, fabric, clothing, and other items related to "Thread City's" textile-driven heritage. Five doors down from the museum is the Mill Café, where the visitor can get coffee, sandwiches, soup, etc.

While You're in the Area

The museum is within easy driving distance of the Prudence Crandall Museum (p. 72) and the Lebanon Historical Society (p. 42).

Windsor Historical Society

96 Palisado Avenue
Windsor, CT 06095
(860) 688-3813
www.historicalsocietyct.com/windsor/

Overview

The Windsor Historical Society allows visitors to enter the early days of America's heritage with the 1756 John and Sarah Strong House and the 1765 Dr. Hezekiah Chaffee House. Both houses have furnishings from the seventeenth, eighteenth, and nineteenth centuries. The society has a hands-on learning center where visitors can milk a cow, cook a colonial meal, and more. The family history library is visited by patrons nationwide.

Directions and Hours

From I-91: Take exit 37 and turn east to the center of town. Take Route 159 north into the Historic District and turn right on North Meadow Road. The society is on the corner, opposite the historic 1794 First Church, just across the Farmington River Bridge. Drive into the parking lot and ring the doorbell. Park on the street or in small parking lot in rear. The society is open year-round but is closed on major holidays. It is partially handicap accessible.

Hours: 10:00 A.M. to 4:00 P.M. Tuesday through Saturday.

Admission and Membership

Adults $3, students $1, members free. Membership costs range from $18-$405.

What to See

The Hands-on-History Learning Center allows families to go to school in the nineteenth century, drive a horse-drawn wagon, milk a cow, churn cream into butter, and to cook a colonial meal and serve it on period plates while wearing period costumes. Families can also sniff spices imported from the West Indies, build a brick wall, and design a stained-glass window. The society has a Windsor history gallery, ca. 1633-1920, and three changing exhibit galleries.

The society offers programs for scout troops, as well as for public and private schools.

There is a gift shop. A café (Bart's) is located within walking distance on Route 159.

While You're in the Area

Other places to visit while in the area include the Oliver Ellsworth Homestead (p. 103), the Windsor Riverwalk, and Northwest Park.

Yale Center for British Art

1080 Chapel Street
New Haven, CT 06520
(203) 432-2800
www.yale.edu/ycba

Overview

The Yale Center for British Art is the largest and most comprehensive collection of British art outside the United Kingdom, housing about 1,500 paintings, 30,000 prints, and 2,000 drawings. The gift of Paul Mellon to Yale University, the museum and its collections of paintings, sculpture, prints, drawings, and rare books are houses in an award-winning building designed by Louis I. Kahn. The collection relates the story of the development of English art from the Elizabethan period to the present.

Directions and Hours

From I-91 and I-95: Take the Downtown New Haven exit onto 34 west. Take exit 3 and turn right at the first stoplight onto York Street. Proceed 2½ blocks to the British Art Center parking lot on the right. Parking is available for a small fee. The Center is also near the Metro North train station.

The Center is open year-round and is handicap accessible.

Hours: Tuesday-Saturday 10:00 A.M. to 5:00 P.M., Sunday 12:00-5:00 P.M. Closed Mondays and major holidays.

Admission and Membership

Admission is free. School group tours are 45-60 minutes in length. Reservations should be made four weeks in advance. Groups can visit the Center without a guided tour, but please register two weeks in advance to avoid conflicts. Chaperones must accompany students at all times. For membership cost please call (203) 432-9658.

What to See

The principal schools and masters of British art from Tudor times to the present are featured with notable holdings from the eighteenth and nineteenth century, including works by William Hogarth, Thomas Gainsborough, Joshua Reynolds, J.M.W. Turner, John Constable, and Richard Parkes Bonington. In addition continental European and American artists who worked in Britain for extended periods are represented: Peter Paul Rubens, Anthony Van Dyck, John Singleton Copley, Antonio Canaletto, and James Abbott MacNeil Whistler, among others. Increasingly the center collects and exhibits twentieth century and contemporary British art. For example, the museum includes impressive holdings by the Camden Town and Bloomsbury groups, as well as large-scale works by living artists such as Damien Hirst and Rachel Whiteread.

The extensive holdings of both the Department of Prints and Drawings and the Department of Rare Books may be consulted by prior appointment in the Study Room.

The Yale Center offers a changing schedule of exhibitions throughout the year, as well as a wide range of free public programs including films, concerts, lectures, and gallery talks. In addition to serving as a public art museum, the Yale Center functions as a resource for scholarly research and participates actively in the academic programs of Yale University.

The Yale Center for British art has children's programming which includes guided thematic tours of paintings and sculptures and can work with education staff to design tours to meet specific needs. Tours for small groups can also take place in the collections of prints, drawings, and rare books.

There is a gift shop. There are numerous cafés and restaurants located a few feet from the museum.

While You're in the Area

Other interesting attractions nearby include the Yale University Art Gallery (p. 104) and the Peabody Museum (p. 69).

Other Museums in Connecticut

Name	Phone	Town
Academy Hall Museum	860-563-6704	Rocky Hill
Adams Schoolhouse	203-261-2090	Easton
Anguilla Gallery	860-535-4399	Stonington
Akus Gallery at Eastern Connecticut State University	860-465-4659	Willimantic
Aldrich Museum of Contemporary Art	203-438-4519	Ridgefield
Allis-Bushnell House and Museum	203-245-4567	Madison
Amasa Day House	860-247-8996	Moodus
American Radio Relay League/Museum of Amateur Radio	860-594-0200	Newington
Artworks Gallery	860-247-3522	Hartford
Atrium Gallery (Quinebaug Valley Community College)	860-774-1130	Danielson
Atrium Gallery at the University of Connecticut	860-486-3930	Storrs
Bellamy-Ferriday House and Garden	203-266-7596	Bethlehem
Bethel Firefighters Museum	203-794-8500	Bethel
Betts-Sturgess Blackmar Museum	203-762-7257	Wilton
Bittersweet Farm	203-488-4689	Branford
Blacksmith Shop and Schoolhouse	860-569-0166	East Hartford
Boothe Memorial Park and Museum	203-381-2046	Stratford
Brick School House	860-742-1419	Coventry
Chaplin Museum	860-455-9209	Chaplin
Charles Ives Birthplace	203-743-5200	Danbury
Charles Ives Center for the Arts	203-837-9226	Danbury
Charter Oak Cultural Center	860-249-1207	Hartford
Chartier Gallery	860-779-1104	Brooklyn
Cheney Homestead	860-643-5588	Manchester
Children's Museum of Hartford	203-236-2961	West Hartford
City Pier	860-447-5270	New London
Connecticut Audubon Center of Glastonbury	860-633-8402	Glastonbury
Connecticut Audubon Society	203-259-6305	Fairfield
Connecticut Audubon Birdcraft Museum	203-259-0416	Fairfield
Connecticut Antique Machinery Association	203-927-0050	Kent
Connecticut Children's Museum	203-562-5437	New Haven

Connecticut College Arboretum . . . . .860-439-5020 . . . . . .New London
Connecticut Fireman's Historical Society Museum . . . . .860-649-9436 . . . . . . .Manchester
Connecticut Fire Museum . . . . .860-623-4732 . . . . . .East Windsor
Connecticut Sports Museum and Hall of Fame . . . . .860- 724-4918 . . . . .Hartford
Connecticut State Museum of Natural History at UConn . . .860-486-4460 . . . . .Mansfield
Connecticut Historical Society Museum . . . . .860-236-5621 . . . . .Hartford
Connecticut Resources Recovery Authority . . . . .860-247-4280 . . . . .Hartford
County Historical Society . . . . .203-790-9277 . . . . .Danbury
Cummings Art Center . . . . .860-439-2740 . . . . . . .New Lodon
Danbury Muscum and Historical Society . . . . .203-743-5200 . . . . .Danbury
Danbury Railway Museum . . . . .203-778-8337 . . . . .Danbury
Danbury Scott-Fanton Museum . . . . .203-743-5200 . . . . .Danbury
Danielson Art Museum . . . . .860-774-4215 . . . . .Danielson
Day-Lewis Museum . . . . .860-678-1645 . . . . . . .Farmington
Denison Society . . . . .860-536-9248 . . . . .Mystic
Derrin House . . . . .860-678-7621 . . . . .Avon
Discovery Museum,The . . . . .203-372-3521 . . . . .Bridgeport
Dudley Farm Museum . . . . .203-457-0770 . . . . .Guilford
East Haddam Historical Museum . . . . .860-873-8144 . . . . . .East Haddam
East Lyme Art League . . . . .860-739-3263 . . . . .Niantic
Ebenezer Avery House . . . . .860-446-9257 . . . . .Groton
Edward E. King Museum . . . . .860-289-6429 . . . . . .East Hartford
Edward Waldo House . . . . .860-456-0708 . . . . .Scotland
Eli Whitney Museum . . . . .203-777-1833 . . . . .Hamden
Eliot Beardsley Homestead . . . . .203-261-1383 . . . . .Monroe
Enoch Kelsey House . . . . .860-666-7118 . . . . .Newington
Essex Steam Train & Riverboat . . . . .860-767-0103 . . . . .Essex
Farm Implement Museum . . . . .860-242-1130 . . . . .Bloomfield
Farmington Valley Arts Center . . . . .203-678-1867 . . . . .Avon
Fenton River Gallery . . . . .860-429-3646 . . . . .Willington
Fire Museum . . . . .203-649-9436 . . . . . . .Manchester
Flanders Nature Center and Land Trust . . . . .203-263-3711 . . . . .Woodbury
Fyler House . . . . .860-688-3813 . . . . .Windsor
Garbage Museum, The . . . . .203-381-9571 . . . . .Stratford
General David Humphreys House .203-735-1908 . . . . .Derby
General William Hart House . . . . .860-388-2622 . . . . . .Old Saybrook
Gillette Castle State Park . . . . .860-526-2336 . . . . . .East Haddam
Glebe House Museum . . . . .203-263-2855 . . . . .Woodbury
Greenwich Arts Center . . . . .203-622-3998 . . . . .Greenwich
Haight Wine Education Center . . . . .800-577-9463 . . . . .Mystic
Harrison House . . . . .203-488-4828 . . . . .Branford
Hartford Exhibit, The . . . . .860-278-2044 x295 . . . . .Hartford
Hartford Steam Boiler . . . . .860-722-5175 . . . . .Hartford
Hitchcock Museum . . . . .860-738-4950 . . . . .Riverton
Horse Cavalry Museum . . . . .203-528-8882 . . . . .Avon

Housatonic Museum of Art .... .203-332-5000 .... .Bridgeport
Hoyt-Barnum House .... .203-329-1183 .... .Stamford
Huguenot House .... .860-569-0166 ...... .East Hartford
Hurlbut-Dunham House .... .860-529-7656 .... .Wethersfield
Hurlbutt Street Schoolhouse .... .203-762-7275 .... .Wilton
Hygienc Galleries .... .860-442-4020 ...... .New London
IMAX Theater .... .203-852-0700 .... .Norwalk
Institute for American Indian Studies .... .860-868-0518 .... .Washington
Jabez Smith House .... .860-445-6689 .... .Groton
Jillson House Museum .... .860-423-3857 .... .South Windham
John Stanton House .... .860-669-2132 .... .Clinton
Joshua Hempstead House .... .860-443-7949 ...... .New London
Judson House and Museum .... .203-378-0630 .... .Stratford
Kellogg-Eddy House .... .860-666-7118 .... .Newington
King House Museum .... .860-668-5256 .... .Suffield
Lebanon Art Gallery .... .860-886-2477 .... .Lebanon
Leffingwell House Historic Museum .... .860-889-9440 .... .Norwich
Litchfield Historical Society Museum .... .860-567-4501 .... .Litchfield
Living Museum of Avon .... .860-678-7621 .... .Avon
Lock 12 Historical Park Museum .... .203-272-7923 .... .Chesire
Lockwood-Mathews Mansion Museum .... .203-838-9799 .... .Norwalk
Lonetown Farm Museum .... .203-938-9095 .... .Redding
Lutz Children's Museum .... .860-643-0949 .... .Manchester
Lyme Academy of Fiine Arts, Art School and Gallery ...... .860-434-5232 .... .Old Lyme
Manchester Historical Museum .... .203-647-9983 .... .Manchester
Maple Sugar House and Tobacco Cultural Museum .... .860-285-1888 .... .Windsor
Matthew Curtiss House .... .203-426-5937 .... .Newtown
McLean Game Refuge .... .860-653-7869 .... .Simsbury
Middlesex County Historical Society .... .860-346-0746 ...... .Middletown
Military Museum of Southern New England .... .203-790-9277 .... .Danbury
Millstone Information and Science Center .... .860-691-4670 .... .Niantic
Monroe Historical Society .... .203-261-1383 .... .Monroe
Monte Cristo Cottage .... .860-443-0051 ...... .New London
Mr. Seward's Museum of Curiosities .... .860-522-6766 .... .Hartford
Museum of American Political Life .... .860-768-4090 ..... .West Hartford
Museum of Connecticut History .... .203-566-3056 .... .Hartford
Museum of Fife & Drum .... .860-767-2237 .... .Ivoryton
Nathan Hale Schoolhouse .... .860-443-7949 ...... .New London
Nathan Lester House .... .860-464-8662 .... .Gales Ferry
National Helicopter Museum .... .203-375-5766 .... .Stratford
NCTC Art Gallery .... .203-857-7000 .... .Norwalk
New Britain Museum of American Art .... .860-229-0257 .... .New Britain
New Canaan Historical Society .... .203-966-1776 ...... .New Canaan
New Canaan Nature Center .... .203-966-9577 ...... .New Canaan
New England Carousel Museum .... .860-585-5411 .... .Bristol

New England Center for Contemporary Art	860-774-8899	Brooklyn
New London County Historical Society	860-443-1209	New London
New England Civil War Museum	860-871-1552	Vernon
New Haven's Historic Green	203-432-2300	New Haven
New England Hobby Supply (train display)	860-646-0610	Manchester
Noden-Reed House	860-627-9212	Windsor Locks
Northeast Audubon Center	860-364-0520	Sharon
Norwalk Museum	203-866-0202	South Norwalk
Norwalk Seaport Association (Sheffield Lighthouse)	203-838-9444	Norwalk
Nut Museum	860-434-7636	Old Lyme
Old Lighthouse Museum	860-535-1440	Stonington
Old State House	860-522-6766	Hartford
Old Stone Schoolhouse	860-678-1645	Farmington
Olde Mistick Village	860-536-4941	Mystic
Oliver Ellsworth Homestead	860-688-8717	Windor
Pardee-Morris House	203-562-4183	New Haven
Phelps Homestead	860-658-2500	Simsbury
Price Fine Arts Gallery	860-691-0223	East Lyme
Portersville Academy/Mystic River Historical Society	860-536-4779	Mystic
Pump House Gallery	860-722-6536	Hartford
Purple Heart Museum	203-745-1729	Enfield
Putnam Cottage	203-869-9697	Greenwich
Putnam Memorial State Park	203-938-2285	Redding
Railroad Museum of New England	860-283-RAIL	Thomaston
Real Art Ways	860-232-1006	Hartford
Revolutionary War Office	860-642-6579	Lebanon
Stanley L. Richter Association for the Arts	203-792-5606	Danbury
Ridgefield Military Museum	203-438-3459	Ridgefield
Palmer Arboretum	860-928-1035	Woodstock
Rowayton Arts Center	203-866-2744	Norwalk
Sarah Whitman Hooker House	860-523-5887	West Hartford
Sawmill Park	860-464-8740	Ledyard
Science Center of Eastern Connecticut	860-442-0391	New London
Shore Line Trolley Museum	203-467-6927	East Haven
Silas Deane House	860-529-0612	Wethersfield
Silvermine Guild Arts Center	203-966-5617	New Canaan
Simsbury Historical Society museum	860-658-2500	Simsbury
Slater Memorial Museum	860-887-2506	Norwich
Smith-Harris House	860-739-0761	Niantic
Somers Mountain Indian Museum	860-749-4129	Somers
Somers Museum of Natural History and Primitive Technology	860-749-4129	Somers
Special Joys Antique Doll and Toy Museum	860-742-6359	Coventry
Stamford Historical Society	203-329-1183	Stamford
Stamford Museum and Nature Center	203-322-1646	Stamford

Name	Phone	Town
State Capitol	860-240-0222	Hartford
Stonington Vineyards	860-535-1222	Stonington
Talcott Mountain State Park	860-658-4000	Simsbury
Tantaquidgeon Indian Museum	860-848-9145	Uncasville
Tapping Reeve House and Law School	860-567-4501	Litchfield
Thomas Lee House and Little Boston School	860-739-6070	East Lyme
Timexpo Museum	800-367-8463	Waterbury
Tourtellotte Memorial Room	860-923-9303	Thompson
Travelers Tower/Towers Museum	860-277-4208	Hartford
Unionville Museum	860-673-2231	Unionville
Vernon Historical Society Museum and Library	860-875-4326	Vernon
Waldo Homestead	860-456-0708	Windham
Watermark, The	860-535-2529	North Stonington
Weston Historical Society	203-226-1804	Weston
White Memorial Foundation	860-567-0857	Litchfield
Whitlock Farm Book Barn	203-393-1240	Bethany
Whitney Museum of American Art at Champion	203-358-7630	Stamford
Willimantic Camp Meeting Association (Putnam Cottage)	860-423-9448	Willimantic
Winchester Center Kerosene Lamp Museum	860-379-2612	Winchester Center
Woodcock Nature Center	203-762-7280	Wilton
Wood Memorial Library and Museum	860-289-1783	South Windsor
Woodstock Historical Society	860-928-1035	Woodstock
Wooster Community Art Center	203-744-4825	Danbury
WAP Murals	203-866-0202	Norwalk
Yale Collection of Musical Instruments	203-432-0822	New Haven
Yale University Art Gallery	203-432-0600	New Haven
Ye Olde Towne Mill	860-447-5270	New London

MAINE

Abbe Museum

PO Box 286
Bar Harbor, ME 04609
(207) 288-3519

Overview

Founded in 1927, the Abbe Museum at Sieur de Monts Spring is the only museum devoted solely to the history, cultures, and archaeology of all Native Americans in Maine. The museum's exhibitions and educational programs are designed to develop an understanding and appreciation of Maine's Native American heritage. Its collection comprises 50,000 objects from 10,000 years ago to the present. Also, a year-round museum in downtown Bar Harbor will be opening in September, 2001.

Directions and Hours

The museum is located off Route 3, south of Bar Harbor, and is also accessible from the Park Road Loop. The downtown facility is located on Mount Desert Street (Route 3), a main corridor through Bar Harbor.

The Sieur de Monts Spring facility is seasonal, and is handicap accessible.

Hours for the Sieur de Monts facility: daily in May, June, September, and October 10:00-4:00; daily in July and August, 9:00-5:00.

Hours for the year-round facility will be announced.

Admission and Membership

$2 for adult admission to the Sieur de Monts facility; $0.50 for children. Membership is $25/year for individuals and $50/year for families.

Groups receive ½-price admission with reservations. The museum is free to members.

What to See

The Abbe's most significant collections are its holdings of archaeological artifacts and basketry. It has the largest and best documented collection of baskets made by Native Americans, with more than 1,000 pieces dating back to the early 19th century.

Hands-on programs include workshops taught by Native American artists and archaeological field schools. The annual Native American Festival, co-sponsored with the Maine

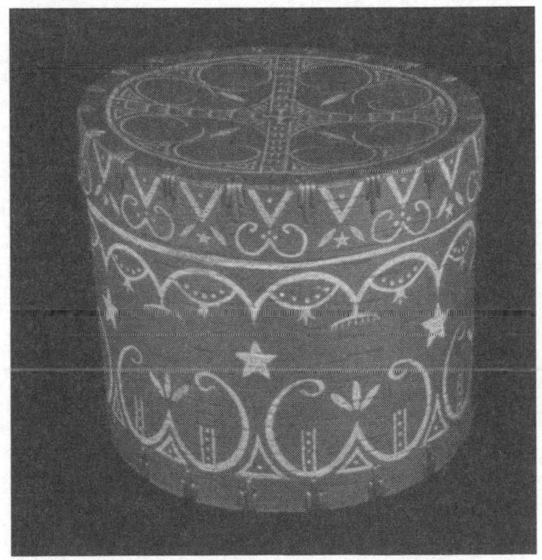

Cylindrical birch bark basket by David Bridges. Abbe Museum, Bar Harbor, Maine. Photo by Stephen Bicknell.

Indian Basketmakers Alliance, is held on the Saturday after the Fourth of July.

The opening exhibition in the new museum will be "Four Mollys: Women of the Dawn," a look at four centuries of history in the Northeast through the lives of four Native American women.

Educational programs for children include hands-on crafts workshops and mock archaeological digs.

The Abbe Museum Store offers crafts made by Maine Native Americans, such as baskets and carved wooden walking sticks, along with a wide selection of books on Native American cultures.

Visitors can eat at local restaurants.

While You're in the Area

The Acadia National Park is located nearby, which attracts more than 3 million visitors annually. Also nearby is the Natural History Museum at the College of the Atlantic (p. 158), Wendell Gilley Museum of Bird Carving (p. 201), Bar Harbor Historical Society (p. 110), Mount Desert Island Historical Society (p. 156), and the Islesford Historical Museum (p. 138).

Acadian Village

Van Buren, ME 04785
(207) 868-5042
www.themainelink.com/acadianvillage/

Overview

The village is made up of 16 reconstructed buildings dating from 1790 to 1900, and depicts Maine life in those years. The Acadian Village was built by La Societe Historique-Heritage Vivant (L'Heritage Vivant), the Living Heritage Society of Van Buren. It opened in July 1976, just in time for the Bicentennial.

Directions and Hours

The village is five miles north of Van Buren, on Route 1. It's located five miles from the the Trans-Canada Highway and Port St. Leonard, New Brunswick.

The museum is open from June 14 to September 15 (and is available for tours two weeks before and after those dates as well). Hours are noon-5:00 in the summer and by appointment at other times.

Admission and Membership

$3.50 for adults, $1.25 for children. membership in L'Heritage Vivant is $5/year. Discounts are offered for seniors, group tours, and students under 12.

What to See

The village has collections of telephones, furniture, and religious artifacts. There is an original one-room schoolhouse, and a new art museum that has rotating displays every season.

The last weekend in July the village features a special musical program, meal, and a Catholic Mass in the Chapel.

The Acadian Village is child-friendly, and lends itself to a history lesson that can't be taught in books.

There is a gift shop. The village does not have a café, but there are interesting restaurants in Van Buren.

While You're in the Area

The St. John Valley is filled with seasonal attractions, and every town has at least one museum.

Alexander-Crawford Historical Society

216 Pokey Road
Alexander, ME 04694-6012
(207) 454-7476

Overview

The Alexander-Crawford Historical Society has a collection of artifacts representing two centuries of living in a place with poor soil, cold winters, and isolation.

Directions and Hours

Take I-95 north to Bangor, Maine then Route 9 east to Alexander (90 miles). Turn onto South Propriety Road North (one mile) and then take Pokey Road North (one mile). The Historical Society is on the left with a "Tree Farm" sign in the drive.

Open by appointment only from mid-June to mid-October. The museum is not handicap accessible.

Admission and Membership

Admission is free; membership costs $7.50/year, which includes a quarterly newsletter.

What to See

The Alexander-Crawford Historical Society collection is made up mostly of grave and house sites scattered over 63 acres. Programs include tours of these sites with stories of the people who lived and died there. The Historical Society also has an archive.

There is no café although there are many eating establishments 5-15 miles away.

While You're in the Area

There are many attractions in the area, including Holmes Cottage (p. 208), Charlotte County Museum, Burnham Tavern (p. 116), and Grand Lake Stream Museum.

Androscoggin Historical Society

County Building
2 Turner Street
Auburn, ME 04210-5978
(207) 784-0586
www.rootsweb.com/~meandrhs

Overview

The purpose of the Androscoggin Historical Society is to preserve and disseminate the history of Androscoggin County, Maine.

Directions and Hours

Take the Maine Turnpike to exit 12 (Auburn). Go left and drive about five miles to Minot Avenue. Take a right onto Court Street, and go about half a mile. The museum is located in the County Building.

The museum is open year-round, Wednesday through Friday, 9:00-noon and 1:00-5:00. The museum closes at 4:00 on Fridays during the winter. It is handicap accessible.

Admission and Membership

Admission is free. Membership is $15/year for individuals, $25/year for families, $150 for life; there are four levels of corporate membership.

What to See

The collection includes dishes and household goods, memorabilia from local soldiers in the American Revolution, Aroostook War, and Civil War, family bibles, cemetery records, and genealogical information.

Speakers appear every month on topics of regional interest, such as "Maine Hooked Rugs" and "Nineteenth Century Maine Through the Photographs of Chansonetta Stanley Emmons."

There is no gift shop or café, although the museum does sell postcards. There are local restaurants within walking distance.

While You're in the Area

Nearby attractions include the Knight House and Downing Shoe Shop (p. 143), the Auburn-Lewiston Sports Hall of Fame, and the History Room at the Auburn Public Library.

Aroostook Historical and Art Museum

109 Main Street
Houlton, ME 04730
(207) 532-4216
www.greaterhoulton.com

Overview

The Aroostock Historical and Art Museum was founded to collect, preserve, store, and exhibit artifacts relating to Houlton, Aroostock, and the State of Maine.

Directions and Hours

From I-95: take exit 62. Go right off the exit, about 1 mile and 50 feet after crossing the bridge, turn left into Houlton Historic District. Go through the square and then after two blocks, the museum and chamber of commerce is on the right.

From Route 1: Follow to center of business section (square), turn right on Main Street. Go one block. The museum and Chamber of Commerce will be on the right.

From Route 2: Enter Houlton Historic District (square), go two blocks. The museum and Chamber or Commerce is on the right.

Open Memorial Day-Labor Day, Monday-Friday, 1:00-4:00. The museum is not handicap accessible.

Admission and Membership

Suggested donations from $2-$5 are accepted. School groups and Scout groups are free.

What to See

Listed on the National Register of Historic Places, the White Memorial Building, a 1903 Colonial Revival edifice, holds the museum and its vast collection of pioneer tools, household furnishings, quilts, vintage fashion, account books, maps, and pictures. On display is a baby tender that had a variety of uses. Other displays feature the 1900 Northern Maine Map and the 1895 Bangor and Aroostock game record. Among the Aroostock, Civil, and Spanish-American War artifacts are guns, maps, and broadsides. In the lobby, one can find band pictures and musical instruments from 1860.

Also in the museum are various Indian artifacts such as moccasins, baskets, dishes, sinkers used for fishing, tomahawks, arrowheads, and daggers. Most of the Indian artifacts on display have been found in the surrounding areas. The Houlton Academy, Ricker Classical Institute, and Ricker College exhibit has yearbooks, diplomas, trophies, and pictures. Housed at the museum is the bell from Wording Hall. The Ricker College Room also contains a scale model, day book, and artifacts (including coins recently unearthed by metal detectors) from Hancock Barracks, where federal troops were stationed from 1828-1845, during northern border controversy and the "bloodless Aroostock War."

In the upstairs children's room, there are different dolls from such places as Norway, Leningrad, and Copenhagen. There is an old doll cradle and children's clothing and books.

There is no gift shop or café, but there is a restaurant only a block away.

While You're in the Area

The Cedric Shaw Pastime Museum is five miles from the museum and the Watson Settlement Covered Bridge is also only four miles away. Two miles away from Houlton is the U.S.-Canadian border.

Bachelder's Inn

Route 126 and Hallowell Road
Litchfield, ME 04350
(207) 268-3100
www.bachelderinn.com

Overview

Bachelder's Inn was a stagecoach stop on the Bangor to Portland route. Its main feature is the Moses Eaton Room, hand-painted by artist Moses Eaton who traveled throughout New England painting rooms with his unique and bright designs. Only a few of his painted walls remain in existence.

Directions and Hours

Take Route 95 to exit 28, and travel 6.5 miles to the flashing light at the intersection of Route

126 and Hallowell Road.

The inn is open from April 1-December 15, but is not handicap accessible.

Hours: Wednesday 1:00-4:00, and by reservation.

Admission and Membership
$1 donation to the local historical society. Visitors should be 10 years old or older.

What to See
The Moses Eaton Room at the Bachelder's Inn was painted by Eaton in 1824. It was discovered by Olympia Snow (aunt of Senator Snow) and has been fully restored.

There is no gift shop. The Wee Otter restaurant is on site and open for dinner from 5:00-9:00. There is also a café across from the Inn.

While You're in the Area
Old Fort Western (p. 167), Cumston Hall (p. 208), and the Theater at Monmouth State Capital are also in the area.

Bangor Police Museum
35 Court Street
Bangor, Maine 04401
(207) 234-2394

Overview
The Bangor Police Museum was created from the collection of retired police sergeant Fred Bryant and his wife, Debbie, who have accumulated law enforcement items from the late 1700s to the present. It includes an original police uniform from the turn of the century as well as a rare one man jail chair. There are also collections of badges, handcuffs and photographs as well as other items of interest.

Directions and Hours
From I-95 North, take Hammond Street Exit. Head toward downtown. Turn left on Court Street. The Museum is in the Police Station.

The museum is open year around during normal business hours or by arrangement. It is handicap accessible.

Admission and Membership
There is no admission but donations to the Bangor Police Relief-Museum are appreciated.

What to See
In addition to the various collections, visitors will see a Civil War Diary kept by a soldier-turned-police officer and his police diary kept in the same book. Two of his badges from the Civil War era are also on display as well as early flashlights, billies, and old police call boxes.

There is no gift shop or café, but downtown Bangor and several restaurants are nearby.

While You're in the Area
The Museum is within walking distance to downtown Bangor, the Bangor Historical Society Museum (p. 207), and the Hose 5 Fire Museum (p. 208).

A "tramp chair," or one-man jail, at the Bangor Police Museum. Photo courtesy of Fred Bryant.

Bar Harbor Historical Society

33 Ledgelawn Avenue
Bar Harbor, ME 04609
(207) 288-0000
www.barharborhistorical.org

Overview

Listed on the National Register, the museum building of the Bar Harbor Historical Society has many displays and scrapbooks on the "gilded age" of Bar Harbor.

Directions and Hours

Take Route 3 into Bar Harbor. Driving down Mount Desert Street, take a right at the Catholic Church. The Society is the seventh building on the right. Open from mid-June to mid-October, Monday-Saturday 1:00-4:00. The museum is not handicap accessible.

Admission and Membership

Admission is free although donations are accepted. Membership costs $20/year.

What to See

In addition to the numerous exhibits, the museum features a display on George B. Dorr, the first superintendent of Acadia National Park in 1916. The society also hosts two to three programs each year on area history.

Visitors may purchase books about the history of the area at the museum. There is no café although there are eating establishments within walking distance.

While You're in the Area

Nearby is the Abbe Museum (p. 105), devoted to Maine Indians and Stone Age artifacts.

Bates College Museum of Art

Olin Arts Center
75 Russell Street
Lewiston, ME 04240
(207) 786-6158
www.bates.edu/acad/museum

Overview

The Bates College Museum of Art has two galleries devoted to the exhibition of a wide range of art. The museum's collection includes the nationally renowned Marsden Hartley Memorial Collection.

Directions and Hours

The museum is located approximately three miles from Maine Turnpike exit 13 (Lewiston Exit). Northbound travelers: take exit 13 and turn left onto Alfred A. Plourde Parkway at the stop sign at the end of the ramp. Southbound travelers: take exit 13 and bear right onto Plourde Parkway. Continue on Plourde straight through the stop light at the intersection of Plourde and Pleasant; continue on Plourde .6 miles to the stop light on Webster Street. Turn left onto Webster and travel one mile to the stop light at Farwell Street. Turn right onto Farwell and follow .6 miles to stop light. Continue straight across the intersection onto Russell and follow for .7 miles through two stop lights. Turn left onto Bardwell Street and into the Olin Arts Center parking lot adjacent to the museum.

The museum is open Monday-Saturday, 10:00 A.M.-5:00 P.M., Sunday 1:00 P.M.-5:00 P.M. Closed major holidays. The museum is handicap accessible.

Admission and Membership

Admission is free. Membership: $15 Student, $25 Individual, $35 Family, $100 Contributing, $250 Sponsor, $500 Donor, and $1,000 Benefactor.

What to See

Prints, drawings, photographs, paintings, and important collections of sculpture make the museum a working laboratory in the arts for visitors. Catalogues, posters, and notecards are available for purchase at the museum desk.

Educational programs and lectures by artitsts and scholars accompany special exhibitions. Family events for children are also held.

The museum is a stop on the Maine Art Museum Trail.

There is no café but food service is available in the campus Den or in conveniently located places in Lewiston and Auburn.

While You're in the Area

The Edmund S. Muskie Archives (p. 124) are also on the Bates College campus.

Baxter Museum

71 South Street
Gorham, ME 04038
(207) 839-3878

Overview

The Baxter Museum was the boyhood home of James Phinney Baxter, four-time mayor of Portland, Maine.

Directions and Hours

From the Maine Turnpike: Take exit 8 and follow the signs to Gorham on Route 25. At the intersection of Route 25 and Route 114 turn left. The museum will be on your right about 500 yards away. The building sits a little behind the Baxter Memorial Library.

The museum is open in July and August.

Hours: Tuesdays and Thursdays 10:00 A.M. to 2:00 P.M.

Admission and Membership

Donations are accepted.

What to See

Known as a benefactor and industrialist, James Phinney Baxter was also the father of Percival Baxter, who was the governor of Maine and created Baxter State Park. The house is filled with articles relating to Gorham history.

While You're in the Area

Nearby attractions and museums include the Portland Public Library, the Portland Museum of Art (p. 176) and the Children's Museum of Maine (p. 207), the Maine Narrow Gauge Railroad Company & Museum (p. 148), the Museum of African Tribal Art (p. 157), the Victoria Mansion (p. 200), the Maine Historic Museum (p. 209), the Longfellow House, the Portland Cultural Center, the Harrington House (and Pettingill Farm (p. 129), the Desert of Maine (p. 122), and the Portland Harbor Museum (p. 175).

Bethel Historical Society's Regional History Center

10-14 Broad Street
PO Box 12
Bethel, ME 04217-0012
(207) 824-2908 or (800) 824-2910
http://orion.bdc.bethel.me.us/~history

Overview

The Bethel Historical Society's Regional History Center is a major research center located in the middle of a well-preserved village center. It offers historical and genealogical resources, conferences, workshops, exhibits, lectures, and programming related to the region, as well as publishing works about the area.

Directions and Hours

Come to Bethel Common from Routes 2, 5, 26, or 35. The center is on the common.

The center is open year-round, Tuesday-Friday from 1:00-4:00. In July and August the center is also open from 1:00-4:00 on Saturday and Sunday. It is partially handicap accessible.

Admission and Membership

$3 adults, $1.50 children 6-12, $7 families. Membership is $10, or $3 for students. Discounts are offered to members, as well as to AAM or AAA members.

What to See

The center is located in two adjoining proper-

Bethel Historical Society's Moses Mason House. Photo by F. Lucille Johnstone.

ties, the 1821 O'Neil Robinson House (remodeled in the Italianate style in 1881) and the 1813 Dr. Moses Mason House (a Federal-style house with Rufus Porter murals and home of a former congressman). Both buildings are listed in the National register of Historic Places. The research library is a rich repository of materials relating to northern New England, with major concentrations on western Maine and the White Mountains. The center offers more than a dozen period rooms ans exhibition galleries as well as areas for craft demonstrations and research library operations.

The center sponsors school programs and special events, such as the 15oth anniversary of railroad service in the area.

There is a gift shop but no café. Visitors can eat at many restaurants within walking distance.

While You're in the Area

The Artist's Covered Bridge nearby is worth visiting.

Boothbay Railway Village

Route 27
PO Box 123
Boothbay, ME 04537
(207) 633-4727
www.railwayvillage.org

Overview

Nowhere else in New England can visitors experience a steam train ride, early village exhibits, and an outstanding collection of over 50 antique vehicles in one museum. The Boothbay Railway Village offers a peaceful village, beautiful gardens, and a village green surrounded by historic structures such as the 1847 Town Hall and the 1923 Spruce Point Chapel.

Directions and Hours

From Portland take I-95 to Coastal Route 1 then take Route 27 South for 8 miles to the museum.

Open Memorial Day through Columbus Day, 9:30-5:00. The museum is partially handicap accessible.

Admission and Membership

$7/adult, $3/child. Family membership is $30. Group rates are available.

What to See

The Village exhibits are evocative of the rich New England heritage. Situated on 30 acres and housed in 28 exhibit buildings, the large collection of exhibits includes all aspects of rural town life, from various types of transportation to lessons taught in a one-room schoolhouse. A variety of special events bring history to life with demonstrations and activities.

Frequent special events are offered, including Model T rides, demonstrations of early life, entertainment and food. Several special events, such as Children's Day and Father's Day, are specifically tailored to children.

The museum store is stocked with unique times and books related to the village's area of concern. There is no café, but there are many fine restaurants and small roadside eating establishments nearby.

While You're in the Area

Nearby museums include the Maine Maritime Museum (p. 209) and the Owls Head Transportation Museum (p. 170).

Boothbay Region Historical Society

72 Oak Street
PO Box 272
Boothbay, ME 04538-0272
(207) 633-0820

Overview

The society is housed in an 1874 captain's home, filled with seven rooms of artifacts and local historical material. The society's main role is as a research facility.

Directions and Hours

Following Route 1 north, take Route 27 at Edgecomb and follow it about 12 miles to Boothbay Harbor. Just a quarter mile past the shopping center/mall area with its stop light and intersection with Route 96, the museum is located on Route 27 (which is also Oak Street).

The Society is open year-round, Saturdays from 10:00-2:00. It is not handicap accessible.

July and August hours: Wednesday, Fridiay, and Saturday from 10:00-4:00

Admission and Membership

Admission is free. Memberships start at $10.

What to See

The museum exhibits cover all areas—home, shipyards, fishing, art schools. Many people enjoy seeing the Ram Island lighthouse lens.

The society sells books on local history. There is no café, but many restaurants are within easy walking distance.

While You're in the Area

Boothbay Railway Village (p. 112) is nearby.

Bowdoin College Museum of Art

9400 College Station
Brunswick, ME 04011
(207) 725-3275
www.bowdoin.edu/artmuseum

Overview

Housed in a beautiful 1894 McKim, Mead, and White building, the Bowdoin College Museum of Art is one of the oldest college art museums in the United States. Its extensive art collection represents a broad range of cultures and time periods and the museum's temporary exhibitions of art come from around the nation and the world.

Directions and Hours

The Bowdoin College Museum of Art is located on the quadrangle of Bowdoin College in Brunswick, Maine, 25 miles from Portland and 120 miles from Boston.

From the south: Take the Maine Turnpike to exit 9 (I-95 to Coastal Route 1). Continue on I-95 to exit 22 (Brunswick, Route 1). Proceed to the business district and turn right on Maine Street, following signs to Bowdoin College.

From the north: Take exit 14 off the Maine Turnpike. Take I-95 to exit 22 (Topsham-Brunswick, Route 1 north). Proceed to the business district and turn right on Maine Street, following the signs to the college.

The museum is open year-round and is handicap accessible.

Hours: Tuesday-Saturday 10:00 A.M. to 5:00 P.M.; Sunday from 2:00-5:00 P.M.

Admission and Membership

Admission is free. Donations are accepted.

What to See

The museum houses more than 14,000 art objects, selections of which are rotated frequently. Among the highlights are a group of Greek, Roman, and Egyptian antiquities; a body of colonial and federal American portraits by artists such as Stuart, Copley, and Feke; Old Master drawings and graphics; European paintings from the Renaissance and Baroque periods; nineteenth century American and European paintings; and a broad representation of the history of photography from its invention to the present. In addition to its own collections, the museum presents temporary exhibition programs that feature contemporary art.

Tours are available with two weeks notice.

The museum has a museum shop. There is a café on the Bowdoin College campus that is open to the public.

While You're in the Area

While on campus visitors can check out the Peary-MacMillan Arctic Museum (p. 172).

The Brick Store Museum

117 Main Street
Kennebunk, ME 04043
(207) 985-4802
www.brickstoremuseum.org

Overview

The Brick Store Museum is located in the 1825 William Lord's Brick Store building and three adjacent nineteenth century restored buildings. The museum is dedicated to preserving the cultural heritage of the Kennebunks through rotating exhibits and architectural walking tours of historic neighborhoods.

Directions and Hours

The museum is located at the intersection of Routes 1 and 35 in the center of downtown Kennebunk.

The museum is open March-December, and has limited handicap accessibility.

Hours: Tuesday-Saturday 10:00-4:30; walking tours are available June through Labor Day.

Admission and Membership

$5 for adults, $2 for children and students, children under six are admitted free. Walking tours are $4 per person. Membership is $20/year for seniors and students, $25/year for individuals, $35/year for senior families, and $40/year for families.

Members are admitted free, and AAA members and groups receive a discount rate.

What to See

The museum is home to 45,000 objects, including paintings, works on paper, furniture, photographs, costumes, maritime-related objects, and other archival material spanning the mid-seventeenth century to the twenty-first century. There is also a 3,000-volume library of books on history and genealogy available for use during museum hours by appointment.

There are interactive displays for children and adults.

There is a gift shop. There is no café, but there are local restaurants and sandwich shops.

While You're in the Area

Also nearby are Kennebunkport, Walker's Point (summer home of President George Bush), the 1,600 acre Wells National Estuarine Research Walk (including Laudholm Farm, a unique nineteenth century saltwater farm), the Rachel Carson National Wildlife Refuge. There are also many shops and beaches in the area.

Bridgton Historical Society

Gibbs Avenue
Bridgton, ME 04009
(207) 647-3699

Overview

The Bridgton Historical Society's collection includes local genealogies and railroad artifacts and memorabilia. The society also owns and operates a historical farm, Narramissic, and a research room.

Directions and Hours

Take Route 302 west from Portland, Maine. At the traffic light in Bridgton, turn left, then turn left onto Gibbs Avenue.

The museum and research center are open year round, but are not handicap accessible.

Hours: Monday 2:00-5:00; Thursday 2:00-4:00; Saturday 1:00-4:00 (winter only). The Narramissic farm is open during July and August, Friday-Sunday 10:00-4:00.

Admission and Membership

$1 for adults to the museum; $4 for adults to Narramissic farm. Membership is $10/year for individuals, $15/year for families, $5/year for students and retired individuals, and there are various levels of contributing membership.

What to See

The society houses a large collection of narrow gauge railroad materials, and artifacts from the local area.

In July, the society hosts a woodworkers show. There is also a harvest festival in the fall.

There are some children's programs at the Narramissic farm in the summer.

There are small gift shops at the museum and Narramissic. There is no café, but there are several restaurants within walking distance.

While You're in the Area

Nearby attractions and museums include the Harrison Historical Society Museum (p. 134), the Spratt-Mead Museum (p. 210), the Waterford Historical Society, and the Norway Historical Society (p. 210).

Brooksville Historical Society Museum

150 Coastal Road
Brooksville, Maine 04617
(207) 326-8681

Overview

The Brooksville Historical Society Museum contains archives and artifacts of nineteenth and early twentieth century life in Brooksville. This coastal town was a typical Maine farming, fishing, and boatbuilding community and tourist destination for "rusticators." Unusual industries included a copper mine and a large ice-harvesting operation on nearby Walker Pond.

Directions and Hours

Brooksville is on the DeLorme Maine Atlas and Gazetter Map number 15. Take Route 15 from Blue Hill toward Stonington, and turn right on Coastal Road, Route 175-176. Stay on Coastal Road until you come to the museum, a small, white building set back from the road on the left.

The Museum is open during July and August, Wednesday and Sunday afternoons, and other hours by appointment. There is a short set of steps leading to the front door, on which a temporary ramp could be placed for wheelchair access. Please telephone ahead for this service.

Admission and Membership

Admission to the museum is by donation. Membership in the Brooksville Historical Society is open to anyone, and current dues are $5 annually.

What to See

The museum grounds have an interesting garden of historically important plants, divided into four beds representing medicinal, household, decorative, and culinary uses, and a brochure describing them. The Society has developed a video, "Summering in Brooksville," that engagingly describes the life of the "rusticators" during the early 1900s. On display is an unique machine that was invented locally and used to produce postcards for the tourists.

While You're in the Area

Brooksville is the home of the Holbrook Island Sanctuary, a Maine state nature preserve with beach and picnic area. South Brooksville is a charming, tiny town with a grocery and cafe. There are no gas stations in Brooksville, so visitors are advised to fill their tanks beforehand.

Burnham Tavern Museum

Main Street
Machias, ME 04654
(207) 255-4432

Overview

The Burnham Tavern Museum is the oldest building in eastern Maine, and the only one with a Revolutionary War history. The wounded were taken to the tavern after the first naval action of the American Revolution, fought on June 12, 1775 in Machias Bay.

Directions and Hours

Burnham Tavern is just off Route 1 on Route 192 (there are signs for the museum on Route 1 in both directions). Park in the municipal parking lot across the street.

The museum is open mid-June through September, Monday-Friday 9:00-5:00. Winter hours are by appointment. Burnham Tavern is not handicap accessible.

Admission and Membership

$2.50 for adults, $0.25 for children.

What to See

The museum, built in 1770, is preserved as a memorial to the early settlers of the area. The building was a tavern and the family home of Job and Mary (O'Brien) Burnham, who raised 11 children there. The articles in the museum reflect life in the late 1700s and early 1800s.

There is no gift shop, although a few items are for sale. There are several restaurants nearby.

While You're in the Area

The town of Machias is the county seat and home of the University of Maine at Machias. Nearby Machiasport contains the Gates House museum (p. 131) and Fort O'Brien (p. 128). Campobello International Park, the summer home of Franklin D. Roosevelt, is about 20 miles away.

Caribou Historical Society

PO Box 1058
Caribou, ME 04736

Overview

The museum's two buildings contain a broad and quirky collection of local historical material and slices of Maine life from the Revolutionary War era to the present. There is also an extensive audiocassette oral history collection on Caribou's early history.

Photo courtesy of the Caribou Historical Society.

Directions and Hours

The museum is on Route 1 three miles south of Caribou, on the right side of the highway.

The museum is open

from June through August, Wednesday-Saturday 11:00-5:00. It is partially handicap accessible.

Admission and Membership

Donations are accepted. Memberships are $5/year or $25 for a lifetime membership.

What to See

The museum includes everything from a Revolutionary War era plow, to an excellent Civil War collection from early Caribou citizens, to unusual human hair and an actual caul from the 1800s. The museum's smaller building is a complete replica of a one-room schoolhouse, and includes furnishings from the 1920s and 1930s.

The museum hosts an old-fashioned ice cream social every summer, and gives frequent children's tours of the museum.

The gift shop sells t-shirts, mugs, hats, and Society and local publications. There is no café, but there are two good restaurants within ¼ mile.

While You're in the Area

The Nylander Natural History Museum (p. 210) is also in Caribou, about three miles away.

The Castine Historical Society

PO Box 238
Court Street
Castine, ME 04421
(207) 326-4118 summer
(207) 326-8786 winter

Overview

The Castine Historical Society is located on the Town Common in historic Castine. Its headquarters is the former Abbott School, an 1859 building listed in the National Registry of Historic Houses. The present Historical Society was formed in 1966 and in 1996 purchased the Abbott School to provide a central location for the gathering and preserving of materials that illustrate the unique history of the area.

Directions and Hours

From Route 1, 1½ miles north of Bucksport, turn onto 175 south. Follow eight miles to Route 166. At the junction of 166 and 166A, follow either route into Castine. The historical society is located in the northwest corner of the town common on Court Street.

The museum is open from July 1 through September 15. It is handicap accessible.

Hours: Tuesday-Saturday 10:00-4:00; Sunday 11:00-3:00.

Admission and Membership

Admission is free. Membership is $15/year for individuals and $25/year for families.

What to See

Castine was a fortified trading post in 1629 and in its early years was the center of struggle between the British, French, and Dutch for control of the peninsula. Because of its deep water harbor, it was an important seaport. It was also the scene of what was reputed to be the worst naval disaster in American history, the Penobscot Expedition. It played an important role in the early days of the Colonies. Some present-day residents of the town can trace their family history back to these early days.

"Castine in the 20th Century," a temporary exhibit, will be on view during the summer of 2001. In 2002, a permanent exhibit called "Penobscot Expedition" will open. Of special note is the Bicentennial Quilt, a 24-foot wall hanging with seven quilted panels that recall the colorful history of Castine. It was designed by a local artist and completed by members of the community, including children. A free copy of the walking tour of Castine is available and will help visitors identify points of historic interest and their locations. Many homes mentioned in the brochure date back to the eighteenth and nineteenth century.

There is a gift shop but no café on the premises. Several restaurants and delis are nearby.

While You're in the Area

Other local attractions are historic homes dating from the eighteenth century, the John Perkins House—a pre-Revolution house located at the Wilson Museum (p. 211), town signs citing historic events, and the Maine Maritime Academy.

Castle Tucker (SPNEA)

Lee Street at High Street
Wiscasset, ME 04578
(207) 384-2454
www.spnea.org

Overview

Built on the top of a hill overlooking the Sheepscot River, Castle Tucker presents a record of Wiscasset history. Judge Silas Lee built his Federal-style mansion at the peak of prosperity, when the town was the busiest port east of Boston. Lee's death in 1814, combined with the stunning effect of the Jefferson Embargo, forced his widow to sell.

Directions and Hours

From I-95: Take Maine exit 22 (Route 1, Brunswick). Follow Route 1 to Wiscasset. Turn right on Lee Street and proceed to the intersection with High Street. The house is on the right.

The house museum is open June 1 to October 15. It is not handicap accessible.

Hours: Wednesday-Sunday, 11:00 A.M. to 5:00 P.M. Tours are at 11:00 A.M., 12:00, 1:00, 2:00, 3:00 and 4:00 P.M.

Admission and Membership

$5 for adults, $4.50 senior citizens, ½ off for students and children 6-12. Children 5 and under, SPNEA members, and residents of Wiscasset are free. AAA members receive a 2 for 1 discount. SPNEA membership is $35/year for individuals and $45/year for a household. Membership includes free admissions to 35 properties and museums across New England.

What to See

The house passed through a succession of hands until 1858, when Captain Richard Tucker, scion of a Wiscasset shipping family, bought the property, updated the interiors, and added a dramatic two-story porch to the front. Shortly after, he brought a shipload of fashionable furnishings and moved in with his young bride. In 1871, however, his fortunes collapsed. Renovations and family entertainments gave way to subsistence farming and taking in paying guests. After Tucker's death, his daughter Jane returned from New York, bringing with her a passion for Japanese and exotic decoration. She, and later her niece, took an interest in preserving the house and contents, making few changes to the decorating schemes, preserving the house much as it appeared in the late nineteenth century.

The house has a small gift shop. There are several restaurants within walking distance.

While You're in the Area

Attractions and museums nearby include SPNEA's Nickels-Sortwell House (p. 162).

Cherryfield-Narraguagus Historical Society

Main Street
PO Box 96
Cherryfield, ME 04622

Overview

The Cherryfield-Narraguagus Historical Society museum displays a collection of artifacts and photographs of Cherryfield, including the homes, farms, and businesses from the 1800s to the mid-1900s. Genealogical information is available in the public library.

Directions and Hours

The historical society is located at the intersection of Route 1 and state Route 193, which is Main Street.

The historical society is open during the

summer, but is not handicap accessible.

Hours: last Saturday in June 10:00-4:00; July and August, Wednesday and Friday 1:00-4:00.

Admission and Membership

Admission to the historical society is free. Membership is $3/year for individuals, and $100 for a lifetime membership.

What to See

The historical society houses a collection of locally made quilts, some of which are over 100 years old. There are displays on the Cherryfield Band that started in 1869 and on the blueberry industry that began in Cherryfield in the 1860s.

A brochure is available that gives an overview and maps to the historic homes in town, two of which are over 200 years old.

There is no gift shop, but historic publications are available. There is no café, but restaurants and sandwich shops are nearby.

While You're in the Area

The Milbridge Historical Museum is nearby. The blueberry fields, known as "Blueberry Barrens," are located several miles out of town on Route 193.

Colby College Museum of Art

5600 Mayflower Hill
Waterville, ME 04901
(207) 872-3228
www.colby.edu/museum

Overview

The Colby College Museum of Art showcases eighteenth, nineteenth, and twentieth century American art. It features the John Marin collection as part of the permanent collection, and it also has an active temporary exhibition program.

Directions and Hours

Take 95 to exit 33, and follow the signs to Colby College.

The museum is open year round, and is handicap accessible.

Hours: Monday through Saturday 10:00-4:30; Sunday 2:00-4:30.

Admission and Membership

Admission to the museum is free.

What to See

In addition to the John Marin collection, the Colby College Museum of Art collection has 100 American Primitive paintings and 98 American Impressionist paintings. There are also examples of European art, Greek ceramics, Roman portrait busts, African masks, Japanese woodcuts, Indian miniatures, and more than 300 Oriental ceramics.

There is also an outreach program for Maine schools.

The Museum Shop offers a wide selection of catalogues, books, posters, and postcards relating to the museum's collection as well as traveling exhibitions.

There is a spa on the Colby campus where visitors can eat.

Cole Land Transportation Museum

405 Perry Road
Bangor, ME 04401
(207) 990-3600
www.colemuseum.org

Overview

The Cole Land Transportation Museum features over 200 vehicles and 2,000 photographs. The museum was established to preserve and display a cross section of Maine's early land transportation history; to honor the hard work, ingenuity and discipline of Mainers who built, maintained and used these vehicles; and to challenge young people to consider what old-timers accomplished for Maine and what they, too, can accomplish for themselves and their communities.

Directions and Hours

Take exit 45B off Route 95. Take a left at the first light and a left on Perry Road. Follow the signs.

The museum is open from May 1 to November 11, and it is handicap accessible.

Hours: Daily, 9:00-5:00.

Admission and Membership

$5 for adults, $3 for seniors 62 and over, and children under 19 are free. AAA members receive $1 discount off the regular adult price. Group rates are also available.

What to See

The museum, which is also the home of the Maine State WWII Veterans Memorial, features a complete train from locomotive to caboose inside the building, along with an actual railroad station. It has the largest collection of snow removal equipment in the country under one roof. Vehicles of every description, from vintage automobiles to antique baby carriages to cement mixers to wagons are also on display.

Children's programming includes guided school field trips and a Veteran/student interview program.

The museum has a gift shop. There are many hotels and fast food restaurants within ½ mile.

While You're in the Area

Attractions nearby include the Bangor Historical Society Museum (p. 207), the Thomas A. Hill House (p. 207), the Hose 5 Fire Museum (p. 208), the Isaac Farrar Mansion (p. 208), the Maine Discovery Museum (p. 209), Nichols Mansion (p. 209), and the Bangor Police Museum (p. 109).

Counting House Museum

Old Berwick Historical Society
PO Box 296
Main and Liberty Streets
South Berwick, ME 03908
(207) 384-0000

Overview

The Counting House Museum is a repository for some 6,000 documents, photographs, and historical curiosities covering a wide spectrum of community life in the region of South Berwick, site of the first permanent settlement in Maine. All that remains of an early nineteenth century textile mill, the Counting House today is a regional treasure containing one of northern New England's last textile mill ballrooms. Years ago the mill entertained dancers each autumn when gas lamps were illuminated for a "Lighting Up Ball."

Directions and Hours

From I-95 in southern Maine, take exit 3 in Kittery to Route 236N. Follow to stop sign in South Berwick and take left onto Route 4. The Counting House is two blocks on your left just before the Salmon Falls River/New Hampshire border.

The museum is open year round, but only by appointment or occasionally in the evening during the winter.

Summer hours: July-September, Saturday and Sunday 1:00-4:00 P.M. Other times by appointment. About half the building, including the exhibit and research areas, are handicap accessible.

Admission and Membership

Admission is free, but donations are welcome. One year's membership in the Old Berwick Historical Society is $15, $25 for family, and $5 senior/student.

What to See

The museum's collection includes exhibits on the nineteenth century cotton factory and its transportation network on the Salmon Falls River; a collection of models of the river's indigenous craft, the gundalows; and artifacts from the 1650-1690 Humphrey Chadbourne homestead, that of one of Maine's earliest pioneering mill families. The museum is a source for genealogy and reference, with its collection of photos, maps, and books.

Special programming includes local history education projects for everyone, and speakers on the last Thursday of the month throughout the winter. A different schedule of programs is available each year. The Old Berwick Historical Society is one of the most active small historical societies in the region. Every summer for two weeks the society sponsors an archeological dig where volunteers can work with a professional archeologist and help discover the seventeenth century Humphrey Chadbourne Homestead. A teen summer scholars program is also offered.

A small inventory of local history books, maps and photos are for sale. There is no café, but in South Berwick by the Salmon Falls River is Fogarty's Restaurant for good family dining.

While You're in the Area

Nearby attractions include the Sarah Orne Jewett House in South Berwick (SPNEA, p. 188), Hamilton House in South Berwick (SPNEA, p. 133), and Salmon Falls Mill Village in Rollinsford, New Hampshire.

Dead River Area Historical Society

170 Main Street
PO Box 15
Stratton, Maine 04982
(207) 246-2271

Overview

The Dead River Area Historical Society museum contains displays of old carpentry tools and logging tools, china, glass, a complete schoolroom, a memorial to the "lost" towns of Flagstaff and Dead River, the lineage of several native familes, and photographs of days gone by.

The Counting House Museum and Salmon Falls. Photo courtesy of the Old Berwick Historical Society.

Directions and Hours

The museum is located at the junction of Routes 16 and 27.

Open every weekend from Memorial to Labor Day, 11:00 A.M. to 3:00 P.M. There is no handicap ramp.

Admission and Membership

Admission is free, but donations are requested. Memberships start at $7.

What to See

Of special interest is the memorial room dedicated to the lost towns of Flagstaff and Dead River.

Society historians also go into local schools and speak about the past.

The museum sells postcards and calendars. There is no café, but downtown area restaurants are nearby.

While You're in the Area

Nearby attractions and museums include the Rangeley Lakes Region Logging Museum (p. 210), the Wilhelm Reich Museum (p. 211), and the Rangeley Lakes Region Historical Society (p. 179).

Desert of Maine

95 Desert Road
Freeport ME 04032
(207) 865-6962
www.desertofmaine.com

Overview

The Desert of Maine is a glacial wash plain that was exposed in the late 1800s. Visitors will learn the history of this area from the time of the glaciers through the eventually doomed farming era of early New England.

Directions and Hours

Take I-95 north or south to Freeport Maine. Take exit 19 and go west two miles.

The Desert of Maine is open from May 5-October 15 and is handicap accessible.

Hours: 9:00 A.M. to 5:00 P.M. daily.

Admission and Membership

$7.50 for adults and $4 for children (5-12). Special discounts are given.

What to See

The 1783 barn, the only remaining structure of the Tuttle Farm, now houses a Farm Museum with relics of the farming past and a Sand Museum with sand samples from all over the world, as well as sand art made by local and international artisans. Visitors can explore many nature trails and go on a narrated history ride of the desert.. Children get to hunt for gemstones (the desert is seeded daily with gem stones for kids to find).

Children's programming is available for school groups.

There is a gift shop. Freeport Village is only two miles away and has more than 15 cafes, restaurants, and sandwich shops.

While You're in the Area

The Maine Maritime Museum (p. 209) is a nearby attraction.

Dexter Historical Society Museums

PO Box 481
Dexter, ME 04930
(207) 924-5721
www.dextermaine.org

Overview

The Dexter Historical Society has three historic buildings that house and display the artifacts and archives that the society has collected for over 50 years. The 1854 Grist Mill, the 1825 Miller's House, and the 1845 one-room Carr Schoolhouse sit along the bank of the stream that passes through town and was the source of power that allowed industrial development.

Directions and Hours

Take I-95 to exit 39 (state Route 7). Take Route 7 north 13 miles to Dexter. Follow the signs to the museums, which are located in the downtown area.

The museums are open from mid-June to mid-September, and all year by appointment. They are not handicap accessible.

Summer hours: Monday-Friday, 10:00-4:00; Saturday, 1:00-4:00.

After Labor Day: Monday-Saturday, 1:00-4:00

Admission and Membership

Admission is free. Membership is $10/year.

What to See

The Grist Mill Museum has displays illustrating many aspects of life in Dexter (settled 1801): the fire department, auto garages, World War I soldiers, farming and lumbering, banking, business advertising signs, and a kitchen area. The grist mill was run by water power for 150 years.

The Miller's House has a photo gallery, maps, and a Victorian parlor. There is also a corner for genealogy research.

The Carr Schoolhouse was moved from three miles out of town and lovingly restored by the society in 2000.

The Dexter Historical Society is negotiating the gift of another historic building, the original 1836 Town Hall, which was used as the office for the Abbott woolen mill from 1857 to 1975. The building will have a gift shop, woolen industry display, research library, and meeting space.

The society offers children "living history" programs utilizing the Carr School, and tours for scout groups and school classes.

There is a small gift shop in the Grist Mill. There is no café, but the Dexter Café is nearby, along with Kasha's Eatery, a pizza place, and several sandwich shops. A lovely town park where visitors can picnic adjoins the museums.

While You're in the Area

The Abbott Memorial Library, built in 1895, is a beautiful building. There is a public beach (and Lakeshore Lunch for meals and ice cream) at Lake Wassookeag, just north of town.

Dixfield Historical Society

PO Box 182
Dixfield, ME 04224
(207) 562-7595

Overview

The Dixfield Historical Society purchased a lovely Victorian home (ca. 1899) in 1997. The house has extensive grounds and is located next to Dixfield's new town park, which features a gazebo and a large carved moose named Bullrock—the town's mascot.

Directions and Hours

The museum is on Maine's Route 2, a main east-west highway.

The museum is during the summer months and is partially handicap accessible. It is open by appointment the rest of the year by calling (207) 562-7595 or (207) 562-8151.

Hours: Saturday 1:00-3:00.

Admission and Membership

Admission to the museum is free, but donations are accepted. Membership to the historical society is $5/year and includes the "Dixfield Star" newsletter.

What to See

The Dixfield Historical Society Museum House features many artifacts and archival materials, which are now being catalogued. The barn hous-

The Mid Maine Association of Historical Societies is dedicated to promoting and preserving the heritage of Northern Central Maine Communities. The association meets quarterly to share ideas, resources, and support efforts to preserve the history of the region. For meeting dates and information contact:

Mary Annis, Secretary,
(207) 564-0820
10 Orchard Road
Dover-Foxcroft, ME 04426

The historical societies that are part of the Mid Maine Association of Historical Societies include:

Abbot Historical Society	(207) 876-3073
Bowerbank Historical Society	(207) 564-7736
Bradford Heritage Museum and Historical Society	(207) 327-1246
Brownville/Brownville Junction Historical Society	(207) 943-2185
Cambridge Historical Society	(207) 277-3091
Corinna Historical Society	(207) 278-3542
Dexter Historical Society	(207) 924-5721
Dover-Foxcroft Historical Society	(207) 564-0820
Garland Historical Society	(207) 924-3925
Guilford Historical Society	(207) 876-2817
Harmony Historical Society	(207) 683-6485
Milo Historical Society	(207) 943-2268
Moosehead Historical Society	(207) 695-2909
Monson Historical Society	(207) 876-3073
Newport Historical Society	(207) 368-5260
Sangerville Historical Society	(207) 876-4579
Sebec Historical Society	(207) 564-8338

es the John L. Towle Antique Tool Museum, which includes over 1,000 small hand tools and specializes in hand planes. It is the largest such collection in western Maine and features a very rare 1700s Chelor plane.

There is no gift shop or café, but visitors can eat at restaurants nearby.

While You're in the Area

A few miles outside of Dixfield on Route 2 is the Mainely Critters Museum (p. 148), a taxidermy museum featuring a display of local animals.

Dr. John Hubbard Office Museum

Corner of Central and Second Streets
Hallowell, ME 04347
(207) 623-4021

Overview

The original mid-nineteenth century doctor's office of John Hubbard Jr., Hallowell doctor and governor of Maine. The collection was left intact after Hubbard's death in 1869, and was moved to the present site in 1989.

Directions and Hours

Take Route 201 (Water Street) north into Hallowell. Turn left onto Central Street and then right onto Second Street.

The museum is open Memorial Day and Old Hallowell Day (third Saturday in July) or by appointment. It is not handicap accessible.

Admission and Membership

Admission is free.

What to See

The collection features nineteenth century medical and surgical instruments, as well as period office furnishings. There is also an eighteenth and nineteenth century medical library.

School tours of the museum are available.

There is no gift shop or café.

While You're in the Area

Across the street from the museum is the 1880 Hubbard Free Library. The museum is two miles away from the Maine State Museum (p. 149) and Maine State Archives (p. 209), and three miles from Old Fort Western (p. 167).

The Edmund S. Muskie Archives and Special Collection Library

70 Campus Avenue
Bates College
Lewiston, ME 04240-6018
(207) 786-6354
www.bates.edu/muskie_archives

Muskie Archives, Bates College. Photo by Phyllis Graber Jensen.

Overview

The Edmund S. Muskie Archives and Special Collection Library collects, preserves, and makes available papers, office files, campaign files, campaign records, and memorabilia of Edmund S. Muskie and James B. Longley and other modern political collections. It also houses the Muskie Oral History Project, maintains rare books and manuscripts relating to Freewill Baptists and local natural history, collects works published by small Maine presses, and administers the Archives of Bates College.

Directions and Hours

From the Maine Turnpike (I-495): Take exit 13, at mile 78, and turn on to the Alfred Plourde Highway heading toward Route 196. At the first traffic light (a Ramada Inn will be across the street to the left), turn left on Pleasant Street. Go about 1½ miles to the first set of traffic lights. Take a right on East Avenue. After the first traffic light, turn left on Campus Avenue (there is a sign for Bates College on the right). Go through one set of lights (at Sabattus Street) go to the next intersection, at Campus and Central Avenues, which has four stop signs. Cross that intersection; the Muskie Archives is the first building on the right.

The museum is open year-round and is handicap accessible.

Hours: Monday-Friday 9:00 A.M. to 4:00 P.M.

Admission and Membership

Admission is free.

What to See

The library has an exhibit in the Edmund S. Muskie Room and holds symposia, lectures, and organized discussions of public policy questions and literature. Occasional workshops and exercises relating to the Muskie collection are also organized.

The museum does not have a gift shop or a café but there is the Bates College Den next door.

While You're in the Area

Museums and other interesting attractions nearby include Bates College campus and Olin Art Museum (p. 110).

The Farnsworth Art Museum and Wyeth Center

356 Main Street
PO Box 466
Rockland, ME 04841
(207) 596-6457
www.farnsworthmuseum.org

Overview

The Farnsworth Art Museum, founded in 1948, is the only museum in the United States dedicated solely to the collection, preservation, exhibition, and interpretation of Maine's role in American Art. The museum is a major art resource for the State of Maine and the Northeastern United States. The museum's collection includes nineteenth- and twentieth-century works by such American masters as Eastman Jackson, Winslow Homer, Frank Benson, John Marin, Fitz Hugh Lane, George Bellows, Edward Hopper, Louise Nevelson, Robert Indiana, Neil Welliver, Alex Katz, N. C. Wyeth, Andrew Wyeth, and Jamie Wyeth, among many others.

Directions and Hours

The museum is located on Route 1 in downtown Rockland, Maine. It is open year round and is handicap accessible.

Summer hours: Memorial Day through Columbus Day: daily, 9:00 A.M. to 5:00 P.M. Winter hours: Tuesday through Saturday, 10:00 A.M. to 5:00 P.M., Sunday, 1:00 P.M. to 5:00 P.M., closed Mondays.

Admission and Membership

$9 for adults, $8 for seniors, $5 for students 18 and over; members, children under 18, and Rockland residents are free. Admission includes the main building, Wyeth Center, and the Farnsworth Homestead. Olson House is $4.

$40 for individual membership, $60 for household membership, $150 for patron membership.

What to See

In addition to the Farnsworth's collection of nineteenth- and early twentieth-century artwork, the museum's Wyeth Center showcases the prodigious works of three generations of Wyeth artists, N. C., Andrew, and Jamie Wyeth. Permanently featured in the Nevelson-Berliawsky Gallery is the artwork of Louise Nevelson (a Rockland native). The museum's beautifully landscaped campus includes an historically accurate Victorian Garden where visitors may stroll to the adjacent Farnsworth Homestead. A registered national historic site, the Homestead tells the story of upper middle-class life in the nineteenth-century coastal Rockland. The Olson House, in nearby Cushing, represents the precarious rural life of shipmasters and saltwater farmers whose descendants became, for three decades, the subject of numerous Andrew Wyeth paintings.

In Summer 2003, the Farnsworth Art Museum will present an exhibition surveying the work of Kenneth Noland who has a studio near Rockland, and it will be the first Maine presentation of this pioneer of color-field painting. In Summer 2004, a Jamie Wyeth/Andy Warhol show is slated, exploring an unlikely but artistically productive friendship between the two artists.

Weekly classes for children and teens and Family Sundays with Art are offered year round as well as special seasonal events. The museum also produces the very successful "Arts Initiative for Maine Schools" (AIMS) program, reaching 20,000 Maine schoolchildren annually.

The Farnsworth has an excellent Museum Store within the main museum. Exhibition-related merchandise including prints, books, cards, jewelry, toys, and exquisite gifts are available in the store as well as on-line at www.farnsworthmuseum.org.

There are many nearby restaurants and cafés, either across the street or within short walking distance from the museum. Look for Market on Main, Park Street Grille, Sea Breeze Café, The Landings, Rockland Café, Waterworks, Amalfi, Café Miranda, and many others.

While You're in the Area

Visit the Owls Head Transportation Museum (p. 170) (receiving $1 off the price of admission if you visit both the Farnsworth and OHTM in the same day) and the Owls Head Lighthouse in nearby Owls Head, Maine. Stop by the Island Institute one block north of the museum on Main Street and check out artwork, crafts, and merchandise made in Maine island communities. Walk the nearly mile-long breakwater to the Rockland Breakwater Lighthouse. And don't miss Rockland's exciting galleries and many excellent shops.

Fifth Maine Regiment Center

45 Seashore Avenue
PO Box 41
Peaks Island, ME 04108
(207) 766-3330
http://fifthmaine.home.attnet

Overview

The Fifth Maine Regiment Memorial Hall was built in 1888 by Civil War veterans as a reunion hall and summer home. Today it serves as a museum and cultural center for the community. The hall is listed in the National Register of Historic Places.

Directions and Hours

Take exit 7 (Franklin Street) off Route 295. Go to the end of Franklin Street, to the Casco Bay Lines terminal. Board a ferry to Peaks Island (15 minute ride). On the island, follow signs to the Fifth Maine. Parking is available at Casco Bay Lines. There's no need to bring a car to the island; the museum is a short walk from the wharf.

Hours: July and August, weekdays 1:00-4:00 and weekends 11:00-4:00; June and September, weekends 11:00-4:00.

The museum is partially handicap accessible.

Admission and Membership

$2 suggested donation. Membership levels range from $10-$250.

What to See

The museum has a large collection of Civil War artifacts with special emphasis on the Fifth Maine Regiment. It also has a growing collection of materials relating to local history. Subject areas include early settlers, tourism between 1880-1920, and World War II.

Visitors can also take the Peaks Island Military Historic Trail administered by the museum, a self-guided tour of the World War II Peaks Island Military Reservation.

The center is hosting a Civil War encampment on August 18-19, 2001, and the rededication of the Alonzo P. Stinson monument in June 2001.

Both in-school and museum children's programs are offered, focusing on Peaks Island history, tourism, and the Civil War.

The museum has a small gift shop but no café. There are several restaurants on the island.

While You're in the Area

Nearby attractions include the Umbrella Cover Museum (p. 211), the Eighth Maine Regimental Hall (p. 208), Greenwood Garden, and Battery Steele (p. 207).

The First Parish Church

9 Cleaveland Street
Brunswick, ME 04011
(207) 729-7331
w3.ime.net/~fpchurch/

Overview

Founded in 1717, the church has a rich history. The building (the parish's third) is an early Richard Upjohn. It became a prototype in American church architecture for 50 years. A number of significant events occurred in the church, and many famous people have been leaders, members, speakers, or visitors. Harriet Beecher Stowe sat in pew 23 when she had her vision of Uncle Tom's death.

Directions and Hours

From U.S. 1, I-95, U.S. 201, or Maine 196: Go to Brunswick downtown, Maine Street. Go south on Maine. Cross the railroad tracks. The church will loom on your left.

The church is open Monday-Friday from 8:00-5:00, but closed holidays.

Admission and Membership

There is no fee for tours, but a donation is appreciated. Monies go to the archives work.

What to See

The church's interior is not only architecturally significant, but has extensive faux-oak painting, one of the best examples of the era.

General Joshua L. Chamberlain was an active member for over 50 years. His father-in-law was minister for over 40 years, and the archives include his journals, covering over 30 years. Researchers use the archives (arranged with two weeks notice) for nineteenth century lives and events, and for early genealogy information.

School group tours may be arranged with two weeks notice.

There is no gift shop or café, but there are restaurants within easy walking distance.

While You're in the Area

There are many other features in the area. Bowdoin College and Art Museum (p. 113), the Peary MacMillan Arctic Museum (p. 172), Hawthorne-Longfellow Library and special collections; Pejepscot Historical Society has a museum (p. 172), the Joshua L. Chamberlain House (p. 172), and the Skolfield Whittier House (p. 172); the Maine Maritime Museum (p. 209) is 10 miles away in Bath; and both Bath and Brunswick have fine small art galleries.

Fort Knox Visitor and Education Center

Route 174
Prospect, ME 04416
(207) 469-6553
www.FortKnox.Maineguide.com

Overview

The Fort Knox Visitor and Education Center is one of the best preserved mid-eighteenth century forts on the East Coast. Fort Knox is a state historic site and a national landmark. The newly opened visitors center showcases local history and military history relating to the region.

Directions and Hours

From Belfast: Proceed north on Route 1, through Searsport and Stockton Springs. Immediately before crossing the Waldo-Hancock County suspension bridge, take a left onto Route 174. Fort Knox will be approximately ¼ mile on the right.

From Bar Harbor: Follow Route 1 south across the Waldo-Hancock County suspension bridge, immediately adjacent to the town of Bucksport. Once over the bridge, take a right onto Route 174. Fort Knox will be approximately ¼ mile on the right.

From Bangor/Route 1A: Follow Route 1A south through the towns of Hampden, Winterport, Frankfort, and Prospect. In Prospect Center, take a left onto Route 174. Follow Route 174 for approximately four miles. Fort Knox will be on your left.

From Bangor/Route 15: Follow Route 15 south through the city of Brewer and the towns of Orrington and Bucksport. In Bucksport, take a right onto Route 1 south and proceed over Waldo-Hancock County suspension bridge. Take a left onto Route 174. Fort Knox will be approximately ¼ mile on the right

The museum is open from May 1 until November 1, and is handicap accessible.

Hours: 9:00 A.M. until sunset.

Admission and Membership

$2 for adults, $.50 for children aged 6-12. Seniors and children under six are free. Membership is $25/year for individuals, $35/year for families, $100 for sustaining, and $1,000 for sponsor membership.

What to See

Opening during the summer of 2001, the Fort Knox Visitor and Information Center will have educational exhibits that depict fort construction, military use, and the history of the Penobscot River region.

As part of the Friends of Fort Knox Summer Series, the Twentieth Marine Civil War Re-enactors will perform July 28-29 and August 25-26, 2001.

There is a small museum gift shop. The museum has no café, but there are many nearby restaurants.

While You're in the Area

The museum is near Acadia National Park, Maritime Museum (p. 209), Abbe Museum (p. 105), and the Johnathan Buck Memorial.

Fort O'Brien State Historic Site

Route 92
Machiasport, ME 04654
(207) 941-4014
www.state.me.us/doc

Overview

The Fort O'Brien State Historic Site displays the earthwork of the old fort, built in 1775.

Directions and Hours

From Route 1 in Machais, take Route 92 to Machaisport. Look for park sign on the right about four miles from Route 1. Grounds are open year round even when the gates are closed. The area is not handicap accessible.

Admission and Membership

Admission is free.

What to See

Fort O'Brien (Fort Machias) was built in 1775 and destroyed by the British in the same year. It was refortified in 1777 and destroyed once again by the British in 1814. Well-preserved earthworks which overlook Machias Bay were erected for a battery of guns in 1863. The first naval engagement of the Revolution was fought offshore in 1775, five days before the Battle at Bunker Hill. The view from the fort is beautiful.

While You're in the Area

In the nearby town of Machias, visitors can see the Burnham Tavern (p. 116).

Franklin Historical Society

PO Box 317
Franklin, ME 04634
(207) 565-2223

Overview

The Franklin Historical Society offers local artifacts celebrating town history, including the local heritage in the shipbuilding and granite industries.

Directions and Hours

Take Route 1 northeast from Ellsworth to Route 182. Follow the fork in the road onto Route 200S. The society is another 2.2 miles, on the right side of the road.

The museum is open from July 4 through Labor Day and should be handicap accessible as of summer 2001.

Hours: First and third Saturdays of the month from 11:00 A.M. to 3:00 P.M. Also open by appointment any time.

Admission and Membership

The museum is free, but donations are accepted. Membership is $3/year.

What to See

The historical society's collection includes assorted family artifacts, kitchen items, tools, granite industry tools, and genealogical information. They occasionally offer children's programming.

The museum sells stationery and postcards, but there is no gift shop. A local store has a lunch counter where visitors can eat.

While You're in the Area

The museum is located in Downeast Maine, only a few miles from Acadia National Park and Bar Harbor.

Freeport Historical Society

45 Main Street
Freeport, ME 04032
(207) 865-3170

Overview

The Freeport Historical Society owns two historic properties, the Harrington House and Pettengill Farm Gardens. Harrington House is a 1830 Federal period building with Transitional Greek Revival and Colonial Revival interior. Pettengill Farm includes a saltbox house ca. 1810 on 140 acres with fields, woods, salt marshes, and apple orchards on the Harraseeket River estuary.

Directions and Hours

Take exit 19 off I-95, north of Portland. Harrington House is located at 45 Main Street in Freeport.

To get to Pettengill Farm Gardens from Main Street in Freeport. Turn east on Bow Street (across from the L.L. Bean main entrance). Go 1½ miles, then turn right onto Pettengill Road. Park at the gate and then walk along the dirt road for about 15 minutes to the farmhouse.

Freeport Historical Society is open year-round and is not handicap accessible.

Hours: Winter: Tuesday-Friday 10:00 A.M. to 2:00 P.M. and by appointment. Summer hours:

to be announced, so contact the museum for up to date information.

Admission and Membership

There is no admission cost. Please contact the museum for membership information.

What to See

The Harrington House was built by merchant Enoch Harrington with locally made bricks. It now houses the Freeport Historical Society library, office, and museum store. Attached to the house is a carriage barn, creating a small courtyard that is encircled with antique roses and more than 20 varieties of plants commonly used during the 1860s such as bee balm, catmint, false indigo, and monkshood. The Pettengill Farm house remains without plumbing and electricity. Around the house are wild roses, lilacs, cedar trees, and other plants, some of which are Native American species, found when colonists arrived. Walking trails for people and dogs offer marsh views.

The Historical Society is expanding their research and library services and is developing permanent Freeport history exhibits.

The 26th annual Pettengill Farm Day will occur on October 14, 2001 with house and garden tours, a horse drawn wagon, and local civil war reenactors.

Educational programs are offered to school groups and scouting groups. Included is Freeport history information, research classes, and life on an 1850s saltwater farm.

The Historical Society has a gift shop. Nearby places to eat are the Corsican Restaurant at 9 Mechanic Street, the Broad Arrow Tavern, and the Jameson Tavern.

While You're in the Area

Nearby place to visit while in area include the Peary-MacMillan Museum (p. 172) and the Pjepscot Historical Society (p. 172).

Friendship Museum, Inc.

1 Martin Point Rd.
Friendship, ME 04547
(207) 832-4337

Overview

The museum is housed in an old one-room brick schoolhouse. Its exhibits represent life in a small fishing village, with over half of the exhibits relating to the famous Friendship sloop.

Directions and Hours

Take Route 220 south to Friendship. The museum is ¼ mile before the center of town on the corner of Route 220 and Martin Point Road.

Open from July 1 through Labor Day, Monday-Saturday 1:00 P.M.-4:00 P.M. and Sunday 2:00 P.M.-4:00 P.M. The museum is not handicap accessible.

Admission and Membership

Admission is free but donations are accepted. Annual membership: $1 students, $5 individual (regular), $10 family, $100 sponsor, $250 patron, and $1,000 Benefactor (lifetime).

What to See

The overall mission of Friendship Museum is to accumulate, organize, and exhibit artifacts and memorabilia relating to the history of the Town of Friendship. This ever-changing collection consists of paintings, drawings, photographs, books, diaries, maps, documents, furniture, textiles, household fixtures and equipment, boat/ship models and many items of maritime equipment.

Approximately half of the collection is maritime related and features the famous Friendship Sloop, first built by Wilbur Morse in 1874. The Friendship Sloop Society, which now represents owners of over 250 sloops, provided much of the exhibit material.

Coinciding with the all-day celebration of Friendship Day, the museum hosts an open house from 10:00 A.M.-4:00 P.M. on the last day of July.

There is no gift shop or café, although the museum sells a few items.

While You're in the Area

The museum is located in the quaint fishing village of Friendship where life is centered around lobstering and other sea-related occupations.

The Fryeburg Public Library

98 Main Street
Fryeburg, ME 04037
(207) 935-2731

Overview

The Fryeburg Public Library houses a collection of Hopalong Cassidy memorabilia, pictures, and books.

Directions and Hours

From Portland, take Route 302 into Fryeburg (about 55 miles). Go past the monument in the center of town (at the junction of Routes 5 and 113). The library is a small granite building two blocks past the monument on 302, on the left hand side.

The library is open year round. It is handicap accessible.

Hours: Monday 9:00-7:00, Tuesday-Thursday 9:00-5:00, Saturday 9:00-2:00.

Admission and Membership

There is no cost for admission into the library. Memberships are not available.

What to See

The Clarence Milford Room plans to be open at the Fryeburg Library in the summer of 2001. Clarence Milford, the author of *Hopalong Cassidy*, lived in Fryeburg for many years. The library is dedicating a room to his memory that includes a small collection of his many books, including first editions. The room will also feature his pictures, personal letters and papers, which have been in storage for many years. These will be organized, catalogued and displayed at the museum.

The first week in October is the Fryeburg Fair ("The Blue Ribbon Classic"), a huge eight-day agricultural fair and one of the biggest fairs in the Northeast.

There is no gift shop. Visitors can eat at nearby cafés.

While You're in the Area

North Conway, New Hampshire, with its many attractions is about 20 minutes away. Nearby Mount Washington has many attractions, including the observatory (p. 363). There is a train ride through the Notch, and polar caves.

Gates House

Machiasport Historical Society
PO Box 301
Machiasport, ME 04655-0301
(207) 255-8461

Overview

The Gates House contains rooms displaying period furniture and clothing, along with extensive genealogies of local families.

Directions and Hours

Take Route 92 from Route 1 in Machias. Follow directional signs to the museum.

The museum is open from mid-June to Labor Day, Tuesday-Saturday from 12:30-4:30. It is not handicap accessible.

Admission and Membership

Donations are requested. Membership is $7.50/year for individuals, $12.50/year for families, and $150 for life.

What to See

In addition to rooms filled with period furniture, clothing, and artifacts, Gates House contains a Marine Room, containing models, photos, and marine artifacts.

There is a privately owned gift shop next to the museum. Visitors can eat at restaurants in nearby Machias.

While You're in the Area

Visitors may also want to explore Fort O'Brien (p. 128), scene of the first naval battle of the American Revolution; Burnham Tavern (p. 116) in Machias; and Jasper Beach.

George I. Lewis and Family Gallery

Portland Public Library
5 Monument Square
Portland, ME 04101
(207) 871-1700
www.portlandlibrary.com

Overview

The Portland Public Library's Lewis Gallery provides an open venue for Maine and New England artists. The gallery features individual and group exhibits of diverse subject matter and media.

Directions and Hours

From Route 295, take exit 7 (Franklin Street). At the fourth traffic light, take a right onto Congress Street. The library is located on the corner of Congress and Elm Streets, across from Monument Square.

The gallery is open year round, and is handicap accessible.

Hours: Monday, Wednesday, Friday 9:00-6:00; Tuesday, Thursday noon-9:00; Saturday 9:00-5:00.

Admission and Membership

Admission to the gallery is free. Memberships are not available.

What to See

In addition to the gallery, the library's Portland Room includes the Maine collection, children's antique books, books on the book arts, and first editions.

There is a children's and young adult's room, and regular children's programming.

There is a book peddler book cart that sells used books and various gift items. There is no café, but the new Portland Public Market is located next door to the library, and there are many restaurants on Congress Street and in the historic Old Port section of Portland within walking distance of the library.

While You're in the Area

The Portland Museum of Art (p. 176) and the Children's Museum of Maine (p. 207) are also in the area.

Great Harbor Maritime Museum

125 Main Street
Northeast Harbor, ME 04662
(207) 276-5262

Overview

The Great Harbor Maritime Museum is the only maritime museum in Hancock County. This informal museum is located in an old firehouse. Nearby Mount Desert Island is peppered with boat builders, which adds to the museum's charm.

Directions and Hours

From the Maine Turnpike: Take Route 3 through Ellsworth, crossing the bridge onto Mount Desert Island. At the Mobil gas station, go left onto Route 198 and follow it to Northeast Harbor. The museum is located in the middle of the village and is grey stucco with dark green trim.

The museum is open from the end of June until Labor Day, Tuesday-Saturday 10:00-5:00. From Labor Day through Columbus Day, the museum is open weekends only. Only the first floor is handicap accessible.

Admission and Membership

Suggested admission is $3.

What to See

In addition to artifacts and a "Learn to Look, Look to Learn" program that takes people to the islands, the Museum is developing an artist in residence program.

Children's programming is offered by arrangement.

The museum has no café, but there are many restaurants within a short walk or drive.

While You're in the Area

The museum is near Acadia National Park, Abbe Museum (p. 105), Wendell Gilley Museum of Birdcarving (p. 201), Mount Desert Island Historical Society (p. 156), and the Natural History Museum at the College of the Atlantic (p. 158).

Hamilton House (SPNEA)

40 Vaughan's Lane
South Berwick, ME 03908
(207) 384-2454
www.spnea.org

Overview

After railroads made the region accessible in the late nineteenth century, coastal Maine became a fashionable destination for wealthy summer people. Many of the newcomers bought and restored the fine old houses built during the prosperous years following the American Revolution. In 1898 Mrs. Emily Tyson and her stepdaughter, Elise, purchased the ca. 1785 Hamilton House, built on a site overlooking the Salmon Falls River. The Tysons restored the house to its former state. Influenced by literary imagery, including the writings of their neighbor and friend, Sarah Orne Jewett, they decorated the house in an interpretation of America's colonial past.

Directions and Hours

From the south: Take I-95 to Maine exit 3.

From the north: After the York tolls, take exit 2. Follow Route 236 for nine miles. After the junction with Route 91 take the first left onto Brattle Street then take the second right onto Vaughan's Lane. Follow to the end.

The house museum is open June 1 to October 15. It is not handicap accessible.

Hours: Wednesday through Sunday, 11:00 A.M. to 5:00 P.M. Tours are at 11:00 A.M., 12:00, 1:00, 2:00, 3:00 and 4:00 P.M.

Admission and Membership

$5 for adults, $4.50 senior citizens, ½ off for students and children 6-12. Children 5 and under, SPNEA members, and residents of South Berwick are free. AAA members receive a 2 for 1 discount. SPNEA membership is $35/year for individuals and $45/year for a household. Membership includes free admissions to 35 properties and museums across New England.

What to See

The house contains a mixture of antiques, painted murals, and simple country furnishings. In addition to the house, the extensive grounds include a formal garden, the site of a summer concert series every Sunday in July, a garden cottage, and planted fields. Paths provide access to a nearby state park.

The Hamilton House offers group tours and public programs throughout the season.

The house does not have a gift shop or a café but visitors can eat in the center of South Berwick, where several restaurants are located.

While You're in the Area

Attractions and museums nearby include the Sarah Orne Jewett House in South Berwick (p. 188), Castle Tucker (p. 118) and the Nickels-Sortwell House (p. 162) in Wiscassett, the Old Berwick Historical Society (p. 120), and the Sayward Wheeler House (p. 189).

Harrison Historical Society Museum

121 Haskell Hill Road
Harrison, ME 04040
(207) 583-6225

Overview

The Harrison Historical Society Museum contains three floors and an annex filled with artifacts of the town of Harrison.

Directions and Hours

Take Route 35 or Route 117 to Harrison Village. From the center of Town, take Dawes Hill Road and turn right onto Maple Ridge Road. Then turn left onto Haskell Hill Road.

The museum is open from April to December, and is handicap accessible.

Hours: meetings are held on the first Wednesday of every month at 7:00; open house every Wednesday in July and August 1:00-4:00.

Admission and Membership

Admission to the museum is free. Membership is $5/year for individuals.

What to See

The museum houses such research materials as Harrison cemetery records from 1810 to the present, obituaries, maps, area town histories, and news clipping scrapbooks from 1900 to the present.

There are programs for groups of school children to visit the museum.

There is no gift shop. There is no café, but there are restaurants in the center of town, three miles from the museum.

While You're in the Area

The Deertrees Theater is also in Harrison. The Historical Society Museums of Bridgton (p. 114), Waterford, and Norway (p. 210) are also in the area.

Head Tide Church

Head Tide Road
Alna, ME 04535

Overview

The Head Tide Church is an early eighteenth-century church with boxed pews that overlooks the village.

Directions and Hours

From route 1 in Wicasset, take route 218 north for about 8 miles to Head Tide Road (on the right). Follow around the church on the right on top of the hill. Park and walk up dirt driveway.

The museum is open in July and August. It is not handicap accessible.

Hours: Saturday 2:00-4:00.

Admission and Membership

Donations are accepted.

What to See

The church features the remnants of the Paul Revere Bell, broken by lightning. There is also a large collection of local historic photographs. The church holds an annual service in August.

There is no gift shop or café, but visitors can eat at a luncheonette in Alna or at restaurants in Wiscasset.

While You're in the Area

Nearby in Alna, visitors can tour the Narrow Gauge Railroad Museum (p. 148), the Alna Meeting House (p. 167), and the Alna Schoolhouse (both on route 218). In Wiscasset there are two SPNEA houses (pp. 118 and 162) and the Lincoln County Jail.

High Country Mission on Hackers Hill

Quaker Ridge
Casco, ME 04015
(866) 310-8445 or (207) 627-6065
www.SilentPreacher.com

Photo courtesy of High Country Mission.

Overview

The High Country Mission is steward of Hackers Hill, a natural landmark and one of Maine's most accessible and panoramic views. On a clear day, visitors can see for 100 miles from east to west and a 360 degree panorama of the area, including Mount Washington in New Hampshire. This natural delight of outdoor landscape is located on a solid rock dome and has much to offer for geologists, stargazers, leaf peepers, and others who want tranquility and peace.

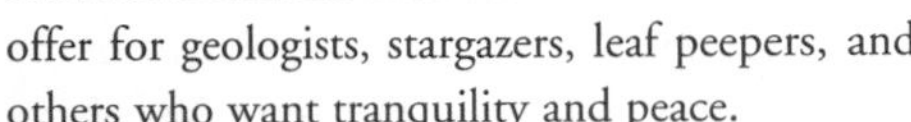

Directions and Hours

From Windham: Take Route 302 west through Raymond to the Casco town line. Go right on Quaker Ridge Road. At the "Cry of Loon" gift shop, go 3½ miles to Hacker's Hill Gate on the right.

From Oxford: Take Route 11 west through Poland into Casco. Pass Route 121 intersection and continue for one mile. Go left at Quaker Ridge Road.

From Naples: Take Route 11 east for 1½ miles beyond Hancock. Go right onto Quaker Ridge Road.

The area is open for autos, trucks, vans, and a limited number of buses from May until November. It is open all year for hikers, snowmobilers and skiers. The Quaker Meeting House is open to interested parties in automobiles. It is located 25 feet from the roadway. The area is handicap accessible.

Summer Hours: 8:30 A.M. until ½ hour past sunset. Closed to traffic on Tuesdays. Closed in inclement and dangerous weather.

Admission and Membership

There is no charge for admission, but there is a Jacob's Well set up for donations.

What to See

This historic area was inhabited by many Quakers. The Friends Meeting House was built in 1804 and can be accessed at any time for no charge. Each Sunday there is an informal, non-denominational church service at 11:00 A.M. The people who attend these simple services support the maintenance and improvement of the Hill. Sunday school is available for children.

There is no museum gift shop, but printed clothing is available by mail order. There are many nearby restaurants in Casco Village, including the Naples Diner.

While You're in the Area

High Country Mission is near Big Sabego Lake and the Naples waterways. There are various local shops and activities including tourist boat trips.

History House Museum

Elm Street
Skowhegan, ME 04976
(207) 474-6632

Overview

The History House Museum is set up as an 1800s house. Tours are given and area genealogy is available.

Directions and Hours

Take 95 north to the exit for Route 201 north to Skowhegan. Elm Street is off of Route 201.

The museum is open from May through September, but is not handicap accessible.

Hours: Tuesday-Friday 1:00-5:00.

Admission and Membership

$2 for adults, $1 for children.

What to See

The History House Museum is a local area history museum. School tours are available.

There is no gift shop. There is no café, but there are sandwich shops nearby.

While You're in the Area

Nearby attractions and museums include the Colby Art Museum (p. 119), the Pittsfield Historical Society (p. 210), the Depot House Museum (p. 210), Waterville Historical Society (p. 211), the Wiscasset, Waterville, and Farmington Railroad Museum (p. 204), and Redington Museum of the Waterville Historical Society (p. 181).

The Holt House

Blue Hill Historical Society
Water Street
Blue Hill, ME 04614

Overview

The Holt House is located in the center of the historic district of a seacoast village. The largely unchanged Holt House played an important role in local history since it was built in 1815.

Directions and Hours

From the south, take Route 1 and 3 through Bucksport. Turn right on Route 15 in Enland to Blue Hill. Turn right at the stop sign entering the village. Take the first left and the house is immediately on the right.

From Down East and Acadia: Take Routes 1 and 3 through Ellsworth. Turn left on Route 172 leaving town. Proceed 14 miles to Blue Hill and take the first left to the house, immediately on the right.

The house is open from July 4 through the first week in September and otherwise by appointment. It is not handicap accessible.

Hours: Tuesday and Friday 1:00-4:00, Saturday 10:00-1:00, and by appointment.

Admission and Membership

Admission is $3. Memberships are $5/year for individuals, $10/year for families, and $25 for continuing memberships. School groups are free.

What to See

The Holt House features stenciled walls in the dining room and a unique hooked/braided rug in the front bedroom, displaying the history of an unknown local family. There is a collection of nineteenth-century toys and children's attire in a back bedroom. During the holidays, the seasonally decorated Holt House hosts annual Christmas tours for local school groups.

There is no gift shop. There is a small café for breakfast and lunch adjacent to the house and several other restaurants within walking distance in the village.

While You're in the Area

The historic Parson Fisher Homestead is one mile away, and the Colonel Black Mansion and Museum (p. 205) in Ellsworth is 14 miles away.

Hudson Museum, The University of Maine

5746 Maine Center for the Arts
University of Maine
Orono, ME 04469
(207) 581-1901
www.umaine.edu/hudsonmuseum

Overview

The Hudson Museum is the gateway for the University and the community to explore and understand the diversity of the human experience. The museum houses artifacts from Micronesia to Maine that excite the imagination and open doors to greater understanding of world cultures.

Directions and Hours

From 95 take exit 51. Follow the signs to the University of Maine, then follow the signs to the Maine Center for the Arts, Hudson Museum.

The museum is open year round, and is handicap accessible.

Hours: Tuesday-Friday 9:00-4:00; Saturday and Sunday 11:00-4:00.

Admission and Membership

Admission to the museum is free. There are fees for guided tours for groups. Membership is $35/year for individuals, $45/year for families, $25/year for students and seniors; donor memberships start at $100.

What to See

The Hudson Museum has hands-on computer-based activities for children, and offers regular family programs and lectures. There are also special events, such as the annual Maine Indian Basketmakers Sale and Demonstration each December.

The Hudson Museum Shop features Maine Indian baskets and gifts from around the world. It offers a 10% discount for University of Maine alumni. Restaurants are located nearby.

While You're in the Area

The University of Maine campus features other museums and attractions nearby. These include the Page Farm and Home Museum (p. 210), the Fay Hyland Arboretum (p. 208), and the Maynard F. Jordon Planetarium (p. 153).

Island History Room

Islesford Library
Little Cranberry Island
Islesford, ME 04646
(207) 244-9565

Overview

The Island History Room exhibits the history of the people of Little Cranberry Island. Little Cranberry Island is the farthest "Down east" of the offshore Maine Islands that still have a year-round population. Isleford is the village on Little Cranberry Island.

Directions and Hours

Take Route 1 to Ellsworth, then follow Route 102 to Southwest Harbor.

Or, take Route 198 to Northeast Harbor. Visitors must take the ferry from Southwest Harbor or Northeast Harbor. A water taxi (207-244-5724) is also available.

The room is open year round whenever the library is open, and is handicap accessible.

Hours: Tuesday and Thursday 11:00-1:00; also during the summer, Wednesday evenings and Saturdays.

Admission and Membership

Admission to the room is free. Membership to the Islesford Historical Society is $8/year for individuals and $10/year for families.

What to See

The Island Historical Room contains exhibits, artifacts, and archives concerning the history of Little Cranberry Island, Maine, and its people.

There is no gift shop, but local publications are available, including a new *History of Little Cranberry Island, Maine*. There is no café, but there is a good restaurant (from late June through early September) on the town dock.

While You're in the Area

Acadia National Park and the Islesford Historical Museum (p. 138) are also on the island.

Islesford Historical Museum

Little Cranberry Island
Islesford, ME 04646
(207) 244-9224
www.nps.gov/acad

Overview

The Islesford Historical Museum is located on an island about a 40-minute boat ride from the mainland. The beautiful setting provides views back to the Mount Desert Island Mountains. The museum houses a collection that includes ship-related items, such as fishing tools and equipment, and boat and ship models. There is also a changing exhibit room.

Directions and Hours

Take Route 3 from Ellsworth to Mount Desert Island, then Route 102 from the head of Mount Desert Island to Somersville. Take Route 198 to Northeast Harbor, from where the boat to Islesford leaves.

The museum is open from mid-June to September, but is not handicap accessible.

Hours: Daily, 10:00-4:30.

Admission and Membership

There is no cost for admission into the museum. Memberships are not available.

What to See

The museum shows tools, household items, books, letters and other correspondence. Recent exhibits in the changing exhibit room have included photographs of island life reproduced from old glass plates, and historic postcards.

The museum has a bookstore.

The closest place to eat is Northeast Harbor.

While You're in the Area

The Abbe Museum (p. 105), Native American Natural History Museum, and William Gilley Museums (p. 201) are nearby.

John E. and Walter D. Webb Museum of Vintage Fashion

Route 2
Island Falls, ME 04747
(207) 463-2404 (mid May-October 4)
(207) 862-3797 (November-mid May)

Overview

The John E. and Walter D. Webb Museum of Vintage Fashion is the result of 50 years of collecting men's, women's, and children's antique clothing. The museum contains 17 rooms, 14 of which hold displays of antique fashions. The structure itself could be deemed historic, having been built in 1894 by A. L. Hamilton and rebuilt after a fire in 1910 by Byron Noyes.

Directions and Hours

This inconspicuous, red, three story structure is located centrally in the village of Island Falls. Follow Route 2 into Aroostook County and into Island Falls—the museum is on Route 2.

The museum is open (in 2001) from June 4 until October 4.

Hours: 10:00-4:00, Monday-Thursday. Weekend visits and group tours are available by appointment. The museum is not handicap accessible.

Admission and Membership

Donations of $3 per person are appreciated. Senior citizens are $2 and children under twelve, $1. AAA members receive a 10 percent discount with card. All tours are guided and cameras, video recorders, food, and drink are not allowed.

What to See

The display rooms evoke a homelike atmosphere and feature themes including a millinery and dressmaker's shop, a "yesteryear" room, a hat boutique, a tea room, a haberdashery shop, a children's room, a bridal room, and an Island Falls room. It is among the largest antique fashion collections in the country.

The museum will not survive the passing of its owner, Francis Webb Stratton, when the collection will be sold and the proceeds donated to helping those with medical needs.

There is a small gift shop. There is no café, but there are two restaurants within the village.

While You're in the Area

The museum is near the Island Falls Historical Society (p. 209), just 10 miles from the Lumberman's Museum (p. 171), and 10 miles from the Railroad Museum (p. 186).

Jonathan Fisher Homestead

Route 15
Blue Hill, ME 04614
(207) 374-2459

Overview

The Parson Fisher House is a living memorial to Blue Hill's first settled minister. Jonathan Fisher was a remarkable scholar who, besides being a parson, was also a farmer, missionary, portrait and landscape painter, a wood engraver, a writer of poetry and prose, a scientist, mathematician and surveyor, and the father of a large family.

Directions and Hours

The Fisher Homestead is located just south of Blue Hill Village on Route 15. Proceed on Route 15 to the point where Routes 172-175 turn left for Sedgwick. (Tradewinds Shopping Center) Continue straight ahead one eighth mile. The Fisher Homestead is on the left side of Route 15.

From Ellsworth: Take Route 172 south to Blue Hill. Continue on Route 15 as above.

From Bangor (or Interstate 95): Take Interstate 395 then take Route 15 south. In Brewer, follow Route 15 to Blue Hill and continue as above.

If coming north on Route 1, Maine 3, go through Bucksport then follow Route 15 south to Blue Hill and continue as above.

The museum is open daily from 1:00-5:00 July 1 until September 30, and is open by appointment only from October 1-June 30. The museum is handicap accessible.

Admission and Membership

$3 per person, children under eight are free. Membership is $10/year for individuals, $15/year for families, $25 for sustaining, $100 for contributing, and $1,000 for endowment membership.

What to See

The Jonathan Fisher Homestead has 40 years of journals written by Mr. Fisher in a code that he devised to save paper. These have all been translated and are in the process of being published. This 1814 home has most of the original contents including books, furniture, tools, and town and church records, most of which were made by Mr. Fisher himself. There is a remarkable collection of artwork including paintings and wood engravings that he used to illustrate the books he wrote. In the house are his mother's bible and wedding shoes and the clock that Mr. Fisher made with his wooden works while he was a student at Harvard College. The museum also has a great deal of Fisher geneology.

Don't miss the Annual Arts and Crafts Festival held every Independence Day weekend.

Call for exact dates for the Children's Summer Festivals in July and August.

There is a small museum gift shop. The museum has no café, but there are many nearby restaurants and a convenient restaurant listing available at the museum.

While You're in the Area

Holt House (p. 136) is also in Blue Hill.

The Jones Museum of Glass & Ceramics

35 Douglas Mountain Road
PO Box 129
Sebago, ME 04029
(207) 787-3370

Overview

Founded in 1978, The Jones Museum of Glass & Ceramics is America's only museum of glass and ceramics. There are over 7,000 objects from ancient artifacts to modern creations. Visitors can also view special exhibits and consult the research library.

Directions and Hours

From Portland, take Route 114 to E. Sebago, and follow it to Route 107. Take Route 107 North to the Dyke Mountain Road to the Douglas Mountain Road, and follow the signs.

The museum is open from mid-May to mid-October, and is partially handicap accessible.

Hours: Monday through Saturday 10:00-5:00, Sunday 1:00-5:00.

Admission and Membership

$5 for adults, $3.75 for seniors and AAA members, $3 for students, children free. Membership levels start at $25/year for individuals and $35/year for families.

What to See

The collection of glass includes ancient, early blown, pattern molded, pressed, cut, engraved, and fancy by companies such as Sandwich, Pittsburgh, Tiffany, and Steuben. There are ceramics by Native Americans, Russians, and companies such as Wedgwood, Redware, Worcester, and Sevres.

The Jones Museum holds new exhibitions every year. Special lectures and seminars are offered monthly, and there is a research library for use by appointment.

There is a volunteer docent program and special treasure hunt tours for children.

The Gallery Shop carries original antique glass, gifts, cards, jewelry, and more.

Visitors can eat at local sandwich shops.

While You're in the Area

The museum is adjacent to the Douglas Mountain Preserve hiking trail and lookout tower with views of Mount Washington, Sebago Lake, and Casco Bay.

Kennebec Historical Society

61 Winthrop Street
PO Box 5582
Augusta, ME 04332-5582
(207) 622-7718
www.geocites.com/kennebec_historical

Overview

First formed in 1891 as the Kennebec Natural History and Antiquarian Society, Kennebec Historical Society is an organization whose mission is to "preserve, protect, and interpret" artifacts relating to the rich history of Maine's capital city.

Kennebec Historical Society. Photo by Linda Violette.

Directions and Hours

From I-95: Take exit 30. Then take Western Avenue to Airport Road (across from Shaw's Plaza). Turn left. Follow Airport Road to the top of the hill, where it turns right, to Winthrop Street. The Historical Society building is 10 blocks down Winthrop Street on the far left corner of Summer Street.

The museum is open year-round and is handicap accessible on the first floor only.

Hours: 10:00 A.M. to 2:00 P.M. Tuesday, Wednesday, and Saturday; 6:00-8:00 P.M. Thursday.

Admission and Membership

Donations are requested. Membership cost is $10/year for a student/senior, $15/year for an individual, $25/year for a family, $50/year for a business, $100/year for a corporate membership, and $100 for a life membership.

What to See

The society presents public lectures and programs, and maintains a collection that includes local newspapers dating back to 1822. The collection consists of: primary sources (documents and manuscripts), reference books, maps, pictorial records from the nineteenth and early twentieth centuries, Augusta Architectural and Historic Buildings survey materials, and the 1938 WPA photographs of all buildings in Augusta.

The museum houses a collection of primarily Augusta-related artifacts, documents, manuscripts, and books, as well as rotating displays of objects and photographs throughout the facility.

There are items for sale at the facility. Cafés are available on nearby Water Street and fast food is located on Western Avenue, four blocks away.

While You're in the Area

Other interesting places to visit while you are in the area include Old Fort Western (a restored eighteenth century fort, p. 167), Maine State Museum (p. 149), the Maine State Library, the Maine State Archives (p. 209), the Maine Military Historical Society Museum (p. 209), Capital Park, and the Blaine House (p. 146).

The Kennebunkport Historical Society

PO Box 1173
125-175 North Street
Kennebunkport, ME 04046-1173
(207) 967-2751
www.kporthistory.org

Overview

The Kennebunkport Historical Society offers guided and self-guided walking tours of the village, and also has two museums. The Nott House, a Greek revival structure, is unique in its original period furniture. The Pasco Exhibit Center features a large textile collection in period settings.

Directions and Hours

Take I-95 north to exit 2 (Route 9 and 1) and follow Route 9 into Kennebunkport. The Nott House is at Spring and Maine Streets. To get to the Pasco Center, go left on Maine and right on North Street.

Or, take I-95 south to exit 4 and take Route 1 south. Go left on Log Cabin Road to reach the Pasco Center at 125 North Street.

The Pasco Exhibit Center is open year round and is handicap accessible.

Hours: Tuesday-Friday 10:00-4:00; Saturday 10:00-1:00, mid-June through mid-October.

The Nott House is open mid-June through mid-October. It is not handicap accessible. Hours: Tuesday-Friday 1:00-4:00; Saturday 10:00-1:00.

Admission and Membership

Nott House tours are $5. Membership is $25/year for individuals, $35/year for families, and $100/year for businesses. Discounts are available for children and groups.

What to See

The Pasco Exhibit Center, located at 125 North Street, features an extensive textile collection of cloth from the mid-1800s through the 1920s displayed in period settings. The Nott House

Photo courtesy of the Kenneth E. Stoddard Shell Museum

features docent-led tours of the mansion, which is completely furnished with the belongings and treasures of four generations of the Perkins and Nott families.

In the spring of 2001, the Nott House gardens will be refurbished. Occasional children's programming is available.

There is a gift shop but no café. There are numerous eating establishments nearby.

While You're in the Area

Visitors may also seek out the many other active historical societies/museums in the neighboring towns of York, Wells/Ogunquit, Kennebunk, Saco, and Old Orchard Beach.

Kenneth E. Stoddard Shell Museum

RR1, Box 452
Boothbay, ME 04537
(207) 633-4828
www.mpdblue.com/dolphin

Overview

The Kenneth E. Stoddard Museum is located inside a 56-foot covered bridge surrounded by outside walkways. The glass-topped display cases are filled with a fascinating array of shells atop pure white sand.

Directions and Hours

From Route 1 north: One mile north of Wiscasset, turn right onto Route 27. Follow for seven miles and go left onto Hardwick Road. Follow for 200 feet and go right into parking lot.

The museum is open from May 1 until October 1, and is handicap accessible.

Museum hours: 10:00 A.M.-10:00 P.M. daily.

Admission and Membership

Donations are appreciated.

What to See

The museum houses one of the largest private shell collections in the world. The property features flower gardens, running water and pools stocked with goldfish and water flowers. Other attractions include miniature golf and an ice cream hut.

A mini-golf tournament is held annually during the second weekend of September. All proceeds from the tournament are donated to the Shriners Hospital for burned and crippled children. Donations average over $3,000 each year for the past six years.

Children's programming is offered by arrangement.

The museum features an ice cream hut and hot dog restaurant within a half mile drive.

While You're in the Area

The museum is less than one mile from the Boothbay Railway Village (p. 112).

Kinsley House Museum

Hampden Historical Society
83 Main Street
Hampden, ME 04444
(207) 862-2027

Overview

The Kingsley House Museum contains an extensive genealogy of early Hampden residents, as well as a collection of Hampden artifacts.

Directions and Hours

Take interstate 95 to exit 44, and follow Route 1A (Main Street) to the museum.

The museum is open daily 10:00-4:00 from April-October, but is not handicap accessible.

Admission and Membership

Admission to the museum is free. Membership is $10/year for individuals, $20/year for families.

What to See

The museum contains artifacts from the Hannibal Hamlin Law Office, as well as items from the Battle of Hampden and the boat that carried passengers from Boston to Bangor until the 1930s.

The museum sponsors Heritage Days in September. There are also house tours for schools and adults.

There is a gift shop. There is no café, but there are restaurants nearby.

While You're in the Area

The Bangor Historical Society (p. 207), Cole's Land Transportation Museum (p. 119), and Leonard's Mills (p. 146) are also in the area.

The Knight House and Downing Shoe Shop

Operated By Auburn Heritage, Inc.
30 Great Falls Plaza
Auburn, ME 04212-3446
(207) 783-0584
www.rootsweb.com/nmeandrhs/auburn/heritage/knight/house

Overview

The Knight House is the oldest frame house in Auburn, Maine, built in 1796.

Directions and Hours

From the Maine Turnpike: Take Exit 12 in Auburn. Proceed north for four miles to Minot Ave. After one half mile, go right onto Court Street. Take a left before the Longly Bridge to the Falls.

The museum is open from July 4 until the Great Falls Balloon Festival, which is usually the third weekend in August. The museum is not handicap accessible.

Hours: Are by appointment only so please call ahead.

Admission and Membership

Donations are gratefully accepted and membership can be purchased for a nominal fee.

What to See

Special features include shoe shop items, tools, and other authentic furnishings that illustrate aspects of local history.

The museum participates in the Liberty Festival over Independence Day weekend and in the Great Falls Balloon Festival during the third week of August.

Children's programming is available by arrangement.

The museum has no café, but there are many delightful local restaurants.

While You're in the Area

The museum is located near the Androscoggin Historical Society (p. 107), the Auburn-Lowiston Sports Hall of Fame and the Begin Chapter of the American-Canadian Genealogical Society.

Lagerstrom House Museum

Woodland Historical Society
251 Beckstrom Road
Woodland, ME 04736

Overview

The Lagerstrom House was built in 1896. The

farm house is furnished with period furniture.

Directions and Hours

Take Route 161 to New Sweden Road. Turn right onto Beckstrom Road and travel for approximately six miles.

The museum is open during July and August, but is not handicap accessible.

Hours: Sunday 1:00-4:00 and by appointment.

Admission and Membership

Admission to the museum is free. Membership is $2/year for working membership, $5 for contributing membership, and $50 for a lifetime membership.

What to See

The farm house is decorated with furnishings of the early 1900s.

There is no gift shop or café, but there are restaurants in nearby Caribou.

While You're in the Area

The Snowman School Museum (p. 193) is also run by the Woodland Historical Society.

Early 1900s schoolroom. Photo courtesy of L. C. Bates Museum.

L. C. Bates Museum

Route 201
Hinckley, ME 04944
(207) 238-4250
www.gwh.org

Overview

The L.C. Bates Museum is an old-fashioned "cabinet of curiosities" museum with diverse and extensive collections of natural history and culture. The museum provides an educational look into the natural environment and Maine culture. The museum has displays of natural history, including 28 dioramas, Americana, art, ethnology and archaeology, an arboretum, and nature trails. The museum is part of the Good Will Home for children, founded by George W. Hinckley in 1889. Today more than 120 children live at Good Will Hinckley, which has grown to become a village comprised of schools, cottages, libraries, a chapel, farms, and a museum.

Directions and Hours

From I-95: Take exit 36. Go north on Route 201 for six miles.

From Route 2 in Skowhegan: Go south on Route 201 for seven miles.

The museum is located in on Good Will-Hinckley campus on the west side of Route 201.

The museum is open from April 1-November 15 and off season by appointment or chance.

Hours: 10:00 A.M. to 4:30 P.M. Wednesday, Thursday, Friday, and Saturday, 1:00-4:30 P.M. on Sunday.

Admission and Membership

Adults $2, child 12-18 $1, youth under 12 $.75. Group rates are available. Membership is $10/year for individuals, $20-$50/year for families, and $50/year for patrons.

What to See

The L.C. Bates Museum has a wide variety of objects including birds, minerals, fossils, art, marine life, archaeology collections, a six foot tall mounted bird, a cassowary, a blue marlin caught by Ernest Hemingway, sea shells, a Rangeley boat, tools, china, iron cooking utensils, plows, harrows, sleighs, printing presses, spinning wheels and looms, carpentry tools, boat models, a dugout canoe, war artifacts, spear points, axes, gouges, and plummets made by the Red Paint People, prehistoric implements, pre-Columbian ceramics heads and figures made by the Chirique Indians of Central America, Maine Native American baskets, an early 1900s school room, and a print shop. A video and display tells the history of the Good Will-Hinckley Homes for children.

Art is displayed in the top floor gallery in changing exhibits of paintings and sculptures with an emphasis on the work of contemporary Maine artists. Older works include paintings by Hubbard, Akers, and Reid.

The museum offers weekly Saturday morning drop-in natural history family programs, seasonal trail hikes and bird walks, a fall "Heritage Day," summer art exhibits with openings, talks, and panel discussions, as well as other special tours and programs. The museum recommends that families bring a picnic and enjoy the arboretum and trails after their museum visit.

The museum's "Museum on Wheels" outreach program visits schools and institutions.

The museum does have a gift shop. Visitors can eat in Waterville, South Kowhegan, Fairfield, and in Hinckley Village.

While You're in the Area

Nearby museums and interesting attractions include the Colby Art Museum (p. 119).

Lincoln County Museum and Old Jail

PO Box 61
133 Federal Street
Wiscasset, ME 04578
(207) 882-6817
www.wiscasset.net/lcha

Overview

The Lincoln County Museum and Old Jail is a three-story 1811 granite structure with original cells and fascinating period graffiti. Attached is a jailer's house furnished with nineteenth century decorative arts from Maine and displays.

Directions and Hours

From the intersection of Routes 1 and 218 in Wiscasset Village take Route 218 north (Federal Street) for approximately ½ mile.

The museum is open on June and September weekends and July 1-Labor Day Tuesday-Sunday. It is not handicap accessible.

Hours: Tuesdays-Saturday 10:00 A.M. to 4:00 P.M. and Sunday 12:00-4:00 P.M.

Admission and Membership

Adults $3, children 7-17 $2, seniors/AAA members $2.50, and a family $8. Groups rates are available. Membership is $20/year for individuals and $30/year for families.

What to See

Room displays in the 1839 Jailer's House include a living room, a dining room, a bedroom, a kitchen, an office, and a tool collection in the shed. Other exhibits change annually so please contact the museum for up to date information.

Children's programming includes an annual Halloween event. The jail tour is very popular with children.

The museum has a gift shop. Visitors can eat ½ mile from the museum in Wiscasset Village, which has a variety of eateries.

While You're in the Area

Attractions and museums in the area include: Castle Tucker (p. 118), Pownalborough Court House (p. 178), the Maine Art Gallery, the Nickels-Sortwell House Museum (p. 162), the Musical Wonder House (p. 160), along with many galleries and antique shops.

Machiasport Historical Society

PO Box 301
Machiasport, ME 04655-0301
(207) 255-8461

Overview

The Machiasport Historical Society features "hands-on" display rooms loaded with period furniture, marine artifacts, ship models, and vintage photographs.

Directions and Hours

Follow Route 1 to Machias. Take Route 92 to Machiasport. After 3½ miles, follow the signs to the Machiasport Historical Society.

The museum is open from mid June until early September.

Hours: Tuesday-Saturday 12:30-4:30. The Historical Society is not handicap accessible.

Admission and Membership

Donations are appreciated. Membership is $7.50 for individuals, $12.50 for families.

What to See

The Machiasport Historical Society features an extensive collection of maritime items, photographs of ships, period costumes and furniture, and early stoves and kitchen utensils.

The museum has no café, but there are several vending machines available.

While You're in the Area

The museum is near Burnham Tavern in Machias (p. 116), Ruggles House in Columbia Falls (p. 210), Jasper Beach in Machiasport, and Machias Bay.

Maine Arts Commission

55 Capitol Street
25 State House Station
Augusta, ME 04333-0025
(207) 287-0025
www.mainearts.com

Overview

The Maine Arts Commission includes visual arts exhibits in the Blaine House, the governor's official residence. Exhibits are also in the Governor's State House Gallery and the commission offices. There are special events, such as readings, performances, lectures, and conferences.

Directions and Hours

From 95, take exit 30 and go east on Route 202. Take the first right off the rotary onto State Street. Turn left at the first light onto Capitol Street. 55 Capitol Street is the first building on the left.

The museum is open year round, and is handicap accessible.

Hours: Monday-Friday 8:00-5:00.

Admission and Membership

Admission to the museum is free.

What to See

The Maine Arts Commission has rotating exhibits. Some recent exhibits have been by the Maine Artists Space, watercolors by Charlotte Joy Chase, and an arts in education exhibit from the O'Farrell Gallery.

There is no gift shop or café, but there are numerous restaurants and sandwich shops within a two-mile radius.

While You're in the Area

Other attractions in the area include the Maine State Museum (p. 149), Old Fort Western (p. 167), and the Maine State House (p. 209).

Maine Forest and Logging Museum

Route 178
Bradley, ME 04411
(207) 581-2871

Overview

Located on 265 acres in Bradley on Blackman

Stream, the Maine Forest and Logging Museum lets visitors step back in time and learn about the forest heritage of Maine. A mill settlement, with a reconstructed stone dam, a water-powered up-and-down sawmill, a blacksmith shop, a log cabin, a covered bridge, and a trapper's cabin provides the setting for reenactments, demonstrations, and school programs highlighting Maine's pioneer and early lumbering eras.

Directions and Hours

Leonard's Mills is located halfway between Milford and Brewer just off Route 178 in the Penobscot Experimental Forest. From I-95 in Bangor take exit 48. Take Broadway across Penobscot River to Brewer. Turn left at the first major intersection onto Route 9 for about four miles. Watch for Leonard's Mills signs. Turn left onto Route 178. The museum is north about four miles. The entrance is on the right. The museum can also be reached from the north via Route 2A/2 in Old Town/Milford (the museum is about two miles south of Bradley Village, with the entrance on the right).

The museum is open year-round for self-guided tours. Public events are held from April to October on several weekends. Please contact the museum for the latest schedule. The museum property and trails are handicap accessible, but the buildings are not. A van is provided on event days for guests who cannot walk between the parking lot and the settlement site.

Hours: Open from dawn to dusk for self-guided walks.

Admission and Membership

There is no admission for daily self-guided tours but donations are welcome. Public events range from $3-$5 for adults, and $1 for children. Reservations are required for educational tours. Membership is $5/year for students, $15/year for individuals, and $30/year for families. Other membership options are available; please contact the museum for details.

What to See

The Museum's home, known as Leonard's Mills, was formed by volunteers over the past 30 years, creating this historical setting. People can walk through the water-powered sawmill and see how their ancestors harnessed energy to build homes and communities. Living history events in early July and October are celebrations of the diverse crafts and skills of the settlers. Women spin, weave, and cook, while the men fire up the forge and do some blacksmithing. Kids can learn how to drive a pair of oxen or can go for a ride in a river bateau. The weekend events also feature volunteers in period dress performing typical tasks for the season, horse-drawn wagon rides, woodworking, hearth cooking, dying of wool, bagpipe or fiddle music, and candle-making.

Woodsmen's Day in the spring features horse-logging and timber-hewing with broad axes, and Blacksmith's Roundup in the fall, sponsored in association with New England Blacksmiths, is a day of fancy forging with time for hands-on learning.

River driver's bateau at the Maine Forest and Logging Museum. Photo by Steve Bicknell.

The museum serves beans cooked in the ground overnight during most of the public events along with reflector oven biscuits and cider.

Children's programming includes school visits in the spring and fall as well as events in spring featuring old-fashioned games, paper making, puppet shows, and plenty of other children's activities.

The museum does have a gift shop. The museum offers a large picnic area and outdoor amphitheatre or visitors can eat in the towns of Brewer, Orono, and Bangor. On event days a lunch wagon is available

While You're in the Area

Nearby museums and interesting attractions include: Bangor Historical Society (p. 207), Cole Land Transportation Museum (p. 119), the Maine Discovery Museum (p. 209), the Hudson Museum (p. 136), the Page Farm and Home Museum (p. 210), the Sunkhaze National Wildlife Refuge (p. 210), and the Penobscot Nation Museum (p. 210).

Mainely Critters Museum

RR2 Box 510
Dixfield, ME 04224
(207) 562-8231

Overview

The Mainely Critters Museum consists of Maine wildlife mounted in lifelike settings. A large part of the animal collection comes from salvaged roadkill.

Directions and Hours

The Mainely Critters Museum is on US Route 2 between Dixfield and Welton.

The museum is open year-round and is handicap accessible.

Hours: 10:00 A.M. to 4:00 P.M.

Admission and Membership

Admission is free. Donations are appreciated.

What to See

The museum hosts talks from wardens, game officers, and teachers of many different kinds. The museum offers films and videotapes about wildlife, both onsite, and to nursing homes and other locations.

Children's programming, including speakers and videos on wildlife, is available.

There is a gift shop. A good café is located within eight miles of the museum.

While You're in the Area

The Norlands Living History Center (p. 209) and Livermore Falls Historical Society (p. 209) are nearby.

Maine Narrow Gauge Railroad Company & Museum

58 Fore Street
Portland, ME 04101-4842
(207) 828-0814; (207) 828-6132 Fax
mngrr.rails.net

Overview

Maine Narrow Gauge Railroad Company & Museum features train rides and a display of Maine industrial history, including two-foot gauge trains run in Maine from 1899 to 1943. The equipment ran as the Edaville Railroad until 1992. Then it was returned to Maine to be run on the waterfront in Portland. The museum is housed in the Portland Company complex, builders of locomotives from the 1850s to 1906.

Directions and Hours

Take Route 495 to exit 7 to Franklin Street. Turn left on Fore Street, to #58, the site of the Portland Company Complex. Follow yellow locomotive signs to a parking lot on the waterside of the complex.

The museum is open year round and seven

days a week. Both museum and train are handicap accessible. The trains run on weekends until May 15 and after October 15.

Hours: daily, 11:00-4:00 from May 15-October 15; weekends only from mid-February to May 15 and after October 15 until Thanksgiving.

Admission and Membership

Admission is free. Adult round trip train ride is $5, seniors $4, children $3. Group rates of $3 for groups of seven or more are available. Memberships start at $35/year.

What to See

The museum features a one-of-a-kind two-foot gauge "Porter Car." Built in 1901 and in original condition, it is the only one in the United States and possibly the world. Visitors who take the train ride can see a lovely view of the Islands of Casco Bay. A walking trail follows the right of way along the train route.

The museum hosts special events such as the annual Steam Fest Day in September. Children's programming includes school visits to the museum for instruction in transportation history and a fun train ride.

There is a gift shop and a snack bar. Visitors can also eat at many local restaurants.

While You're in the Area

The Museum of Art (p. 176), the Portland Children's Museum (p. 207), and local parks and playgrounds are other nearby attractions.

Maine State Museum

83 State House Station
Augusta, ME 04333
(207) 287-2301 TTY: (207) 287-6740
www.state.me.us/museum

Winding yarn for weaving, ca. 1820. Maine State Museum photography by Greg Hart.

Overview

The Maine State Museum exhibits the entire cross section of Maine history. Exhibits feature Maine's natural environment, prehistory, social history, and manufacturing heritage.

Directions and Hours

From the North (Waterville and Bangor area): Head southwest on Interstate I-95. Take exit 30, then turn right on Route 202 (Western Avenue) to the Rotary. Take Route 201 heading southwest for 0.5 miles to the State Capitol. The Museum is located just south of the Capitol building. Free parking is available west and north of the Museum.

From the South (Portland area): Head northeast on Interstate I-95. Take exit 30 (Route 202, Western Avenue.) Take Western Avenue southwest to a rotary. At the rotary take Route 201 South, and the State Capitol will be on your right. The museum is located just south of the Capitol.

From mid-coast Maine (Rockland, Camden, Belfast): Head west on Route 17 or 3. After crossing the Kennebec River take Route 201 South. The museum is directly south of the State Capitol.

From the East (Lewiston): Take Route 202 to Augusta (Western Avenue) to a rotary. At the rotary follow 201 South to the State Capitol.

The Museum is located south of the Capitol on your right.

The museum is open year-round and is handicap accessible. Closed Easter, Thanksgiving, Christmas, and New Year's Day.

Hours: Monday-Friday 9:00 A.M. to 5:00 P.M., Saturday 10:00 A.M. to 4:00 P.M., Sunday 1:00 to 4:00 P.M.

Admission and Membership

Admission is free. Membership is $30/year, $20/year for senior citizens, students, and teachers, $50/year to be a supporting member, $100/year to be a business member, $250/year to be a contributing member, $500/year to be a benefactor, and $1,000/year to be a sponsor.

What to See

The Maine State Museum offers exhibits on all aspects of Maine's history. Some of these exhibits include a lumbering exhibit which features the *Lion*, an 1846 steam locomotive that hauled lumber, a Lombard Log Hauler, and an up-down sawmill; a shipbuilding exhibit with a section of Downeaster *St. Mary* along with some of the products on board when she ran aground in the Falkland Islands; a granite exhibit with a stone wagon that was used to move granite blocks, as well as polished granite from Maine quarries; an ice harvesting section with the equipment used to cut the blocks of ice on the rivers, along with a mural that shows the steps in the ice cutting process; an agriculture exhibit with a barn that includes farming equipment and a cider press; and a fishing section with sardine canning equipment and fishing gear. The museum also has a life-sized natural history scene named "This Land Called Maine" that depicts the animals and plants in the area as well as gems and minerals found in Maine. A "Made in Maine" exhibit, which includes a three-level operating water powered mill, shows how many of the products made at homes, mills, shops, and factories were manufactured and the conditions in which the people worked. An exhibit called "12,000 Years in Maine" chronicles the story of Maine's first inhabitants, which includes a life-sized diorama. Two videos show how stone tools were made by people living in the Paleo-Indian and Archaic periods. The exhibit "Struggle for Identity" describes Maine's story from the 1600s to statehood in 1842, concentrating on the geographical and political process that established the present boundaries of Maine.

Children's programming is available by reservation. The museum offers 25 formal education programs and tours.

The museum does have a gift shop. On weekdays visitors can eat in a nearby state office building cafeteria and on weekends there are many restaurants near the complex.

While You're in the Area

Interesting places in the area include: the Maine State House (p. 209), Blaine House (p. 146), the Governor's Mansion, and Capitol Park.

Maine's Swedish Colony, Inc.

PO Box 50
New Sweden, ME 04762
(207) 896-3199
www.Aroostook.me.us/newsweden/activities.com

Overview

Maine's Swedish Colony, Inc. has three restored buildings on Station Road, New Sweden. The Capitol School Museum is the only remaining one-room schoolhouse in New Sweden. The other two buildings—the restored and fully operational Lars Noak Blacksmith Shop and the only two-story log home in Maine, the Larsson/Ostlund Log House—are both listed on the National Register of Historic Buildings.

Directions and Hours

From Caribou, drive north on Route 161 to the four corners. At Northstar Variety, take a right onto Station Road. Capitol School is located between the New Sweden Historical Museum and the New Sweden cemetery.

Or, take Route 1 (Van Buren Road) left on Emond Road to Station Road.

The museum is open Tuesdays-Saturdays from approximately May 30 to November 16 from noon to 4:00 P.M. Guided tours of the Blacksmith Shop and the Larsson/Ostlund log house are available by appointment. Only the Blacksmith Shop is handicap accessible.

Admission and Membership

There are no admission fees but donations are accepted. Memberships are Association $5/year, Regular Member $50, or Life Member $100.

Children must be accompanied by an adult.

What to See

The Capitol School has original blackboards as well as donated desks from that period. The Blacksmith Shop exhibits forges, carpentry, and wheelright tools. Guided tours of the fully restored Blacksmith Shop and the Larsson/Ostland Log House (under restoration) are available by appointment. During special programs, blacksmithing demonstrations are held.

There are several events during the year in New Sweden including Midsommer celebration, approximately June 21-22; New Sweden Day ("The Coming of the Swedes") July 23, 24; Leif Ericsson Day, October 9; and the Santa Lucia Celebration on December 13.

At the Capitol School, there is a nonprofit shop featuring Scandinavian gifts and decorations. Visitors can dine at the nearby Northstar which has coffee and a variety of sandwiches or at "Stan's" at Madawaska Lake—the home of the 10 cent coffee. Caribou restaurants are also only eight miles away.

While You're in the Area

New Sweden has a variety of attractions including the New Sweden Historical Museum (p. 162), old and new Swedish cemeteries, Thomas Park and Lindsten Stuga. Points of interest in the towns of Stockholm and Woodland are also nearby.

Marrett House (SPNEA)

Route 25
Standish, ME 04084
(207) 642-3032
www.spnea.org

Overview

In 1796, Daniel Marrett, a recent Harvard graduate, moved to Standish to become the town parson. The grand house he purchased reflected his status as the community's leading citizen. Over the years, his children and grandchildren enlarged and updated the house but left unchanged many furnishings and interior arrangements as relics of the past.

Directions and Hours

From I-95: Take Maine exit 8. Follow Route 25 west about 13 miles to the center of Standish. The house is on the right, opposite town hall.

The house museum is open June 1 to October 15.

Hours: Saturday and Sunday, 11:00 A.M. to 5:00 P.M. Tours at 11:00 A.M., 12:00, 1:00, 2:00, 3:00 and 4:00 P.M.

Admission and Membership

$5 for adults, $4.50 senior citizens, ½ off for students and children 6-12. Children 5 and under, SPNEA members, and residents of Standish are free. AAA members receive a 2 for 1 discount. SPNEA membership is $35/year for individuals and $45/year for a household. Membership includes free admissions to 35 properties and museums across New England.

What to See

The southwest parlor is preserved exactly as it appeared on the occasion of a family wedding in 1847. In 1889, the family celebrated the house's centennial by refurbishing several of the rooms with reproduction heirloom wallpapers and bed hangings and organizing a large family reunion to honor the Marrett legacy. Today, visitors can see the layering of eras and tastes that occurs when a family resides in one house for three generations. The Marrett sisters' extensive perennial garden, which they laid out in the 1920s and 1930s, has been restored.

The Marrett House offers group tours and public programs throughout the season. Please call or write for details. Programs include the annual June perennial and herb sale.

While You're in the Area

The Portland area has many attractions to choose from. Some of the nearby museums include the Portland Public Library, the Portland Museum of Art (p. 176), the Children's Museum of Maine (p. 207), the Maine Narrow Gauge Railroad Company & Museum (p. 148), the Museum of African Tribal Art (p. 157), the Victoria Mansion (p. 200), the Maine Historic Museum, the Longfellow House, the Portland Cultural Center, the Harrington House, the Pettingill Farm (p. 129), the Desert of Maine (p. 122), and the Portland Harbor Museum (p. 175).

Marshall Point Lighthouse Museum

Marshall Point Road
PO Box 247
Port Clyde, ME 04855
(207) 372-6450

Volunteers carry pine benches from the museum as a new visitors season begins in May. Photo courtesy of the Marshall Point Lighthouse Museum, Port Clyde, Maine.

Overview

The Marshall Point Lighthouse Museum is dedicated to the preservation of the history of St. George. It contains thousands of pictures, documents, and artifacts relating to the fishing, shipping, lobstering, and quarrying history of the St. George peninsula. The museum is housed in the keepers house, built in 1895. The present light tower and bridge were constructed in 1857.

Directions and Hours

From Thomaston, Maine: Depart U.S. Route 1. Go south on Main State Route 131 toward St. George. It is 16 miles to the village of Port Clyde. Follow the signs, which indicate left turns. The lighthouse stands at the entrance of Port Clyde harbor at the confluence of Muscongas and Penobscot Bays.

The museum is open from May to October and is handicap accessible.

Hours: Saturday and Sunday in May and October from 1:00 to 5:00 P.M., every day from June to September, Sunday-Friday 1:00 to 5:00 P.M., Saturday 10:00 A.M. to 1:00 P.M.

Admission and Membership

Admission is free. Donations are appreciated.

What to See

A cross indexing system of names allows museum visitors to locate any individual listed in the museum's collection of photographs and documents, which is a popular genealogy tool.

In 1995 a replica of the summer kitchen was erected to provide more room for the growing collection.

There is a gift shop. There are restaurants in Port Clyde and Tenants Harbor.

While You're in the Area

Nearby attractions and museums include Colonial Pemaquid State Historic Site and Camden-Rockport Historical Society Conway Homestead (p. 207).

Maynard F. Jordan Planetarium

University of Maine
5781 Wingate Hall
Orono, ME 04469
(207) 581-1341
www.ume.maine.edu/~lookup

Overview

The Maynard F. Jordan Planetarium at the University of Maine, Orono, offers public shows on the weekend, in addition to school and private shows.

Directions and Hours

Take Interstate 95 to exit 51 (Stillwater Avenue). At the third traffic light, turn right onto College Avenue. The planetarium is located on the second floor of Wingate Hall.

The planetarium is open year round, and is handicap accessible.

Hours: Monday-Friday 9:00-5:00.

Admission and Membership

$4 for adults, $3 for children and seniors.

University of Maine students are free. Discount rates for school groups and seniors are available.

What to See

There are children's shows designed to introduce children ages four and up to the night sky.

There is a gift shop. There is a seasonal café next door to the planetarium, as well as restaurants in the Orono area.

While You're in the Area

The Page Farm and Home Museum (p. 210 and the Hudson Museum (p. 136) are also nearby.

The McLaughlin Foundation, Garden and Horticultural Center

97 Main Street
PO Box 16
South Paris, ME 04281
(207) 743-8820
www.mclaughlingarden.org

Overview

The McLaughlin Foundation, Garden and Horticultural Center is a three acre perennial garden and 1840s house and barn that houses major collections of lilacs, wildflowers, ferns, hosta, semprevivums, and day lilies.

Directions and Hours

From the Maine Turnpike: Take exit 11. Go north on Route 26 to South Paris. The garden is located on Route 26. Parking is available along Western Avenue.

The gardens are open from May 1-October 31. The gift shop is open year round. The tea room is open from Memorial Day-Labor Day. The Foundation is handicap accessible.

Hours: Gardens: 8:00 A.M. to 6:00 P.M. Gift shop: Monday-Saturday 10:00 A.M. to 5:00 P.M. Tea Room: Wednesday-Saturday 11:00-4:00.

Admission and Membership

There is no admission cost but donations are requested. Membership begins at $25/year.

What to See

The McLaughlin Garden is a vernacular garden, which is rare to see in Maine. A vernacular garden is formed by a non-professional gardener and uses flowers native to the region. The garden includes the Entry Garden, a perennial garden with varieties of ornamental grasses, and native plants like Joe Pye weed, salvia, thyme, allium, and lamb's ear; the Lilac Border, which usually blooms at the end of May, is a double row of lilacs with a wide variety of lilacs; the Core Garden, with phlox, astilbes, sedum, bugbane, and flowering trees like magnolia, bechtel crab apple, and Japanese viburnum; the Sempervivums Collection; Wildflower Lane with trillium, forget-me-nots, Jack-in-the-Pulpits, ferns, and other wildflowers; and the Shade Garden that is the home to European Ginger, hepatica, Solomon's seal, Jack-in-the-Pulpit, and the toad lily. The wildflowers bloom in May while the Daylilies bloom in July.

Please contact the museum for information about annual events.

Children's programming is available Tuesday and Thursday mornings from 9:00-11:00 A.M., mid-June to mid-August.

There is a gift shop and a tea room. The tea room serves food Wednesday-Saturday from 11:00 A.M. to 4:00 P.M.

While You're in the Area

Other museums or interesting attractions nearby include the Shaker Museum (p. 191), Paris Hill Village, the Moses Mason House Museum (p. 111), and the Jones Glass Museum on Douglas Mountain (p. 139).

Milbridge Historical Museum

South Main Street
Milbridge, ME 04658
(207) 546-4471
www.milbridgehistoricalsociety.com

Overview

The Milbridge Historical Museum displays local history of the people and businesses of the town and region. Rotating displays change each season. Milbridge was once a major shipbuilding center, and the museum chronicles the schooners once built in the area.

Directions and Hours

The museum is located on Route 1, approximately 30 minutes north of Ellsworth.

The museum is open from Memorial Day weekend through September, in the winter by appointment, and is handicap accessible.

Hours: Tuesday, Saturday, Sunday 1:00-4:00.

Admission and Membership

Admission to the museum is free. Membership is $5/year for individuals and $100 for a lifetime membership.

What to See

The museum houses shipbuilding tools and photographs. In the summer, local artists display their work in the museum's meeting room.

On the second Tuesday of each month, the museum sponsors a speaker on local history or cultural topics.

There is a gift shop. Visitors can eat at the Red Barn Restaurant and Milbridge House.

While You're in the Area

McClellan Park, a lovely rocky coast for picnics and camping, is also in the area.

"Montpelier" General Henry Knox Museum

PO Box 326
Thomaston, ME 04861
(207) 354-8062
www.generalknoxmuseum.org

Overview

The "Montpelier" General Henry Knox Museum is a 22-room mansion that is the repository of General Knox (1750-1806) artifacts, family portraits, furnishings, silver, china, and Revolutionary War mementos.

Directions and Hours

Take I-95 north to coastal Route 1. Follow Route 1 to the intersection of Route 131.

The museum is open June-September and by appointment in winter. The museum is not handicap accessible.

Hours: Tuesday-Saturday 10:00 A.M. to 4:00 P.M. The last tour begins at 3:00 P.M. Closed Sundays and Mondays.

Admission and Membership

Admission ranges from $3-$5. Discounts for seniors are available. Children must be accompanied by an adult. Membership is $25/year for an individual, $40/year for a family, and $1,000 for a lifetime membership.

What to See

The museum features an innovative skylight system and stairway design as well an an oval room and a bell cast by Paul Revere.

Children's programming is available through the local school system.

The museum does have a gift shop. Visitors can eat at the Thomaston Cafe.

While You're in the Area

Nearby museums and interesting attractions include: the Farnsworth Art Museum and Wyeth Center (p. 125), the Owls Head Transportation Museum (p. 170), and the Olson House (p. 210).

Moosehead Historical Society

PO Box 1116
Greenville, ME 04441-1116
(207) 695-2909 or (207) 695-3163
www.mooseheadhistory.org

Overview

The Moosehead Historical Society operates the Eveleth-Crafts-Sheridan Historical House, the only restored Victorian mansion in northern Piscataquis County open to the public. The house also has various special exhibits and displays as well as the 1880s kitchen, old-time laundry room, and more. The campus also includes the Carriage House, which contains a Lumberman's Museum and various displays including one of the finest collections of Indian artifacts in northern Maine. The Carriage House also includes the office, where staff is available year-round to help with research questions. The office contains extensive files of what the society calls "People, Places, and Things" to help researchers and those just wanting to know more about the history of the area. The grounds contain a restored sunken garden as well as exotic flora.

Directions and Hours

The Moosehead Historical Society campus is located in Greenville, Maine, and is easily accessible from Route 15. From the south, turn left on Pritham Avenue in downtown Greenville (at the blinking light) and proceed west about 1.5 miles. The Society is on the left (there's a sign out front) across from the Currier's Flying Service.

The Carriage House, the Lumberman's Museum, and the displays in this building are open three days a week during the winter. It's best to call ahead for hours and snow days. From mid-June through September the entire campus is included in a docent-guided tour.

Admission and Membership

Admission to the Carriage House office is free; a $2 fee for adults and $1 for children 12 and under applies for summer guided tours. Members are admitted free of charge. Membership is: $5/year for individuals, $10/year for families, or a one-time $100 Life Membership is available.

What to See

The Moosehead Historical Society is a repository for artifacts relating to northern Piscataquis County, a large geographical area in northern Maine. The museum collects, maintains, and preserves items relating to the early families of the Moosehead region and the lumbering era of the North Woods. The museum is also a state repository for paper ephemera records relating to the towns of Greenville, Shirley, and Rockwood. Visitors are encouraged to conduct research of genealogical records. Tourists are also encouraged to visit the Eveleth-Crafts-Sheridan Historical House as part of the summer docent-guided tours to learn about the way of life in this remote area of northern Maine in the past. The Indian artifacts collection spans time from 9,000 B.C. to the 1700s.

There is a gift shop. There is no café, but there are a number of restaurants nearby.

While You're in the Area

Nearby attractions and museums include the Moosehead Marine Museum (p. 209), the Monson Museum (p. 209), the Tisbury Manor Chapter, DAR (p. 211), and the Dexter Historical Society Museums (p. 122).

The Mount Desert Island Historical Society Somesville Museum

2 Oak Hill Road
PO Box 653
Somesville
Mount Desert, ME 04660
(207) 244-5043
www.ellsworthme.org/mdihsociety

Overview

The Mount Desert Island Historical Society Somesville Museum, built in 1981, overlooks an ancient mill pond and Somes Harbor. Exhibits focus on the settlement of Somesville in 1761 and the development of the Island.

Directions and Hours

From Route 3 in Ellsworth: Go to Mount Desert Island. After the bridge bear right at the fork, following Route 102 and Route 198 for four miles. At the traffic light proceed ahead on Route 102 for ½ mile to the museum parking lot on the corner of Route 102 and Oak Hill Road.

The museum is open from June 15 to September 30. Please contact the museum for handicap accessibility information.

Hours: 10:00 A.M. to 5:00 P.M. Tuesday-Saturday.

Admission and Membership

$1 per person. The museum is free to children and members. Special groups and bus tours are welcome and may arrange for guided tours of the museum or the historic district by contacting the museum director. Membership is $10/year for an individual and $25/year for a family. Other membership options are available; please contact the museum for details.

What to See

The Greek Revival houses, located in a National Historic District, are well preserved and take visitors back to the 1850s. On the museum grounds the MDI Historical Society is proud of its 1780 Selectmen's Building, one of the oldest buildings on the island.

Every year on the second week of July the museum holds an annual Strawberry Festival.

Children's activities are part of every exhibit.

The museum does have a gift shop. Two take out eateries are nearby, and Mother's Kitchen and The Brown Bag are on Route 102.

While You're in the Area

Other interesting places to visit while you are in the area are the Wendell Gilley Museum of Bird Carving (p. 201) and the Sound School House Museum operated by The Mount Desert Island Historical Society (p. 193).

Musée et centre cultural du Mont-Carmel

993 Main Street
PO Box 150
Lille, ME 04746-0150
(207) 895-3339

Overview
The Musée et centre cultural du Mont-Carmel is a restored French baroque church with an ancient Roman interior. It houses a large collection of artifacts and Acadian cultural material.

Directions and Hours
The museum is located on Route 1, 98 miles north from Interstate 95.

The museum is open June 15-September 15, and is partially handicap accessible.

Hours: Sunday-Friday from 12:00-4:00 or by appointment. Closed Saturdays.

Admission and Membership
Donations are appreciated. For a $10 membership fee, a newsletter is provided.

What to See
This very large French church is located on Route 1 and the Saint John River in lovely northern Maine only five hundred feet from the Canadian border. Located in a small village, it is truly a wonderful rural setting. This restored church features twin domes mounted with trumpeting arch angels, many church textiles and religious objects, and a collection of Acadian artifacts. The cultural center offers three performance spaces.

While You're in the Area
Other great places to visit nearby include the Acadian Village (p. 106), Van Buren (seven miles away), Tante Blanche Museum (p. 197), and Madawaska (seven miles away).

The Museum of African Tribal Art

122 Spring Street
Portland, ME 04101
(207) 871-7188
www.africantribalartmuseum.org

Overview
The Museum of African Tribal Art is dedicated to education, to preserving the African humanities and traditions, to serving as a resource for scholars, and to encouraging the celebration of diversity.

Directions and Hours
From the south, take Maine Turnpike (95 North) to exit 6A (295 north). Take exit 4 and stay right following the downtown Portland sign. Turn right on High Street. Go through the first two lights and turn right at the third light. Parking is on the left and the museum is the first building on the left.

From the north, take exit 6A and bear right onto State Street. At the fifth light, turn left onto Spring Street. The museum will be on the right between Spring and High Streets.

The museum is open year round. It is not handicap accessible.

Hours: Tuesday-Saturday 10:30-5:00.

Admission and Membership
Admission to the museum is free. Donations are welcome. Membership is $35/year for individuals and $50/year for families.

What to See
The museum's collection of African masks and artifacts has an inherent power that speaks to visitors. In addition, special exhibits rotate every four to six months. Two upcoming exhibits are "The House of Ancestors" and "The Spirit Masks of the Nigerian Igbos." Children's programming is available.

No gift shop or café are on the premises, but restaurants and cafés surround the museum.

While You're in the Area
The Portland Museum of Art (p. 176), the Victorian Mansion, the Children's Museum of Maine (p. 207), the Maine Historic Museum (p. 209), the Longfellow House, and the Portland Cultural Center are also Portland attractions.

Museum of Natural History

College of the Atlantic
105 Eden Street
Bar Harbor, ME 04609
(207) 288-5015/5395
www.coa.edu/nhm

Overview

The Museum of Natural History at College of the Atlantic exhibits and interprets the natural history of Maine through a human ecological perspective. Detailed dioramas created by COA students depict the plant and animal life of coastal Maine.

Directions and Hours

The Museum is located on Route 3 in Bar Harbor, between downtown and the ferry terminal, approximately 15 miles from Ellsworth.

The museum is open year round: Mid-June through Labor Day, Monday-Saturday 10:00 A.M.-5:00 P.M.; Labor Day through mid-June, Thursday, Friday, Sunday 1:00-4:00 P.M., Saturday 10:00 A.M.-4:00 P.M. The Museum is handicap accessible.

Admission and Membership

$3.50 for adults, $2.50 for seniors, $1.50 for teens, $1 for children 3-12, and free for children 2 and younger. Membership information is available at the Museum. Members of the COA community and NEMA and AAM members are admitted free.

What to See

The museum exhibits are designed and created by students at the College of Atlantic as part of a series of courses in museum work. On display are mounted animals, skeletons, and models of wildlife found in Maine. Many exhibits highlight the affect of humans on the natural environment. Children of all ages can touch, smell, listen, and create while learning about the environment. Objects such as baleen, fur, wings, and skulls are available to touch.

A marine observation tank holds native sea creatures found in local tide pools. Museum staff lead a variety of activities encouraging the entire family to participate in natural history learning. Evening lectures on many topics are offered throughout the summer. In Summer Field Studies, children investigate the ecology of Mount Desert Island. School and community groups can arrange a variety of special programs through the museum. Throughout 2001, a special exhibit entitled "Maine's Endangered Species," will be at the museum.

In the museum shop, a selection of high quality books, toys, cards, shirts, and other keepsakes are offered for sale. The museum does not offer food but there are several restaurants located throughout Bar Harbor.

Museum of Natural History, College of the Atlantic. Photo courtesy of Richard Hill.

While You're in the Area

Several museums are located on Mount Desert Island, including the Abbe Museum (p. 105), the Wendall Gilley Museum (p. 201), the Bar Harbor Historical Society (p. 110), and the Mount Desert Island Historical Society (p. 156). Acadia National Park offers hiking trails, mountains, lakes, and coastlines to explore.

Museum of Yarmouth History

215 Main Street
Yarmouth, ME 04096
(207) 846-6259

Overview

The Museum of Yarmouth History is the only organization in Maine dedicated to the preservation and promotion of Yarmouth's history. The museum exhibits life in Yarmouth from the early years of settlement to the present.

Directions and Hours

Take Route 1 north to the exit for Route 115. Turn left at the end of the off ramp, then turn left into the parking lot of the Merrill Memorial Library.

Or, take Route 1 south to the exit for Route 115. Turn right at the end of the off ramp, then turn right into the Library parking lot.

The museum is seasonal, and is handicap accessible.

Hours: September-June, Saturday 10:00-5:00; Tuesday-Friday 1:00-5:00; July-August, Monday-Friday 1:00-5:00.

Admission and Membership

Admission to the museum is free. Membership levels start at $10/year for individuals.

What to See

The Museum of Yarmouth History features a gallery with changing exhibitions of local art and history. Artifact and research collections document more than two centuries of Yarmouth and Old North Yarmouth's history. The museum sponsors an annual lecture series and special programs such as Heirloom Appraisal Day.

The museum offers in-school and on-site programs about many aspects of Yarmouth's history, including shipbuilding and the mills on the Royal River.

There is a small gift shop. The museum has no café, but there are several restaurants in the area.

While You're in the Area

The Harrington House (p. 129), the Pettingill Farm (p. 129), and the Desert of Maine (p. 122) are ten minutes from the museum in Freeport, in addition to museums fifteen minutes away in Portland.

The Museum on High Street

Vinalhaven Historical Society
PO Box 339
Vinalhaven, ME 04863
(207) 863-4410
www.midcoast.com/~vhhissoc/

Overview

The Vinalhaven Historical Society Museum on High Street was established in 1967 in the former Town Hall. The museum features a variety of exhibits highlighting and interpreting the history of daily life on Vinalhaven Island. Research and educational opportunities are also available at the museum.

Directions and Hours

From Rockland, Maine on US 1, take the state ferry to Vinalhaven Island (1¼ hour trip). From the ferry landing, go along the harbor to High Street, turn left up the hill. The building is on the right at the top.

The museum is open from June 12 through the Sunday of Labor Day and other times by appointment.

Hours: 11:00-3:00.

Admission and Membership

Admission to the museum is free; donations are welcome.

What to See

The museum's exhibits contain artifacts depicting many facets of past Island life, including Native American tools, the granite quarrying industry, fishing, boat building, farming, net making, schools, stores, homes and family life, celebrations, music, churches, and fraternal organizations.

The structure was originally built as a Universalist Church in Rockland, Maine, in 1838. It was sold at auction in 1875 for $300 to the "Young Men's Association" to be used as a new church under William Henry Johnson. It was purchased by the town in 1878 and then used for a variety of purposes, including church, a dance hall, roller-skating rink, local theater, town meetings, a gymnasium, and youth center. Extensive local records from 1789 to the present are available for research, and there is also a small video collection, including interviews and oral histories.

There are gift items on sale; no food is permitted in the museum, but there are restaurants a block away on the harbor.

While You're in the Area

There is a Nature Conservancy Preserve on Lane's Island, within walking distance from the ferry landing

The Musical Wonder House

18 Middle Street
Wiscasset, ME 04578
(800) 336-3725/(207) 882-7163
www.musicalwonderhouse.com

Overview

The Musical Wonder House showcases a private collection of one-of-a-kind and rare music boxes, phonographs, and player pianos. The collection is housed in a furnished 1852 sea captain's home. It is located along a tidy street of similar mansions in an eighteenth century seacoast village.

Directions and Hours

Northbound, take 95 and take the Brunswick exit. Follow Route 1 north signs to Wiscasset. Turn left onto Lee Street, and take the first left onto High Street. Look for the sign at the end of the street.

Southbound, take 95 and take the Augusta exit. Follow Route 27 signs south to Wiscasset. At the intersection of Route 27 and Route 1, turn right. Turn right onto Lee Street, then left onto High Street. Look for the sign at the end of the street.

The museum is seasonal; it is not handicap accessible.

Hours: Memorial Day-October 15, daily, 10:00-5:00.

Admission and Membership

$1 for people who choose not to have a guided presentation. Guided presentations range from $8 to $30 per person. There is a $1 discount for children under 12, accompanied by an adult, for a guided presentation. There is a discount for groups of 20 or more that make reservations.

What to See

The house offers both grand and small—everything from astounding grand format music boxes, the rare Emerald Polyphon, a signed Steinway player grand piano, to tiny whistling birds. To see or hear any of the items in this collection in today's world is a rarity. The museum also offers detailed guided presentations through private rooms in the mansion.

The grand entry houses over 20 antique coin-operated music boxes that visitors are free to play as they choose.

The gift shop offers antique, vintage, and new music boxes, as well as a repair facility. (The Merry Music Box, a year round gift shop, is located in Lexington, Massachusetts.)

There is no café, but there are restaurants within walking distance.

While You're in the Area

The museum is located on the tidal Sheepscot River on the coast of Maine. The entire village is a step back in history. Within a block, SPNEA has two houses (pp. 118 and 162). The Lincoln County Museum and Old Gaol (p. 145) is also within the village of Wiscasset.

The New England Museum of Telephony

166 Winkumpaugh Road
Ellsworth, ME 04605
(207) 667-9491
www.ellsworthme.org/ringring

Overview

The modern telephone network evolved from hand-cranked, wall mounted telephones in wooden boxes that signaled live operators who asked "Number, please?" These "magneto" telephones would be replaced by dial telephones, and the operators by ever more complex electromechanical switching systems. The New England Museum of Telephony traces the history of the telephone network through working exhibits featuring large-scale displays of equipment that originally served communities in Maine and elsewhere. All of the exhibits operating at the museum have been replaced in the present telephone network by digital communications technology.

Directions and Hours

The museum is located 10 miles north of downtown Ellsworth off of Route 1A on the Winkumpaugh Road. From Bangor, follow Rt. 1A south.

The museum is open July-September, Wednesdays and Sundays, 1:00-4:00 and by appointment. During other months, the museum is by appointment only. It is handicap accessible.

Admission and Membership

$4 adult, $2 child. Individual memberships are $20/year. Inquire by phone or e-mail about group rates and special discounts.

What to See

The museum has perhaps the only working example of #3 Crossbar in the country, as well as a substantial portion of a #5 Crossbar office that will be operating soon. Both are Bell System offices. Also on display—and working—is the entire central office of The Island Telephone Company, an independent telephone company from Frenchboro, Maine. Although museum volunteers usually operate the manual switchboards, visitors may don a headset, say "Number, please?" and learn how to connect two "subscribers."

In August 2001 the museum will host Telephone Fair 5, the theme of which is "125 Years of Service: Telephone Workers in New England."

On the drawing board is a Reception Center that will operate year-round, serving school and community groups and providing visitors with an introduction to the museum's extensive collections.

The gift shop offers books, videos, T-shirts, and other items related to the collections.

Museum members (called "subscribers") who volunteer for Work Days are treated to lunch in "The Magneto Cafe," an impromptu affair. Visitors to Telephone Fair (August 11, 2001) may lunch on crab rolls and other snacks at the food tent. At other times, many good restaurants can be found in downtown Ellsworth.

While You're in the Area

There are plenty of things to do nearby, particularly during the summer months. These include visiting Acadia National Park and the villages of downeast Maine. Two other museums are located in Ellsworth: Stanwood Homestead Museum and Birdsacre (p. 210), a wildlife sanctuary, and the Colonel Black Mansion (p. 205), a historic home. To learn more about the area, log on to www.ellsworthme.com.

New Sweden Historical Society Museum

110 Station Road
PO Box 33
New Sweden, ME 04762
(207) 896-3018 or (207) 896-5843
www.state.me.us/museum

Overview

The New Sweden Museum was organized in 1925 for the purpose of collecting items used by the early settlers and their descendents and to promote the heritage of the Swedish settlement. Swedish immigrants arrived in 1870 to settle in the virgin forest area. Their relatives and friends from Sweden followed in several months and years to help establish a growing community.

Directions and Hours

From Caribou: Take Route 161 north about 10 miles to a four-way intersection. There is a service station on the left just before the intersection. Turn sharply right on Station Road, and proceed about one mile. The museum is a large white building on the left. It is just before the cemetery, also on the left. Access to New Sweden is also available by taking Route 1 north from Caribou.

The museum is open from the third Saturday in June to Labor Day and is not accessible in winter. It is partially handicap accessible.

Hours: Tuesday-Sunday, noon-4:00 P.M. Special visiting hours can be arranged by prior appointment during May-October.

Admission and Membership

Admission is free. Donations are appreciated. Adequate adult supervision is requested for children's groups. Membership cost is $7/year for individuals, $20/year for families.

What to See

The museum's collections include: a handmade wood kitchen and other household items, a ski collection (local crafted), trunks brought by the early immigrants, many portraits, books in English and Swedish, a large collection of farm machinery and tools from the early era, the Lindsten Stuga (a restored log cabin with many items used by the family who resided there), and the Memorial Cemetery with a large monument naming those who were buried there.

Annual events include: a Memorial Weekend Breakfast on Saturday (cost is by donation), a Midsommar Celebration (it takes place on Saturday and Sunday nearest to June 21 with decorating and raising the Maypole, Swedish dancing, a traditional bonfire, an Ecumenical church service, a luncheon at noon, and special programs), and on July 23 (the date the immigrants arrived in New Sweden) there is a brief Founders Day commemorative service. Lucia Day is also celebrated on December 13.

Schoolchildren are welcome to tour the museum. Some children are taught Swedish dancing and appear in costume at the Midsommar programs.

The museum does have a small gift shop. Museum attendants can give directions to places to eat within 10 miles.

While You're in the Area

Interesting places in the area include Maine's Swedish Colony, Inc. (p. 150), the Woodland Museum and Stockholm Museum (p. 195), the New Sweden Cemetery, and W.W. Thomas Memorial Park.

Nickels-Sortwell House (SPNEA)

121 Main Street
Route 1
Wiscasset, ME 04578
(207) 882-6218
www.spnea.org

Overview

The Nickels-Sortwell House, whose façade dominates the main street of Wiscasset, was built by Captain William Nickels, a ship owner and trader. The architecture recalls the period when shipbuilding and the maritime trade brought prosperity to this riverside community. Soon after the house was built, however, the Embargo Act of 1807, followed by the War of 1812, crippled the shipping industry, and many coastal families lost their fortunes.

Directions and Hours

From I-95: Take Maine exit 22 (Route 1, Brunswick). Follow Route 1 to the junction with Route 218 at Wiscasset. The house is on the left. Public parking is available behind the shops on Main Street.

The house museum is open June 1 to October 15. It is not handicap accessible.

Hours: Wednesday-Sunday, 11:00 A.M. to 5:00 P.M. Tours are at 11:00 A.M., 12:00, 1:00, 2:00, 3:00 and 4:00 P.M.

Admission and Membership

$5 for adults, $4.50 senior citizens, ½ off for students and children 6-12. Children 5 and under, SPNEA members, and residents of Wiscasset are free. AAA members receive a 2 for 1 discount. SPNEA membership is $35/year for individuals and $45/year for a household. Membership includes free admissions to 35 properties and museums across New England.

What to See

Around 1830, the house was transformed into a hotel. Towards the end of the century, when the Maine coast became fashionable as a summer resort, Alvin Sortwell purchased the building as a summer residence. He and his daughter, Frances, a leader in the local preservation movement, refurbished it in the Colonial Revival manner. The grounds, landscaped in 1926 with period gardens and an elaborate classical fence, are being restored.

The Nickels-Sortwell House offers group tours and programs throughout the season.

The house does not have a gift shop or a café. There are a few restaurants within easy walking distance in the center of Wiscasset.

While You're in the Area

Attractions and museums nearby include SPNEA's Castle Tucker (p. 118), which is within walking distance.

Nobleboro Historical Center

198 Center Street
Nobleboro, ME 04555
(207) 563-5874

Overview

The Nobleboro Historical Society operates the Center, an 1818 schoolhouse now used for holding meetings. It displays artifacts and stores town records.

Directions and Hours

The Center is located halfway between Damariscotta and Waldoboro, at the front of Nobleboro's Elementary Central School.

The school is open in July and August, and by appointment, and is handicap accessible.

Hours: Saturday 1:30-4:30.

Admission and Membership

Admission to the Center is free. Membership is $10/year for individuals, $15/year for families.

What to See

The Center houses Indian relics, a large hand-sewn flag with thirteen stars, paintings, a fully rigged ship model, and town maps of 1813 and 1857. There are also genealogies and cemetery records.

There is an open house in June for school children.

There is a small gift shop. There is no café, but there are several restaurants nearby.

While You're in the Area

Nearby attractions include Fort Edgecomb (p. 208), the Narrow Gauge Railroad Museum (p. 148), the Alna Meeting House (p. 167), the Alna Schoolhouse, the Wiscasset, Waterville, and Farmington Railroad Museum (p. 204), the Head Tide Church Museum (p. 134), the Lincoln County Museum and Old Jail (p. 145), Castle Tucker (p. 118), Pownalborough Court House (p. 178), the Maine Art Gallery, the Nickels-Sortwell House Museum (p. 162), and the Musical Wonder House (p. 160).

Northeast Historic Film

379 Main Street
Bucksport, ME 04615
(207) 469-0924
www.oldfilm.org

Overview

Located in the 1916 Alamo Theatre, Northeast Historic Film is a community cinema dedicated to the film and video heritage of northern New England from 1901 to the present.

Directions and Hours

From Bangor: Take Route 15 south for 20 miles.

From Belfast: Take Route 1 north for 20 miles; after crossing the bridge take a left at the light on to Main Street. Northeast Historic Film is ½ mile up Main Street on the right.

Maine newsreel photographer, 1920s. Northeast Historic Film, Daniel Maher Collection.

The museum is open year-round and is handicap accessible.

Hours: Monday-Friday 9:00 A.M. to 4:00 P.M.. There are additional film event times; please contact Northeast Historic Film for details and up-to-date information.

Admission and Membership

Admission is free but there is a fee for screenings. A school group discount is available for screenings and field trips. Membership is $15/year for an educator/student, $25/year for an individual, and $50/year for a household.

What to See

Northeast Historic Film has film and video of Maine, New Hampshire, Vermont, and Massachusetts from 1901 to the present, specializing in work and rural life. Historic Film has excellent projection facilities with a big picure, digital sound, and live music for silent film presentations.

The Alamo Theatre shows popular movies on Friday and Saturday nights and Sunday afternoons. Please call (207) 469-6910 for a prerecorded message of the week's features and admission information.

In July a Northeast Silent Film Festival, along with a summer film symposium on the use of movies to record culture, is held.

Children's programming is available.

There is a gift shop. Visitors can eat at MacLeod's Restaurant on Main Street.

While You're in the Area

Other interesting places to visit while you are in the area are: Fort Knox in Prospect (p. 128), Abbe Museum in Bar Harbor (p. 105), and Penobscot Marine Museum in Searsport (p. 173).

Northern Maine Museum of Science

181 Main Street
Presque Isle, ME 04769
(207) 768-9482
www.umpi.maine.edu/info/nmms/museum.htm

Overview

The Northern Maine Museum of Science is in Folsom Hall on the campus of the University of Maine at Presque Isle. The museum occupies three floors or hallways and stairwells and includes more than 100 exhibits illustrating science and mathematics concepts. The museum also administers the second largest herbarium in the state of Maine and 200 acres of natural areas. The museum is presently assisting in the construction of the Maine Solar System Model, which will be along the 40 miles of Route 1 between Presque Isle and Houlton (see www.umpi.maine.edu/info/nmms/solar/index.htm for information).

Directions and Hours

The University of Maine at Presque Isle is along Route 1 just south of the city. To see the campus and museum, park near the flagpole and proceed about 100 meters away from Route 1 to Folsom Hall.

The museum is open year round, whenever the campus is open, and is handicap accessible.

Admission and Membership

There is no admission fee.

What to See

The museum entrance includes two full-scale dolphins and a ¼ scale model of a pterosaur, as well as the Sun for the Maine Solar System Model. The third floor covers geology and biology and includes a large leatherback sea turtle, original Passenger Pigeon, coral map and other displays. The second floor covers physics, chemistry, forestry and agriculture and includes a large "Powers of Ten" exhibit and displays about Maine soils and potatoes. The first floor is dedicated to mathematics. The Museum also has a nature trail on campus.

While You're in the Area

The Old Iron Inn (p. 168) is run by the same adminstrator.

Nowetah's American Indian Museum

2 Colegrove Road, Route 27
New Portland, ME 04961-3821
(207) 628-4981
www.mainemuseums.org

Overview

Nowetah's American Indian Museum, located in scenic Maine and surrounded by streams, evergreen trees, and mountains, was established in 1969 by Nowetah Wirick, a descendant of the St. Francis Abenaki and Paugussett Indians. Although Indian art from all parts of the United States, Canada, and South America are displayed, the museum has a special focus on Maine's Abenaki Indians.

Photo courtesy of Nowetah's American History Museum. Photo by Nowetah Wirick.

Directions and Hours

The museum is located just off Route 27, down a 1,000 foot scenic graveled driveway. Watch for large black and white signs in the shape of an eagle with arrows. The building is dark brown with white trim.

The museum is open year-round and is handicap accessible.

Hours: Open seven days a week 10:00-5:00.

Admission and Membership

There is no admission cost but donations are welcome. Schools, scouts, and other groups are welcome to visit by appointment.

What to See

Museum pieces on display include old stone artifacts, moccasins with porcupine quill and moose hair embroidery, quill looms, belts, bear claw-antler necklaces, glass Hudson Bay trade beads, shell Wampum beads, soapstone carvings, corn crushers, gourd bowls/dippers, dream nets, bows and arrows, bone games, spinning wheels, butter churns, brass bed warmers, pierced tin lanterns, candle molds, false-face medicine society masks, turtle rattles, flutes, prehistoric pottery, Indian rugs, drums, a mortar and pestle, war clubs, dolls, Sioux shields, and buffalo horned medicine bonnets. One of the museum rooms features a collection of over 400 old birch bark, quill, and ash splint Maine Indian baskets.

Educational programs are held to teach visitors how Indians of the past lived. Topics focused on include food, homes, adornment, clothing, wild herb and plant medicine, hunting, fishing, family, marriage, divorce, wampum, money, religion, travel, warfare, death, games, legends, words, and music. A question and answer session is included. A Learn-by-Doing Hands On Program consists of Indian dancing (with authentic music recorded at live Pow-wows) with explanations of dances and musical instruments. If time permits, kids take part in the dances and try out the musical instruments.

Indian refreshments are served, including homemade acorn bread.

The museum has a gift shop that offers genuine American Indian homemade arts, crafts, and jewelry, made by Nowetah and her seven daughters, as well as other Indians in the US, Canada, and South America. Visitors can eat at the Wire Bridge Diner, just past the museum on Route 27.

While You're in the Area

Nearby place to visit while in area include the Stanley Museum (p. 194) and the Western Maine Children's Museum (p. 211).

The Ogunquit Museum of American Art

183 Shore Road
Ogunquit, ME 03907
(207) 646-4909

Overview

The OMAA, called "the most beautiful little museum in the world," was founded in 1952. It houses a permanent collection of over 1,500 works of art by some of America's most important twentieth century artists. In addition to its collection, the museum is noted for its beautiful site overlooking the ocean, and for its sculpture gardens.

Directions and Hours

Take Interstate 95 to exit 4, and turn left onto Route 1. Take Route 1 for approximately seven miles into Ogunquit. Turn right onto Bourne Lane. At the first stop sign turn right onto Shore Road. The museum is on the left.

The museum is open from July to October 15 (except for Labor Day and four re-hanging days in mid-August), and all but one gallery is handicap accessible. There are no age restrictions, but children must be accompanied by an adult.

Hours: Monday, Saturday, 10:30-5:00; Sunday 2:00-5:00.

Admission and Membership

$4 for adults, $3 for seniors and students. Members and children under 12 are admitted for free.Membership is $25/year for individuals, $50/year for families, and various levels of contributing memberships.

What to See

The OMAA's collection includes paintings, drawings, and sculptures. Included in the collection are artists such as Benton, Burchfield, Cadmus, Demuth, Hartley, Henri, Homer, Hopper, Kent, Kuhn, Lawrence, Levine, Marsh, Tooker, and Zorach.

Approaching the museum, visitors can look directly through the main gallery to the rocky coast, the ocean, and the far horizon. Inside, four additional galleries house selections from the permanent collection, and special exhibits of American art. The OMAA also has an extensive education program.

There is a museum shop offering art-related gifts. There is no café, but there are fine restaurants in nearby Perkins Cove and Ogunquit Village.

While You're in the Area

Ogunquit Village, Marginal Way, Perkins Cove, and Ogunquit Beach are also nearby.

Old Alna Meetinghouse

PO Box 265
Alna, ME 04535
(207) 586-5313

Overview

Built in 1789, the Old Alna Meetinghouse is the largest and finest meetinghouse in Maine.

Directions and Hours

Take Route 218 north 6.8 miles from US Route 1 in Wiscasset. The building is open July-August, Saturdays from 2:00 P.M. to 4:00 P.M., or by appointment.

Admission and Membership

Admission is free although donations are accepted. The building is not yet handicap accessible.

What to See

The Old Alna Meetinghouse has all its original fixtures and wonderful paint decoration. There is no café although Alna Store is located nearby, north on Route 218.

While You're in the Area

In the Alna area is the Wiscasset, Waterville, and Farmington Railroad Museum (p. 204) and the Head Tide Church Museum (p. 134).

Old Fort Western

16 Cony Street
Augusta, ME 04330
(207) 626-2385
www.oldfortwestern.org

Overview

Old Fort Western is America's oldest surviving wooden military building. The 1754 National Historic Landmark fort, store, and house museum is located on the Kennebec River in downtown Augusta. The year 2004 will be Old Fort Western's 250th anniversary.

Directions and Hours

From 95, take either of the Augusta exits and follow the signs to downtown, riverfront, city center, and Old Fort Western.

The museum is partly handicap accessible.

Old Fort Western is open from the first weekend in May to Columbus Day. May-July 3, 1:00-4:00; July 4-Labor Day, weekdays 10:00-4:00, weekends 1:00-4:00; Labor Day-Columbus Day, daily 1:00-4:00.

Admission and Membership

$4.75 for adults, $2.75 for children 6-16, under 6 is free. Membership levels begin at $25/year.

Discounts are available for seniors and AAA.

What to See

The museum's collections and programs help interpret Old Fort Western's military, storekeeping, and residential history. There is a reproduction of a river bateau similar to those used by Benedict Arnold's Quebec Expedition, and furniture owned by the Howard family at the Fort. There are also archeological artifacts excavated at Old Fort Western.

The museum offers a summer apprentice program for children 8-15, as well as scheduled school and group programs.

There is a gift shop, and visitors can eat at local restaurants.

While You're in the Area

The Maine State Museum (p. 149), the Children's Discovery Museum (p. 207), and the Maine Military Museum (p. 209) are nearby.

The Old Iron Inn Bed and Breakfast

155 High Street
Caribou, ME 04736
(207) 492-4766
www.oldironinn.com

Overview

The Old Iron Inn is a 1913 cape-style house with attractive mission oak interior. The Inn displays a substantial collection of antique laundry or pressing irons.

Directions and Hours

The Old Iron Inn is located on High Street, near downtown Caribou. Take the bypass around Caribou; High Street is located about midway between the two stoplights along Route 1, about a half mile from each of them. Once you have turned onto High Street, the Old Iron Inn will be the fifth house on the left. Watch for the sign in the shape of an antique charcoal iron.

The museum is open year round by appointment.

Admission and Membership

The collection is available for visit, without charge. Please call ahead.

What to See

More than 200 iron are on display, from the typical stovetop flat or "sad" irons to others heated by metal slugs, coal or gasoline. There is a good representative collection of the many unusual irons used during the Victorian Era for hats, sleeves or fancy lacework.

While You're in the Area

The Northern Maine Museum of Science (p. 165) is run by the same adminstrator.

Old Walpole Meeting House

Old Walpole Meeting House Road
South Bristol, ME 04568
(207) 563-5318

Overview

Built in 1772, the Old Walpole Meeting House is still all original. Most of the old glass still remains, and three outside walls still have 1772 shingles. The museum is on the national register of Historic Places.

Directions and Hours

Old Walpole Meeting House Road is between Route 130 and Route 129.

The museum is open by appointment from early spring until late fall, but is not handicap accessible.

Admission and Membership

Admission is free.

What to See

In addition to the exterior details, the box family pews remain intact as well. Services are still conducted each Sunday in August, with a candlelight service held the third Sunday in September at 7:00 P.M. A chamber music concert is held at 7:00 P.M. on the second Sunday in September.

There is no gift shop or café; the nearest place to eat is in Damariscotte, about 3½ miles away on Route 1.

While You're in the Area

Nearby attractions include the Thompson Ice House (p. 198) and the restored Harrington House (p. 129).

Photo courtesy of the Old Walpole Meeting House.

Old York Historical Society

PO Box 312/207 York Street
York, ME 03909
(207) 363-4974
www.oldyork.org

Overview

The Old York Historical Society was founded 100 years ago to preserve the history and artifacts of York, Maine—America's first chartered city (1632) and one of New England's earliest colonial settlements. Offering 37 period room settings and several galleries housed throughout seven historic museum buildings, Old York showcases a wealth of early New England art, architecture, and decorative arts. The exhibits focus on the stories of southern Maine's men, women, and children and the world they created and lived in from the earliest settlement in the 1600s to the present day. The Old Gaol features an exhibit on the history of the jail as a museum from 1900 to 2000.

Directions and Hours

Take exit 4 (The Yorks) off I-95. Follow to intersection and bear right onto Route 1 and head south. At the traffic light, turn left onto Route 1A, York Street. Follow for about ½ mile into the center of York Village. Just before the First Parish Church (the large white church on the left) take a right onto Lindsay Road. Jefferds' Tavern is the reddish-brown salt-box style building on the corner of York Street (Route 1A) and Lindsay Road. Drive past the Tavern to the parking lot located to the right.

The museum is open from mid-June to mid-October, Tuesday-Saturday from 10:00 A.M.-5:00 P.M. and Sunday from 1:00-5:00 P.M. The last tour begins at 4:00 P.M.

The administration office and research library are open year round. Some buildings have limited handicap accessibility.

Admission and Membership

$7 for adults, $6 for seniors and groups over 20, $3 for children under 16, under 4 free. Membership is $35/year for individual, $50/year for family.

What to See

On-site living history demonstrations, gallery talks, guided tours, and self-guided walks introduce the ordinary—and extraordinary—individuals who built and shaped the town. On any given day meet the jailer's family, the Tavern Keeper, or the School Master. Take a picture in the pillory where criminals were once kept for public humiliation in front of the Old Gaol.

Jefferds' Tavern (1754) serves as the museum visitor and education center.

The Old Schoolhouse (1745) is the only remaining one-room schoolhouse in York.

Containing a series of period rooms from 1750-1850, The Emerson-Wilcox House (1742) is furnished with fine American antiques (many with York origin) including the Bulman Bedhangings—the only known complete set of American crewel bedhangings.

The Old Gaol housed prisoners from 1719-1860 and is one of the oldest British public buildings in the U.S. It has dungeons, cells, and a gallery.

The John Hancock Warehouse (ca. 1740) stands along the York River and was owned by John Hancock. Visitors can experience early seafaring days in the ancient building.

The Elizabeth Perkins House (1730) was the former house of York's pioneer preservationist and contains Miss Perkins's eclectic collections from around the world.

Once serving as the customs house for York and a general store, the George Marshall Store (1869) now contains an art gallery with changing exhibits.

The York County Trust Building houses the research library and administrative offices.

The museum shop is located across the street from the Old Gaol and features many fine reproductions, gifts, cards, books, and old-time toys. There is no café, but visitors can eat at local restaurants within walking distance.

While You're in the Area

The museum buildings are within walking distance to charming York Village shops, restaurants, and art galleries. A walking tour throughout the historic district leads to the sparkling tidal waters of the York River and an 18-acre nature preserve. From the center of York Village, it is a short drive to beautiful sandy beaches and the famous Nubble Lighthouse.

Owls Head Transportation Museum

117 Museum Lane (Route 73)
Owls Head, ME 04854
(207) 594-4418
www.ohtm.org

Overview

The Owls Head Transportation Museum is home to a collection of antique autos, motorcycles, engines, bicycles, and carriages. The museum's collection includes the largest motorcycle ever made and luxury autos from the silent film era.

Directions and Hours

Take 95 to Augusta, then Route 17 west from Augusta. The museum is located on Route 73.

The museum is open year round, and is handicap accessible.

Hours: daily, April-October 10:00-5:00; daily April-October 10:00-4:00.

Admission and Membership

$16 for families, $6 for adults, $4 for children younger than twelve, children under five are free. Tours are $4 per person.

Event admission: $7-$8 for individuals, $5-$6 for children under twelve, $20-$24 for families, children under five receive free tours; group rate is $4 per person.

School groups and other nonprofit groups are free.

What to See

The Owls Head Transportation Museum displays the world's only Scripps-Booth Bi-Autogo, the largest motorcycle ever made. The museum also displays one of only five Stout Scarabs in existence, a minivan-like vehicle from 1935. There is also the 1962 Mustang II, which was the prototype for the Mustang line.

Also at the museum is a collection of antique airplanes, including an original 1917 Curtiss Jenny, a 1918 Standard J-1, and a 1923 Folker C.IV. The Folker C.IV is powered by the world's only Rolls Royce Eagle Engine V-12.

The museum holds a series of special events in the summer. These transportation jamborees attract antique airplanes, automobiles, motorcycles, engines, trucks, tractors, and commercial vehicles from throughout New England. These special events are highlighted by the museum's Antique Aeroplane Show, ground vehicle demonstrations, engine demonstrations, and guided tours.

The museum also offers a winter series of workshops and presentations. Dramatic offerings address airplane and automobile restoration, and transportation history and science.

Children's programs have included a reading hour of books illustrating transportation in the past, and a workshop in model building.

There is a gift shop, but there is no café. Visitors can eat at local restaurants, and a concession stand operates during special events.

While You're in the Area

Many lighthouses are within several miles of the museum. Also, the Farnsworth Art Museum (p. 125) and Shore Village Museum (p. 192) are nearby.

The Patten Lumberman's Museum

PO Box 300
Shin Pond Road
Patten, ME 04765
(207) 528-2650
www.lumbermenssmuseum.org

Overview

The Patten Lumbermen's Museum was established in 1962 to preserve a record of the lumber industry as it existed in the forests of Northern Maine before the second World War. It is located just west of Patten on the Shin Pond Road, which for over 175 year has been the highway over which thousand of woodsmen have passed to cut the pine, spruce, firs, and hardwoods in the upper valley of the East Branch of the Penobscot. In more recent years an endless stream of trucks loaded with logs and pulpwood pass the museum daily. The Patten Lumbermen's Museum presents a nostalgic view back into the bygone days of the "Great North Woods." Located in 9 buildings are artifacts of the past that show the hard work and the hard life, as well as the leisure times of the men who perfected the "Art of Logging." These men were so respected in their craft developed in the wood and on the rivers of Maine that they became known as the "Penobscot Tigers" when they pushed westward to New Hampshire and then on to Michigan and Minnesota, and even into the great Northwest. Washington and Oregon lumbering was jump started by "Penobscot Tigers."

Directions and Hours

From the South: Take I-95 to exit 58 (Sherman). Proceed north on Route 11 to Patten, then take a left onto Route 159. The museum is ½ mile from there.

From the North (Houlton): Take I-95 to exit 59 (Island Falls). Go west on Route 159 through Patten to the museum ½ mile from Patten.

From the North (Fort Kent): Proceed south on Route 11 to Patten. Turn right on Route 159. The museum is ½ mile away.

The museum is open Memorial Day-Columbus Day. and is partially handicap accessible.

Hours: Tuesday-Sunday 10:00-4:00.

Admission and Membership

$3.50 age 12 and up, $1 age 6-11, and under 6 are free. Special discounts are made by arrangement. Membership is $10/year for an individual, $20/year for a family, $25/year for a Friend, $75/year for a Supporter, and $200/year for a Patron.

What to See

The museum maintains 1,000 early logging photographs, a Steam Log hauler, handcrafts from the logging camps, 3 log buildings recreating early logging camps, 1 restored log farmhouse with dovetailed corners, and 9 buildings full of logging artifacts.

The museum does have a gift shop. There is no café but local downtown Patten has restaurants, pizza, and a fast food bar next door.

While You're in the Area

Other interesting places to visit while you are in the area are the Ashland Logging Museum (p. 207) and the Clothing Museum in Island Falls (p. 138).

Peary-MacMillan Arctic Museum

Bowdoin College
9500 College Station
Brunswick, ME 04011-8495
(207) 725-3416
www.bowdoin.edu/dept/arctic

Overview

The Peary-MacMillan Arctic Museum is named for Arctic explorers (and Bowdoin graduates) Robert E. Peary and Donald B. MacMillan. The museum and center studies the culture and natural environment of the Arctic region. Collections include exploration gear suitable for the arctic, natural history specimens, drawings, and artifacts made by Inuit and North American Indians.

Directions and Hours

The museum is located on the quadrangle of Bowdoin College in Brunswick, Maine, 25 miles from Portland and 120 miles from Boston.

From the south: Take the Maine Turnpike to exit 9 (I-95 to Coastal Route 1). Continue on I-95 to exit 22 (Brunswick, Route 1). Proceed to the business district and turn right on Maine Street, following signs to Bowdoin College.

From the north: Take exit 14 off the Maine Turnpike. Take I-95 to exit 22 (Topsham-Brunswick, Route 1 north). Proceed to the business district and turn right on Maine Street, following the signs to the college.

The museum is open year-round and is handicap accessible through the library.

Hours: Tuesday-Saturday, 10:00 A.M. to 5:00 P.M.; Sunday, 2:00-5:00 P.M. Closed Mondays and national holidays.

Admission and Membership

Admission and tours are free. Donations are appreciated.

What to See

The museum is a place where families can learn about the Arctic, its explorers, and the people and animals that inhabit the region. Visitors can play Inuit games, hold a walrus tusk, view stuffed Polar Bears, and see the actual dog sledge used in 1909 by Admiral Peary in the Arctic. All ages of children visit the Arctic Museum and participate in numerous activities, from preschool to high school. A popular activity lets guests feel things in a "Touch Box." A climate change exhibit will be opening in the Fall of 2001.

School tours are given by appointment, with at least four weeks notice.

The museum does have an Arctic Museum Gift Shop. There is a café on the Bowdoin College campus that is open to the public and Jack Magee's Grill is also nearby.

While You're in the Area

While on campus visitors can check out the Bowdoin College Museum of Art (p. 113), the Chamerberlain House (p. 172), the Pejepscot Museum (p. 172), and the Skolfield-Whittier House (p. 172).

Pejepscot Historical Society

159 Park Row
Brunswick, ME 04011
(207) 729-6606

Overview

The Pejepscot Museum offers changing exhibits and research collections for local history of Brunswick, Topsham, and Harpswell. The Society also operates two historic house museums, the Skolfield-Whittier House and the Joshua Lawrence Chamberlain Museum.

Directions and Hours

From I-95: Take exit 22. From the exit ramp go straight to downtown Brunswick. From there follow the signs to Maine Street and turn left. Head toward the big First Parish Church and park anywhere on Maine Street along the mall and the open space bordered by Park Row and Maine Street. The museum is located in the big brick double house on Park Row (#159). Please contact the museum for detailed directions to the two historic house museums.

The museum is open year-round while the two houses are seasonal, open approximately from June 1 to mid-October. The Pejepscot Museum is handicap accessible. The Skolfield-Whittier House is not handicap accessible and the Joshua Lawrence Chamberlain Museum is handicap accessible first floor only.

Hours: Pejepscot Museum: Tuesday, Wednesday, and Friday 9:00 A.M. to 5:00 P.M., Saturday 9:00 A.M. to 4:00 P.M. and Thursday 9:00 A.M. to 8:00 P.M. The Skolfield-Whittier House and the Joshua Lawrence Chamberlain Museum are open Tuesday-Saturday 9:00 A.M. to 4:00 P.M., closed Sundays, Mondays, and holidays. The Skolfield-Whittier House offers tours at 10:00, 11:30, 1:00, and 2:30. The Joshua Lawrence Chamberlain Museum offers tours twice per hour with the last tour leaving at 3:15.

Admission and Membership

The Pejepscot Museum is free. The two historical houses are $4 for adults and $2 ages 6-16. Combination tickets are $6 for adults and $3 for ages 6-16. Membership is $20/year for an individual and $35/year for a family. Other categories of membership are available but please contact the historical society for more information. Discounts are available for members of AAM, NEMA, and AAA.

What to See

The Historical Society is best known for their two historic houses, one of which, the Joshua Lawrence Chamberlain Museum, was the home of a four-term governor of Maine and hero of the Civil War. The other, the Skolfield-Whittier House, is the home of three generations of sea captains (the Skolfields) and physicians (Whittiers), and is virtually unchanged since a redecoration of the house in 1885. The house remains in the shape that the family left it, and is not a recreation.

The Historical Society conducts a four-day event in odd-year summers (2001, 2003, etc.) called Chamberlain Days featuring lectures, concerts, field trips, and special tours about Joshua Lawrence Chamberlain. The dates in 2001 are July 18, 19, 20, and 21.

The Historical Society has worked closely with the Brunswick Junior High School "History Huskies Club" since 1989 and sponsors a junior museum in a carriage barn, open Fridays in July and August.

The museum has a gift shop and is surrounded by a dozen eateries ranging from fast food to gourmet delis to sit-down restaurants, in all price ranges.

While You're in the Area

Brunswick is the home of the Bowdoin College Museum of Art (p. 113) and the Peary-MacMillan Arctic Museum (p. 172).

Penobscot Marine Museum

Church Street and Route One
Searsport, ME 04843
(207) 548-2520
www.penobscotmarinemuseum.org

Overview

The Penobscot Marine Museum is dedicated to the preservation, documentation, and exhibition of the history of Penobscot Bay and the maritime history of the state of Maine. The museum's 12-building complex houses a collection that includes marine paintings, ship models, nautical instruments, China trade artifacts, and artifacts of the nineteenth century age of sail.

The Thomas and James Buttersworth galleries of Marine Paintings at the Penobscot Marine Museum at Searsport. Photo by Benjamin Magro.

Directions and Hours

The museum is located on Route 1 in Seaport. Take Route 1 to Route 90 interesection, then Route 90 to Route 1 in Rockport. Or, take 95 to Augusta, then take Route 3 to Route 1. From Bar Harbor, take Route 3 to Route 1.

Most major exhibitions in the museums are handicap accessible.

The museum is open from Memorial Day weekend to mid-October.

Hours: Monday-Saturday 10:00-5:00, Sunday noon-5:00. The museum's Stephen Philips Memorial Library is open year round; call for hours.

Admission and Membership

$6 for adults, $5 for senior citizens, and $2 for children. Membership is $25/year, $40/family. Lifetime memberships are available.

Discounts are available for groups and AAA members, and all Maine schoolchildren are admitted free.

What to See

The museum has the country's largest collection of works by Thomas and James Butterworth, nineteenth century father and son painters. The museum's Fowler-True-Ross House is the recreation of a sea captain's home with fine oil portraits, furniture, and marine paintings. In each building there are interpreters to explain the exhibitions and answer questions.

Yard-in-the-Yard and capstan are popular outdoor exhibits for the whole family and give adults and children a hands-on experience. There is also an active Education Program that includes visits to schools, hosting school groups, and exhibitions done by local school children. The ongoing "Tea and Talk" series takes place in the Education Center and presents different facets of the collection and exhibitions. In 2001, the museum will offer a series of workshops on ship modeling.

The museum has a new Museum Store in the historic Whitcomb-Pendleton building in Main Street. Museum members receive a 10% discount at the gift shop.

Visitors can eat at local restaurants.

While You're in the Area

The museum is within walking distance to antique shops, and is within an hour's drive to Owls Head Transportation Museum (p. 170), Maine State Museum (p. 149), and the Farnsworth Art Museum (p. 125).

Phillips Historical Society

Pleasant St.
Phillips, ME 04966

Overview

Phillips Historical Society is located in Vose House, built in the early 1830s and an example of the beautiful architecture of that time period. The building houses a vast collection of household and work objects from the nineteenth to early twentieth century and is ever-expanding.

Directions and Hours
From Route 4, go to Main Street in Phillips. The society is open most major holidays in the summer and is open in the winter by appointment only. The facilities are not presently handicap accessible but will be in the near future.

Admission and Membership
Admission is free but donations are accepted. Membership is $10/year per person or $15/year per family.

What to See
Built on land owned by Joel Whitney, a prominent businessman in the 1830s, the Vose House has a variety of rooms with exhibits from nineteenth- to early twentieth-century life. In the front of the house, visitors can view a kitchen as it would appear in the 1800s, complete with a wood stove and butter churn among other items likely found in that era. In the parlor, there are many more displays including a priceless Portland Glass collection, examples of Victorian furniture, and even a bellows-type organ in good working condition. Other collections of special interest include a display of every tool available to farmers, loggers, and carpenters from the 1800s to the early 1900s and the document room with a vast collection of printed material and photos. With great pride, the Historical Society presents an display in the Railroad Room about the Sandy River, Rangeley Lakes Narrow Gauge Railroad. The Griscom Gallery holds many items from days long gone by—sports memorabilia, World War II objects, children's toys, an antique telephone switchboard, and hundreds of donated items. More recently, the Society has an ongoing project at the old agriculture building to display various horse-drawn implements including a hearse and an antique snow roller.

Photo courtesy of the Phillips Historical Society.

There is no café, but there is a restaurant a mile away at Avon Mall.

While You're in the Area
Nearby attractions and museums include the Sandy River & Rangeley Lakes Railroad, the Rangeley Lakes Region Logging Museum (p. 210), and the Stanley Museum (p. 194).

Portland Harbor Museum
SMTC campus, Fort Road
South Portland, ME 04106
(207) 799-6337
www.portlandharbormuseum.org

Overview
The Portland Harbor Museum is located at the entrance to the harbor with views of three lighthouses and three forts. It is dedicated to preserving and interpreting the maritime heritage of Portland Harbor, its islands, and the surrounding communities. The bow of the only surviving clipper ship, *Snow Squall*, brought from the

Photo of Spring Point Ledge Lighthouse, courtesy of Portland Harbor Museum.

Falklands Islands in 1987, forms the centerpiece of an exhibit on this ship and nineteenth century wooden shipbuilding.

Directions and Hours

Take Route 295 to exit 6A. follow Route 77 over the Casco Bridge to South Portland. After the bridge, go straight onto Broadway and follow it to the end. Follow the signs to the museum.

The museum is open from April to December, and is handicap accessible.

Hours: July, August, September, daily 10:00-4:30; call for hours of other months.

Admission and Membership

$3 for adults, $1 for children six to sixteen, younger children and members are free. Membership is $25/year for families, and there are various levels of contributing membership.

The museum offers a 2-for-1 discount for AAA members and a group rate for 40 or more people is $2.

What to See

In addition to the *Snow Squall* exhibit, the museum also has an exhibit featuring the Lighthouses of Casco Bay. On site are historic Fort Preble, the Spring Point Ledge Lighthouse, and the signed Shoreline Walkway to Willard Beach.

The museum offers group tours with lunch, a maritime lecture series, and historical walking tours. It maintains collections of maritime artifacts and archival material.

There is a museum gift shop. There is no café, but there are numerous restaurants and sandwich shops in the Portland area.

While You're in the Area

The Portland Harbor Museum is close to Portland Head Light, the Liberty Ship Memorial at Bug Light Park, and many other Portland attractions.

Portland Museum of Art

Seven Congress Square
Portland, Maine 04101
(207) 775-6148 or (207) 773-ARTS
www.portlandmuseum.org

Overview

Celebrate art in Maine at the Portland Museum of Art, the state's oldest and largest arts institution, founded in 1882. The Museum's extensive collection of fine and decorative arts dates from the eighteenth century to the present. Works by Winslow Homer, John Singer Sargent, Rockwell Kent, Marsden Hartley, and Andrew Wyeth showcase the unique artistic heritage of the United States and Maine. The major European movements, from Impressionism through Surrealism, are represented by the Joan Whitney Payson, Albert Otten, and Scott M. Black collections, which include works by Auguste Rodin, Edgar Degas, Claude Monet, Pablo Picasso, Edvard Munch, and René Magritte. Special exhibitions complement those holdings. The Museum is housed in an award-winning building, which opened in 1983, designed by I.M. Pei & Partners.

Directions and Hours

The Museum is located at Seven Congress Square on the corner of High and Congress Streets. Follow signs to the Downtown Arts

District from major routes. From I-295, take exit 6A (Forest Avenue South). Bear right off the exit and drive through the park. Proceed on State Street to the light at the top of the hill. Turn left onto Congress Street and proceed 2/10 of a mile to the museum, located on your right.

The museum is open year round, and is handicap accessible.

Hours: Tuesday, Wednesday, Saturday, and Sunday, 10:00 A.M. to 5:00 P.M.; Thursday and Friday, 10:00 A.M. to 9:00 P.M.; closed Mondays in the winter.

Memorial Day thru Columbus Day: Open Mondays from 10:00 A.M. to 5:00 P.M.

Admission and Membership

$6 for adults, $5 for seniors and students with I.D., $1 for youths 6-12, children under 6 free. The Museum is free on Friday evenings from 5:00 P.M. to 9:00 P.M. Groups of 15 or more receive a discount admission of $4. School groups are $1 per student. Seniors are $5 ($1 off regular admission).

Membership: Individual $35, Family/ Household $50, Contributing $100, Donor $250, Patron $500, Committee of One Hundred $1,000-$5,000.

What to See

The museum highlights works by Marsden Hartley, Winslow Homer, Rockwell Kent, and Andrew Wyeth, among other Maine artists. There is an extensive glass collection.

A Jazz Breakfast series is offered in Fall/Winter/Spring.

In the fall of 2002, the museum will open the newly renovated Federal-style McLellan-Sweat House and the Beaux-Arts L. D. M. Sweat Memorial Galleries. These exceptional structures will be restored to their past elegance and make them welcoming spaces for the preservation of the museum's fine collections of nineteenth-century American paintings and decorative arts. The museum will provide visitors with rich experiences in architecture, painting, sculpture, and decorative objects that will span two centuries of American culture and make this complex of buildings unique among American museums.

Frequent children's programming is offered. The museum has a gift shop and a café.

The Portland Museum of Art is part of The Maine Art Museum Trail along with the Bates College Museum of Art (p. 110), Bowdoin College Museum of Art (p. 113), Colby Museum of Art (p. 119), Farnsworth Art Museum (p. 125), Ogunquit Museum of American Art (p. 166), and the University of Maine Museum of Art (p. 211).

Since Frederic Edwin Church, Fitz Hugh Lane, Thomas Cole and others first came here in the mid-nineteenth century, Maine has inspired many renowned artists, including Winslow Homer, Edward Hopper, George Bellows, Marguerite Zorach, and three generations of Wyeths. It was through the work of artists such as these that the world first glimpsed the distinct light that shines on Maine. Seven distinguished art museums invite you to see it for yourself by exploring The Maine Art Museum Trail.

Offering over 53,000 magnificent works of art, the trail's collections feature works by the many artists associated with Maine, as well as masterpieces by Pierre-Auguste Renoir, Edgar Degas, Mary Cassatt, and Pablo Picasso, among others. The trail also showcases ancient pottery and sculpture, early American silver and furniture, as well as contemporary textiles, prints, ceramics and sculpture.

On this Trail, all roads lead to treasure: in the museums that comprise it, as well as in the vibrant communities in which they reside. For more information on the trail, visit www.maineartmuseums.org

While You're in the Area

Nearby attractions include Victoria Mansion (p. 200), the Center for Maine History's Maine History Gallery and Wadsworth-Longfellow House (p. 207), Portland Headlight, Old Port shopping area, the Children's Museum of Maine (p. 207), art galleries, the Portland Stage Company, the Portland Symphony, and the Portland Observatory (p. 178).

Portland Observatory

138 Congress Street
Portland, ME 04101
(207) 774-5561
www.portlandlandmarks.org

Overview

The Portland Observatory was built in 1807 by Captain Lemuel Moody. It is the only remaining maritime signal tower on the east coast. The observatory offers views of Portland, Casco Bay, and the islands, and a glimpse of Portland's rich maritime history.

Directions and Hours

Take the Maine Turnpike to exit 6A (Route 295). Take exit 7 off Route 295. Travel on Franklin Artery to intersection with Congress Street. Take a left onto Congress Street and travel to the top of Munjoy Hill—the obeservatory will be on your right.

The observatory is open from Memorial Day through Columbus Day, but only the first floor is handicap accessible.

Hours: daily at 10:00.

Admission and Membership

$3 for adults, $2 for children. Members of the Greater Portland Landmarks are admitted free.

What to See

Visitors to the observatory should be sure to ask tour guides to show them the ballast that has held the building steady for nearly 200 years.

The observatory offers weekly sunset tours. Visitors should call ahead for specific dates and times. Children's programming includes Halloween at the observatory.

There is a gift shop. There is no café, but Portland's historic Old Fort district offers many restaurants and cafes.

While You're in the Area

The Lewis Gallery (p. 132) and Museum of African Tribal Art (p. 157) are both nearby, as are many other Portland-area museums and attractions.

Pownalborough Court House

Route 128
PO Box 61
Dresden, ME 04578
(207) 882-6817
www.wiscasset.net/lcha

Overview

The Pownalborough Court House was built in 1761 and features a restored courtroom, kitchen, parlor, a tavern room, a judge's chambers, and displays of ice harvesting and eighteenth century rural life.

Directions and Hours

From Routes 1 and 27 in Wiscasset follow Route 27 nine miles north to Route 128 and go 2½ miles to the site.

The museum is open on June and September weekends and July 1-Labor Day Tuesday-Sunday. It is not handicap accessible.

Hours: Tuesdays-Saturday 10:00 A.M. to 4:00 P.M. and Sunday 12:00-4:00 P.M.

Admission and Membership

Adults $3, children 7-17 $2, seniors/AAA members $2.50, and a family $8. Group rates are available. Membership is $20/year for individuals and $30/year for families.

What to See

The museum features an ice harvesting model and a large assortment of ice tools, along with nature trails, a picnic area, a cemetary, spinning and weaving tools, wood-working tools, and 12 period rooms.

Exhibits, programs, and reenactments change annually so please contact the museum for up to date information. The museum hosts an annual Memorial Day observation.

The museum has a gift shop. Eateries are limited in Dresden so a packed lunch might be a good idea.

While You're in the Area

Attractions and museums in the area include: the Dresden Schoolhouse Museum (p. 208), the Lincoln County Museum and Old Jail (p. 145), Castle Tucker (p. 118), and the Musical Wonder House (p. 160).

Rangeley Lakes Region Historical Society

PO Box 521
Rangeley, ME 04970

Overview

The Rangeley Lakes Region Historical Society focuses on the famous hotel area and the region's outdoor sporting heritage.

Directions and Hours

Take Route 4 to Main Street in Rangeley.

Open July 1-September 1, Monday-Saturday from 10:00 A.M. to noon.

Admission and Membership

Admission is free and a newsletter is available at no cost. The basement is handicap accessible.

What to See

The Rangeley Lakes Region Historical Society has an outstanding collection of flies and mounts as well as memorabilia from the Rangeley Lake House Hotel and other hotels from the 1920s to the 1950s. The society also houses an early collection of blown eggs from eighty species, including the now-extinct passenger pigeon.

The Historical Society hosts a variety of events every year including the annual meeting in a potluck supper in June, the annual meeting in July, and Outdoor Sporting Heritage Day in August.

Visitors may purchase books at the Historical Society. There is no café although there are several restaurants nearby.

While You're in the Area

Rangeley Logging Museum (p. 210) is nearby.

Raye's Old Stone Mustard Mill

83 Washington Street
PO Box 2
Eastport, ME 04631
(207) 853-4451
www.rayesmustard.com

Overview

This operating mustard mill is the last nineteenth century stone mill still in operation in this

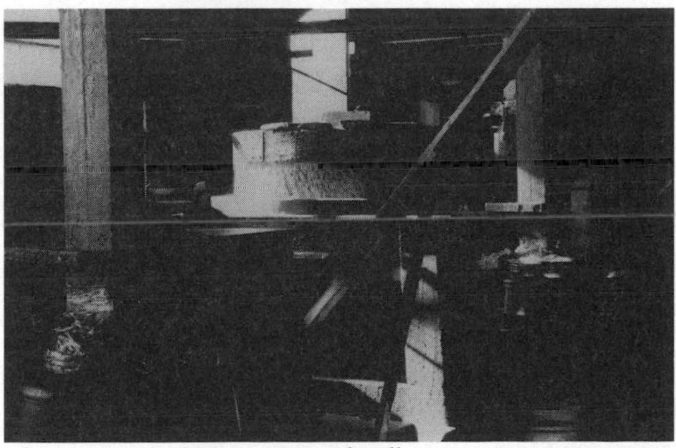

Photo courtesy of Raye's Mustard Mill.

country. The process used dates back to the middle ages and would be lost if not represented by this mill and its distinctive mustards. The Raye family has been grinding mustard in the same location since 1903, when J. W. "Wes" Raye set up his first mill in the family smokehouse to grind mustard sauces for the growing sardine industry.

Directions and Hours

From Route 1 north: Turn right on Route 190 in Perry and continue to Eastport (7-8 miles).

From Route 9 north: Take the Alexander turnoff to Route 191. Turn left at the "T" and bear right at the "Y." Continue to Route 1 and turn left (north). Follow the directions from Route 1.

The museum is open year-round and is handicap accessible.

Mill tours: When the mill schedule allows, tours run on weekdays on the hour from 10:00-4:00, and on weekends by arrangement.

Shop hours: Summer: 8:00 A.M. to 5:30 P.M. Monday-Wednesday, 8:00 A.M. to 6:30 P.M. Thursday and Friday. Closed Saturday and Sunday. Winter: 8:00 A.M. to 5:00 P.M. Monday-Wednesday, 8:00 A.M. to 5:00 P.M. Thursday and Friday. Closed Saturday and Sunday.

Photo courtesy of the Readfield Union Meeting House Co., Inc.

Admission and Membership

There is no admission cost and guided tours are free. Children under 12 must be accompanied by an adult.

What to See

Raye's Mill, a working museum, has produced distinctive and unique mustards that have won many international awards. Most mustards today are either cooked or ground at high speeds. Raye's mustard, however, used a process first developed in the seventeenth century and uses the slow cold-grind method, with a series of large granite stones that slowly grind the mash to a creamy consistency before leaving it to age.

There is a gift shop which includes local and Maine-made foods, gifts, crafts, and arts. There is also a café with limited seating inside and picnic tables outside. Also prepared is food to go for picnics on the breakwater or at the Shackford Head State Park.

While You're in the Area

Other interesting places to visit while you are in the area are: the Eastport Historical "Barracks Museum" (p. 207), the Tidal Dam Model, whale watching rides, a ferry to Canadian islands, Roosevelt Park, and Shackford Head State Park.

The Readfield Union Meeting House

PO Box 8
Readfield, ME 04355-0008
(207) 685-3831

Overview

The Meeting House's primary attraction is the beautiful and realistic trompe l'oeil artwork of Charles J. Schumacher, a Prussian immigrant, painted in 1867 and covering the entire interior. The building also has original unique windows painted on both sides and baked in the 1800s, along with some stained glass windows of later date, a clock, and the excellent brick made in a farmyard in Readfield in 1827 at the time the Meeting House was built. The museum is on the National Record of Historic Places.

Directions and Hours

The Meeting House is on Church Road, at the intersection where Route 17 (traveling west from Augusta and manchester) meets Route 41 (traveling north from Winthrop). Go north on Church Road at the intersection; the museum is a large brick building on the left within one block.

The museum is open for open house days during the summer, or by appointment year yound. The building is handicap accessible.

Admission and Membership

The museum is free, but a donation is requested.

What to See

The trompe l'oeil artwork covering the entire interior is of the highest quality and is the work of an expert in that style (which was popular in this country from about 1860-1880). The painted windows are also very valuable in their area of art. Both the artwork and the windows are in their original state and well preserved. The big clock on the tower is also well preserved, but now operates from electric motors rather than large weights.

The Meeting House hosts frequent musical concerts.

There is no gift shop, but visitors can buy prints, cards, and a book of the museum artwork. There is no café, but there is a restaurant on the lake less than a mile away.

While You're in the Area

The Maine State Museum is only 12 miles away in Augusta.

Redington Museum of the Waterville Historical Society

64 Silver Street
Waterville, ME 04901
(207) 872-9493

Overview

The Redington Museum offers a comprehensive view of life in Waterville during the past two centuries. Its collection includes furniture, accessories, household artifacts, toys, tools, and weapons. The museum is located in the Federal-style home built by Asa Redington, a Revolutionary War veteran and member of George Washington's honor guard, in 1814.

Directions and Hours

Take 95 to exit 33. Follow Route 11 north about two miles and turn right onto Silver Street.

The museum is open from Memorial Day week to Labor Day, but is not handicap accessible.

Hours: Tuesday-Saturday, tours are at 10:00, 11:00, 1:00, and 2:00.

Admission and Membership

$3 for adults, $2 for children under twelve. Membership is $15/year for individuals.

School tours by appointment are $1 per student.

What to See

In addition to the artifacts of daily life in Waterville, the LaVerdiere apothecary building houses a large collection of pharmaceutical antiques typical of the early twentieth century, including a matching set of mahogany, brass, and glass cases.

The Waterville Historical Society will be celebrating its centennial in 2003.

There is no gift shop. Local sandwich shops and restaurants are nearby.

While You're in the Area

The Redington Museum is located near the Colby College Museum of Art (p. 119).

Reverend Daniel Merrill House

Sedgwick Brooklin Historical Society
Route 172
Sedgwick, ME 04676
(207) 359-4447

Overview

The museum was the home of Daniel Merrill, the first minister in Township #4 of the Marsh Grant, which is now Sedgwick, Brooklin, and parts of Brooksville and Penobscot.

Directions and Hours

From US Route 1 take Route 15 to Blue Hill and then Route 172 to the museum.

The museum is open in July and August. The first floor is handicap accessible.

Hours: Sunday afternoons 2:00-4:00 P.M. or by appointment.

Admission and Membership

Donations are encouraged.

What to See

The Reverend Daniel Merrill House is one of the buildings in the Sedgwick Historic District. It was built in the late 1700s as was the original Town Meeting House and the Town Pound. Other buildings include a one room schoolhouse, a barn for storage, a display of old hearses, and a new barn to store large items on display.

During the summer there will be a theme on small, native boats and a costume display.

While You're in the Area

Nearby attractions and museums include the Holt House (p. 136) and Jonathan Fisher Homestead (p. 139).

Robbins House

Union Historical Society
343 Common Road
Union, ME 04862
(207) 785-5444
www.midcoast.com/comespring

Overview

The Union Historical Society collects and preserves historical documents, relics, and records of Union, and makes these items available to the community and visitors to the Robbins House. The house, built in 1849, has been restored to its modified Greek Revival architecture. The parlors and bedrooms are furnished in the Early Victorian style featuring locally produced pieces and early artifacts from the first families in 1776.

Directions and Hours

Take Route 17 to Route 235 south in Union, to Union Common and Common Road. Turn left onto Common Road and follow the signs.

Or, take Route 1 to Route 235 north in Waldoboro to Common Road. Turn right onto Common Road and follow the signs.

The house is open year round, and is handicap accessible.

Hours: Wednesday and Saturday 10:00-noon, and by appointment.

Admission and Membership

Admission to the house is free. Membership is $5/year for individuals.

What to See

The house contains a large collection of early local photographs and postcards. A recent project has been to document the old houses and buildings of the town through photos and oral histories. The genealogy of some families of the area is also a focus of the Union Historical Society.

The inventor of Moxie, first promoted as a nerve tonic, was Augustin Thompson, a local resident. Some Moxie memorabilia is on display at the museum.

School groups tour such Union memorabilia as the pump organ, telephone exchange desk, old textiles, and the furnishings of the house. Monthly programs are held from March through December at 7:30 on the first Wednesday of the month.

There is a gift shop. There is no café in the Robbins House, but nearby cafés include Hannibal's Café on the Common and Come Spring Café on Route 17.

While You're in the Area

The Old Town House, Matthews Farm Museum and One Room School (p. 209), Yellow Schoolhouse Museum, Flea Market at Thompson Community Center, and an Antique Show at Union Fairgrounds are also in the area.

Rumford Historical Society

Municipal Building
145 Congress Street
Rumford, ME 04276

Overview

The Rumford Historical Society's museum building is an unusual two story, two room schoolhouse with distinct architectural features. Two backhouse type toilets, one for boys and one for girls, connect the museum to the main building.

Directions and Hours

The museum is located at 1378 US Route 2 in the village of Rumford Center.

The museum is open June through August and by appointment, but is not handicap accessible.

Hours: daily 10:00-4:00.

Admission and Membership

Admission to the museum is free.

What to See

The museum exhibits old hand tools, medical and surgical equipment, period furniture and clothing.

The museum conducts tours for school children.

There is a gift shop. There is a café across the street.

While You're in the Area

The Dixfield Historical Society Museum (p. 123) and the Bethel Historical Society Museum (p. 111) are also in the area.

Saco Museum

Dyer Library
371 Main Street
Saco, ME 04072
(207) 283-0958 or (207) 283-3861
www.sacomaine.org

Overview

Founded in 1867, the Saco Museum is one of the oldest in the state of Maine. Housed in a 1926 building by John Calvin Stevens, the collection comprises a rich wealth of folk art master works, decorative arts, period room settings, natural history specimens, and nineteenth century curiosities. Changing exhibitions explore contemporary art and historic themes of the Saco River Valley.

Directions and Hours

From the Maine Turnpike (I-95): Take exit 5 to Route 195. Take exit 2A to Route 1 south. The museum is 8/10 of a mile on the left.

The museum is open year-round and is handicap accessible.

Hours: Monday, Tuesday, Wednesday, Friday: 12:00-4:00 P.M. Thursday noon-8:00 P.M. Closed Saturday and Sunday.

Admission and Membership

Adults $4, seniors $3, students $1; children 6 and under are free. Group discounts are available for half price. Students are $1.50 for educational programs. The Dyer Library Association Membership is $20/year for an individual, $25/year for a senior citizen family, $30/year for a family, $50/year for a Contributor, and $100/year for a donor.

What to See

Aside from the museum's permanent collections, the museum hosts changing exhibitions of contemporary art and historic themes approximately every three months. The Dyer Library (located adjacent to the Saco Museum), provides a Maine History Room for local history research and a children's room with regular children's programming.

Upcoming 2001 exhibitions include "All in a Day's Work" (featuring tools and processes of fabrication from the past, including old-time demonstrations of various crafts), "Beddeford High School Student Artists" (student art work will be presented), "Inspired by Saco: Artists Reflect on the Collection of the Saco Museum" (artists will choose a piece from the museum collection and create an artwork in response), "Miniatures" (examines the psychology of the miniature, including paintings, books, furniture, and ceramics), and "Dealing with Death" (addresses the customs and attitudes concerning death and dying).

Children's programming at the museum includes art classes, family fun nights, and summer discovery programs.

There is a gift shop. There are many shops and cafés located in downtown Saco as well as fast food and restaurants along Route 1.

While You're in the Area

Other interesting places to visit while you are in the area include the Seashore Trolley Museum (p. 191), the Brick Store Museum (p. 114), the Portland Art Museum (p. 176), and the Children's Museum in Portland (p. 207).

St. Croix Historical Society

PO Box 242
245 Main Street
Calais, ME 04619
(207) 454-2604

Overview

This museum, started in 1954, is the home of the first three doctors to practice in Calais. The house was built in 1800 and restored to be the office and home of Dr. Job Holmes. The museum, complete with furnishings and medical office, offers the public a glimpse of a way of life in a small town at that period.

Directions and Hours

Main Street Calais is also Route 1, the coastal Maine route. The museum can also be reached at the Canadian border crossing from Route 9 and St. Stephen, Canada. The museum is located in the center of Calais, one mile from the Canadian border and 90 miles northeast of Bangor, Maine.

The museum is open July 1 to Labor Day. There are no winter hours but the museum will open for special groups up to December and after June 1. It is not handicap accessible.

Hours: Monday-Friday 1:00-4:30, and by appointment.

Admission and Membership

Donations are requested. Annual dues of $10 includes 4 issues of a local history newsletter.

What to See

The house features post and beam construction with split lath walls, demonstrated through viewing holes, and the rooms are decorated with period textiles, furnishings and toys. Toy models of a steam lumber hauler and steam lake boat to move lumber are displayed in the boy's room. The doctor's office features Dr. Holmes's traveling medicine box, drying herbs, mortise and pestle, and diploma from Bowdoin Medical School. The museum offers Dutch oven cooking demonstrations and a talk on fire fighting methods, displaying fire buckets and bags for the local Fire Club. The historical society has a junior membership and gives talks on Calais history in the middle schools.

In 2004, the museum will celebrate the anniversary of the landing of DeMonts and

Champlain in 1604 on the island of St. Croix in Calais. Programs will be held on both the Canadian and American sides starting June 25 and continuing through the summer. Lectures will cover the history of the landing and the navigation techniques of that period.

There is no gift shop or café, but many dining opportunities are available within a mile. The museum does sell books of local history and photographs from glass plate negatives.

While You're in the Area

Moosehorn National reservation is located in Calais, offering nature trails and guided programs. Twenty miles east on Route 1, the town of Eastport has a museum and exhibit of the Quoody tidal power project of the 1930s. The Charlotte County Museum in St. Stephen, New Brunswick, features a Victorian house with many displays.

The Salmon Brook Historical Society Museums

PO Box 71
Washburn, ME 04786
(207) 455-4339

Overview

The Salmon Brook Historical Society exhibits material and information of the area and includes the Benjamin C. Wilder House, a restored 1852 home now listed on the National Register of Historical Places. A recently constructed barn, holding an extensive collection of old farm machinery and equipment, is attached to the house.

Directions and Hours

Take Route 164 to Washburn from either Presque Isle or Caribou. The museum is located in the center of Washburn next to Story Park on 17 Main Street.

The buildings are open to the public from mid-June to mid-September, every Wednesday 8:00-11:00 A.M. and Sunday 1:00-4:00 P.M. The museum is handicap accessible.

Admission and Membership

There is no admission although donations are gratefully accepted to help with maintenance and other operating expenses. Yearly membership is $2/year.

What to See

The Benjamin C. Wilder House has been renovated with furniture and other pieces from the mid-to-late 1800s. There are two especially interesting exhibits in the barn: "Don & Barb's Country Corner" is a display of old and rare pottery, iron, copper, and brass culinary items, and many other fine pieces, and "The Fox's Den" holds a fine old Craftsmans Chest, numerous types of wooden planes, and many rare shop tools.

During the Washburn festival in August, the museums host an open house each year on the third weekend in August. The society also schedules tours for classes from local schools.

There is no café but visitors will find places to dine in neighboring towns.

While You're in the Area

Nearby attractions and museums include the Caribou Historical Society (p. 116), the Nylander Natural History Museum (p. 210), the New Sweden Historical Museum (p. 162), Maine's Swedish Colony, Inc. (p. 150), as well as the Woodland Historical Society and the Snowman School Museum (p. 193).

The Salt Gallery

The Salt Institute for Documentary Studies
110 Exchange Street
Portland, ME 04101
(207) 761-0660
www.salt.edu

"Father Seamus and Brother Nicholas." From The Salt Gallery exhibits. Photo by Patrick Winkelman.

Overview

The Salt Gallery is an integral part of the Salt Institute for Documentary Studies in Portland, Maine. The gallery exhibits the best work of graduates of the institute: documentary photography, writing, and radio, all of which focus on Maine people, places, and industries. Visitors to the student exhibits will find black and white prints accompanied by nonfiction text panels and stations for listening to radio documentaries. The Salt Gallery also exhibits the work of other documentary photographers throughout the year.

Directions and Hours

To get to the gallery from 295, take the Franklin Street Exit and go through three lights, up the hill. At the fourth light, turn right onto Congress Street. Go straight and then take your second left on Exchange Street. The gallery is on the right corner, one block down on Federal Street.

The Salt Gallery is open Monday through Saturday from noon to 5:00, and is handicap accessible.

Admission and Membership

Admission is free.

What to See

The Salt Institute has an annual publication, *Salt Omnibus*, which showcases the photographs and stories of the institute's graduates. Also, Salt has an archive that includes photos, negatives, tape-recorded interviews, and transcripts from the past 28 years of documenting contemporary Maine.

While You're in the Area

The Salt Gallery is located in the Old Port area of Portland, near excellent shopping, dining, and sightseeing spots.

Sandy River & Rangeley Lakes Railroad

PO Box B
Phillips, Maine 04966
(207) 779-1901
www.srrl-rr.org

Overview

The railroad is an operating museum dedicated to the preservation and restoration of the two foot gauge Sandy River & Rangeley Lakes RR and its predecessor lines which served Franklin County, Maine, from 1879 through 1935. Your conductor on the short ride will also be your guide through the history of the Railroad and a tour of our roundhouse and restoration efforts.

Directions and Hours

From the Portland area: Follow the Maine Turnpike north to exit 12 in Auburn. From exit 12, take Route 4 north all the way to Phillips (about 70 miles from exit 12). You will pass through Auburn/Lewiston, Turner, Livermore, Livermore Falls, Jay, Wilton, Farmington, and the edge of Strong on your way. As you pass through Avon, watch for the grass runway of the Raymond Airport on your left. Take the next right turn onto Pleasant Street. If you take no further turns, you will cross the Sandy River on a concrete bridge and head up the hill on Bridge Street. After you come down the other side of the hill, the SR&RL Sander's Station is on your left. The driving time from exit 12 to Phillips should be about 90 minutes.

From the Augusta area: Take Route 27 north

to Farmington, about 37 miles. At Farmington, take Route 4 north to Phillips, about 18 miles. As you pass through Avon, watch for the grass runway of the Raymond Airport on your left. Take the next right turn onto Pleasant Street. If you take no further turns, you will cross the Sandy River on a concrete bridge and head up the hill on Bridge Street. After you come down the other side of the hill, the SR&RL Sander's Station is on your left. Driving time from Augusta should be about 75 minutes.

From the Waterville area: From Waterville, take Route 104 North to Route 139, about 4 miles. Follow Route 139 west to Route 2 at Norridgewock, about 11 miles. Follow Route 2 west to Farmington, about 21 miles. At Farmington, take Route 4 north to Phillips, about 18 miles. As you pass through Avon, watch for the grass runway of the Raymond Airport on your left. Take the next right turn onto Pleasant Street. If you take no further turns, you will cross the Sandy River on a concrete bridge and head up the hill on Bridge Street. After you come down the other side of the hill, the SR&RL Sander's Station is on your left. Driving time from Waterville should be about 70 minutes.

Directions from Newport, Bangor and points North: Take I-95 South to exit 39 at Newport. Take Route 11 north to Route 2, less than 0.5 mile. Take Route 2 west to Farmington, about 49 miles. At Farmington, take Route 4 north to Phillips, about 18 miles. As you pass through Avon, watch for the grass runway of the Raymond Airport on your left. Take the next right turn onto Pleasant Street. If you take no further turns, you will cross the Sandy River on a concrete bridge and head up the hill on Bridge Street. After you come down the other side of the hill, the SR&RL Sander's Station is on your left. Driving time from Bangor should be about 100 minutes.

From Rangeley: Take Route 4 south to Phillips, about 22 miles. Slow down where Route 142 North departs from Route 4. Less than 0.5 mile further down Route 4, take the left turn onto Pleasant Street. If you take no further turns, you will cross the Sandy River on a concrete bridge and head up the hill on Bridge Street. After you come down the other side of the hill, the SR&RL Sander's Station is on your left. Driving time should be about 35 minutes.

The railroad is open June through September on the first and third Sundays.

On the Friday and Saturday of Phillips Old Home Days (the week including the third Friday in August) the railroad operates the daytime schedule plus a Night Train at 9:00 P.M. The railroad also runs on additional dates, which change from year to year. See www.srrl-rr.org for schedule.

Operating dates for 2001: June 3, 17; July 1, 2, 14, 15; August 5, 17, 18, 19; September 2, 3, 16, 22, 23, 29, 30; Octer 6, 7. All operations are subject to the availability of equipment and manpower.

Locomotive #4, coach #6, and caboose #559 on the occasion of #4's return to service after rebuilding on August 18, 2000. It shows Conductor Tom Moore boarding passengers after a roundhouse tour. Photo by R. Troup, SR&RL.

Trains run approximately hourly, from 11:00 A.M. to 3:00 P.M. The ride and tour takes 45-55 minutes. Handicapped visitors are welcome, but there are some difficulties with wheelchairs and walkers. Wheelchairs and walkers cannot access the coach, but the museum can load a wheelchair with occupant into the caboose. Wheelchairs may not be able to navigate the roundhouse area due to loose sand and projecting rails and loading/unloading wheelchairs at the roundhouse is not currently provided for. Please call in advance to insure the caboose will be on the train, and/or discuss particular needs.

Admission and Membership

$3.00 for age 13 and over. Under age 13 rides free. Young children should be under the close supervision of a responsible adult.

Membership: $10/year for Junior (under 18), $20/year for Individual, $50/year for Family, $100/year for Corporate, $200 for 15-year membership

What to See

The museum has have the largest collection of original SR&RL equipment and buildings. It operates Sandy River RR coach #6, and is actively restoring her sister #5. Both were built by Laconia Car Co. in 1884. There are six box cars including the oldest survivor, SRRR #55 (later SR&RL Tool Car #562) that dates from 1882.

Tickets are sold from the Phillips Freight Station (built 1900), which stands next to the second Sanders Station.

Recent acquisitions include Flanger #505 (built 1894) and the Maplewood Depot (built 9/1906) which both await restoration work.

Operations run over 0.5 miles of the original Phillips & Rangeley roadbed to the site of the abutments of the Phillips Covered Bridge (1890-1939). The museum stores its equipment and conducts restoration work at its roundhouse. The roundhouse is a reconstruction on the foundations of the P&R "Old Stone Fort." There is a working steel turntable in the original pit of the P&R wooden turntable.

There are no special programs, but there is always a preservation/restoration project in progress. The railroad can find work for all skill levels from paint stirrer and nail banger to cabinet maker. The museum is always looking for new members to participate in the preservation, restoration, and operation of the museum and its equipment.

There is a gift shop, and soft drinks are available at the ticket counter. The closest restaurant is a pizza/sandwich shop on Main Street in Phillips. There is a small restaurant in Avon (about a mile south on Route 4, adjoining gas station) that provides a hearty meal, and another sandwich shop across from it.

While You're in the Area

Rangeley Lakes Region Logging Museum (p. 210) and The Stanley Museum (p. 194) are both nearby.

Sarah Orne Jewett House (SPNEA)

5 Portland Street
South Berwick, ME 03908
(207) 384-2454
www.spnea.org

Overview

Writer Sarah Orne Jewett spent most of her life in this stately Georgian residence, owned by her family since 1819. The view from her desk in the second-floor hall surveys the town's major intersection and provided her with material for her books, such as *The Country of the Pointed Firs,* which describes the character of the Maine countryside and seacoast with accuracy and affection.

Directions and Hours

From the south: Take I-95 to Maine exit 3.

From the north: After the York tolls, take exit 2. Follow Route 236 north for 10 miles to South Berwick. At the intersection with Route 4, turn right. The house is in the center of town where Routes 236 and 4 divide.

The house museum is open June 1 to October 15. It is not handicap accessible.

Hours: Wednesday-Sunday, 11:00 A.M. to 5:00 P.M. Tours are at 11:00 A.M., 12:00, 1:00, 2:00, 3:00 and 4:00 P.M.

Admission and Membership

$5 for adults, $4.50 senior citizens, ½ off for students and children 6-12. Children 5 and under, SPNEA members, and residents of South Berwick are free. AAA members receive a 2 for 1 discount. SPNEA membership is $35/year for individuals and $45/year for a household. Membership includes free admissions to 35 properties and museums across New England.

What to See

In decorating the house for their own use, Jewett and her sister expressed both a pride in their family's past and their own tastes. The result is an eclectic blend of eighteenth-century architecture, antiques, and old wallpapers with furnishings showing the influence of the Arts and Crafts movement. Jewett was also instrumental in preserving the Hamilton House (also owned by SPNEA), which she used as the setting for her historical romance, *The Tory Lover.*

The Jewett House offers group tours and public programs throughout the season. Please call or write for details.

The house does have a gift shop. Visitors can eat in nearby restaurants in Downtown South Berwick, most of which are within easy walking distance.

While You're in the Area

Attractions and museums nearby include Hamilton House (p. 133), the Sayward Wheeler House (p. 189), and the Old Berwick Historical Society (p. 120).

Sayward-Wheeler House (SPNEA)

79 Barrel Lane Extension
York Harbor, ME 03911
207-384-2454
www.spnea.org

Overview

Overlooking a once-thriving waterfront, the Sayward-Wheeler House was the home of Jonathan Sayward, a local merchant and civic leader, who remodeled and furnished the house in the 1760s according to his own conservative taste. Sayward participated in the attack on the French fortress at Louisbourg, Nova Scotia, in 1745, served in the Massachusetts legislature, and despite outspoken loyalist views, retained the respect of his neighbors during the Revolution.

Directions and Hours

From I-95: Take Maine exit 4, "The Yorks." Bear right onto Route 1 south then left onto Route 1A. Follow Route 1A for 1½ miles through York Village then turn right on Route 103 (Lilac Lane) and then left on Barrell Lane. Take the next right onto Barrell Lane Extension.

The house museum is open June 1 to October 15.

Hours: Saturday and Sunday, 11:00 A.M. to 5:00 P.M. Tours are at 11:00 A.M., 12:00, 1:00, 2:00, 3:00 and 4:00 P.M.

Admission and Membership

$5 for adults, $4.50 senior citizens, ½ off for students and children 6-12. Children 5 and under, SPNEA members, and residents of York Harbor are free. AAA members receive a 2 for 1 discount. SPNEA membership is $35/year for individuals and $45/year for a household. Membership includes free admissions to 35 properties and museums across New England.

What to See

After Sayward's death, his heirs made few changes to the house. In part, this was due to the depressed economy following Jefferson's trade embargo of 1807, but the family's reverence for its founding patriarch was an equally important factor in preservation. As early as the 1860s, Sayward's descendants opened the house to visitors to show how their forebears had lived in bygone colonial days. In the early twentieth century, the house was refurbished for use as a summer residence, with fresh wallpapers and white-painted woodwork, but the original furnishings and family portraits remained in place. Today, the house mirrors the fortunes of a coastal village in the transition from trade to tourism.

The Sayward Wheeler House offers tours and programs throughout the season. Please call or write for details.

While You're in the Area

Nearby attractions and museums include the Hamilton House (p. 133), the Sarah Orne Jewett House in South Berwick (p. 188), Castle Tucker (p. 118) and the Nickels-Sortwell House (p. 162) in Wiscassett, and the Old Berwick Historical Society (p. 120).

Scarborough Historical Society and Museum

PO Box 156
Scarborough, ME 04070-0156
(207) 883-3539; (207) 883-2371

Overview

The Scarborough Historical Society and Museum, an all-volunteer museum, has a diverse collection ranging from fishing and farming tools, to household and military items, to photographs, books, and genealogy. All artifacts relate to some period of Scarborough's history (dating from the 1600s). The museum occupies a former trolley generator house next to a new addition.

Directions and Hours

From the Maine Turnpike, take exit 6. Turn right on Payne Road. Turn right onto Route 1 South and follow ¼ mile to the next intersection. The museum is on the right next to Engine 6 Fire Station and across from Dunstan Ace Hardware.

The museum is open year round and it is handicap accessible.

Hours: Tuesday 9:00-12:00 or by appointment.

Admission and Membership

Admission is free; donations are accepted.

What to See

The museum features Roger Deering murals, painted in the 1930s and formerly displayed at the Atlantic House Hotel. The murals depict Scarborough's early history and are on permanent display. The museum also has a genealogy and history library with a large computer database index of family names. A trunk that serves as a time capsule of the King family, ancestors of William and Rufus King, is on semi-permanent display. Bog shoes are also special regional artifacts.

The museum hosts monthly evening programs from September to May on some aspect of history. The meetings are held on the first Wednesday of the month at 7:30 pm. Children's programming is available for Scarborough public schools only.

There is no gift shop, but the museum sells a few incidental items. Visitors can eat at local restaurants, including one seasonal establishment ¼ mile away, several seasonal take-outs three miles away, and fast-food restaurants six miles away.

While You're in the Area

The Winslow Homer Studio (p. 211) and the Hunnewell House (p. 208) are local attractions open by appointment only. The Audubon Marsh Nature Center and other nature preserves are also in the area.

Seashore Trolley Museum

195 Log Cabin Road
Kennebunkport, ME 04046
(207) 967-2800
www.trolleymuseum.org

Overview

The Seashore Trolley Museum is the world's oldest and largest museum of its type. It collects, preserves, restores, and interprets artifacts of the mass transit industry. The museum was founded in 1939 and displays more then 250 vehicles.

Directions and Hours

Take 95 north to exit 3. Turn left onto Route 35, then turn left onto Route 1. Turn right at the traffic light onto Log Cabin Road.

Or, take 95 south to exit 4. Cross Route 111 and turn right onto Route 1. Turn left at the traffic light onto Log Cabin Road.

The museum is open from Memorial Day to Columbus Day, and is handicap accessible.

Hours: daily 10:00-5:00.

Admission and Membership

$7.25 for adults, $5.25 for seniors, $4.75 for children 6-16, free for children under 6. Memberships are $25/year for individuals.

There are discounts for AAA members, MBTA employees, and groups of twelve or more.

What to See

The Seashore Trolley Museum houses "The National Collection of American Streetcars." There is an exhibit of photographs of local trolleys and landmarks of the early twentieth central. A timeline traces streetcar development from an 1880 horse car to a 1940 PCC.

Special cars in operation or display are #31 (Biddeford), "City of Manchester" (NH), "Golden Chariot" (Montreal), Streetcar named "Desire" (New Orleans), "Liberty Bell Limited" (Philadelphia, "Red Rattler" (Chicago), "breezer" (New Haven), and more.

The Town House (restoration) Shop allows visitors to see work in progress.

There is a museum gift shop. There is no café, but there are sandwich shops in the area.

While You're in the Area

The Kennebunkport Historical Society (p. 141), the Nott House (p. 141), the Brick Store Museum (p. 114), Rachael Carlson Preserve, Laudholm Farm Estuarine Preserve, and the Wells Auto Museum (p. 211) are also in the area.

Shaker Museum

707 Shaker Road
New Gloucester, ME 04260
(207) 926-4597
www.shaker.lib.me.us

Overview

The Shaker Museum is located in an active community of Shakers that has been a center of work and worship since 1783. The museum complements this history with tours, exhibits, and special programs.

Directions and Hours

From Boston/Portland, take the Maine Turnpike to exit 11 and follow Route 26 to the museum. Or, from Augusta/Bangor, take the Maine Turnpike to exit 12 and follw Route 26 west to the museum.

The museum is open from Memorial Day to Columbus Day, but is not handicap accessible.

Hours: Monday-Saturday 10:00-4:30.

Admission and Membership

$6 for adults, $2 for children, children under six are free. Membership is $15/year for individuals.

Group discounts are available with reservations.

What to See

The museum displays special collections of Shaker furniture, artifacts, farm implements, and other aspects of Shaker material culture.

Programs include crafts workshops and

demonstrations, concerts, Apple Saturdays, Christmas Fair, and lectures. The museum also offers adult education course on the Shaker way of life and an exhibit on Shaker architecture.

There are two gift shops. There is no café, but there are restaurants and sandwich shops within a ten minute drive.

While You're in the Area

The State of Maine Building, Outlet Beach, Range Pond State Park, McLaughlin Gardens, Olin Arts Center (p. 110), and Poland Spring Bottling are also nearby.

Shore Village Museum

104 Limerock Street
Rockland, ME 04841
(207) 594-0311
www.lighthouse.ccshorevillage

Overview

Also known as "Maine's Lighthouse Museum," the Shore Village Museum displays the largest collection of lighthouse lenses and artifacts in the Unites States. There are also Civil War artifacts and a library.

Directions and Hours

Take Route 1 east to Route 1A in Rockland. At the next traffic light, take a right onto Limerock Street.

Or, take Route 1 west and continue to Union Street. At the first traffic light, turn right onto Limerock Street.

The museum is open from June to October 15, and by appointment. Only the main floor is handicap accessible.

Hours: daily 10:00-4:00.

Admission and Membership

Admission to the museum is free. Membership is not available.

What to See

Lighthouse lenses are extremely beautiful, and are known as the gems or jewels of the lighthouses. In addition to the collection of lighthouse lenses and artifacts, the museum offers guided tours for school children and bus tours.

There is a large gift shop specializing in lighthouse things. There is no café, but there are many restaurants in the area.

While You're in the Area

The Farnsworth Art Museum (p. 125) and the Owl's Head Transportation Museum (p. 170) are also nearby.

Sieur de Monts Springs Nature Center

Acadia National Park
PO Box 177
Bar Harbor, ME 04609
(207) 288-3003
www.nps.gov/acad

Overview

This nature center was established to interpret the natural history of Acadia National Park.

Directions and Hours

Located on Mount Desert Island on Park Loop Road.

The museum is open from May until September and is handicap accessible.

Hours: daily, 9:00-5:00.

Admission and Membership

Admission to the nature center is included with the entrance fee to the park.

What to See

Exhibits illustrate the natural history of Acadia National Park. Current scientific studies being conducted are also explained.

Children's educational programs are offered for school groups, as well as interpretive programs for families.

The nature center has a bookstore, but no café.

While You're in the Area

Be sure to explore Acadia National Park, Park Loop Road, the Abbe Museum (p. 105), George B. Dorr Museum of Natural History (p. 158), Wendell Gilley Museum of Birdcarving (p. 201), Mount Desert Island Historical Society (p. 156), Bar Harbor Historical Society (p. 110), and the Tremont Historical Society (p. 211).

Snowman School Museum

Woodland Historical Society
423 Woodland Center Road
Woodland, ME 04736

Overview

The Snowman School Museum is a one room schoolhouse, the only original one room schoolhouse remaining in the community of Woodland.

Directions and Hours

From Caribou take Woodland Center Road. The museum is approximately four miles on the right, across from Thibodeau Road.

The museum is open from Memorial Day weekend to the end of June.

Hours: Sunday 1:00-4:00; and by appointment.

Admission and Membership

Admission to the museum is free. Membership is $2/year for active membership, $5 for contributing membership, and $50 for a lifetime membership.

What to See

The museum contains the school history and photographs, and town history and photographs. It has the original slate blackboards and outhouses, including a period stove in the center of the room.

There is a very small gift shop. There is no café, but there are restaurants in nearby Caribou.

While You're in the Area

The Lagerstrom House Museum (p. 143) is also run by the Woodland Historical Society.

Sound School House Museum

373 Sound Drive
PO Box 653
Mount Desert, ME 04660
(207) 276-9323
www.ellsworthme.org/mdihsociety

Overview

The Sound School House Museum was built in 1892 for the children of the quarrying and farming village of Sound. The building was only used as a school for 34 years, closing in 1926. For most of its life it has been a community center. In 1999 the Mount Desert Island Historical Society restored the building. During the summer rotating exhibits focus on a variety of island history themes.

Directions and Hours

From I-95: Take Route 395 to Route 1A to Route 3. Take Route 3 to Mount Desert Island. After crossing the bridge bear right and go four miles to the traffic light in Somesville. At the light turn left and go 2.2 miles to the School House, which will be on the left.

The museum is open year-round (in winter only by appointment). It is handicap accessible.

Hours: Summer: 10:00 A.M. to 5:00 P.M. Tuesday-Saturday. Winter by appointment.

Admission and Membership

$1 per person. The museum is free to children and members. Special groups and bus tours are welcome and may arrange for guided tours of the museum or the historic district by contacting the museum director. Membership is $10/year for an individual and $25/year for a family. Other membership options are available; please contact the museum for details.

What to See

The School House Museum houses a research library featuring a large collection of historic preservation books. Visitors can see the old blackboards, ring the bell, and sit on the original benches.

Summer, 2001 will feature an exhibit on the history of the Granite Industry on Mount Desert Island.

Local school children attend living history programs in the winter.

The museum does not have a gift shop. Two take out eateries are nearby, and Mother's Kitchen and The Brown Bag are on Route 102.

While You're in the Area

The Mount Desert Island Historical Society Somesville Museum (p. 156) is nearby, and the Great Harbor Maritime Museum (p. 132) is a five minute drive.

South Portland and Cape Elizabeth Historical Society

Braeburn Avenue
South Portland, ME 04106
(207) 799-1977

Overview

The South Portland and Cape Elizabeth Historical Society is a local history museum covering the communities of South Portland and Cape Elizabeth.

Directions and Hours

After exiting the Maine Turnpike at exit 7 turn left on Route 1 (Main Street) and then turn left at the next traffic light onto Westbrook Street. Take the next street on the right (Braeburn Avenue). The museum is the second brick building on the right (a former school annex).

Open May through October. Closed in winter, November to May.

Hours: 1:00-4:00 P.M. first and third Saturday of each month May through October.

Admission and Membership

There is no admission cost. Membership is $5/year.

What to See

The South Portland and Cape Elizabeth Historical Society, a museum pertaining only to local history, displays hundreds of photos of old South Portland and Cape Elizabeth, as well as newspaper clippings dating back to 1900, antique historical documents such as old deeds, tax bills, graduation programs, diplomas, school yearbooks, city and town reports, books on the history of South Portland and Cape Elizabeth, and other memorabilia.

The museum does not have a café or a gift shop. There are several restaurants nearby on Main Street and Route 1 as well as a Dunkin Donuts right at the corner of the street.

While You're in the Area

Also in South Portland is the Portland Harbor Museum (p. 175).

Stanley Museum

40 School Street
Kingfield, ME
(207) 265-2729
www.stanleymuseum.org

Overview

The Stanley Museum showcases the Yankee ingenuity of the Stanley twins, innovators in transportation, industry, and the arts. The museum's collection includes steam cars and photographs from the early nineteenth century.

Directions and Hours

Northbound, take the Maine Turnpike to exit

12, then Route 4 to Route 27 to Kingfield. Or, take 95 to Belgrade exit to Route 27.

Or, take Route 2 to Farmington, north on Route 27.

The museum is open year round, but is not handicap accessible.

Hours: May 1-October 31, Tuesday-Sunday 10:00-4:00; November 1-April 30, Monday-Friday 8:00-5:00.

Admission and Membership

$2 for adults, $1 for children and seniors. Membership is $25/year for individuals, $40/year for families.

School groups may attend for 50 cents/person. Members attend the museum for free.

What to See

The Stanley Museum is located in a school building built in 1903 and designed by the Stanleys. It currently exhibits steam cars from 1905, 1909, 1910, 1916, and 1924.

An exhibit shows a photography timeline of the Stanleys' innovations, including their patented dry plate photographing process. One of the twins invented the airbrush and used this process to paint portraits. The museum has several of these on display.

There is a gift shop. The museum does not have a café, but there are restaurants in town.

While You're in the Area

While in the area, people can also visit the Wire Bridge in New Portland, which is the oldest suspension bridge in Maine. Sugarloaf Mountain and Rangely Lakes Regions are also nearby.

Stockholm Historical Society Museum

280 Main Street
Stockholm, ME 04783
(208) 896-3177
www.aroostook.me.us

Overview

Stockholm Historical Society Museum is part of "The Swedish Colony," a group of related historical institutions in the towns of Stockholm, New Sweden, Woodland, and Westmanland in northern Maine. The Stockholm Museum contains artifacts used in the area for the past 120 years as well as items brought to America by immigrants. The museum encourages celebration of the town's heritage and wants to keep the culture and heritage of the area alive for future generations. The museum building was the first store in Stockholm and now houses photographs of the boom and bust times, Stockholm's unique history, family histories, house histories, genealogy records, and other artifacts.

Directions and Hours

Watch for the blue and yellow "Gateway" signs.

From the south: Take Route 1 to Caribou. Exit to Sweden Street, Route 161. Take Route 161 north approximately 13 miles. Turn right after Lil's Grocery. Go down the hill to the center of Stockholm. From Van Buren go south on Route 1 to the Stockholm turnoff, which is approximately 10 miles. Turn right and proceed down Schooland Road to the heart of town.

The museum is open from July 4-Labor Day and is handicap accessible.

Hours: Wednesday-Sunday 1:30-4:30 P.M. or by appointment.

Admission and Membership

Admission is free but donations are accepted. The museum is open to all, but children under 12 must be accompanied by an adult. The Stockholm Historical Society meets on the last Monday of each month April-November. Membership is Active $2, Contributing $5, Life $100, Student $2, and Business $25.

What to See

The museum houses trunks that the first Swedes used to transport their household goods to American, as well as other early Swedish memo-

Stockholm Historical Society Museum. Photo courtesy of John Hede.

rabilia. The museum includes a Veterans Room, featuring pictures and service histories of Stockholm's military from WWI to now; a living room, kitchen, and bedroom circa 1920-30; handmade skis, snowshoes, and ice-skates; farming and forestry exhibits; and changing displays throughout the summer months.

The museum will be hosting a special "Scandinavian Root—American Lives" exhibit at the museum from July 1 to July 21, 2001. A web page about this exhibit can be accessed at www.migrationinstitute.fi.nordic.

Visitors can eat at Eureka Hall in Stockholm (call 207-896-3196 for reservations).

While You're in the Area

In winter months visitors can snowmobile or ski on several trails, and in the summer people can bike, walk, kayak, canoe, swim, and fish.

Sullivan-Sorrento Historical Society

PO Box 44
Sullivan, ME 04664
(207) 422-6816
www.downeast.net

Overview

The museum collects and displays artifacts of local history, industry, and life.

Directions and Hours

The museum is on Route 1, across the street from the fire station in the Sullivan-Sorrento Recreation/Library Building.

The society is open each Tuesday year round from 1:00 to 3:00 P.M., and is handicap accessible.

Admission and Membership

Admission is free. Membership dues range from $5 for individual membership to $100 for life membership.

What to See

The collection includes material on the granite and silver mining industry, shipbuilding, fishing, Customs Port of entry, Summer Colony, local sports, Lodges, and Grange. Over 15,000 items are exhibited.

There is no gift shop or café, but visitors may eat at the local inns and restaurants.

While You're in the Area

Visitors can also see the Ellsworth Historical Society Museum at the Old County Jail, Ellsworth (p. 208); The Abbe Museum, Bar Harbor (p. 105) as well as the Bar Harbor Historical Society (p. 110); the MDI Historical Society Museum, Somesville (p. 156); the Hancock Historical Society, Hancock (p. 208); and the Milbridge Historical Society in Milbridge (p. 154), east of Sullivan.

Swan's Island Lobster and Marine Museum

4 Quarry Road
Swan's Island, ME 04685
(207) 526-4423

Overview

The Swan's Island Lobster and Marine Museum is dedicated to the commercial fisheries of Maine. This is a recently formed museum, so call to ask about new and expanded programs.

Directions and Hours

Swan's Island is reached by ferry from Bass Harbor (Mount Desert Island).

The museum is open from June 1 to September 30, but is not handicap accessible.

Hours: Thursday, Sunday 11:00-4:00.

Admission and Membership

Admission to the museum is free.

What to See

The museum has a large collection of boat types, equipment, and photographs displaying a way of life in Maine's past and present. There is also a 45-minute boat ride across Penobscot Bay.

Marine biology exhibits are also on display.

There is no gift shop or café, but there are restaurants within walking distance.

While You're in the Area

Mount Desert Island and Acadia National Park are also in the area.

Tante Blanche Museum Complex

393 Main Street, Library Building
Madawaska, ME 04756

Overview

The Tante Blanche Museum Complex is a log cabin that holds local artifacts of French Heritage Culture. French and English are spoken.

Directions and Hours

The museum is two miles from Madawaska on on US #1.

The museum is open June 10-September 10 or by appointment.

Maine Archives and Museums (MAM)

60 Community Drive
Augusta, ME 04330
(207) 623-8428
www.mainemuseums.org

The purpose of Maine Archives and Museums is to develop and foster a network of individuals and institutions who collect, interpret, and/or provide access to materials relating to history and culture. The state is divided into regions to facilitate communication at local and regional levels. Regional Representatives sit on the MAM Council to advocate for their regions.

Maine Archives and Museums offers spring workshops on topics of interest to museum and historical society staff and other interested persons. MAM also sponsors Maine Heritage Day, a statewide event designed to showcase the great work Maine's cultural institutions engage in to preserve the state's rich heritage. This year Maine Heritage Day will take place on Saturday, September 15, 2001. MAM publishes a quarterly newsletter. An annual fall conference is also held, and topics can include collection care, membership and development, disaster planning, exhibit design and building on a budget, educational programming, local history writing and research, registration methods, legislation that affects museums, recruiting and retaining volunteers, board development, grant writing, preservation planning, museum shop management, accessibility issues, and care for archives and artifact collections. Regional workshops are also available with the topics listed above. Membership ranges from $20 to $250.

Hours: 10:30-3:30—closed for lunch.

Admission and Membership

Donations only. Membership is $10/year or $50 for a lifetime membership.

What to See

On display are an Acadian historic cross, local artifacts, a monument, and different trees planted by reunion families, wooden statues carved with a chainsaw, and a single room schoolhouse.

On June 28, 2001 a reenactment of the Acadian landing will take place on St. John River. This is in conjunction with the Acadian Festival, which runs from June 28-July 1.

There is a gift shop. There are places to eat in town, about two miles away.

While You're in the Area

The Musée et centre cultural du Mont-Carmel (p. 156) is about seven miles away.

Thomaston Historical Society Museum

80 Knox Street
Thomaston, ME 04861
(207) 354-2295
www.mint.net/thomastonhistoricalsociety

Overview

The Thomaston Historical Society Museum is housed in the last remaining original building of General Henry Knox. It contains paintings, photographs, documents, and artifacts from the mid-seventeenth century.

Directions and Hours

Take 95 north to exit 22, then take Route 1 north. Take a right turn onto Knox Street.

The museum is open from June through August, and is handicap accessible.

Hours: Tuesday-Thursday 2:00-4:00. The museum is also open the first Thursday night of each month from April-November at 7:30.

Admission and Membership

Admission to the museum is free. Membership is $10/year for individuals, $18/year for families, $50/year for corporate membership, and $100 for a lifetime membership.

What to See

The museum contains records of the town of Thomaston from the time of the first landing of Captain George Weymouth in 1605 to the present. It has several collections of letters from the Cilley family, as well as documents from the estate of Senator John Ruggles. There are also artifacts of area archeological digs and histories of men from the area who fought in the Civil War.

Special programs include Maine's Historic Boat-Building, the Overlock Homes of Thomaston, and the Annual Reading of Jonathan Cilley Family Letters. The historical society also has special programs for school classes.

There is a gift shop. The museum has no café, but there is a café and bakery down the street.

While You're in the Area

Montpelier-General Henry Knox Museum (p. 154), Owl's Head Transportation Museum (p. 170), and the Farnsworth Art Museum and Library (p. 125) are nearby.

Thompson Ice Harvesting Museum

Route 129
South Bristol, ME 04568
(207) 644-8551

Overview

Naturally frozen ice has been harvested at this site since 1826 when Asa Thompson dammed a small brook flowing from natural springs on his property to create Thompson Pond, thus providing a source of ice for his farm. Five generations of Thompsons ran a commercial ice business from the site of the present ice house until 1985.

During its commercial life Thompson Pond ice was regularly delivered to the surrounding community, used for making ice cream, and sold to yachtsmen and local fishing vessels. Since 1990 the ice house has been a working museum. The Thompson Ice Harvesting Museum cuts ice, usually in mid-February, and stores it in an old fashioned ice box. The ice is also used to make ice cream for an ice cream social in July.

Directions and Hours

From U.S. Route 1 (Newcastle from the South or Damariscotta from the north) take State Route 129 for about 12 miles. The museum is on the left side of the road.

The museum is open from July 4 to Labor Day and is not handicap accessible.

Hours: Wednesday, Friday, and Saturday from 1:00 to 4:00 P.M.

Admission and Membership

Admission is by donation. Suggested contributions are $1 for adults and $.50 for children. Special discounts must be arranged ahead of time. The ice house site and the Amthor Stone Shelter Outdoor Museum display board are open to visitors at all daylight hours at no charge.

What to See

The Thompson Ice Harvesting Museum includes the ice tool collection of Herbert and Gwen Thompson with an explanation of how each tool is used. Summer visitors may view the stored ice cakes, as long as they last, through a double glass window between the Ice Harvesting Museum and the main room. The south shed is a viewing area for dynamic visual displays.

The museum has a collection of ice cutting tools and shows a video of the ice cutting done in February for the summer visitors.

An Ice Cream Social is held the Sunday nearest July 4. Both homemade and commercial ice cream is available. There is usually live music along with sundaes and root beer floats. The ice pond has fish, turtles and frogs—the kids are usually more interested in these than ice.

School groups are given tours by special arrangement.

The museum has a few items for sale: T-shirts, sweatshirts, photos, notepaper, etc. There is a small restaurant in town a mile or so beyond the museum.

While You're in the Area

Other interesting places to visit while you are in the area are the Old Walpole Meeting House (p. 168) and the Harrington House (p. 129).

Vance-Dorothy Hammond Historical Society

Upper Main Street
Strong, ME 04983
(207) 684-2975

Overview

This house museum has a kitchen, dining room, and living room filled with historical furniture and memoribilia, as well as a room of objects once owned by the Hammond Family. The museum also contains objects pertaining to the history of Strong, Maine.

Directions and Hours

Take Route 4 north out of Farmington to Route 145 in Kingfield. The historical society is located on Main Street across from the Nazarene church.

The public is welcome to the Historical Society's regular meetings that are held every month except December on the first Wednesday night at 5:15 P.M., with potluck supper at 6:00 P.M. Otherwise, the house is open by appointment. Call President Wendell Voter at (207) 684-5612 or Program Guide Charlene White at (207) 684-4137.

Admission and Membership

$3 for couples, $2 for single. Open to all ages; young people are especially encouraged to visit.

Reception Room, Victoria Mansion (Morse-Libby House), Portland, Maine. Photo courtesy of J. David Bohl.

What to See

Each room of the museum is furnished with donated and loaned period pieces. Visitors can learn about the Hammond family as well as the history of Strong, Maine. Outside of the house is a barn with an attic set up like a classroom with desks and books.

The Society has a variety of special programs each year with an eye toward educating children. In the past, they have hosted a demonstration on the "Lost Arts" which included tanning cow hides and making soap. Call or write for information about future events.

There is no café although two restaurants, Adams Rib and Lunchbox, are located nearby.

While You're in the Area

At one time, Strong, Maine, was the toothpick capital of the world, and people can still visit Fosters Mill where they were made.

Victoria Mansion (Morse-Libby House)

109 Danforth Street
Portland, ME 04101
(207) 772-4841
www.victoriamansion.org

Overview

The Victoria Mansion, also known as the Morse-Libby House (1858-1860), is one of New England's finest historic house museums of the Victorian Era. Visitors can have a guided tour of the house and view its Italianate architecture and Gustave Herter furnishings.

Directions and Hours

Victoria Mansion is located at 109 Danforth Street in Portland's Arts District, minutes from the Old Port.

From Interstate 295 north or south: Take exit 6A. Bear right and drive through Deering Oaks Park. At the light proceed straight up the hill on State Street. Turn left at the fourth light onto Danforth Street. Victoria Mansion is located on the left at Park Street.

Victoria Mansion is open for public tours May through October, Monday-Saturday 10:00 A.M. to 4:00 P.M. and Sunday 1:00 P.M. to 5:00 P.M. Special Christmas tours are available in December. The house is not handicap accessible.

Admission and Membership

Summer: $7 adults, $3 ages 6-17, free for kids under age 6. Christmas: $8 adults, $5 ages 6-17, free for kids under age 6. Group tours of 10 or more, seniors, AAA members, and AAM/NEMA members are given special discounts. Membership is $30-$50/year for an individual, $60-$100/year for a family, $125-$225/year for supporting, $250-$475/year for a donor, $500-$750/year for a patron, and $1,000 and up for a morse associate.

What to See

Victoria Mansion has the first and only surviving commission by interior designer Gustave Herter.

Ninety percent of the original contents have survived, including furniture, gas lighting fixtures, wall paintings, artwork, carpets, stained glass, and porcelain. In Spring 2001 a stained glass skylight, missing from the three-story stairhall since 1938, will be reinstalled.

The Victoria Mansion offers lectures and educational program as well as special school tours.

There is a gift shop called The Carriage House. There is no café on site but the Portland CVB guide is free in the shop and has a full listing of places to eat.

While You're in the Area

Other places to visit while you are in the area include the Portland Museum of Art (p. 176), the Wadsworth-Longfellow House and the Center for Maine History (p. 207), the Tate House (p. 210), and the Greater Portland Landmarks and Center for Cultural Exchange.

Wendell Gilley Museum of Bird Carving

PO Box 254
4 Herrick Road
Southwest Harbor, ME 04679
(207) 244-7555
www.acadia.net/gilley

Overview

The Gilley Museum connects art with nature with its collection of woodcarvings, from miniature shorebirds to life-size birds of prey. Visitors can step inside the Gilley workshop to try carving or watch demonstrations. Changing wildlife art exhibits complement the bird carvings, along with nature videos. Lectures on environmental topics are offered year-round in association with local conservation organizations.

Directions and Hours

The museum is located at the corner of Route 102 and Herrick Road.

The museum is open from June through October: Tuesday-Sunday 10:00 A.M. to 4:00 P.M. (close at 5:00 P.M. during July and August), closed on Monday and July 4; May, November, and December (until Christmas): open Friday-Sunday 10:00 A.M. to 4:00 P.M., closed Monday-Thursday; January-April: the workshop is open to museum members every Friday 1:00-4:00 P.M. Groups are welcome by appointment. The museum is handicap accessible.

Admission and Membership

$3.25 for adults, $1 for children 5-12. Museum members and children under 5 are admitted free. Special rates are available for prepaid, reserved groups of 25 or more. Membership is $35/year for individuals and $50/year for a family.

What to See

A Carver-in-Residence gives demonstrations and leads workshops, ranging from one day to 10 weeks in duration. There is an introductory video about Wendall Gilley, Maine's pioneer in the field of decorative bird carving. Natural history and art programs are available along with touring art exhibits of local and international interest.

Children's programming is available—please call ahead for a current schedule.

The museum does have a gift shop. There are many local restaurants where visitors can eat, but they vary by season.

While You're in the Area

Attractions in the area include the Abbe Museum (p. 105), the Mount Desert Island Historical Society, (p. 156), the Islesford Historical Museum (p. 138), Sieur de Monts Springs Nature Center (p. 192), the Bar Harbor Historical Society (p. 110), and the Great Harbor Maritime Museum (p. 132).

William Otis Sawtelle Collections and Research Center

c/o Acadia National Park
PO Box 177
Bar Harbor, ME 04609
(207) 288-5463
www.nps.gov/acad

Overview

The Sawtelle Collections and Research Center was established in 1999 to house the Acadia National Park artifact collection that contains over a million pieces. It provides access to the public to conduct research on the items in the collection.

Directions and Hours

The center is located on Route 233 (Eagle Lake Road) on Mount Desert Island.

The center is open year round, and is handicap accessible.

Hours: Tuesday-Friday 8:30-3:30, and by appointment.

Admission and Membership

Admission to the center is free.

What to See

The collection includes natural and cultural historical artifacts as well as genealogical information. These artifacts pertain to Acadia National Park, Saintcroix Island International Historic Site, Cranberry Isles, Mount Desert Island, Maine, New France, and the Carroll Family of Southwest Harbor.

There is no gift shop or café, but there are places to eat within driving distance.

While You're in the Area

There are many other museums in and around Acadia National Park, including the Abbe Museum (p. 105), Isleford History Museum (p. 138) and Island History Room (p. 137).

Willowbrook at Newfield

PO Box 28
Newfield, ME 04056
(207) 743-2784
www.willowbrookmuseum.org

Overview

Willowbrook is the largest nineteenth century museum village in New England. There are 37 buildings housing artifacts and exhibits restored to their date of manufacture—everything from a grand ballroom and costume room to small shops and restored homesteads.

Directions and Hours

Take the Maine Turnpike to exit 3 into Newfield. Willowbrook is located just off Route 11 in Newfield.

The museum is open May 15-September 30, and is partially handicap accessible.

Hours: daily 10:00-5:00.

Admission and Membership

$8 for adults, $4 for students and children 6-18. Children under six are admitted for free.

Discount rates for groups are available.

What to See

Willowbrook has over 60 horse drawn carriages and sleighs, including an 1849 Concord coach. There is also an 1894 carousel, the last one in Maine.

Guided tours are available.

There is a gift shop, and there is also a café.

While You're in the Area

The nearest attractions are the Maine Narrow Gauge Railroad Company & Museum (p. 148) and the Museum of African Tribal Art (p. 157).

Wilton Historical Society Farm and Home Museum

10 Canal Street
Wilton, ME 04294

Overview

The Wilton Historical Society's museum, located in the "Bass Boarding House," contains a collection of memorabilia from farms and businesses of the past. Wilton is on the Coos Trail, the original path from Hallowell which opened up Western Maine to settlement.

Directions and Hours

Take Route 4 north from Jay to Wilton village, or Route 2 east from Rumford.

The museum is open in July and August, Saturdays from 1:00-4:00 P.M. It is handicap accessible.

Admission and Membership

Admission is free but donations are requested.

What to See

There is an exhibit on Sylvia Hardy, Maine Giantess, who grew to nearly eight feet tall, became a circus performer, and then retired back to Wilton where she became a spiritualist; a working iron forge in the cellar with which iron shaping classes are conducted; a G. H. Bass and Company display; an old farm tools room; Wilton Academy memorabilia; and Joe Knowles paintings.

An open house is held during the Blueberry Festival each August. Wilton will be celebrating its bicentennial in 2003.

Children's programming includes school tours.

There is no gift shop, but mugs and stationery are for sale at the museum. Visitors can eat at two nearby restaurants, Mario's and The Boiler Room.

While You're in the Area

The Titcomb House (p. 211) in Farmington is open during the summer, as is the museum in Jay.

Winterport Historical Association

183 Main Street
Winterport, ME 04496
(207) 223-5556

Overview

The Winterport Historical Association Museum is located in the center of the village and was constructed by the Congregational Church in 1864. The collection includes tools used by local artisans, journals, and books. There are also records and photos of well-known families, and town records from 1885. The museum is in a beautifully restored area; building details include a four-faced steeple clock installed in 1861 and a restored 1859 Mason & Hamlin organ.

Directions and Hours

The museum is located on Route 1A.

The museum is open from July through September, but is not handicap accessible.

Hours: Tuesday 2:00-4:00, and by appointment.

Admission and Membership

Admission to the museum is free. Membership is $5/year for individuals.

What to See

The museum houses American Civil War documents and correspondence of Medal of Honor winner Captain Albert Fernald, and copies of other Civil War documents relating to local figures and history. There are also Winterport High School yearbooks, school photos, and programs, Town of Winterport Annual Reports, and personal journals of prominent local figures. A bicentennial quilt made by local residents is also on display, as are photographs depicting town life in the 1800s and a collection of postcards. There is also an architectural inventory of the Winterport Historic District.

There is no gift shop or café, but there are restaurants nearby.

While You're in the Area

There are walking tours of Winterport, "An Old River Town," including the Union Meeting House, Colonial Winterport Inn, Theophilus Cushing House, Abbott House, Philo Washburn House, the Benjamin Thompson House, and others.

Wiscasset, Waterville & Farmington Railway Museum

Sheepscot Station
Alna, ME 04535
(207) 882-4193
http://www.wwfry.org

Overview

The WW&F Railway Museum is dedicated to the preservation and restoration of the WW&F Railway, a two-foot gauge railroad that operated between the towns of Wiscasset and Albion Maine from the years 1895-1933. The Museum has restored some railroad cars and is in the process of restoring the oldest two-foot gauge steam engine in Maine. It has built nearly a mile of track and is building more every year. The museum's role is to educate the visiting public about the impact of the Maine Two-Footers on their community, and to provide a good time to all visitors.

Photo courtesy of James C. Patten/WW&F Railway Museum.

Directions and Hours

From Route 1/Wiscasset (from the west and south), take Route 218 north for 4.5 miles, then turn left at Cross Road. Look for the directional signs on Route 218.

From Route 1/Newcastle (from the east), take Sheepscot Road. Follow the directional signs.

From the north, follow Route 218 south from Route 17 in Cooper's Mills.

The museum is open 9:00-5:00 every Saturday of the year, and 9:00-5:00 on Sundays between Memorial Day and Columbus Day. It is handicap accessible

Admission and Membership

There is no cost for admission to museum, but there is a cost for the train rides. Membership is $20 for an annual membership, $200 for a life membership. Senior citizens and members of the museum receive a $0.50 discount on train rides.

What to See

Locomotive #9: built in 1891, the locomotive worked on the Sandy River Railroad for many years before making its way to the WW&F. This locomotive is now in the beginning stages of restoration to operation.

Locomotive #10: the museum's in-service steam locomotive was built in 1904 for a Louisiana sugar plantation. This engine was purchased in 1999.

Coach #3: the last remaining coach car from the railroad, built in 1894 by the Jackson & Sharp company.

Flatcar #118: the last remaining flatcar from the WW&F, it helped to dismantle the railroad and now is helping to rebuild it.

There are also replicas of one of the railroad's freight sheds (used as a gift shop) and the railroad's station building that was on site.

Current programs include the restoration of Locomotive #9 and the laying of enough track to reach the next station on the line, Alna Center, which is 1.6 miles from Sheepscot Station.

The museum does have a gift shop. There is no café, but there is the Alna Store, about two miles north of the Museum on Rt 218.

While You're in the Area

Boothbay Railway Museum (p. 112), which has a two-foot gauge loop of track, an antique auto collection, and some antique buildings, is located in Boothbay on Route 27.

Maine Narrow Gauge Railroad and Museum (p. 148), located on Front Street in Portland, has on display and in use much of the Maine two-footer collection from Edaville.

Woodlawn Museum/The Black House

19 Black House Drive
PO Box 1478
Ellsworth, ME 04605
(207) 667-8671
www.ellsworthme.org/cbmm

Overview

Visit the Woodlawn Museum and step into the past. Discover the story of the Black Family, one of Maine's most prominent and wealthy families. Built by Colonel John Black in 1824-27, the federal-styled Black House reflects the tastes and interests of three generations of one family in original furnishings and decoration.

Directions and Hours

Take I-95 north to Bangor, then I-395 to 1A to Ellsworth. Turn right onto Route 1/Main Street. Bear left on 172, then turn right onto Black House Drive. Look for road signs.

The museum is open May through October, Tuesday through Saturday, 10:00-5:00, and Sunday 1:00-4:00.

Admission and Membership

$6 adults, $3 children. There is a discount for AAA members. Memberships: student $10, $35 individual, $60 family.

What to See

Gifted to the region by George Nixon Black, Jr. in 1930, the Woodlawn Museum/Black House collection consists of fine examples of American and European decorative and fine arts, including paintings by George Loring Brown. The extensive collection also includes rare books, china, textiles, and other personal belongings. The Carriage and Sleigh Barns contain excellent examples of American and European coaches and sleighs. The museum is situated on a 180-acre estate and features 2 miles of walking trails and formal gardens, which were designed with the help of famed landscape architect Beatrix Farrand.

The museum offers weekly teas and special concerts throughout the summer, family Discovery Days, and a special Christmas event. Children's programming is also offered.

There is a gift shop on the premises, but no café.

While You're in the Area

The museum is close to Bar Harbor and Acadia National Park and the Blue Hill Peninsula. Ellsworth is the Gateway to Down East Maine.

Woodstock Historical Society Museum

Main Street
Bryant Pond, ME 04219
(207) 665-2450

Overview

The Woodstock Museum is a local historical and cultural center as well as a representative New

England town museum.

Directions and Hours

Take Route 26 into Bryant Pond. The museum is on Route 26.

The museum is opened from 1:00-4:00 on Saturdays during the summer, and is handicap accessible.

Admission and Membership

Admission is free, but donations are accepted. Membership costs $2 /year.

What to See

The collection includes local memoribilia, antiques, art, and New England books and antiques.

There is a gift shop, but no café. Visitors can eat at local restaurants within walking distance.

While You're in the Area

The nearby towns of Bethel and Norway also have museums.

Woolwich Historical Society

PO Box 98
Woolwich, ME 04579
(207) 443-4833
www.woolwichhistory.org

Overview

The Woolwich Historical Society maintains a small, intimate nineteenth-century home that helps visitors appreciate the independent, self-sufficient lifestyle of earlier generations.

Directions and Hours

The house is located in the corner of Route 1 and the Nequasset Road, 2.5 miles north of Bath and 7.5 miles south of Wiscasset.

The house is open from July 1-September 1 and by appointment. It is not handicap accessible.

Hours: Tuesday-Saturday 10:30-2:30.

Admission and Membership

Admission is by donation. Memberships are available at $10/year for individuals, $15/year for families, and $300 for honorary life.

What to See

Visitors can view early nineteenth- to early twentieth-century artifacts such as quilts, costumes, farm equipment, tools, and home furnishings. Local history and genealogy information is also available. The historical society, along with other town organizations, participates in Woolwich Day. Children's programming is scheduled for local fourth graders and other school groups as requested.

Local history books, postcard, and maps are available for purchase. There is no café, but the Taste of Maine restaurant is located 2 miles south on Route 1.

While You're in the Area

Nearby attractions and museums include the Maine Maritime Museum (p. 209), Fort Edgecomb (p. 208), the Auburn Fire Dept. Museum (p. 207), the Knight House and Downing Shoe Shop (p. 143), Androscoggin Historical Society (p. 107), the Auburn-Lowiston Sports Hall of Fame, Bowdoin College Museum of Art (p. 113), the Peary MacMillan Arctic Museum (p. 172), and the Hawthorne-Longfellow Library.

Other Museums in Maine

Name	Phone	Town
Abbot Historical Society	207-876-3073	Abbot
Acton-Shapleigh Historical Society	207-636-2606	Shapleigh
Adm. Robert E. Peary Home	207-624-6081	Eagle Island
Alfred Village Museum	207-324-5823	Alfred
Allagash Historical Society	207-398-3335	Allagash
Apple Acres Farm	207-625-4777	South Hiram
Ashland Logging Museum	207-435-6039	Ashland
Arnold Expedition Historical Society	207-582-7080	Pittston
Aroostook County Historical Center	207-764-0311	Presque Isle
Art Association of Sanford-Springvale	207-490-1075	Sanford
Athens Historical Society Museum	207-654-2647	Athens
Atlantic Brewing Company	207-288-9513	Bar Harbor
Auburn Fire Dept. Museum	207-784-5433	Auburn
Bangor Historical Society Museum (Thomas A. Hill House)	207-942-5766	Bangor
Bar Harbor Whale Museum	207-288-2025	Bar Harbor
Barracks Museum (Border Historical Society)	207-853-6630	Eastport
Battery Steele	207-766-2211	Peaks Island
Belfast Museum	207-338-2078	Belfast
Biddeford Historical Society, McArthur Library	207-283-4706	Biddeford.
Blacksmith Shop Museum	207-564-8618	Dover-Foxcroft
Blaine House	207-287-2301	Augusta
Brewer Historical Society's Clewley Museum	207-989-7468	Brewer
Brownfield Historical Society	207-935-4392	Brownfield
Brownville/Brownville Junction Historical Society	207-943-2185	Brownville
Bryant Pond Telephone Museum	207-665-2960	Bryant Pond
Bryant Stove and Music Museum	207-568-3665	Thorndike
Bucksport Historical Society Museum	207-469-2591	Bucksport
Cambridge Historical Society	207-277-3091	Cambridge
Camden-Rockport Historical Society Conway Homestead	207-236-2257	Rockport
Captain Josiah A. Mitchell House	207-865-3289	Freeport
Center for Maine History	207-774-1822	Portland
Chebeague Island Historical Society	207-846-5140	Chebeague Island
Children's Discovery Museum	207-622-2209	Augusta

Children's Museum of Maine	207-828-1234	Portland
Children's Theatre of Maine	207-878-2774	Portland
CHTJ Southard House Museum	207-737-8202	Richmond
Colonial Pemaquid State Historic Site, Fort William Henry	207-287-4975	Pemaqid
Corinna Historical Society	207-278-3542	Corinna
Cumston Hall and Public Library	207-933-4788	Monmouth
Deer Isle-Stonington Historical Society	207-348-2897	Deer Isle
Dinsmore Grain Co. Mill	207-993-2496	Palermo
Dover-Foxcroft Historical Society	207-564-0820	Dover-Foxcroft
Dresden Brick School House Museum	207-737-2839	Dresden
Eastland Gallery	207-775-2227	Portland
Easton Historical Society	207-488-6846	Easton
Eight Maine Regimental Hall	207-766-5086	Peaks Island
Ellsworth Historical Society	207-667-4468	Ellsworth
Embden Historical Society	207-643-2434	Embden
Fay Hyland Arboretum	207-581-2978	Orono
Fayette Historical Society	207-685-4702	Fayette
First Parish Church (1825)	207-729-7331	Portland
Fort Edgecomb	207-882-7777	Edgecomb
Fort Fairfield Blockhouse	207-472-3802	Fort Fairfield
Fort Halifax	207-585-2261	Winslow
Fort Kent Blockhouse	207-941-4014	Fort Kent
Fort Mc Clary Blockhouse	207-384-5160	Kittery
Fort Popham	207-389-1335	Phippsburg
Fort Williams Park Museum at Portland Head Light	207-799-2661	Cape Elizabeth
Francis M. Malcolm Institute	207-488-5451	Easton
Friends Schoolhouse/Raymond/Casco Historical Society	207-655-4231	Casco
Frontier Heritage History	207-768-4777	Fort Fairfield
Fryeburg Fair Farm Museum	207-697-3484	Fryeburg
Fryeburg Historical Society Museum	207-697-3484	Fryeburg
Garland Historical Society	207-924-3925	Garland
Gray Historical Society	207-657-4297	Gray
Greater Portland Landmarks	207-774-5561	Portland
Greenhut Galleries	207-772-2693	Portland
Guilford Historical Society	207-876-2817	Guilford
Hamlin Memorial Library and Museum	207-743-2980	Paris
Hampden Historical Society	207-862-2027	Hampden
Hancock Historical Society	207-422-3080	Hancock
Harmony Historical Society	207-683-6485	Harmony
Hay Gallery	207-773-2513	Portland
Haystack Historical Society	207-764-4717	Mapleton
Heartwood College of Art	207-967-8444	Kennebunkport
Hebron Historical Society	207-846-5683	Hebron
Hiram Historical Society	207-625-4794	Hiram
Holbrook Island Sanctuary	207-326-4012	Brooksville

Holmes Cottage	207-454-2604	Calais
Hose 5 Fire Museum	207-945-3229	Bangor
Hunnewell House	207-883-8427	Scarborough
Hussey Seating Company Museum	207-676-2271	North Berwick
Isaac Farrar Mansion	207-941-2808	Bangor
Island Falls Historical Society	207-463-2264	Island Falls
Islesboro Historical Society	207-734-6733	Islesboro
Jacqueline Designs—The 1840 House	207-883-5403	Scarborough
Jay Historical Society (Holmes-Crafts Homestead)	207-645-2732	Jay
John Paul Jones Memorial State Historic Site	207-384-5160	Kittery
Katahdin Iron Works	207-941-4014	Brownville
Kingfield Historical Society	207-265-4871	Kingfield
Kittery Historical and Naval Museum	207-439-3080	Kittery
Lawrence Public Library	207-453-6867	Fairfield
Lee Historical Society Museum	207-738-5014	Lee
Lincolnville Historical Society Museum	207-789-5445	Lincolnville
Lisbon Historical Society	207-353-4326	Lisbon
Livermore Falls Historical Society	207-897-4695	Livermore
Lovell Historical Society	207-925-3234	Lovell
Maine Archives and Museums	207-623-8428	Portland
Maine College of Art's Institute of Contemporary Art	207-879-5742	Portland
Maine Discovery Museum	207-262-7200	Bangor
Maine Historical Society	207-879-0427	Portland
Maine Maritime Museum	207-443-1316	Bath
Maine Military Historical Society Museum	207-626-4472	Augusta
Maine State Archives	207-287-5793	Augusta
Maine State Building and All Souls Chapel	207-998-4142	Poland Spring
Maine State Police Museum	207-624-7000	Augusta
Maine Tribal Museum	207-948-3131	Unity
Margaret Chase Smith Library	207-474-7133	Showhegan
Marine Resources Aquarium	207-633-9542	Boothbay
Matthews Farm Museum	207-785-3321	Union
Meddybemps Historical Society	207-454-3216	Meddybemps
Meetinghouse Museum	207-646-4775	Wells
Millinocket Town Museum	207-723-5766	Millinocket
Milo Historical Society	207-943-2268	Milo
Monhegan Museum	207-594-5646	Monhegan Island
Monmouth Historical Society, Monmouth Museum	207-933-2287	Monmouth
Monson Museum	207-997-3792	Monson
Moosehead Marine Museum	207-695-2716	Greenville
Mount Desert Oceanarium/The Lobster Hatchery	207-288-5005	Bar Harbor
Mountain Museums of Western Maine	207-265-2729	Kingfield
Naples Historical Society Museum	207-693-6790	Naples
Nathaniel Hawthorne's Boyhood Home	207-655-3268	Casco
Neal Dow Memorial	207-773-7773	Portland

Name	Phone	Town
Newport Historical Society	207-368-5260	Newport
Nichols Mansion	207-945-9774	Bangor
Nordica Homestead Museum	207-778-2042	Farmington
Norlands Living History Center	207-897-4366	Livermore
Norridgewock Historical Society	207-634-4243	Norridgewock
Northern Timber Cruisers Snowmobile Museum	207-723-9720	Millinocket
Norway Historical Society	207-743-7377	Norway
Nott House	207-967-2571	Kennebunkport
Nylander Natural History Museum	207-493-4209	Caribou
Oakfield Railroad Museum	207-757-8575	Oakfield
Old Church on the Hill	207-336-2191	Buckfield
Old Jail Museum	207-463-2264	Island Falls
Old Ledge School	207-846-6259	Yarmouth
Old Orchard Beach Historical Society Museum	207-934-4485	Old Orchard Beach
Old Town Museum	207-827-7256	Old Town
Olson House	207-596-6457	Cushing
Orland Historical Society	207-469-2476	Orland
Page Farm and Home Museum	207-581-4100	Orono
Parsonfield-Porter Historical Society	207-625-4667	Porter
Pemaquid Point Lighthouse and Fisherman's Museum	207-677-2494	Bristol
Penobscot Nation Museum	207-276-3940	Northeast Harbor
Phippsburg Historical Museum	207-442-7606	Phippsburg
Pittsfield Historical Society, Depot House Museum	207-487-2254	Pittsfield
Portland Fire Museum	207-772-2040	Portland
Portland Parks and Recreation	207-766-2970	Portland
Presque Isle Historical Society	207-762-1151	Presque Isle
Quoddy Head State Park	207-733-0911	Lubec
Railway City U.S.A., Model Railroad Museum	207-439-1204	Kittery
Rangeley Lakes Region Logging Museum	207-864-3939	Rangeley
Red Schoolhouse Museum	207-778-4215	Farmington
Roosevelt Campobello International Park Commission	506-752-2922	Lubec
Ruggles House	207-483-4637	Columbia Falls
S.O.J. School House	207-372-8012	Tenents Harbor
S.S. *Katahdin* (Moosehead Marine Museum)	207-695-2716	Greenville
Salome Sellers House	207-348-2886	Deer Isle
Sangerville Historical Society	207-876-4579	Sangerville
Scribner's Mill Preservation	207-583-4298	Harrison
Sea Side Hall Museum	207-526-4350	Swans Island
Seal Cove Auto Museum	207-244-9242	Seal Cove
Sebec Historical Society	207-564-8338	Sebec
South Salon Meeting House	207-474-8274	Solon
Spratt-Mead Museum	207-647-3469	South Bridgton
St. Croix Island International Historic Site	207-288-3338	St. Croix Island
Standish Historical Society	207-642-4443	Standish
Stanwood Homestead Museum and		

Wildlife Sanctuary—Birdsacre	207-667-8460	Ellsworth
State Capitol Building	207-289-1615	Augusta
Ste. Agatha Historical Society	207-543-6364	Ste. Agatha
Stein Gallery	207-772-9072	Portland
Stewart Free Library	207-278-2454	Corinna
Stewart M. Lord Memorial Historical Society	207-732-4121	Burlington
Sunkhaze National Wildlife Refuge	207-827-6138	Old Town
Tate House Museum	207-774-9781	Portland
Taylor-Barry House (Brickstore Museum)	207-985-4802	Kennebunkport
Temple Historical Society	207-778-2841	Temple
Thomas Heritage House	207-493-3188	Caribou
Tisbury Manor Chapter, DAR	207-997-3792	Monson
Titcomb House	207-778-2835	Farmington
Tory Hill Meeting House	207-929-8573	Buxton
Town House School	207-967-2751	Kennebunkport
Tremont Historical Society	207-244-3410	Tremont
Umbrella Cover Museum	207-766-4496	Casco Bay
Union Meeting House	207-685-3831	Portland
University of Maine Museum of Art	207-581-3255	Orono
Vassalboro Historical Society Museum	207-923-3533	Vassalboro
Waponahki Resource Ctr. & Sipayik Museum	207-853-4001	Passamoquoddy
Waterville Historical Society	207-872-9439	Waterville
Weld Historical Society	207-585-2586	Weld
Wells Auto Museum	207-646-9064	Wells
Wells Historical Society	207-646-4775	Wells
Westbrook Historical Society	207-797-2455	Westbrook
Western Maine Art Group	207-743-5411	Norway
Western Maine Children's Museum	207-235-2211	Carrabassett Valley
Whitefield Historical Society	207-549-5064	Whitefield
Wilhelm Reich Museum	207-864-3443	Rangeley
Wilson Museum, John Perkins House	207-326-8545	Castine
Windham Historical Society	207-892-5388	Gray
Winslow Homer Studio	207-883-2249	Scarborough
Women's Christian Temperance Union	207-773-7773	Portland

MASSACHUSETTS

Adams National Historical Park

135 Adams Street
Quincy, MA 02169
(617) 773-1177
Visitor Center: (617) 770-1175
www.nps.gov/adam

Overview

The Adams National Historical Park, consisting of 11 historic structures and 14 acres, tells the story of five generations of the Adams family. The park includes the birthplace of John Adams, the second president of the United States, as well as that of his son, John Quincy Adams, the sixth president of the United States. The park's Old House has been the home of four generations of Adamses. Visitors can begin their tour at the Visitor Center, where a trolley will pick them up and take them to the Birthplaces and then to the Old House to view the house and grounds.

Directions and Hours

Visitors can take the MBTA Red Line "T" to the Quincy Center station. Visitors then simply cross Hancock Street to the Visitor Center at 1250 Hancock.

Traveling south by car on Route 128: Take exit 7 to Route 3 south. Take the first exit, #18, off of Route 3 south. Follow Burgin Parkway through six sets of lights and at the seventh turn right onto Dimmock Street. Turn right off of Dimmock onto Hancock Street. The Visitor Center is located in the Galleria at Presidents Place at 1250 Hancock Street.

Traveling north on Route 3: Take exit 19 onto Burgin Parkway and follow the instructions above.

The park is open from April 19 until November 10. The Visitor Center is open limited hours during the winter season. All of the sites are handicap accessible.

Hours: The park is open seven days a week, 9:00 A.M. to 5:00 P.M.

Admission and Membership

Admission to the park is $2. Admission is discounted for seniors and children. The special programs do not charge a fee. Tours of the houses are limited to groups of 10 at a time.

What to See

The birthplaces of John Adams and John Quincy Adams are both saltbox style colonial homes that are furnished with period pieces and reproductions. At the Old House, visitors can see original furnishings used by the Adamses during their occupancy of the Old House, including furniture, portraits, and china dating to the eighteenth, nineteenth, and twentieth centuries. The Stone Library, built in 1870, houses about 14,000 volumes that were owned by John Quincy Adams. Visitors are welcome to enjoy the park's grounds, including a beautiful nineteenth-century formal garden at the Old House.

Programming includes National Park Week, a Mother's Day Celebration, Patriots at Fort Independence, Flag Day Parade, Patriots at Bunker Hill, Father's Day Celebration, a June lecture series with topics that include Women and the American Revolution, Liberty or Loyalty: Take a Stand!, Fourth of July: Independence Forever!, the Birthday of John Quincy Adams, and many others. Please contact the park for up-to-date information regarding these programs.

There is a gift shop in the Visitor Center on Hancock Street. There are numerous cafés and restaurants in Quincy Center where visitors can get something to eat.

While You're in the Area

Other area attractions include the United First Parish Church in Quincy Center, the Hancock Cemetery in Quincy Center, the Quincy Historical Society (p. 335), the Dorothy Quincy Homestead, and the Josiah Quincy House (p. 308).

American Sanitary Plumbing Museum

39 Piedmonth Street
Worcester, MA 01610
(508) 754-9453

Overview

The American Sanitary Plumbing Museum traces the history of American plumbing from outhouses to modern day fixtures. It is a tribute to the history of the American plumbing industry.

Directions and Hours

From Boston, take the Mass Pike (I-90) to Route 495 north to I-290 west toward Worcester. From the North Shore, take I-495 south to I-290 west toward Worcester. From Connecticut, take Route 84 north to the I-90 east toward Boston. Take exit 10 in Auburn onto I-290 east toward Worcester. Call for directions from I-290.

The museum is open September through June and closed July and August. It is handicap accessible.

Hours: Tuesday and Thursday 10:00-2:00 or by appointment.

Admission and Membership

Admission to the museum is free. There are no memberships. The museum can only accommodate small groups and children ages 7 and up.

What to See

The upstairs of the 3,000-square-foot, two-story facility features major fixture displays and an extensive reference library. Downstairs are exhibits of tools, different types of old piping, trap arrangements, and so on, which are displayed so that visitors can examine them in detail. The museum also features the first "electric sink" (dishwasher) and a display comparing 1889 and 1999 versions of prison toilets. The museum adds to its displays regularly and encourages schoolchildren to visit.

There is no gift shop or café, but there are many restaurants in the area.

While You're in the Area

The Worcester Art Museum (p. 327), the Worcester Historical Museum (p. 336), and the Higgins Armory (p. 260) are other sites worth visiting in Worcester.

American Textile History Museum

491 Dutton Street
Lowell, MA 01854-4221
(978) 441-0400
www.ATHM.org

Overview

The art of spinning and weaving comes to life in the American Textile History Museum as visitors view exhibits ranging from the interior of an eighteenth century Pennsylvania weaver's log cabin to a working 1870s wool mill. Guests explore the realities of America's premier manufacturing industry from colonial times to the

Photo courtesy of American Textile History Museum.

present. The museum has an extensive collection of textile tools and machinery with finished textiles displayed. Visitors can also observe fabric being woven and made into products used around the house.

Admission and Membership

$6 for adults 17 and over, $4 for children 6-16, seniors, and students with ID, and free for children under 6 and museum members. Additional admission fees may be applicable with some special programs and exhibitions. Parking is free. Membership is $30/year for individuals, $20/year for seniors and students, $50/year for a family, and $100/year for Museum Leadership Circle. Other options are available; please contact the museum for details.

Directions and Hours

35 miles north of Boston, the museum is adjacent to Lowell's National Historical Park. Take Route 495 north or south to the Lowell Connector, exit 35C. Then take exit 5B (Thorndike Street). Follow Thorndike Street through four sets of lights. The museum entrance and parking lot will be on the immediate left after the fourth set of lights. The museum is a red brick building with green and yellow banners.

The museum is open year-round except for Thanksgiving, Christmas, and New Year's Day. Closed Mondays except on Monday holidays. It is handicap accessible with wheelchair access and an elevator.

Hours: Tuesday-Friday 9:00 A.M. to 4:00 P.M. Saturday, Sunday, and holidays 10:00 A.M. to 5:00 P.M. Hours may vary for special programs and exhibitions.

What to See

The museum's collection consists of hand-powered tools and equipment, machinery, and garments from the eighteenth century to the mid-1900s. The museum library houses books, manuscripts documenting the history of textile production in the United States, trade catalogues, photographs, and prints.

The Webster Education Center has activities for adults and children which includes hands-on workshops, a lecture series, classes, and community outreach programs.

There is a gift shop and a café.

While You're in the Area

Other interesting attractions in the area are: The Brush Gallery (p. 332), the Whistler House (p. 336), Lowell Historical National Park (p. 223), and the New England Quilt Museum (p. 334).

Arnold Arboretum of Harvard University

125 Arborway
Jamaica Plain, MA 02130
www.arboretum.harvard.edu
(978) 369-9609

Overview

Founded in 1872, the Arnold Arboretum is the oldest public arboretum in the United States, with 265 acres and 14,000+ specimens of temperate woody plants, all of which are labeled and identified.

Directions and Hours

By public transportation: Take the Orange Line to the Forest Hills Station. The Arboretum's Frost Hills Gate is a one-block walk northwest along the Arborway from the station. Visitors can also take the #39 bus to the Monument stop in Jamaica Plain, then walk five blocks south along Centre Street to the Arborway. The Hunnewell Building is located inside the main gate.

From Boston and Cambridge: Take Storrow Drive to the Fenway Park Drive exit. At the top of the ramp, follow signs to the Riverway, which becomes the Jamaicaway and the Arborway. Follow signs to the Arnold Arboretum, located at the junction of the Arborway (Route 203) and Centre Street (Route 1).

From Route 95/128: From either the north or the south exit onto Route 9 east. Follow Route 9 for 7 miles to the Riverway. Exit to your right onto the Riverway (Route 1 south) toward Dedham and Providence. Follow the signs along the Riverway, Jamaicaway, and Arborway to the Arboretum, located at the intersection of Centre Street (Route 1) and the Arborway (Route 203).

Fom Route 93: Take exit 11 (Granite Ave./Ashmont) onto Route 203 west. Follow Route 203 through Dorchester, past Franklin Park to the Arnold Arboretum. The Arboretum is on your left just beyond the Forest Hills Subway Station. At the rotary (near the western edge of the grounds) turn left at the lights, go around the rotary 360 degrees onto Route 203 in the opposite direction. The main gate will be on your right, 50 yards beyond the rotary.

The Arboretum is open year-round and is handicap accessible.

Hours: Monday through Friday 9:00 A.M. to 4:00 P.M., weekends 12:00-4:00 P.M. Closed holidays. November-March: 10:00 A.M. to 2:00 P.M.

Admission and Membership

There is no cost for admission. Membership is \$20/year for a student/teacher, \$35/year for an individual, \$50/year for a household, \$100/year for a sustaining membership, \$200/year for a sponsor membership, \$500/year for a patron, \$1,000/year for a benefactor membership, and \$150/year for an organization membership.

What to See

The arboretum houses a bonsai collection, a lilac colection (in May), a rose garden (in Spring and Summer), a conifer path, and "Science in the Pleasure Grounds," an indoor exhibit in the Hunnewell Building that describes the development of the Arnold Arboretum.

Special programs include Lilac Sunday annually in mid-May and the annual fall plant sale on the third Sunday in September.

Children's programming includes field studies experiences for third-fifth grade groups.

The museum has a gift shop. Visitors can eat in restaurants in Jamaica Plain, a 10 minute walk.

While You're in the Area

Other places of interest nearby include the Franklin Park Zoo and the Frederick Law Olmsted National Historic Site (p. 245).

Arthur Griffin Center for Photographic Art

67 Shore Road
Winchester, MA 01890
(781) 729-1158
www.griffincenter.org

Overview

The Arthur Griffin Center for Photographic Art was started in 1992, built by local resident Arthur Griffin (now 97 years old). The center was built to look like an old grist mill. It has a 1,500 foot gallery which holds exhibits as well as displaying Griffin's legacy of photos taken over 60 years, primarily of New England. Griffin was one of the first photographers to use 35mm film, and he took the first color photos of baseball legend Ted Williams in 1939.

Directions and Hours

From Routes 128/95: Take exit 36 (Washington Street/Woburn) or exit 37A (Route 93S). From the Washington Street exit go up the ramp and take a right. Follow Washington Street 3½ miles to Winchester Center (going through 6 sets of lights). At the seventh light bear right, keeping town hall on your left. This is Mount Vernon Street. Follow to the rotary. Take a right just before the rotary (you'll see a sign for Griffin Center). This is Shore Road. Go ¼ mile. The Griffin Center will be on your right.

The museum is open year round and is handicap accessible.

Hours: Tuesday-Sunday noon-4:00 P.M.

Admission and Membership

Adults $5.00, Seniors $2.00. Students and children are free. All visitors are free on Thursdays. Membership is $25/year for individuals, $45/year for families.

What to See

Griffin was a photojournalist on the cutting edge of the new medium, photography. He has past covers of *Life* and the *Saturday Evening Post*. The photography gallery changes exhibitions six times a year (with exhibitions chosen through open juried competitions). In the year 2000 the center hosted an exhibition of the work of Edward Weston and his sons, Cole and Brett Weston.

There is a gift shop. There is no café but there are restaurants within walking distance in downtown Winchester.

While You're in the Area

Nearby attractions and museums include the Lexington Historical Society (p. 271), the Museum of Our National Heritage (p. 286), and the Minuteman National Historic Park.

Arthur M. Sackler Museum (Harvard University Art Museums)

485 Broadway Street
Cambridge, MA 02138
(617) 495-9400
www.artmuseumes.harvard.edu

Overview

The Sackler houses collections of ancient, Asian, Islamic, and later Indian art. Among its particular treasures are the world's finest collection of Chinese jades, Korean ceramics, Chinese cave temple painting and sculpture, a significant collection of Japanese woodblock prints, one of America's most important collections of Indian and Persian miniature paintings, an outstanding group of Chinese bronzes, Greek and Roman sculpture and vases, and ancient coins. The Sackler Museum building also contains the Art Museum's largest special exhibition gallery, an auditorium, the offices of Harvard's Department of Fine Arts, and Rubel Library, a research center for Asian art.

Directions and Hours

From the West: On Mass Pike eastbound (Route 90) take the Cambridge/Allston Exit on the left side of the road. Proceed through the toll booth toward Cambridge/Somerville. At the end of the ramp is the intersection of River Street and Soldier's Field Road. Cross Soldier's Field Road and go over the Charles River to Memorial Drive. Make a left onto Memorial Drive to J.F.K. Street. Take a right onto J.F.K. and follow J.F.K.

through Harvard Square. Bare right at the lights after Harvard Square into a tunnel. Stay in the right lane onto Broadway. The Fogg is on the right and the Sackler is on the left. Quincy Street is the first right outside of the tunnel.

From the East and South: Take Route 93/3 north to the Mass Pike—90 West. Take the Allston/Cambridge Exit to Memorial Drive to J.F.K. Street. Follow the West instructions from here.

From the North: Take I-93/Route 1 south to the Cambridge Memorial Drive Exit. From Memorial Drive go to J.F.K. Street. Follow above directions from here.

The museum is open year round except on national holidays. The entrance to the Sackler is handicap accessible. Hearing assistants are available for lectures, gallery talks, and other events. Please make arrangements beforehand by calling Visitor Services at (617) 495-8286.

Hours: Monday through Saturday 10:00 A.M. to 5:00 P.M., Sunday 1:00-5:00 P.M.

Admission and Membership

Admission is $5, free for individuals all day Wednesday and Saturday morning 10:00 A.M. to noon. Groups of 8 or more must schedule in advance and pay regular admission fees. Admission discounts are $4 for seniors, $3 for students, and free for children under 18. Membership information: if you join the Friends of the Harvard Art Museums visitors get free admission to three museums, invitations to openings and other special events, subscriptions to the Calendar and the Review, as well as reduced rates for lectures, seminars, concerts, and other events. Membership categories are: Individual $35/year, Senior Citizen and Students $25/year, Dual $50/year, Contributor $100/year, Junior Fellow for ages 21 to 40 single $100/Dual $150/year, Forbes Fellow $500/year, Patron $1,000/year, and Corporate or Institutional $1,000/year.

What to See

The ancient art collection comprises Greek, Roman, Etruscan, Egyptian, and Near Eastern Art, and includes vases, sculpture in stone, metalwork, terracottas, glass, glyptics, some wood, ivory and bone, and a very large and important collection of ancient coins. Particular strengths of the collection lie in Greek red and black figure vases of the classical period, Greek and Roman bronzes, stone sculpture, and ancient coins. The time span covered is roughly the following: Greek vases date from circa eighth century B.C. to second century B.C.; bronzes date from eighth century B.C. to third century A.D.; and stone sculptured date from circa 2,500 B.C. to fourth century A.D.

The Asian art collection's greatest strength is in Chinese art, specifically early Chinese art. The collection of ancient Chinese jades is unrivaled in the United States. The ritual bronze vessels, ceremonial weapons, mirrors, and chariot fitting, combined with the numerous early stone and gilt bronze sculptures, the clay bodhisattva and wall-painting fragments from Tun-huang make this collection among the most important in the county. The holdings of Chinese ceramics are both comprehensive and impressive, with recognized strengths in Liang-chu culture pottery, Sung- and Yuan-period Chum and temmoku wares, and late Ming enameled porcelains. The rhinoceros horn carvings are the best in the United States. The Chinese painting collection includes 30 masterworks, of which 10 rank among the most important examples of the genre.

The Sackler Museums have the most impressive holdings outside Korea of Korean ceramics and archaeological materials. The Henderson Collection spans the entire history of Korean ceramics from the 1st century A.D. through the nineteenth century A.D. It has great strengths in all three major areas of the field: robust stonewares from the archaeological period (through the ninth century A.D.); the celadons from the Koryo dynasty (918-1392); and the porcelains and punch'ong stonewares from the Chosin dynasty (1392-1910).

The Japanese collections are preeminent in the field of surimono prints and strong in other Japanese prints, woodblock-printed books, calligraphy, and certain types of painting. The Art Museum's Asian collections are strong in Thai and other Southeast Asian illustrated manuscripts and also include first-rate Indian (traditional Buddhist, Hindu, and Jain) and Southeast Asian sculptures.

The Islamic and Later Indian Art collection also includes a number of pottery shards as well as some ivory and wood objects. The collection consists mostly of works on paper in three major groupings: Safavid (mostly seventeenth century Iran); Ottoman (seventeenth century and later Turkey and Empire); and Indian (the contemporary Mughal empire). Indian paintings includes both Islamic and non-Islamic holdings. The department's object holdings include some important Iranian and Central Asian carpets as well as Ottoman Iznik ceramic ware.

The collection of miniatures from the 14th-century Tabriz "Book of Kings" (Shahnama) is unrivaled. The holdings of Persian paintings and drawings from the Safavid and Uzbek periods rank in terms of quality with those of the British Library, the British Museum, and the Bibliotheque Nationale. The museum's Muslim calligraphies, illuminations, and marbling rank high in this field. The collection is also moderately rich in the rare schools of Deccani painting.

Arthur M. Sackler Museum does occasionally have children's programming.

There is a museum shop located in the Fogg courtyard that is open daily until 4:45 P.M. The shop offers reproductions of many of the images in the collection, as well as catalogues, art books, and related merchandise. The Sert Gallery Café presents art museum visitors with a relaxing atmosphere overlooking the Harvard campus and a variety of fresh and unique sandwiches, pasta and rice salads, and scones, cookies, and other sweet tooth's delights. It is open 8:30 A.M. to 3:30 P.M. Monday through Friday.

While You're in the Area

Harvard Square and the city of Cambridge are rich in history and filled with multiple activities from museums and historical sites to cafés and restaurants.

Atwood House Museum

Chatham Historical Society
347 Stage Harbor Road
Chatham, MA 02633
(508) 945-2493
www.atwoodhouse.org

Overview

Sea Captain Joseph C. Atwood built the Atwood House in 1752. It was occupied by five generations of his family until 1926. The museum began with the purchase of the house by the Chatham Historical Society, who then made it available to the public. The house remains essentially unchanged since it was built. Over the years, six rooms have been added to provide display space for the extensive collection of art, decorative arts, maritime objects and artifacts, and paintings relating to the history of Chatham. Its museum rooms are virtually in their original condition.

Directions and Hours

From Route 6 take exit 11 onto Route 137 South to the intersection with Route 28. Turn left and take Route 28 East to the rotary on Waltham Main Street. Turn right on to Stage Harbor Road. The museum is ¾ mile on the left.

The museum is open from June 10 to September 30 and is mostly handicap accessible.

Hours: Tuesday-Friday 1:00-4:00 P.M.

Admission and Membership

$3 for adults, $1 for students, children under 12 and members free. Membership is $15/year for individuals, $20/year for families.

What to See

The Joseph C. Lincoln Wing of the Atwood House is a memorial to the author of many novels, stories, and poems about Cape Cod. It contains manuscripts, first editions, and other memorabilia. Also displayed are reminders of the times and people that Lincoln wrote about. The Durand Wing is a memorial to Samuel Durand. It contains collections of worldwide seashells, including those of Cape Cod, special threaded Sandwich Glass, and Parian Ware vases, figurines, and busts. It was designed to display the portraits of Cape Cod sea captains. The Nickerson Wing is named for Chatham's first settler and displays a Bicentennial Quilt, toys, dolls, costumes, pictures, maritime art and artifacts, china, and furniture. An Antique Tool Room has a collection of old tools and equipment used in the area to earn a living.

The museum houses many portraits of Chatham sea captains, mainly of the nineteenth century. It also has a maritime collection and a mural barn painted by local and noted artist Alice Stallknacht that is referred to as the "Spoon River Anthology" and is seen as a picture of a small town during that time period, featuring paintings of local people during the 1930s and 1940s. The murals have been exhibited in major areas around the country. The nationally known Stallknecht Murals were presented to the Chatham Historical Society in 1977 by the artist's son.While you can still enter the barn, the murals were sent to Los Angeles for conservation. The Old "Chatham Light" Turret can also be viewed.

In 2001 paintings by local artists will comprise a special program called "Picturing Chatham." The museum runs special exhibits every summer.

There is a small gift shop. There is no café but there are many restaurants in the village center about a mile away.

While You're in the Area

Interesting attractions nearby include the Chatham Railroad Museum (p. 332), the Mayo House, and the Cape Cod Museum of Natural History (p. 332).

Battleship *Massachusetts*

Battleship Cove
Fall River, MA 02721
(508) 678-1100
www.battleshipcove.com

Overview

Battleship *Massachusetts* has the world's largest collection of retired naval fighting vessels. The star attraction is the battleship USS *Massachusetts,* a veteran of the Atlantic and Pacific theaters of World War II. Standing over 18 stories tall and 680 feet long, the *Massachusetts* is accompanied by the destroyer *Joseph P. Kennedy, Jr.*, the submarine *Lionfish,* two PT Boats, and the Russian missile corvette *Hiddensee.*

Photo courtesy of Battleship Massachusetts

Directions and Hours

From points north take I-93 south to 128 south; take Route 24 south to Fall River, Massachusetts; take exit 7 (State Route 79) to the Davol Street exit and follow the signs (Waterfront, Heritage State Park, or Battleship Cove) along the waterfront to Battleship Cove.

From points south or west take I-95 north to 195 east for approximately 14 miles; take exit 5 from the Braga Bridge in Massachusetts, bear left at the fork in road, turn left at the first stop sign and left at the first traffic light onto Central Street; proceed down the hill to Battleship Cove.

From points east take Interstate 195 west to Fall River, Massachusetts; take exit 5 (before the Braga Bridge); bear right at the first two forks in the road and then take the first left underneath the overpass onto Davol Street; follow Davol Street to Battleship Cove.

The museum is open year round, and has limited handicap access.

Hours: winter 9:00-4:30, spring/fall 9:00-5:00, and summer 9:00-6:00.

Admission and Membership

$9 for adults, $4.50 for children (6-14), $6.75 seniors and AAA members.

Group admission is $6.75 and school admission is $3.

What to See

The battleship houses several special collections, including model airplane and PT Boat memorabilia exhibits.

For families there are interactive programs that enable children to assume the roles of former crew members. An overnight camping program allows over 30,000 scouts from all over the region to spend the night on board the battleship and destroyer and learn about life on a Navy ship.

There is a gift shop, and the battleship has a snack bar (during the summer there is also an outdoor snack bar).

While You're in the Area

The Marine Museum of Fall River (p. 334) is nearby.

Beauport (SPNEA)

Sleeper-McCann House
75 Eastern Point Boulevard
Gloucester, MA 01930
(978) 283-0800
www.spnea.org

Overview

Beauport, summer home of interior designer Henry Davis Sleeper, is a fantasy house built on the rocks overlooking Gloucester Harbor. The eclectic-style shingle house contains a labyrinth of rooms decorated to evoke different historical and literary themes. Beauport was Sleeper's escape, a backdrop for entertaining, and a professional showcase. The house drew attention through publication in books and magazines, and its romanticized images of the past were widely accepted and often imitated.

Directions and Hours

Take Route I-95/128 north to the end. At the second set of lights after the second rotary, go straight onto East Main Street. Travel 1½ miles to the stone gates at the entrance to Eastern Point Boulevard. Follow Eastern Point Boulevard ½ mile to Beauport.

The house museum is open May 15 through September 15.

Hours: Monday-Friday, 10:00 A.M. to 5:00 P.M. Tours are at 10:00, 11:00, 12:00, 1:00, 2:00, 3:00 and 4:00 P.M. Please note: Beauport's extended weekend hours run September 15 through October 15, Monday through Sunday, 10:00 A.M. to 5:00 P.M. Tours are at 10:00, 11:00, 12:00, 1:00, 2:00, 3:00, and 4:00 P.M.

Admission and Membership

$10 for adults, $9.50 senior citizens, ½ off for students and children 6-12. Children 5 and under, SPNEA members, and residents of Gloucester are free. AAA members receive a 2 for 1 discount. SPNEA membership is $35/year for individuals and $45/year for a household. Membership includes free admissions to 35 properties and museums across New England. Visit SPNEA's website at for more information.

What to See

Every nook displays curiosities, paintings, folk art, china, or colored glass. The settings are playful constructs, such as a sea captain's retreat or an early American kitchen, arranged for visual delight rather than historical truth. After Sleeper's death, Beauport was purchased by Mr. and Mrs. Charles McCann. They refurnished the China Trade Room as a parlor and added items from Mrs. McCann's noted collection of Chinese export porcelain but left most of Sleeper's arrangements untouched. The house and its contents were donated to SPNEA by the McCanns' children in 1942.

Beauport offers group tours and public programs throughout the season. Summer programs include teas on the terrace and specialty tours. Please call or write for details.

The Sleeper McCann House has a gift shop.

While You're in the Area

Nearby attractions and museums include the Cape Anne Historical Museum (p. 225), the Gloucester Fisherman's Museum (p. 333), the Patron's Museum and Educational Center (p. 335), and the Sargent House Museum (p. 335).

Benjamin Nye Homestead

The Nye Family of America Association
85 Old County Road
East Sandwich, MA 02537
(508) 888-4213

Overview

The Benjamin Nye Homestead features period furnishings, circa 1750s. It was the home of seven generations of Millers. Many were seafarers, whalers, and captains. Their history is captured in the Marine Room.

Directions and Hours

The museum is located on Cape Cod. Take Route 6 to Hyannis and get off at exit 4, Chase Road. Turn left at the end of the ramp. After a half-mile, go left on Old County Road. The homestead is a mile on the right.

The museum is open from June 15-October 15. It is not handicap accessible.

Hours: Monday-Friday 12:00-4:30.

Admission and Membership

$3 for adults, $1 for children under 12. Membership is $10/year for individuals, $15/year for family, and $150 for single/life.

Discounts are available for groups and AAA members, and local schoolchildren are admitted free.

What to See

Special events include Christmas in Sandwich (held in early December), and bi-annual reunions. Open hearth cooking and spinning during events are attractions for children.

There is no gift shop or café. Visitors can eat at local restaurants within one mile on route 6A.

While You're in the Area

The Sandwich Glass Museum (p. 310), the Heritage Plantation (p. 333), and Greenbriar Nature Center (p. 253) are other area attractions.

Beverly Historical Society and Museum

117 Cabot St.
Beverly, MA 01915
(978) 922-1186
www.beveryhistory.org

Overview

The Beverly Historical Society maintains three

Photo courtesy of The Bidwell House.

While You're in the Area

The Peabody/Essex Museum (p. 303) is about three miles away.

historical houses: the John Cabot House (1781), the John Balch House (1636), and the Hale House (1694). The society also houses a large collection of nineteenth century research books for genealogical and historic research.

Directions and Hours

From 128, take the Beverly exit. Follow Route 1A until you reach the Balch and Cabot houses.

The Cabot house is open year round, and the Balch and Hale Houses are open from May-October. Hours of operation are Tuesday-Friday 10:00-4:00, and Saturday 12:00-4:00. The first floors are handicap accessible, but there is no handicap bathroom.

Admission and Membership

Admission is $4/adults, $3/seniors, and children under the age of 12 are $1. Memberships are $30/year for a family, $20/year for an individual, $15/year for seniors, and $5/year for students.

What to See

The Cabot House gives visitors a chance to view a eighteenth century Federal decor, and houses the research library. There are rotating exhibits in the main gallery which change three times a year. Items related to the Walker Transportation Company are also on display.

The museum has a gift shop, and there are restaurants within walking distance.

The Bidwell House

Art School Road
Box 537
Monterey, MA 01245
(413) 528-6888
www.bidwellhousemuseum.org

Overview

Based on the estate inventory of Reverend Bidwell, the Bidwell House offers a collection of quality country furnishings and decorative arts of the eighteenth and early nineteenth cenuries, housed in a 1750 Georgian saltbox in the Berkshire hills.

Directions and Hours

From New York or Boston: Take exit 2 off Route 90 (Mass Pike). Turn left off the exit ramp and then right onto Route 102. Take an immediate left onto Tyringham Road. Go 5.3 miles then turn right onto Monterey Road for 2.2 miles. Go right onto Art School Road, which ends at the museum.

From Great Barrington: Take Route 23 east. In Monterey village take a left onto Tyringham Road. Travel past Lake Garfield and then take a left onto Art School Road and follow to the end of the road, which ends at the museum.

The museum is open from Memorial Day weekend to mid-October and is handicap accessible.

Hours: 11:00 A.M. to 4:00 P.M. Tuesday through Sunday.

Admission and Membership

Adults $5, seniors/students $4, children under 16 $1. Group rates are available. Membership costs range from $25 to $1,500+. Please contact the museum for more information on membership.

What to See

The Bidwell House has an extensive assortment of earthenware and china that includes many pieces of redware and slipware along with Delft that fill the cupboards and shelves. Early samplers, linsey-woolsey coverlets, and patchwork quilts narrate domestic artistry of the times. A wide display of domestic hand tools and lighting devices rounds out the portrait of early New England life.

The house is surrounded by hiking trails.

The museum does not have a gift shop or a café. A country store is located nearby, howerver, and there are many restaurants in the area.

While You're in the Area

Other interesting places to visit while you are in the area are the Mission House (p. 277), the Norman Rockwell Museum (p. 292), and Jacob's Pillow.

Boott Cotton Mills Museum at Lowell National Historical Park

400 Foot of John Street
Lowell, MA 01852
(978) 970-5000
www.nps.gov/lowe

Overview

The history of America's Industrial Revolution is commemorated in Lowell, Massachusetts. The Boott Cotton Mills Museum, with its operating weave room of 88 power looms, "mill girl" boardinghouses, the Suffolk Mill Turbine Exhibit, and guided tours, tell the story of the transition from farm to factory while chronicling immigrant and labor history and tracing industrial technology. The park includes textile mills, worker housing, 5.6 miles of canals, and nineteenth-century commercial buildings. The museum has interactive exhibits and video programs about the Industrial Revolution, labor, and the rise, fall, and rebirth of Lowell.

Directions and Hours

Take the Lowell Connector from either Route 495 (exit 35C) or Route 3 (exit 30A Southbound, exit 30B northbound) to Thorndisk Street (exit 5B). Follow the brown and white "Lowell National and State Park" signs. Fee parking is available in the Visitor Parking Lot next to Market Mills.

The museum is open year round and is handicap accessible.

Hours: 9:30-5:00 P.M. daily.

Admission and Membership

$4 for adults, $2 for youths 6-16 and students, children 5 and under free. Senior discounts are available.

What to See

Discover the story of Lowell's mills, their machinery, and their workers through the Boott Discovery Trail during your visit to the Boott Cotton Mills Museum. Children of all ages can pick up their work aprons and time cards at the museum entrance and through hands-on activities explore how cotton cloth was made from raw cotton to finished cloth. Visitors can try their hand at carding, spinning, drawing in, and weaving, experiencing the roar of the 1920s weave room, and learning what it was like working in a textile mill.

There is a gift shop. There is no café but there are many restaurants in the immediate area.

While You're in the Area

Interesting attractions nearby include: the American Textile History Museum (p. 213), the New England Quilt Museum (p. 334), the Whistler House Museum of Art (p. 336), and the Brush Art Gallery and Studios (p. 332).

Busch-Reisinger Museum (Harvard University Art Museums)

32 Quincy Street
Cambridge, MA 02138
(617) 495-9400
www.artmuseums.harvard.edu

Overview

The Busch-Reisinger Museum is devoted to the art of German-speaking countries and related cultures of central and northern Europe. Its collections of German expressionism, Vienna Secession art, 1920s abstraction, and the work of Joseph Beuys rank with the finest in the United States. The Busch-Reisinger Museum also has important collections of medieval, Renaissance, and baroque sculpture, sixteenth-century paintings, and porcelain. The museum's permanent display of modern works of art and design is housed in the galleries of its new building, Werner Otto Hall (opened in 1991), which also houses Harvard's Fine Arts Library.

Directions and Hours

From the West: On Mass Pike eastbound (Route 90) take the Cambridge/Allston Exit on the left side of the road. Proceed through the Toll Booth toward Cambridge/Somerville. At the end of the ramp is the intersection of River Street and Soldier's Field Road. Cross Soldier's Field Road and go over the Charles River to Memorial Drive. Make a left onto Memorial Drive to J.F.K. Street. Take a right onto J.F.K. and follow J.F.K. through Harvard Square. Bear right at the lights after Harvard Square into a tunnel. Stay in the right lane onto Broadway. The Fogg is on the right and the Sackler is on the left. Quincy Street is the first right outside of the tunnel.

From the East and South: Take Route 93/3 North to the Mass Pike—90 West. Take the Allston/Cambridge Exit to Memorial Drive to J.F.K. Street. Follow the West instructions from here.

From the North: Take I-93/Route 1 south to the Cambridge Memorial Drive Exit. From Memorial Drive go to J.F.K. Street. Follow above directions from here.

The museum is open year round except on national holidays. Handicap access to the Busch-Reisinger is on Prescott Street at the entrance of the Fine Arts Library. Hearing assistants are available for lectures, gallery talks, and other events. Please make arrangements beforehand by calling Visitor Services at (617) 495-8286.

Hours: Monday through Saturday 10:00 A.M. to 5:00 P.M., Sunday 1:00-5:00 P.M.

Admission and Membership

Admission is $5, free for individuals all day Wednesday and Saturday morning 10:00 A.M. to noon. Groups of eight or more must schedule in advance and pay regular admission fees. Admission discounts are $4 for seniors, $3 for students, and free for children under 18. Membership information: if you join the Friends of the Harvard Art Museums visitors get free admission to three museums, invitations to openings and other special events, subscriptions to the Calendar and the Review, as well as reduced rates for lectures, seminars, concerts, and other events. Membership categories are: Individual $35/year, Senior Citizen and Students $25/year, Dual $50/year, Contributor $100/year, Junior Fellow for ages 21 to 40 single $100/Dual $150/year, Forbes Fellow $500/year, Patron $1000/year, and Corporate or Institutional $1000/year.

What to See

Housed in Werner Otto Hall, the Busch-Reisinger Museum is the only institution in the Americas exclusively devoted to the arts of Central and Northern Europe. The collection spans the Romanesque to the present day, with special emphasis on art after 1880. It is 95% German and includes art from other countries in Central and Northern Europe. The Busch collection is particularly strong in the late Gothic central European art, eighteenth-century porcelains, late nineteenth century, the Austrian

Secession, Expressionism, the Bauhaus, and 1945 to the present.

The collection of Expressionist drawings, sculpture, prints, and paintings is considered outstanding in Germany itself. The museum holds the largest collection of Bauhaus materials in Germany and one of the largest collection of the work of Joseph Beuys, as well as the archives of Walter Gropius and Lyonel Feininger. The museum also has extensive materials on the impact of the Bauhaus on American art education and design.

Busch-Reisinger Museum sometimes has children's programming.

There is a museum shop located in the Fogg courtyard that is open daily until 4:45 P.M. The shop offers reproductions of many of the images in the collection, as well as catalogues, art books, and related merchandise. The Sert Gallery Café presents art museum visitors with a relaxing atmosphere overlooking the Harvard campus and a variety of fresh and unique sandwiches, pasta and rice salads, and scones, cookies, and other sweet tooth's delight. It is open 8:30 A.M. to 3:30 P.M. Monday through Friday.

While You're in the Area

Harvard Square and the city of Cambridge are rich in history and filled with multiple activities from museums and historical sites to cafés and restaurants.

Cape Anne Historical Museum (SPNEA)

27 Pleasant Street
Gloucester, MA 01930
(978) 283-0455
www.spnea.org

Overview

The Cape Anne Historical Museum houses art collections from many artists. There are also fisheries and maritime galleries, a granite quarrying gallery, historic vessels and a furnished 1804 sea captain's house.

Directions and Hours

Take Route 128 to the rotary and take the exit for Washington Street. Take a left turn onto Prospect Street, then turn right onto Pleasant Street.

The museum is open year round, except February, and is handicap accessible.

Hours: Tuesday-Saturday 10:00-5:00.

Admission and Membership

$5 for adults, $4.50 for seniors, and $3.50 for students. Membership is $20/year for individuals. Groups and most children's programs are free. Members can visit any of SPNEA's 35 New England properties at no charge.

What to See

The Cape Anne Historical Museum showcases collections by Fitz Hugh Lane, Maurice Prendergast, Stuart Davis, John Sloan, Marsden Hartley, and Milton Avery.

There is also various children's programming.

There is a gift shop.

The museum does not have a café, but people can eat at nearby restaurants in downtown Gloucester.

While You're in the Area

Nearby attractions and museums include the Gloucester Fisherman's Museum (p. 333), the Patron's Museum and Educational Center (p. 335), and the Sargent House Museum (p. 335).

Cape Museum of Fine Arts

PO Box 2034
60 Hope Lane
Dennis, MA 02638
(508) 385-4477
www.cmfa.org

Overview

The Cape Museum of Fine Arts is dedicated to

preserving the contribution of the Cape and the Islands to American Art. A newly completed $1.5 million addition includes seven galleries, a glass enclosed scupture gallery, a 92-seat auditorium with state-of-the-art projection equipment, and a sculpture garden.

Directions and Hours

From the west: Take exit 8 off Route 6 and turn left off the ramp onto Union Street. Continue unitil it ends at Route 6A. Turn right onto 6A and follow for four miles. Turn left at the entrance of the Cape Playhouse Center for the Arts and follow the signs to the CMFA.

From the east: Take exit 9 off Route 6 and turn right off the ramp onto Route 134 north. Continue until it ends at Route 6A. Turn left onto 6A and follow Route 6 and Route 6A.

The museum is open year-round and is handicap accessible with an elevator and ramps.

Hours: October through May: Tuesday-Saturday 10:00 A.M. to 5:00 P.M., Sunday 1:00-5:00 P.M. May-October: Monday-Saturday 10:00 A.M. to 5:00 P.M., Sunday 1:00-5:00 P.M.

Admission and Membership

Adults $5, children under 18 free. A group discount of $3 per person with docent tour is available to groups of 15 or more. Membership is $40/year for individual, $60/year for family, $150/year for sponsor, and $250/year for patron.

What to See

The Cape Museum of Fine Arts conserves and exhbits the work of artists in the Cape Cod area. It has holdings of more than 1,000 objects that display the Cape role in American art since 1899. The museum offers changing exhibitions and displays, such as paintings by Robert Douglas Hunter, works from the Fleet collection, the Twelfth National Exhibition of the American Society of Marine Artists, Bronze Medals by Ralph Menconi, "Stealing the Show II: Cape Playhouse Set Designs" by Herbert Senn and Helen Pond, "Scandinavian Imagery and Mythological Themes" by Anita Askild, "Patterns of Thought" by Haynes Ownby, and the paintings of C. Arnold Slade. The permanent collections include "The Expressive Figure," an exhibition that highlights paintings, sculptures, and works on paper that focus on the human figure; "Drawn to the Lights," that illustrates the ways in which artists use physiological perception of color and pigment to reflect the Cape's light, which drew so many painters to the area; and "Beauty and the Beasts," a presentation that features mammals, and includes Ross Moffett's "Blue Heron on Pilgrim Lake" and Del Filardi's "Golden Eagle."

The museum offers summer art workshops for kids. Each workshop is four days in length and is taught by an artist.

There is a gift shop. There are two restaurants within walking distance.

While You're in the Area

Other interesting attractions in the area are: the Cape Playhouse Center of the Arts, and Dennis Village, a village with art galleries, restaurants, and assorted small businesses.

Captain Bangs Hallet House

11 Strawberry Lane
PO Box 11
Yarmouth, MA 02675
(508) 362-3021
hsoy.org

Overview

This historic captain's house highlights maritime history and Cape Cod family life during the nineteenth century. Special theme tours and exhibits changes annually.

Directions and Hours

Take Route 6 to exit 7. Turn right on Willow Street. Turn right on Route 6A and follow one mile to Yarmouth Port Common on the right. The museum is the second house on the common.

The museum is open June 1 through October 15. It is not handicap accessible.

Hours: Thursday-Sunday, tours on the hour from 1:00-3:00, and off-season tours by appointment.

Admission and Membership

$3 for adults and $0.50 for children under 12. Memberships are $15/year for individuals and $25/year for families.

What to See

The Captain Bangs Hallet House has a library and archives of historical materials and images, a collection of objects related to the maritime industry and the China trade, and 50 acres of nature trails, with rare and unique botanical specimens such as the largest Weeping Beech tree in the United State. The house features an old cellar kitchen, filled with nineteenth- and twentieth-century kitchen antiques, and a children's room.

Children's programming is limited to local school programs.

There is no gift shop but local history publications are for sale. Visitors can eat at Hallets Store and Soda Fountain on route 6A in Yarmouth Port.

While You're in the Area

Nearby on Route 6A are other local attractions such as Hallet's Store and Museum, the Winslow Crocker House (an SPNEA property, p. 326), and Yarmouth New Church historic site. Visitors can also see the Judah Baker Windmill in South Yarmouth and Baxter's Gristmill in West Yarmouth.

Centerville Historical Museum

513 Main Street
Centerville, MA 02632
(508) 775-0331
www.ATHM.org

Overview

The Centerville Historical Museum is an 1840 historic house with 14 rooms. It houses a maritime gallery, period rooms, and collections including historic gowns, quilts, Civil War uniforms, weaponry, a maritime collection, historic tools, and domestic items.

Directions and Hours

Take Route 3 south toward Cape Cod. Continue on Route 6 all the way and it will lead you right into a rotary at the head of the Upper Cape. Continue around the rotary and follow the signs for Route 6 and the Sagamore Bridge. From the Sagamore Bridge take Route 6 to exit 6 and take Route 132 south to the first traffic light. Turn right onto Phinney's Lane and follow it to Route 28. Cross Route 28 and continue on Phinney's Lane until it merges with Main Street. Pick up Main Street, bearing left at the juncture. The museum is a short distance ahead, on the left. Parking is available directly across the street from the museum.

The museum is open from Memorial Day weekend to the end of October and is handicap accessible.

Hours: Monday-Saturday noon-5:00 P.M.

Admission and Membership

$4 adults, $3 seniors, $2 students and children.

Photo courtesy of the Centerville Historical Museum.

Kids under 12 and NEMA members are free. Membership is $20/year for individuals, $30/year for a family, $50/year for Patrons, and $100/year for a Benefactor.

What to See

The museum houses Victorian period objects, a Colonial Revival Kitchen, a Civil War collection, ship models, historic costume exhibits, and the "Portland Wheel."

The museum also offers Main Street Walking Tours in August and a Centerville Old Home Week from August 4-12. In Summer 2001 an exhibition of historic wedding gowns will be displayed and in Summer 2002 there will be an exhibit featuring historic gowns and photographs.

Family programs are available.

There is a gift area. Visitors can eat at the famous Four Seas Ice Cream shop.

While You're in the Area

Other interesting attractions in the area are: the Cahoon Museum of American Art in Cotuit (p. 332), Heritage Plantation in Sandwich (p. 333), and the JFK Memorial Museum in Hyannis (p. 333).

Children's Museum of Boston

300 Congress Street
Boston, MA 02210
(617) 426-8855
www.bostonkids.org

Overview

The Children's Museum of Boston is the second largest and oldest museum of its kind in the nation, and houses many exhibitions that focus on early childhood development. Four themes that the museum concentrates on are art, culture, science, and technology. Its cultural collection has approximately 30,000 objects representing the daily lives of diverse people and cultures around the world. The natural history collection contains over 10,000 specimens of rocks, fossils, shells, minerals, birds, mammals, and reptiles. The museum's mission is to help children understand and enjoy the world in which they live, and develop respect for others and the natural world.

Directions and Hours

From north: Take I-93 south to exit 23. At the end of the ramp, make your first left onto High Street. Go left at the second light onto Congress Street. Go two blocks, cross the bridge, and the museum will be on your left. Continue two more blocks to Farnsworth Street, where you can turn left for the parking garage.

From south: Take I-93 north to the Downtown/Mass Pike/Chinatown exit. Bear left toward downtown Boston. At the end of the ramp, turn left onto Kneeland Street. Go one block and make a right onto Surface Street. Go through several lights, past the Federal Reserve Building, then make a right onto Congress Street. Cross the bridge, and the museum will be on your left. Continue two more blocks to Farnsworth Street, where you can turn left for the parking garage.

From west: take I-90 (Mass Pike) east to the end. Take the Downtown Boston/ South Station exit. At the end of the ramp, go straight onto Surface Street. Go through several lights, past the Federal Reserve Building. Make a right onto Congress Street. Cross the bridge, and the museum will be on your left. Continue two more blocks to Farnsworth Street, where you can turn left for the parking garage.

The use of public transportation is strongly recommended because the museum is located in a busy part of the city. If you choose to drive, discounted parking is available with validation at the Farnsworth Garage. Rates are $8 Monday-Friday, and $5 on weekends.

The museum is open year round 10:00-5:00 Sunday-Thursday, and 10:00-9:00 on Friday. It is handicap accessible.

Admission and Membership

$7 for adults, $6 for seniors, $5 for children over 2, $2 for one-year-olds, and free for infants under one. Membership is $45/year for a family.

What to See

In addition to their permanent collections, four to six new displays are added annually. There are exhibits on environmental issues and New England's Native Americans. The museum also has a Japanese house and a representation of what grandparents' houses might have looked like when they were growing up. Hands-on activities include a bubble display, a kidstage, weaving, and Supermercado (a Spanish grocery store). Playgrounds include the New Balance Climb, the Smith Family Playscape, the Science Playground, Arthur's World, and Boats Afloat.

The museum has a gift shop, and visitors can eat at McDonald's (next door) and Bethany's.

While You're in the Area

The Boston Tea Party Ship (p. 331) and The Boston Aquarium (p. 291) are both nearby.

Civil War Museum at Memorial Hall

198 Main Street
Monson, MA 01057
(413) 267-4100

Overview

The Civil War Museum at Memorial Hall is one of the most intact G.A.R. (Grand Army of the Republic) meeting houses in the state. It was dedicated in 1884.

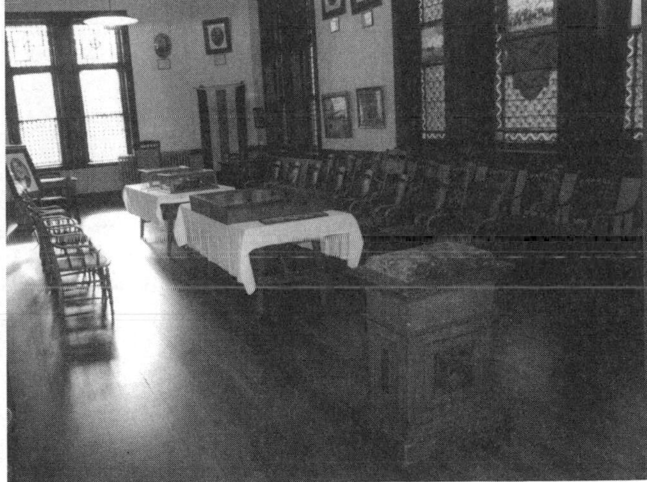

Interior of G.A.R. Hall. Photo by Dennis Swierad.

Directions and Hours

Take Route 90 (Massachusetts Turnpike) to exit 8, Palmer, and turn right onto Route 32. Follow Route 32 into Monson. Route 32 is Main Street.

Or, take Route 84 to the exit for Route 32. Follow Route 32 into Monson.

The museum is open Memorial Day, Fourth of July, Veteran's Day, and by appointment, and will be handicap accessible by the fall of 2001.

Hours: 1:00-3:00.

Admission and Membership

Admission to the museum is free.

What to See

The G.A.R. hall still has all of its original furnishings and decorations. It is a time capsule of the 1884-1924 period when the Civil War veterans had their meetings there. There is also a small collection of Civil War memorabilia.

There is no gift shop or café, but there are restaurants within walking distance.

While You're in the Area

The Keep Homestead Museum (p. 268), Jacob Thompson House (p. 333), Bellman's Antique Fire Apparatus Museum, and the Norcross Wildlife Sanctuary (p. 334) are also in the area.

Codman House "The Grange" (SPNEA)

36 Codman Road
PO Box 429
Lincoln, MA 01773
(781) 259-8843
www.spnea.org

Overview

Overlooking farms and pleasure grounds, this gentleman's country seat was a powerful force in the lives of five generations of the Codman family. In the 1790s, John Codman carried out extensive improvements to the original Georgian house and surrounding grounds. Each generation of Codmans to live here left their mark, and the estate that was originally a country retreat gradually came to symbolize the family's distinguished past.

Directions and Hours

Take Route I-95/128 to Route 2 west. Travel 4.5 miles then turn left on Route 126 south. After crossing the railroad bridge, turn left onto Codman Road. The house is on the left. The property may also be reach by Commuter Rail from North Station in Boston.

The house museum is open June 1 through October 15. The museum tour requires climbing stairs, walking, and standing. Please contact the museum to make any special arrangement.

Hours: Wednesday through Sunday, 11:00 A.M. to 5:00 P.M. Tours are at 11:00, 12:00, 1:00, 2:00, 3:00 and 4:00 P.M.

Admission and Membership

$5 for adults, $4.50 senior citizens, ½ off for students and children 6-12. Children 5 and under, SPNEA members, and residents of Lincoln are free. AAA members receive a 2 for 1 discount. SPNEA membership is $35/year for individuals and $45/year for a household. Membership includes free admissions to 35 properties and museums across New England.

What to See

The interior, richly furnished with portraits, memorabilia, and art works collected in Europe, preserve the decorative schemes of every era, including those of noted interior designer Ogden Codman, Jr. The grounds feature a hidden Italianate garden, ca. 1900, with perennial beds, a sunken fence, fountains, statuary, and a pool filled with water lilies, as well as an English cottage garden, ca. 1930.

Codman House offers school programs, group tours, and public programs. Summer programs include an Antique Vehicle Show in July and an Artisans' Fair in September. Please call or write for details.

While You're in the Area

Nearby attractions and museums include the SPNEA's Gropius House (p. 254) and the DeCordova Museum and Sculpture Park (p. 239).

Coffin House (SPNEA)

14 High Road
Route 1A
Newbury, MA 01951
(978) 462-2634
www.spnea.org

Overview

Coffin House chronicles the evolution of domestic life in rural New England over three centuries. The structure began as a simple dwelling built in the post-medieval style. Tristram Coffin and his family lived, cooked, and slept in two or possibly three rooms; their possessions were few. About 1700, the house was more than doubled in size to provide living space for a married son and his family. As the family grew, partitions were added and lean-tos built so that different generations could continue to live together under one roof.

Directions and Hours

From I-95: Take Route 113, Newburyport, which turns into Route 1A (High Road). Follow Route 1A for 3.3 miles. The house is on right, before the church.

The house museum is open June 1 through October 15.

Hours: Saturday and Sunday, 11:00 A.M. to 5:00 P.M. Tours are at 11:00, 12:00, 1:00, 2:00, 3:00 and 4:00 P.M.

Admission and Membership

$5 for adults, $4.50 senior citizens, ½ off for students and children 6-12. Children 5 and under, SPNEA members, and residents of Newbury are free. AAA members receive a 2 for 1 discount. SPNEA membership is $35/year for individuals and $45/year for a household. Membership includes free admissions to 35 properties and museums across New England.

What to See

In 1785, two Coffin brothers legally divided the structure into two separate dwellings, each with its own kitchen and living spaces. With rooms from the seventeenth, eighteenth, and nineteenth centuries, Coffin House depicts the impact of an expanding economy and new concepts, such as the notion of privacy, architecture, and modes of living.

Coffin House offers school programs, group tours, and public programs.

While You're in the Area

Nearby attractions and museums include the SPNEA's Spencer-Peirce-Little Farm (½ mile away) (p. 315), the old burying ground of Newbury across the street, the Parker River National Wildlife Refuge on Plum Island (an excellent place for bird watching), the Custom House Maritime Museum (p. 332), and the Cushing House Museum (p. 332).

Cogswell's Grant (SPNEA)

60 Spring Street
Essex, MA 01929
(978) 768-3632
www.spnea.org

Overview

Cogswell's Grant was the summer home of Bertram K. and Nina Fletcher Little, preeminent collectors of American decorative arts in the mid twentieth century. Through her research and innumerable publications, Mrs. Little charted new areas of American folk art (which she preferred to call "country arts"), such as decorative painting, floor coverings, boxes, and New England pottery.

Directions and Hours

From Route 128: Take exit 15. Turn left onto School Street and follow to the junction with Route 133. Turn left onto 133 west (Main Street). Pass the intersection of Route 22, then turn right onto Spring Street and go to the end of the street.

The house museum is open June 1 to October 15.

Hours: Wednesday-Sunday, 11:00 A.M. to 5:00 P.M. Tours are at 11:00, 12:00, 1:00, 2:00, 3:00 and 4:00 P.M.

Admission and Membership

$10 for adults, $9.50 senior citizens, ½ off for students and children 6-12. Children 5 and under, SPNEA members, and residents of Essex are free. AAA members receive a 2 for 1 discount. SPNEA membership is $35/year for individuals and $45/year for a household. Membership includes free admissions to 35 properties and museums across New England.

What to See

In 1937, the Littles purchased this eighteenth-century farmhouse overlooking the Essex River as a family retreat and place to entertain. They restored it carefully, trying to preserve original eighteenth-century finishes and faithfully documenting their work. In over 50 years of collecting, they sought works of strong character, and in particular favored objects with their original finishes and New England histories. They decorated the house for visual delight rather than historical accuracy. The result is rich in atmosphere and crowded with collections of things—primitive paintings, redware, painted furniture, stacked Shaker boxes, weathervanes and decoys—that have since come to define the country look.

Cogswell's Grant offers group tours and public programs. Please call or write for details.

Cogswell's Grant does have a gift shop.

While You're in the Area

Nearby attractions and museums include the Salem Witch Museum (p. 335), the Salem Maritime National Historic Site (p. 309), the House of Seven Gables (p. 333), and the Phillips Trust House (p. 319).

Collection of Historical Scientific Instruments

Science Center, B-06, 1 Oxford Street
Cambridge, MA 02138
(617) 495-2779
www.fas.harvard.edu/~hsdept/chsi

Overview

The Science Center's collection contains approximately 20,000 artifacts, including early scientific instruments dating back to the fifteenth century. It also houses a collection of rare books and prints related to scientific instruments and their history.

Directions and Hours

The museum is located on the Harvard College campus in Harvard Square, Cambridge. The museum is open year round and is handicap accessible.

Hours: daily 9:00-5:00 and by appointment for research.

Admission and Membership

Admission is free.

What to See

The Collection of Historical Scientific Instruments is composed of instruments purchased by Harvard for teaching and research, but others have been added since 1949 to cover subjects important in the history of science. The core of the collection is the considerable number of instruments that survived from a large order placed with London makers in 1764 after a disastrous fire destroyed the philosophical (scientific) apparatus and the College Library. This collection is one of three in the world where the majority of the instruments can be identified by their date of purchase and and their use; Harvard Archives has bills, correspondence with the makers, lecture notes, and research reports that combine to establish their history. The instruments illustrate the development of a broad range of subjects, including astronomy, surveying, horology, meteorology, physics, electricity, biology, geology, and navigation.

There is a café on the first floor of the Science Center.

While You're in the Area

The Harvard Natural History Museum (p. 258), the Peabody Museum of Archaeology and Ethnology (p. 335), and several other museums are located on the Harvard campus.

The Colonel John Ashley House (Trustees of Reservations)

Cooper Hill Road
Sheffield, MA 01222
(413) 298-3239 or (413) 229-8600
www.thetrustees.org

Overview

The Colonel John Ashley House was a center of social, political, and economic life in Western Massachusetts during the 1700s. The abolition of slavery in America was strengthened in the celebrated 1781 court battle that freed the Ashleys' slave Mumbet.

Directions and Hours

From Route 7 south in Sheffield: Turn right onto Route 7A and follow for ½ mile. Turn right onto Rannapo Road and follow for 1½ miles then turn

Trustees of Reservations

Who we are: The Trustees of Reservations is a member-supported nonprofit organization formed for charitable purposes to preserve, for public use and enjoyment, landscapes of exceptional scenic, historic, and ecological value in Massachusetts and to protect special places across the state. The organization was founded in 1891 by a small group led by landscape architect Charles Eliot, a protégé of Frederick Law Olmsted. Witnessing the dramatic loss to development of large amounts of land in the Boston area, this group successfully campaigned for the establishment of what became the first private, statewide conservation and preservation organization in the nation.

What we do: The Trustees of Reservations works to enhance and extend the Commonwealth's system of protected lands through acquisition of new reservations and lands associated with existing reservations, conservation restrictions on private land, landowner assistance, statewide planning, collaboration, and legislative advocacy.

Management of reservations is guided by a three-fold commitment to protecting scenic, historic, and ecological resources, providing public access, and maintaining a high quality visitor experience. Natural resource protection is achieved through inventory, monitoring, and research, habitat conservation and management, habitat restoration, and rare species protection. Protection of cultural resources entails research, preservation, exhibition, and interpretation of historic buildings, structures, landscape features, and fine and decorative arts.

What we protect and why: The Trustees of Reservations conserves over 22,000 acres of land across the state comprising 87 reservations and protects nearly 13,000 acres of private land on which the organization holds conservation restrictions.

These landscapes include hills, mountains, and ridges; forests and woodlands; lakes, ponds, and bogs; river gorges, waterfalls, and flood plains; islands, rocky coastline, beaches, and sand dunes; marshes, grasslands, heath, and swamp; farms and agricultural land; prehistoric and relic industrial sites; and historic houses, designed landscapes, and gardens.

Together, these reservations offer a wide range of recreational opportunities, such as bird watching, nature study, canoeing and kayaking, boating and sailing, cross-country skiing, snow shoeing, fishing, hiking, horseback riding, picnicking, swimming, pond skating, and tours. Over 200 public events, programs, and activities are held year-round. Several reservations offer overnight B&B accommodation and can be rented for meetings and functions.

How we are supported: As a nonprofit organization, we rely for support entirely upon membership dues, contributions, grants, reservation receipts, special events, and endowments. We enjoy the support of hundreds of volunteers and over 25,000 members. For membership information, call (978)921-1944 or join online at www.thetrustees.org.

right onto Cooper Hill Road.

The house is open from Memorial Day weekend-Columbus Day weekend and on holidays. It is not handicap accessible.

Hours: Saturday-Sunday 1:00 to 5:00 P.M.

Admission and Membership

Adults $5, children $2.50. There is a .50 cent discount for seniors. Free for Trustees of Reservations members. Membership is $40/year for an individual, $60/year for a family, $30/year for students and senior citizens, and $50/year for a family of students and senior citizens. Benefactor membership is $100/year for a contributing, $150/year for a supporting, $300/year for a sustaining, and $600/year for a sponsor.

What to See

The Ashley House has a collection of antique furniture, tools, and redware that illustrates how America gained independence from England. In the Ashley Study in 1773, local residents drafted a statement of individual rights known as the Sheffield Declaration. Visitors can enjoy 400 acres of neighboring Bartholomew's Cobble.

There is a small gift shop but no café. Visitors can eat in the center of Sheffield or bring a picnic and eat on the grounds.

While You're in the Area

Other museums or interesting attractions nearby include other Trustees of Reservations properties such as The Mission House (p. 277) and Naumkeag (p. 289), as well as Sheffield Historical Society (p. 312) and Bartholomew's Cobble (p. 331).

Lantern hung in the North Church on the night of Paul Revere's ride in April 1775. Photo courtesy of the Concord Museum.

Concord Museum

200 Lexington Road
PO Box 146
Concord, MA 01742
(978) 369-9609 or (978) 369-9763
www.concordmuseum.org

Overview

The Concord Museum is the one place where all of Concord's remarkable past is brought to life through artifacts from the museum's outstanding collection, rarely seen images, period room settings, and audio presentations, and creative hands-on activities. Concord was the site where the American Revolution began, and the home of some of the most important writers of the American literary renaissance. Museum highlights include "Why Concord?"—six history galleries accompanied by a film—and *Exploring Concord*; a nationally significant collection of decorative arts, featuring Concord-made clocks, silver, and furniture. Changing exhibitions on Concord history and American culture are offered throughout the year.

Directions and Hours

The Concord Museum is easily accessible from

Route 495, Route 128 via Route 2. It is located at the intersection of Lexington Road and Cambridge Turnpike, ¼ mile East of Concord Center. The Museum's entrance is on Cambridge Turnpike; parking is free.

The museum's hours for January-March are Monday-Saturday 11:00-4:00, and Sunday 1:00-4:00 P.M. From April-December, hours are Monday-Saturday 9:00-5:00, and Sunday 12:00-5:00. The museum is closed on Thanksgiving, Christmas, and Easter. It is handicap accessible.

Admission and Membership

Admission is $7/adults, $6/seniors and students with a valid ID, $3/children, and $16/families. Membership is $35 for an individual, $45 for a family, $100 for Associates, and $500 for benefactors; corporate rates are available on request. Admission is free for members.

A joint ticket for the Concord Museum, Orchard House, and the Old Manse is available for $17/adult, $14/senior or student, $8/child, and $45/family. Not all museums have to be visited on the same day.

What to See

The Concord Museum collection includes the lantern that signaled Paul Revere's famous ride; Emerson's study where he wrote his influential essays; the world's largest Thoreau's possessions, including the desk on which he wrote *Civil Disobedience* and *Walden*; and native American stone tools.

Special programs include lectures and discussions with renowned speakers; family-oriented Sunday afternoon concerts, walking tours, storytelling, crafts, living history, and other children's programming (for over 13,000 children a year); a holiday "Family Trees" exhibition; and a "Picnic in the Park" on the Fourth of July. A summer camp, vacation week activities, and Summer teacher training workshops are also sponsored annually.

The Concord Museum Shop features reproductions and adaptations of American decorative arts, many from the museum's collection. The museum offers a café during the holiday exhibition and living history teas during the winter months.

While You're in the Area

Other area attractions include the Minutemen National Historical Park; the Orchard House, home of the Alcotts and *Little Women* (p. 335); the Old Manse, Emerson House (p. 335), and Walden Pond.

Connecticut Valley Historical Museum

Springfield Museums at the Quadrangle
Corner of State and Chestnut Streets
Springfield, MA 01103
(413) 263-6800, ext. 312
www.quadrangle.org

Overview

The museum exhibits decorative objects and domestic artifacts highlighting the history of the Connecticut River Valley since 1636. The museum's Genealogy and Local History Library contains tens of thousands of books, photos, and microforms, and literally millions of manuscripts and documents.

Directions and Hours

From the North: Take I-91 south to exit 7. Turn left onto State Street, and proceed for three blocks.

From the South: Take I-91 north to exit 4. Stay on Columbus Avenue to State Street. Turn right, and proceed for three blocks.

From the East: Take the Massachusetts Turnpike (I-90) to exit 6 (I-291). Exit at Dwight Street (exit 2B), and turn left. Follow Dwight to State Street. Turn left, and proceed for three blocks.

From the West: Take the Massachusetts Turnpike to I-91 south and follow I-91 south to exit 7. Turn left on State Street, and proceed for three blocks.

Parking is free in the Springfield Library and Museums' lots on State Street and on Edwards Street. The first floor of the museum is handicap accessible.

Hours: Wednesday-Friday, noon-5:00 P.M. (also Tuesdays in July and August), Saturday and Sunday, 11:00 A.M.-4:00 P.M.

Admission and Membership

Museum Admission: $6 for adults; $3 for seniors and college students with ID; $2 for children ages 6-18; free for children under 6 and members. Admission fee includes entry into all four Quadrangle museums. Group tours/rates are available by appointment: 413-263-6800, ext. 472. Membership: Single $35; dual $45; household $60.

The Springfield Museums at the Quadrangle

220 State Street
Springfield, MA 01103
(413) 263-6800
www.quadrangle.org

At Springfield's historic Quadrangle, four distinctive museums and a major urban resource library are clustered around a tree-shaded green. Visitors can explore masterpieces of American, European, and Asian paintings; sculpture and decorative arts; plus dinosaurs, wildlife exhibits, arms and armor, "please touch" exhibits for children, an aquarium, a planetarium, a genealogy research library, early aviation artifacts, and much, much more. Museums at the Quadrangle include the Springfield Museum of Fine Arts (p. 316), the George Walter Vincent Smith Art Museum (p. 248), the Springfield Science Museum (p. 318), and the Connecticut Valley Historical Museum (p. 235). Admission ($6 for adults; $3 for seniors and college students with ID; $2 for children ages 6-18; free for children under 6 and members) includes entrance to all four museums.

What to See

Collections of furniture, manufactured goods, toys and games, paintings and graphics tell the stories of the people who have settled and developed the region since 1636. Changing exhibitions highlight the artists, industrialists, financiers, craftsmen, politicians, and workers whose spirit of innovation has shaped the history and traditions of Springfield, the Connecticut River Valley, and the nation.

The genealogy and local history library includes 30,000 books, 40,000 photographs, 36,500 microforms and 2,500,000 manuscripts and documents. New England family histories, local business records, photographs, diaries and maps illustrate the region's past. An extensive collection of French Canadian genealogical research materials, the Church of Jesus Christ of Latter Day Saints' family search collection on CD-ROM, and census and immigration records attract researchers and family historians from around the country.

Exhibitions include "Looking Backward to the Future: Springfield Visions and Visionaries" (through July 15, 2001), an exhibition celebrating the vision, creativity, and inventiveness of Springfield in honor of the Millennium; "Growing Your Family Tree: Sources of Family History" (through September 2, 2001), which explains how to construct a family tree, where to look for information, what kinds of information you can expect to find, how to use census and immigration records, and reliable genealogy resources on the Internet.

Each summer the four Museums on the Quadrangle and the library present a six-week series of "Meet Your Neighbors Days"—programs celebrating the traditions of some of the cultural communities in the region. Activities include music and dance performances, storytelling, and traditional crafts. Programs are offered Tuesday through Friday beginning the second week of July.

From mid-November 2001 to mid-January 2002, the four Springfield Museums will display "Holiday Enchantment," an exhibit containing Victorian dollhouses and room boxes loaned by private collectors; early-twentieth-century cast iron toys; mirrors decorated in holiday style by area artists; and toy soldiers including lead figures, cardboard stand-ups, and handmade soldiers arranged in a variety of set-ups. Also a selection of early-nineteenth-century to mid-twentieth-century dolls, including milliners' dolls, American folk dolls, ethnic figures, and character dolls such as Teddy Roosevelt, Uncle Sam, Charlie Chaplin, and Shirley Temple will be on view.

From October through April, the four Springfield Museums present a series of Sunday programs which feature exciting live performances, art-making workshops, gallery games, special guests and more. Themes include dinosaurs, Dr. Seuss's birthday party, seasonal holidays, and more. Programs are offered approximately twice a month. For information, call 413-263-6800, ext. 312.

During each of the three weeks of school vacation (December, February, and April), the museums offer extended hours and a variety of craft and art workshops, performances, and demonstrations for children and families. The Museum School offers a wide range of courses for children and adults. Children's classes include hands-on science programs, studio art classes, and summer art and science camps. Adult classes include art history courses and studio art classes in painting, sculpture, calligraphy, drawing, and much more. History-related courses include genealogy and traditional American crafts.

There is no gift shop. Lunch and snacks are available in the Café on the Quadrangle.

While You're in the Area

Also on the Quadrangle are the Springfield Museum of Fine Arts (p. 316), the George Walter Vincent Smith Art Museum (p. 248), and the Springfield Science Museum (p. 318). Other nearby museums include the Springfield Armory National Historic Site (p. 335) and the Basketball Hall of Fame (p. 288).

Crane Museum of Papermaking

30 South Street
Dalton, MA 01226
(413) 684-6380

Overview

Crane & Co. is a 200-year-old family owned and operated business on the banks of the Housatonic River which produces fine cotton papers. The museum, housed in the company's historic 1844 stone mill, was first opened as a museum in 1930. The building's interior, with its rough-hewn oak beams, colonial chandeliers,

Photo courtesy of Crane Museum of Papermaking, Dalton, Massachusetts.

multi-paned windows, and wide oak floorboards fastened with wooden dowels, resembles the Old Ship Church in Hingham, Massachusetts with its distinctive "ship's hull" architecture.

Directions and Hours

From the Mass Pike, take exit 2 to Route 8 north. Follow Housatonic Street until you see the museum on your left.

The museum is open from June to mid October, Monday-Friday 2:00 to 5:00 P.M.

It is partially handicap accesible.

Admission and Membership

Admission is free.

What to See

In addition to making the paper used for US currency since 1879, Crane makes papers intended for bonds, stock certificates, and correspondence. The museum houses collections of photographs and paper related items. On display is a papermaking mold and a video about the company and the making of paper. Also of interest is a ledger with an entry noting the sale of currency paper in 1775 to Paul Revere. This paper was used to print the continental currency that financed the American Revolution.

The museum does not have a gift shop or a café, but there are restaurants nearby.

While You're in the Area

Other museums nearby include the Norman Rockwell Museum (p. 292), the Berkshire Museum (p. 331), and the Massachusetts Museum of Contemporary Art (MOCA, p. 276).

Danforth Museum of Art

123 Union Avenue
Framingham, MA 01702
(508) 620-0050

Overview

Established as a grassroots organization in 1975 by a committed group of citizens, the Danforth Museum of Art is housed in a retired school building and features a collection of primarily nineteenth and twentieth century art. There is also a fine arts school for children and adults. The museum is dedicated to the celebration and creation of art and to educating the public through its collection of American art, temporary exhibits of contemporary artists, classes, workshops, and a variety of community outreach programs.

Directions and Hours

From Mass Pike west: Get off at exit 13 (Framingham and Natick). After the tollbooth bear right onto Route 30 west; continue on Route 30 about 1 mile (you will pass Lechmere/Filene's Basement, Shoppers World, then McDonalds and Burger King) until you reach a light at the junction with Route 126. Make a left turn onto Route 126 (Concord Street) and continue 1 mile until you reach downtown Framingham (approximately four or five traffic lights). On your right you will see the town hall (called the Memorial Building), a large cream colored building with pillars in front. Take a sharp right turn around the building at the three-way intersection in front of the building onto Union Avenue (you will be going back north). Go two blocks to the first light, take a right onto Lexington Street and another quick right into the museum parking lot in front of the building. Enter the museum through the main entrance in the center of the building facing Union Avenue.

From Worcester and points West: Take the Mass Pike east. Get off at exit 12 and make a right turn after the toll booth onto Route 9 east toward Boston. You'll come to a set of lights at Temple Street, with Finally Michael's restaurant on your right; continue straight through on Route 9 for another ½ mile to the Framingham/Edgell Road exit. At the end of the off ramp, turn right at the light onto Main Street. This becomes Union Avenue after you pass the Minute Man statue on your left in the small square. Proceed on Union Avenue about 1 mile; make a left turn onto Lexington Street and then a quick right into the museum parking lot in front of the museum. Enter the museum through the main entrance in the center of the building facing Union Avenue.

The museum is open year round. There is handicap access to the museum.

Hours: 12:00-5:00 P.M. Wednesday-Sunday.

Admission and Membership

Adults $3, $2 for seniors, and children under 12 free. Special group rates are available. Membership is $30/year for individuals and $45/year for families.

What to See

The permanent collection specializes in nineteenth and twentieth century American art, featuring well-known artists such as Gilbert Stuart, James McNeill Whistler, Albert Beirstadt, Yves Tanguy, Karl Knaths, Thomas Hart Benton, and Faith Ringgold. The Danforth is also home to the Marks Fine Arts Library, with holdings of over 4,000 volumes of art reference books and materials.

Throughout the year the museum welcomes the public to various special events, such as the renowned Danforth Craft Festival, Spring Gala, and Dan4th Fridays concert series. Public programs such as Family days provide families with opportunities for hands-on experience in the arts. The interactive Ballou Family Junior Gallery offers families a place to learn and play together. The museum also offers Art on the Move curriculum kits and tour programs for hundreds of area school children throughout the year. An active Gallery Educator program involved interested volunteers in learning about art and leading tour groups through one of many available interpretive programs.

Nearly 5,000 children and adults participate in 350 day and evening fine arts and art appreciation classes and workshops offered annually at the Danforth Museum School. Special full-day art programs are available for children during school vacations.

There is a small gift shop. There is no café but there are several restaurants in walking distance located in downtown Framingham.

While You're in the Area

Other interesting places to visit while you are in the area are the Framingham Historical Society's Old Academy Museum (p. 334) and the Mazmanian Gallery at Framingham State College (p. 334).

DeCordova Museum and Sculpture Park

51 Sandy Pond Road
Lincoln, MA 01773
(781) 259-8355
www.decordova.org

Overview

The DeCordova Museum and Sculpture Park is the only major art museum in New England dedicated exclusively to the exhibition, interpretation, and collection of modern and contemporary American art. The Museum accomplishes this mission by focusing primarily, though not exclusively, on the art of the New England region. With nearly 4,000 students annually, DeCordova's Museum School is the most extensive non-degree granting studio art program in the state. DeCordova's year-round outdoor sculpture park is the largest in New England and one of the few in America committed to the changing exhibition of large-scale contemporary sculpture.

Directions and Hours

Take the Mass Pike or I-93 to Route 128/I-95. Head north to exit 28B, Trapelo Road/Lincoln. You will drive approximately 3 miles to Lincoln center, a five road intersection. Sandy Pond Road is directly ahead. The DeCordova Museum is approximately half a mile on your right.

Take 495 to Route 2. Take Route 2 to Route 126 South. Take a left on Baker Bridge Road. At the end of Baker Bridge Road, take a right. DeCordova is less than a quarter mile on the left. The museum also has large "trailblazing" signs on I-128/95 and Route 2 to help guide visitors to the Museum.

The museum is open year round, Tuesday to Sunday from 11:00 A.M. to 5:00 P.M. The Museum is fully handicapped accessible. The Park has a natural terrain and some areas may be difficult for physically challenged individuals.

Admission and Membership

Admission is $6 per person, $4 for senior citizens, students, and youth 6-12. Children age 5 and under and Lincoln residents are free.

What to See

DeCordova's permanent collection features more than 2,200 works primarily by New England artists. In addition to these exhibitions, DeCordova curates exhibitions of national and regional artists (individual and group) and shows traveling exhibitions. In addition to these interior exhibitions, the Sculpture Park features more than 75 works that are changed regularly.

Normally held the second Sunday in June, DeCordova's Art in the Park Festival and Art Sale features more than 100 artists and craftspeople selling their work. In addition, family hands-on art activities, special performances, and a variety of food complete this large festival. Art in the Park is scheduled for June 10, 2001 and June 9, 2002.

DeCordova offers ongoing studio art classes, workshops, and a Summer Art Camp for children. In addition, in-school programs, field trips, and Sculpture Park activities are offered.

The Store@DeCordova features an array of one-of-a-kind gifts, jewelry, wearable art, children's hands-on art items and other creative products, artist supplies, and glassware. With spectacular views of Flint's Pond, The Café@DeCordova provides light lunches, desserts, and coffee specialty drinks.

While You're in the Area

The town of Lincoln has many walking trails.

The Dickinson Homestead

280 Main St.
Amherst, MA 01002
413-542-8161
www.amherst.edu/~edhouse

Overview

The Dickinson Homestead (c.1813), was home to Emily Dickinson, one of America's most intriguing and remarkable poets. She was born there on December 10, 1830, and lived there for all but 15 years of her life. Visitors can walk through the house and grounds where she attended to her domestic chores, cultivated plants in her garden and conservatory, and composed almost 1800 poems. Emily Dickinson died at the Homestead on May 15, 1886.

Directions and Hours

From points South: Take I-91 north to exit 19. Turn right onto Route 9 East. Go about five miles to Amherst town limits. Once in Amherst continue straight on Route 9 (about one mile) to the traffic light at the top of the hill. Turn left onto south Pleasant Street toward Amherst Center. At next light, turn right onto Main Street. Homestead is 3/10 mile ahead on the left at 280 Main Street.

From points North: Take I-91 south to exit 25. Follow Route 116 south about 11.5 miles to the junction of Route 9 east and 116 south. Turn left onto Route 9E /116S. Continue ½ mile into Amherst town limits and follow the directions above.

From the Boston area: take the Mass Pike (I-90) west to exit 4. Take I-91 North. Follow directions above from I-91 North.

Admission to the Homestead is by guided tour only. Reservations are advised, especially on Saturdays, but walk-ins are welcome, space permitting. Grounds are open daily, 10:00-5:00. The first floor of the Homestead is handicap accessible.

Admissions and Membership

Admission is $5/adults, $4/seniors and students, and $3/children 6-18. Children under 6 are free. There are no provisions for membership.

What to See

The house and grounds offer an intimate glimpse of Emily Dickinson's life.

There is a poetry walk on the second Saturday in May, during which participants visit various sites in Amherst associated with Emily Dickinson, and hear her poetry read aloud. A special open house is held in honor of the poet's birthday each year.

While You're in the Area

Other Dickinson related sites in Amherst include the West Cemetery at Triangle Street, the Jones Library, and the Frost Library at Amherst College. Additional places of interest in the area include the Mead Art Museum (p. 334), Pratt Museum of Natural History (p. 335), Amherst History Museum (p. 331), the National Yiddish Book Center (p. 336), and The Evergreens.

The Discovery Museums

177 Main Street
Acton, MA 01720
(978) 264-4200
www.ultranet.com\~discover

Overview

The Discovery Museums are two separate but complementary museums filled with exciting, interactive exhibits for children of all ages using focused spaces and hands-on activities inviting exploration and discovery. The Children's Museum is a 100-year-old Victorian home with 10 theme rooms especially for pre-schoolers and toddlers. The Science Museum invites exploration and experimentation designed for school age children through adults.

Directions and Hours

From Route 2 west: Continue on Route 2 as you go around the Concord rotary for about 2 miles. You will see the exit for Route 27. Take Route 27 south toward Maynard—not Acton. The museums are one mile down on the left.

From Route 495 heading south: Take Route 2 east. After approximately 5 miles there is an exit for Route 27, Acton/Maynard. Take Route 27 south toward Maynard—not Acton. The museums are one mile down on the left.

From Route 495 heading north: Take exit 28 for Route 111 Boxborough/Harvard. Take a left toward Boxborough. Go approximately 5 miles to the second set of lights which is the intersection of Route 27. Turn right onto Route 27. The museums are about ½ mile down on the left.

From Route 27 heading north: Go straight on Route 27. Go through Maynard, watching for signs to Acton. Entering Acton you will go over a small bridge. On your left you will notice a large building that appears to be a church but is really a music store. The museums are about ¼ mile further on your right.

MBTA Commuter Rail: The Discovery Museums are located a short walk from the South Acton MBTA Commuter Rail (the "purple" line). From the parking lot, take a right onto Central Street, and a left onto Route 27 (North). The museums are about ¼ mile further on your right.

The museum is open year round. The Children's Museum is partially handicapped accessible and the Science Museum is fully accessible.

School year hours: Tuesday, Thursday, and Friday 1:00-4:30 P.M., Wednesday 9:00 A.M. to 6:00 P.M., and Saturday and Sunday 9:00 A.M. to 4:30 P.M. Closed Monday. Summer hours:

Tuesday-Sunday 9:00 A.M. to 4:30 P.M. Closed Monday. Group visit hours are by reservation only. Call (978) 264-4200 ext. 11.

Admission and Membership

Children's Museum *or* Science Museum: $7 per person age 1 and older, seniors $6. Both museums, same day: $10 per person, $9 for seniors. Memberships: $55/year for a two person membership, $15/year for each additional family member.

What to See

The Children's Discovery Museum is a wonder-filled Victorian house with rooms, corridors, and even closets creatively transformed into ten hands-on exhibit areas especially for toddlers and pre-school children and their families. There are theme areas: in the Dinosaur Room you will find real fossils to touch and puppets to create your own dinosaur adventure, in the Chain Reaction Room balls roll along the walls, in the Water Discovery Room kids splash away and experiment, in the Ocean Space area children add to the wall-sized mural, in the Woodland Room a New England forest is recreated with animals and trees, and in the Safari Room guests climb in native thatched roof huts. Other areas are the Adventure Fort Room, a Rainbow Room, Bessie's Play Diner, a Discovery Ship, and the Infant Corner.

The Science Discovery Museum is a creative and challenging interactive experience designed especially for school aged children and is filled with innovative theme spaces for hands-on experimenting with the basic sciences and math. The exhibits begin outside with the large parabolic whisper dishes and a variety of sound and music exhibits. Inside are water and vapor whirling vortexes as well as rock and mineral explorations. As you enter the museum the Tower Court rises three stories up. The Inventor's Workshop is an area where children can put together their own creations and inventions with recycled materials. The Light and Color Room explores kaleidoscopes, optical illusions, colored shadows, reflections, and filters. There is also a Science Circus where kids test physical phenomena, a Math Room that contains wall-sized probability boards, an Electricity Room with circuit tables to explore the basic concepts of electricity and magnetism, a Sound and Communications Area, and the Earth Science Area that looks at minerals and fossils.

Scout Workshops are available for groups of 10-15 scouts and up to 3 adults for $135.00, and $5.00 for each additional person. This price includes one workshop and a visit to the Science Museum. If you have more than 18 scouts, you must purchase an additional workshop for $45.00.

There is a small gift shop at the Science Museum. The museum does not have a café but provides visitors with a list of nearby restaurants.

While You're in the Area

The Acton Arboretum is a lovely garden/walking area, about 1.5 miles from the Discovery Museums. Other nearby attractions include the Fruitlands Museum (p. 246) and the Concord Museum (p. 234).

Fisher Museum of Forestry

Harvard Forest
324 North Main Street (Route 32)
Petersham, MA 01366-0068
(978) 724-3302
www.lternet.edu/hfr

Overview

The Fisher Museum was built to house the Harvard Forest dioramas, 23 three-dimensional models depicting the changes in the central New England landscape and forest during the past 300 years, as well as forest management practices and conservation. The dioramas not only illustrate landscape history and conservation but are also examples of the art of modeling.

Fisher Museum Diorama, Harvard Forest, Petersham, Massachusetts.

Directions and Hours

Take Route 2 to exit 17 (Route 32). Take Route 32 south toward Petersham Center. Go three miles to the sign for the Fisher Museum/ Harvard Forest on the left.

From the Worcester area take Route 122 north to Petersham then Route 32 north. Go three miles north to Petersham Center; signs for Fisher Museum/Harvard Forest will be on the right. The Fisher Museum is a brick building up a short driveway.

The museum is open year round and is handicap accessible.

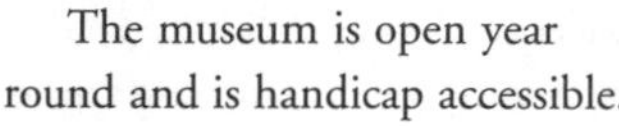

Hours: Year round: Monday-Friday 9:00 A.M. to 5:00 P.M. Closed holidays. In addition: May-October Saturday and Sunday 12:00-4:00 P.M.

Admission and Membership

Donations are requested.

What to See

In addition to the dioramas, the museum features many exhibits about the history, ecology, and conservation of New England forests based on results of past and current research at Harvard Forest. Two self-guided nature trails and miles of hiking trails wind through the adjacent 1,000 acre forest. These trails connect the dioramas and exhibits in the museum to the landscape outside and provide examples of some of the ways the forests are being studied.

The museum also contains a visitor-operated video station. These videos, which are changed monthly, focus on different aspects of the local environment.

There is a small shop with items related to Harvard Forest. Sandwiches and soup are available at Petersham Country Store, three miles down Route 32 in the center of Petersham.

While You're in the Area

Also in Petersham are several properties with hiking trails owned and maintained by the Trustees of Reservations (p. 234), including the Swift River Reservation, North Common Meadow, and the Brooks Woodland Preserve.

Fogg Art Museum (Harvard University Art Museums)

32 Quincy Street
Cambridge, MA 02138
(617) 495-9400
www.artmuseumes.harvard.edu

Overview

The Fogg Art Museum, which opened to the public in 1895, is Harvard's oldest art museum. Around its Italian Renaissance courtyard, based on a sixteenth-century façade in Montepulciano, Italy, are galleries illustrating the history of Western art from the Middle Ages to the present, with particular strengths in Italian early Renaissance, British pre-Raphaelite, and nineteenth-century French Art. The Wertheim Collection, housed on the second floor of the Fogg, is one of America's finest collections of Impressionist and post-Impressionist work, and contains many famous masterworks. The Boston area's most important collection of Picasso's work is also to be found at the Fogg, as well as outstanding collections of photographs, prints, and drawings.

Directions and Hours

From the West: On Mass Pike eastbound (Route 90) take the Cambridge/Allston Exit on the left side of the road. Proceed through the Toll Booth toward Cambridge/Somerville. At the end of the ramp is the intersection of River Street and Soldier's Field Road. Cross Soldier's Field Road and go over the Charles River to Memorial Drive. Make a left onto Memorial Drive to J.F.K. Street. Take a right onto J.F.K. and follow J.F.K. through Harvard Square. Bear right at the lights after Harvard Square into a tunnel. Stay in the right lane onto Broadway. The Fogg is on the right and the Sackler is on the left. Quincy Street is the first right outside of the tunnel.

From the East and South: Take Route 93/3 North to the Mass Pike—90 West. Take the Allston/Cambridge Exit to Memorial Drive to J.F.K. Street. Follow the West instructions from here.

From the North: Take I-93/Route 1 South to the Cambridge Memorial Drive Exit. From Memorial Drive go to J.F.K. Street. Follow above directions from here.

The museum is open year round except on national holidays. Handicap access to the Fogg is on Prescott Street at the entrance of the Fine Arts Library. Hearing assistants are available for lectures, gallery talks, and other events. Please make arrangements beforehand by calling Visitor Services at (617) 495-8286.

Hours: Monday through Saturday 10:00 A.M. to 5:00 P.M., Sunday 1:00-5:00 P.M.

Admission and Membership

Admission is $5, free for individuals all day Wednesday and Saturday morning 10:00 A.M. to noon. Groups of 8 or more must schedule in advance and pay regular admission fees. Admission discounts are $4 for seniors, $3 for students, and free for children under 18. Membership information: if you join the Friends of the Harvard Art Museums visitors get free admission to three museums, invitations to openings and other special events, subscriptions to the Calendar and the Review, as well as reduced rates for lectures, seminars, concerts, and other events. Membership categories are: Individual $35, Senior Citizen and Students $25, Dual $50, Contributor $100, Junior Fellow for ages 21 to 40 single $100/Dual $150, Forbes Fellow $500, Patron $1000, and Corporate or Institutional $1000.

What to See

The drawings collection is the finest and most comprehensive of any university art museum in the United States. It ranks among the three most important public collections in this country along with the Metropolitan Museum of Art and the Morgan Library. The paintings collection consists of nearly 2,000 Western paintings with Italian Renaissance, nineteenth-century French, nineteenth-century British, and American paintings, including the largest holdings of Copley in the country.

The sculpture collections consists of just over 1,000 works of sculpture and includes significant holdings of French and Spanish Romanesque stone pieces, Italian Renaissance placquettes, an important group of seventeenth-century Roman terracotta studies by Bernine and others, and nineteenth-century French sculpture, notably Rodin and Barye.

The museum's collection of Decorative Arts comprises approximately 3,750 works. The main strengths in this collection are seventeenth- and eighteenth-century American and English silver, eighteenth century Wedgewood pottery, seventeenth- and eighteenth-century clocks, Renaissance Limoges enamels, tapestries, and considerable quantities of European and American furniture.

The collection of photography contains 8,700

photographs, 4,000 of which are by Ben Shahn. Other holdings include over 400 "imperial" size photographic portraits by Mathew B. Brady, Ansel Adams, Sarah Choate Sears, Edward Steichen, and Aaron Siskind. The collection also houses extensive collections of nineteenth century portraiture in the form of cartes-de-visite and cabinet photographs, numbering 17,700 images, made by hundreds of European and American studios.

The print collection is particularly strong in Old Master etchings, engravings, and woodcuts, with extensive representation of the works of masters such as the early Italian engravers, Schongauer, Dürer, Rembrandt, Ostade, Castiglione, Ribera, Testa, Canaletto, and Goya.

The museum also has one of the best collections in the country of reproductive engravings of the sixteenth and nineteenth centuries. The nineteenth- and twentieth-century collections include outstanding examples by Blake, Turner, Constable, Daumier, Manet, Degas, Toulouse-Lautrec, Picasso, and Munch.

In the twentieth century the museum's particular strength is in German Expressionist works, with substantial representations of Kirchner, Nolde, Heckel, and Schmidt-Rottloff. The Fogg is also beginning to assemble a selection of post-WWII prints, especially of the American School of the 1960s to the present.

There is a museum shop located in the Fogg courtyard that is open daily until 4:45 P.M. The shop offers reproductions of many of the images in the collection, as well as catalogues, art books, and related merchandise. The Sert Gallery Café presents art museum visitors with a relaxing atmosphere overlooking the Harvard campus and a variety of fresh and unique sandwiches, pasta and rice salads, and scones, cookies, and other sweet tooth's delight. It is open 8:30 A.M. to 3:30 P.M. Monday through Friday

While You're in the Area

Harvard Square and the city of Cambridge are rich in history and filled with multiple activities from museums and historical sites to cafés and restaurants.

Frederick Law Olmsted National Historic Site

99 Warren Street
Brookline, Massachusetts 02445
(617) 566-1689
www.nps.gov/frla/home.htm

Overview

Frederick Law Olmsted (1822-1903) is recognized as the founder of American landscape architecture and the nation's foremost parkmaker. Olmsted moved his home to suburban Boston in 1883 and established at "Fairsted" the world's first full-scale professional office for the practice of landscape design. Over the course of the next century, his sons and successors expanded and perpetuated Olmsted's design ideals, philosophy, and influence.

Directions and Hours

From Boston and points east: Follow Huntington Avenue SW from the area of Copley Square. As you cross from Boston into Brookline beneath the Jamaicaway overpass, Huntington Avenue becomes Route 9/Boylston Street. Continue on Route 9/Boylston. At the third major intersection, turn left onto Warren Street and follow 1/8 mile to intersection of Warren and Dudley Streets. Olmsted NHS is on right-hand corner with NPS sign and distinctive archway at house front.

From I-95/Rt.128 and points west: From I-95/Route 128, take exit 20 (Route 9 East, Boston/Brookline). Follow Route 9/Boylston St. for approximately 5 miles. Pass through a major intersection with Lee Street and continue on Boylston, passing the Brookline Reservoir on right side. At next intersection, turn right from Boylston onto Warren Street and follow 1/8 mile to intersection of Warren and Dudley Streets. Olmsted NHS is on right-hand corner with NPS sign and distinctive archway at house front.

By Bus: Use MBTA Bus #60 and exit at intersection of Boylston and Warren Streets in Brookline. Follow Warren Street 1/8 mile to Olmsted NHS.

By Subway: Use MBTA Riverside "D" Green Line and exit at Brookline Hills station. Turn right out of station and follow sidewalk to Cypress Street. Continue on Cypress across the Boylston Street intersection. Turn right on Walnut Street. Turn left on Warren Street and continue to the intersection with Warren and Dudley Street where Olmsted NHS is located.

The site is open year round, Friday-Sunday 10:00-4:30. Groups may visit at other times by advance notice. The site is partially handicap accessible.

Admission and Membership

Admission is free.

What to See

Visitors may tour the recently restored "Fairsted" historic landscape and a century-old design office that remains virtually unchanged from the days when the Olmsted firm's activity was at its height. Housed within the office complex are nearly 1,000,000 original design records detailing work on many of America's most treasured landscapes including the U.S. Capitol and its House Grounds; Great Smoky Mountains and Acadia National Parks; Yosemite Valley; New York's Central Park; and whole park systems in cities such as Seattle, Boston, and Louisville. The Olmsteds also played an influential role in the creation of the National Park Service.

Upcoming special programs include the Olmsted Celebration of July 4, both at Olmsted NHS and Jamaica Pond, a segment of Olmsted's "Emerald Necklace" of parks in Boston.

The site has a gift shop, but no café. There are many restaurants located in nearby Brookline Village.

While You're in the Area

The John F. Kennedy National Historic Site (p. 266), Museum of Transportation (p. 334), and Longyear Museum (p. 233) are all nearby.

Fruitlands Museums

102 Prospect Hill Road
Harvard, MA 01451
(978) 456-3924
www.fruitlands.org

Overview

Located in rural Harvard, Massachusetts, Fruitlands has an unparalleled view across the Nashua River valley. The successive landscapes covering 210 acres contain direct evidence of human interactions with the land for at least 5,000 years as well as ecological history dating back 250 million years. The collections in four museum buildings and along three miles of meadow and woodland trails tell stories and explore evidence about New England cultures and their expression in the landscape. These stories are based on local geology, ecology, Native American evidence before and after colonization, colonial settlers, market farmers, and the religious, utopian and aesthetic seekers who populated New England during the turbulent nineteenth century. Each of these stories represents a distinct and defining moment in the evolving history of New England culture, and of New England landscapes.

Directions and Hours

Fruitlands is located 30 miles west of Boston, approximately six miles from the junction of Routes 495 and 2. From points east and west take Route 2 to exit 38A, bear right off the ramp, take first right onto Old Shirley Road. Fruitlands is ahead two miles on the right.

Open daily 10:00 A.M.-5:00 P.M. from mid-May through October. Fruitlands has limited handicap accessibility.

Admission and Membership

$8 for adults, $6 for seniors and students with a valid college I.D., $4 for children ages 4-17, and free for children under age 4. Discounts are given for groups of 10 or more. Members are admitted free of charge. Membership is $25/year for seniors/students, $40/year for individuals, $65/year for families, $125/year for Fruitlands Patrons, and $350/year for Fruitlands Benefactors.

WGBH members receive $2 off admission; AAA members receive $1 off admission.

What to See

Fruitlands Farmhouse is the site of the utopian community founded by Concord philosopher Bronson Alcott, who brought his family here in 1843 to "live off the fruit of the land." The Willard Farm Site is an archaeological site that explores how frontier farmers cleared and cultivated the land.

Visitors can explore the world's first Shaker museum and learn how Harvard's Shakers sought to live a heavenly life in an earthly world.

The Indian Museum focuses on the lifeways of native New England peoples from over 10,000 years ago to the present, while the Native American Hunting/Gathering Ground explores Native land management and manufacturing practices in this recreated landscape of the Native homeland pre-1656.

The Picture Gallery displays dramatic Hudson River School landscapes and the distinctive portraits of New England's nineteenth-century rural folk.

More than three miles of walking trails lead through varied terrain, showcasing diverse ecosystems, plant and animal life, and intriguing geologic formations. Visitors can also enjoy unparalleled views of the Nashua River Valley, the Oxbow National Wildlife Refuge, Mount Wachusett (to the west) and Mount Monadnoc (to the north) from the Pergolas, the site of founder Clara Endicott Sears' former estate and gardens.

Guided museum tours are offered at select times. Other attractions include craft demonstrations, family activities, and changing exhibits. Special programs include Founder's Day the first Saturday in June; a Summer Concert Series with The Concord Band, Thursday evenings mid-June through July; and the Harvest Festival the third Sunday in September.

A museum store is located in the reception center. The store has a selection of Museum related gifts, books, games, toys, and reproductions. Luncheon, drinks, desserts, and Sunday brunch are served in the Tea Room. Picnic facilities are also available for use with museum admission.

While You're in the Area

Fruitlands is located in the midst of the Freedom's Way Heritage Area, the geographic region comprised of the central Massachusetts uplands and river valleys and six New Hampshire towns. These 40 towns are unique in their contributions toward the evolution of the landscape of American history with proposed cultural heritage trails which will link these towns from Arlington to Gardner, Massachusetts and Nashua, New Hampshire. Harvard's many fruit orchards are also located within a short distance of the museum.

Fuller Museum of Art

455 Oak Street
Brockton, MA 02301
(508) 588-6000
www.fullermuseum.org

Overview

The Fuller Museum of Art is the largest visual arts organization in southeastern Massachusetts. Established in 1969, the museum's mission is "to teach and inspire the awareness, knowledge, and creation of art as a unifying force in a changing society." It is housed in an award-winning contemporary building that includes five exhibition

Photo courtesy of the Fuller Museum of Art

galleries, a library, a café, an auditorium, and two art studios where classes for adults and children are offered.

Directions and Hours

From Boston: Take Route 93 south to 24 south. Take exit 18B to Route 27 north. Turn right onto Oak Street at the light. The Museum is located one mile down on the left.

From Cape Cod: Take Route 495 north to Route 24 north. Take exit 18B to Route 27 north. Turn right onto Oak Street at the light. The Museum is located one mile down on the left.

From Providence: Take I-95 north to Route 495 south to Route 24 north. Take exit 18B to Route 27 north. Turn right onto Oak Street at the light. The Museum is located one mile down on the left.

The museum is open year round, Tuesday-Sunday, noon-5:00, and is handicap accessible.

Admission and Membership

$5/adults, $3/seniors and students, under 18 free. Parking is free. Membership is $30/year for Individuals, $40/year for a household.

What to See

The FMA holds a permanent collection of nearly 5,000 objects focusing on American art of the nineteenth and twentieth centuries, with an emphasis on regional art of New England. Included are paintings, sculpture, prints, drawings, photographs, and decorative arts. The museum hosts as many as 12 exhibitions each year, featuring contemporary art, historical American art, craft and art from outside mainstream traditions.

Upcoming programs include a site-specific installation dealing with the environment and history of the FMA and an exhibition featuring major print works from the collection of Dr. Eli Goldman and Judith Strull, which showcases some of the best print work in contemporary art.

The FMA has an active Education Department that plans programs at the museum and in the community. Lectures, field trips, concerts, and family programs are offered frequently. Kid's Corner provides activities for preschoolers at a free weekly drop-in program. Special after-school activities are offered to elementary and middle school youngsters in theater and studio arts.

There is a gift shop and a café (open Thursday and Friday noon-2:00).

While You're in the Area

The FMA is adjacent to D.W. Field Park, overlooking Upper Porter's Pond.

George Walter Vincent Smith Art Museum

Springfield Museums at the Quadrangle
Corner of State and Chestnut Streets
Springfield, MA 01103
(413) 263-6800, ext. 312
www.quadrangle.org

Overview

Opened in 1896 in the style of an Italian palazzo, the museum houses the huge collection of its Victorian namesake. Displays include Japanese arms and armor, screens, lacquers and ceramics; Islamic rugs and decorative arts; one of the largest collections of Chinese cloisonné outside Asia; a Shinto wheel shrine; a Classical Casts gallery; and nineteenth century American paintings.

Directions and Hours

From the North: Take I-91 south to exit 7. Turn left onto State Street, and proceed for three blocks.

From the South: Take I-91 north to exit 4. Stay on Columbus Avenue to State Street. Turn right, and proceed for three blocks.

From the East: Take the Massachusetts Turnpike (I-90) to exit 6 (I-291). Exit at Dwight Street (exit 2B), and turn left. Follow Dwight to State Street. Turn left, and proceed for three blocks.

From the West: Take the Massachusetts Turnpike to I-91 south and follow I-91 south to exit 7. Turn left on State Street, and proceed for three blocks.

Parking is free in the Springfield Library and Museums' lots on State Street and on Edwards Street. The museum is handicap accessible.

Hours: Wednesday-Friday, noon-5:00 P.M. (also Tuesdays in July and August), Saturday and Sunday, 11:00 A.M.-4:00 P.M.

Admission and Membership

Museum Admission: $6 for adults; $3 for seniors and college students with ID; $2 for children ages 6-18; free for children under 6 and members. Admission fee includes entry into all four Quadrangle museums. Group tours/rates by appointment only: 413-263-6800, ext. 472. Membership: Single $35; dual $45; household $60.

What to See

The museum features stained glass windows by the Louis Comfort Tiffany Company, along with the exquisite decorative arts and paintings collected by G.W.V. Smith and his wife, Belle, during the late nineteenth century. A continuously running video introduces visitors to the Smiths and their museum.

Through July 1, 2001, the museum is displaying "Style and Symbol: Chinese Cloisonné from the Permanent Collection." The museum's collection of 150 examples of cloisonné is one of the largest outside of China. The Smith collection includes examples from the Ming Dynasty (1368-1644), considered to be the golden age of cloisonné, as well as fine pieces from the Ching Dynasty (1644-1912). The exhibit includes household objects such as vases, candlesticks, dishes, and jars, as well as religious items such as incense burners, altar sets, and Buddhist figures.

From October through April, the four Springfield Museums present a series of Sunday programs which feature exciting live performances, art-making workshops, gallery games, special guests and more. Themes include dinosaurs, Dr. Seuss's birthday party, seasonal holidays, and more. Programs are offered approximately twice a month. For information, call 413-263-6800, ext. 312.

From mid-November 2001 to mid-January 2002, the four Springfield Museums will display "Holiday Enchantment," an exhibit containing Victorian dollhouses and room boxes loaned by private collectors; early-twentieth-century cast iron toys; mirrors decorated in holiday style by area artists; and toy soldiers including lead figures, cardboard stand-ups, and handmade soldiers arranged in a variety of set-ups. Also a selection of early-nineteenth-century to mid-twentieth-century dolls, including milliners' dolls, American folk dolls, ethnic figures, and character dolls such as Teddy Roosevelt, Uncle Sam, Charlie Chaplin, and Shirley Temple will be on view.

Each summer the four Museums on the Quadrangle and the library present a six-week series of "Meet Your Neighbors Days"—programs celebrating the traditions of some of the cultural communities in the region. Activities include music and dance performances, storytelling, and traditional crafts. Programs are offered Tuesday through Friday beginning the second week of July.

During each of the three weeks of school vacation (December, February, and April), the museums offer extended hours and a variety of craft and art workshops, performances, and demonstrations for children and families. The Museum School offers a wide range of courses for children and adults. Children's classes include hands-on science programs, studio art classes, and summer art and science camps. Adult classes include art history courses and studio art classes in painting, sculpture, calligraphy, drawing, and much more. History-related courses include genealogy and traditional American crafts.

There is no gift shop. Lunch and snacks are available in the Café on the Quadrangle.

While You're in the Area

Also on the Quadrangle are the Springfield Museum of Fine Arts (p. 316), the Springfield Science Museum (p. 318), and the Connecticut Valley Historical Museum (p. 235). Other nearby museums include the Springfield Armory National Historic Site (p. 335) and the Basketball Hall of Fame (p. 288).

The Gibson House Museum music room. Photo courtesy of the Gibson House Museum.

The Gibson House Museum

137 Beacon Street
Boston, MA 02116
(617) 267-6338

Overview

Built in 1859, The Gibson House Museum is an amazingly detailed Victorian townhouse complete with the Victorian and Edwardian era furnishing of three generations of Gibsons who lived there from 1860-1954. The museum offers an "upstairs-downstairs" tour featuring servants' areas, a laundry room, a butler's pantry, and a kitchen along with formal interiors.

Directions and Hours

Take the Mass Pike (I-90) east to the Copley Square exit (Dartmouth). Take a right on Boylston, a left on Berkley, and then a right on Back Street. Take a right on Beacon Street or take Storrow Drive to the Arlington exit and then take a right onto Beacon Street.

The museum is open Wednesday-Sunday from May 1-October 31, with tours at 1:00, 2:00, and 3:00 P.M. From November 1 to April 30 the museum is open Saturday and Sunday only at 1:00, 2:00, and 3:00 P.M. The museum is not handicap accessible.

Admission and Membership

$5 per person. Children under 10 must be accompanied by an adult. Groups of 12 or more must make prior arrangements. Please call the museum for group rates. Membership is $35/year for an individual, $50/year for two individuals who live at the same address. For more membership options please contact the museum.

What to See

The Gibson House Museum has an outstanding collection of textiles including wallpapers, upholstered furniture from the late nineteenth to the early twentieth century, as well as a painting collection including works by William Morris Hunt, Samuel T. Coleman, and Jane Stuart, and unsigned mid-nineteenth century copies of old master paintings. The museum also has a collection of porcelain and a small collection of clothing from the 1870s to the 1920s and over 1,000 nineteenth and early twentieth century books (many of which are first editions), period lighting fixtures, and kitchen utensils.

The museum holds an annual Summer Twilight Talk Series every Thursday evening from late June to early August. Topics include Architecture, decorative arts, costumes, photography, and book collecting. The reception is at 5:30 P.M., with the talk starting at 6:15 P.M.

The museum does not have a gift shop or a café but Café de Paris is on Arlington Street, between Newbury and Boylston.

While You're in the Area

Other museums or interesting attractions nearby include the Nichols House Museum (p. 335), the Prescott House, and the First Harrison Gray Otis House (p. 257).

Gore Place

52 Gore Street
Waltham, MA 02453-6866
(781) 894-2798
www.goreplace.org

Overview

Gore Place, an early nineteenth century estate and house museum, was the home of Christopher Gore—the seventh governor of Massachusetts, a U.S. senator, and the first district attorney of Massachusetts—and his wife Rebecca Amory Payne Gore. Visitors may tour the 1806 mansion, visit the working farm with its heritage breeds of sheep, goats, chickens, and turkeys, and walk the grounds and gardens of this 45 acre estate. Gore Place offers a year-round calendar of concerts, festivals, lectures, and educational programs.

Directions and Hours

Gore Place is located in Waltham, Massachusetts just off Route 20. From I-90 (Mass Pike) take exit 17 to Watertown Square. Turn left onto Route 20 (Main Street) and drive 1¼ miles to Gore Street.

From Route 128/I-95 exit 26 to Route 20 east (Main Street) 3½ miles to Gore Street.

The mansion is shown by guided tour April 15-November 15, Tuesday through Saturday, 11:00-5:00, and Sunday, 1:00-5:00 (last tour begins by 4:00 P.M.). It is partially handicap accessible. Tours may be arranged Mondays and in the off-season by calling the office.

Admission and Membership

Tours: $7 adults, $6 seniors and students, and $5 children 5-12. Group rates available. Grounds open free to the public during posted hours.

Discounts are offered to seniors, WGBH Members, groups of 20 or more, Massachusetts Teachers Association members, and for Waltham and Watertown Library passes.

Membership is $25 Individual, $40 Dual/Family, $100-249 Sustaining, $250-999 Sponsor (or Corporate), $1000 Patron.

The 1806 mansion at Gore Place, south front. Reprinted by permission of Gore Place Society, Waltham, MA.

What to See

The grounds and gardens of this 45 acre estate are available free of charge during posted hours. The 1806 mansion is available for guided tours and offers viewings of 21 rooms decorated and furnished in period style. The working farm has heritage breeds of sheep, goats, chickens, and turkeys. In addition, Gore Place offers a full roster of concerts, festivals, lectures, and educational programs.

The Sheepshearing Festival, the last Saturday in April, is an outdoor event now in its fourteenth year featuring demonstrations of shearing, herding, spinning, weaving, a large crafts fair, and live music. Last year's attendance was over 4,000. The Candlelight & Holly Celebration in December features a ground floor, self-guided tour of 12 rooms decorated for the holidays, live music, refreshments, and a holiday gift boutique.

The Education Department offers special programs for Scouts and local schools and homeschoolers. In addition, there are children's concerts and puppet shows.

The Museum Shop offers publications and merchandise related to the mission. There is no café, but Waltham is famous for its ethnic restaurants including Mother India and Ciro's on Moody Street.

While You're in the Area

Gore Place is located just a few miles from the Lyman Estate (p. 272), The Robert Treat Paine House (p. 322) and the Charles River Museum of Industry (p. 332).

The Great House at Castle Hill (Trustees of Reservations)

The Crane Estate
290 Argilla Road
Ipswich, MA 01938
(978) 356-4351
www.thetrustees.org

Overview

The Great House at Castle Hill was the summer home of Chicago industrialist Richard Teller Crane Jr. and family. The 59-room Stuart-style mansion was designed by Chicago architect David Adler. The mansion is the focal point of the greater complex of early twentieth century buildings and designed landscapes to create one of America's grandest and most intact Country Place Era estates. In 1998, Castle Hill was designated a National Historic Landmark.

The Crane Estate is comprised of more than 2,100 acres along the the Ipswich and Essex River estuaries, including Crane Beach, Crane Wildlife Refuge, and the National Historic Landmark, Castle Hill. All are open to the public year-round for outdoor study, leisure and recreation. The Great House hosts private functions, such as weddings, and offers numerous seasonal and year-round public events, such as concerts, lectures, and house tours. It also serves as the Northeast Regional Office of The Trustees of Reservations, a member-supported, nonprofit conservation organization which owns some 87 reservations across the state of Massachusetts.

Directions and Hours

Route I-95/Route 128 North to exit 20A, Route 1A North. Follow 1A eight miles to Ipswich. Right onto Route 133 East for 1.5 miles to Northgate Road. Left on Northgate .5 mile to Argilla Road. Right on Argilla 2.3 miles. Follow signs to Crane Beach/Castle Hill.

House tours are offered seasonally, Wednesdays and Thursdays from the end of May through early October. Historic landscape tours are offered on Thursdays, June through August. Weddings/functions take place April-November. Offices are open year-round, Monday-Friday from 9:00-5:00. The museum is partially handicap accessible.

Admission and Membership

Adult $7, child (6-12) and senior/student $5. Group rates are available. Free for Trustees of

Reservations members. Membership is $40/year for an individual, $60/year for a family, $30/year for students and senior citizens, and $50/year for a family of students and senior citizens. Benefactor membership is $100/year for a contributing, $150/year for a supporting, $300/year for a sustaining, and $600/year for a sponsor.

What to See

The Great House library has an overmantel carving by English Baroque sculptor Grinling Gibbons; throughout the house is other salvaged architectural woodwork from English homes Cassiobury Park and 75 Dean Street, London. The home and interiors were designed by Chicago architect David Adler, rare for this area of the country. Also not to miss are the state-of-the-art Crane Co. bathrooms, all with marble and sterling fixtures, that best reflect the 1928 period of the house.

Surrounding the house are designed landscapes by such noted landscape architects as The Olmsted Brothers and Arthur Shurcliff. A complex of other outbuildings on the property were designed by Shepley, Rutan & Coolidge in the Italian style.

Castle Hill offers special "Afternoon Tea and Tour" programs at The Great House. Visitors can enjoy an hour-long tour of The Great House followed by high tea in the formal Dining Room. Please call for dates, times, and reservations.

In the summer, the museum offers Thursday night picnic concerts on the lawn, a Fourth of July family celebration, and other events. In September, Castle Hill hosts the "Concourse d'Elegance" antique car show.

Children's parties are offered at Christmas, and the Fourth of July celebration and picnic concerts are family oriented.

There is no gift shop or café. Visitors can find a variety of eateries in downtown Ipswich.

While You're in the Area

The Ipswich Historical Society (p. 333) has two House museums, the Whipple House and Heard House. The Trustees owns The Paine House at Greenwood Farm (p. 322) in Ipswich, a First Period House on its original site surrounded by salt marsh farm. Interpretation focuses on American First Period Architecture, archaeology at The Paine House, and the Colonial Revival.

Green Briar Nature Center and Jam Kitchen

6 Discovery Hill Road (Off Route 6A)
East Sandwich, MA 02537
(508) 888-6870
www.thorntonburgess.org

Overview

The Green Briar Nature Center and Jam Kitchen, located in a rural setting on the shores of Boiling Springs Pond in East Sandwich, offers live animal exhibits, an award-winning wildflower garden, nature trails, and a 1903 jam kitchen. Today the jam kitchen is a "living museum," where visitors may view jams, jellies, and preserves still being made using century-old methods.

Directions and Hours

Take Route 6 (Mid-Cape Highway) to exit 3. Turn east on Quaker Meetinghouse Road and go ½ mile to Route 6A. Turn left onto Route 6A and go ½ mile to Discovery Hill Road on the left. The Green Briar sign is right there on Route 6A.

Green Briar Nature Center is open year round. The building is handicap accessible. Hours: Monday-Saturday 10:00 A.M. to 4:00 P.M., Sunday 1:00-4:00 P.M. from mid-April through December. Winter hours from January to mid-April are Tuesday-Saturday 10:00 A.M. to 4:00 P.M.

Green Briar Jam Kitchen is open mid-April through December. Hours: Monday-Saturday 10:00 A.M. to 4:00 P.M., Sunday 1:00-4:00 P.M.

Gropius House. Photo courtesy of the Society for Preservation of New England Antiquities.

Admission and Membership

Admission is by donation, with a suggested donation is $1 per person. Bus tours are welcome with advance reservations. The fee is $1 per person. Green Briar is owned and operated by the Thornton W. Burgess Society. Membership in the society is $20/year for an individual, $30/year for a family.

What to See

In addition to the natural history exhibits and the working jam kitchen, Green Briar Nature Center offers a variety of programs for children, families, and adults throughout the year. Unique among these programs are jam-making workshops in the old-fashioned kitchen. Special events during the year include the annual Herb Festival, Strawberry Festival, Farmer's Market, and Thanksgiving Celebration. A complete schedule of programs is available upon request.

There is a gift shop that offers jams, jellies, and preserves made at Green Briar as well as a variety of nature-related items. Sun-cooked jams are a special product.

While You're in the Area

Green Briar Nature Center and Jam Kitchen is two miles from Sandwich Village, where three museums are located: the Thornton W. Burgess Museum (p. 323), the Sandwich Glass Museum (p. 310), and Heritage Plantation (p. 333).

Gropius House (SPNEA)

68 Baker Bridge Road
Lincoln, MA 01773
(781) 259-8098
www.spnea.org

Overview

Walter Gropius (1883-1969), founder of the Bauhaus and a leading proponent of modern architecture, built this house in 1938 as his family home after coming to the United States to teach at the Graduate School of Design at Harvard. Though modest in scale, the house was revolutionary in impact. Gropius combined traditional elements of New England vernacular architecture—clapboard, brick and fieldstone—with innovative material rarely used in domestic settings—glass block, acoustical plaster, chromed banisters, and welded steel. Every detail of the house, from its careful siting on a rise overlooking orchard and fields, to the arrangement of furniture and works of art, was planned to form an integrated whole. The interior features furniture designed by Marcel Breuer and produced at the Bauhaus and works of art by friends Lazslo Moholy-Nagy, Josef Albers, and Henry Moore.

Directions and Hours

From Route 2 west: Take Route 126 south. Turn left onto Baker Bridge Road.

From Route I-95/128: Take the Trapelo Road exit. Continue on Trapelo Road toward Lincoln. Cross Lincoln Road onto Sandy Pond Road then turn left onto Baker Bridge Road.

The Gropius House is open year round: June

1 to October 15, Wednesday-Sunday; October 16 to May 31, Saturday and Sunday. Tours are at 11:00 A.M., 12:00, 1:00, 2:00, 3:00, & 4:00 P.M.

Admission and Membership

$8 for adults, $7.50 senior citizens, ½ off for students and children 6-12. Children 5 and under, SPNEA members, and residents of Lincoln are free. AAA, WGBH, and Massachusetts Teachers Association members receive a 2 for 1 discount. SPNEA membership is $35/year for individuals and $45/year for a household. Membership includes free admissions to 35 properties and museums across New England.

What to See

The Gropius House has remained virtually unaltered over the years. It retains its furnishings, works of art, its decorative treatments, and its finish materials. The collection consists of one of the largest collections of Bauhaus furnishings outside of Germany. Among these are the double desk in the study, the furniture in the master bedroom and guest room, and the desk from Gropius's Bauhaus office. Other pieces were designed at the Bauhaus by faculty and students. These include the dining room set made by Marcel Breuer in the carpentry workshop in 1925. In addition, there are objects that the Gropiuses collected over time by other significant designers, including Eero Saarinen and Alvar Aalto.

Throughout the house artworks from the Gropius' collection are displayed. Like the furniture, the works on display evolved over time as the Gropiuses acquired new works or as they refined or shifted their presentation. There are works by Bauhaus masters, Joseph Albers, Alexander Schawinsky, Lazlo Moholy-Nagy, and Herbert Bayer, as well as works by well known artists of the modern movement Henry Moore, Juan Miro, and Dimitri Hadzi.

The Gropius House offers group tours, public programs, and special tours throughout the year. Please call or write for details.

A Visitor Center and museum shop are housed in the former garage. The museum has no café but there are a number of restaurants in the area.

While You're in the Area

Nearby attractions and museums include the Codman House (p. 230) and the DeCordova Museum and Sculpture Park (p. 239).

Hancock Shaker Village

Route 20
PO Box 927
Pittsfield, MA 01202
(413) 443-0188 or (800) 817-1137
www.hancockshakervillage.org

Overview

Hancock Shaker Village is a 200-year-old restored Shaker site situated on 1,200 acres of woodland, pasture, farm, and meadow. Twenty historic buildings contain the most comprehensive collection of Shaker furniture, tools, personal items, art, and artifacts of any Shaker site. Rural life in primarily the eighteenth and nineteenth centuries is presented through an interactive program of presentations, talks, tours, demonstrations, character portrayals, and changing exhibitions. The famous 1826 Round Stone Barn is the centerpiece of the working historic farm with heritage breeds of livestock and herb and heirloom vegetable gardens. To accommodate non-English speaking visitors, an orientation is subtitled and a walking tour is published in French, German, Spanish, and Japanese.

Directions and Hours

Hancock Shaker Village is located on Route 20, just west of the junction of Routes 20 and 41 in Pittsfield, Massachusetts. From the Mass Pike (I-90) take exit 1 to Route 41 north. Follow 41 until it meets with Route 20 west. The entrance to Hancock Shaker Village is about one mile west from the junction of Routes 20 and 41.

The museum is open year round but is closed on Thanksgiving, Christmas, and New Years Day. It is partially handicap accessible. Wheelchairs are available at no cost on a first-come first-served basis.

Hours: Late May-late October open daily from 9:30 A.M. to 5:00 P.M. Late October-Late May open daily from 10:00 A.M. to 3:00 P.M.

Admission and Membership

From late May-late October adults $13.50, children under 18 $5.50, children under 6 free, families (2 adults and any number of children under age 18) $33.50. Late October-Late May adults $10 for a guided tour and gallery access, $5 for gallery only, children under 18 free. Group rates are available. Membership is $50/year for a family/joint membership (2 adults and any number of children in your household under 18), and $35/year for an individual membership.

What to See

Hancock's collection of Shaker furniture artifacts is the largest of any Shaker site. Room setting exhibitions in 20 historic buildings show the daily life of the Shakers from the late eighteenth through the mid-twentieth centuries. The village's collection of rare Shaker art—or gift drawings, as they are known—includes *Tree of Life* by Hannah Cohoon. During the self-guided season (late May-late October) visitors explore the 20 historic buildings at their own pace. Staff give tours and talks about various aspects of Shaker life—daily life, religious practices, music, technology—in each of the Village's buildings. Traditional Shaker trades such as blacksmithing, spinning and weaving, oval box making, basket-making, chair seat weaving, and wood working are demonstrated in original workshops.

Hancock Village is the only site with a working water power system. Visitors can see a reproduction 1858 water turbine operate nineteenth century woodworking equipment in the recently restored Laundry/Machine Shop. Hands-on activities abound in the historic area including the kitchen, dairy, and woodworking shop.

Visitors should not miss the Hands-on History Discovery Center located in the 1910 barn. Visitors try Shaker crafts such as spinning and weaving, try on Shaker-style clothing, play with nineteenth century toys, or milk Mary Jane, a life-size replica of a Holstein cow. During guided tour season (late October-late May) visitors learn about Shaker life through a guided tour of selected buildings including the 1830 Brick Dwelling, Laundry/Machine Shop, Round Stone Barn, gallery exhibitions, video presentations, and a daily craft demonstration.

Special season events happen throughout the year such as ice harvesting in winter, plowing day and sheep shearing in spring, crafts and antiques in summer, and harvest activities in the fall.

Children's programming includes the Discovery Room and the Schoolhouse where kids meet an early twentieth century Shaker schoolteacher and take lessons.

There is a gift shop, a seasonal café, and a picnic area.

While You're in the Area

Other museums or interesting attractions nearby include the Berkshire Museum (p. 331), Arrowhead, the Berkshire Opera, Williams College Museum of Art (p. 326), Sterling and Francine Clark Art Institute (p. 320), the Williamstown Theatre Festival, the Massachusetts Museum of Contemporary Art (p. 276), Jacob's Pillow Dance Festival, the Tanglewood Music Festival, Shakespeare and Co., The Mount (p. 281), the Norman Rockwell Museum (p. 292), the Berkshire Botanical Gardens, Chesterwood, and the Berkshire Theatre Festival.

Harlow Old Fort House

119 Sandwich Street
Plymouth, MA 02360
(508) 746-0012

Overview

Sergeant William Harlow built this house in 1677 for his family of 10 and worked as a cooper, farmer, and soldier. Harlow House is one of three historic properties operated by the Plymouth Antiquarian Society, reflecting Plymouth life in the seventeenth, eighteenth, and nineteenth centuries.

Directions and Hours

Take Route 3 south to Route 44 east. Then take Route 3A south.

The museum is open in July and August and is not handicap accessible.

Hours: 10:00 A.M. to 4:00 P.M. Fridays only. Also open for special events and by appointment.

Admission and Membership

$4 adults, $2 children. Plymouth Antiquarian Society members and Plymouth residents are free. AAA Members get 50% off. Group rate is $6 per person. Memberships: $25/year for individuals, $40/year for families.

What to See

Costumed interpreters offer tours and demonstrate daily activities of Colonial American Life. Visitors can learn to dip candles, spin wool, or weave textiles.

An Annual Pilgrim Breakfast will be held on Sunday, July 8 2001 from 8:30-11:30 A.M. A hearty New England breakfast will be served al fresco on the grounds of an authentic Pilgrim era homestead. Costumed servers dish out fishcakes, eggs, baked beans, cornbread, and other tasty fare while strolling singers share songs, riddles, and seventeenth-century cheer. The admission fee benefits historic preservation.

A Children's Colonial Life Field Trip is available by reservation only and includes spinning, weaving, candle dipping, and other period activities. The recommended time is 1½ hours. The trip is suitable for children ages 7-13. Other children's programming includes Corn Planting and the Colonial Life Program.

The museum does have a gift shop. There are several restaurants within walking distance.

While You're in the Area

The Plymouth Antiquarian Society also operates Spooner House (p. 315) and Hedge House (p. 259) in Plymouth. Plymouth Rock, the Sparrow House Museum, and the *Mayflower II* (p. 306) are located nearby.

Harrison Gray Otis House (SPNEA)

141 Cambridge Street
Boston, MA 02114
(617) 227-3956
www.spnea.org

Overview

The Otis House, SPNEA's headquarters, exemplifies the elegant life led by Boston's governing class after the American Revolution. Harrison Gray Otis made a fortune developing nearby Beacon Hill, served as a representative in Congress, and later was mayor of Boston; he and his wife Sally were noted for their frequent and lavish entertaining. This was the first of three houses designed for the Otises by their friend Charles Bulfinch, the architect of the Massachusetts State House. Its design reflects the proportions and detail of the Federal style, which Bulfinch introduced to Boston.

Directions and Hours

From 93 north: Take exit 25. At the bottom of the exit ramp turn right and go up New Chardon Street to Cambridge Street. At Cambridge Street turn right. The Otis House is 1½ blocks ahead on the right next to the Old West Church.

From 93 south: Take exit 25. At the bottom of the ramp take a left onto Causeway Street. Go past North Station. At the Fleet Center set of lights go straight up the hill on Stamford Street. Turn right onto Cambridge Street. The Otis

House will be ½ block ahead on the right.

The house museum is open year round. It is not handicap accessible.

Hours: Wednesday-Sunday 11:00 A.M. to 5:00 P.M. Tours are at 11:00, 12:00, 1:00, 2:00, 3:00 and 4:00 P.M. The last tour is at 4:00 P.M.

Admission and Membership

$5 for adults, $4.50 senior citizens, ½ off for students and children 6-12. Children 5 and under, SPNEA members, and residents of Boston are free. AAA and WGBH members receive a 2 for 1 discount. SPNEA membership is $35/year for individuals and $45/year for a household. Membership includes free admissions to 35 properties and museums across New England.

What to See

The interior of the Harrison Gray Otis house provides insights into social, business, and family life, as well as the role played by household servants. The restoration of the Otis House, with its brilliantly colored wallpapers, carpeting, and high-style furnishings, is based on historical and scientific research.

Bengal Tiger, Harvard Museum of Natural History

The building houses SPNEA's Library and Archives (open to the public by appointment; free to SPNEA members).

Otis House offers group tours and public programs throughout the season. Programs include evening tours, walking tours of Beacon Hill, and special tours during Boston's Harborfest and First Night Celebrations. From May through October the house has a tour called "Magnificent and Modest: Beacon Hill Walking Tour." The tour runs every Saturday from 11:00 A.M. to 1:00 P.M. Reservations are required.

Otis House offers two school programs: "Unknown Hands" (social history of the early 1800s), and "Classical Times" (classical architecture).

There is a museum shop with books, reproductions, and gifts. There are several restaurants, bars, and cafés on Cambridge Street.

While You're in the Area

The Otis House is within easy walking distance of the Museum of Afro-American History (p. 282), the Nichols House Museum (p. 334), the State House, Quincy Market, and Faneuil Hall.

Harvard Museum of Natural History

26 Oxford Street
Cambridge, MA 02138
(617) 495-3045
www.hmnh.harvard.edu

Overview

The Harvard Museum of Natural History has 21 million specimens—ranging from one of the first discovered *Triceratops* to a 1,642 pound amethyst geode. Visitors can explore 17 galleries and a "garden" of glass flowers.

Directions and Hours

Take Route 93 or Route 1 south toward Boston, and take the exit for Storrow Drive/Cambridge. Storrow Drive west becomes Soldiers Field Road. Stay in the right lane to the exit for Harvard Square/Cambridge. Go straight through the lights at Memorial Drive onto JFK Street. Stay to the left of the fork and then get in the right lane to Massachusetts Avenue. At the lights at Everett Street, turn right and go to the next set of lights at Oxford Street.

Or, take Route 3 north and follow the above directions for Storrow Drive west.

Or, take Route 90 (Massachusetts Turnpike) east to the Cambridge/Allston exit, and follow the signs for Cambridge bearing to the right. Move to the left lane passing a 10-story hotel, then go straight through the light at the corner of the hotel. Turn left before the bridge onto an entrance ramp leading onto Storrow Drive. Then follow Storrow Drive to the Harvard Square/Cambridge exit on the right. Go straight through the lights at Memorial Drive onto JFK Street. Stay to the left of the fork and then get in the right lane to Massachusetts Avenue. At the lights at Everett Street, turn right and go to the next set of lights at Oxford Street.

The museum is open year round, and is handicap accessible.

Hours: daily 9:00-5:00.

Admission and Membership

$6.50 for adults, $5 for seniors and students, and $4 for children 3-18.

There are discounts for groups of ten or more when reservations are made.

What to See

The museum collections on view include the Mineralogical Museum, the Botanical Museum, and the Museum of Comparative Zoology. The botanical galleries feature the Ware Collection of Blaschka Glass Models of Plants.

Education programs for the family, include children's classes and adult education courses.

There is a gift shop. There is no café, but Harvard University and Harvard Square offer many places to eat.

While You're in the Area

Admission to the Harvard Museum of Natural History also grants admission to the Peabody Museum of Archaeology and Ethnology (p. 335).

Hedge House

126 Water Street
Plymouth, MA 02361
(508) 746-0012

Overview

The Hedge House is a Federal style home overlooking Plymouth Harbor built in 1809 by a merchant shipowner. Its unusual octagonal rooms are furnished with China Trade treasure along with American furniture, toys, and costumes reflecting Plymouth maritime history. Hedge House is one of three historic properties operated by the Plymouth Antiquarian Society, reflecting Plymouth life in the seventeenth, eighteenth, and nineteenth centuries.

Directions and Hours

From Expressway south on Route 3: take exit 6 to Route 44 east to Water Street.

The museum is open from June through October 6, 2001 and is not handicap accessible.

Hours: 10:00 A.M. to 4:00 P.M. Thursday, Friday, and Saturday.

Admission and Membership

$4 adults, $2 children. Plymouth Antiquarian Society members and Plymouth residents are free. AAA Members get 50% off. Group rates are available. Memberships: $25/year for individuals, $40/year for families.

What to See

Guided tours of Hedge House are available and

last for 30 minutes. An Antiquarian Summer Fair will be held at Hedge House on Saturday, August 4, 2001 from 10:00 A.M. to 3:00 P.M. The old fashioned summer fair on the Plymouth waterfront will allow visitors to hunt for bargains. Delicious baked goodies, attic treasures, gifts, jewelry, and children's activities will be available. A lobster luncheon will be served in the garden.

The museum does not have a gift shop or a café. Guests can eat anywhere on the Plymouth waterfront.

While You're in the Area

The Plymouth Antiquarian Society also operates Spooner House (p. 315) and Harlow Old Fort House (p. 256) in Plymouth. Plymouth Rock and Pilgrim Hall Museum (p. 304) are located nearby.

Higgins Armory Museum

100 Barber Avenue
Worcester, MA 01606
(508) 853-6015
www.higgins.org

Overview

The Higgins Armory Museum is the only institution in the Americas solely dedicated to arms and armor. The exterior of the building is an extremely rare example of an Art Deco glass and steel frame structure. The main gallery, the Great Hall, is fashioned after the medieval castles of Europe, with Gothic arches, a cobalt blue vaulted ceiling, and secretive archways.

Directions and Hours

From East: Take I-495 to I-290 West. Get off I-290 at exit 19, I-190 north. Take exit 1 onto Route 12 north. Follow Route 12 north on West Boylston Street for ¼ mile past the Greendale Mall. Stay in the right lane over the railroad bridge. Take the next right (sharp right) onto Barber Avenue. Travel less than ¼ mile to the Museum, a tall glass and steel building with pennants on the roof.

From South or West: Take Mass Pike to exit 10, I-290 east. Get off I-290 at exit 19, I-190 north. Take exit 1 onto Route 12 north. Follow Route 12 north on West Boylston Street for ¼ mile past the Greendale Mall. Stay in the right lane over the railroad bridge. Take the next right (sharp right) onto Barber Avenue. Travel less than ¼ mile to the Museum, a tall glass and steel building with pennants on the roof.

From North: Take I-190 south to exit 1. Follow Route 12 south a few yards to the Route 12 north turnaround on left. Pass the Greendale Mall on right. Stay in the right lane over the railroad bridge and follow directions above.

The armory is open year round, and is handicap accessible.

Hours: Tuesday through Saturday, 10:00-4:00; Sunday, noon-4:00; closed Mondays and select holidays.

Admission and Membership

$6.75 adults, $6 seniors, $5.75 ages 6-16, ages 5 and under free. Individual membership: $35. Family/dual membership: $45. Student/senior membership: $15. Group discounts are available.

What to See

Areas of the collection not to be missed include the fourth floor gallery, which contains a 4,000 year old rare Egyptian axe; Roman horse armor made of metal scales, which is one of only 3 surviving examples of Roman scale horse armor; and the most complete collection of Corinthian helmets in the USA.

The Great Hall contains 100 suits of armor in "castle" setting; jousting, foot combat, and Crusader displays; an extremely rare folding spetum (staff weapon) which belonged to the Rothschilds, was seized by the Nazis, and was eventually returned and sold to the Higgins; a small sword from late eighteenth century designed by Josiah Wedgwood and Matthew Boulton, with hilt decorations of jasperware and beaded, faceted steel cut to resemble diamonds; horse armor; rare staff weapons; and examples of Japanese, Tibetan, and African armor and weapons.

The Quest Gallery is a hands-on gallery where children can try on helmets and costumes, play chess and other period games, make a brass rubbing, and explore a medieval cottage.

Regular program offerings include "Saturdays at the Higgins," with a rotating schedule of scavenger hunts, films, costumed characters, and demonstrations/perfomances like Joan of Arc, Arms & Armor, fencing, and a re-enactment group of a medieval knight and his entourage.

Special events throughout the year include Founders Day in January, featuring special programs and free admission; Winter Ball in February; "Higgins Faire" medieval festival in May; "Haunted Days and Knights" Halloween celebration in October; "Live Birds of Prey" falconry demonstration in November; and a holiday festival in December.

Recent and upcoming programs include

"Romance in Steel: the Heritage of Armor" (January-June 2001), "Russian Icons: The Warrior Saints" (June-August 2001), "The Age of Armor" (September-May 2002), "The Connecticut Yankee in King Arthur's Court" (In association with Mark Twain House, September-May 2003), "The Last Crusaders: Hospitallers and Turks at the Siege of Rhodes" (September-February 2004), and "Empire of the Sultans: Ottoman Art from the Khalili Collection" (in partnership with the Worcester Art Museum, March-May 2004)

Children's programming includes scavenger hunts, arms and armor demonstrations, jousting demonstrations, swordplay demonstrations, costumed characters, craft workshops, films about dragons and castles, birthday parties, "overknights," and other special events throughout the year.

There is a gift shop, but no café. Visitors can eat at Eddy's Pub (diner), King Buffet (Chinese buffet), Barber's Crossing (family restaurant), or D'Angelo's (deli), all within walking distance.

While You're in the Area

Nearby features include the Worcester Art Museum (p. 327), Worcester Historical Museum (p. 336), EcoTarium (p. 332), Tower Hill Botanical Garden (p. 336), and Mechanics Hall (p. 334).

Indian Motorcycle Museum

Hall of Fame
33 Hendee Street
PO Box 90003, Mason Square Station
Springfield, MA 01139
(413) 737-2624
www.sidecar.com

Overview

Indian was the first commercially marketed gasoline-powered motorcycle manufacturing company in the U.S. The Indian Motorcycle Museum is an on-site viewing museum located in the last building owned by the company (manufacturing ceased in 1953). The museum has the finest collection of Indian motorcycles and other Indian products, as well as a superb collection of toy motorcycles, an extensive photo gallery, and showcases filled with memorabilia. Other American-made motorcycles are also on display.

Directions and Hours

Take I-91 or the Mass Pike to Route 291. Take exit 4 (St. James Avenue) off 291. Go right on Page Boulevard and right on Hendee Street.

Hours: March-November, open daily 10:00-4:00; December-February, open daily 1:00-4:00. Closed Thanksgiving, Christmas, and New Years.

Admission and Membership

Admission is $3.

What to See

In its heyday, Indian also manufactured airplane engines, bicycles, outboard motors, home air conditioning units, and many other items that are on display at the museum.

While You're in the Area

Also nearby are the Springfield Museum of Fine Arts (p. 316), the George Walter Vincent Smith Art Museum (p. 248), the Springfield Science Museum (p. 318), and the Basketball Hall of Fame (p. 288).

Isabella Stewart Gardner Museum

280 The Fenway
Boston, MA 02115
(617) 566-5643
www.isgm.org

Overview

Isabella Stewart Gardner collected the museum's impressive collection and opened her house to the public in 1903, believing that works of art should be displayed in settings that would inspire the imagination. As a result she designed "Fenway Court" in the style of a Venetian Palace. The Isabella Stewart Gardner Museum has three floors of galleries (all of which open into a interior courtyard with horticulture displays) that feature more than 2,500 paintings, sculptures, tapestries, textiles, rare books, photographs, correspondence and other interesting objects. The museum has a large Italian Renaissance art collection, including works by Titian, Botticelli, and Raphael, as well as works by French, German, and Dutch painters like Rembrandt and more modern artists such as Degas, Matisse, Sargent, and Whistler.

Directions and Hours

From south of Boston: Take Route 93 north to the Massachusetts Avenue exit (exit from the right lane only). Continue straight at the end of the exit ramp onto Melnea Cass Boulevard. Follow Melnea Cass Boulevard to Tremont Street. At Tremont Street turn left. At the next intersection turn right onto Ruggles Street. Continue on Ruggles Street, crossing Huntington Avenue. The Museum is two blocks down on your left. To park at the Museum of Fine Arts garage or surface lot, turn right at the first set of lights after crossing Huntington Avenue. Continue straight behind the Museum of Fine Arts, turning right onto Forsyth Way. Take a right at the light onto Huntington Avenue. Continue on Huntington Avenue in front of the Museum of Fine Arts, taking the first right (a block before the next light) onto Museum Road. The garage is on the left side of the street and the surface lot entrance is on the right.

From north of Boston: Take the Storrow Drive exit from Route 93 South (exit from right lane). Follow ramp signs to Storrow Drive. Follow Storrow Drive to the Fenway/Kenmore exit (exit from the left lane). Stay to the left (Fenway) at the exit ramp fork. At the end of the ramp turn right onto Boylston Street at the lights. Continue on Boylston Street for approximately ½ mile until you arrive at the intersection of Boylston Street and Park Drive. Bear right onto Park Drive—do not take a sharp right onto Brookline Avenue! Merge into the left hand lane, taking the first left that takes you around a parking lot (you've just made a U-turn). Cross Brookline Avenue onto The Fenway. Continue past Emmanuel College and Simmons College on your right. The Museum is the next building on your right after Simmons College. To park at the Museum of Fine Arts garage or surface lot, continue past the Museum bearing to the left at the first light. Continue straight behind the Museum of Fine Arts, turning right onto Forsyth Way. Take a right at the light onto Huntington Avenue. Continue on Huntington Avenue in front of the Museum of Fine Arts, taking the first right (a block before the next light) onto Museum Road. The garage entrance is on the left side of the street and the surface lot entrance is on the right.

From west of Boston: Take the Mass Pike eastbound to exit 22. Once on the off ramp choose the Prudential Center exit; this exit will put you right on Huntington Avenue traveling west. Stay on Huntington Avenue (you will pass Symphony Hall, Northeastern University, and the Museum of Fine Arts). Turn right onto Louis Prang Street (the Museum of Fine Arts subway stop is on your left at this corner). The Museum is on the left two blocks down. To park at the Museum of Fine Arts garage or surface lot, turn off Huntington Avenue one block before Louis Prang onto Museum Road. The garage entrance is on the left side of the street and the surface lot entrance is on the right.

From Cambridge: Take Massachusetts Avenue toward Boston. Cross the Charles River. Follow Massachusetts Avenue to Huntington Avenue (Symphony Hall will be on the right). Turn right. Follow Huntington Avenue to Louis Prang (you will pass Northeastern University and the Museum of Fine Arts). Turn right and continue for two blocks. The Museum is on the left. To park at the Museum of Fine Arts garage or surface lot, turn off Huntington Avenue one block before Louis Prang onto Museum Road. The garage entrance is on the left side of the street and the surface lot entrance is on the right.

From Boston: Take Huntington Avenue westbound past the Museum of Fine Arts. Turn right onto Louis Prang Street (the Museum of Fine Arts subway stop is on your left at this corner). The Museum is on the left two blocks down. To park at the Museum of Fine Arts garage or surface lot, turn off Huntington Avenue one block before Louis Prang onto Museum Road. The garage entrance is on the left side of the street and the surface lot entrance is on the right.

Public Transportation: Take the Green Line E train outbound or No. 39 bus to the Museum of Fine Arts stop. Cross Huntington Avenue (towards the Texaco gas station) to Louis Prang Street. Walk down Louis Prang Street for two blocks. The Museum is on the left.

The museum is open year round.

Hours: Tuesday-Sunday 11:00 A.M. to 5:00 P.M. (Galleries begin closing at 4:45 P.M.) Open all holidays except Thanksgiving, Christmas, and New Year's Day.

Admission and Membership

$10 adults ($11 on weekends), $7 seniors, $5 college students with current ID. Members and children under 18 are admitted free. Guided tours can be arranged 3 weeks before the visit. Discounted group rates with 15 or more people are available to adults, seniors, and students. For more information contact the tour coordinator at (617) 278-5147. Membership is $55/year for individuals, $75/year for a family, $150/year to be a Friend, and $300/year to be a Contributor.

What to See

The museum has an Artist-in-Residence program where artists share their range of disciplines through lectures, exhibitions, and other programs. The museum also offers adult education courses, hosts classical and jazz concerts, lectures, family activities, and tours.

Visitors can take a self-guided audio tour of the museum (for an extra $4) in English and Spanish. This audio guide allows guests to pick out objects of interest in any order that they wish. This tour includes each of the gallery rooms and their objects and describes the life of Isabella Stewart Gardner and the history of her Fenway Court. Music plays an important role at the museum and as a result there are classical and jazz concerts in the Tapestry Room Saturdays and Sundays during the Spring and Fall.

On Saturday mornings the museum offers a Family Fun program that allows families to engage in active gallery exploration before the museum opens to the public. This is followed by art-making in the studio. Children 6-10 must be accompanied by an adult. The cost for each adult and child pair is $20 for non-members, $15 for members (with an additional $5 per person for

The Jackson Homestead. Photo by Steve Rosenthal.

an extra child or adult) and registration is required in advance. To register please call the Education Department at (617) 278-5147.

The museum has a café and a museum shop. The café is open Tuesday-Friday 11:30 A.M.-4:00 P.M. and Saturday-Sunday 11 A.M. to 4:00 P.M. The museum shop is open during regular museum hours.

While You're in the Area

Nearby attractions and museums include the Boston Athenaeum (p. 331), the Boston Tea Party Ship and Museum (p. 331), the Children's Museum of Boston (p. 228), the Bunker Hill Museum (p. 332), the Longyear Museum (p. 333), and the Museum of Bad Art (p. 334).

The Jackson Homestead

Newton's Museum and Historical Society
527 Washington St.
Newton, MA 02458
(617) 552-7238
www.ci.newton.ma.us/jackson

Overview

The Jackson Homestead serves as a nationally accredited museum and center for Newton history with exhibitions and programs highlighting Newton as one of the country's first railroad suburbs. The home was also once a station on the Underground Railroad.

Directions and Hours

From Massachusetts Turnpike (Route 90), take exit 17. Follow signs for West Newton and stay on Washington St. The museum is one mile from exit 17.

Open in the winter, Monday-Thursday 12:00-5:00 and most Sundays 2:00-5:00. Summer hours are Monday-Thursday 12:00-5:00 and other hours by appointment. The museum is handicap accessible.

Admission and Membership

Admission is $2/adults and $1/seniors and children. Newton Historical Society and WGBH members receive discounts. Membership is $15/student and older adult, $20/individual, $30/household, $50/supporting, $100/sustaining, and $500/life. Business membership levels are $100/friend, $250/associate, and $500/sponsor.

What to See

The Jackson Homestead is home to the Newton Historical Society and Newton's City Museum. The 1809 Federal-style farmhouse was a station on the Underground Railroad and the collection houses documents as well as an abolition exhibition in the children's gallery. The collection also pertains to Newton's cultural, economic, and physical development including paintings, decorative arts, photographs, maps, manuscripts, and building histories.

The historical society hosts many functions throughout the year including the "Heritage of Faith" tour in the fall, an annual house tour in May, Children's Sunday and Interracial Harmony Day in June, "Halloween Happening" in October, an open house in December, and also in December, "Stories at the Homestead." Other programming for children includes monthly history hunts, vacation programs, and holiday events, as well as events prepared for school groups.

The museum has a gift shop. There is no café, but there are many nearby eating establishments such as delis, bakeries, and cafés.

While You're in the Area

Visitors can also tour the Gore Place Museum (p. 251) and Our Lady's Catholic Church at Boston College. Other areas include Wellesley College, Brandeis University, and the Adams Street Synagogue.

John Alden House Museum

105 Alden Street
Duxbury, MA 02331
(781) 934-9092
www.alden.org

Overview

Arriving in Plimoth Colony in 1620 on the Mayflower (and marrying two years later), John Alden and Priscilla Mullins moved to land in Duxbury and eventually built the present house there in 1653. The John Alden House is the only building still standing that is known to have housed original Pilgrims.

Directions and Hours

From Route 95 or Route 128: get on State Route 3 south from Boston or from Plymouth and Cape Cod. Get off Route 3 at exit 11 (the Duxbury/Pembroke exit). At the end of the ramp head east toward Duxbury on Route 14. Bear right on Route 14 just beyond the police station. When Route 14 intersects with Route 13A (about 2 miles) continue straight through the traffic light. In less than a mile you will come to a small group of stores. Just past Millbrook Market watch for Railroad Avenue, which will be on the right. Turn right onto Railroad Avenue which will end shortly at Millbrook Market. Then turn right onto Railroad Avenue which will shortly end at Alden Street. Almost directly across from Alden Street is the entrance to the John Alden House.

The House is open from mid-May to mid-October.

Hours: Monday-Saturday 12:00-4:00 P.M. Closed on Sundays.

Admission and Membership

Adults $2.50, under 12 $1. Special group rates are available. Membership is $20/year for individuals, $40/year for a family, and $50/year for a business/group.

What to See

The John Alden Homestead has remained in the Alden family since it was built and has escaped the "improvements" common in most old houses like plumbing, electricity, and modern kitchens. The house is post and beam construction, each piece having been fitted into the next and pinned with wooden pegs. The kitchen seems to be older than the rest of the house in size, style, and cut of boards. While the furniture, kitchen equipment, and personal items don't date back to the first Alden owners, they do represent 300 years of Alden occupation. There is, however, a bonnet that is believed to have been Priscilla's and which has been proven to have originated from that time period. A well sweep has been restored for interest only, as the water is now too low to use it. The Alden Kindred are building a barn on the same location that photographs from the 1800s show it to be. This barn will have modern conveniences, including heat, which will allow the museum to extend programming throughout the year.

Before the barn was built the University of Massachusetts did archaeological surveys to make sure that nothing historically significant would be lost. The dirt collected is preserved and will be sifted by Duxbury school children who can discover shards of pottery, small implements, and glassware.

There is a gift shop but no café.

While You're in the Area

Attractions nearby include King Caesar's House, The Captain Bradford Gersham House, the Ellison Art Center, and the Duxbury Art Museum Complex (p. 332).

John F. Kennedy Library and Museum

Columbia Point
Boston, MA 02125
(617) 929-4523 or (877) 616-4599 (toll free)
www.jfklibrary.org

Overview

The John F. Kennedy Library and Museum allows visitors to step into the early 1960s and to experience firsthand the life and legacy of President John F. Kennedy. The national memorial to President Kennedy sits on a 10-acre waterfront site on Columbia Point. Period settings from the White House and 25 multimedia exhibts create an account of President Kennedy's thousand days in office.

Directions and Hours

From the South: Take Route 3/I-93 North (Southeast Expressway). Take exit 14 onto Morrissey Boulevard. Turn right at the first traffic light onto the University of Massachusetts and JFK Library perimeter road. This is for cars only, not buses.

From the North: Take Route I-93 South or Route I-95 South to Boston and onto Route 3/I-93 South (Southeast Expressway).Take exit 15. At the traffic light turn left onto Columbia Road. Travel to the rotary and turn right onto Morrissey Boulevard. Bear right onto the access road. Travel on the access road to the traffic light. Turn left onto the University of Massachusetts and JFK Library perimeter road. This is for cars only, not buses.

From the West: Take Route I-90 East (Massachusetts Turnpike) to Route 3/I-93 South (Southeast Expressway) and follow the directions from the North.

Exiting the JFK Library and Museum: Follow the perimeter road to the traffic light. Turn right onto Morrissey Boulevard. Travel to the rotary. Take the third right off the rotary onto Columbia Road. Go straight and ahead are ramps to 3/I-93 North and South.

Please contact the Library and Museum for bus directions; buses are restricted from using exit 14.

Public transportation: Take the MBTA Red Line to the JFK/UMASS stop. A free shuttle bus to the Kennedy Library runs every 20 minutes from the T station.

The library and museum are open year-round. The museum is handicap accessible.

Hours: Daily from 9:00 A.M. to 5:00 P.M. Closed Thanksgiving, Christmas Day, and New Years Day.

Photo courtesy of John F. Kennedy Library.

Admission and Membership

Adults $8, seniors and students $6, youth 13-17 $4, children 12 and under free. Groups of 10 or more: adults $6, seniors and students $4, and youth 13-17 $3. Parking is free. Membership is $25/year for individuals, $40/year for families, $100 for a Contributor, $250/year for a Benefactor, $500/year for the Leadership Circle, and $1000/year for the President's Circle.

What to See

Visitors can witness the first televised presidential debate, see life during the Cold War and the Cuban Missile Crisis, and relive the first manned exploration of space. Guests can also see first lady Jacqueline Bouvier Kennedy give her televised tour of the White House and sit in on Oval Office meetings as President Kennedy prepares to address the nation on the need for civil rights legislation.

There is a museum store and a café. The café is open from 9:00 A.M. to 4:00 P.M. A box lunch is available for groups (advance notice required).

While You're in the Area

The museum is accessible to all major Boston-area attractions.

Josiah Dennis Manse Museum

77 Nobscusset Road
PO Box 963
Dennis, MA 02638
(508) 385-2232

Overview

This 1736 saltbox was home of the town's first minister (and the man for whom the town of Dennis is named). The house contains artifacts of early life in Dennis, a children's room, a spinning and weaving exhibit, and a Dennis maritime wing. A one-room schoolhouse is also on the property as well as a Colonial-style garden. Costumed docents demonstrate colonial skills.

Directions and Hours

From Cape Cod: Take Route 6 to exit 8. Go 1.4 miles north on Union Street until you reach Route 6A. Turn right then go 3.2 miles and turn left on Nobscusset Road. Follow the signs. The museum is at the end of the block on the left.

The museum is open from mid-June through September and is handicap accessible.

Hours: Tuesday 10:00 A.M. to 12:00 P.M. and Thursday 2:00-4:00 P.M. From April through December the Josiah Dennis Manse Museum is open for group tours. Please call (508) 385-3528 for more information.

Admission and Membership

A $2 donation is suggested.

What to See

The Josiah Dennis Manse Museum houses artifacts belonging to the first settlers in 1639. Part of the current house dates back to 1670. Of note is a beehive oven in the keeping room, a spinning and weaving exhibit in the back chamber with demonstrations, a children's room with early Dennis samplers, a maritime wing with a diorama of Shiverick Shipyard (the only place on Cape Cod to build clipper ships), ship models, paintings, and artifacts that tell the story of 360 years of Dennis maritime history. The one-room schoolhouse, used from 1770-1859, shows a 1700s school on one side and an 1800s one on the other side.

Photo courtesy of the Josiah Dennis Manse Museum.

Photo Courtesy of the Keep Homestead Museum.

Every year during the Dennis Festival in mid-August the manse hosts a Colonial Open House, featuring many early American skills that encourages some audience participation. The Yarmouth Colonial Militia also holds an encampment on the grounds, performing drills and a mock battle.

As part of the manse's interactive commentary, the life of children in the 1700s is explored and children can play some early games and write on slates in the schoolhouse.

There is a gift shop. A list of nearby cafés and restaurants is available upon request.

While You're in the Area

Other interesting places to visit while you are in the area are the 1801 Jericho House and Barn, the Cape Museum of Fine Arts (p. 225), the Cape Playhouse and Cinema, Scargo Tower, as well as golf courses and beaches.

Keep Homestead Museum

35 Ely Road
Monson, MA 01057
(413) 267-5210
www.keephomesteadmuseum.org

Overview

When Myra Keep Lovell Moulton died in 1988, the last of a long line of Keeps in Monson, she willed her property, its contents, and an endowment fund to the town. Myra was an avid collector and her button collection is considered one of the largest in the U.S. She mastered many forms of needlework and many of her works are on display, as are examples of her work in oil, watercolor, and ceramics. History was also important to Myra and the museum contains many examples of this interest: history of her family, her town, her church, rocks and minerals of the area—to name only a few. In addition, there are 75 acres with marked trails for hiking and cross-country skiing.

Directions and Hours

From the East or West: From the Massachusetts Turnpike (I-90) take exit 8 (Palmer). At the end of the ramp, turn right onto Route 32. Follow Route 32 for approximately five miles into Monson. At the white church on the hill, turn right onto Ely Road. The Keep Homestead is at the top of the hill on the right.

From the South: In Stafford Springs, follow Route 32 for approximately 10 miles to the Massachusetts line. After about five more miles, go past the Civil War Monument, the library, and the white church on the hill. Then turn left onto Fountain Street. Take the next left onto High Street, then the first right onto Ely Road. The Keep Homestead Museum is at the top of the hill on the right.

The Museum is open on the first Sunday of the month from April-December, from 1:00-3:00. Special tours are available by appointment.

The museum is handicap accessible, except for four rooms on the second floor.

Admission and Membership

Admission is free, but donations are accepted. Anyone interested may join the Friends of the Keep Homestead Museum for $5/year.

What to See

The collections are the personal belongings of a family that lived for nearly 200 years in the same house. Rooms represent several periods: a 1920s dining room, a 1930s bedroom, an 1890s bedroom.

The museum contains the largest collection of antique and vintage buttons on display in the Northeast. The buttons are exhibited on a rotating basis, but on permanent display is the fantastic collection of mosaic buttons. They depict flowers, birds, animals, people, common buildings and not-so-common building scenes. Presently, along with the mosaic buttons, are buttons from the Art Nouveau era. There are Gibson Girl buttons, enamels and Gay Nineties buttons as well as opera buttons, storybook buttons, and other figural buttons manufactured during this time period. Also, there are buttons of historical significance, military, political, and Colonial buttons.

Special programs include "Welcoming Spring" in April, "Storybooks and the Button Collection" in May, "Old-fashioned Ice Cream Social" in July, "Make Your Own Corn Husk Doll" in October, "Costumes from History,"and "Christmas Tree Showcase" in December. All programs are from 1:00- 3:00, and some are geared to children.

There is a gift shop, but no café. Nearby restaurants include Captain's Inn and Norcross House (both on Main Street) as well as Mug n'Muffin and Guesapina's (on Palmer Road).

While You're in the Area

Other places of interest nearby include the Civil War Museum (p. 229), the Jacob Thompson House (p. 333), the Norcross Wildlife Sanctuary (p. 334), Old Sturbridge Village (p. 297), and the Basketball Hall of Fame (p. 288). The Eastern States Exposition (the Big E) is held in West Springfield every September.

The Kendall Whaling Museum

27 Everett Street
PO Box 297
Sharon, MA 02067
(781) 784-5642
www.kwm.org

Overview

The Kendall Whaling Museum houses a collection of whaling artworks and artifacts, including impressive collections of scrimshaw (the indigenous sailors' art of carving and etching whale ivory and bone), Old Masters paintings and decorative arts from the Dutch "Golden Age," rare eighteenth century Japanese whaling scrolls and ukiyo-e prints, African, African-American, Native American, and Pacific Island exhibitions, British and American paintings, ship models, figureheads, wood carvings, and whaling gear. The exhibits in its 10 galleries span seven continents and over 10 centuries of maritime heritage.

Directions and Hours

There are blue-and-white Kendall Whaling Museum directional signs on all major roads and at all intersections along the way.

From Boston and the North/I-95 South towards Providence: Take exit 10 (Coney Street, Sharon/Walpole). At the exit stop sign turn left onto Coney Street, toward Sharon. Coney Street crosses I-95 and becomes Route 27 south where the name changes to Norwood Street. Take this 1.8 miles to where the road divides to form a middle island (there is a house on the island and

Photo courtesy of the Kendall Whaling Museum

a blinking yellow CAUTION signal). Just after the road divides turn right onto Upland Road. Take Upland Road and travel .3 miles to a T intersection with Everett Street. Travel on Everett Street for .2 miles directly to the museum.

From Providence and the south: Take I-95 north toward Boston and get off at exit 8 (South Main Street, Sharon/Mechanic Street, Foxboro). At the exit stop sign turn right onto South Main Street, toward Sharon. Travel on South Main Street for 3 miles to Station Street (this takes you past four traffic signal lights, past Shaw's shopping plaza, Sharon Heights shopping plaza, and past the Police Station on your left and the Fire Station on your right). The junction of South Main Street and Station Street is not clearly marked but it is just past the Fire Station on the right and an old school building on the left with three downtown church steeples visible several blocks ahead. Turn left onto Station Street and travel for two blocks to the stop sign junction of Depot Street (Route 27). Turn left onto Depot Street and travel for .4 miles, across a railroad overpass and up Moose Hill, to where the road divides to a middle island. Just past the island turn left 180 degrees, reversing direction on Route 27. Immediately turn right onto Upland Road and go for .3 miles to a T intersection with Everett Street. Travel on Everett Street for .2 miles directly to the museum.

Sharon is served by commuter rail on the Boston-Attleboro-Providence line from South, Back Bay, and Route 128 Stations in Boston and from the Amtrak station in Providence. The museum is about .6 miles from the Sharon Station, and local taxi service is available: (781) 784-9195.

The museum is open year round. All galleries are handicapped accessible, and served by a wheelchair accessible entrance. Some special programs are planned for non-accessible spaces, so advance notice of special needs is advised when attending a program.

Hours: Tuesday-Saturday 10:00 A.M. to 5:00 P.M., Sunday 1:00-5:00 P.M. Also open Monday holidays 10:00 A.M. to 5:00 P.M.

Admission and Membership

Adults $4, seniors/students $3, children 6-16 $2.50, family rate $10. Children under 6, members, and Massachusetts public school teachers are admitted free. An introductory program and tour is free with admission for groups of 6 or more, reserving in advance. Membership is $25/year for individuals, $35/year for families, and $50/year for a contributing member.

What to See

The museum has an international and multicultural focus, with an abundance of New England art and history, a Japanese Gallery, a Dutch Gallery, a Northwest Coast Native American Gallery, an Arctic Gallery, an "Ancient Treasures" exhibit, and an African American exhibit, all of which show the influence of whales and whaling in many cultures.

The museum offers monthly evening programs that include lectures, concerts, and films, as well as an Annual Whaling History Symposium on the second weekend of October.

The museum offers many tours and programs for children as young as 5 by arrangement. There are also family films and programs scheduled during school vacations. Please call ahead for information.

There is a gift shop. Restaurants are located within one mile, in Sharon center, and within two-four miles on Route 1. There are picnic tables on the museum grounds.

While You're in the Area

Other interesting attractions nearby include the Sharon Historical Society museum and the Moose Hill Wildlife Sanctuary of the Massachusetts Audubon Society (it borders the museum and offers hiking trails and programs). The town of Sharon also offers Lake Massapoag for swimming and boating.

Lawrence Heritage State Park

1 Jackson Street
Lawrence, MA 01840
(978) 794-1655
www.state.ma.us/dem/parks/lwhp.htm

Overview

Lawrence Heritage State Park includes a visitor center housed in a restored 1840s textile workers' boarding house, and over 70 acres of greenspace and walkways in the city. The visitor center features a permanent exhibit on the history of Lawrence, a planned industrial city which became the center of the American woolen textile industry, an "Immigrant City" of over 40 nationalities, and the location of one of the landmark events in American labor history, the "Bread and Roses" Strike of 1912. There is also a Gallery with changing art and historical exhibits.

Lawrence Heritage State Park Visitor Center.

Directions and Hours

From Boston: Route 93 north to Route 495 north

From Salem: Route 114 west to Route 495 north

From Portsmouth: Route 95 south to Route 495 south

From Route 495: Take exit 45 (Marston Street). Take the first left onto Canal Street. Go straight through the lights then take the second right onto Jackson Street. The Visitor Center is on right, on the corner of Jackson and Canal. A small parking lot is in back on Mill Street.

The Visitor Center is open seven days a week, from 9:00 A.M. to 4:00 P.M., and the facility is fully accessible.

Admission and Membership

Admission to the museum and all events is free.

What to See

In addition to the regular exhibits at the visitor's center, tours, concerts, lectures, and other programs are offered.

The Park's greenspaces include adjacent Visitor Center Park, a mile-long canal walkway, four-acre Pemberton Park along the river, and 47-acre Riverfront State Park, all in Lawrence.

While You're in the Area

Lawrence Heritage State Park serves as a visitor center for the State of Massachusetts and for the Essex National Heritage Area, a National Park Service designation for Essex County, an area rich in cultural offerings. The area's three themes are Early Settlement, Maritime History, and the Industrial Revolution. Numerous art, historical, and recreational resources are within easy reach.

Lexington Historical Socicty

PO Box 514
Lexington, MA 02420
(781) 862-1703
www.lexingtonhistory.org

Overview

The Lexington Historical Society maintains three historic houses: Hancock-Clarke House, Paul Revere's destination on that fateful night of April 18, 1775; Buckman Tavern, Minuteman headquarters, where Captain Parker's troops assembled before the battle with the British on the Common (now known as the Lexington Battle Green); and Munroe Tavern, headquarters and field hospital for British troops on the afternoon of April 19, 1775, and where President Washington dined in 1789. Visitors may view the Garden of Colonial Flowers at Munroe Tavern, a collection of flowering plants and culinary herbs grown in the Boston area before 1830. (Garden viewing is free.)

Also onsite is the Antique Fire Equipment Museum, located in the Fire Barn behind the Hancock-Clarke House (by appointment only).

Directions and Hours

The society is located near three major highways, Route 3, Route 95 and Routes 2 and 2A. The houses and fire museum are near each other, but directions to each vary slightly. Please call for directions.

Buckman Tavern is open in mid-March from 11:00 A.M. to 3:00 P.M.; from April-November, the tavern is open 10:00-5:00.

Hancock-Clarke and Munroe Tavern open for Patriot's Day weekend only, 10:00 A.M. to 5:00 P.M., then reopen June, July, August, and October, noon-4:00 P.M.

Admission and Membership

Adults, $5 per house; Ages 6-16, $3; under age 6 is free. A three house combination ticket is $12 for adults, $11 for seniors, and $7 for children. Members are admitted free.

What to See

The historic houses have many extraordinary features, such as the restored taproom at Buckman Tavern and the musket ball hole in the door, William Diamond's drum and John Pitcairn's pistols at Hancock-Clarke House, the chair and table where George Washington sat to eat at Munroe Tavern, and the tapestries made by Munroe women.

The Old Belfry, which sounded the alarm on April 19, 1775, was erected by the Society in its original location on the hill in sight of the Battle Green.

The Lexington Historical Society archives are housed at Hancock-Clarke house and are open by appointment.

The Antique Fire Equipment Museum contains Hose 1, the town's first motorized fire engine, along with a wide variety of unusual firefighting equipment: a fully restored 1940s vintage paper tape alarm system; a collection of old hoses, including a leather one for use with the pumper; a collection of nozzles, including one that can shoot a spray of water 250 feet; photographs of major fires in Lexington as well as past and present fire apparatus; a collection of badges from all over Massachusetts; a collection of portable fire extinguishers from the baking-soda throw sticks to carbon bombs to modern canister extinguishers; tools carried on past and present trucks include special picks and axes, a wrecking bar, a "can opener," wrenches, a special screw jack, and a line gun; firemen's clothing, such as boots, hats, and coats from various eras; and a Davies escape mechanism used to lower people out of an upper window during a fire.

While You're in the Area

As visitors stroll through Lexington Center for plenty of shopping and dining, they can take a peek at the Old Depot (the big white building), which was purchased by the Society and is slowly being renovated for use as headquarters and welcoming center. Also nearby are the Museum of Our National Heritage (p. 286) and the Minuteman National Historic Park.

Lyman Estate/Greenhouse at The Vale (SPNEA)

185 Lyman Street
Waltham, MA 02452
(781) 891-4882 ext. 244
www.spnea.org

Overview

The Lyman Estate is one of the finest examples in the United States of a country estate laid out according to the principles of eighteenth-century English naturalistic design.

Directions and Hours

From I-95/Route 128: Take exit 27A. Turn east onto Totten Pond Road. Go to the end then turn right onto Lexington Street then left onto Beaver Street. At the traffic circle go partway around, then bear right through stone pillars to the gravel drive.

The Lyman Estate Greenhouses are open year round for sales and tours.

Hours: Greenhouses: Monday-Saturday 9:30 A.M. to 4:00 P.M. Grounds: 9:00 A.M. to 5:00 P.M.

Admission and Membership

$5 for adults, $4.50 senior citizens, ½ off for students and children 6-12. Children 5 and under, SPNEA members, and residents of Waltham are free. AAA members receive a 2 for 1 discount. SPNEA membership is $35/year for individuals and $45/year for a household. Membership includes free admissions to 35 properties and museums across New England.

What to See

The estate's historic greenhouses are evidence of a fascination with horticulture common among Boston gentry in the early years of the Republic. They contain century-old camellia trees and grapevines, along with a large collection of orchids, herbs, and exotic fruits, many of which are for sale. Specialized plant sales are held throughout the year. The house, designed in the Federal style in 1793 by Salem architect Samuel McIntire, is available for private events.

Plant sales include annual camellia, herb, hosta, and perennial sales. Call for more information.

While You're in the Area

Nearby attractions and museums include the Gore Place (p. 251), the Charles River Museum of Industry (p. 332), and the Rose Art Museum (p. 335) of Brandeis University.

Lynn Museum

125 Green Street
Lynn, MA 01902
(781) 592-2956
www.lynnmuseum.org

Overview

The Lynn Museum is dedicated to preserving, interpreting, and promoting the fascinating and diverse cultural heritage of Lynn, Massachusetts.

Directions and Hours

Take Route 128 north to exit 44B. Follow signs for Lynn, 129. Follow Route 129 to Chestnut Street. Turn right onto Broad Street then right onto Green Street. The museum is on the left.

The museum is open year round, and it is partially handicap accessible.

Hours: Monday-Saturday 1:00-4:00.

Admission and Membership

$4 for adults. Membership is $20/year for individuals, $30/year for families, $10/year for students, $12/year for seniors over 65, $60/year for sustaining memberships and $150/year for supporting memberships.

What to See

The Lynn Museum has over 17,000 artifacts relating to Lynn as well as a research library with over 600 linear feet of primary documents and 20,000 photographs. The museum has a rotating schedule of exhibits that explore a number of topics in Lynn history. Exhibits in 2001 include "Cityscapes: Investigating Our Urban Envirnonment, 1850 to 2000" (May 6 to August 18) and "May Useful Arts Imploy My Youth": Lynn Samplers and the Education of Young Women, 1750 to 1910" (June 3-December 29)

Children's programming includes seasonal

workshops, school programs, and vacation week programs.

The museum does have a gift shop.

While You're in the Area

Visitors can also visit the Lynn Heritage State Park or any number of sites in the north Shore.

McMullen Museum of Art

Boston College
140 Commonwealth Avenue
Chestnut Hill, MA 02467
(617) 552-8100
www.bc.edu/artmuseum

Overview

The McMullen Museum of Art is a small museum presenting one large or two to three small exhibitions at a time. The museum focuses on high-quality temporary exhibitions, especially of medieval, Irish, and modern art. Boston College faculty from a variety of disciplines contribute to the informative texts that accompany the exhibitions.

Directions and Hours

From 95/128: Take exit 24. Proceed east on Route 30 (Commonwealth Avenue) for five miles to Boston College.

From 90 east: Take exit 17. At the first set of lights after the exit ramp turn right on Centre Street. At the fourth set of lights, turn left on Route 30 (Commonwealth Avenue). Follow Commonwealth Avenue for about 1½ miles to Boston College.

From 90 west: Take exit 17. Continue straight past the Sheraton Hotel. Turn left onto the bridge, and then take the first right on Centre Street. At the fourth set of lights, turn left on Route 30 (Commonwealth Avenue). Follow Commonwealth Avenue for about 1½ miles to Boston College.

The museum is open year round and is handicap accessible.

Hours: September-May, Monday-Friday 11:00 A.M. to 4:00 P.M., Saturday and Sunday noon-5:00 P.M.; June-August, Monday-Friday 11:00 A.M. to 3:00 P.M., Sunday noon-5:00 P.M.

Admission and Membership

Admission is free. Membership: $50 to become a Friend of the Museum.

Interior of the McMullen Museum of Art, Boston College, during the exhibition "Fragmented Devotion: Medieval Objects from the Schnutgen Museum, Cologne." Photo courtesy of Steven Vedder, Boston College.

What to See

The McMullen Museum's permanent collection features American Landscape paintings, sixteenth and seventeenth century Italian paintings, and Japanese prints. During larger exhibitions the permanent collection may not be on display.

A series of public lectures, concerts, and films accompanies each exhibition.

Free tours are available with advance notice, including school groups. Call (617) 552-8587 to schedule a tour.

The museum does not have

a gift shop or a café but visitors can eat at Boston College cafeterias and snack shops.

While You're In the Area

Nearby attractions and museums include the Frederick Law Olmsted National Historic Site (p. 245), the John F. Kennedy National Historic Site (p. 266), the Museum of Transportation (p. 334), and the Longyear Museum (p. 333).

Marblehead Historical Society

170 Washington Street
Marblehead, MA 01945
(781) 631-1768

Overview

The Marblehead Historical Society has three properties: the 1768 Jeremiah Lee Mansion (a historic house museum), the J.O.J. Frost Folk Art Gallery (with changing exhibits), and the G.A.R. Civil War Museum. The story of Marblehead's history is told through arts and artifacts of 100 years of collection and preservation.

Directions and Hours

From I-95 or I-93: Get on Route 128 north. Then take Route 114 east into Marblehead. Take Lafayette Street to Pleasant Street to Washington Street. Turn right on Washington Street. The society headquarters are one block on the left.

The properties are open year-round except for the Jeremiah Lee Mansion, which is open from June 1-October 15. The Civil War Museum is open by appointment. They are not handicap accessible.

Hours: Jeremiah Lee Mansion: Tuesday-Saturday 10:00 A.M. to 4:00 P.M., Sunday 1:00-4:00 P.M. The office, archives, and research library are open Tuesday-Friday 10:00 A.M. to 4:00 P.M. Appointments are requested.

Admission and Membership

Admission to the Lee Mansion is $5, $4.50 for students, seniors, and groups, children under 13 free. The J.O.J. Frost Folk Art Gallery and the Civil War Museum are free. Fees to research in the Historical Society office are $5. Staff research by written request is $10/hour. Membership is $20/year for an individual and $30/year for a family.

What to See

The Marblehead Historical Society's archives include: genealogical records, documents, photographs, children's furniture and toys, folk art, maritime and military artifacts, women's and children's shoes that were a specialty of the town's small factories and cottage shoe industry, and colonial furnishings. The society's exhibition galleries offer changing exhibits and paintings of Marblehead and the sea by folk artist J.O.J. Frost.

The 1768 Jeremiah Lee Mansion is an example of pre-Revolutionary Georgian architecture, which emulated the architectural fashions of the English gentry and aristocracy. The mansion has a wood façade, stone ashlar blocks, and has newly refurbished rooms with original architectural features that include a grand entrance hall and carved woodwork. The mansion also has original hand-painted wallpaper. Its 15 rooms are decorated with collections of furniture, ceramics, textiles, paintings, folk art, utilitarian objects, and maritime and other artifacts from the 1700s and 1800s. Eighteenth century gardens surround the mansion and are open to the public and are available for functions.

The Civil War Museum is located on the second floor of Marblehead's 1727 Old Town House, which was a meeting place of The John Goodwin Jr. Post #82 of the Grand Army of the Republic. It houses objects, paintings, swords, rifles, canteens, flags, banners, leather accessories, uniforms and blankets, pamphlets, photographs, books, account books, documents, about 50 portraits and other pictures, furnishings including chairs, tables, ceremonial stands, and several display cases. The room is still set up the

Catherine Chalmers, "The Food Chain," in MASS MoCA's Tall Gallery. Photo by Arthur Evans.

way it was actually used in the late 1800s. The museum is open by appointment to serve as an educational resource for school groups and other.

The Historical Society is hosting the following exhibitions: "Dory Fishing in Old Marblehead" from April-November 2001, "A Marblehead Childhood" from November 2001-March 2002, and "Elegance of Bygone Eras: Costumes" from April 2002-November 2002. Lecture series and family events are also available; please contact the historical society for more information.

There is a gift shop and many charming restaurants and shops nearby.

While You're in the Area

Other interesting attractions and museums in the area include the Robert "King" Hooper Mansion (p. 333), Abbot Hall (p. 331), the Historic District, and Harborside parks and vistas.

MASS MoCA (Massachusetts Museum of Contemporary Art)

87 Marshall Street
North Adams, MA 01247
(413) 664-4481
www.massmoca.org

Overview

MASS MoCA, located in a renovated nineteenth-century factory building, juxtaposes a restored icon of American industrial past with today's art. The museum offers a performing arts program, which varies from Robert Wilson and Robert Lepage to dance parties or the "silent film/live music" series. The museum emphasizes art that charts new territory and ignores traditional boundaries between the performing and visual arts.

Directions and Hours

From Eastern Massachusetts: Take Route 2 west to North Adams. Alternate route: take the Mass Turnpike to exit 2 in Lee. In Lee take Route 7 north to Williamstown then take Route 2 east to North Adams.

From Connecticut: Take Route 7 north and follow the directions above.

From New York City: Take the Taconic Parkway to Route 295 east (in Chatham NY) to Route 22 north to Route 43 east, which will end in Williamstown. Take a right onto Route 2 east and continue to North Adams.

From Vermont: Take Route 7 south to Williamstown, then take Route 2 east to North Adams.

The museum is open year round and is handicap accessible.

Hours: Daily 10:00 A.M. to 6:00 P.M. June 1-October 31; 11:00 A.M. to 5:00 P.M. November 1-May 31, closed Tuesdays.

Admission and Membership

$8 per person summer and fall, $7 per person winter and spring. Student and senior discounts are available in the winter and spring. Group discounts are available by contacting the marketing department at extension 8111. Membership is $40/year for individuals and $70/year for a dual/family membership. Other membership categories are available but please contact the museum for more information.

What to See

MASS MoCA features several permanent sound installations, and its "Tree Logic"—six upside-down live maple trees. Exhibitions change frequently so please check the museum's web page for up to date information and upcoming events.

Children's programming is available.

The museum has a gift shop and a café.

While You're in the Area

Museums and interesting attractions nearby include the Williams College Museum of Art (p. 326), the Clark Art Institute (p. 320), the Williamstown Theatre Festival, Hancock Shaker Village (p. 255), and the Norman Rockwell Museum (p. 292).

Merwin House "Tranquility" (SPNEA)

14 Main Street
Stockbridge, MA 01262
(413) 298-4703
www.spnea.org

Overview

At the end of the nineteenth century, railroads opened the Berkshires, which soon became a summer destination for wealthy New Yorkers. This handsome brick structure, which dates from the late Federal period, was purchased by William and Elizabeth Doane as a summer home in 1875. Situated in the heart of the charming resort town of Stockbridge, the house reflects a leisurely summer existence, with afternoons spent relaxing on the capacious back porch or strolling through the gardens and down the lawn to the Housatonic River.

Directions and Hours

From I-90: Take exit 2 (Route 102 west) to Stockbridge. Merwin House is the seventh house on the left after the Red Lion Inn.

The house museum is open June 1 through October 15.

Hours: Saturday and Sunday, 11:00 A.M. to 5:00 P.M. Tours are at 11:00, 12:00, 1:00, 2:00, 3:00 and 4:00 P.M.

Admission and Membership

$5 for adults, $4.50 senior citizens, ½ off for students and children 6-12. Children 5 and under, SPNEA members, and residents of Stockbridge are free. AAA members receive a 2 for 1 discount. SPNEA membership is $35/year for individuals and $45/year for a household. Membership includes free admissions to 35 properties and museums across New England.

What to See

Around 1900, the Doanes doubled its size by adding a shingle-style ell and remodeled the interior of the main house. They decorated the house in an eclectic manner with European and American furnishings, much of which they collected during their extensive travels. The house was preserved by the Doanes' daughter, Vipont Merwin, who added her own memorabilia to the decorative schemes.

Merwin House offers tours and public programs. Programs include a walking tour of the local cemetery and a town-wide Holiday Stroll. Please call or write for details.

While You're in the Area

Nearby attractions and museums include the Mission House (p. 277), Naumkeag (p. 289), the Norman Rockwell Museum (p. 292), and other historic sites in the Stockbridge area.

The Mission House Museum and Gardens (Trustees of Reservations)

19 Main Street
Stockbridge, MA 01262
(413) 298-3239
www.thetrustees.org

Overview

The Mission House Museum and Gardens began as a home for the first missionary to the Stockbridge Mohegan Indians in 1739. Surrounded by perennial gardens on Main Street in Stockbridge, a tour of the Mission House is a passage back to Colonial life.

Directions and Hours

From the intersection of Route 7 and Route 102 (at the Red Lion Inn) in Stockbridge, take Route 102 (Main Street) west for two long blocks. The Mission House is located on the right at the corner of Main Street and Sergeant Street.

The museum is open from Memorial Day weekend-Columbus Day and is not handicap accessible.

Hours: Daily from 10:00 A.M. to 5:00 P.M. The last tour is at 4:00 P.M.

Admission and Membership

Adults $5, children $2.50. Free for Trustees of Reservations members. Senior and group discounts are available. Membership is $40/year for an individual, $60/year for a family, $30/year for students and senior citizens, and $50/year for a family of students and senior citizens. Benefactor membership is: $100/year for a contributing, $150/year for a supporting, $300/year for a sustaining, and $600/year for a sponsor.

What to See

The Mission House is a National Historic Landmark. The museum's collection of antique furnishings, tools, and decorative woodwork is one of the finest in America.

Children are welcome. Tours give information on colonial life.

There is a small gift shop but no café. Visitors can eat in Stockbridge.

While You're in the Area

Other museums or interesting attractions nearby include other Trustees of Reservations properties such as The Colonel John Ashley House (p. 232) and Naumkeag (p. 289), as well as Chasterwood, Rockwell, and The Mount (p. 281).

MIT List Visual Arts Center

20 Ames Street E15-109
Cambridge, MA 02139
(617) 253-4400
web.mit.edu/lvac/www/

Overview

The List Visual Arts Center is a contemporary art gallery affiliated with the Massachusetts Institute of Technology. Exhibitions change three times a year. One upcoming exhibit will be a major retrospective of Yoko Ono's artwork.

Directions and Hours

By T Subway, take the red line to the Kendall/MIT stop. Follow Main Street west to Ames Street, turn left.

By car, coming across the Longfellow Bridge or Memorial Drive, follow the signs for Kendall Square.

The gallery is open September through June, and is handicap accessible.

Hours: Tuesday-Thursday, Saturday, Sunday noon-6:00; Friday noon-8:00.

Admission and Membership

Admission to the gallery is free.

What to See

The List Visual Arts Center's temporary exhibitions include six room-size installations by artists engaging the language of architecture, photographs made with non-photographic means by Marco Breuer, film installations by Isaac Julien, and new work by Paul Pfeiffer.

Food, souvenirs, and MIT gifts are available at Kendall Square.

While You're in the Area

The gallery is located within a reasonable distance to all the major attractions in Boston and Cambridge. These include the MIT Museum (p. 279), the Museum of Fine Arts (p. 284), the Isabella Stewart Gardner Museum (p. 262), the Institute of Contemporary Art (p. 333), the Fogg Art Museum (p. 243), the Sackler Museum

(p. 216), and the Busch-Reisinger Museum (p. 224).

MIT Museum

265 Massachusetts Avenue
Cambridge, MA 02139
(617) 253-4444
http://web.mit.edu/museum

Overview

MIT Museum features a host of changing science and technology exhibitions including "Robots & Beyond," "Holography: The Light Fantastic," and "Thinkapalooza." One of the museum's most popular exhibitions features the whimsical work of MIT artist-in-residence Arthur Ganson, an inventor who combines the artistic vision of a choreographer and the precision of a mechanical engineer in his creation of unforgettable mechanical sculptures.

Directions and Hours

MIT Museum is located near Central Square in Cambridge at 265 Massachusetts Avenue at the intersection of Front Street. From Boston or Harvard Square, take the #1 MBTA bus to the NECCO Factory stop. Via subway, take the MBTA Red Line to Central Square and walk down Massachusetts Avenue toward the Boston skyline for seven minutes. The Museum is on the left.

From I-90, take the Cambridge/Brighton exit (exit 18). Following the signs to Cambridge, cross the River Street Bridge, and continue straight about 1 mile to Central Square. Turn right onto Massachusetts Avenue and follow Massachusetts Avenue for about a half mile. The main entrance to MIT will be on your left. If you cross the river again, you have gone too far.

From I-93, take exit 26, and follow the signs to Back Bay along Storrow Drive West, approximately 1.5 miles, to the exit for Route 2A. The exit will be on the left, just before the Harvard Bridge (more appropriately called the Massachusetts Avenue Bridge). The Charles River will be on your right. As you cross the bridge, you will be looking at MIT—the Great Dome and academic facilities are on the right, the dormitories and athletic facilities are on the left. Parking is available at the 55 Franklin Street Garage.

The museum is open year-round, and all facilities are wheelchair accessible.

Hours: Tuesday-Friday 10:00-5:00 and Saturday-Sunday 12:00-5:00

Admission and Membership

\$5 adults, \$2 students and seniors, \$1 children under 18. Two-for-one admission discounts are offered to members of WGBH and the Massachusetts Teachers Association.

What to See

MIT Museum has something to engage adventurous minds of all ages and interests. Watch a woman turn into a tiger in "Holography: The Light Fantastic." Watch a chair explode and reassemble itself in "Gestural Engineering: The Sculpture of Arthur Ganson." Watch your own

Rodney Brooks, head of MIT's Artificial Intelligence Laboratory, interacts with the robot Cog. From the MIT Museum exhibition "Robots & Beyond." Photo by Sam Ogden.

shadow freeze in "Flashes of Inspiration." Or try to keep your virtual marble from falling through the virtual hole of the lifesize MetaField Maze game.

The museum has a shop with puzzles, games, and technological whimsy. There is no café, but MIT Museum is surrounded by a variety of small restaurants serving everything from New American to Indian food.

While You're in the Area

The List Visual Arts Center (p. 278) is also on the MIT campus.

Mount Holyoke College Art Museum

Lower Lake Road
South Hadley, MA 01075-1499
(413) 538-2245
www.mtholyoke.edu/offices/artmuseum/

Overview

The Mount Holyoke College Art Museum is one of the oldest teaching museums in the country. Its founding in 1876 was marked by the gift of Albert Bierstadt's majestic painting *Hetch Hetchy Canyon*. Dedicated to providing firsthand experience with works of significant aesthetic and cultural value, the museum develops exhibitions and programs that aim to provide aesthetic enjoyment, stimulate inquisitive looking, and encourage understanding of the artistic achievements represented by a diversity of cultures.

Directions and Hours

The museum is located on the campus of Mount Holyoke College, 12 miles north of Springfield and 10 miles south of Amherst, Massachusetts.

From Route 91: Take exit 16 (Route 202 Holyoke/South Hadley). Turn right and proceed on Route 202 north through Holyoke and across the Connecticut River. Continue on Route 202 north and take the second exit marked South Hadley Center/Amherst to Route 116 north. The college is approximately two miles north of the exit. At the north corner of the campus, turn right onto Church Street. Take the second right onto Lower Lake Road. The museum is on the right adjacent to the greenhouse.

From the Massachusetts Turnpike: Take the West Springfield exit. Turn onto Route 91 north and follow the above direction.

The museum is currently undergoing substantial renovation and expansion and is closed to the public. The museum will re-open in February 2002. The museum offices remain open during the project Monday through Friday 8:30 A.M. to 5:00 P.M. The museum entrance, all galleries, and restroom facilities are handicap accessible.

Admission and Membership

Admission is free. Group visits are welcome by appointment, scheduled at least three weeks in advance. Membership to Friends of Art is $25/year for individuals, $100/year for a Patron, $250/year for a Sponsor, $500 for a Benefactor, and $1000 for the Director's Circle membership.

What to See

The museum maintains a comprehensive collection of approximately 13,000 objects ranging from antiquity to the present. Primary strengths include Asian art; nineteenth- and twentieth-century European and American paintings and sculpture; Egyptian, Greek, and Roman art; Medieval sculpture; early Italian Renaissance paintings; and an extensive collection of prints, drawings, and photographs.

Notable objects include a statuette of a youth, a very significant example of Greek bronze sculpture from the Classical period; a red-figure column krater by the Eupolis Painter, of great interest to students of Greek religion, costume, and cult performance; a bronze bust of Isis that has been described as one of the finest to have survived from the Roman period; a rare fragment of Duccio's celebrated Maestà altarpiece; a panel painting by Guariento, acknowledged by scholars to be the finest work in America by this Paduan master; and the only known pair of screens by Yukinobu, the most distinguished Japanese woman painter of the Edo period. In 1997 the museum added to its strong collection of antiquities an important portrait of the second-century Empress Faustina, wife of Antoninus Pius. Seen alongside the museum's outstanding wall paintings of Pompeii and its ancient coins—some with Faustina's likeness—this sculpture contributes substantially to the picture of the Roman material environment that our collection provides for visitors.

In Fall 2003 the museum presents Sally Mann at Work—an exhibition of photographs by Sally Mann, many never previously exhibited.

A three part educational program entitled "Daily Life and Afterlife: Ancient Egypt, Greece, and Rome" is usually offered to school groups each spring. During the construction project the museum is providing an abridged version of the program. A Mount Holyoke student can visit a classroom in the school (if located within a 30-mile radius of South Hadley) to present a participatory lesson on archaeology. A volunteer docent can also present an introduction to the museum's collections in the classroom, using color slides. Materials and follow up activities will also be available. There is no charge for the program, but the museum does suggest a $25 donation to the museum, which would be much appreciated.

The museum does not have a gift shop but catalogues of current and past exhibitions as well as notecards are available for sale. Several restaurants are located within easy walking distance at The Village Commons, located across from the college on College Street (Route 116).

While You're in the Area

The Hampshire College Art Gallery (p. 333), the Mead Art Museum at Amherst College (p. 334), the Smith College Museum of Art (p. 335), the University Gallery at the University of Massachusetts Amherst (p. 336), and Historic Deerfield are all within a 10-15 mile drive of the Mount Holyoke College Art Museum.

The Mount, Home of Edith Wharton

Edith Wharton Restoration, Inc.
PO Box 974
2 Plunkett St.
Lenox, MA 01240
(413) 673-1899
www.edithwharton.org

Overview

The Mount is an American Classical mansion designed and built by Edith Wharton, the first woman to receive the Pulitzer prize for fiction. The design was based on the precepts of her influential book, *The Decoration of Houses.* The house is one of only 5 percent of National Historic Landmarks dedicated to a woman.

The East Elevation of The Mount. Photo by David Andersen. Courtesy of Edith Wharton Restoration at The Mount.

Directions and Hours

From the Mass Pike take exit 2. Get on Route 20 west, and go through the town of Lee. After seeing the sign "Entering Lenox," watch for Plunkett Street on the left. Turn onto Plunkett Street and go one mile to The Mount's entrance on the left.

From Route 7, the mount is at the Southern junction of Routes 7 and 7A in Lenox (5-6 miles North of Stockbridge, MA).

The Mount is open daily from 9:00-5:00 from May through October and is handicap accessible. Please call for confirmation of hours before you visit.

Admission and Membership

Current admission rates are $6/adult, $5.50/seniors, $4.50/13-18, free under 12. Group discounts are available. Rates will increase, however, as new phases of construction are completed. There is currently no membership program, but contributions are accepted.

What to See

Newly restored interior rooms offer visitors a representation of the turn -of-the-century splendor Wharton surrounded herself in. She designed her own gardens, which are being restored to their former state.

The Edith Wharton Restoration annually presents a Women of Achievement lecture series in July and August. The speakers are published authorities on their subjects. The events are held on Mondays at 4:00, and include tea and book signing.

During the school year, The Mount works with local schools to teach children about the author.

The museum has a book and gift shop, and is planning to serve food from carts in the near future.

While You're in the Area

Other nearby places of interest include Tanglewood, the Clark Art Institute (p. 320), the Mission House (p. 277), and the Shaker Village (p. 255).

Museum of Afro-American History

14 Beacon Street, Suite 719
Boston, MA 02108
(617) 725-0022
(508) 228-9833 Nantucket
www.afroammuseum.org

Overview

The museum of Afro-American History is a not-for-profit cultural institution dedicated to preserving, conserving, and accurately interpreting the contributions of African Americans. Through educational workshops, youth camps, special events, and unique partnerships with professional organizations and educational institutions, the Museum places the African American experience in an accurate social, cultural, and historical perspective.

Directions and Hours

The Museum of Afro-American History's Abiel Smith School and African Meeting House are located at 8 Smith Court and 46 Joy Street on Beacon Hill, Boston.

Public Transportation: The museum is accessible by MBTA at the Park Street Station on the Red or Green lines. From the Park Street Station, walk up Park Street to the State House with the gold dome. The State House is on Beacon Street. Turn left on Beacon and then turn right on Joy Street. Walk up the hill and start back down again. Smith Court is the fourth street on the left toward the bottom of the hill.

By car: Take the Government Center exit off Storrow Drive (east or west). Proceed down Cambridge Street toward downtown Boston. Pass Massachusetts General Hospital and the Holiday Inn on your left. After you pass the fire station on your right, you will see Joy Street which runs one way into Cambridge Street.

Smith Court is the first right up Joy Street.

Parking: Parking on Beacon Hill is limited to Beacon Hill residents. You can park at a meter on Cambridge Street or in the Cambridge Street Garage or in the Charles River Plaza parking lot on Cambridge Street across from Joy Street. For weekend and evening events $5 validated parking is available at the Cambridge Street Garage, under the Holiday Inn. Bring the ticket to the museum for validation.

The museum is open year round and is handicap accessible.

Boston hours: Memorial Day-Labor Day: Monday-Sunday 10:00 A.M. to 4:00 P.M. Labor Day-Memorial Day: Monday-Saturday 10:00 A.M. to 4:00 P.M. Nantucket hours: By Appointment.

Admission and Membership

Museum admission is free. Suggested donation is $5 per adult, $3 for students and senior citizens.

What to See

The museum began its first exhibitions and public gatherings in 1963. Today the museums houses permanent, interactive exhibits that include "The Times We Had," "Separate Schools, Unequal Education," and the film presentation "Building on a Firm Foundation," as well as historic artifacts and works of art. The Museum of Afro-American History's other assets are: The African Meeting House on Beacon Hill, the oldest extant black church building in the US built in 1806 by free African American artisans; The Abiel Smith School on Beacon Hill, the first public school in the country for African American children constructed in 1835 Boston; The African Meeting House on Nantucket Island, the only public building constructed and occupied by African Americans in the nineteenth century still standing on Nantucket Island; and The Black Heritage Trail®, a 1.6 mile walking tour encompassing the largest collection of historic sites in the country relating to the life of a free African American community prior to the Civil War. The history of these buildings and sites is national in scope. The MAAH treasures its resources and preserves the remarkable and vivid history of free African Americans and white abolitionists whose effort changed a nation.

Touchscreen computer interactives are also available. In one program 10 different animations explore the Atlantic Slave Trade and the ideas of freedom and proposals for self-determination that were communicated across the seas. Another computer interactive explores the idea of courage and heroes while still another allows the visitor to act as the editor of one of two famed abolitionist newspapers. Historical

Boston African American National Historic Site

14 Beacon Street, Suite 503
Boston, MA 02108
(617) 742-5415
www.nps.gov/boaf

The National Park Service offers free guided tours of the Black Heritage Trail® through the historic neighborhood of Beacon Hill for groups with advance reservations Tuesday through Saturday at 10:00 A.M., twelve noon, and 2:00 P.M. Reservations for groups are required with 24 hours advance notice.

The two hour walking tour is 1.6 miles and departs from the Shaw Memorial at the corner of Beacon and Park Street, across from the gold-domed State House. Fourteen different sites are viewed. The African Meeting House (Site 14), the oldest extant black church in America, and the Abiel Smith School are open daily 10:00 A.M. to 4:00 P.M. The Museum of Afro-American History and the National Park Service operate the Black Heritage Trail®, the African Meeting House, and the Abiel Smith School under a cooperative agreement.

speeches and articles from the 1800s can be viewed.

There is a museum store. There is no café but there are restaurants on Cambridge Street and Beacon Street and visitors can picnic on Boston Commons.

While You're in the Area

Interesting attractions nearby include the SPNEA State House (p. 257), Boston Commons, and the Black Heritage Trail® (owned and operated by the museum).

Museum of Fine Arts, Boston

Avenue of the Arts
465 Huntington Avenue
Boston, MA 02115-5523
(617) 267-9300
www.mfa.org

Overview

The Museum of Fine Arts, Boston, has one the finest collections of artwork in America, ranging from ancient Egyptian sculptures to paintings from all over the world. The works are grouped by country rather than chronologically. The museum has a huge body of art which includes 38 works by Monet, a crucifixion of 1310 by Duccio, and works by Gaugin and Renoir, to name only a few. Short essays written by the museum's curators describe each painting.

Directions and Hours

From the Mass Pike (I-90): Take the Prudential Center exit (exit 22) and bear right. At the Prudential/Copley sign bear left and follow the Prudential signs; you will come out on Huntington Avenue. Stay on Huntington, going under the underpass. The museum will be on the right Go past the museum and make a right on Museum Road to reach parking.

From Route 128: Take Route 3 (Fitzgerald Expressway) to Massachusetts Avenue (exit 18). Follow Mass Ave. until it crosses Columbus Avenue. Make a left onto St. Botolph Street and follow it for one block. Make a right onto Gainsborough and go one block to Huntington Avenue. Turn left on Huntington; the museum will be on your right. Make a right into the parking area.

The museum is open year-round and is handicap accessible. The museum is closed Thanksgiving and Christmas but open Mondays and on all Monday holidays.

Hours: Monday and Tuesday 10:00 A.M. to 4:45 P.M., Wednesday, Thursday, and Friday 10:00 A.M. to 9:45 P.M. (Thursday and Friday West Wing only after 5:00 P.M.), and Saturday and Sunday 10:00 A.M. to 5:45 P.M. Please note that Gund Gallery closes 15 minutes before the museum. The Musical Instruments Collection is open from 11:00 A.M. to 4:00 P.M. 7 days a week.

Admission and Membership

Adults $12 (fee reduced to $2 during West Wing-only hours—Tuesday and Friday after 5:00 P.M.), senior citizens and college students, $10 (fee reduced to $1 during West Wing-only hours—Thursday and Friday after 5:00 P.M.), and youth 7-17 $5 or free ($5 on school days until 3:00 P.M. admitted free at all other times). Children under 7 are free at all times. Wednesday evenings 4:00-9:45 P.M. general admission is by voluntary contribution. Please note that there may be an additional charge for some special exhibitions. Groups by appointment only—adults call (617) 369-3368 and youth/school groups call (617) 369-3310. Membership is $60 for an individual, $40 for a special rate for museum friends living outside of New England, $80 for a dual/family membership, $135 for a family plus membership, $135 to be an Associate, $250 to be a Universal member, $600 to be a Supporting member, $900 to be a Sustaining member, and $2,000 to be a Patron.

What to See

Children's programs include the Children's

Room, a free gallery and workshop program for kids age 6-12. Children are involved in active exploration of the museum's collections through art projects, dramatics, poetry, and music. Classes meet Monday through Friday from October to May from 3:30-4:45 P.M. in July and August. No preregistration is required. A Family Place is also available, where puzzles, games, and other activities send children on a self-guided tour of art from around the world. Art classes and workshops are offered as well, which include drawing, painting, sculpture, and weaving. Preregistration is required. School Vacation Week Adventures in February and April public school vacation has activities ranging from hands-on art making and self-guided activities to films and performances. No preregistration is required but children must be accompanied by an adult.

There is a gift shop and dining available.

While You're in the Area

Other interesting attractions in the area include the Boston Tea Party Ship (p. 331) and the Boston Aquarium (p. 291).

Museum of Madeiran Heritage

1 Funchal Place
New Bedford, MA 02746
(508) 994-2573
www.portuguesefeast.com

Overview

The Museum of Madeiran Heritage (Madeira is a semi-tropical island that lies 600 miles southwest of Portugal) is the only museum dedicated to the preservation of art and artifacts from the island of Madeira. The museum houses Madeiran art, homemade embroidery, lace, linens, and carvings. The museum also has an archive of Madeiran-American families.

Directions and Hours

From Providence and points west: Take I-195 east to exit 16 (Washburn Street/Belleville Avenue). Take a right on Washburn Street and then another immediate right on Belleville Avenue. Follow Belleville Avenue for .8 miles to Hathaway Street. Take a left on Hathaway Street and an immediate right onto Funchal Place.

From Boston and points north: Take Route 24 south to Route 140 south to I-195 east to exit 16. Follow the directions above.

From Cape Cod and points east: Take I-195 west to exit 17 (Coggeshall Street). Take a left on Coggeshall Street to the first set of lights (Belleville Avenue). Take a right on Belleville Avenue and follow it for .7 miles to Hathaway Street. Take a left onto Hathaway Street and then an immediate right on Funchal Place.

The museum is open from April-November and is handicap accessible.

Hours: Sundays 10:00 A.M. to 4:00 P.M. or by appointment.

Admission and Membership

Adults $4, seniors $3, children under 14 $1. Special or group discounts are available. Student (group) tours are available.

What to See

On display is a *corca*, or sled, used to transport visitors downhill from a hill in Funchal (the capital of Madeira), a *carro de bois* (a canopied carriage without wheels), and a three dimensional model of Madeira showing its topographical features (a gift from the island's government). Next to the museum is a Madeira garden with a grape arbor and a central fountain.

Held during the first full weekend of August every year since 1915, New England's largest ethnic festival (300,000 visitors are expected in 2001) is the Feast of the Blessed Sacrament. Featured is a parade, live entertainment, authentic cuisine, a barbecue pit, and traditional *carne d'espeto*. There is no charge. Also available, through agreement with the Madeiran government, is Madeira wine.

Special events, lectures, and exhibits are

scheduled thoughout the year. Please contact the museum for more details.

There is a gift shop. The New Bedford area has a large variety of places to eat. The museum opens a quiet covered outdoor café during the annual Feast of the Blessed sacrament.

While You're in the Area

Other interesting attractions nearby include: the New Bedford Art Museum (p. 334), the New Bedford Whaling Museum (p. 289), the Rotch-Jones-Duff House and Garden Museum (p. 335), and the Schooner *Ernestina* Museum (p. 335).

The Museum of Our National Heritage

33 Marrett Road
Lexington, MA 02421
(781) 861-6559
www.monh.org

Overview

The museum presents a wide range of exhibitions on American history and popular culture. As many as 12 different shows per year are presented. It is known as "Lexington's premier museum."

Directions and Hours

From 128 north or south, take exit 30A. The museum is 2.5 miles off the exit on Route 2A.

The museum is open year round. It is handicap accessible.

Hours: Monday-Saturday, 10:00-5:00, Sunday 12:00-5:00.

Admission and Membership

Admission is free. Membership is $40/year for households, $30/year for singles, and $20/year for seniors and students.

What to See

The museum has a permanent exhibition, "Lexington Alarm'd," showing how and why Lexington became the launch site for the Revolutionary War. Visitors can find out what exactly happened on the Battle Green the morning of April 19, 1775. The museum also displays a fully restored 15-star American flag. The only similar flag is at the Smithsonian.

Special annual events include the Heritage Festival, held each September, and special programming on Patriot's Day Weekend. In October of 2002, the museum will present "Enterprising Women" in conjunction with the Schlesinger Library. A permanent exhibit "To Build and Sustain: Freemason in American Community" will open in October 2002.

Children's programming includes a series of "Second Saturday" programs for children and families. Other programs are presented during vacation weeks and throughout the summer.

There is a gift shop and a café will be opening soon.

While You're in the Area

Lexington, the town known as the birthplace of the American Revolution, offers many other historic sites to visit. Also nearby is the Lexington Historical Society (p. 271).

Museums on the Green

Falmouth Historical Society
55-65 Palmer Avenue
Falmouth, MA 02540
(508) 548-4857
www.FalmouthHistoricalSociety.org

Overview

The Falmouth Historical Society, founded in 1900, is the oldest and largest historical society on Cape Cod. It maintains two historic eighteenth century homes as museums, connected by a colonial garden, in the center of Falmouth's historic district just off the Village Green. The 1790 Julia Wood House, with one of the town's few remaining "Widow's Walks," features period rooms which offer an intimate look at the Falmouth of yesteryear. The Conant House, a typical eighteenth century Cape Cod "half-house," is noted for its exhibits on nineteenth century whaling. Trained guides lead visitors through the museums, sharing highlights of 300 years of Falmouth history.

The Julia Wood House. Photo courtesy of the Falmouth Historical Society.

Directions and Hours

The Museums are 14 miles south of the Cape Cod Canal. Cross the Bourne Bridge onto Cape Cod and follow Route 28 to Falmouth. Stay on Route 28 at the Jones Road traffic lights and continue half a mile. Turn left on Palmer Avenue toward Falmouth Center and the Village Green where the museums are on the left.

The Museums are open during the summer, weekends in the fall, and by appointment the rest of the year. The Archives, Library and Office are open year round. The museums are not handicap accessible. (Note: The 100 year old Hallett Barn, currently under restoration and scheduled for future use in 2002 as an educational center with hands-on exhibits, will be handicap accessible.)

Summer hours: Tuesday through Saturday, 10:00 A.M. to 4:00 P.M.

Fall hours: Saturday and Sunday, 1:00-4:00.

Admission and Membership

$4 per person. Children under 12 and members are free. Group rates are available, and there is a AAA discount. Individual, family and business memberships are available.

What to See

Not to be missed is a room chronicling the life of Katharine Lee Bates, author of "America the Beautiful," who was born and raised in Falmouth. Also, learn about the British brig *Nimrod*, which opened fire on the village during the War of 1812 and see one of its cannon, which is carefully being restored by the Museum.

Special attention is given to exhibits of Falmouth's golden age of whaling, which occurred between 1830 and 1870 when whaling masters took their families on four-year cruises in the Pacific.

Changing exhibits showcase unique aspects of Falmouth's growth, such as evaporating salt from seawater, the expansion of the railroad, and the turning of open meadow into a major cranberry and strawberry-growing center.

During the summer, special programs include Trolley Tours of Falmouth History, Teas in Julia's Garden on the museum grounds, and free Walking Tours of Falmouth Village. Free public lectures with guest speakers are held in the spring and fall. The Hallett Barn on the museum grounds will offer special hands-on educational exhibits upon completion of a current restoration project.

Summer family programs include a Colonial Fair in July with demonstrations of eighteenth century life and crafts and the Annual Katharine Lee Bates Poetry Fest in August. An October Halloween program takes place in Falmouth's Old Burying Ground when spirits of the town's early settlers are brought back to life by members of the Falmouth Historical Society.

The Museum Store features distinctive gifts, unique collectibles, books, and unusual items for children. The Museums have no café but are just a short walk away from the many restaurants and shops on Main Street.

While You're in the Area

Falmouth harbor, beaches, Beebe Woods for a quiet woodland stroll, and the Shining Sea

Bikepath are within walking distance, as are shops, restaurants, and historic bed and breakfast inns. Historic Nobska Lighthouse and Woods Hole with its museums, Oceanographic Exhibit Center (p. 331), aquarium, and the ferries to Martha's Vineyard are nearby.

Naismith Memorial Basketball Hall of Fame

1150 West Columbus Avenue
Springfield, MA 01105
(413) 781-6500 or (877) 4HOOPLA
www.hoophall.com or www.basketball-halloffame.com

Overview

The Naismith Memorial Basketball Hall of Fame houses memorabilia and exhibits that celebrate the game of basketball and the great players who have played over the years. The Hall of Fame was founded by the National Association of Basketball Coaches in 1949. Its first class was honored in 1959, starring the early legends of basketball. The original Basketball Hall of Fame was opened on the Springfield College Campus on February 17, 1968 and remained there until June 30, 1985, when the current Hall of Fame was opened in Springfield. By the end of 2002 a new Basketball Hall of Fame is expected to be opened, nearly doubling the size of the existing Hall.

Directions and Hours

From the east or west: Take the Massachusetts Turnpike (Route 90) to exit 4 (91 south). Take exit 7. Continue straight off exit 7 for one mile. The Hall of Fame appears on the right.

From the north (Vermont): Take 91 south. Follow above directions.

From Maine: Take 95 south to 495 south to Massachusetts Turnpike west (route 90) to exit 4 and follow above directions.

From New York City and South: Take 95 north to exit 47 (91 north). Continue straight on 91 north for 60 miles until exit 4 (Broad Street exit). Go to your second light and take a left. At the next light turn left. The Hall of Fame will appear on your right.

The Hall of Fame is open year 362 days a year and is fully handicap accessible. Closed on Thanksgiving, Christmas, and New Year's Day.

Hours: Open seven days a week from 10:00 A.M. to 5:00 P.M.

Admission and Membership

$10 for adults, $6 for youths 7-14, children free with parent. Group rates are available for 15 or more people at $7 a person for adults and $4 per person for youths. Parking is free.

What to See

The Hall of Fame has a 208 seat theater with a 20 by 30 foot screen. The Edward J. and Gena G. Hickox Library at the Hall of Fame is a public facility that collects and displays items about basketball from the high school, college, and professional levels that document the history of basketball and attempts to preserve the game. A full-time staff is available to assist visitors. For guests who want to learn more about the game, the library has over 5,000 books, 100 periodicals, archival material, scrapbooks, photographs, and film and oral histories. The oral histories consist of either cassette or video recorded interviews which are then transcribed, but are available for research purposes by appointment only.

The Hall of Fame offers many children's programs. During Spring Vacation 2001, for example, the Hall of Fame plans a week's worth of activities, including live demonstrations, safety messages, mounted police, motorcycles, movies in the Converse Theater, official NASCAR cars, drivers, and pit crews along with video highlights. Kids can shoot baskets, as well as play video and basketball arcade games. The Hall of Fame also has ongoing exhibits like the Classic NBA photo exhibit and "Freedom to Play."

There is an extensive gift shop with many college and professional team items plus Hall of

Fame merchandise. The Hall of Fame has a food court (special group rates are available).

While You're in the Area

Attractions in the area include the Connecticut Valley Historical Museum (p. 235), the George Walter Vincent Smith Art Museum (p. 248), the Springfield Museum of Fine Arts (p. 316), the Springfield Science Museum (p. 318), the Springfield Armory National Historic Site (p. 335), the Indian Motorcycle Museum and Hall of Fame (p. 261), and Symphony Hall.

Naumkeag House and Gardens (Trustees of Reservations)

5 Prospect Hill Road
Stockbridge, MA 01262
(413) 298-3239
www.thetrustees.org

Overview

Designed by the firm McKim, Mead & White in 1885, the Naumkeag House is one of the true "country cottages" of the Berkshires. Visitors can view original furnishings owned by the Choate family from 1886-1958.

Directions and Hours

From the intersection of Route 7 and Route 102 (at the Red Lion Inn) in Stockbridge take Pine Street north. Bear left onto Prospect Hill Road and follow for ½ mile to the House's entrance on the left.

The house is open from Memorial Day weekend-Columbus Day.

Hours: Daily 10:00 A.M. to 5:00 P.M. The last tour is at 4:00 P.M.

Admission and Membership

Adults $8 for a house tour, $6 for a self-guided garden tour. Free for Trustees of Reservations members. Group and senior discounts are available. No strollers or backpacks are allowed. Membership is $40/year for an individual, $60/year for a family, $30/year for students and senior citizens, and $50/year for a family of students and senior citizens. Benefactor membership is: $100/year for a contributing, $150/year for a supporting, $300/year for a sustaining, and $600/year for a sponsor.

What to See

Built in 1885 for Joseph and Caroline Choate, Naumkeag is filled with a fine collection of Asian, European, and American ceramics, rugs, and furniture. The interiors were left intact when the house became a property of the Trustees of Reservations in 1959. Eight acres of landscaped gardens designed by Fletcher Steele surround the property.

There is a gift shop but no café. Visitors can eat in the center of Stockbridge.

While You're in the Area

Other museums or interesting attractions nearby include other Trustees of Reservations properties such as The Mission House (p. 277) and the Colonel John Ashley House (p. 232), as well as Rockwell, Chesterwood, and the Berkshire Museum (p. 331).

New Bedford Whaling Museum

18 Johnny Cake Hill
New Bedford, MA 02740
(508) 997-0046
www.whalingmuseum.org

Overview

The Whaling Museum was established in 1907 to tell the story of American whaling and to describe the role New Bedford played as the whaling capital of the world in the nineteenth century. The Museum is the largest in America devoted to the history of the American whaling industry and its greatest port. Through exhibits, publications, and programs, the museum brings to life the whaling era and the history of the local area. It houses the most extensive collection of art, artifacts, and manuscripts pertaining to American whaling in the age of sail—late eighteenth century to the early twentieth, when sailing ships dominated merchant trade and whaling.

Directions and Hours

New Bedford is located one hour south of Boston and 35 minutes east of Providence. From the west: Take the Mass. Turnpike to exit 11A to Rte. 495 south to exit 7B. Then take Rte. 24 south to New Bedford, exit 12. Take Rte. 140 south to exit 2E, which is Rte. 195 East Cape Cod. Get off exit 15, Route 18, the New Bedford Historic District. Take the downtown exit. Turn right on Elm Street and take the second left onto Bethel Street, which becomes Johnny Cake Hill. Museum is on the second block.

From north/central: Take either Rte. 495 south or Rte. 128 south (whichever is closest to Route 24) and follow directions listed above. From the south: Take Route 95 North to Route 195 East, then follow directions above. From Cape Cod: take Route 495 North to Route 25 to Route 195 to exit 15, Route 18, then follow directions above.

Street parking is available, as well as a parking garage on Elm Street.

The museum is open year round. There is handicap access to most of the museum.

Hours: Open daily 9:00-5:00; until 9:00 P.M. the second Thursday of each month. Closed Thanksgiving, Christmas, and New Year's Day.

Admission and Membership

Adults $6, senior citizens and students with ID $5, children (6-14) $4. Admission is free for members of the museum and children under 6. Group rates are available for 10 or more visitors, with a reservation made at least two weeks in advance. There is a 10% discount for AAA members. Membership is $30/year for individuals, $45/year for a dual membership, and $60/year for a family.

What to See

The museum houses an 89-foot half-scale model and interactive exhibits about whales and life aboard a whale ship. Also on display are paintings, photographs, and logbooks. The museum is one of only three locations in the United States where the public can view a complete blue whale skeleton.

A research library is open to the general public, students, and scholars by appointment. The Research Library contains the world's largest collection of printed and manuscript material on American whaling, as well as information on maritime and local history. Open hours are Monday-Friday 10:00 A.M. to 12:00 P.M. and 1:00 P.M. to 4:00 P.M. on the first Saturday of the month. Closed all holidays. Please call for an appointment: (508) 997-0046, Ext. 14.

The museum has many exhibitions, including: "New Bedford and the Sea" and "A Whaling Voyage 'Round the World: Melville's Inspiration Revisited."

Children's programming includes "Saturdays at Sea" from 2:00-4:00 P.M. and various other children's activities throughout the year.

There is a museum store. There is no café but there are many cafés and restaurants within walking distance of the museum.

While You're in the Area

The museum is the centerpiece of the New Bedford Whaling National Historical Park, which was established to preserve and interpret America's nineteenth century whaling and maritime history. It consists of a 13-block Waterfront Historic District. Visitors should also stop by the Schooner Ernestina, the New Bedford Art Museum (p. 334), and the Rotch-Jones-Duff House and Garden Museum (p. 335), and the famous Seameus Bethel, depicted in Melville's *Moby Dick*.

New England Aquarium

Central Wharf

Boston, MA 02110-3399
(617) 973-5200
www.neaq.org

Overview

The Aquarium's Giant Ocean Tank holds 200,000 gallons and is home to hundreds of different species of marine life including sharks, eels, and sea turtles. Divers enter the tank several times a day to feed the animals. The Aquarium Medical Center exhibit is a behind-the-scenes look at the Aquarium's animal care facility. Visitors can watch actual medical procedures being administered to fish, penguins, turtles, frogs, and a host of other aquatic features. In addition, the Aquarium houses three species of penguins: rockhopper penguins, African penguins, and the world's smallest, little blue penguins.

Directions and Hours

From West—Storrow Drive: Take Storrow Drive west to the end and follow signs to Interstate 93 south. Take the Callahan Tunnel exit. At the bottom of the ramp, there is a very busy intersection. (Ahead and to the left is the entrance to the Tunnel. *Do not* take the tunnel to the airport.) Go through the intersection and follow the sign for "Waterfront Surface Artery." Continue along underneath the elevated highway with Faneuil Hall on your right. Stay in the left lane and watch for Aquarium signs. The Aquarium is ahead about three blocks on the left.

From West—Mass Pike: Follow the Mass Pike to its end, and follow signs for Route 93 north. Take exit 22, Atlantic Avenue. At the stop sign, bear left so the Northern Avenue Bridge is on your right. Follow Atlantic Avenue past Rowes Wharf, a large hotel on the right. Continue straight two more blocks and turn right at the 7-Eleven. The Aquarium is directly ahead.

From North—Interstate 93 south: Take Interstate 93 south to the Callahan Tunnel exit. At the bottom of the ramp, there is a very busy intersection. (Ahead and to the left is the entrance to the Tunnel. *Do not* take the tunnel to the airport.) Go through the intersection and follow the sign for "Waterfront Surface Artery." Continue along underneath the elevated highway with Faneuil Hall on your right. Stay in the left lane and watch for Aquarium signs. The Aquarium is about three blocks on the left.

From South—Interstate 93 north: From Interstate 93 north, take exit 22, Atlantic Avenue. At the stop sign, bear left so the Northern Avenue Bridge is on your right. Follow Atlantic Avenue past Rowes Wharf, a large hotel on right. Continue straight two more blocks and turn right at the 7-Eleven. The Aquarium is directly ahead.

From East—Airport: Take the Sumner Tunnel to Boston. Once out of the tunnel, bear right onto Cross Street. Follow signs for Interstate 93 south, but *do not* get onto the highway (which will be ahead and to the left) Watch for Dock Square sign and head diagonally across, bearing right. Haymarket and the Bostonian Hotel will be on the right. Follow the sign for "Waterfront Surface Artery," which takes you under the expressway. The Aquarium is straight ahead, about three blocks on left. Watch for a 7-Eleven on the corner.

The Aquarium is open year round, and is handicap accessible.

Winter hours (Day after Labor Day-June 30): Monday-Friday, 9:00-5:00; weekends and holidays: 9:00-6:00. Closed Thanksgiving Day and Christmas Day. Open at noon on New Year's Day.

Summer hours (July 1-Labor Day): Monday, Tuesday, Friday: 9:00-6:00; Wednesday, Thursday: 9:00-8:00; weekends and holidays: 9:00-7:00.

Admission and Membership

Adults $13, Senior Citizens $11, Juniors (3-11 years) $7. Members and children younger than 3 are admitted free. For group rates, please call our reservations department at (617) 973-5206. Seniors also get discounted admission rates.

African penguins. Photo courtesy of the New England Aquarium.

Membership rates range from $40-$250. In addition to free admission, other benefits of membership include discounts on parking, educational programs, and whale watches. Members also receive invitations to special events, lectures and members-only exhibit viewings. Keep your admission receipt when you visit the Aquarium and you have up to two weeks to use the admission fee as a credit toward the cost of membership. Membership is fully tax-deductible.

What to See

The centerpiece of the Aquarium is the Great Ocean Tank, which holds 200,000 gallons of water and hundreds of species of marine life. The Aquarium's Medical Center is also a must-see. The museum's divers give informative talks several times a day while feeding the penguins and sea otters.

"Nyanja! Africa's Inland Sea" is an exhibit focusing on Africa's Lake Victoria, the world's second largest lake and the source of the Nile River. This two-story exhibit features a great variety of animals native to the lake: three huge pythons, weaver birds, hairy baboon tarantulas, lungfish, a ten-foot Nile crocodile, and hundreds of species of cichlids, a small fish that is the fastest evolving species in the world. Nyanja will close in early 2002.

A new exhibit will open around April, 2002 and will invite visitors to "travel" with sea turtles, frogs and fish through an interconnected mosaic of habitats.

The aquarium is opening an IMAX theater in late 2001.

Children's programs include an Exploration Center located adjacent to the aquarium. It houses an Activity Center, which features hands-on science and art projects for kids ages 0-10, and an interactive Immersion Theater.

The Aquarium has a gift shop and a café.

While You're in the Area

The Aquarium is located in downtown Boston, near the Children's Museum (p. 228), Museum of Science (p. 334), and the historic Quincy Market, which is part of the Freedom Trail.

The Norman Rockwell Museum at Stockbridge

9 Glendale Road Route 183
PO Box 308
Stockbridge, MA 01262-0308
(413) 298-4100
www.normanrockwellmuseum.org

Overview

Norman Rockwell captured both everyday and historic events throughout most of the twentieth century. His images were a defining influence on generations of Americans. The museum houses the world's largest and most significant collection of Rockwell's work, including 574 original paintings and drawings. Rockwell's Stockbridge studio, moved to the museum site, is open to the public from May through October, and features original art materials, his library, furnishings, personal items, and changing exhibitions of Rockwell's work and that of other noted illustrators, both past and present.

Directions and Hours

From the east: Boston (2½ hours) or Springfield (1 hour): Take the Massachusetts Turnpike, getting off at exit 2 (Lee). Take Route 102 west into Stockbridge center, about five miles. Follow directions from The Red Lion Inn, below.

From New York City: (2½ hours) Take either the Taconic Parkway or Route 22 north to Route 23 east. Proceed to Great Barrington and pick up Route 7 north. Follow Route 7 north to Stockbridge center and follow the directions from The Red Lion Inn, below.

From Hartford: (1½ hours) Go north on I-91 to the Mass Pike and follow directions from the east.

From Albany and west: (1 hour) Take Route I-90 east to Route 22, exit B3. Go south on NY Route 22 to Mass Route 102. Follow Route 102 through West Stockbridge and travel approximately 5.5 miles to the flashing light at the intersection of Route 183. Turn right and proceed .6 miles to the museum entrance on the left.

From the north or south: Route 7 runs north to south through the Berkshires. Follow Route 7 to Stockbridge and The Red Lion Inn. Follow Directions from The Red Lion Inn.

From The Red Lion Inn, Stockbridge Center: (5 minutes) Go west on Route 102 (Main Street). Turn right onto Church Street (102) for about 1.8 miles. At the flashing light, turn left onto Route 183 (south) and go .6 miles to the museum entrance.

The museum is open year round and is handicap accessible.

Hours: May-October 10:00 A.M. to 5:00 P.M. November-April 10:00 A.M. to 4:00 P.M. weekdays and 10:00 A.M. to 5:00 P.M. on weekends and holidays. The museum is closed on Thanksgiving, Christmas, and New Year's Day. Norman Rockwell's Studio is open from May through October, 10:00am-4:45 P.M.

Admission and Membership

Museum admission is $10 for adults, $7 for students. Visitors age 18 and under are admitted free with an adult (up to 4/adult). Special discounts are available for groups of 15 or more at a rate of $9. Seniors are half price on Wednesdays from November-April only. Membership is $35/year for individuals and $50/year for a dual membership. Call (413) 298-4100 x230 for more information.

What to See

The Norman Rockwell Museum at Stockbridge holds the world's largest collection of original Norman Rockwell art. The museum also houses the Norman Rockwell Archives, a collection of over 100,000 items, including working photographs, letters, personal calendars, fan mail, and business documents as well as sculptures by Peter Rockwell (Norman's son).

The Norman Rockwell Museum at Stockbridge has recently celebrated its thirtieth anniversary, and is moving in new directions, with a national touring exhibition and ongoing forays into the field of illustration.

Programs for everyone from students to scholars use active learning that is inspirational for people of all abilities and backgrounds. Children's programming includes a school vacation week with special classes for all ages, but the museum has innovative offerings available year round.

There is a gift shop on the premises, and snacks are available from summer-fall. Places to eat nearby include the Red Lion Inn, Once Upon a Table, and Michael's Restaurant.

While You're in the Area

There are many interesting attractions nearby. They include the Berkshire Museum (p. 331), Chesterwood, Berkshire Botanical Garden (p. 331), Naumkeag Mission House (p. 289), Merwin House, Tanglewood, the Berkshire

Theatre festival, Arrowhead, MASS MOCA (p. 276), Jacob's Pillow, Williams College Art Museum (p. 326), Clark Art Museum (p. 320), Shakespeare & Co., Edith Wharton (p. 281), Ventfort Hall, and Canyon Ranch.

North Andover Historical Society

153 Academy Rd.
North Andover, MA 01845
(978) 686-4035
www.essexheritage.org

Overview

The North Andover Historical Society owns five historic buildings on three sites and maintains a collection that documents life in North Andover/ Eastern Massachusetts from the seventeeth to the twenty-first century. The Historical Society also runs a library/ archive.

Directions and Hours

Take 495 to exit 43 (Massachusetts Ave.) Follow Massachusetts Ave. toward North Andover for approximately two miles. After passing two traffic lights, begin looking for the Museum Gallery, which is located two blocks down on the left.

The Museum Gallery and 1789 Johnson Cottage is open from Wednesday through Friday, 10:00-12:00 and 2:00-4:00. Call for inquiries regarding Spring and Fall hours for the Parson Bernard House. The main gallery is handicap accessible.

Admission and Membership

Tour rates are $3/adults, $2/seniors, $1/children under 12, and $5 for research. Call for group rates. Membership is $20/year for individuals, $30/year for families, and $15/year for seniors.

What to See

The Society maintains two sites that have museums featuring furniture, tool, and household collections, which were started by the founder, Samuel D. Stevens. The Parson Barnard House (1715) features gardens, a ca. 1812 barn with nineteenth-century farming equipment, vehicles, and a schoolroom. The Johnson Cottage showcases the daily life of men and women in the mid-nineteenth century. The archive/library houses personal, town, and church records, as well as genealogies, photographs, ephemera, and an inventory of historically and architecturally significant North Andover buildings. In addition, the society sits within an historic district that evokes life in Federal America.

Annually, the first Sunday in October is Harvest Day at the Parson Barnard House. Children's programming includes workshops on historic crafts throughout the year, "Adventures in Time" Summer programs, and school programs for second, third, fourth, and seventh grades.

There is a gift shop, and visitors can eat at the "Top of the Scales" restaurant, which is within walking distance.

While You're in the Area

The Museum of Printing (p. 334) is right next door.

Old Greenfield Village

386 Mohawk Trail (Route 2)
PO Box 1124
Greenfield, MA 01302
(413) 774-7138
www.crocker.com/greenfield/ogr.html

Overview

Waine Morse began gathering fixtures over 37 years ago and his passion for antiques led to the development of Old Greenfield Village, a museum of Americana. Old Greenfield Village is the setting for a replica of a New England town as it appeared in 1895.

Directions and Hours

From I-91: Take exit 26 in Greenfield, MA and

drive ½ mile west on the Mohawk Trail.

The museum is open from May 15-October 15 and is handicap accessible.

Hours: 10:00 A.M. to 4:00 P.M. Wednesday-Monday. Closed on Tuesdays.

Photo courtesy of Old Greenfield Village.

Admission and Membership

$5 adults, $4 seniors, $3 youth ages 6-16, age 5 and under no charge. Group discounts are available.

What to See

Old Greenfield Village consists of the following shops and settings: A General Store, a church/schoolhouse perched on a hill overlooking the village, a Drug Store, a Blacksmith and Tinsmith Shop, an Ice Cream Parlor with an original Italian marble soda fountain, a Candy Counter, a Toy Shop, a Doctor's Office, a Dentist's Office, an Eye Specialist, a Barber Shop, a Drygood Shop, a Woodworker and Wheelwright's Shop, a Steamfitter's Shop, machine equipment, thread cutting tools, a Builder's Shop, a Print Shop, and a nineteenth century fire engine. The village also houses a collection that traces the development of taps and dies back to 1872. The production of these taps and dies made Greenfield the thread-cutting capital of the world. A collection of murals by artist Thurston Munson also resides in Old Greenfield Village.

There is a gift shop. Visitors can eat at restaurants or fast food only ¼ mile away.

While You're in the Area

The Shelburne Falls Trolley Museum (p. 313) is nearby.

Old South Meeting House

310 Washington Street
Boston, MA 02108
(617) 482-6439
www.oldsouthmeetinghouse.org

Overview

The Old South Meeting House, built in 1729, was the largest building in colonial Boston. It is in this building that the Boston Tea Party began, and where colonists came to challenge British rule. It is still used today as a showcase for controversial debate. The Meeting House has a permanent exhibit called Voice of Protest where the story of the Old South Meeting House and the people who have spoken there over the years is told.

Directions and Hours

From the north: Take 93 south to the North Station exit. At the end of the exit ramp, take a right onto Causeway Street. At the lights turn right onto North Washington Street. Follow North Washington Street to the end. Turn right at the lights onto New Chardon Street. At the next set of lights turn left onto Congress Street. Continue straight on Congress Street to Franklin Street. Take a right onto Franklin Street and follow it to Arch Street. Take a right onto Arch Street and follow to the end then take a left to Milk Street. Old South Meeting House is on the right. For the main entrance take a right onto Washington Street and enter through the large wooden red doors.

From the south: Take 93 north to the Downtown/South Street exit. *Bear left at the end of the exit ramp and cross Kneeland Street at the lights. You are on Surface Road. Go through the next set of lights. At the third set of lights take a left onto South Street. Go through the first set of lights onto High Street. At the next set of lights there is no choice but to turn left onto Federal Street. Follow to Franklin Street. Turn left on Franklin Street, then turn right on Arch Street. At the end of Arch Street, turn left on Milk Street. The Old South Meeting House is on the right.

The Old South Meeting House, Boston. Photo by Sam Sweezy.

From the west: Take the Mass Turnpike (I-90) into Boston to the Downtown/South Street exit. Follow directions from the * above to the Old South Meeting House.

From the west via Storrow Drive: Take the Government Center/Kendall Square exit. Go straight at the lights, then follow the Government Center sign (you are on Cambridge Street). Go through eight sets of lights. At the ninth light take a left onto School Street. Meeting House is in front of you at the corner of Milk Street.

Parking: The Meeting House validates parking at 275 Washington Street Garage and the Post Office Square Parking Garage.

The museum is open year round and is handicap accessible.

Hours: Open daily. April-October 9:30 A.M. to 5:00 P.M. and November-March 10:00 A.M. to 4:00 P.M. Closed on Thanksgiving, Christmas Eve Day, Christmas Day, and New Year's Day.

Admission and Membership

Adults $3, seniors/students $2.50. Kids under 6 free. Discounted admission rates are available for school and adult groups with reservations. One adult is required for every 10 children and is admitted free. Additional adults will be charged $3. For the "Tea is Brewing" program additional adults will be charged $5. Group reservations must be made at least three weeks ahead of time. Membership is $30/year for individuals, $50/year for families, $100/year for Friends, $250/year for Contributors, $500/year for Donors, and $1,000/year for Patrons.

What to See

The Old South Meeting House has programs that consist of concerts, lectures, walking tours, and special events. Visitors get to learn about historical figures in their struggle for free speech such as Phillis Wheatley, George Robert Twelves Hewes, Mayor James Michael Curley, and Margaret Sanger. The Meeting House offers a Thursday lunchtime lecture and concert series

October through April from 12:15-1:00 P.M. Music is incorporated into ongoing programs.

Children's programming is available; many educational programs are offered such as "Short Stop on the Freedom Trail," "Tea is Brewing," "Tea Party Meeting," "Slave to Poet: Phillis Wheatley, Speaking Out!" People and Place Programs, and Teacher Workshops. All programs vary in cost, grade level, and time, so please contact the Meeting House for more information.

There is a gift shop. There are many places to eat in Boston.

While You're in the Area

Interesting attractions nearby include the State House, the Old State House, the Paul Revere House (p. 302), the U.S.S. *Constitution* Museum (p. 336), and the Bunker Hill Museum (p. 332).

Old Sturbridge Village

1 Old Sturbridge Village Rd.
Sturbridge, MA 01566
(508) 347-3362 or (800) SEE-1830
www.osv.org

Overview

Old Sturbridge Village is a re-created village where historically costumed staff demonstrate the daily life, work, and community celebrations of a rural New England town of the early nineteenth century. The museum covers over 200 acres with more than 40 exhibits, including restored houses, gardens, meetinghouses, mills, a district school, a working farm, a country store, and craft shops such as a blacksmith shop and a tin shop.

Directions and Hours

Old Sturbridge Village is located off Route 20 in Sturbridge, exit 9 off the Mass Pike (I-90); exit 2 off I-84.

Old Sturbridge Village is open year round, and is handicap accessible. Hours for 2001 are as follows:

February 19-March 30, 2001 Open daily, 10:00-4:00.

March 31-October 28, 2001 Open daily, 9:00-5:00.

October 29-January 1, 2002 Open daily, 10:00-4:00. (closed Christmas Day, December 25)

January 1-February 17, 2002 Open Saturdays and Sundays, 10:00-4:00. (open New Year's Day, January 1)

February 18-March 29, 2002 Open daily, 10:00-4:00.

March 30-October 27, 2002 Open daily, 9:00-5:00.

Admission and Membership

$20 for adults, $18 for seniors (65 and over), $10 for youths (ages 6-15). Children under age 6 are admitted free. Seniors aged 65 and over receive discounted admission rate ($18) and Group rates are available for parties of 15 or more with advance reservation. For more information on groups, call 508-347-3362, ext. 291.

Admission tickets may be credited toward Museum Membership, which offers free admission and other benefits. Individual membership is $50 per year. Family membership is $80 per year. Call 508-347-3362, ext. 212 for information about other membership levels and benefits. Membership in the Old Sturbridge Village Kids' Club, geared toward children ages 8-12, is $10 per child.

What to See

A trip to Old Sturbridge Village, the largest outdoor history museum in the Northeast, is a journey through time to a rural New England town of the 1830s. Visitors are invited into a historical landscape of more than 40 buildings, including many original eighteenth- and nineteenth-century structures carefully researched and brought to the museum site from towns throughout New England. These restorations and authentic reproductions include a working farm, homes, meetinghouses, a district school, country store, bank, law office, printing office, carding mill, sawmill, gristmill, pottery, blacksmith shop, shoe shop, and cooper shop.

Authentically costumed staff, called history interpreters, carry out the daily activities of an early nineteenth-century community. Visitors may wander country roads and talk with a farmer plowing fields, hear the blacksmith's rhythmic hammering, smell the aroma of bread baking in a fireplace oven, or help the tinner with his work. With four unique seasons and more than 200 acres to explore, there is always something new to see at Old Sturbridge Village.

The period portrayed by Old Sturbridge Village, 1790-1840, was an important time in American history when everyday life was being transformed by revolutions in commerce and manufacturing, westward migration and the growth of cities, improvements in farming and transportation, and the tides of social and cultural change. The Village's portrayal of the past is based on its extensive collections, ongoing research, archaeology, and painstaking study of historical documents.

Samson's Children's Museum opened in 1999 to provide new hands-on learning opportunities for children ages three to seven. Activities include a play kitchen with a pretend hearth and fireplace cooking tools, a one-room school with benches and slates, a costume try-on space, a book corner, an area for games and toys, and a computer station where children can design their own quilt blocks. Additional activities, led by museum staff, are frequently available. Samson's Children's Museum is open each day from 10:00 A.M. to museum closing.

Due for completion in Fall 2001, the Tavern at Old Sturbridge Village will offer a nineteenth-century dining experience that's both unique and educational. The decor, the entertainment, the furnishings, the table settings, and the menu are all designed to transport the diner to an earlier time in our nation's history. In addition to being open for lunch and dinner every day, the tavern will be the setting for hearthside cooking demonstrations and other special events, and will be available for private functions.

The Shops at Old Sturbridge Village include the Museum Gift Shop and the New England Bookstore. The expanded New England Bookstore, which re-opened in its new spacious quarters in June 2000, has a broad selection of books on a variety of topics, including local and American history, cooking, gardening, crafts of all kinds, and a children's section. There is also a section on poetry and early American literature as well as recordings. The Museum Gift Shop offers items made at Old Sturbridge Village by tinsmiths, potters, and blacksmiths, accents for the home, a selection of specialty New England foods, accessories, toys and games, and t-shirts.

Within the Village, the Bullard Tavern offers a seasonal buffet of New England fare, while its year-round cafeteria offers a menu of à la carte items including hot entrées, soups, salads, and snacks. The Village also maintains a picnic grove accessible from the main parking lot. From Memorial Day through Columbus Day, The Pantry, a scenic patio café near the Museum Gift Shop and Herb Garden, offers fresh deli sandwiches, salads, and gourmet coffee. No admission is required to tour the Herb Garden, lunch at The Pantry, or shop at the Museum Gift Shop and New England Bookstore.

For overnight accommodations, the Old Sturbridge Village Lodges and Oliver Wight House are located near the museum on Route 20 in Sturbridge, Mass. The OSV Lodges offer a range of accommodations, including wheelchair-accessible rooms, smoke-free rooms, and special packages. For reservations or additional information, call or write Old Sturbridge Village Lodges, Route 20, PO Box 481, Sturbridge, MA 01566; 508-347-3327. TTY: 508-347-2235. FAX: 508-347- 3018. e-mail: osvlodge@osv.org. A charming Bed & Breakfast in Sturbridge is the Commonwealth Cottage. For other lodging options, visit www.sturbridge.org.

While You're in the Area

Sturbridge has a wealth of shopping and dining. The Publick House, a New England inn dating from 1777, is located not far away, on the common of the Town of Sturbridge. Yankee Candle, Hebert's Candies, and Country Curtains each have a store in town, and there are many places to shop for antiques as well. Hyland Orchards and Brewery offers tours and beer-making demonstrations. Stageloft Repertory Theater is an excellent local theater troupe. Salem Cross Inn, located 20 minutes away in West Brookfield, is an historic inn that offers unique dining experiences (Fireplace Feasts in winter, Maple Gathering dinners in March, Herbal Dinners in summer, Drover's Roast in spring and fall). Other excellent restaurants in Sturbridge include the Cedar Street Restaurant, the Whistling Swan (and its casual alter-ego The Ugly Duckling) and the Hearthstone Inn. The town of Brimfield, famous for its flea markets, is located just west of Sturbridge on Route 20.

Osterville Historical Society and Museum

PO Box 3
155 West Bay Road
Osterville, MA 02655
(508) 428-5861
www.osterville.org

Overview

The Osterville Historical Society Museum has five historical buildings on its grounds, which make up three separate museums. The Captain Jonathan Parker House sits on its original site and contains the majority of the Osterville Historical Society's arts and antiques. The Boat Shop Museum traces the development of the renowned local style of wooden boat building and features Crosby Catboats, a Wianno Senior and Junior, a Crosby Striper, and several smaller boats. The Cammett House is furnished as a farmhouse in the 1790s.

Directions and Hours

Conveniently located in the center of Osterville the museum can be accessed by both Routes 28 and 6 (follow the signs for Osterville, and then the Historic Museum signs).

The museum is open from mid-June through mid-October, and by appointment other times of the year.

Hours: Thursday-Sunday 1:30-4:30.

Admission and Membership

$2 for adults; children and members are free.

What to See

The Cammett House (c. 1790) was saved from demolition and moved to the museum grounds in 1981. It is one of the few examples existing of a "one room deep" dwelling of post and beam construction. The kitchen has a beehive oven, root cellar, and an herb garden is outside.

Inside the Captain Parker House are exhibits of Pairpont glass, Chinese Export ceramics, textiles and fans, historical portraits, paintings, and heirlooms. The Children's Room holds a unique

The Boat Shop Museum. Photo Courtesy of the Osterville Historical Society.

collection of dolls, doll houses and toys.

The Colonial Garden, designed and maintained by the Osterville Garden Club offers a changing panorama of seasonal flowers.

The museum gift shop carries Osterville-related items, including Sandwich cup plates and nautical motif stationary.

While You're in the Area

There are other historic museums in each of the seven villages of Barnstable.

The Paine House (Trustees of Reservations)

Greenwood Farm
Jeffrey's Neck Road
Ipswich, MA 01938
Phone number
(978) 356-4351
www.thetrustees.org

Overview

The Paine House at Greenwood Farm is a rare example of a First Period House sited on its original location, surrounded by hundreds of acres of salt marsh and islands. Interpretive signage explains what The Trustees of Reservations has done with archaeology at this site. The Paine House also explains its history as an early twentieth century guest house for the Dodge family's summer estate, Greenwood Farm. Colonial Revival furnishings decorate rooms of the house and describe this once-fashionable movement.

Directions and Hours

Route I-95/Route 128 North to exit 20A, Route 1A North. Follow 1A eight miles to Ipswich. At Ipswich Town Green, stay straight (do not bear left into town center). Follow this road (County Road which turns into East Street). Pass Ipswich Town Landing on right. At approximately 1 mile bear left onto Jeffrey's Neck Road. Travel .7 miles until fieldstone pillars on right mark entrance to property. Parking halfway down on left.

The museum is opening in June 2001. Guided tours are offered on Sundays, 1:00-5:00 P.M.; groups tours are by appointment. The museum is not handicap accessible.

Admission and Membership

Call for price and hours. Free for Trustees of Reservations members. Membership is $40/year for an individual, $60/year for a family, $30/year for students and senior citizens, and $50/year for a family of students and senior citizens. Benefactor membership is $100/year for a contributing, $150/year for a supporting, $300/year for a sustaining, and $600/year for a sponsor.

What to See

The Paine has in it a rare example of a colonial dairy, or buttery, probably dating to the third quarter of the eighteenth century. This is left partially exposed, with examples of the redware pottery found on site.

The collection includes examples of Essex County redware and other redware; late seventeenth, eighteenth and nineteenth century furniture and decorative arts; and some dolls.

There is no gift shop or café. Visitors are close to many Ipswich restaurants and cafes.

While You're in the Area

The Ipswich Historical Society (p. 333) has two House museums, the Whipple House and Heard House. The Trustees own The Great House at Castle Hill (p. 252) in Ipswich.

Paper House

52 Pigeon Hill Street
Rockport, MA 01966
(978) 546-2629
www.rockportusa.com

Overview

Paper House is a house, including furniture, made out of newspaper. Approximately 100,000 newspapers were used in the construction of the

Photo courtesy of Paper House.

house and furniture, which was constructed as a 20 year hobby from 1922-42 by a Swedish couple who liked to experiment. (The house is not all paper: there is a wooden frame, roof, and floor.) Ellis F. Stenman thought of the idea after experimenting with newspaper to use as insulation for the cottage he was building. The material was so hardy that he varnished it to make it waterproof. The cottage was used as a summer cottage from 1924-1929.

Directions and Hours

Take Route 128 north to Route 127 north. Follow Route 127 north to Pigeon Cove. Turn left onto Curtis Street and then left again onto Pigeon Hill Street.

The museum is open from April 1 through October 31 and is not handicap accessible.

Hours: 10:00 A.M. to 5:00 P.M. daily.

Admission and Membership

There is no cost but donations are accepted.

What to See

The furniture consists of a table, chairs, lamps, a settee, a desk made of the *Christian Science Monitor*, a cot with some papers saved since the First World War, a piano covered with paper rolls, a radio cabinet, a writing desk made up of Charles Lindbergh's flight, a bookshelf, a grandfather's clock made of newspapers from each of the then 48 states, and a fireplace mantel.

While You're in the Area

Attractions and museums located nearby include the Sandy Bay Historical Society (p. 311), and many art galleries in a seaside town.

Parson Capen House & Gould Barn

#1 Howlett Street, PO Box 323
Topsfield, MA 01983
(978) 887-3998
www.tiac.net/users/topshist

Overview

The Parson Capen House dates from 1683 and is furnished in the style of the late seventeenth century. The Gould Barn dates from 1710 and retains the flavor of the early eighteenth century. The property is on the National Historic Register.

Directions and Hours

Take I-95 north of Boston to exit 50. Go north on Route 1 for three miles. Turn left onto Route 47 at the light. Proceed one-half mile to East Common Street. Go right 200 yards to sign and parking space.

The museum is open from mid-June to mid-September. It is partially handicap accessible.

Hours: Wednesday, Friday, and Sunday 1:00 to 4:30.

Admission and Membership

Donations are accepted. Membership is $10/year for an individual and $15/year for couple.

Children under 12 must be supervised by an adult.

What to See

The Parson Capen House is one of a few rare surviving examples of Elizabethan architecture in the United States. Herb tea is served on Wednesdays. The museum sponsors an annual visit of local fourth graders to the house.

There is a modest gift shop. Visitors can eat at the Day Break Café, the Topsfield House of Pizza, and other restaurants in the area.

While You're in the Area

While in Topsfield, visitors can also see the Topsfield Common (ca. pre-1775), a witchcraft marker in memory of three victims, and the Pine Grove Cemetery (dating from the 1600s). The Massachusetts Audubon's Ipswitch River Wildlife Sanctuary features 2,600 acres two miles away, and the historic town of Salem is 10 miles to the east.

The Paul Revere House

19 North Square
Boston, MA 02113
(617) 523-2338
www.paulreverehouse.org

Overview

The Paul Revere House (ca. 1680) is the oldest building in downtown Boston and the only building left from the original wooden city. The house was also Paul Revere's home from 1770 to 1800. It is one of Boston's 16 Freedom Trail sites.

Directions and Hours

From the north: Take Route 93 to the Callahan Tunnel/Dock Square exit. Take an immediate left onto North Street and stay to the left.

From the west: Take I-90 to Route 93 north to the Atlantic Avenue/Northern Avenue exit. Go north on Atlantic Avenue and turn left on Richmond Street. Turn right on North Street and stay to the left.

From the south: Take Route 93 north to the Atlantic Avenue/Northern Avenue exit. Go north on Atlantic Avenue and turn left on Richmond Street. Turn right on North Street and stay to the left. (See the website for map and parking information.)

The museum is open year round. It is partially handicap accessible.

Daily hours: November 1-April 14, 9:30-4:15; April 15-October 31, 9:30-5:15; closed Mondays from January-March.

Admission and Membership

$2.50 adult, $2 for college students with an ID and for seniors 62 and up, $1 for children ages 5-17. Group rates are available with two-week advance reservation. Memberships range from $15 to $250.

What to See

The Paul Revere House features four rooms that are furnished with seventeenth and eighteenth-century American and European pieces, including seven Revere family pieces. Also exhibited are some examples of Revere silver.

Seasonal events and programming are scheduled throughout the year, such as special programs for Patriot's Day held in April, Saturday living history programs from May-October, a fall lecture series in September, and holiday tours on the first weekend in December. Children's programming is also available.

There is a gift shop, and the surrounding neighborhood (the North End) is known for its many fine Italian restaurants.

While You're in the Area

Other Boston sites worth visiting include Faneuil Hall/Quincy Market to the south, the Old North Church to the north, and many other museums and attractions.

Peabody Essex Museum

East India Square
Salem, MA 01970
1 800 745 4054, ext. 3011
www.pem.org

Overview

The Peabody Essex Museum offers an extraordinary blend of art, architecture, and culture. It is one of New England's largest museums, with renowned collections of maritime art and history, American decorative art, folk art, portraits, costumes, and furniture, Native American art, art from Africa, and art from China, Japan, Korea, India, and the Pacific Islands. It also displays one of the world's largest and most important collections of Asian decorative arts produced for the west.

Directions and Hours

Via I-95 or U.S. 1 to Route 128 north: Take exit 26 (Lowell Street, Peabody). Proceed through Peabody center 2.4 miles; turn left after Dunkin Donuts onto Bridge Street (Route 107). Proceed 1.2 miles to Winter Street (1A). Turn right. Follow 1A past Salem Common (on the left) to Essex Street (opposite Hawthorne Hotel). Take a right onto Essex Street, then another for municipal parking.

Via 1A north: Follow Route 1A north one mile past Salem State College. Continue on Route 1A until it becomes Derby Street. Bear right onto Derby Street. Turn left onto Hawthorne Boulevard. Take a left onto Essex Street opposite the Hawthorne Hotel, then a right for municipal parking.

Via 1A south: Go through Beverly over the bridge into Salem. Follow 1A signs past Salem Common (on the left) to Essex Street (opposite Hawthorne Hotel). Take a right onto Essex Street. At the mall, take a right for municipal parking.

Via MBTA Commuter Rail: From the North Station take the Rockport/Ipswich Line to Salem. For MBTA information, call (617) 722-3200 (Boston only) or 1-800-392-6100.

Via Boston-Salem Ferry Service (From Boston's Long Wharf to historic Salem waterfront): Daily service begins in June and runs through October. Ferry passengers receive $1 off museum admission. Call Boston Harbor Cruises at (617) 227-4321 for tickets or more information.

Hours of operation are: Tuesday-Saturday, 10:00 A.M.-5:00 P.M., and Sunday noon-5:00 P.M. The museum is handicap accessible, but the historical houses are not.

Admission and Membership

Admission to the museum is $10/adults, $8/seniors and students over 16, and free for students 16 and under. House tours are $6 without admission to the museum. Rates for groups of 15 or more are $6/adults and $5/seniors. Groups of 14 or less are $8.50/adults and $7.50/seniors. Membership is $30/year for students and seniors, $40/year for one adult, $65/year for two adults, and $35/year for non-New England residents.

What to See

The museum collections include maritime arts and history, Asian arts, American decorative arts and architecture, and Native American and Oceanic art.

Upcoming exhibits include "Splendors from China's Imperial Palace" (July-September, 2001), "Edward Curtis" (October 2001-January 2002), and "Treasures of the Musee National de la Marine, Paris" (March 2002-June 2002).

Children's programming includes a nature culture room, and free Lowell Institute programs.

There is a gift shop and a café.

While You're in the Area

The Salem Witch Museum (p. 335), the Salem Maritime National Historic Site (p. 309), the House of Seven Gables (p. 333), and the Phillips Trust House (p. 319) are located nearby.

Pilgrim Hall Museum

75 Court Street
Plymouth, MA 02360-3891
(508) 746-1620
www.pilgrimhall.org

Overview

The Pilgrim Hall Museum, located in the center of historic Plymouth, is the oldest continuously operating museum in the country. Through its exhibition of Pilgrim and Native American artifacts, Pilgrim Hall tells the stories of America's founding and traditions. Among the treasures on display are William Bradford's *Bible*, the cradle in which Susanna White rocked her son Peregrine, the Loara Standish sampler (the first sampler made in America), the Jennie Brownscombe's painting "The First Thanksgiving," and the great chair of William Brewster. You'll see the skeleton of the eighteenth-century transatlantic vessel *Sparrow-Hawk* as well as the only portrait of a Pilgrim—Edward Winslow—actually painted from life. You will also learn the story of the Wampanoag, "People of the Dawn" who inhabited this area for 10,000 years before the arrival of the new settlers.

Directions and Hours

Take Route 3 to exit 6 (Rt. 44 East). Turn right at the end of the ramp and follow Rt. 44 toward the waterfront. At the intersection of Rt. 44 and Rt. 3A (Court Street) turn right, the museum is 2½ blocks on your left-hand side at 75 Court Street. Free parking is adjacent to the museum. The museum is open year round except for Christmas Day, New Year's Eve Day, and the month of January.

Hours: Seven days a week, 9:30-4:30, except for Christmas Eve and New Years Eve 9:30-12:00.

Admission and Membership

$5 for adults, $4.50 for senior citizens (62+) and AAA members, $3 for children 5-17, $15 for families. Plymouth residents are admitted free. Guided tours are offered to schools and other large groups, but must be reserved in advance by calling (508) 746-1620, ext. 3. Group rates are $2.50 per person.

Membership is Senior/Individual $20, Dual/Family $40, Sustaining $100, Supporting $1,000, and Family/Dual Life $1,500. Membership entitles you to a range of benefits including free admission, 10% discount in the Museum Shop, newsletters, invitations to exhibit openings, special events, and the annual celebration of Forefather's Day on December 21.

What to See

In addition to the permanent exhibitions, the museum presents 2-3 temporary exhibitions per year. In 2001, it will host Arms and Armour of the Pilgrims, April 6-October 31, 2001, and Patriots and Pilgrims: Plymouth and the Revolution from June 8 to April 30, 2002. A year-long series of special events including Paul Revere and Deborah Sampson presentations, a re-enactment of an American Revolution "recruiting party," an evening of dancing with Captain Magee, walking tours and several lectures will be held in conjunction with the Patriot and Pilgrim special exhibition. The first annual *Mayflowers* event will open on May 5, 2001. This weeklong special event will feature "floral interpretations" of museum artifacts. In 2002, the museum will host Three Hundred Years of Childhood and Samplers: A Stitch in Time featuring some of the earliest and finest samplers in America.

Pilgrim Hall Museum offers interactive educational programs designed to acquaint visitors of all ages with Pilgrim History. For instance, series of Treasure Hunt/Activity Sheets have been developed to guide visitors through the exhibit halls.

There is a gift shop. The museum doesn't have a café, but many cafés and waterfront restaurants are within walking distance in historic Plymouth.

While You're in the Area

Plymouth is home to several major historic landmarks. Visitors can follow the Pilgrim Path, a self-guided walking tour, to visit Plymouth Rock, the *Mayflower*, Burial Hill and several historic homes including the Hedge House (p. 259), the Spooner House (p. 315) and the Mayflower Society Museum (p. 334). Whale-watching cruises and Duck/Amphibious tours of Plymouth in addition to numerous boutiques and gift shops make Plymouth a great destination for visitors of all ages.

Pilgrim Monument and Provincetown Museum

High Pole Hill Road
PO Box 1125
Provincetown, MA 02657
(508) 487-1310
www.pilgrim-monument.org

Overview

The 252-foot granite Pilgrim Monument was erected between 1907-1910 to commemorate the "first" landing of the Mayflower Pilgrims in Provincetown Harbor. The town's skyline can be viewed from the top. The Provincetown Museum building houses artifacts from Provincetown's history, including maritime history and the Mayflower Pilgrims as well as exhibits on the birth of modern drama and Eugene O'Neill.

Directions and Hours

Take I-95 to Route 3 south to the Sagamore Bridge at the entrance to Cape Cod. After Bridge Road is Route 6, which leads through Cape Cod to Provincetown. Take the Shank Painter Road exit, then take the first left, followed by a right onto the next road (Winslow Road). Follow signs to the museum.

The museum is open from April-June and September-November between 9:00 A.M. and 5:00 P.M.; in July and August, hours are 9:00 A.M. to 7:00 P.M. Admission ends 45 minutes prior to the final closing. The museum building is handicap accessible, but the monument is not.

Admission and Membership

Admission to the museum is $6/adults, $3/children 4-12, and free for children under 4. Groups of 15 or more get discounted admission of $3/adults and $2.50/students.

What to See

The exhibits and collections of the Pilgrim Monument and Provincetown Museum reflect the long and varied history of Provincetown. Exhibits showcase the first landfall of the Mayflower Pilgrims and the signing of the Mayflower Compact in Provincetown Harbor in

The Pilgrim Monument

1620, through the development of the town as a major whaling and fishing center in the 1800s, to the development of Provincetown as a major art and theater mecca that continues today.

There is a gift shop but no café. There are many restaurants, sandwich shops, and fast food stands in the vicinity.

While You're in the Area

The Whydah Pirate Museum and the Provincetown Art Association and Museum (p. 335) are located nearby.

Plimoth Plantation & Mayflower II

PO Box 1620
137 Warren Ave
Plymouth MA 02362
(508) 746-1622
www.plimoth.org

Overview

The plantation features a living history museum of seventeenth century Plymouth. It includes a Pilgrim village where costumed role-players take visitors back in time to 1627, seven years after the Pilgrims arrived in Plymouth. There is also a Wampanoag homesite where contemporary Wampanoag people talk about their history and customs both in the seventeenth century and today. The craft center features some of the trades of early seventeenth century England, such as pottery, joinery, basketry and leatherwork. On the Plymouth waterfront is a recreation of the *Mayflower*, the ship that brought the Pilgrims to New Plymouth. Costumed role-players and modern guides tell about the first voyage and the history of the *Mayflower II*, built in 1956.

Directions and Hours

From Route 3 south, take exit 4 to Plimoth Plantation Highway and follow the signs. From Route 3 north, take exit 5, then circle back to Route 3 south, take exit 4 to Plimoth Plantation Highway, and follow the signs.

The plantation is open seasonally, from April to early December, seven days a week from 9:00-5:00. It is wheelchair accessible in some areas.

Admission and Membership

A combination ticket to Plimoth Plantation and *Mayflower II* is $22/adults, $14/children 6-12. Plimoth Plantation only is $20/adults, $12/children 6-12. *Mayflower II* only is $8/adults, $6/children 6-12. Children 5 and under admitted free. Levels of museum membership are available. Discounts for seniors, students, and AAA are offered at certain times.

What to See

Conversations with Pilgrim role-players and Wampanoag interpreters are a wonderful way to enjoy the museum and to learn about the early seventeenth century. The museum also has an indoor exhibit hall that currently tells the story of the Wamanoag and English relationship from 1627-1690 called "Irreconcilable Differences."

The indoor exhibit will change in July 2001 (pending funding) to an exhibit about Thanksgiving, dispelling myths and legends and describing the evolution of the holiday we now know.

Programming for school groups includes seventeenth-century games. There is also a summer camp for kids.

The museum has six gift shops. Cafeteria-stylemeals are offered, and there are many restaurants in Plymouth.

While You're in the Area

There is Pilgrim Hall Museum, the country's oldest museum of its kind, Cranberry World, a museum telling the history of the cranberry, an several other small museums in town. Plymouth has a beautiful walkable harbor where Mayflower II is docked. There is whales watching, sightseeing and fishing excursions all from Plymouth Harbor, some of the freshest seafood in

Massachusetts in quaint New England seafood shacks, many restaurants, a lovely downtown area with shopping and several antique shops.

Porter-Phelps-Huntington Museum

130 River Drive
Hadley, MA 01035
(413) 584-4699

Overview

Through the words, spaces, and possessions of women, the Porter-Phelps-Huntington Museum, containing the belongings of six generations of one extended family, portrays the activities of a wealthy and productive eighteenth-century household and its evolution into a nineteenth-century rural retreat and mid twentieth-century example of historic preservation.

Directions and Hours

Take Route 91 to exit 19. Follow Route 9 east to Route 47. Follow 47 north two miles. The museum is on the left.

The museum is open from May 15 through October 15. It is not handicap accessible.

Hours: Saturday-Wednesday 1:00-4:30.

Admission and Membership

$4 for adults, $1 for children 12 and under. There are various levels of contributing membership, starting at $25.

What to See

The museum exhibits the words, spaces, and possessions of three generations of women. Members of this household along with numerous artisans, servants, and slaves made "Forty Acres" an important social and commercial link in local, regional, and national cultural and economic networks.

The museum offers a Folk Tradition Concert Series every Wednesday in July and August. A Perfect Spot of Tea is held each Saturday in July and August, featuring tea and pastries with musical accompaniment by area performers and served on the Museum's back veranda. Children's programming includes Re-enactors Weekend in May and a performance series in September.

There is a small gift shop. The museum has no café, but tea is served on Saturdays in July and August and there are many restaurants in the Amherst/Northampton area.

While You're in the Area

Other local attractions include the Summit House at Mount Holyoke Range, Emily Dickinson Homestead (p. 240) and the Evergreen in Amherst, the Wistiriahurst Museum (p. 336), and historic districts in Deerfield and Northampton.

Porter Thermometer

49 Zarahemla Road
Box 944
Onset, MA 02558
(508) 295-5504
http://members.aol.com/thermometer-man/index.html

Overview

Onset is named the Thermometer Capital of the World thanks to Richard T. Porter, who's been collecting thermometers for 20 years, since retiring from teaching junior high science. In

Photo courtesy of Porter Thermometer Museum.

October 2000 the old record number of 3,500 thermometer devices was surpassed for entry into the *Guinness Book of World Records*.

Directions and Hours

I-495 ends at the intersection of I-195, about 50 miles south of Boston. It becomes State Route 25 toward the Bourne Bridge over Cape Cod Canal. Take a right off exit 1 (Onset) and take a right at the third red light (Depot Street). Cross the railroad tracks and veer left. Take the sixth left off Onset Avenue (Zarahemla Road). The museum is the sixth building from the end of the dead end, on the right (#49).

The museum is almost always open, year-round. The museum is shown at any hour, but it is best to call ahead.

Admission and Membership

Admission is free. Motto: Always FREE and almost always OPEN with over 3,500 to see.

What to See

Porter Thermometer museum collects all kinds of thermometers, including art deco, lab, fever, weather, marine, souvenir, rare, antique, unusual, and advertising thermometers. The museum also has eight thermometers used in Oliver Stone's film *U-Turn*, Deep Sea Reversing devices used by Wood Hole for El Nino in the Pacific, an 1830 French woodcut thermometer, a Galileo Thermometer, an Admiral Fitzroy Storm Glass, a 100-year-old Doctor's house call-type thermometer that has been in 5,000 armpits, an Alaskan thermometer that reads to -100 degrees, gift devices from around the world (Australia, Korea, China, Finland, Turkey, and England), the kind of thermometer that John Glenn used in space (pill-sized, swallowed with an external sensor), the type sewn into all spacesuits to prevent frostbite on space walks, and other worldwide souvenirs. The thermometers have been collected in 75 major trips taken to four continents, 20 countries, and all 50 states in the last 16 years.

Special programs include a traveling lecture series and interactive display table.

Porter Thermometer caters to visits by scouts and brownies for weather badge work, students working on science fair projects, home school families, and attends kid's and family fairs and festivals.

There is a small gift shop. There are many good and varied restaurants featuring seafood, pizza, and fast food within walking distance.

While You're in the Area

The museum is within five miles of the Cape Cod Canal and welcomes picnickers. It has an eight-mile walking and biking trail (no hills). Onset is a Victorian Village with gingerbread houses, red-brick sidewalks, and colonial lamps with gift shops, a Canal Cruiser, a Whale Watch boat, and antique shops.

Quincy House (SPNEA)

20 Muirhead Street
Quincy, MA 02170
(617) 471-4508
www.spnea.org

Overview

Built as a country estate, Quincy House was originally surrounded by fields and pasture overlooking Quincy Bay. Its elegant architectural details, including a Chinese fretwork balustrade and classical portico, befit the status of the man who built it, the Revolutionary leader Colonel Josiah Quincy. For generations, the Quincys, like the Adamses, to whom they were related, played important roles in the social and political life of Massachusetts. The family produced three mayors of Boston and a president of Harvard.

Directions and Hours

From the north: Take I-93 to exit 12, Route 3A (Hancock Street) to Wollaston Center. After 2.2 miles, turn left on Elm then turn left on Staunton. Jog right to Muirhead Street.

From the south: Take I-93 to exit 19, to Burgin Parkway. At the sixth traffic light, turn right on Dimmock, turn left on Hancock, right on Elm, left on Staunton, and right on Muirhead.

The museum is open June 1-October 15.

Hours: Saturday and Sunday, 11:00-5:00. Tours on the hour, from 11:00-4:00.

Admission and Membership

$3 for adults, $2.50 senior citizens, ½ off for students and children 6-12. Children 5 and under, SPNEA members, and residents of Quincy are free. AAA members receive a 2 for 1 discount. SPNEA membership is $35/year for individuals and $45/year for a household. Membership includes free admissions to 35 properties and museums across New England.

What to See

Much of the historical information pertaining to the house and family was documented in the early 1880s by Eliza Susan Quincy. She kept journals, inventoried the contents of the house, commissioned photographs of the interior, and persuaded relatives to return heirlooms so that the house could become a repository of Quincy family history.

Quincy House offers tours and public programs. School programs are available in the spring and fall.

While You're in the Area

Nearby attractions and museums include the Adams National Historic Site (p. 212) and the Birthplaces of John and John Quincy Adams.

Salem Maritime National Historic Site (NHS)

174 Derby Street
Salem, MA 01970
(978) 740-1660
www.nps.gov/sama

Overview

Salem Maritime NHS was the first NHS designated by Congress in 1937. The site tells the story of early American commercial shipping and trade to international ports from 1783-1807. The only three surviving pre-Revolutionary War wharves are part of the site, as are several historic buildings—the Custom House (1819), the Derby House (1782), and the Narbonne House (1671). A replica tall ship called the East Indian *Friendship* is open in summer.

Directions and Hours

From Route 128 North: Take exit 26 (Lowell Street) to Boston Street. Turn left on Bridge Street and follow the signs to the waterfront.

From Route 128 North (alternate Route): Take exit 25A (Route 114) to Downtown Salem and follow the waterfront signs.

Route 1A North and South will bring you to the Downtown Salem/Waterfront area as well.

From I-95 and I-93: Take the Route 128 North exit and follow the above directions.

The museum is open every day except Thanksgiving, Christmas, and New Year's Day. The orientation center is handicap accessible.

Hours: September-June 9:00-5:00, July-August 9:00-6:00.

Admission and Membership

There is no admission to the site, but there is an interpretive fee for guided tours of the historic buildings: $3 for adults, seniors and children $2.

What to See

The Salem Maritime National Historic Site shows a 17-minute movie every thirty minutes in the Orientation Center called "To the Farthest Part of the Rich East." The movie covers the early Salem maritime history from 1626 to modern day. The nine acre site has a spectacular view of Salem Harbor. A half mile walk down Derby Wharf takes you to the Lighthouse and is a favored walking trail. There is free entrance into the Custom House Warehouse, the Scale House, and the West Indian Goods Store. A picnic area and restrooms are available. Central Wharf gives visitors a view of replica tall ships and a reminder of what a busy port looked like during its trade heyday.

Children's programming is geared toward elementary school grades and some higher level education grades. Education programs are free but reservations are required..

There will be a Annual Maritime Festival from July 1-15, 2001. There will be arts, crafts, music, and food along with family fun. The Peabody Essex Museum is participating this year with programs from Alaska to Hawaii.

The museum does have a gift shop. There is no café but many local restaurants surround the site.

While You're in the Area

Other museums nearby are: the Peabody Essex Museum (p. 303) the Salem Wax Museum of Witches and Seafarers (p. 335), and the House of the Seven Gables (p. 333).

Sandwich Glass Museum

PO Box 103
129 Main Street
Sandwich, MA 12563-0103
(207) 265-2729
www.sandwichglassmusuem.org

Overview

The Sandwich Glass Museum, located in the heart of historic Sandwich Village, displays blown, pressed, cut, and decorated glassware that was made in Sandwich from 1825 to 1907. Fourteen galleries comprise the museum.

Directions and Hours

Take exit 2 off Route 6. Turn left at the end of the ramp onto Route 130 North. The museum is 1.5 miles on the right. Parking is behind the museum off Tupper Road.

The museum is open from February to December and closed Thanksgiving, Christmas, and the month of January. It is handicap accessible.

Hours: February-March, Wednesday-Sunday 9:30-4:00; April-December, daily 9:30-5:00.

Admission and Membership

$3.50 for adults, $1 for children 6-16, $2.50 each for groups of 10 or more. Walking tours are free to the public. Membership is $20/year for individuals, $30/year for families. There are various levels of contributing memberships also.

What to See

Exhibits include Sandwich glass made by more than 10 glass companies. Videos demonstrate the traditional methods of making glass.

Free walking tours that depart from the museum are offered during June, July, and August. "Stones of Time" features the town's oldest cemetery, which dates to the seventeenth century, and is scheduled mostly on Tuesdays. A "Lantern Tour of Historic Sandwich Village" is led by a costumed guide and is scheduled for Wednesday evenings. A "Lantern Tour of Historic Town Hall Square" is scheduled for Saturday, December 1. Tours range from 1-1½ hours and may be canceled by inclement weather.

The fourteenth annual Cape Cod Glass Show will be held September 15-16, 2001 at Cape Cod Community College. Glass dealers offering all manner of antique glassware as well as reference material and resources are highlights.

Children can participate in a "Treasure Hunt" by using an activity sheet to help them locate special pieces of glassware in the museum.

There is a gift shop that features both contemporary and older glassware. Visitors can dine at the Daniel Webster Inn, the Dunbar Tea Room, and Marshlands nearby.

While You're in the Area

Other local attractions are the Heritage Plantation of Sandwich (p. 333), the Thornton

Burgess Museum (p. 323) and Green Briar Jam Kitchen (p. 253).

Sandy Bay Historical Society and Museums, Inc.

PO Box 63
Rockport, MA 01966
(978) 546-9533

Overview

The Sandy Bay Historical Society and Museums owns and operates the Sewall-Scripture House, built in 1832 by Levi Sewall, on 40 King Street and the Old Castle, a 1715 saltbox built by Jethro Wheeler, located in Pigeon Cove Center.

Directions and Hours

Take Route 128 north to Route 127 north. Follow Route 127 north to Rockport. The society is on Route 127, at the corner of Granite and King Streets.

The Sewell Scripture House is open mid-June to mid-September and other times by appointment. It is partly handicap accessible. Hours: Monday-Saturday 2:00-5:00. The library is open Monday 9:00-1:00.

The Old Castle is open July and August on Saturday from 2:00-5:00 and by appointment.

Admission and Membership

$3 for adults includes admission to both museums. Children 12 and under are free. Discounts are available by special arrangement.

What to See

The Sewall-Scripture House was built with granite from Levi Sewall's own quarry. It was lived in by his descendants until purchased by the historical society in 1957. A library with extensive holdings of local history and genealogical information is located in a new addition. The house also features a Victorian Parlor, the Marine Room, Keeping Room, Children's Room, and Military Room. The Hatchet Gang Exhibit and local artwares are other attractions.

The Old Castle contains Dogtown exhibits, quarry tools, and North Village history.

There is no gift shop but the society sells books of local interest.

While You're in the Area

The Paper House (p. 300) on Curtis Street is another local attraction.

Semitic Museum of Harvard University

6 Divinity Avenue, Cambridge MA 02138
(617) 495-4631
www.fas.harvard.edu/~semitic

Overview

The Semitic Museum, founded in 1889, is Harvard University's repository for its ancient Near Eastern archaeological collections and home to the university's Department of Near Eastern Languages and Civilizations. The Museum uses its collections for teaching, research, and publication of Near Eastern archaeology, history, and culture.

Directions and Hours

Driving: From I-95 (Route 128) North or South, follow the Massachusetts Turnpike toward Boston. Exit at Allston/Cambridge, exit 18. Bear right on the exit ramp for Cambridge. At the end of the ramp, cross the Charles River on the River Street Bridge. After the bridge turn left onto Memorial Drive. At the third traffic signal, turn right onto JFK Street and follow JFK Street through Harvard Square. Continue through Harvard Square, keeping the Harvard Coop on your left. At the traffic signal in front of the Johnson Gate, the main gate into Harvard Yard, bear right through the underpass, staying in the left lane. At the intersection beyond the underpass, turn left onto Quincy Street. Travel one block. At the next intersection (Quincy and

Kirkland), turn right at the traffic signal, then immediately left onto Divinity. The Museum is at 6 Divinity Avenue. *Note*: There is no parking on Divinity Avenue, but there is limited street parking on Kirkland. The nearest commercial parking lots are in Harvard Square.

Walking: From the Harvard Square T station cross Massachusetts Avenue and walk a short distance down Massachusetts Avenue toward the Cambridge Common. At the Johnson Gate, the main gate into Harvard Yard, turn right into the Yard and face University Hall, a large, gray granite building with the statue of John Harvard in front of it. Turn diagonally left and exit the Yard through the North Gate. Outside the gate is the Science Center, large modern complex; to the right is Memorial Hall, a large Victorian-style brick building. Follow the walkway diagonally between the Science Center and Memorial Hall onto Kirkland Street. Walk one block down Kirkland and turn left onto Divinity Avenue. The Semitic Museum is halfway down the road on the right.

The museum is open year round, 10:00-4 :00 Monday-Friday, 1:00-4:00, Sunday; closed Saturdays and University holidays. It is not handicap accessible.

Admission and Membership

Free of charge; donations are accepted.

Membership (annual): $35 (member), $50 (donor), $100 (contributor), $250 (supporting), $500 (sustaining), $1000 (benefactor). Members receive the Museum Newsletter, regular announcements of Museum-sponsored lectures, and a discount in the museum shop.

What to See

The collections comprise over 40,000 artifacts from museum-sponsored expeditions to Iraq, Jordan, Israel, Egypt, Cyprus, and Tunisia. The Museum uses these collections for teaching, exhibition, research, and publication of ancient Near Eastern archaeology, history, and culture.

Ongoing exhibits include "the Sphinx and The Pyramids: 100 Years of American Archaeology at Giza," "Ancient Cyprus: The Cesnola Collection at the Semitic Museum," and "Nuzi and the Hurrians: Fragments from a Forgotten Past." Docent-led tours are available by appointment. The Museum sponsors an annual free public lecture series by visiting scholars on ancient Near Eastern topics. The Museum also sponsors archaeological field research in the Near East, with special emphasis on those ancient cultures related to the world of the Bible. The Museum publishes results of these and other investigations of the archaeology, history, languages, and cultures of the ancient Near East in its publications, the Harvard Semitic Series, Harvard Semitic Monographs, and Studies in the History and Archaeology of the Levant.

The Museum has an active public outreach program featuring tours for school groups and teacher training workshops. Through its educational efforts, the Museum seeks to promote a wider public understanding of the civilizations of the Near East and their great cultural legacies.

There is a gift shop, but there is no café on the premises. Biolabs Café is next door (open 8:00-3:00, Monday-Friday).

While You're in the Area

Harvard Peabody Museum (p. 335), Harvard Museums of Natural History (p. 258), and the Harvard University Art Museums (p. 333) are all on the Harvard University campus.

Sheffield Historical Society

159-161 Main Street
PO Box 747
Sheffield, MA 01257
(413) 229-2694
sheffieldhistory.org

Overview

The Sheffield Historical Society maintains several historic structures: the 1774 Dan Raymond

House, the 1820 Parker Hall Law Office, the nineteenth-century Carriage House and Tool Exhibit, and the 1876 Brick Learning Center. The Mark Dewey Research Center also features genealogical and local history sources.

Directions and Hours

The Sheffield Historical Society is located on Route 7, just north of the Connecticut state line and south of Great Barrington.

The Dan Raymond House is open from Memorial Day through October 31 on Thursday through Saturday, 11:00-4:00. It is open from November through Memorial Day by appointment.

The Mark Dewey Research Center is open year round, Monday-Friday, 1:30-4:00 and by appointment.

Handicap accessibility is very limited.

Admission and Membership

Regular admission to the Dan Raymond House is $5 for adults, $4 for seniors, and $1 for children 6-16. Monthly meetings are free. Special event fees vary. Memberships range from $10/year for individuals to $100 or more for lifetime memberships.

What to See

The Mark Dewey Research Center is free and open to the public. Its collections relate to the social and genealogical history of Sheffield and surrounding towns in Berkshire County. An extensive collection of documents dates back to 1730 and includes house histories, maps, photographs, cemetery records, and family histories.

The Dan Raymond House is a brick structure that remains nearly the same as it was during the Revolution, when it was one of Sheffield's finest homes. It is furnished with artifacts representative of Dan Raymond's time.

The Parker Law Office is a two-room office that served three lawyers throughout the nineteenth century. The building was rescued and moved by the society in the mid-1970s.

The Carriage House is a two-story clapboard structure that showcases a variety of ingenious tools and devices used in rural farms and in households of generations past.

The Sheffield Historical Society's collection housed in the above historic structures includes furniture, ephemera, portraits, ceramics, toys, textiles, and tools. The buildings are open for guided tours, school programs, special events and workshops. An extensive calendar of events and programs scheduled throughout the year is offered.

Educational programming in the Brick Learning Center, formerly a Victorian vegetable growing house, includes "A Place in Time," a three-phase experiential learning program and that focuses on children's activities in a historic environment. These programs are geared toward specific grade levels and address topics in the Massachusetts "Social Studies Framework."

There is a small museum gift shop. Visitors can eat in local establishments in Great Barrington, 10 minutes from Sheffield center.

While You're in the Area

Sheffield has numerous antique shops, nature centers, and cultural attractions as well as several historic sites within a half hour.

Shelburne Falls Trolley Museum

PO Box 272
14 Depot Street
Shelburne Falls, MA 01370
(413) 625-9443
www.sftm.org

Overview

The Shelburne Falls Trolley Museum gives rides on a restored 1896 trolley car for the public on weekends and holidays, and has a display of local railroad and trolley related information, artifacts, and pictures. A Baldwin 0-4-0T steam engine and a 1910 CV caboose are also under restoration.

Directions and Hours

From I-91: Take exit 26 to Route 2 West (The Mohawk Trail). From Route 2 take the first exit into Shelburne Falls. Follow the signs for the Bridge of Flowers and the Trolley Museum. Cross the Iron Bridge (notice the Bridge of Flowers on your right) over the river. Turn left toward the Salmon Falls Artisans Showroom and follow the signs to the museum. Then take the middle road (Depot Street, but unmarked—it will be the second left) at the three-way fork. Depot Street passes in front of the Salmon Falls Market Place and turns to dirt in the railroad yard. Drive to the far end of the yard, about ¼ mile, or walk to the Salmon Falls Market Artisan's Showroom and ride the trolley to the museum.

The museum is open from Memorial day to mid-October and is not completely handicap accessible although wheelchairs can be accommodated on the trolley car.

Hours: 12:00-5:00 P.M. on weekends and holidays, or by appointment. A complete tour will be provided, including trolley rides, outside of the scheduled hours and/or days for a fee.

Admission and Membership

$2, children under 6 are free. Memberships: $15 and up. See website for membership form.

What to See

Restored Trolley No. 10 was the first trolley of the Shelburne Falls and Colrain Street Railway, and ran from 1896 to 1927 over the nearby Bridge of Flowers. This is one of the oldest operating trolleys in the country. A ride on this car is very nearly identical to what people experienced 100 years ago. The car has been beautifully and meticulously restored. The museum is hoping to acquire the Buckland Freight Yard and restore the freight house.

Children's programming includes hosting field trips from schools. The children enjoy playing with and watching the model and toy trains.

There is a gift shop on the premises, but no café. Visitors can eat at nearby McCuster's Market, Subway, Copper Angel, Ten Bridge Street, Mother's Café, Buckland Pizza, Keystone Market, and Bottle of Bread.

While You're in the Area

Other attractions in the area are the Buckland Historical Society, the Shelburne Historical Society (p. 335), the Bridge of Flowers, the Glacial Potholes, and several artisans' showrooms and studios.

Spellman Museum of Stamps & Postal History

235 Wellesley Street
Weston, MA 02493
(781) 768-8367
www.spellman.org

Overview

The Spellman Museun of Stamps & Postal History is the first museum in the United States devoted to stamps and postal history. Rotating exhibits feature international rarities, worldwide and United States material, and featured collectors.

Directions and Hours

The museum is located on the campus of Regis College. From Interstate 95, 128, or the Mass Pike, take the exit for Route 30 west. Travel approximately two miles on Route 30 and turn right onto Wellesley Street. Turn left at the sign for the museum.

The museum is open year round, and has limited handicap accessibility.

Hours: Thursday-Sunday noon-5:00.

Admission and Membership

$5 for adults, $3 for seniors and students. Members and children sixteen and under are free. Membership is $30/year for individuals and $50/year for households.

What to See

In addition to the exhibition galleries, there is a premier philatelic research library.

There are programs for adults and children, such as stamp hunts, designing stamps, and boxes of stamps that visitors may peruse. Visitors may also send a postcard anywhere in the world free of charge. All children receive a free packet of stamps to take home.

There is a gift shop. Visitors may eat at the Regis College food service cafeteria or at area restaurants.

While You're in the Area

The Davis Museum and Cultural Center (p. 332), the Golden Ball Tavern, the DeCordova Museum and Sculpture Park (p. 239), the Charles River Museum of Industry (p. 332), Museum of Our National Heritage (p. 286), and Gore Place (p. 251) are also in the area.

Spencer Peirce Little Farm (SPNEA)

5 Little's Lane
Newbury, MA 01951
(978) 462-2634
www.spnea.org

Overview

This 230 acre farm features a unique stone and brick manor house built circa 1690. Newly installed period rooms portray life on the farm from the seventeenth century through today.

Directions and Hours

Take I-95 to Route 113, Newburyport, which turns into Route 1A (High Road). Follow Route 1A for 3.7 miles, then turn left onto Little's Lane.

The house museum is open June 1 to October 15.

Hours: Wednesday-Sunday, 11:00 A.M. to 5:00 P.M. The Eliza Little Walking Trail is open year round.

Admission and Membership

$5 for adults, $4.50 senior citizens, ½ off for students and children 6-12. Children 5 and under, SPNEA members, and residents of Newbury are free. AAA members receive a 2 for 1 discount. SPNEA membership is $35/year for individuals and $45/year for a household. Membership includes free admissions to 35 properties and museums across New England.

What to See

Viewports into the walls and floors reveal 300 years of construction technique and state of the art preservation. The Eliza Little Trail through the farmlands is available from dawn to dusk for walking, birdwatching, and snowshoeing.

While You're in the Area

Nearby attractions and museums include the ca. 1654 Coffin House museum (p. 230) ½ mile away, the Parker River National Wildlife Refuge on Plum Island, the Custom House Maritime Museum (p. 332), and the Cushing House Museum (p. 332).

Spooner House

27 North Street
Plymouth, MA 02361
(508) 746-0012

Overview

The 1749 Spooner House is the home to five generations of family history set in an elegant colonial house with an enclosed "secret" garden. Spooner House is one of three historic properties operated by the Plymouth Antiquarian Society, reflecting Plymouth life in the seventeenth, eighteenth, and nineteenth centuries.

Directions and Hours

Take Route 3 south to Route 44 east. Take a right onto Court Street and then a left onto North Street.

The museum is open from June through

early October, and is not handicap accessible.

Hours: 10:00 A.M. to 4:00 P.M. Thursday, Friday, and Saturday.

Admission and Membership

$4 adults, $2 children. Plymouth Antiquarian Society members and Plymouth residents are free. AAA Members get 50% off. Group rates are available. Memberships: $25/year for individuals, $40/year for families.

What to See

Visitors learn how one American family adapted to changing tastes and technologies over the centuries.

The museum does not have a gift shop or a café. Guests can eat anywhere on the Plymouth Waterfront.

While You're in the Area

The Plymouth Antiquarian Society also operates Hedge House (p. 259) and Harlow Old Fort House (p. 256) in Plymouth. Plymouth Rock, the Sparrow House Museum, and the *Mayflower II* (p. 306) are nearby.

Springfield Museum of Fine Arts

Springfield Museums at the Quadrangle
Corner of State and Chestnut Streets
Springfield, MA 01103
(413) 263-6800, ext. 312
www.quadrangle.org

Overview

Collections include six galleries of American art from the eighteenth through the twentieth centuries. The museum also exhibits fourteenth to twentieth century European paintings with strengths in French, Italian, and Dutch—including works by Degas, Pissarro, Gauguin, Monet, and Gericault.

Directions and Hours

From the North: Take I-91 south to exit 7. Turn left onto State Street, and proceed for three blocks.

From the South: Take I-91 north to exit 4. Stay on Columbus Avenue to State Street. Turn right, and proceed for three blocks.

From the East: Take the Massachusetts Turnpike (I-90) to exit 6 (I-291). Exit at

Dwight Street (exit 2B), and turn left. Follow Dwight to State Street. Turn left, and proceed for three blocks.

From the West: Take the Massachusetts Turnpike to I-91 south and follow I-91 south to exit 7. Turn left on State Street, and proceed for three blocks.

Parking is free in the Springfield Library and Museums' lots on State Street and on Edwards Street. The museum is handicap accessible.

Hours: Wednesday-Friday, noon-5:00 P.M. (also Tuesdays in July and August), Saturday and Sunday, 11:00 A.M.-4:00 P.M.

Admission and Membership

Museum Admission: $6 for adults; $3 for seniors and college students with ID; $2 for children ages 6-18; free for children under 6 and members. Admission fee includes entry into all four Quadrangle museums. Group tours/rates by appointment: 413-263-6800, ext. 472.

Membership: Single $35; dual $45; household $60.

What to See

The Museum of Fine Arts features 14 galleries of paintings, sculpture, and works on paper. Six galleries are devoted to American art from the eighteenth through the twentieth centuries. Special highlights of this collection are Winslow Homer's *The New Novel*, Frederic Church's *New England Scenery*, and Erastus Salisbury Field's *Historical Monument of the American Republic*. Among the twentieth-century American artists represented are O'Keeffe, Calder, Sheeler, and Frankenthaler.

Visitors will also find European paintings, including stunning works by Chardin, Tiepolo, Gericault, and Corot. The Impressionist Gallery boasts works by Degas, Pisarro, Gauguin and Monet. A fine Dutch and Flemish collection includes paintings by Ferdinand Bol and one of the earliest signed works by Jacob van Ruisdael.

Current and forthcoming exhibitions include "Janet Rickus: Still Life" (May 24-August 27, 2001), photorealistic oil paintings on board of fruits, vegetables, crockery and fabric; "Dale Chihuly: Seaforms" (June 6-August 19, 2001), an exquisite collection of work from the master glass artist who was declared "America's First National Living Treasure"; "Italian Watercolors from the Permanent Collection" (through July 1, 2001), a selection of brightly colored nineteenth-century paintings by Raffaele Mainella that reflect a degree of realism not usually seen in watercolors of their time; "Brother Thomas Ceramics" (September 26, 2001-January 6, 2002), a selection of works by Brother Thomas Bezanson, a self-taught potter and former Benedictine monk whose hand-thrown pottery does not rely on elaborate surface decoration but attains its beauty through its simple forms and the unique color and depth of its glazes; "American Impressionism: Treasures from the Smithsonian American Art Museum" (February 17-April 14, 2002), including landscapes, domestic scenes, and elegant figure compositions that reveal the freedom and sparkling qualities of the Impressionist style; and "Out of Time: Twentieth Century Design" (October 5 to December 1, 2002), a Smithsonian Institution traveling exhibition of watercolors, oil paintings, pen-and-ink drawings and other renderings that explore American's hypothetical "tomorrow."

From mid-November 2001 to mid-January 2002, the four Springfield Museums will display "Holiday Enchantment," an exhibit containing Victorian dollhouses and room boxes loaned by private collectors; early-twentieth-century cast iron toys; mirrors decorated in holiday style by area artists; and toy soldiers including lead figures, cardboard stand-ups, and handmade soldiers arranged in a variety of set-ups. Also a selection of early-nineteenth-century to mid-twentieth-century dolls, including milliners' dolls, American folk dolls, ethnic figures, and character dolls such as Teddy Roosevelt, Uncle Sam, Charlie Chaplin, and Shirley Temple will be on view.

From October through April, the four Springfield Museums present a series of Sunday programs which feature exciting live performances, art-making workshops, gallery games, special guests and more. Themes include dinosaurs, Dr. Seuss's birthday party, seasonal holidays, and more. Programs are offered approximately twice a month. For information, call 413-263-6800, ext. 312.

Each summer the four Museums on the Quadrangle and the library present a six-week series of "Meet Your Neighbors Days"—programs celebrating the traditions of some of the cultural communities in the region. Activities include music and dance performances, storytelling, and traditional crafts. Programs are offered Tuesday through Friday beginning the second week of July.

During each of the three weeks of school vacation (December, February, and April), the museums offer extended hours and a variety of craft and art workshops, performances, and demonstrations for children and families. The Museum School offers a wide range of courses for children and adults. Children's classes include hands-on science programs, studio art classes, and summer art and science camps. Adult classes include art history courses and studio art classes in painting, sculpture, calligraphy, drawing, and much more. History-related courses include genealogy and traditional American crafts.

There is a gift shop. Lunch and snacks are available in the Café on the Quadrangle.

While You're in the Area

Also on the Quadrangle are the George Walter Vincent Smith Art Museum (p. 248), the

Springfield Science Museum (p. 318), and the Connecticut Valley Historical Museum (p. 235). Other nearby museums include the Springfield Armory National Historic Site (p. 335) and the Basketball Hall of Fame (p. 288).

Springfield Science Museum

Springfield Museums at the Quadrangle
Corner of State and Chestnut Streets
Springfield, MA 01103
(413) 263-6800, ext. 312
www.quadrangle.org

Overview

The museum features a Dinosaur Hall dominated by a life-sized replica of Tyrannosaurus Rex; the multilevel R. E. Phelon African Hall with a mounted elephant, giraffe and other animals, as well as exhibits on traditional African cultures; the Solutia Eco-Center, an aquarium and live animal center; a new Mineral Hall; the Exploration Center with hands-on exhibits investigating natural and physical science; Native American Hall; a 100-seat planetarium; an observatory; and an exhibit on the Springfield-based aviation pioneers, the Granville Brothers.

Directions and Hours

From the North: Take I-91 south to exit 7. Turn left onto State Street, and proceed for three blocks.

From the South: Take I-91 north to exit 4. Stay on Columbus Avenue to State Street. Turn right, and proceed for three blocks.

From the East: Take the Massachusetts Turnpike (I-90) to exit 6 (I-291). Exit at

Dwight Street (exit 2B), and turn left. Follow Dwight to State Street. Turn left, and proceed for three blocks.

From the West: Take the Massachusetts Turnpike to I-91 south and follow I-91 south to exit 7. Turn left on State Street, and proceed for three blocks.

Parking is free in the Springfield Library and Museums' lots on State Street and on Edwards Street. The museum is handicap accessible.

Hours: Wednesday-Friday, noon-5:00 P.M. (also Tuesdays in July and August), Saturday and Sunday, 11:00 A.M.-4:00 P.M.

Admission and Membership

Museum Admission: $6 for adults; $3 for seniors and college students with ID; $2 for children ages 6-18; free for children under 6 and members. Admission fee includes entry into all four Quadrangle museums. Group tours/rates by appointment: 413-263-6800, ext. 472. Membership: Single $35; dual $45; household $60.

What to See

The Underwater World of the Connecticut River, a new, permanent exhibit, features underwater photographs and artifacts that explore the biology, geology, and historical uses of the river. The exhibit is a joint project of the Science Museum and the University of Massachusetts at Amherst.

Planetarium Shows are offered daily. Show times are at 2:45 P.M. on Wednesdays, Thursdays, and Fridays (also Tuesdays in July and August); and 1:00, 2:00, and 3:00 P.M. on Saturdays and Sundays.

Public stargazing evenings are held at 7:30 P.M. on the first Friday of each month at the Science Museum. Participants view the sky through the museum's large rooftop telescope and smaller telescopes set up outdoors on the Quadrangle. Programs are geared for families with children age eight and older, but younger children are also welcome. For information, call 413-263-6800, ext. 318.

The museum offers live animal demonstrations and Transparent Anatomical Manikin shows on Saturdays and Sundays. Times vary; call for information.

Recent and forthcoming exhibitions include "Tricking Fish" (May 5-July 29, 2001), an exhibit that unravels the mystery of what makes fish bite or not bite by showing the angler the world as the fish sees, hears, feels, tastes and smells it; "Places of Power: Objects of Veneration" (September 8-October 28, 2001), photographs of sacred Inuit sites—both natural and man-made—in the Canadian arctic, plus Eskimo artifacts from the Science Museum's collection; "Women and Flight" (March 9-April 21, 2002); and "The Bicycle Takes Off: From Boneshaker to Boom" (April 6-June 30, 2002)

From October through April, the four Springfield Museums present a series of Sunday programs which feature exciting live performances, art-making workshops, gallery games, special guests and more. Themes include dinosaurs, Dr. Seuss's birthday party, seasonal holidays, and more. Programs are offered approximately twice a month. For information, call 413-263-6800, ext. 312.

From mid-November 2001 to mid-January 2002, the four Springfield Museums will display "Holiday Enchantment," an exhibit containing Victorian dollhouses and room boxes loaned by private collectors; early-twentieth-century cast iron toys; mirrors decorated in holiday style by area artists; and toy soldiers including lead figures, cardboard stand-ups, and handmade soldiers arranged in a variety of set-ups. Also a selection of early-nineteenth-century to mid-twentieth-century dolls, including milliners' dolls, American folk dolls, ethnic figures, and character dolls such as Teddy Roosevelt, Uncle Sam, Charlie Chaplin, and Shirley Temple will be on view.

Each summer the four Museums on the Quadrangle and the library present a six-week series of "Meet Your Neighbors Days"—programs celebrating the traditions of some of the cultural communities in the region. Activities include music and dance performances, storytelling, and traditional crafts. Programs are offered Tuesday through Friday beginning the second week of July.

During each of the three weeks of school vacation (December, February, and April), the museums offer extended hours and a variety of craft and art workshops, performances, and demonstrations for children and families. The Museum School offers a wide range of courses for children and adults. Children's classes include hands-on science programs, studio art classes, and summer art and science camps. Adult classes include art history courses and studio art classes in painting, sculpture, calligraphy, drawing, and much more. History-related courses include genealogy and traditional American crafts.

There is a gift shop. Lunch and snacks are available in the Café on the Quadrangle.

While You're in the Area

Also on the Quadrangle are the Springfield Museum of Fine Arts (p. 316), the George Walter Vincent Smith Art Museum (p. 248), and the Connecticut Valley Historical Museum (p. 235). Other nearby museums include the Springfield Armory National Historic Site (p. 335) and the Basketball Hall of Fame (p. 288).

The Stephen Phillips Trust House

34 Chestnut Street
Salem, MA 01970
(978) 744-0440
www.salemweb.com/org/phillipshouse

Overview

Mrs. Stephen Phillips established the Trust House in 1973 as a memorial to her husband and the sailing ship era of Salem of which his family was a part. The house's collection reflects the accumulated belongings of five generations of a Salem family. The tour offers a unique look at life in the early twentieth century.

Directions and Hours

From 128 or I-95, take Route 114 east to Salem. Take a right onto Essex Street. Turn left at the first stoplight onto Flint Street. Take the first left onto Chestnut Street. The house is #34, the fifth house on the left. There is free on-street parking.

The Museum is open from Memorial Day weekend to the end of October. Hours are Monday-Saturday, 10:00-4:30, with the last tour given at 4:00. It is not handicap accessible.

Admission and Membership

$3 for adults, $2 for students, seniors, and groups. Ages 6 and under are free. Please make reservations for group tours.

What to See

The house's collection includes fine export porcelain, antique furniture, and carpets. Representative of the Phillips's extensive travels and interests, the collection also includes artifacts as diverse as Fiji throwing clubs, African woodcarvings, and Native American pottery. The front four rooms were originally part of a larger house in Danvers, until being moved to the present location by oxcart in the 1820s.

The carriage house exhibits horse-drawn carriages, sleighs, a Model A Ford, and two Pierce Arrow automobiles.

A special tour, "The Home at the Crossroads of Technology," highlights the emergence of early modern conveniences such as electricity, plumbing, and the advances in locomotion. Tours are also offered for school groups.

There is no gift shop or cafe, but there are places to eat in downtown Salem.

Photo courtesy of The Stephen Phillips Trust House

While You're in the Area

Chestnut Street was said to be the most beautiful street in Americ by P. D. Jamesa. It contains some of the finest examples of federal architecture in the country, built by the town's sea captains and merchants. Related trails and historic areas include the McIntire Historic District Walking Trail, the Women's Heritage Trail, the Salem Crescent Architectural Trail (an architectural trail of Salem, Beverly, and Marblehead), and part of the Essex National Heritage Area. Other museums of interest are the Peabody Essex Museum (p. 303), the House of Seven Gables (p. 333), and the Witch Museum (p. 336).

Sterling and Francine Clark Art Institute

225 South Street
Williamstown, MA 01267
(413) 458-2303
www.clarkart.edu

Overview

The Clark Art Institute is an art museum and research center welcoming visitors year-round to experience its outstanding collections, including French Impressionist, American, and Old Master paintings, in the lovely pastoral setting of its 130-acre campus. The Clark has built upon the personal collection of founders Sterling and Francine Clark to become a beloved museum.

Directions and Hours

From Massachusetts Turnpike (westbound) take exit 2 (Lee/Pittsfield) to U.S. 20. Take U.S. 20 to U.S. 7 North. Take US 7 into Williamstown center to the junction of routes 7 and 2. The Clark is located ½ mile from the intersection on South Street.

Hours: September 1-June 30: Tuesday through Sunday, 10:00-5:00; July 1-August 31: Daily 10:00-5:00; President's Day, Memorial Day, Labor Day, Columbus Day, 10:00-5:00; Closed Thanksgiving, Christmas, New Year's

Day

Admission and Membership

From November-June, admission is free. From July 1-October 31, adult admission is $5. Children 18 and under, members, and students are free every day. Admission is free to everyone on Tuesdays. Additional fees may apply for special exhibitions and events.

Membership starts at $25 for an individual membership. Benefits include free admission, shop discounts, discounts on public programs, special events and travel opportunities, and our members' calendar/newsletter.

What to See

Collection highlights include paintings by Auguste Renoir (more than 30), Claude Monet, Edgar Degas, Camille Pissarro, Winslow Homer, John Singer Sargent, Frederic Remington, Piero della Francesca, and Sir Lawrence Alma-Tadema, as well as English and American silver, American furniture, prints, drawings, and photographs.

Special exhibitions and public programs are offered year-round.

The museum shop is open during gallery hours. A courtyard cafe serves snacks and beverages during gallery hours year-round. In July and August, the museum also offers lunch service (call ahead for hours and menu).

While You're in the Area

Other area attractions include the Williams College Museum of Art (p. 326), MASS MoCA (p. 276), and the Williamstown Theatre Festival.

The Stevens-Coolidge Place (Trustees of Reservations)

139 Andover Street
North Andover, MA 01845
(978) 682-3580
www.thetrustees.org

Overview

An exquisite and intact example of a neo-Georgian Colonial Revival estate, complete with house and garden designs by early twentieth century preservation architect Joseph Everett Chandler. For generations, the 91-acre property had served as the Stevens family farm, then known as Ashdale Farms. It later became the gentlemen's farm and summer home of Helen Stevens and her husband John Gardner Coolidge. The house still boasts their original furnishings and art objects, as well as hand-painted wall murals. The beautifully maintained gardens, or "garden rooms," still reflect life on this early twentieth century estate. These include perennial garden beds, a rose garden with fountain, and the site of a former French potager garden, which is slated for restoration in the near future.

Directions and Hours

From I-93: Take Route 125 north 7.3 miles. At lights (Merrimack College) turn right onto Andover Street (still 125) and follow for .2 miles. Turn right at lights, continue .5 miles. House and gardens are on the left, with parking across the street in the field.

The grounds are open year round, 8:00 A.M. to sunset. House tours are offered from Mother's Day Sunday to Columbus Day weekend, on Sundays from 1:00-5:00 P.M. The office is open year round at Stevens-Coolidge Place and Trustees Northeast Regional Office.

The museum is not handicap accessible.

Admission and Membership

The grounds are free. House tours are $5 adult, $2 children and students. (Children must have adult supervision.) Group rates are available. Free for Trustees of Reservations members. Membership is $40/year for an individual, $60/year for a family, $30/year for students and senior citizens, and $50/year for a family of students and senior citizens. Benefactor membership is $100/year for a contributing, $150/year for a supporting, $300/year for a sustaining, and $600/year for a sponsor.

What to See

The collection includes American eighteenth and nineteenth century furniture and decorative art, Chinese porcelains, oriental rugs, Anglo-Irish cut glass, and Asian art, along with other eclectic, exotic, and sentimental of objects collected by the Coolidges for their summer house.

There is an annual plant sale on the third Saturday in May.

The museum has a small gift shop, but no café. Visotors can eat at restaurants in North Andover.

While You're in the Area

Nearby attractions include the North Andover Historical Society (p. 294) and the Addison Gallery of American Art at Phillips Andover (p. 331).

Stonehurst/The Robert Treat Paine Estate

100 Robert Treat Drive
Waltham, MA 02452
(781) 893-0381

Overview

Designed by Henry Hobson Richardson and Frederick Law Olmsted, "Stonehurst" is the only museum devoted to these two pioneering figures in American architectural and landscape design history. In addition to early modern interiors that presage those of Frank Lloyd Wright, visitors can enjoy the Olmsted-designed grounds and woodland trails. Stonehurst is owned by the City of Waltham.

Directions and Hours

From Route 128 north or south: Take Route 128 to the Totten Pond Road/Waltham exit (27A). Following the signs, take Totten Pond Road into Waltham. At the end of Totten Pond Road where there is a set of traffic lights, turn right onto Lexington Street. At the first traffic light about 100 yards down Lexington Street, take a left onto Beaver Street. Follow Beaver Street to a rotary. Take the second right off of the rotary to continue on Beaver Street. Approximately 100 yards from the circle, turn left at the sign for "Stonehurst," and follow the driveway for about ¼ mile to a large house of shingles and boulders.

The museum is open year round and is handicap accessible.

Guided tours are offered Tuesdays and Wednesdays at 1:00, 2:00, and 3:00 P.M. or by appointment. Public hours will increase in 2002.

Admission and Membership

Admission is a recommended donation of $5. For information on the affiliated nonprofit group, the Friends of Stonehurst, call (781) 893-0162.

What to See

The quintessential shingle style house by one of America's master architects, Stonehurst draws architectural enthusiasts from far and wide. Its Great Hall, widely recognized as Richardson's best interior domestic space, features one of the most famous staircases in American architecture. This convention-breaking home contains its original Victorian furnishings.

There is a gift shop. There are many unique, independently owned restaurants on Moody and Main Streets in downtown Waltham, about a mile away.

While You're in the Area

The estate is surrounded by 109 acres of Storer Conservation Lands. Within a few miles of Stonehurst are Gore Place (p. 251), the Lyman Estate (p. 272), the Charles River Museum of Industry (p. 332) and the Rose Art Museum (p. 335) of Brandeis University.

Thornton W. Burgess Museum

4 Water Street, Route 130
Sandwich (Cape Cod), MA 02563
(508) 888-6870
www.thorntonburgess.org

Overview

The Thornton W. Burgess Museum, located in the Deacon Eldred House in Historic Sandwich Village, preserves the life, spirit, and works of the renowned children's author and naturalist. Burgess wrote 170 books teaching young and old about the natural world and conservation. The museum has an extensive collection of Burgess's books about "Peter Rabbit," "Jimmy Skunk," "Reddy Fox," "Grandfather Frog," "Johnny Chuck," "Hooty Owl," and many others from stories which have enthralled generations of children.

Directions and Hours

Take Route 6 (Mid-Cape Highway) to exit 2 at Route 130. Turn north onto Route 130 and go one mile until you reach Shawme Pond on the left. The museum is the older house located along the shores of the pond.

The museum is open mid-April through October. There is limited handicap accessibility due to the historic nature of the house.

Hours: Monday-Saturday 10:00 A.M.-4:00 P.M., Sunday 1:00-4:00 P.M.

Admission and Membership

Admission is by donation. Suggested donation: $2 per adult, $1 per child. Bus tours are welcome with advance reservations. The fee is $1 per person. Membership is $20/year for individuals and $30/year per family.

What to See

In addition to the collection of Burgess books and memorabilia, the museum has changing exhibits on the natural history of the area and a small children's activity room. The museum grounds overlook Shawne Pond and the center of Sandwich Village, where ducks, geese, and swans abound.

During July and August, a Burgess Animal Story Time takes place out on the lawn every Monday, Wednesday, and Saturday at 10:30 A.M.

The museum does have a gift shop offering the Burgess books and a variety of nature-related items. Members receive a discount on certain purchases.

The Museum does not have a café, but there is a charming tea room across the street and there are many good restaurants throughout the town.

While You're in the Area

The museum is within walking distance of the Sandwich Glass Museum (p. 310) and the Hoxie House (p. 333), which is the oldest house on Cape Cod. It is also within a half-mile of Heritage Plantation (p. 333) and two miles from the historic Green Briar Nature Center and Jam Kitchen (p. 253).

The *Titanic* Museum

208 Main Street
Indian Orchard, MA 01151
(413) 543-4770
www.titanic1.org

Overview

The Titanic Historical Society collection at The *Titanic* Museum was established to preserve the history of the *Titanic* and the White Star Line. On display is an Englehardt collapsible lifeboat, a 27-foot reproduction loaned from 20th Century Fox's film *Titanic*. Many of the rare and one-of-a-kind pieces were donated by survivors and their families. These documented pre-discovery artifacts bring the true story of the ship and her passengers to life.

Directions and Hours

East/West: Take 90 (Mass Pike) and take exit 7. Take a left turn onto Route 21, cross a bridge, then take a right turn onto Main Street.

North/South: Take 91 and take the exit for

interstate 291. Then take exit 5A (Indian Orchard), and take Route 20. Turn left onto Berkshire Avenue, turn left onto Oak Street, then turn right onto Main Steet.

The museum is open year round, but is not handicap accessible.

Hours: Monday-Friday 10:00-4:00; Saturday 10:00-3:00; Saturday during July and August 11:00-2:00.

Admission and Membership

$4 for adults, children under six are free. Membership is $50/year for individuals.

Members are admitted for free.

What to See

The *Titanic* Museum's collection includes authentic elements from the ship, such as the ice message that never made it to the bridge, lookout Fred Fleet's rendition of the fatal iceberg, plus luncheon and dinner menus.

Other personal effects include letters written by passengers, a lifeboat seat support, and a railing section from the ship. A *Titanic* blueprint by Harland and Wolff is also on display, as well as artifacts from the *Carpathia* and *Olympic*.

There is a small gift shop.

There is no café, but visitors can eat at a small luncheonette down the street or a Portuguese restaurant a block further down.

While You're in the Area

The village of Indian Orchard has many antique shops within walking distance. Also nearby are Six Flags, the Basketball Hall of Fame (p. 288), Indian Motorcycle Museum (p. 261), the Springfield Armory National Historic Site (p. 335), Connecticut Valley Historical Museum (p. 235), George Walter Vincent Smith Art Museum (p. 248), Museum of Fine Arts (p. 316), Springfield Science Museum (p. 318), and the Zoo in Forest Park (p. 336).

Wenham Museum

132 Main Street
Wenham, MA 01984
(978) 468-2377
www.wenhammuseum.org

Overview

The Wenham Museum contains social history. Visitors may explore how inhabitants of Wenham lived, worked, dressed, and played from the seventeenth century to the present. The museum also houses the International Doll Collection, the largest continuously held collection in the world.

Directions and Hours

Take Route 128 north to exit 20A (Route 1A north, also Main Street). Follow Route 1A north for approximately two and a half miles.

The museum is open year round, and is handicap accessible.

Hours: Tuesday-Sunday 10:00-4:00.

Admission and Membership

$5 for adults, $4 for seniors, $3 for children 2-16. Membership is $30/year for individuals, $25/year for seniors, and $55/year for families.

Discount group rates are also available.

What to See

The International Doll Collection contains period dolls of French, German, American, and English manufacture. There are also American cloth dolls and rare nineteenth century Native American dolls. It also contains dolls donated by celebrities and royalty at the turn of the twentieth century. Miss Columbia, the museum's most famous doll, traveled around the world by herself from 1900-1902.

The museum has a the finest display of British toy soldiers in the world.

The Train Room has six operating train layouts. The Arnott model train layout is an exceptional HO gauge.

There is an annual summer craft fair during the third weekend in August. An Annual

Holiday Gift Boutique happens the weekend before Thanksgiving. The Annual Railroad Hobby Show is the first weekend in January.

There are new programs quarterly for children, adults, and families.

There is a gift shop. There is no café, but the Wenham Tea House is located across the street.

While You're in the Area

The Peabody Essex Museum (p. 303), the Beverly Historical Society (p. 221), Ipswich Historical Society (p. 333), and the Bradley-Palmer State Park are located in the area.

Westford Historical Society, Inc.

2-4 Boston Road
PO Box 411
Westford, MA 01886
(978) 692-5550
www.westford.com/museum

Overview

Just 10 miles from Lowell, the Westford Historical Society is home to the Westford Museum and is located just a few steps from the town common in the Historic District of Westford, Massachusetts. The museum building itself is the original Westford Academy, built in 1792. It now houses a comprehensive collection of Westford Academy and town artifacts. Special emphasis has been given to founding families—Hildreth, Fletcher, Prescott, and Wright.

The Parish Center for the Arts is also part of the museum complex and has a whole array of programs for all ages and abilities. See their website at westford.com/parishcenter

Directions and Hours

From Route 495, take exit 32 (Boston Road) to the town center. The museum and office are located on the right, just before the town common.

The museum is open every Sunday 2:00-4:00 P.M. or by special appointment and has a handicap ramp for access to the first floor. The museum office is open Monday/Wednesday/Friday 9:00-1:00.

Admission and Membership

Admission is open to all. Donations are appreciated. Family membership is $40; individuals $25; seniors $5.

What to See

As well as housing yearbooks of Westford Academy and Nashoba Valley Technical High School, on the first floor of the museum there is a country store display including post office boxes and wall crank telephone. There are also displays of early fire equipment, the Dr. Benjamin Osgood medical display, and military memorabilia, including a button from the uniform of the town patriot, Col. John Robinson.

The second floor includes both permanent and revolving exhibits. The Westford Knight is a very popular exhibit. Reflecting Westford's heritage are exhibits featuring the granite and woolen industries as well as our agricultural past.

Materials for genealogical research on Westford families and histories of houses in Westford are available.

On the third Friday night of each month there are special programs of folk and chamber music. Be sure and reserve early as these programs are very popular. As part of the Strawberry Festival in June, the museum hosts a gigantic barn and attic sale. All Westford third graders get an introduction to town history during the year, and the museum club at Westford Academy maintains the Academy collection. In November, the Veteran's Roundtable is a touching and memorable event. Skinner Auctions also has an appraisal program at the museum—another event that sells out quickly.

The society has an excellent collection of town-related items available for sale: postcards, notecards, books, posters, and t-shirts of the Westford Knight.

While You're in the Area

There are many museums in the Lowell area, including the Boott Cotton Mills Museum (p. 223) and the American Textile History Museum (p. 213).

Williams College Museum of Art

15 Lawrence Hall Drive, Suite 2
Williamstown, MA 01267
(413) 597-2429
www.williams.edu/WCMA

Overview

The Williams College Museum of Art's (WCMA's) collection of approximately 12,000 objects spans the history of art and includes important ancient works, Chinese and Japanese scrolls, medieval sculpture, and American art. As the only museum in the area with significant holdings in twentieth century and non-Western art, WCMA offers its community the opportunity to experience this art without having to travel to distant metropolitan centers.

Directions and Hours

In Williamstown, the museum is centrally located on the Williams campus on Route 2 (Main Street) between Spring Street and Route 43 (Water Street), across from Thompson Memorial Chapel. The museum is about one hour's drive from the Massachusetts Turnpike and Interstates 91, 90, and 87. Driving time from Boston or New York is about three hours; from Albany, NY, about one hour.

Parking in front of the museum is limited. Additional parking is available across the street in the lower lot behind the Thompson Memorial Chapel and in other lots on campus.

The museum is open year round. Museum hours are 10:00-5:00 Tuesday through Saturday, and 1:00-5:00 on Sunday. Closed Mondays (except Memorial Day, Labor Day, and Columbus Day), and closed New Year's, Thanksgiving, and Christmas.

Admission and Membership

Admission is free. Membership levels range from $25 to $2,500.

What to See

The Museum's Prendergast collection serves as a national center for the study of the context and culture of the Prendergasts and their era. WCMA is guided by its mission to "serve as a laboratory for the production and exhibition of works by living artists." WCMA's contemporary art programming attempts to balance the work of emerging and regional artists with that of nationally known artists. The Museum maintains a strong connection to its local community, particularly to young audiences, and has developed an engaging educational program geared to children of all ages. WCMA regularly presents lectures, symposia, films, gallery talks, and other programming in conjunction with its exhibitions.

There is a gift shop. The museum does not have a café, but it's steps away from quaint Spring Street, which has several eating establishments.

While You're in the Area

The museum is within minutes from the Sterling and Francine Clark Art Institute (p. 320) and MASS MoCA (p. 276).

Winslow Crocker House (SPNEA)

250 Main Street, Route 6A
Yarmouth Port, MA 02675
(508) 362-4385
www.spnea.org

Overview

The Winslow Crocker House was the home of wealthy eighteenth-century trader and land speculator, Winslow Crocker. In 1936, Mary Thatcher, an avid collector of antiques, moved the house to its present location in Yarmouth.

Thatcher's primary goal was to provide a backdrop for the display of her collection of furniture and decorative arts.

Directions and Hours

Take Route 3 to the Sagamore Bridge, to Route 6 East. From exit 7 turn right onto Willow Street, go 1½ miles and turn right onto Route 6A. The house is ½ mile on the left.

The museum is open from June 1 through October 15, but it is not handicap accessible.

Hours: Tours are held hourly, on the hour, Saturday and Sunday from 11:00-4:00.

Admission and Membership

$5 admission; SPNEA members and Yarmouth Port residents free. SPNEA membership is $35 for individuals, $45 for household, and includes free admissions to 35 properties and museums across New England.

What to See

Considering that Cape Cod in the eighteenth century was a region of small farms and fishing ports, the house is surprisingly elaborate, with rich paneling in every room. Thatcher took a non-historical approach to the house's restoration, stripping woodwork, installing smaller-paned windows, and rebuilding a fireplace to contain a beehive oven. The result is a colonial Cape Cod with a twentieth-century flavor. Thatcher's collection includes colorful hooked rugs, ceramics, and pewter. It presents a thorough survey of early American styles from Jacobean, William and Mary, and Queen Anne, to Chippendale.

The museum offers educational family programs and walking tours.

While You're in the Area

The Captain Bangs Hallet House (p. 226) is also in Yarmouth Port.

Worcester Art Museum

55 Salisbury Street
Worcester, MA 01609
(508) 799-4406
www.worcesterart.org

Overview

Opened to the public in 1898, the Worcester Art Museum is the second largest art museum in New England. Its exceptional 35,000-piece collection of paintings, sculpture, decorative arts, photography, prints, and drawings is displayed in 36 galleries and spans 5,000 years of art and culture, ranging from Egyptian antiquities and Roman mosaics to Impressionist paintings and contemporary art. Throughout its first century, the Worcester Art Museum was the first American museum to purchase work by Claude Monet (1910) and Paul Gauguin (1921), the first museum to bring a medieval building to America (1927), a sponsor of the first major excavation at Antioch (one of the four great cities of ancient Rome) (1932), the first museum to create an Art All-State program for high school artists (1987), and was the originator of the first exhibition of Dutch master Judith Leyster (1993).

Directions and Hours

From East-West-South: From the Mass Turnpike (Interstate 90) go to exit 10 (Auburn); follow I-290 heading east to Worcester to exit 17 (Route 9 exit). At the top of the ramp turn left onto Route 9. At the third set of lights at the top of the hill turn right onto Harvard Street. The museum is on the left at the second traffic light (Salisbury Street).

From East (alternate): From the Mass Turnpike go to exit 11-A; follow I-495 north to I-290 west to Worcester, exit 18. Take a right at the light at the bottom of the exit ramp (Lincoln Street). Take the first right (before the lights) onto Concord Street. Go straight (Concord becomes Salisbury Street). At the third light, turn left onto Lancaster Street. The museum will be on your left.

From North: Take I-495 to I-290 west to Worcester, exit 18. Take a right at the light at the bottom of the exit ramp (Lincoln Street). Take the first right (before the lights) onto Concord Street. Go straight. At the third light, turn left onto Lancaster Street. The museum is on your left.

From I-90: Take I-90 South to I-290 west to Worcester. Take exit 18. Take a right at the light at the bottom of the exit ramp (Lincoln Street). Take the first right before the lights onto Concord Street. Go straight. At the third light, turn left onto Lancaster Street.

Free parking is available in front of the museum in the Salisbury lot along Lancaster and Tuckerman Streets, and in the second lot on Lancaster Street.

Via train from Boston: Take the Framingham/Worcester line on the MBTA from South Station in Boston and arrive in Worcester for $4.75 one way. The trip takes about an hour and runs four or five times a day during the week and about three times a day on weekends. For actual times call the MBTA at (617) 222-5000 and ask for the information center.

Via bus from Boston: Take the Peter Pan Bus Lines from South Station in Boston to Worcester. These lines run more frequently than the trains and cost $10.95 one-way. The trip takes about an hour. Call Peter Pan directly at (800) 434-9999 for specific times.

The museum is open year round and is handicap accessible.

Hours: Wednesday-Friday 11:00 A.M.-5:00 P.M., Saturday 10:00 A.M.-5:00 P.M., and Sunday 11:00 A.M.-5:00 P.M.

Admission and Membership

$8 adults, $6 seniors/college students with current ID, and free to children 17 and under. Free for all Saturdays 10:00 A.M.-12:00 P.M. Memberships: $45/year individual, $35/year for individual value (a discounted rate offered to senior citizens 65+ and full-time students), and $55/year for a family/household.

What to See

Collections include: John Chandler Bancroft Collection of Japanese prints, American Paintings of Seventeenth-Twentieth Centuries, British Paintings of the Eighteenth and Nineteenth Centuries, Dutch Seventeenth and Nineteenth Century Paintings, Egyptian, Classical, Oriental, and Medieval Sculpture, French Paintings of the Sixteenth-Nineteenth Centuries, Flemish Sixteenth-Seventeenth Century Paintings, Italian Paintings of the Thirteenth-Eighteenth Centuries, Mosaics from Antioch, Pre-Columbian Collections, and Twelfth Century French Chapter House.

Children's programming includes youth art classes, school vacation classes, and family days.

There is a gift shop on the premises, as well as a café. The café is open from Wednesday to Sunday 11:30 A.M. to 2:00 P.M., but closed Saturdays and Sundays June-September.

While You're in the Area

The museum is close to Mechanics Hall, the Higgins Armory Museum (p. 260), the American Antiquarian Society, Music Worcester, the Foothills Theatre, Arts Worcester, and the Worcester Center for Crafts.

Yankee Candle® Company Candlemaking Museum

PO Box 110
Route 5
South Deerfield, MA 01373-0110
(877) 636-7707 ext. 1206
www.yankeecandle.com

Overview

The Yankee Candle® Company Candlemaking Museum gives demonstrations by costumed interpreters of the 1830s era. The Yankee Candle® Company is an 80,000 square foot store featuring candles of nearly 2,000 fragrances. Visitors can also view the Bavarian Christmas Village, the Black Forest, Village

Square, Glockenspiel Tower, Nutcracker Castle, Santa's Toy Factory, Kringle Market, the Nordic Fountain, and the Oompah Boys (an animatronic German band).

Directions and Hours

The Yankee Candle® Company is located off Mass Interstate 91, at exit 24. At the exit, take Route 5 and 10 north for ¼ mile, and Yankee Candle® will be on your left.

The museum is open year-round, every day but Thanksgiving and Christmas. It is handicap accessible.

Hours: 9:30 A.M. to 6:00 P.M. Call for information regarding extended Fall through Christmas holiday hours. Demonstrations of antique candlemaking are at 11:30, 1:30, and 3:30 daily.

Admission and Membership

Admission is free.

What to See

The museum has a large collection specific to candlemaking and storage. Visitors can dip their own candle for personal candle souvenirs ($1 per person). A 25-foot Christmas tree, a suit of armor, and a toy train are also on display.

Special programming is ongoing so please call for up to date information.

Yankee Candle® is the world's largest candle store. Items besides candles and candle accessories are also sold, including New England crafts, collectibles, toys, and gifts. Yankee Candle® has a full service restaurant, a cafeteria style coffee house, and a Candlewick Café ice cream parlor.

While You're in the Area

The Yankee Candle® Company Car Museum (p. 329) is in the same location. Other interesting attractions nearby include the Norman Rockwell Museum (p. 292), Old Sturbridge Village (p. 297), and Basketville.

Photo courtesy of the Yankee Candle® Company Candlemaking Museum

Yankee Candle® Company Car Museum

PO Box 110
Route 5
South Deerfield, MA 01373-0110
(877) 636-7707 ext. 1700
www.yankeecandle.com

Overview

Attached to the Yankee Candle® flagship store, the Car Museum has an ever-changing display of 80-100 vehicles from every era of automotive transportation. Whether visitors' memories involve brass-era cars, pre-World War II classics, icons from the 1950s, 1960 muscle cars, exotic dream cars from overseas, or classic motorcycles they will find something to enjoy. Most vehicles are on loan from area collectors and are displayed in a well-lit showroom.

Directions and Hours

The Yankee Candle® Car Museum and Yankee

Candle® Company are located off Mass Interstate 91, at exit 24. At the exit, take Route 5 and 10 North for ¼ mile, and Yankee Candle® will be on your left.

The museum is open year round and is handicap accessible. Closed on Thanksgiving and Christmas Day.

Hours: Open daily from 9:30 A.M.-6:00 P.M. Call for Holiday hours in November and December.

Admission and Membership

$5 for adults, $4 for seniors (60+), and children 4 through 11 $2.Children under 4 are admitted free. Call for bus and tour group rates. Season passes are available: $25 for adults, $20 for seniors, and $10 per child. Special discounts are available. Please call ahead to arrange tours.

What to See

Vehicles come and go from the museum on a regular basis so something new will be seen on repeat visits. While there is no central theme to the museum except a varied and interesting collections of cars and motorcycles, each season there are various sub-themes to the vehicles on display. Visitors might find anything from Ferraris, Fords, Bentleys, MGs, Chevies, Mopars to race cars to street rods—not to mention Harleys. To find out what is on display, check the Yankee Candle® website

Each year car clubs make the Yankee Candle® Car Museum a destination and are given a designated parking area near the museum.

The museum welcomes school, church, or camp groups for guided tours. Museum guides will tailor their presentation to be age appropriate. Staff will also work with teachers to tie in their presentation to classroom programs, since the automobile is integral to the history, sociology, industry, economy, ecology, and art of the twentieth century. Please call to arrange a tour.

The museum does have a gift shop offering car enthusiast merchandise as well as fun mementos like logo accessories, scale die-cast models, NASCAR collectibles, clothing, prints posters, and car care products.

The Coffee Haus café is located near the museum entrance from the candle shop. There is also a full service restaurant called Chandler's Tavern.

While You're in the Area

The Yankee Candle® Company Candlemaking Museum (p. 328) is in the same location. Other attractions nearby include Historic Deerfield, Mount Sugarload, Old Greenfield Village (p. 294), Long Hollow Bison Farm, Shelburne Bridge of Flowers, and Glacial Potholes.

OTHER MUSEUMS IN MASSACHUSETTS

Name	Phone	Town
Abbot Hall	781-631-0528	Marlbehead
Abigail Adams Birthplace	781-335-7065	Weymouth
Addison Gallery of American Art	978.749.4015	Andover
American Jewish Historical Society	781-891-8110	Waltham
American Marine Model Gallery	978-745-5777	Salem
Amherst History Museum	413-256-0678	Amherst
Ancient & Honorable Artillery	617-227-1638	Boston
Andover Historical Society	978-475-2236	Andover
Aptucxet Trading Post and Museum	508-759-9487	Bourne
Arlington Historical Society and Smith Museum	508-648-4300	Arlington
Art Complex Museum at Duxbury	781-934-6634	Duxbury
Attleboro Area Industrial Museum	508-222-3918	Attleboro
Attleboro Museum	508-222-2644	Attleboro
Bartholomew's Cobble	413-229-8600	Sheffield
Bartlett Museum	978-388-4528	Amesbury
Becket Arts Center of the Hilltowns	413-623-6635	Becket
Bell School House	508-636-6011	Westport
Berkshire Art Association	413-528-5235	Pittsfield
Berkshire Museum	413-443-7171	Pittsfield
Berkshire Scenic Railway Museum	413-637-2210	Lenox
Beverly Historical Society	978-922-1186	Beverly
Willard House and Clock Museum	508-839-3500	North Grafton
Blindiana/Tactual Museum/ Museum on the History of Blindness	617-924-3434	Watertown
Blue Hills Trailside Museum	617-333-0690	Milton
Boston Athenaeum	617-227-0270	Boston
Boston Public Library	617-536-5400	Boston
Boston Tea Party Ship and Museum	617-338-1773	Boston
Bradley House/Woods Hole Historical Museum	508-548-7270	Woods Hole
Brockton Historical Society Museums	508-583-1039	Brockton
Brooks Free Library	508-430-7562	Harwich

Brush Art Gallery and Studios	978-459-7819	Lowell
Bunker Hill Museum	617-242-1843	Boston
Cahoon Museum of American Art	508-771-3800	Cotuit
Caleb Lothrop House	781-383-1434	Cohasset
Cape Cod Children's Museum	508-539-8788	South Mashpee
Cape Cod Conservatory of Music and Arts	508-362-2772	Barnstable
Cape Cod Museum of Natural History	508-896-3867	Brewster
Cape Cod Discovery Museum	508-398-1600	Dennisport
Captain Forbes House Museum	617-696-1815	Milton
Captain John Wilson House	781-383-1434	Cohasset
Captain Samuel Brocklebank Museum	978-352-8526	Georgetown
Carnegie Library, Artifacts Loft	413-863-3214	Montague
Clara Barton's Birthplace Museum	508-987-2056	North Oxford
Charles River Museum of Industry	781-893-5410	Waltham
Chatham Railroad Museum	508-945-2809	Chatham
Children's Museum at Indian House Memorial	413- 772-0845	Deerfield
Children's Museum at Holyoke	413-536-KIDS	Holyoke
Charles River Museum of Industry	617-893-5410	Waltham
Cohasset Historical Society	781-383-6930	Cohasset
Colonel Josiah Quincy House	781-545-1083	Quincy
Commonwealth Museum—Massachusetts State Archives	617-727-9268	Boston
Connecticut Valley Historical Museum	413-263-6800	Springfield
Cushing House Museum	978-462-2681	Newburyport
Custom House Maritime Musuem	978-462-8681	Newburyport
Cyrus E. Dallin Art Museum	781-641-0747	Arlington
Danvers Historical Society: Memorial Hall and Museum	978-777-1666	Danvers
Davis Museum and Cultural Center	781-283-2051	Wellesley
Deerfield Museums	413-774-7476	Deerfield
Dickinson Memorial Library	413-498-2455	Northfield
Dighton Rock Museum	508-822-7537	Berkley
D. L. Moody Museum	413-498-3227	Northfield
Donald G. Trayser Memorial Museum	508-362-2092	Barnstable Village
Dorchester Historical Society	617-265-7802	Dorchester
Dracula's Castle	978-745-4777	Salem
Duryea Transportation Society Museum	413-783-5624	Springfield
Duxbury Art Museum Complex	781-934-6634	Duxbury
Eastham Historical Society	508-255-4968	Eastham
EcoTarium	508-929-2700	Worcester
Ervng Historical Engine House	508-544-7422	Erving
Essex Shipbuilding Museum	978-768-7541	Essex
Fairbanks House	781-326-1170	Dedham
Nantucket Historical Association	508-228-1894	Nantucket
Fall River Historical Society	508-679-1071	Fall River
Firehouse Center for the Performing and Visual Arts	978-462-7336	Newburyport
Fitchburg Art Museum	978-345-4207	Fitchburg

Name	Phone	Town
French Cable Station Museum	508-240-1735	Orleans
General Artemus Ward Home	508-842-8900	Shrewsbury
General Sylvanus Thayer Birthplace	781-848-1640	Braintree
Glen Magna Farms	978-774-9165	Danvers
Gloucester Fisherman's Museum	978-281-1820	Gloucester
Golden Ball Tavern Museum	781-894-1751	Weston
Hadley Farm Museum	413-586-1812	Hadley
Hadwen House	508-228-1894	Nantucket
Hammond Castle Museum	978-283-2080	Magnolia
Hampshire College Art Gallery	413-559-5544	Amherst
Hart Nautical Galleries (MIT)	617-253-5942	Cambridge
Harvard University Art Museums	617-495-0350	Cambridge
Haverhill Historical Society	978-374-4626	Haverhill
Heritage Plantation Museum	508-888-3300	Sandwich
Hetty Green; A Frugal Woman's Museum	508-996-0326	New Bedford
Hingham Historical Society	781-749-0013	Hingham
Historic Deerfield	413-774-5581	Deerfield
Historic North Hampton Museum	413-584-6011	North Hampton
Historical Society Building and Johnson Cottage	978-686-4035	North Andover
Historic Society of Santuit and Cotuit	508-428-0461	Cotuit
Hooper-Lee-Nichols House	617-547-4252	Cambridge
House of Seven Gables	978-744-0991	Salem
Hoxie House	508-888-1173	Sandwich
Hull Lifesaving Museum	781-925-5433	Hull
Old Indian Meeting House	508-477-0208	Mashpee
Institute of Contemporary Art	617-266-5152	Boston
Ipswich Historical Society	978-356-2811	Ipswich
Jabez Howland House	508-746-9590	Plymouth
Jacob Thompson House Museum	413-267-4292	Monson
Jenney Grist Mill	508-747-5959	Plymouth
Jethro Coffin House	508-228-1894	Nantucket
John Adams Birthplace	617-773-1177	Quincy
John Cabot House	978-922-1186	Beverly
John F. Kennedy Hyannis Museum	508-790-3077	Hyannis
John Greenleaf Whittier Home	978-388-1337	Amesbury
John Hale House	978-922-1186	Beverly
John Heard House	978-356-2811	Ipswich
John Quincy Adams Birthplace	617-773-1144	Quincy
John Whipple House	978-356-2811	Ipswich
Jonathan Young Windmill	508-240-1329	Orleans
"King" Hooper Mansion	781-631-2608	Marblehead
Kingsman Tavern Historical Museum	413-634-5527	Cummington
Lizzie Borden Bed & Breakfast/ Museum	508-675-7333	Fall River
Longfellow House National Historic Site	617-876-6014	Cambridge
Long Hill	978-921-1944	Beverly

Longyear Museum - . . . . .617-267-6688 . . . . .Boston
Lowell National Historical Park . . . . .978-459-1000 . . . . .Lowell
Macy-Christian House . . . . .508-228-1894 . . . . .Nantucket
Magnolia Historical Society Museum . . . . .978-525-3070 . . . . .Magnolia
Maria Mitchell Birthplace and Science Library . . . . .508-228-9219 . . . . .Nantucket
Maria Mitchell Science Center . . . . .508-228-0898 . . . . .Nantucket
Marine Museum at Fall River . . . . .508-674-3533 . . . . .Fall River
Martin House Farm . . . . .617-277-7569 . . . . .Swansea
Mary Baker Eddy House . . . . .978-388-1361 . . . . .Amesbury
Massachusetts Institute of Technology Museum . . . . .617-253-4444 . . . . . . .Cambridge
Massachusetts Museum of Contemporary Art . . . . .413-664-4481 . . . . .North Adams
Mayflower Society Museum . . . . .508-746-2590 . . . . .Plymouth
Mazmanian Gallery at Framingham State College . . . . .508-626-4985 . . . . . .Framingham
Mead Art Museum—Amherst College . . . . .413-542-2335 . . . . .Amherst
Mechanics Hall . . . . .508-752-5608 . . . . .Worcester
Memorial Hall Museum . . . . .413-774-3768 . . . . .Deerfield
Middleboro Historical Museum . . . . .508-947-1969 . . . . . . .Middleboro
Milton Art Museum . . . . .617-696-1145 . . . . .Milton
Mattapoisett Historical Society . . . . .508-758-2844 . . . . . .Mattapoisett
Museum of Bad Art . . . . .617-325-8224 . . . . .Boston
Museum of Comparative Zoology . . . . .617-495-3045 . . . . . . .Cambridge
Museum of Fine Arts . . . . .617-267-9300 . . . . .Boston
Museum of Printing . . . . .978-686-0450 . . . .North Andover
Museum of Science . . . . .617-723-2500 . . . . .Boston
Museum of the National Center of
Afro-American Artists, Inc. . . . . .617-442-8614 . . . . .Roxbury
Museum of Transportation . . . . .617-522-6547 . . . . .Brookline
Museum of Truro Historical Society (Highland House) . . . . .508-487-3397 . . . . .Truro
Nantucket Life Saving Museum . . . . .508-228-1885 . . . . .Nantucket
National Plastics Center and Museum . . . . .978-537-9529 . . . . . . .Leominster
New Bedford Art Museum . . . . .508-961-3072 . . . . . .New Bedford
New Bedford Fire Museum . . . . .508-992-2162 . . . . . .New Bedford
New England Fire and History Museum . . . . .508-896-5711 . . . . .Brewster
New England Pirate Museum . . . . .978-741-2902 . . . . .Salem
New England Quilt Museum . . . . .978-452-4207 . . . . .Lowell
New England Sports Center . . . . .508-229-2700 . . . . . .Marlborough
Nichols House Museum . . . . .617-227-6993 . . . . .Boston
Norcross Wildlife Sanctuary . . . . .413-267-9654 . . . . .Monson
Northfield Historical Museum . . . . .413-498-5565 . . . . .Northfield
Oceanographic Exhibit Center . . . . .508-548-1400 . . . . . .Woods Hole
Ocean Spray . . . . .508-946-5790 . . . . . . .Middleboro
Old Academy Museum . . . . .508-872-3780 . . . . . .Framingham
Old Colony and Fall River Railroad Museum . . . . .508-674-9340 . . . . .Fall River
Old Colony Historical Society . . . . .508-822-1622 . . . . .Taunton
Olde School House Museum . . . . .508-255-0333 . . . . .Eastham

Bostonian Society Old State House	617-720-1713	Boston
Old Schwamb Mill	781-643-0554	Arlington
Orchard House	978-369-4118	Concord
Patron's Museum and Educational Center	978-281-6437	Gloucester
Peabody Museum of Archaeology and Ethnology	617-496-1027	Cambridge
Peter Foulger Museum	508-228-1894	Nantucket
Pickering House	978-744-1647	Salem
Pioneer Valley Museum of Industry	978-544-2749	Orange
Salem 1630: Pioneer Village	978-744-0991	Salem
Plymouth National Wax Museum	508-746-6468	Plymouth
Pratt Museum	413-542-2165	Amherst
Rebecca Nurse Homestead	978-774-8799	Danvers
Rotch-Jones-Duff House and Garden Museum	508-997-1401	New Bedford
Platts-Bradstreet House (Rowley HS)	978-948-7483	Rowley
Pratt Museum of Natural History	413-542-2165	Amherst
Provincetown Art Association and Museum	508-487-1750	Provincetown
Provincetown Heritage Museum	508-487-7098	Provincetown
Quincy Historical Society	617-773-1144	Quincy
Ralph Waldo Emerson House	978-369-2236	Concord
Richard Sparrow House	508-747-1240	Plymouth
Robert Cole Museum of Natural History	413-527-4805	Holyoke
Robert S. Peabody Museum of Archaelogy	978-749-4490	Andover
Rockport Art Association	978-546-6604	Rockport
Rocky Hill Meeting House	978-462-2634	Amesbury
Rose Art Museum (Brandeis University)	781-736-2000	Waltham
Saint Anne Shrine	508-347-7461	Fiskdale
Salem's Museum of Myths and Monsters	978-745-7283	Salem
Salem Wax Museum of Witches and Seafarers	800-298-2929	Salem
Salem Witch Museum	978-744-1692	Salem
Sargent House Museum	978-281-2432	Gloucester
Saugus Iron Works National Historic Site	617-233-0050	Saugus
Schooner Museum	508-992-4900	Pemaquid Point
Shelburne Museum	413-625-2026	Shelburne
Shooting Sports Center at Smith and Wesson Academy Museum	413-846-6400	Springfield
Shovel Museum	508-565-1396	North Easton
Swift-Daley House, Tool Museum and 1940 Beach Shack	508-240-1247	Eastham
Smith College Museum of Art	413-585-2760	Northampton
South Shore Art Center	781-383-ARTS	Cohasset
Springfield Armory National Historic Site	413-734-8551	Plymouth
Springfield Arts Festival	413-736-ARTS	Springfield
Spooner House Museum	508-746-0012	Plymouth
Storrowton Village Museum	413-787-0136	Springfield
Sports Museum of New England	978-452-6775	Lowell
Stow West School Museum	978-897-7417	Stow

Strobe Alley (MIT)	617-253-4629	Cambridge
Toy Cupboard Puppet Theatre and Museum	978-365-9519	South Lancaster
Tower Hill Botanical Garden	508-869-6111	Boylston
Trask House	978-526-7230	Manchester
Tsongas Industrial History Center	978-970-5080	Lowell
Tufts University Art Gallery	617-627-3518	Medford
University of Massachusetts Fine Arts Center	413-545-2511	Amherst
U.S. Naval Shipbuilding Museum	617-479-7900	Quincy
USS *Cassin Young*	617-242-5601	Charlestown
USS *Constitution* Museum	617-426-1812	Charlestown
USS *Salem*	617-479-7900	Quincy
Vineyard Museum/ Dukes County Historical Society Museum	508-627-4441	Edgartown
Wellfleet Historical Society Museum	508-349-9157	Wellfleet
West Fort House	508-888-3591	East Sandwich
Whaling Museum	508-228-1736	Nantucket
Whately Historical Museum	413-665-3609	Whately
Whistler House Museum of Art	978-452-7641	Lowell
Willard House and Clock Museum	508-839-3500	North Grafton
William Cullen Bryant Homestead	413-634-2244	Cummington
Wistariahurst Museum	413-534-2216	Holyoke
Witch Dungeon Museum	978-741-3570	Salem
Witch History Museum	978-741-7770	Salem
Witch House	978-744-0180	Salem
Worcester Historical Museum	508-753-8278	Worcester
Yesteryears Doll Museum	508-888-1711	Sandwich
Yiddish Book Center	413-256-4900	Amherst
Zoo in Forest Park	413-733-2251	Springfield

New Hampshire

Albacore Park

600 Market Street
Portsmouth, NH 03801
(603) 436-3680

Overview

Albacore Park is the home of the USS *Albacore*, the prototype for modern submarines. The park also contains the Port of Portsmouth Maritime Museum. The park is a National Historic Landmark.

Directions and Hours

From I-95, take exit 7. Head toward Portsmouth, and the sub will be on your right.

From Memorial Day-Columbus Day, the museum is open seven days a week 9:30- 5:00. From Columbus Day-Memorial Day, hours are 9:30-3:30, and the museum is closed Tuesday and Wednesday. The museum is handicap accessible, but the submarine is not.

Admission and Membership

Admission to the museum is $5/adults, $3.50/seniors, and $2/children. An adult must accompany children.

What to See

The *Albacore* is a historical mechanical engineering landmark and a historic welded structure, while the museum explores the region's rich maritime tradition.

There is a gift shop, and there are many restaurants in Portsmouth.

While You're in the Area

Another attraction in the area is the Portsmouth Children's Museum (p. 343).

Amos J. Blake Museum

66 NH Route 119 West
PO Box 87
Fitzwilliam, NH 03447
(603) 585-7742

Overview

Built in 1837 on the Common, next to the historic Fitzwilliam Inn, the house in later years became the residence and law office of Amos J. Blake, a community leader, town official, and state legislature. Rooms available for viewing include Mr. Blake's law office, the town physician's consulting room, and a schoolroom. There is also a military display and firefighting memorabilia.

Directions and Hours

The museum is located on Route 119, across from the common.

From Memorial Day through Columbus Day, the house is open on Saturdays from 1:00-4:00 P.M. It is not handicap accessible.

Admission and Membership

Admission is free, but donations are accepted. Fitzwilliam Historical Society memberships are available.

Potter Place Railroad Station, Andover, NH. Courtesy of the Andover Historical Society Museum.

What to See

Special programs include a Spring program in late April, a Strawberry Festival the last Saturday in June, an antique show the third Saturday in July, and a Fall program in early October.

There is no gift shop or café, but food is available at the Fitzwilliam Inn across the street.

While You're in the Area

The entire common and all the buildings around it are on the National Register of Historic Places, and a walking tour map is available from local shops. Rhododendron State Park is also in Fitzwilliam.

Andover Historical Society Museum

Village of Potter Place
Andover, NH
(603) 735-5694

Overview

The Andover Historical Society Museum is housed in a beautiful stick-built Victorian station. The building is listed on the National Registry of Historic Places.

Directions and Hours

Take Route 93 north to Route 89 and take exit 11. Travel east on Route 11 to the intersection of Route 4 and Route 11. The museum is located on Route 4 at this intersection.

The museum is open June-September, but is not handicap accessible.

Hours: Saturday 10:00-3:00; Sunday 1:00-3:00.

Admission and Membership

Admission to the museum is free. Membership is $5/year for individuals and $8/year for families.

What to See

The museum has a fully furnished station master's office and a collection of railroad memorabilia. Also on display are an early settler's log boat and early farm implements.

A second building is an early post office and general store, also authentically furnished.

On the first Sunday in August the museum holds a nineteenth-century fair, flea market, craft market, and auction. There are also children's games, antique rail hand car rides, music, and entertainment.

There is a gift shop. Visitors can eat at Potter Place Inn, and there is also a public picnic area.

While You're in the Area

There are two covered bridges in Andover, and many hiking trails and Mount Kearsarge to climb in the area. Nearby New London also has a collection of early buildings and a museum, and there are public beaches.

Annalee Doll Museum

44 Reservoir Road
Meredith, NH 03253
(603) 279-6542
www.annalee.com

Overview

The Annalee Doll Museum traces the history and career of doll maker Annalee Thorndike. There are hundreds of Annalee Dolls on display from the 1940s to the present.

Directions and Hours

Take Route 93 north to exit 23 (Route 104). Travel approximately eight miles, and turn right onto Hemlock Drive for a quarter of a mile. Follow the signs to the parking lot.

The museum is open from Memorial Day to Labor Day, and weekends and by appointment in October. The museum is handicap accessible.

Hours: daily 9:00-5:00.

Admission and Membership

Admission to the museum is free.

What to See

The museum displays a small collection of Annalee Thorndike's earliest dolls from the 1940s. These dolls are very rare and few are still in existence. There is also a display of life-size dolls including Santa Claus and the Easter Bunny.

There is a gift shop. There is no café, but there are restaurants in downtown Meredith and along the shore of nearby Lake Winnipesaukee.

While You're in the Area

There are wonderful shops in downtown Meredith and lake recreation on Winnipesaukee.

The Art Gallery, University of New Hampshire

Paul Creative Arts Center
30 College Road
Durham, NH 03824
(603) 862-3712
www.unh.edu/art-gallery

Overview

The Art Gallery at the University of New Hampshire houses a wide variety of exhibitions, including faculty and student exhibitions. Wednesday noon programs complement the exhibitions. Weekly programs include artist lectures and demonstrations, readings, concerts, theatrical performances, and panel discussions.

Directions and Hours

Take 95 to exit 4 (Spaulding Turnpike). Continue across the bridge and take exit 6W (Route 4). Take Route 4 west to the exit for Route 155A and turn left onto Main Street. At the traffic light, take a right onto College Road.

The gallery is open from September through May, but is not handicap accessible.

Hours: Monday-Wednesday 10:00-4:00; Thursday 10:00-8:00; Saturday and Sunday 1:00-5:00.

Admission and Membership

Admission to the gallery is free. Memberships range from $15/year to $1,000/year.

What to See

The gallery has a collection of 200 Japanese woodblock prints and many works on paper.

It has a 25-year-old outreach program that lends out slide packets and videos to primary and secondary schools. This program enhances the curriculum to make art lessons more interesting and complete. There are also school tours. Family programs incorporate art activities for parents and children to do together.

There is a small gift shop. There is no café, but there are many restaurants and sandwich shops nearby.

While You're in the Area

The Strawbery Banke Museum (p. 378) and historic Portsmouth, New Hampshire, are also nearby.

Ashland Railroad Station Museum

Ashland Historical Society
69 Depot Street
Ashland, NH 03217
(603) 968-3902

Overview

The Ashland Railroad Station Museum is a

Photo courtesy of the Ashland Railroad Station Museum.

restored 1891 passenger station, used by the Boston, Concord & Montreal Railroad, that retains its original character. This station was the central point for the development and growth of the Squam Lakes and Ashland area region. Today the Ashland Railroad Station is one of the best preserved nineteenth century railroad stations in New Hampshire and houses a collection of railroad artifacts, pictures, and documents.

Directions and Hours

From Route 93: Take exit 24 to Ashland. Turn right on Winter Street. The station will be in front of you.

From Route 3: Take Route 3 to Ashland then turn onto Route 132. The Station will be ½ away on the left.

The museum is open every Saturday in July and August, for special train events, and on request. It is handicap accessible.

Hours: 1:00-4:00 P.M. Any time on request April 1 to foliage time.

Admission and Membership

Admission is free. Donations are welcome. Membership to the Ashland Historical Society is $10 per year, $100 for lifetime membership. Group tours are welcome any time with an appointment.

What to See

The Railroad Station's collection includes a ca. 1960 maintenance car, a 1896 velocipede handcar, local railroad memorabilia, and a diorama of the 1891 railroad station done by an eighth grade class.

Children's programming includes teaching the elementary school grades the importance of the railroad in the development of the local area and industry. The station is looking forward to revising the Railroading Merit Badge for the Boy Scouts of America.

The museum does not have a gift shop or a café but John's Restaurant, the Alias Smith and Jones Restaurant, and the Common Man Restaurant are nearby.

While You're in the Area

Other interesting places to visit while you are in the area include the George Hoyt Whipple House Museum (p. 379) and the Glidden Toy Museum (p. 367).

Barrett House (SPNEA)

79 Main Street
New Ipswich, NH 03071
(603) 878-2517
www.SPNEA.org

Overview

According to tradition, Barrett House was built by Charles Barrett Sr. for his son, Charles Jr., on the occasion of his marriage. Its grand scale was encouraged by the bride's father, who promised to furnish the house in as lavish a manner as it could be built. The interiors, which are decorated with many of the family's furnishings, are indeed elegant and must have presented a fine backdrop for the young couple.

Directions and Hours

Take Route 2 west to Route 13 north to Townsend, Mass. Go left on Route 119 to West Townsend. Turn north (right) on Canal Street; at the fork bear left. This becomes Route 124. Go 10 miles to New Ipswich. Turn left onto Main Street (Route 123A). The house is .25 miles on the right.

The museum is open from June 1 to October 15. It is not handicap accessible.

Hours: Saturdays and Sundays there is a tour on the hour from 11:00 A.M. to 5:00 P.M.

Admission and Membership

$4 for adults, $3.50 for senior citizens, children 12 and under $2. SPNEA members are free. Please call for group tours. SPNEA membership is $35 at the Individual level, $45 at the Household level, $65 at the Contributing level, $100 at the Sustaining level, $250 at the Supporting level, $25 at the National level, $1000 for the Appleton Circle, and $3000 for the Appleton Circle Patron.

This Gothic Revival summer house was constructed shortly after Barrett House was built. Photograph courtesy of SPNEA. John Cooke, photographer.

What to See

Used as the setting for the Merchant-Ivory production of *The Europeans*, Barrett House features family furnishings, French scenic wallpaper, and a third floor ballroom with antique musical instruments. The distinctive landscape includes gardens and a Gothic Revival summer house that crowns the terraced hillside behind the museum.

Each year Barrett House hosts a series of programs which include an open house, lectures, and family programming.

The museum does not have a gift shop or a café but there is a pizza shop on Main Street, the Depot restaurant is located in nearby Greenville, and Pickety Place, located in Mason, is also close.

While You're in the Area

Other interesting places to visit while you are in the area are Frye's Measure Mill, Peterborough with historic buildings and old mills, and West Townsend with numerous antique shops. Hiking and camping are available at Monadnock State Park.

The Belknap Mill Society

The Mill Plaza
Laconia, NH 03246
(603) 524-8813

Overview

Built in 1823, the Belknap Mill is the only remaining brick mill representing the first stage of America's Industrial Revolution. It was one of the first mills to convert from weaving to knitting, during the Civil War. In 1971, the Society made national headlines to preserve the mill and convert it into a cultural center. Today the Mill houses the nation's first industrial knitting museum. The Society also offers changing exhibits on art and history.

Directions and Hours

The Belknap Mill is about 2 hours north of Boston. From I-93 in New Hampshire, take exit 20. Proceed north on routes 3 and 11, about 6 miles. Pass Belknap Mall on the left and continue straight on what is now routes 11A East and route 3. Continue 1-2 miles to a traffic light at the junction of routes 3, 11A, and 106. Turn left onto 106 north and immediately turn right at the blinking left. The Mill is on the right.

The museum is open year round and it is handicap accessible.

Hours: weekdays 9:00-5:00; other times for special events.

Admission and Membership

Admission is free. Membership is $25/year for individuals and $40/year for families.

What to See

The Belknap Mill may be the nation's only industrial knitting museum, with machines that operate and a 1918 hydroelectric power system. Self-guided tours are available, but guided tours are recommended and arranged by calling in advance.

The Belknap Mill hosts an annual Quilt Show every Columbus Day Weekend. It is closed for tours during that event. Another featured event is the Motorcycle Week Exhibit, which begins the week preceding Father's Day.

Children's programming is seasonal. For example, there is a tree trimming party on the first Saturday in December. Call extension 3 for more information.

The mill does have a gift shop and there are several café s within walking distance.

While You're in the Area

Lake Winnipesaukee and the White Mountains are two nearby New Hampshire features not to be missed.

Bell Cove Caboose Museum

Route 103
Newbury, NH 03255
(603) 763-4940
www.town.newbury.nh.us

Overview

The Bell Cove Caboose Museum has an extensive collection of donated and purchased railroad memorabilia which includes signal lights and lanterns, bells, whistles, brochures, timetables, a clock, a desk, and a stove. The site for this museum is part of the original railroad line that ran from Concord to Claremont from the 1870s to the 1950s.

Directions and Hours

Take I-89 to exit 9 to Route 103. The museum is on Route 103 in Newbury.

The museum is open from Memorial Day-Columbus Day weekend (June, July, and August) and is handicap accessible.

Hours: 10:00 A.M. to 4:00 P.M.

Admission and Membership

Admission is free.

What to See

The site is enhanced by an illustrated interpretive sign placed near the caboose that gives visitors information about the site and the area in general.

The museum does not have a gift shop or a café but there is a restaurant and a sandwich shop across the street. There is also a picnic area at the site.

While You're in the Area

Other museums and interesting attractions nearby include the Mount Kearsarge Indian Museum (p. 378), the Musterfield Farm (p. 378), Lake Sunapee, Mt. Sunapee Resort, and the John Hay National Wildlife Refuge.

The Children's Metamorphosis Museum

217 Rockingham Road
Londonderry, NH 03053
(603) 425-2560
www.discoverthemet.com

Overview

The Children's Metamorphosis Museum, or "the Met," is a hands-on museum for children ages 1-8 years. It is a small, family environment offering 14 different exhibits that encourage learning and exploration through play.

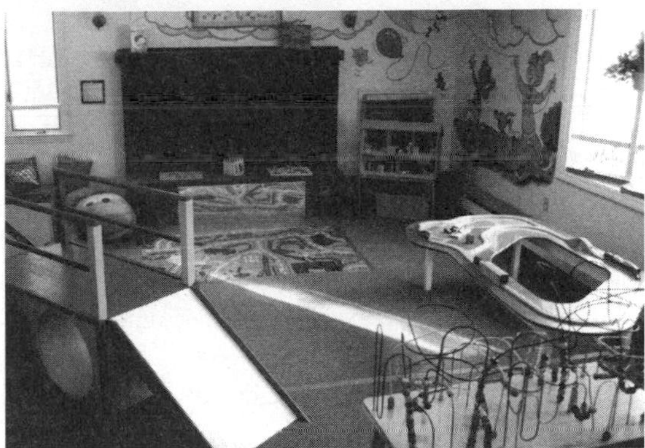

The Children's Metamorphosis Museum Toddler Room. Met Staff Photo.

Directions and Hours

Take Route 93 to exit 5. Take a left off the ramp onto Route 28 if coming from Route 93 north, take a right off the ramp onto Route 28 if coming from Route 93 south. Route 28 is also Rockingham Road.

The museum is open year round, and is handicap accessible.

Hours: Tuesday-Saturday 9:30-5:00; Sunday 1:00-5:00; Friday 9:30-8:00; July 5-August 31 also Monday 9:30-5:00.

Admission and Membership

$5 per person, children under 1 are free. Membership is $75/year for families.

There is a field trip discount rate (at least ten people) of $4 per person.

What to See

Exhibits include the Toddler Room, Sticky Room, Climbing Wall, Dr. Smile's Office, and the Dinosaur Room. There is also a Nature Center with live animals, a grocery store, a water play area, and a construction site. There is a family resource lending library in the Toddler Room. Outside is a play area with a climbing structure, sandbox, grassy hill, butterfly garden, picnic tables, and a train.

Many additional children's programs are offered, including toddler programs and a story hour for preschoolers. The museum also offers an afterschool art program for 6-10 year olds. During the summer the Met runs a Summer Enrichment Program. Themes vary, and have included science, community helpers, music, and animals. Every September, the Met holds a huge childrens' clothing, toy, and equipment sale.

There is no gift shop, but the museum sells t-shirts and ice cream treats. There is no café, but a small area is available for families to snack, and there are many restaurants nearby.

While You're in the Area

The Robert Frost Farm (p. 378), the SEE Museum (p. 378), the Christa McAuliffe Museum and Planetarium (p. 377), the Manchester Historical Society Museum (p. 378), and the Curner Gallery of Art (p. 347) are also in the area.

The Children's Museum of Portsmouth

280 Marcy Street
Portsmouth, NH 03801
(603) 436-3853

Overview

The Children's Museum of Portsmouth is an arts and science museum. It features more than 19 hands-on exhibits housed in a historic building.

Exhibit themes range from dinosaurs, space, and lobstering to music, sound, literature, and world cultures.

Directions and Hours

Take 95 to exit 7. From the south take a right off the ramp onto Market Street, from the north take a left onto Market Street. Turn left onto Bow Street, and at the second stop sign turn left onto State Street. Take the last right before the harbor onto Marcy Street.

The museum is open year round, and is handicap accessible.

Hours: Tuesday-Saturday 10:00-5:00; Sunday 1:00-5:00; summer and school vacations Monday 10:00-5:00, also.

Admission and Membership

$4 for adults and children, $3 for seniors, children under one are admitted for free. Family membership is $45/year for the first member and $5 for each additional family member.

AAA members, Massachusetts Teachers Association, and groups of 10 or more receive a discount.

What to See

The Children's Museum of Portsmouth's exhibits include Space Shuttle, Step into a Story, Poetry in Pieces, Magicam, Yellow Submarine, Dino Detective, and Shape Scape.

The museum offers seasonal, after school, and family workshops, as well as preschool classes. There are also special performances and events throughout the year, and the museum conducts a daily activity in the project area.

The museum offers outreach programs to schools, including the Animation Station unit. School groups can also participate in Focused Group Visits that include special activities.

There is a museum gift shop. There is no café, but there are many places to eat within walking distance.

While You're in the Area

Prescott Park, Peirce Island, the Strawberry Banke Museum (p. 378), the USS *Albacore* Submarine Park (p. 337), and several historic homes are located nearby.

Christies' Maple Farm and Maple Museum

US Route 2, 246 Portland Street
Lancaster, NH 03584
(800) 788-2118
www.RealMaple.com

Overview

Christies' Maple Farm and Maple Museum is an authentic sugaring operation in New Hampshire's White Mountains. Created to offer an inside look to New England's maple heritage, this hands-on museum offers visitors insights on how Native Americans first made maple syrup, the practices of early colonists, and a fresh look at today's progressive and innovative maple industry.

Photo courtsy of Christies' Maple Farm and Maple Museum.

Directions and Hours

Take Route 93 to Route 3 north to Route 2 East.

Or, take 91 to Route 2 East.

The museum is open every day from 9:00-5:00 from May-October. It is closed on Sundays in November and December. January-April: call ahead for winter hours. The museum is handicap accessible.

Admission and Membership

Admission is free.

What to See

Visitors become maple connoisseurs by tasting each of the four grades of maple syrup at the "taste-testing" bar. The self guided tour includes a walk through the family's authentic working sugarhouse, a classic post-and-beam structure with unbeatable views of New Hampshire's spectacular Presidential Range. Visitors can see the Christie family's steam-powered evaporator (one of only a handful in the U.S.) and its state-of-the-art sap collection system.

A Kid's Maple Madness Harvest Fest is held the last weekend in September, featuring hayrides, off-the-wall maple contests such as the "pancake discus throw," live music, and scarecrow building. The museum's Spring Maple Fest is held each spring on the third weekend in March, and offers free "sugar on snow" and tastes of new syrup straight from the evaporator.

The museum includes a farmhouse gift shop featuring a full line of maple products and gifts, accessible bathroom facilities, ample parking for RV's and buses, and a picnic area with some of the most spectacular views of the White Mountains.

While You're in the Area

The museum is a three-minute drive from Weeks State Park and the John W. Weeks historic site, and minutes from two classic New England covered bridges. It is adjacent to a New Hampshire State historic marker commemorating the fastest winds recorded by man on nearby Mount Washington.

Clark's Trading Post

PO Box 1
Lincoln, NH 03251
(603) 745-8913
www.clarkstradingpost.com

Overview

Clark's Trading Post was established in 1928 as "Ed Clark's Eskimo Sled Dog Ranch" for raising Eskimo sled dogs. Today, Clark's Trading Post entertainment includes a bear show with North American Black Bears (who work unmuzzled and unleashed) and a ride on a White Mountain Central Railroad standard gage wood burning

Clark's Trading Post. Photo courtesy of Maureen Clark.

locomotive steam train ride through a 1904 covered bridge.

Directions and Hours

From I-93: Take exit 33. The post is one mile south on Route 3.

Clark's Trading Post is open in 2001 from May 26-June 17 and September 8-October 14 weekends, and daily June 23-September 3. The post is partially handicap accessible.

Hours: 10:00-5:00 preseason and postseason days; 9:30-6:00 June 23-September 3.

Admission and Membership

$9 ages 6 and up, $3 ages 3-5, $8 seniors 65+, children under 3 free. A season pass is $35. Group rate for 10 or more with one person paying is $8/each.

What to See

Early firefighting equipment, such as antique horse-drawn fire engines, is on display along with early typewriters, cameras, toy trains, dolls, children's games, railroad memorabilia, early telephones, soda water advertising, sewing machines, coin operated pianos, early light bulbs, steam and gas engines, antique cars, motoring memorabilia, Clark family history and information on Eskimo sled dogs, and trained North American Black Bears. Featured attractions include Avery's Garage with antique cars and motorcycles, Old Mill Pond Water Bumper Boats, the Clark Museum, the Florence Murray Museum, Merlin's Mystical Mansion, a guide of Tuttle's Rustic House, an Americana Museum and 1884 Fire Station, Liberty Press where visitors can get their name in print, and Kilburn's Photo Parlor where guests can get their picture taken dressed in old-time costumes.

The trading post has a large gift shop and a dairy bar, a Popcorn Wagon, Peppermint Saloon, and Pullman's Pizza and Subs.

While You're in the Area

Other interesting places to visit while you are in the area include Conway Scenic Railroad (p. 377), Loon Mountain (p. 378), Polar Caves Park (p. 378), Santa's Village (p. 378), Six Gun City (p. 378), Story Land (p. 378), the Whale's Tale (p. 379), and Attitash Bear Peak (p. 378).

The Cornish Colony Gallery and Museum

"Mastlands," Route 12-A
RR-3, Box 292
Cornish, NH 03745
(603) 675-6000
www.almagilbert.com

Overview

The Cornish Gallery and Museum at "Mastlands" is the only museum in New Hampshire that displays a collection of original paintings by American artist Maxfield Parrish, whose home was in the neighboring town of Plainfield. The museum is housed in a historic 1857 farmhouse which was the home of Elizabeth and Arthur Nichols, sister and brother-in-law of Augustus Saint-Gaudens. The Nichols's eldest daughter was one of the earliest woman garden designers in America, and her signature garden at the museum has been restored and is open to the public.

Directions and Hours

Take 89 north to exit 20, then south on local route 12-A for approximately eleven miles.

The museum is open Memorial Day-October, and is partially handicap accessible.

Hours: Tuesday-Saturday 10:00-5:00; Sunday noon-5:00.

Admission and Membership

$5 per person, $3 for students and seniors. Membership is $25/year for individuals, $50 for families.

What to See

In addition to the Maxfield Parrish collection,

The Cornish Gallery and Museum exhibits the works of approximately 20 other artists, writers, architects, and sculptors who lived and worked in the Cornish, New Hampshire, area.

Visitors can also walk through the restored, turn-of-the-century walled garden designed by Rose Nichols, niece of Augustus Saint-Gaudens. The garden is next door to the gallery.

There is a gift shop. There is also a café that serves lunches and afternoon tea on a screened porch with a view of the gardens.

While You're in the Area

While in the area, people can visit Saint-Gaudens National Historic Site (p. 378), American Precision Museum (p. 486), Vermont State Craft House (p. 487), and the Old Constitution House (p. 366).

The Currier Gallery of Art

201 Myrtle Way
Manchester, NH 03104
(603) 669-6144
www.currier.org

Overview

The Currier is an intimate and internationally renowned art museum featuring European and American paintings, decorative arts, photographs and sculpture. The permanent collection includes works by Picasso, Matisse, Monet, O'Keeffe, Calder, and Wyeth. A lively schedule of exhibitions has recently included the photographs of Linda McCartney and the paintings of Maxfield Parrish. The Currier Gallery of Art also owns the Zimmerman House, designed in 1950 by Frank Lloyd Wright and meticulously preserved and restored, complete with the original furnishings and the owners' fine art collection. Reservations are required for Zimmerman House tours, which depart from the museum.

Directions and Hours

Take 293 to exit 6. Bear right across the bridge and follow the signs for Route 3 and Business District to Elm Street. At the traffic light, cross Elm Street and turn right onto Beech Street. The Currier is half a mile in the left.

Or, take 93 to exit 8. Bear right onto Bridge Street, then turn right onto Ash Street. The Currier will be a quarter mile ahead on the left.

The museum is open year round.

Hours: Monday, Wednesday, Thursday, Sunday 11:00-5:00; Friday 11:00-8:00; Saturday 10:00-5:00.

Admission and Membership

$5 for adults, $4 for seniors and students, children under 18 are free. Free admission on Saturday from 10:00-1:00. Membership is $30/year for individuals, and there are additional levels of membership available.

What to See

The Currier is especially well-known for its substantial holdings in American art. John Singer Sargent, Georgia O'Keeffe, Edmund Tarbell and Augustus Saint-Gaudens are a few of the major American artists represented in the Currier's collection. The Currier also has an important collection of early American decorative arts.

Annually, the Currier produces four to five "Family Days" which include activities and programs for all ages, and are often designed to enhance the special exhibitions on view at that time (for example, a recent exhibition of prints

The Currier Gallery of Art. Photo courtesy of Rixon Photography.

by John James Audubon produced a Family Day at which a naturalist introduced children to live birds).

In October, 2001, the Currier Gallery of Art will mount the most important traveling exhibition to date devoted to Edmund C. Tarbell (1862-1938), a major American Impressionist from the Boston School who spent many years in New Castle, New Hampshire. The show will include about 45 paintings demonstrating the range of Tarbell's work, from portraits, figure and family scenes, to interiors, riding pictures and still lifes. The exhibition will travel to the Delaware Art Museum and the Terra Museum of Art, Chicago.

The gallery has a gift shop, a café, and a children's room.

While You're in the Area

The Currier Gallery of Art is located about five minutes from downtown Manchester and the city's adjacent Millyard district, where there are several small shops and restaurants ranging from a 1930's diner to an upscale bistro. Other attractions in Manchester include the Manchester Historic Association's new Millyard Museum (p. 378), the New Hampshire Institute of Art (an art school located downtown, p. 365), the SEE Science Center (learning experiences for children) (p. 348), the Palace Theatre (featuring plays, musicals, live music, comedy, etc.), and the Franco-American Association (p. 377).

Diocesan Museum of Manchester

140 Laurel St.
Manchester, NH 03103
(603) 624-1729
www.CatholicChurchnh.org

Overview

The museum was founded in 1988 to collect and preserve the history of New Hampshire's Catholic community. It is housed in the Chapel of the Annunciation, which was the convent chapel of the Sisters of Mercy motherhouse until 1990.

Directions and Hours

From Route 93, take the Bridge Street exit and turn right onto Bridge Street, and follow it to Union Street. Turn left onto Union Street. Laurel Street is nine blocks down; turn left onto Laurel Street. The museum is on the left.

Open year-round, from 10:00-4:00 Tuesdays to Fridays, and by appointment. In December the museum is also open on Saturdays and Sundays from 1:00-4:00. Museum tours are available upon request. Handicap accessible.

Chapel of the Annunciation, Manchester, New Hampshire. Photo by Gerald L. Durette.

Admission and Membership

Admission is free.

What to See

The museum collects artifacts from throughout the Diocese. The collections reflect the history of New

Hampshire's parishes, clergy, religious orders, schools, and lay organizations. There are also exhibits of the works of current religious artists, and the museum offers a spring lecture series. Each year, from mid-November to January, the museum displays over a hundred nativity sets from around the world.

The museum has no gift shop. There is no café, but the museum is located three blocks from Elm Street, the main business street in Manchester. There are many restaurants within easy walking distance there.

While You're in the Area

Other Manchester museums include the Currier Gallery of Art (p. 347), the Lawrence L. Lee Scouting Museum (p. 358), and the New Hampshire Institute of Art (p. 365).

Eastman Lord House

100 Main St.
PO Box 1949
Conway, NH 03818
(603) 447-5551
www.geocities.com/conhist

Overview

The Eastman Lord House was the 1818 residence of mill owner William K. Eastman. Rooms are furnished in periods from 1818-1945.

Directions and Hours

The house is located on Route 16 in Conway Village, across from the fire station.

Open Memorial Day-Labor Day, Tuesday 6:00-8:00, Wednesday 2:00-4:00, Thursday, 6:00-8:00 and by appointment. In May, September, and October, the house is open by appointment only. Please call ahead. The house is not handicap accessible.

Admission and Membership

Admission is $3/person and $6/family. Groups are welcome by advance arrangement, and the historical society offers group rates.

What to See

The Eastman Lord House, which was extensively renovated in 1845, includes two "borning rooms," an authentic Victorian parlor, and a reconstructed sleeping loft. It has been home to a millinery shop and a general store. The museum now houses thousands of fine antiques, paintings, and collectibles. Other points of interest include a 1940s kitchen, examples of period clothing, and a research library.

The museum has a gift shop. There is no café, but there are several restaurants within walking distance.

While You're in the Area

Other attractions in the area include the Remick Museum (p. 368), the Chester Eastman Homestead (p. 377), and the Mount Washington Observatory (p. 363).

Enfield Historical Society Museum

Route 4A
PO Box 612
Enfield, NH 03748
(603) 632-7740

Overview

The Enfield Historical Society Museum is located in one of the few two-story one-room schoolhouses in New England.

Directions and Hours

Take I-89 to Route 4 to Route 4A. The Museum is located in Enfield center.

The museum is open mid-June through Labor Day. It is not handicap accessible.

Hours: Saturday 2:00-4:00.

Admission and Membership

Admission is free, but donations are accepted.

What to See

The Enfield Historical Society Museum features general town history.

There is no gift shop, but there are items for purchase. Visitors can dine at the Shaker Inn on Route 4A, or Janet's Roadside Café on Route 4.

While You're in the Area

The Enfield Shaker Museum on Route 4A (p. 350), the Lockehaven Schoolhouse Museum (p. 360), the Hood Museum at Dartmouth College (p. 377), and the LaSallette Shrine on Route 4A are other attractions in the area.

Enfield Shaker Museum

24 Caleb Dyer Lane
Enfield, NH 03748
(603) 632-4346
www.shakermuseum.org

Overview

Founded in 1793, this village was the ninth of 18 Shaker communities to be established in this country. At its peak in the mid-nineteenth century, the community was home to three "Families" of Shakers. Brothers, Sisters, and children lived, worked, and worshipped and practiced equality of the sexes and races, celibacy, pacifism, and communal ownership of property. Striving to create a heaven on earth, the Enfield Shakers built more than 200 buildings (including the Great Stone Dwelling, the largest Shaker dwelling ever built), farmed over 3,000 acres of fertile land, educated children in model schools, and followed the "Shaker Way" of worship. In 1923, after 130 years of farming, manufacturing, and productive existence, declining membership forced the Shakers to close their community and put it up for sale. In 1927, forgoing a much more lucrative offer from a New York syndicate, the Shakers sold the site to the LaSalettes, an order of Catholic priests, ensuring the continued tradition of spiritual, communal life on the site. The LaSalettes also continued the very active agricultural use of the land as well as establishing a seminary and high school. In 1985 the property changed hands again when the remaining buildings and grounds were purchased by a group of private investors.

The Enfield Shaker Museum interprets a 192 year period of communal, religious residence beginning with the Shakers from 1793 to 1923, and followed by the Catholic La Salette order which owned the property from 1927 to 1985. The site offers spectacular architecture, a beautiful lakeside setting, and interpretive analysis of the unique history of the site. Located between Mount Assurance and Lake Mascoma, the setting is idyllic for an afternoon at the museum followed by a hike or a cross-county ski or a picnic in the herb gardens. The Shaker six-story granite dwelling house, completed in 1841, houses the Shaker Inn where visitors can dine and stay in the same rooms the Shakers inhabited a century ago. Dana Robes Wood Craftsmen maintains a Shaker-inspired furniture woodshop and showroom next to the museum.

Directions and Hours

From I-89: Take exit 17. Go right at the end of the ramp onto Route 4. Travel 1½ miles on Route 4 then turn right onto Route 4A. The museum is 3½ miles down Route 4A on the left.

The museum is open daily from Memorial Day through October and in winter on weekends. It is partially handicap accessible.

Summer hours: Monday-Saturday 10:00 A.M. to 5:00 P.M., Sunday noon-5:00 P.M. The Museum store in the Great Stone Dwelling will be open daily 8:00 A.M. to 10:00 P.M. Winter hours: Saturday 10:00 A.M. to 4:00 P.M., Sunday noon-4:00 P.M. In addition, the Museum Store in the Great Stone Dwelling will be open Tuesdays through Saturdays from 8:00 A.M. to 10:00 P.M.

Admission and Membership

Adults $7, $6 for seniors, $3 for children. Discounts are offered to AAA members, seniors, students with ID, youths, and groups (groups must make reservations in advance). Membership is $30/year for individuals and $40/year for families.

What to See

In addition to preserving spectacular religious and residential architecture, the museum offers a permanent collection of illustrative artifacts and exhibits, and maintains an herb garden with over 125 varieties of plants the Shakers grew on the site.

The Enfield Shaker Museum will host a series of five contra dances during the spring and summer of 2001. These events will encourage Museum visitors to participate in a traditional form of New England dancing while enjoying live music performed by New Hampshire's most respected dance bands and being instructed by the region's finest callers. Contra dancing is a form of community-based participatory dance that has been practiced continually in Northern New England for at least 200 years. The dances will be held in a historic Shaker building erected in 1849. All dances in the series will begin at 7:00 pm in the Stone Mill on Route 4A in Enfield. Admission will be $5 for adults and $3 for children under 15. The Enfield Shaker Museum offers year-round opportunities for families and individuals, including a full schedule of events, workshops, tours, exhibits, and craft demonstrations.

There is a small gift shop. There is also a restaurant in the Shakers dwelling house.

While You're in the Area

Other interesting places to visit while you are in the area include the Billings Farm and Museum (p. 435), the Montshire Museum of Science (p. 459), the Hood Museum of Art (p. 377), the American Precision Museum (p. 486), and the Saint Gaudens National Historic Site (p. 378).

Exeter Historical Society

47 Front St.
PO Box 924
Exeter, NH 03833
(608) 778-2335

Overview

The Exeter Historical Society has many permanent displays, mainly focusing on the history of Exeter. There is also a library for genealogy research and an extensive photo collection.

Directions and Hours

From Route 95, take exit 2 to Route 101 west. Take exit 10 and bear left onto Route 88 (this becomes Water Street). Follow all the way into town bearing to the left. At town center, take a right at the bandstand. The Historical Society will be on the right in a yellow brick building.

Open year-round on Saturday, Tuesday, and Thursday, 2:00-4:30. The museum is not handicap accessible.

Admission and Membership

Admission is free and membership costs $20/individual, $30/family, and $10/student or senior.

Photo courtesy of the Exeter Historical Society.

What to See

The Exeter Historical Society features displays about New England printing and the Civil War. The society is in the process of developing special programming for children.

There is a small gift shop where visitors may purchase books including a walking tour of Exeter booklet for $2. While the society does not have a café, there are plenty of lovely bakeries and coffeeshops in downtown Exeter.

While You're in the Area

The town of Exeter is beautiful and very good for walking. Visitors can see such local sites including the American Independence Museum (p. 377) and the Gilman-Garrison House (p. 353).

Franklin Pierce Homestead

Hillsborough, NH 03244
(603) 478-3165

Overview

The Franklin Pierce Homestead is being appropriately furnished for 1824 when future-president Franklin graduated from Bowdoin College and his father Benjamin was running for governor. The house has stenciled walls that are fully restored, and the parlor has the original 1824 French wallpaper.

Directions and Hours

From Concord: Take Route 9 west toward Keene and through Hillsborough. Turn right on 31 north; the homestead is on the right. From Keene, on Route 9 go east.

Open daily July and August. In June and September, weekdays and Saturday, 10:00 to 4:00, Sundays 1:00 to 4:00. Also open on Memorial Day weekend, July 4, and September 5. The first floor is handicap accessible.

Admission and Membership

Admission is $3/person, free for children and seniors. Memberships are available.

What to See

Listed as a National Historic Landmark, the Franklin Pierce Homestead displays many period items and rooms including the Franklin Pierce sleigh and the ballroom on the second floor.

In addition to the exhibits, the historical society hosts a scavenger hunt for children. There will be a Bicentennial celebration in 2004 at the homestead and many other events such an original pig roast that was an annual event for Benjamin Pierce to entertain his friends from the town, from politics and from the Revolutionary War.

The Homestead has a gift shop, and while there is no café, there are many eating establishments nearby.

While You're in the Area

Visitors can view many attractions in Old Hillsborough Center which includes the old schoolhouse, Town Pound, Pewter Shop, and historic churches and houses. There is also a walking tour from the Homestead.

Photo courtesy of the Franklin Pierce Homestead.

Gilman Garrison House (SPNEA)

12 Water Street
Exeter, NH 03833
(603) 436-3205
www.spnea.org

Overview

From the first English settlements of the 1630s to the Treaty of Paris in 1763, the frontier towns of New England lived with the threat of Indian attack. The Gilman Garrison House, described in 1719 as "the old logg house," was built as a fortified house, strategically sited to protect the valuable sawmills and waterpower sites owned by John Gilman.

Directions and Hours

Take I-95 to New Hampshire exit 2. Follow Route 101 west 3½ miles to Route 108 south. Continue 1 mile into Exeter. Turn right on High Street. The house is 3 blocks ahead, just after a small bridge.

The house museum is open June 1 through October 15.

Hours: Saturday and Sunday, 11:00 A.M. to 5:00 P.M. Tours at 11:00 A.M., 12:00, 1:00, 2:00, 3:00 and 4:00 P.M.

Admission and Membership

$5 for adults, $4.50 senior citizens, ½ off for students and children 6-12. Children 5 and under, SPNEA members, and residents of Exeter are free. AAA members receive a 2 for 1 discount. SPNEA membership is $35/year for individuals and $45/year for a household. Membership includes free admissions to 35 properties and museums across New England.

What to See

The interior of this unique building reveals walls constructed of massive sawn logs and a pulley above the main entrance that was used to operate a portcullis, or reinforced door. In the mid eighteenth century Peter Gilman substantially remodeled the house, adding a wing with elegantly paneled rooms. The building was restored in the 1950s by local preservationist William Dudley to reveal its early architecture and to commemorate the lives of its varied occupants over the centuries.

Gilman Garrison offers group tours and special programs. Summer programs include the annual townwide Exeter Revolutionary Festival in July. Please call or write for details.

While You're in the Area

Nearby attractions and museums include the American Independence Museum (p. 377).

Governor John Langdon House (SPNEA)

143 Pleasant Street
Portsmouth, NH 03801
(603) 436-3205
www.spnea.org

Overview

John Langdon, son of one of Portsmouth's oldest families, became a sea captain, merchant, shipbuilder, Revolutionary leader, signer of the United States Constitution, and three-term governor of New Hampshire. The house he built for his family expresses their status as Portsmouth's leading citizens. George Washington, who visited there in 1789, praised its grand reception rooms, which are ornamented by elaborate wood carving in the rococo style. After Langdon's death in 1819, the house was occupied by other leading families.

Directions and Hours

Take I-95 to exit 7 (Market Street). Bear right after the railroad tracks. Turn right onto Deer Street then left on Maplewood Avenue, left on State Street, and right on Pleasant Street. The house is one block down on the left.

The house museum is open June 1 through October 15.

Wednesday-Sunday, 11:00 A.M. to 5:00 P.M.

Tours are at 11:00, 12:00, 1:00, 2:00, 3:00 and 4:00 P.M.

Admission and Membership

$5 for adults, $4.50 senior citizens, ½ off for students and children 6-12. Children 5 and under, SPNEA members, and residents of Portsmouth are free. AAA members receive a 2 for 1 discount. SPNEA membership is $35/year for individuals and $45/year for a household. Membership includes free admissions to 35 properties and museums across New England.

What to See

At the end of the nineteenth century, Langdon descendants purchased the house and restored it as a memorial to their ancestor. A substantial wing, designed by McKim, Mead, and White, was added to house modern conveniences and an elegant dining room in the Colonial Revival style. The garden, dating from the same era, features restored perennial beds, a rose and grape arbor, and a pavilion. The grounds may be rented for weddings and other occasions.

Langdon House offers group tours, educational and family programs, including special tours, concerts, and lecture series. Please call or write for details.

While You're in the Area

Nearby attractions and museums include the Wentworth-Coolidge House (p. 376), the Albacore Submarine (p. 337), the Strawberry Banke Museum (p. 378), the Children's Museum (p. 343), the Warner House (p. 379), and the Seacoast Science Center (p. 371).

Horatio Colony House Museum and Nature Preserve

199 Main Street
Keene, NH 03431
(603) 352-0460

Overview

The 1806 Federal style house was the home of Horatio Colony, descendent of one of Keene's historic families. Handed down through the generations, this old-time New England home is filled with original family furnishings and collections, which offer a view of a vanishing lifestyle of refinement and travel. The house is framed by a city garden. At the Horatio Colony Nature Preserve 415 acres of woodlands, streams, and upland swamps are open to the public for nature study and recreation.

Northeast bedroom, Horatio Colony House Museum and Nature Preserve. Photo courtesy of Anita Carroll-Weldon.

Directions and Hours

From Interstate 91 in Brattleboro: Head east on Route 9. Route 9 becomes Route 101 in Keene; from Route 101 turn left onto Main Street (Route 12) heading north. Pass Keene State College on your left and go through the stop light at the intersection of Winchester and Marlboro Streets. The museum is the second building (yellow with green shutters) on the left. Go past the museum and turn left into the driveway between the museum and Saint Bernard's Church. Park in the church lot and enter the museum at the front door.

The museum is open from May 1-October 15, Wednesday through Sunday, 11:00 A.M. to 4:00 P.M. Winter hours are by appointment. The museum is not handicap accessible.

Admission and Membership

House tours and trail use are free. Children must be accompanied by an adult.

What to See

Horatio Colony, being a world traveler and antique collector, filled his home with extensive categories of collections, as well as family heirlooms. The 3,300 piece collection includes early eighteenth to late nineteenth century American and European furniture, antique oriental rugs, European paintings, Japanese prints, family portraits, tall clocks, 1,300 volumes of rare and antique books, antique silver, European china and crystal, letters and diaries, and a collection of nineteenth century inkwells, paperweights, andirons, doorstops, walking sticks, cribbage boards, porcelain figurines, silver napkins rings, and glass bottles.

On Thursday July 19, 2001 (rain date July 20th), the museum offers *Old-Time Children's Games in the Garden* which includes rolling hoops, game of graces, and shuttle cock. The museum does regular school programs with local third and fourth grade classes both at the museum and the Nature Preserve.

The museum does not have a gift shop or a café but the 176 Main Street Tavern is across the street. There are also a number of cafés and restaurants within walking distance on Main Street.

While You're in the Area

Other interesting places to visit while you are in the area are the Historical Society of Cheshire County Archives Center (p. 377), the Wyman Tavern Museum (p. 379), and the Colony Mill Marketplace.

Jackson House (SPNEA)

76 Northwest Street
Portsmouth, NH 03801
(603) 436-3205
www.spnea.org

Overview

The oldest surviving wood frame house in New Hampshire and Maine was built by Richard Jackson, a woodworker, farmer, and mariner, on his family's 50-acre plot. At that time, timber from the region's abundant pine forests formed the basis of the economy. The extensive Piscataqua riverway powered scores of sawmills and linked the hinterlands to the sea and distant ports. SPNEA's founder, William Sumner Appleton, acquired the house for SPNEA in 1923 from a member of the seventh generation of Jacksons to live there.

Directions and Hours

Take I-95 to exit 7 (Market Street). Bear right after the railroad tracks then turn right on Deer Street, right on Maplewood Avenue, and then right again on Northwest Street.

The house museum is open June 1 through October 15.

Hours: Saturday and Sunday, 11:00 A.M. to 5:00 P.M. Tours are at 11:00 A.M., 12:00, 1:00, 2:00, 3:00 and 4:00 P.M.

Admission and Membership

$5 for adults, $4.50 senior citizens, ½ off for students and children 6-12. Children 5 and under, SPNEA members, and residents of Portsmouth are free. AAA members receive a 2 for 1 discount. SPNEA membership is $35/year for individuals and $45/year for a household. Membership includes free admissions to 35 properties and museums across New England.

What to See

Jackson's house resembles English post-medieval prototypes, but is notably American in its extravagant use of wood. Succeeding generations added a lean-to and more rooms to the east to accommodate several different family groups sharing the property at once. Despite pressure to remove post-seventeenth-century additions, Appleton limited his restoration to stripping off twentieth-century lath and plaster and replacing eighteenth-century sash with diamond-paned casements where evidence of the original fenestration was too compelling to ignore.

Jackson House offers special tours and family programs.

While You're in the Area

Nearby attractions and museums include the Exeter Historical Society (p. 351), the Portsmouth Athenaeum (p. 378), the USS *Albacore* Park and Port of Portsmouth Maritime Museum (p. 337), the John Paul Jones House (p. 356), the John Langdon House (p. 353), the Warner House (p. 379), and the Wentworth-Coolidge Mansion (p. 376).

Portsmouth Historical Society, John Paul Jones House Museum. Photograph by Ralph Morang

John Paul Jones House

43 Middle Street
Portsmouth, NH 03801
(603) 436-8420
www.johnpauljones.org

Overview

The John Paul Jones House, the home of the Portsmouth Historical Society, has something to please everyone, all interpreted through an informal and entertaining tour. Some highlights are marine artifacts, women's textiles, and antique toys.

Directions and Hours

Take Interstate 95 north to Portsmouth at exit 7. Turn right at the end of the ramp onto Market Street. Bear right at the fork at the Sheraton Hotel. Turn right at the stop sign onto Deer Street. Turn left at the traffic light onto Middle Street.

The museum is open mid-May through mid-October, and is partially handicap accessible.

Hours: Monday through Saturday 10:00-4:00, Sunday 12:00-4:00.

Admission and Membership

$5.00 for adults, $2.50 for children.

Group rates are available. Seniors and AAA members receive a discount. Military personnel and clergy are free.

What to See

The museum includes hundreds of artifacts representing Portsmouth history and stories from three centuries. The collection includes an extensive array of Portsmouth-built furniture, nineteenth-century textiles, portraits, china, and a diverse selection of oddities brought back from nineteenth-century sea captains.

There is a summer lecture series and an annual Candlelight Tour in cooperation with other local historic houses.

There is a gift shop. There is no café, but

dozens of nearby restaurants and other establishments for refreshment.

While You're in the Area

The Albacore Submarine (p. 337), Strawberry Banke Museum (p. 378), Children's Museum (p. 343), Warner House (p. 379), Seacoast Science Center, and SPNEA houses (pp. 353 and 355) are some of the many other attractions in the area.

Karl Drerup Art Gallery

Plymouth State College
MSC #21B 17 High St.
Plymouth, New Hampshire 03264-1595
535-2614
www.aroundcampus.com

Overview

Plymouth State College's Karl Drerup Art Gallery is a significant regional center for art, visual culture, and new media.

Directions and Hours

From points south: take I-287 north to I-684 north to I-84 east to the Mass Pike (90 east) to I-495 north to I-93 north. Take exit 25 to Plymouth and follow the signs to the college. From Portland, Maine area: take I-95 to exit 8 (Route 25 west) to Meredith to Route 3 north to Ashland, then I-93 north. Take exit 25 to Plymouth and follow the signs to the college.

The museum is closed on college and legal holidays. It is handicap accessible.

Hours of operation are: noon-5:00 daily (open until 8:00 on Wednesday), noon-5:00 on Saturday, and by appointment.

Admission and Membership

Admission is free. Membership levels range from $10-$1000 and above.

What to See

The gallery hosts frequent special exhibitions, such as "African American Works on Paper," which runs from August 17-October 6, 2001. There are also regular exhibitions, such as "Art in Bloom," which showcases creations by members of the Ashland Garden Club. Additionally, there is a juried student exhibition each year. The gallery extends beyond its own walls and exhibits in the school's Silver Cultural Arts Center and Alumni Hall in Lamson Library, as well as other locations around campus.

There is no gift shop or café, but there are many good places to eat in the area.

While You're in the Area

There are several other school galleries nearby, as well as the attractions of Manchester and Concord. Dartmouth is about an hour away.

Kendall Shop

Bedford Historical Society
24 N. Amhearst Road
Bedford, NH 03110
(603) 472-5242, ask for Martha

Overview

The Kendall Shop displays a variety of items from Bedford's past as well as many photographs.

Directions and Hours

From Route 93 take the 293/101 west exit. Stay on Route 101 when 293 and 101 split. Follow 101 west to the light at Meetinghouse Road. Turn right, go past the library, to the left of the church, down the hill and bear right at the fork, then take the second left.

The museum is open upon request. It is handicap accessible.

Admission and Membership

Admission to the museum is free, but donations are accepted. Children are welcome with supervision.

What to See

The town of Bedford recently celebrated its 250th anniversary. The museum can tailor programs to accommodate children.

The museums sells a variety of items, but there is no café or eating establishment nearby.

While You're in the Area

The Currier Gallery of Art (p. 347) is located in Manchester, about five miles away.

Lawrence L. Lee Scouting Museum

Bodwell Road
PO Box 1121
Manchester, NH 03105
(603) 669-8919
www.scoutingmuseum.org

Overview

The Lawrence L. Lee Scouting Museum collects, preserves, and displays artifacts of the Boy Scout Movement both in the United States and around the world. Conceived by Max I. Silber and Lawrence L. Lee, the museum was brought into existence as a memorial to Mr. Lee after his death.

Directions and Hours

From I-95: Take exit 5 and follow the signs.

From 101/293: Take exit 1 and follow the signs.

The museum is open year round, and is handicap accessible.

Hours: Daily during July and August 10:00 A.M. to 4:00 P.M., Saturdays the rest of the year and by arrangement.

Admission and Membership

Admission is free. A Friends Program exists for membership and has several levels of participation: Friend $25/year, Associate $50/year, and Advocate $100/year.

What to See

The museum contains colorful and historic exhibits such as Scouts on Stamps, the Joseph Moyer World Jamboree collection, a complete display of Max Silber buckles, original paintings of *Boy's Life* covers, and a flag carried to the moon by America's first astronaut and New Hampshire scout Alan Shephard. The Baden-Powell display of sketches, letters, and Boer War memorabilia is one of the finest. Extensive exhibits of international items includes the personal collection of Richard T. Lund, former Director of World Bureau, a complete display of awards donated by Chief Scout Joseph Lawlor of the Catholic Boy Scouts of Ireland upon his visit to the museum, and two of the original Wood Badge beads from the necklace of Chief Dinizulu.

The library has complete collections of Scouting periodicals, yearbooks, fiction, and nonfiction series of interest to Scouters and researchers. A Braille and visually impaired library of Scout and Cub handbooks is available. Indian lore, pioneering, camp craft, nature study, and handicraft are a few examples of the topics included in the book collection.

There is a gift shop. The museum does not have a café, but visitors may picnic on the grounds.

While You're in the Area

Attractions and museums nearby include the the Currier Gallery of Art (p. 347), the Diocesan Museum of Manchester (p. 348), the Centre Franco-Americain (p. 377), and the New Hampshire Institute of Art (p. 365).

The Libby Museum

PO Box 629
Wolfeboro, NH 03894-0629
(603) 569-1035
www.wolfeboroonline.com/libby

Overview
The Libby Museum was established in 1912 and is on the registry of national historic places. It is a museum of natural history featuring an Abenaki Native American collection and the Governor Wentworth collection.

Directions and Hours
Take Route 1 Bypass south to Beaches/Hampton. After one mile the road connects with Route 1 south. Follow Route 1 south approximately one mile to the traffic light just past Yoken's Restaurant. Elwyn Road will be on the left. Turn left on Elwyn Road, go past the Urban Forestry Center (on your left), then go approximately 1.3 miles to the stop sign at Foyes Corner. Go straight at the stop sign onto Route 1A south. Continue for 1.8 miles, over the wood bridge, past Odiorne boat launching ramp (on left), to the main entrance of Odiorne Point State Park (on left).

The museum is open from June-Labor Day.

Hours: 10:00 A.M. to 4:00 P.M. Tuesday-Saturday. 12:00-4:00 Sunday. Closed Mondays.

Admission and Membership
Adults $2, 12 and under $1. Group discounts are available.

What to See
The Libby Museum offers summer day camp programs for children four and up. The museum also features various artists throughout the season.

The museum does not have a gift shop or a café but downtown Wolfeboro is only three miles away.

While You're in the Area
Attractions and museums nearby include the Wright Museum (p. 379), the Clark House, and the Wolfeboro Historical Museum (p. 379).

The Little Nature Museum Inc.

216 Tucker Drive
Hopkinton, NH 03229
(603) 746-6121

Overview
The 46-year-old nature center contains collections of nature-related items from all over the world, and especially from New England. When it partially reopens in the summer of 2001, it will be housed in the historic barn of Gould Hill Orchards, Contoocook, off Route 103. Most collections are hands-on. There are interpretative exhibits as well. One or more interpretive trails will be established on the property by late August 2001. The museum's exhibits relate nature and history and the museum's director or other volunteers give visitors of all ages a very personal visit.

Directions and Hours
From I-89: Take exit 4 and follow Route 103 out of Hopkinton Village to Gould Street Road. Look for the Gould Hill Orchards sign.

The museum should be open by July 1. Call 746-6121 for the latest information. The museum is handicap accessible to a limited degree.

Admission and Membership
Admission cost has not been established yet. Membership is $5/year for an adult, $8/year for a family, $8/year for a recognized organization, and $4/year juniors (up through age 16).

What to See
The museum contains a large collection of invertebrate fossils, rocks and minerals, and shells. Other collections include insects, corals, birds' nests, lichens, galls, cones, Indian artifacts, arachnids, mounted birds, sea life, and bird's eggs. Visitors should not miss the fluorescent mineral collection and fossils, seldom seen in New Hampshire. There are also several interpretive exhibits relating nature and history as well as several interpretive trails.

On August 25-26, 2001, from 1:00-5:00 P.M.

"A Celebration of Nature and Agriculture at Gould Hill" will have exhibits, demonstrations, trail walks, a live raptor program hosted by the New Hampshire Audubon, and other programs.

Children's programming includes an outreach traveling nature/science program in addition to nature/science programming on-site for homeschoolers, youth groups, and individuals. Programs are also suitable for adults and seniors.

There is a small gift shop area when the museum is open. The museum doesn't have a café but visitors can eat at Louis Pizza, The Riverfront Restaurant, or Dimitri's Pizza in Contoocook about a mile from the Orchard.

While You're in the Area

Other museums and attractions nearby include the New Hampshire History Museum in Concord (p. 378), the Mount Kearsarge Indian Museum in Warner (p. 378), and the New Hampshire Audubon in Concord.

Lockehaven Schoolhouse Museum

5 Ibey Road
PO Box 612
Enfield, NH 03748
(603) 632-7740

Overview

The Lockehaven Schoolhouse Museum is a one-room schoolhouse that lets visitors observe a classroom atmosphere of the past. It features an extensive photograph collection and schoolbooks.

Directions and Hours

Take I-89 to Route 4 to Route 4A to Shaker Hill Road to Crystal Lake Road. Turn right onto Lockehaven Road. The museum is about a ¼ mile on the left.

The museum is open mid-June through Labor Day. It is not handicap accessible.

Hours: Sunday 2:00-4:00.

Admission and Membership

Admission is free, but donations are accepted.

What to See

The Lockehaven Schoolhouse was built in 1864. Some artifacts include schoolbooks, desks, photos, and scrapbooks.

There is no gift shop, but there are items for sale at the museum. Visitors can dine at the Shaker Inn on Route 4A, Janet's Roadside Café on Route 4, or the Enfield House of Pizza on Route 4.

While You're in the Area

The Enfield Shaker Museum on Route 4A (p. 358), the Enfield Historical Society Museum (p. 349), the Hood Museum at Dartmouth College (p. 377), and the LaSallette Shrine on Route 4A are other attractions in the area.

Mont Vernon Historical Society

PO Box 15
Main Street
Mont Vernon, NH 03057
[no phone written]

Overview

Mont Vernon Historical Society maintains a museum of artifacts associated with the history of Mont Vernon, New Hampshire. It is located in the Mont Vernon Town Hall.

Directions and Hours

Take Route 13 north from Milford, New Hampshire. The town hall is about 5 miles north of the Milford Post Office. It is at the top of the hill on the left. The museum is on the second floor. Parking is available between the town hall and the fire station, as well as at the McCollam building parking lot across the street.

The museum is open from mid-May through September. It is not handicap accessible.

Hours: The last full weekend of each month, 10:00-2:00 and by appointment.

Admission and Membership
Admission is free. Membership is $10/year.

What to See
The historical society has a variety of publications available (published by the society) about many aspects of Mont Vernon's history and life in Mont Vernon in the past.

While You're in the Area
While in the area, visitors can go to Purgatory, a well-known picnic area in the late 1800s and early 1900s. It is located two miles west of town hall and features a gorge, interesting rock formation, and trails.

Moses-Kent House Museum

One Pine Street
Exeter, NH 03833
(603) 772-2044
www.Moses-Kent.org

Overview
The Second Empire house and its landscape were created in 1868 by wool merchant Henry Clay Moses. George and Adelaide Kent bought the property in 1901 and remodeled the interior. The house still contains the Colonial Revival furnishings purchased at that time. The landscape was designed by Robert Morris Copeland (1830-1874) and maintained by the second owner Adelaide Kent much in its original layout.

Directions and Hours
Directions: From I-95 and Route 101, take the Exeter exits. At the gazebo on Water Street in downtown Exeter turn onto Front Street. Follow Front Street to its junction with Pine and Linden Streets. The Moses-Kent House Museum is on the corner and parking is in the first drive on the left off of Linden.

The museum is near both Route 101, the East-West route through southern New Hampshire, and I-95, which runs North-South along the seacoast.

The house is open from June through September. The gardens are open year round free of charge. The house is not yet handicapped accessible, but the garden is.

Hours: The museum landscape is open every day from dawn to dusk. The interior is open June-September, Thursdays from 1:00-4:00 and by appointment.

Admission and Membership
Groups of four or more may request a special tour by appointment. The garden is free, and there is a $5 charge per person for a tour of the downstairs rooms of the house. Membership in

Photo courtesy of the Moses-Kent House Museum.

Friends of the Moses Kent House Museum is available. Friends of the Moses-Kent House Museum may tour the house free.

What to See

Museum rooms contain furnishings from 1903 and Kent family treasures. Photographs taken from 1901 to 1942 show family members in the garden during its prime.

The garden is being conserved with reference to both the 1868 layout and the glory of the early twentieth century garden. This ongoing effort will be interpreted to visitors at the site by the gardeners. There will also be opportunities for involvement in the restoration process (i.e. a garden archeology field school, garden clinics).

Special Programs: The garden is the site of a yearly sculpture show which opens in 2001 with a ticketed reception on June 27; the show may be visited through September 3. The garden is also the scene of children's art classes, puppet shows, and storytelling for children of all ages.

There is no gift shop or café but the Exeter Inn, directly across Pine Street, offers fine food in pleasant surroundings. There are several good places to eat nearby in downtown Exeter.

While You're in the Area

Exeter and the New Hampshire Seacoast offers many fascinating historic sites, museums, and art galleries.

The Mount Washington Museum

The Summit of Mount Washington
PO Box 2310
North Conway, NH 03860
(603) 356-2137
www.mountwashington.org

Overview

The Mount Washington Museum, operated by the Mount Washington Observatory, chronicles the natural history of Mount Washington and the White Mountains with particular emphasis on the unique sub-arctic environment on the summit. Exhibits on the flora, fauna, geology, weather, and cultural history are joined by interactive exhibits on weather and scientific work of the Mount Washington Observatory.

Directions and Hours

From I-95 north: Take I-95 to exit 4 onto the Spaulding Turnpike, which becomes Route 16. Take Route 16 to the base of the mountain. A mode of ascent must then be chosen: hiking, driving, stage, or cog railroad.

From Route 302 west: Take Route 16 north to the base of Mount Washington.

From Route 89 south: Take Route 302 east to Route 16 north to the base of Mount Washington.

The museum is open from May through October, weather permitting, and is handicap accessible.

Hours: 9:00 A.M. to 9:00 P.M. seven days a week..

Admission and Membership

$1 for everyone over 6. Six and under are free. When the state run Tip Top House is open the museum sells joint tickets which are $2 for people 12 and over, $1 for kids 6-12, and kids under 6 are free. Membership is $65/year for families, $40/year for individuals, $35/year for seniors, and $30/year for students.

What to See

Visitors will find displays about the weather on the mountain—which ranks with the worst in the world—and the reasons for the severe meteorological conditions. A special feature of the Museum is the new Weather Discovery Room, which helps visitors explore the weather phenomena of Mount Washington and how they are observed and recorded. There are exhibits on the geological history of the Presidential Range, with rock strata which date back 400,000,000 million years, and, more visible, the effects of continental ice sheets which scoured the landscape several times over the last million years. There is also a unique exhibit of alpine flowers preserved in synthetic resin, which hint at the variety of adaptations to the mountain's different habitats. The types of wildlife on the mountain are also considered, as well as the impact of the most common animal observed on the mountain—man.

There is a gift shop. The museum doesn't have a café but there is a state run concession in the building.

While You're in the Area

Other museums and attractions nearby include the Tip Top House (within 100 yards, p. 378), which is an 1853 Hostelry restored by the State of New Hampshire. It is the oldest surviving building on the Summit of Mount Washington.

The Mount Washington Observatory's Weather Discovery Center

2936 Main Street (Route 16)
PO Box 2310
North Conway, NH 03860
(603) 356-2137
www.mountwashington.org

Overview

The Mount Washington Observatory's Weather Discovery Center is a state-of-the-art, hands-on science museum dedicated to weather and meteorology. There are interactive exhibits on the weather in general as well as exhibits that connect the visitor with the work being done at the Mount Washington Observatory, a continuously staffed weather observatory on the summit of Mount Washington since 1932 and the site of the world's highest recorded wind speed of 231 m.p.h. on April 12, 1934.

Directions and Hours

Take I-95 north to Portsmouth, NH. Bear left in Portsmouth (exit 4) onto the Spaulding Turnpike. The Spaulding Turnpike will turn into Route 16 after passing through two 50¢ tolls. Route 16 will take you to Conway Village. As you enter the village, you will pass Route 112 (the Kancamagus Highway) on your left and then will travel over a set of railroad tracks. Continue through Conway and turn left at the first set of lights to follow West Side Road or continue to the second set of lights and turn left to follow Route 16 north into the village of North Conway. The Weather Discovery Center is located two-tenths of a mile on the left after the railroad tracks just north of the village of North Conway.

From Portland: Take Route 302 (Forest Avenue) from Portland through Naples, Bridgton, and then Fryeburg. Continue on Route 302 across the Maine/NH border and through Center Conway. Shortly after Center Conway take a right at a flashing light to follow Route 302 into North Conway. Take a right at the intersection of Route 302 and Route 16 and continue west on 302 (north on 16) to the village of North Conway. The Weather Discovery Center is located ⅕ mile on the left after the railroad tracks just north of the village of North Conway.

From Burlington: Take I-89 south from Burlington. Take exit 7 (Barre) from I-89 onto Route 62 and follow the signs for Route 302. Route 62 goes through a number of lights after which you turn right onto Route 302 East. Follow Route 302 to Wells River, cross the Vermont/New Hampshire border into Woodsville, and continue on Route 302 through Littleton, Bethlehem, Twin Mountain, and then

The Mount Washington Observatory's Weather Discovery Center.

through Crawford Notch. Route 302 joins Route 16 in Glen, NH which then continues east (south on 16) for another 3 miles and passes by the Scenic Vista on the right. The Weather Discovery Center is a mile south from the Scenic Vista and is located opposite and just past the Memorial Hospital.

The museum is open year round and is handicap accessible.

Hours: 10:00 A.M. to 5:00 P.M. seven days a week. Closed Thanksgiving and Christmas.

Admission and Membership

$2 for everyone over 12, $1 for children, kids under 6 are free. Membership is $65/year for families, $40/year for individuals, $35/year for seniors, and $30/year for students.

What to See

Visitors can experience what it was like to be in a wooden shack on top of Mount Washington when the world record wind of 231 mph was recorded on April 12, 1934. Visitors can also talk to an Observer on top of Mount Washington via teleconferencing.

There is occasional children's programming on special holidays.

There is a gift shop. The museum doesn't have a café but there are plenty of restaurants a half mile or less downtown. There are also a couple of places to eat within walking distance.

While You're in the Area

Other museums and attractions nearby include Story Land (p. 378), Heritage New Hampshire (p. 377), Squam Lakes Science Center (p. 373), and lots of outdoor activities in surrounding parks and forests.

The Museum of Childhood

2784 Wakefield Rd
Wakefield, NH 03872
(603) 522-8073

Overview

The Museum of Childhood gives visitors a chance to reminisce about childhood throughout the past 100+ years. It features an 1890 schoolhouse and a large collection of teddy bears, music boxes, toys, dolls, and dollhouses from around the world.

Directions and Hours

Take Route 16 north to Palmer's Motel, and take a left. The museum is just around the corner.

The museum is open from Memorial Weekend through Labor Day week. It is handicap accessible.

Hours: Monday 11:00A.M.-4:00 P.M., Wednesday- Saturday 11:00 A.M.- 4:00 P.M., Sunday 1:00-4:00 P.M.

Admission and Membership

Rates are: $3 for adults; $1.25 for children 9 and under. For groups of 12 or more, admission is $2 for adults and $1 for children 9 and under.

What to See

In addition to the 1890 schoolhouse, the museum has a child's room and kitchen from the same period. There are also many exhibits, including one featuring old children's sleds, trains, and over 4,000 dolls from 1860-2000. In all, there are 12 rooms filled with various toy collections.

Changing special events are held on many Fridays. Past special days have included events such as a "Teddy Tea Party," observance of Mickey Mouse's and Barbie's birthdays, and a one-room school reunion.

There is a small gift shop. There are restaurants nearby.

While You're in the Area

Other interesting places to visit while you are in the area are the New Hampshire Farm Museum (p. 378) and the Wakefield Heritage Museum.

New Hampshire Antique and Classic Boat Museum

397 Center Street
Wolfeboro Falls, NH 03896
(603) 569-4554
www.nhacbm.org

Overview

The New Hampshire Antique and Classic Boat Museum honors New Hampshire's boating heritage and its role in the cultural and social fabric of the state. There are displays of traditional and nontraditional small watercraft, outboards, runabouts, and speedboats.

Directions and Hours

Take Route 16 to Route 28, which is Center Street, to Wolfeboro.

The museum is open from Memorial Day to Columbus Day, and is handicap accessible.

Hours: Monday-Saturday 10:00-4:00; Sunday noon-4:00.

Admission and Membership

$4 for adults, $3 for seniors, admission for children is free. Membership is $25/year for individuals, $40/year for couples, $75/year for families, and $100 for a donor membership.

There are group discounts.

What to See

The museum houses a collection of finely crafted contemporary and vintage models of boats.

Photo courtesy of the New Hampshire Antique and Classic Boat Museum.

Vintage race photography and trophies form the backdrop for a changing collection of race boats.

There is a gift shop. The museum has no café, but there are restaurants two miles from Wolfeboro.

While You're in the Area

The Wright Museum (p. 379), the Clark House, and the Libby Museum (p. 358) are located nearby.

New Hampshire Institute of Art

148 Concord Street
Manchester, NH 03104
(603) 623-0313
www.nhia.edu

Overview

The New Hampshire Institute of Art is the state's first and only independent college of art granting a Bachelor of Fine Arts degree. On display is artwork of students and faculty, as well as local artists.

Directions and Hours

Take Route 93 to exit 8 (Bridge Street), and turn right off the exit ramp. Turn left at the third set of lights onto Union Street, then take the third right onto Concord Street.

Or, take 293 to exit 6. Go around the rotary and bear right at the Ramada Inn. Take the fourth right onto Union Street. The first set of lights is a Bridge Street. Proceed as above.

The institute is open year round, but is closed when classes are not in session. The institute is handicap accessible.

Hours: Monday-Friday 9:00-7:30, Saturday 9:00-5:00, Sunday 1:00-5:00.

Admission and Membership

Admission to the institute is free.

What to See

The institute offers changing exhibits of regional and national importance. There are two historical landmark buildings. Each has two galleries featuring changing exhibitions.

There is a gift shop. There is no café, but there are sandwich shops and restaurants in the downtown area surrounding the museum.

While You're in the Area

The city library, Historical Center, and the Franco-American Gallery (p. 377) are all within walking distance.

The New London Historical Society

Little Sunapee Road
PO Box 965
New London, NH 03257
(603) 526-6564

Overview

A village of original and reproduction buildings located on seven acres near the center of town houses a collection of period nineteenth-century artifacts. Volunteer hosts and hostesses guide visitors through exhibits and craft demonstrations in the village during the summer months. A calendar of activities is scheduled throughout the year.

Directions and Hours

From I-89 take exit 12 and head east about 1.5 miles. Turn left at the yellow blinking light and head up the hill. Turn right at the first cross street. The village is the second drive on the right.

Events and activities are scheduled May through December. Winter evening lectures are held monthly. The village is partially handicap accessible.

Hours: The buildings are open July and August on Wednesdays, 10:00-2:00.

Admission and Membership

Admission is charged only for special events and varies accordingly. Basic membership is $30/year, life membership is $2,000, and other levels of contributing membership are also available. Children are welcome with adult supervision.

There are discounts for groups when advance reservation is made.

What to See

The society also hosts many annual events such as an art show each June featuring work of many local artists. A holiday open house—with period decorations, food, music, and crafts for sale—is held in early December. All the buildings are open for this event. A retrospective of paintings by local artist Laurids "Bud" Lauridsen is scheduled for September 8, 2001.

In October, works of local school children are exhibited in a "Young at Art" show. All the buildings are open and period children's (and adult) activities are held. May brings the annual "4th Grade Day," when children from local schools spend the day in the village engaged in nineteenth-century children's activities. The children also assume the identities of important people in New London's history.

The society plans to open a new 5,000 square foot building with exhibits of horse-drawn vehicles and related artifacts in June 2001.

Although a café or gift shop are not on premises, food is served and crafts are sold during major events. New London offers many choices for eating nearby.

While You're in the Area

Musterfield Farm Museum in Sutton (p. 378) is located ten minutes away. Dartmouth College in Hanover and the city of Concord are both 35 minutes from New London.

Old Sandown Meeting House

Fremont Road
Sandown, NH 03873
(603) 887-3453

Overview

The Old Meeting House in Sandown, New Hampshire, is completely original in structure and furnishings.

Directions and Hours

Take 495 to route 125 to route 121-A. Fremont Road is located in Sandown across from the Methodist Church. The Meeting House is a quarter mile on the right.

The museum is open by appointment year round except when there's too much snow. It is handicap accessible.

Admission and Membership

Admission to the museum is free. Membership is $1/lifetime.

What to See

The Meeting House attraction consists only of the building; there are no exhibits or programs. It hosts a third grade tour annually.

There is no gift shop or café, but visitors can eat at several restaurants in Hampstead.

While You're in the Area

Sandown Depot Museum (p. 378) is another local attraction.

Pauline E. Glidden Toy Museum

Pleasant Street
Ashland, NH 03217
(603) 968-7289

Overview

The Pauline E. Glidden Toy Museum has a collection of over 1,000 mostly antique toys by P.E. Glidden. The museum consists of five rooms, including a kitchen and a schoolroom. Mrs. Glidden, who assembled the collection over many years, is 96 years old as of 2001.

Directions and Hours

From Route 93: Take exit 24 into Ashland. Take a left onto Pleasant Street. Walk through the grounds of the Ashland Historical Society's Whipple House Museum.

From Route 3 and Route 25 into Ashland: Cross Main Street onto Pleasant Street.

The museum is open July 4-August 31 and is not handicap accessible.

Hours: 1:00-4:00 P.M. Wedndesday, Thursday, Friday, and Saturday.

Admission and Membership

$1 per adult. Children 12 and under are free. Membership is $10/year.

What to See

Visitors can view collections of rare penny toys, litho tin, Shirley Temple, games, books, doll furniture, china, tin dishes, and more. The museum holds a Young Ladies Tea each July for girls age 12 and under.

Christmas in Ashland Museum is held every other year, where the houses are decorated by the Ashland Garden Club. Next held in 2002, on the first two weekends in November (the 2nd and the 9th). Cost is $7.

Children's programming includes local schools visiting the museum.

The museum does not have a gift shop or a

Pauline E. Glidden Toy Museum. Photo courtesy of the Ashland Historical Society.

café. People can nearby at Common Man Restaurant, John's Restaurant, Ashland House of Pizza, and Alias Smith and Jones Restaurant.

While You're in the Area

The Ashland Historical Society also operates the Whipple House Museum (home of the only New Hampshire Nobel Prize Winner, Dr. George Whipple) (p. 379) and the Ashland Railroad (p. 339).

Pepi Hermann Crystal Inc.

3 Waterford Place
Gilford, NH 03249-6661
(603) 528-1020
www.handcut.com

Overview

Pepi Hermann Crystal displays unique hand-cut and engraved crystal, from ancient to modern glass. There is also an educational eight-minute video presentation showing the various steps of making hand-cut crystal.

Directions and Hours

Take I-93 toward Laconia. Turn right onto the Laconia bypass and go to the very end. At the light turn left, at the next light turn left again. The museum is ¾ of a mile on the left.

The museum is open year round. It is not handicap accessible.

Hours: Tuesday through Saturday 9:30-5:00.

Admission and Membership

Admission is free.

What to See

Besides the museum, Pepi Hermann Crystal Inc. offers studio tours with a demonstration of how crystal is cut. During the winter months, hands-on tours are available by request that are geared toward high school students who might seek a career in a related field.

A limited amount of children's programming is offered on request.

There is a gift shop and a café.

While You're in the Area

Attractions and museums nearby inlcude the Carpenter Museum of Antique Outboard Motors (p. 377), the County Braid House (p. 377), and the Belknap Mill Society (p. 341).

Remick Country Doctor Museum & Farm

58 Cleveland Hill Road
PO Box 250
Tamworth, NH 03886
(800) 686-6117
www.remickmuseum.org

Overview

The museum was established through the support of Dr. Edwin C. Remick, who along with his father provided the town of Tamworth and surrounding communities with 99 consecutive years of medical service. There are three buildings, which house the Remick collection—the Edwin Crafts Remick House, the Captain Enoch Remick House, and Hillsdale Farm's barn and stable. The museum contains comprehensive displays interpreting the tools and equipment of everyday life on a family farm.

Directions and Hours

Take I-93 to Route 25 to Route 113. Turn left onto Great Hill Road, then left onto Cleveland Hill Road.

The museum is open year round, Monday-Friday, 10:00-4:00. In the summer, it is also open on Saturdays from 10:00-4:00. Please call for holiday hours.

Admission and Membership

Admission is free.

What to See

Visitors can explore the family's home with its

antique period furnishings, learn about early medical history, and see what a doctor's office looked like in the days of the horse and buggy and Model T's.

In addition to the displays of tools and equipment, the museum offers many hands-on activities. Guests are encouraged to try their hands at grinding corn, pitching hay, pumping water, buttermaking, and woodworking. There are a variety of farm animals on the premises, and many good spots for picnicking. Also, there are special event days, such as: Traditional Tea (July), Tamworth History day (August), Pumpkin Fest (October), Historic Thanksgiving (November), and Victorian Christmas (December).

The Remick Museum offers customized educational programs and workshops, and will tailor programs to the specific needs of school groups, clubs, or organizations.

While You're in the Area

Tamworth, where the Remick Museum is located, has a rich history, great scenic beauty, and a well-preserved architectural heritage. It is nestled between New Hampshire's Lake Region and the White Mountains.

Rundlet-May House (SPNEA)

364 Middle Street
Portsmouth, NH 03801
(603) 436-3204
www.spnea.org

Overview

The merchant James Rundlet acquired his wealth as an importer and manufacturer of textiles. He erected a mansion for his family on a terraced rise above the street and filled it with the finest furnishings available. He imported his wallpapers from England and purchased his furniture from local cabinetmakers, whose work was noted for its fine craftsmanship.

Directions and Hours

From I-95: Take exit 7 (Market Street). Bear right after the railroad tracks then turn right onto Deer Street and left onto Maplewood Avenue. In 3 blocks follow the right curve onto Middle Street. The house is three blocks down on the right.

The house museum is open June 1 through October 15.

Hours: Saturday and Sunday, 11:00 A.M. to 5:00 P.M. Tours are at 11:00, 12:00, 1:00, 2:00, 3:00 and 4:00 P.M.

Admission and Membership

$6 for adults, $5.50 senior citizens, ½ off for students and children 6-12. Children 5 and under, SPNEA members, and residents of Portsmouth are free. AAA members receive a 2 for 1 discount. SPNEA membership is $35/year for individuals and $45/year for a household. Membership includes free admissions to 35 properties and museums across New England.

What to See

Fascinated by the sciences, Rundlet saw to it that his house was equipped with the latest technologies. The kitchen boasts both a Rumford roaster and a Rumford range, as well as a set kettle and an elaborate venting system that services a smoke room on the third floor. There is an early coal-fired central heating system and an indoor well. The house is shown as it came to SPNEA from Rundlet's descendants, with most of its original furnishings, as well as some pieces added by later generations. The formal gardens, orchard, and attached outbuildings remain largely as designed by Rundlet.

Rundlet-May House offers group tours and family programs, including special tours.

While You're in the Area

Nearby attractions and museums include the Exeter Historical Society (p. 351), the Portsmouth Athenaeum (p. 378), the USS *Albacore* Park and Port of Portsmouth Maritime

Museum (p. 337), the Portsmouth Historical Society Museum (p. 356), the John Langdon House (p. 353), the Warner House (p. 379), and the Wentworth-Coolidge Mansion (p. 376).

Sandwich Historical Society

4 Maple Street.
Center Sandwich, NH 03227
(603) 284-6269

Overview

In addition to the Elisha Marston House which holds the collections and museum offices, the Sandwich Historical Society also maintains the Grange Hall, the Lower Corner one-room schoolhouse, and the Quimby Barn with its collection of early transportation equipment.

Directions and Hours

Take Route 93 to exit 24 then Route 3 to Holderness. Take a left on 113 to Center Sandwich (13 miles) and then a left on 113 (Maple Street).

The museums are open from mid-June to September, Tuesday-Saturday, 11:00-5:00. The first floor is handicap accessible.

Admission and Membership

Admission is free and memberships are available. Members receive quarterly newsletters and an annual bulletin containing original research.

What to See

Collections in the Sandwich Historical Society Museum in the Elisha Marston House are remarkable for their quality and variety. The museum houses objects which were originally owned by early Sandwich families. Particularly extensive collections include early tools, house furnishings, and textiles. Most of the furnishings are appropriate to the modest homes of the artisans and shopkeepers of the last century who lived and worked in Sandwich. The work of early local artists, Albert Gallatin Hoit, Fred G. Quimby, and summer resident E. Wood Perry, are well represented in our current collection.

Each winter a major exhibit utilizing the museum's collections is prepared and is open throughout the summer. Recent exhibits have featured the Quimby School of Sandwich, the development of spinning, early maps, and early twentieth-century crafts. The society also maintains a non-circulating reference library with extensive holdings centered on Sandwich people and history, in genealogy, family and local history, town and state records, manuscripts, documents, publications, and photographs of use to private and professional researchers. A photocopier is available.

There is an active Junior Historical Society which local and summer-vacationing children from six to sixteen are welcome to join without fee. They work on local history projects, genealogy, oral history, early crafts, and clean-ups of cellar holes and early cemeteries.

The museum shop carries a variety of items of interest to younger visitors as well as to their parents or grandparents. The shop also carries the publications of the society including *Sandwich, New Hampshire, 1763-1990*, the Sandwich essays of Cornelius Weygandt, local historical maps, and all the past issues of the society's annual research bulletin from 1920 to present. There is also a café.

While You're in the Area

Attractions and museums nearby inlcude the Karl Drerup Art Gallery (p. 357) and the Annalee Doll Museum (p. 338).

Sandy Point Discovery Center

89 Depot Road
Stratham, NH 03885
(603) 778-0015
www.greatbay.org

Overview

In 1993 the Sandy Point Discovery Center was

constructed on the shores of Great Bay. Located in Stratham, it serves as the conservation-education headquarters for the Great Bay National Estuarine Research Reserve. An accessible trail and boardwalk allow visitors to explore a variety of habitats including upland hardwood forests, freshwater wetlands, salt marsh, and mudflats. Visitors can stand on the deck of a nineteenth-century gundalow replica or wander through the native gardens surrounding the center. Birders find Sandy Point to be an excellent location to watch for Great Bay's wintering eagle population, migratory warblers and waterfowl, and locally nesting pairs of osprey.

Directions and Hours

From I-95: Take exit 3B off Interstate 95. Depot Road is 5 miles west on Route 33. From Exeter, New Hampshire, Depot Road is four miles east on Route 33.

The museum is located at the end of Depot Road on the town line between Stratham and Greenland. The brown signs on Route 33 direct you to the center.

The museum is open from May through October, Wednesday through Sunday, and is handicap accessible. The grounds are open year round.

Hours: 10:00 A.M. to 4:00 P.M.

Admission and Membership

There is no admission cost.

What to See

Visitors can view interpretive exhibits about the Great Bay Estuary and the amazing creatures that call it home. Children can get their hands wet in an estuarine touch tank as they learn about lobsters, horseshoe crabs, mud snails, and more. Interactive displays about salt marsh farming, salmon migration, plankton, tides, and research on the Bay allow children and adults alike to learn about the Estuary.

Visitors can also kayak the Great Bay Estuary and join Discovery Center Interpretive Naturalists as they guide you through the habitats found throughout the estuary. Guests can view secluded tidal creek, rocky shores, osprey diving for fish, and salt marshes. The four hour program will include basic instruction such as how to safely enter and exit your kayak, paddling techniques, and how to do a "wet-exit" should the occasion arise. All kayaks and necessary accessories and safety items are included.

Each summer the reserve hosts Bay Views, an adult speaker series featuring local presenters discussing a variety of issues relevant to coastal and decision makers. Bay Views are free and open to the public. These speeches are held on Wednesday evenings in July and August at the Sandy Point Discovery Center.

The Center also hosts summer programs for children age 7-11. Each week topics change, with themes like "Creature Features" and "Adventures in Aquaculture." Programs are generally held on Wednesdays and Fridays. Preschool programs are also offered on Saturdays.

There is a gift shop called the Discovery Store. The museum doesn't have a café but there is fare in the local towns.

While You're in the Area

Nearby attractions and museums include the Exeter Historical Society (p. 351), the Portsmouth Athenaeum (p. 378), the USS *Albacore* Park and Port of Portsmouth Maritime Museum (p. 337), the Portsmouth Historical Society Museum (p. 356), the John Langdon House (p. 353), the Warner House (p. 379), and the Wentworth-Coolidge Mansion (p. 376).

Seacoast Science Center

570 Ocean Blvd.
Rye, NH 03870
(603) 436-8043
www.seacentr.org

Overview

The Seacoast Science Center is located on over

300 scenic coastal acres at Odiorne Point State Park. Visitors can explore the Center's many exhibits on cultural and natural history that interpret the seven distinct habitats of Odiorne and the coastal history of New Hampshire, dating from the 1600s to the present.

Directions and Hours

Take Route 1 Bypass south to Beaches/ Hampton. After one mile the road connects with Route 1 south. Follow Route 1 south approximately one mile to the traffic light just past Yoken's Restaurant. Elwyn Road will be on the left. Turn left on Elwyn Road, go past the Urban Forestry Center (on your left), then go approximately 1.3 miles to the stop sign at Foyes Corner. Go straight at the stop sign onto Route 1A south. Continue for 1.8 miles, over the wood bridge, past Odiorne boat launching ramp (on left), to the main entrance of Odiorne Point State Park (on left).

The Center is open daily year round. The Center and many of the park trails are wheelchair accessible; and some of the Center's exhibits are Braille interpreted.

Center hours: 10:00 A.M. to 5:00 P.M.

Park hours: open from 8:00 A.M. to dusk daily. For information call NH State Parks at (603) 436-1552 or www.nhparks.state.nh.us

Admission and Membership

Center admission: Adults $1, children under age 2 are admitted free.

Park admission: $2.50/person; children 12 and under and New Hampshire residents 65 and over are free.

Membership to the Seacoast Science Center is available at several levels: individuals $30/year, families $40/year, and contributors $70/year.

What to See

Exhibits interpret the history of the cod fishing industry in the Gulf of Maine, aquaculture, and the first successful undersea rescue of the submarine crew on board *Squalus* that sank off Odiorne in 1939. Visitors can participate in one of the many programs that take place during weekends and summer. Programs include beach combing, exploring tide pools, and nature walks. The Tide pool touch tank, the Gulf of Maine aquarium, as well as interactive exhibits allow visitors to explore Odiorne Point without having to step outside.

The Center also offers camps during the summer and school vacations. Schools also take part in our popular Rocky Shore program in the spring and fall.

For the more adventuresome visitor, there is Odiorne, known as "The Birthplace of New Hampshire" (the site of the first European settlement in New Hampshire). Miles of trails wander through seven habitats ranging from woodland meadows to salt marshes to the rocky shore. Many of the seaside trails offer dramatic coastal views of the mouth of the Piscataqua River, out to the well-known Isles of Shoals. The diversity of habitats in the park and being located along migratory flyways make Odiorne one of the best coastal birding sites in northern New England.

The Seacoast Science Center also offers programs for pre-school children. Children explore nature thru walks, stories, and activities. The Center offers year-round programs including naturalist guided or unguided explorer programs for schools, visitor programs on the natural and social history of Odiorne Point and the Gulf of Maine, and a variety of indoor exhibits highlighting some of the fascinating features of coastal New Hampshire.

Music by the Sea occurs every Thursday in July from 6:00 P.M. to 8:30 P.M.

The Center's gift shop offers a large selection of gifts, books, and teaching resources as well as items for children and fine jewelry.

While You're in the Area

Nearby attractions and museums include the Exeter Historical Society (p. 351), Portsmouth Athenaeum (p. 378), USS *Albacore* Park and Port of Portsmouth Maritime Museum (p. 337), the Portsmouth Historical Society Museum (p. 356), the John Langdon House (p. 353), the Warner House (p. 379), and the Wentworth-Coolidge Mansion (p. 376).

Squam Lakes Natural Science Center

PO Box 173, Route 113
Holderness, NH 03245
(603) 968-7194
www.nhnature.com

Overview

This 200-acre nature center hosts four self-guided trails, including the Gephart Trail with live New Hampshire wildlife in natural trailside enclosures and interactive exhibits. The center also has cruises on Squam Lake.

Photo courtesy of the Squam Lakes Natural Science Center

Directions and Hours

Take I-93 to exit 4. Head east on Route 25/3 for four miles and take a left onto Route 113 in downtown Holderness. The center is on the left.

The nature center is open from May 1 to November 1, and it is handicap accessible.

Hours: 9:30-4:30.

Admission and Membership

$8 for adults, $5 for children 5-15, children 4 and under are free. Memberships are $20/year for individuals and $35/year for families. Discounts are available.

What to See

The Squam Lakes Natural Science Center is a unique outdoor classroom with hands-on exhibits, games, and puzzles designed for people of all ages. Visitors can also enjoy the creatively landscaped Kirkwood Gardens on the grounds of the historic Holderness Inn.

The center holds live animal programs during July and August and nature cruises on Squam Lake from May 28-October 15. There is also a summer Day Camp, Natural Adventures, and weeklong Guided Discoveries special programming for children throughout the year.

The center has a Nature Store, featuring gifts with nature and education in mind. It also provides food service in July and August. Other eating opportunities are within a half-mile.

While You're in the Area

The Lakes Region hosts a variety of attractions.

Sugar Hill Historical Museum

Main Street, Route 117
Sugar Hill, NH
(603) 823-5336
www.franconia.notch.org

Overview

The Sugar Hill Historical Museum contains a reproduction of a local tavern kitchen with a loom. There is also a barn of wagons, sleighs, and buggies, and a blacksmith shop.

Directions and Hours

Take Route 93 to exit 38, then take a right onto Route 16. Route 117 will be a left turn to the town of Sugar Hill.

The museum is open June 20-October 20, and is handicap accessible.

Hours: Thursday, Friday, Saturday 1:00-4:00.

Admission and Membership

Admission to the museum is free.

What to See

In addition to the tavern kitchen and barn, there is also a 1936 town fire engine.

The main exhibit changes every year and features local history.

Children's History Day is in September, 2001. There are also spring and fall school programs for area schools.

There is a gift shop. There is no café, but there is a picnic area.

While You're in the Area

The Sugar Hill Sampler and the Franconia Heritage Museum are also in the area.

Swanzey Historical Museum

Route 10 West Swanzey
PO Box 416
West Swanzey, NH 03469
(603) 352-4579

Photo courtesy of the Tuck Museum.

Overview

The Swanzey Historical Museum features a 1901 steam fire pumper and Denman Thompson homestead memorabilia.

Directions and Hours

The museum is located on Route 10, five miles below Keene, on the east side of the highway (look for the signs).

The museum is open from the end of May to mid-October, and it is handicap accessible.

Hours: Monday-Friday 1:00-4:30, Saturday and Sunday 10:00-4:30.

Admission and Membership

Admission is free; no memberships are offered.

What to See

Denman Thompson wrote an 1886 melodrama about small town life at that time that was an instant success. The play is staged by locals annually in July.

There is a gift shop and visitors can eat at two cafes on Route 10 in Swanzey.

While You're in the Area

Four covered bridges are another attraction in the area.

Tuck Museum

40 Park Avenue
PO Box 1601
Hampton, NH 03843-1601
(603) 929-0781

Overview

The Tuck Museum was started in 1925 to honor the early settlers of Hampton. The main museum houses early documents, manuscripts, artifacts, furniture, and art of the area. The museum is operated by the Hampton Historical Society.

Directions and Hours

From Route 1, turn onto Park Avenue; at the

corner is the professional building "One Park Avenue." The museum is the third building on the left; it is a white building, and it shares a sign with Tuck Field.

Open from late June to early September, Wednesdays, Fridays, and Sundays 1:00-4:00. Other times are available by appointment. Most areas of the building are handicap accessible.

Admission and Membership

Admission is free.

What to See

The featured exhibit changes biannually. In addition to the main museum, there are other buildings to visit. The Farm Museum has early agricultural implements, tools, and ice-harvesting equipment. The Fire Museum has an antique hand pumper. Also on the grounds is an 1850s one-room schoolhouse. Across the street from the Tuck Museum is Founders Park, which features stones showing early families and daughter towns.

There is a crafts fair held at the museum on the first Saturday in August; please call to confirm the date. Children's programming is coordinated through schools.

There is a small museum shop, and there are many great restaurants in the area. Adjacent to the museum, there are playgrounds for children, which have picnic facilities available.

While You're in the Area

Local sites of interest include Hampton Beach, Fuller Gardens, the American Independence Museum (p. 377), and the Seacoast Science Center at Odion (p. 371).

Webster Cottage Museum

32 North Main Street
Hanover, NH 03755
(603) 646-3371

Overview

The Webster Cottage was built in 1780 as a farmhouse. Daniel Webster was a roomer there when he was a senior at Dartmouth College in 1801. It is one of Hanover's oldest houses.

Directions and Hours

Take 91 to exit 13. Travel east on West Wheelock Street to the Main Street traffic light. Continue around the campus green and then take a right onto North Main Street.

Or, take Route 89 to exit 18. Travel north on Route 120 and turn right at the traffic light onto Main Street. Take a right at the next traffic light, then right onto North Main Street.

The museum is open Memorial Day to Columbus Day, but is not handicap accessible.

Hours: Wednesday, Saturday, and Sunday 2:30-4:30.

Admission and Membership

Admission to the museum is free. Membership is not available.

What to See

The museum displays collections including furniture typical of the region. The desk that Daniel Webster used while he was Secretary of State is also at the cottage.

There are paper archives and photographs stored nearby at Dartmouth's Rauner Special Collections Library.

There are programs available to second and fourth grade students at local schools during the school year.

There is no gift shop. There is no café, but there are many sandwich shops nearby.

While You're in the Area

Dartmouth College is in Hanover. At Dartmouth is the Hood Museum of Art (p. 377) and the Rauner Special Collections of archives. The Orozco murals in Baker Library are also in the area.

Wentworth-Coolidge Mansion

375 Little Harbor Road
Portsmouth, NH 03801
(603) 436-6607

Overview

The Wentworth-Coolidge Mansion was built in the 1750s and was the home of New Hampshire Royal Governor Benning Wentworth. A unique example of eighteenth-century architecture, the museum has over 30 partially furnished rooms. An artists' colony in the tweentieth century, it is surrounded by North America's first lilacs.

Directions and Hours

Take 95 to the exit for Portsmouth Traffic Circle, and proceed on Route 1 Bypass South. At the third set of lights turn left onto Greenleaf Avenue. Turn left at the stop sign, then take the first right onto South Street. Turn right onto Route 1A (Sagamore Avenue), and take the first left after the cemetery onto Little Harbor Road.

The mansion is open from May to mid-October, but is not handicap accessible.

Hours: Tuesday and Thursday-Saturday 10:00-3:00, Sunday noon-5:00.

Admission and Membership

$2.50 for adults, admission is free for children 12 and under. Membership is $25/year for individuals, $40/year for families.

Members and New Hampshire seniors are admitted for free.

What to See

The mansion offers guided tours. There are changing exhibits featuring works of local contemporary artists. There is an annual New Hampshire Furniture Masters Exhibit in midsummer, and the Lilac Festival in May.

From April through June there are art classes for adults and children. There are also fall, winter, and spring museum studies internship programs available in conjunction with the University of New Hampshire.

There is a gift shop. There is no café, but there are restaurants in downtown Portsmouth two miles away.

While You're in the Area

There are several other historical houses in the Portsmouth area.

Other Museums in New Hampshire

Name	Phone	Town
American Independence Museum	603-772-2622	Exeter
Attitash Bear Peak	603-374-2368	Bartlett
Bear Brook State Park	603-485-9874	Allenstown
Brattleboro Museum and Art Center	802-257-0124	Brattleboro
Brentwood Museum	603-642-8944	Exeter
Canterbury Shaker Village	603-783-9511	Canterbury
Carpenter Museum of Antique Outboard Motors	603-524-7611	Laconia
Centre Franco-Americain (gallery)	603-669-4045	Manchester
Chapel Art Center (Saint Anselm College)	603-641-7470	Manchester
Charles Bartlett House	603-437-8969	Derry
Chester Eastman Homestead	603-694-3388	Conway
Christa McAuliffe Planetarium	603-271-7827	Concord
Claremont Historical Society Museum	603-543-1400	Claremont
Colonial Dames House	603-436-8221	Portmouth
Conway Scenic Railroad	603-356-5251	North Conway
County Braid House	603-286-4511	Tilton
Crossroads of America	603-869-3919	Bethlehem
Daniel Webster Birthplace Historic Site	603-934-5057	Franklin
Dorchester Historical Society Museum	603-786-9363	Dorchester
Durham Historical Museum	603-868-5436	Durham
Federated Arts of Manchester	603-686-6186	Manchester
Fells Historic Site at the John Hay National Wildlife Refuge	603-763-2452	Newbury
Fort at No. 4 Living History Museum	603-826-5700	Charlestown
Fort Constitution Historic Site	603-436-1552	New Castle
The Frost Place Museum	603-823-5510	Franconia
Greater Derry Arts Council	603-427-0505	Derry
Hartmann Model Railway and Toy Museum	603-356-9922	Intervale
Heritage—New Hampshire	603-383-9776	Glen
Historical Society of Cheshire County	603-352-1895	Keene
Hood Museum of Art	603-646-2808	Hanover

Jefferson Historical Museum . . . . .603-586-7021 . . . . .Jefferson
John Hay National Wildlife Refuge . . . . .603-763-4789 . . . . .Newbury
Littleton Historic Sites . . . . .603-444-6561 . . . . .Littleton
Loon Mountain . . . . .603-745-8111 . . . . .Lincoln
Manchester Historic Association (Millyard Museum) . . . . . .603-622-7531 . . . . . . .Manchester
Mary Baker Eddy House . . . . .603-786-9943 . . . . .Rumney
Melville Academy Museum . . . . .603-532-7455 . . . . .Jaffrey Center
Millyard Museum (Manchester Historic Association) . . . . . .603-524-8831 . . . . . . .Manchester
Moffatt-Ladd House . . . . .603-436-1118 . . . . . . .Portsmouth
Mount Kearsarge Indian Museum . . . . .603-456-3244 . . . . .Warner
Mount Sunapee Resort . . . . .603-763-2356 . . . . .Newbury
Mount Washington Cog Railway and Museum . . . . .800-922-8825 . . . .Bretton Woods
Mt. Kearsarge Indian Museum,
Education & Cultural Center . . . . .603-456-2600 . . . . .Warner
Museum Complex—Bear Brook State Park . . . . .603-485-3782 . . . . . . .Allenstown
Museum Lodges . . . . .603-569-1551 . . . . .Wolfeboro
Museum of American Weather . . . . .603-989-3167 . . . . .Haverhill
Museum of Family Camping (Bear Brook State Park) . . . . . .603-485-9874 . . . . .Allentown
Museum of New Hampshire History . . . . .603-226-3189 x200 . . . . . .Conroy
Musterfield Farm Museum and Harvey Homestead . . . . . . .603-927-4276 . . . . .North Sutton
New England Ski Museum . . . . .603-823-7177 . . . . .Franconia
New Hampshire Art Association/Lassonde Gallery . . . . .603-796-6414 . . . . .Boscawen
New Hampshire Farm Museum . . . . .603-652-7840 . . . . .Milton
New Hampshire Historical Society Museum . . . . .603-226-3189 x 219 . . . .Concord
New Hampshire State House . . . . .603-271-2154 . . . . .Concord
Old Sandown Railroad Depot . . . . .603-887-6100 . . .Sandown Center
Old Webster Meeting House . . . . .603-796-2211 . . . . .Boscawen
Polar Caves Park . . . . .603-536-1888 . . . . .Plymouth
Portsmouth Athenaeum . . . . .603-431-2538 . . . . . . .Portsmouth
Recycling and Environmental Visitors Center . . . . .603-332-2386 . . . . .Rochester
Red Hook Ale Brewery . . . . .603-430-8600 . . . . . . .Portsmouth
Robert Frost Farm . . . . .603-432-3091 . . . . .Rye Beach
Ruggles Mine: The Mine in the Sky . . . . .603-523-4275 . . . . .Grafton
Saint-Gaudens National Historic Site . . . . .603-675-2175 . . . . .Cornish
Sandown Historical Society and Museum . . . . .603-887-3259 . . . . .Sandown
Santa's Village Amusement Park . . . . .603-586-4445 . . . . .Jefferson
Science and Nature Center at Seabrook Station w/ Museum .603-474-9521 . . . . .Seabrook
SEE Science Center . . . . .603-669-0400 . . . . . . .Manchester
Six Gun City . . . . .603-586-4592 . . . . .Jefferson
Spaulding and Frost Cooperage Museum . . . . .603-895-4703 . . . . .Fremont
Stonyfield Farm Yogurt . . . . .603-437-4040 . . . . . .Londonderry
Story Land . . . . .603-383-4186 . . . . .Glen
Strawberry Banke Museum . . . . .603-433-1100 . . . . . . .Portsmouth
Tip Top House . . . . .603-356-2137 . . . .North Conway
Tuftonboro Historic Soc. Museum . . . . .603-544-7225 . . . . .Melvin Village

US Marconi Museum, The	603-472-8312	Bedford
Warner House	603-436-5909	Portsmouth
Weather Discovery Center	603-356-2137	North Conway
Wentworth-Gardner House	603-436-4406	Portsmouth
Whale's Tale Water Park	603-745-8810	Lincoln
Whipple House Museum	603-968-7716	Ashland
Wolfeboro Historical Museum	603-569-4997	Wolfeboro
Woodman Institute Museum	603-742-1038	Dover
Wright Museum	603-569-1212	Wolfeboro
Wyman Tavern Museum	603-352-1895	Keene

Rhode Island

Artillery Company of Newport Military Museum

23 Clarke Street
Newport, RI 02840
(401) 884-0556
www.newportartillery.org

Overview

The Artillery Company of Newport, chartered in 1741 by King George II of Great Britain, is the oldest continually active military unit in the United States. Today it is a ceremonial unit of the Rhode Island Militia, Council of Historic Military Commands. The Company provides cannon salutes, color guards, and honor guards for official state and local ceremonies. Members of the company put on Colonial uniforms and do parades, concerts, and participate in area events.

Photo courtesy of the Artillery Company of Newport.

Directions and Hours

From I-95 North or South follow the signs to Downtown Newport.

The museum is open on Saturdays May through October. The first floor of the museum is handicap accessible.

Hours: Saturday 10:00 A.M. to 4:00 P.M.

Admission and Membership

Admission to the museum is by donation. Membership costs range from $25-$35.

What to See

The Museum houses one of the country's most extensive collections of military uniforms and memorabilia, including uniforms worn by His Royal Highness Prince Phillip, Lord Louis Mountbatten, Field Marshal Sir Bernard Montgomery of Alamein, President Anwar Sadat of Egypt, Fleet Admiral Chester Nimitz, Generals of the Army Dwight Eisenhower and Mark Clark, Generals William Westmoreland, Creighton Abrams, Alexander Haig, and Colin Powell, as well as other American Commanders. The Museum collection also includes four bronze cannons cast by Paul Revere in 1797 for the State of Rhode Island, three Civil War artillery pieces, a letter written to the men of the Artillery Company in 1794 by George Washington, and a Gilbert Stuart portrait of Washington, as well as numerous artifacts of significance to the history of the State of Rhode Island and the Artillery Company of Newport.

While You're in the Area

Attractions and museums nearby include the Kingscote (p. 410), Astor's Beechwood Mansion (p. 381), the Doll Museum (p. 395), and the International Tennis Hall of Fame Museum (p. 405).

The Astors' Beechwood Mansion

Victorian Living History Museum
580 Bellevue Avenue
Newport, RI 02840
(401) 846-3772
www.astors-beechwood.com

Overview

This Victorian Living History Museum recreates the vivid past of Newport in the year 1891. Visitors can interact with history as they step back in time for a 45-minute guided tour given by professional actors in costume recreating members of Newport high society. Reservations are suggested for The Astor Ball, an evening of 1890s songs and dances; Murder Mystery Tour, an interactive murder mystery; and Victorian Christmas events. Beechwood Mansion is also available for special events and weddings.

Directions and Hours

Follow I-95 South to exit 9 (Route 4). Route 4 merges into Route 1 at a sharp right-hand curve. Follow Route 1 (for less than a mile) and you will see a sign for 138 east and first right hand exit. Follow 138 east and it will bring you over the Jamestown Bridge and then Newport Bridge ($2 Toll). At the first exit off the Newport Bridge, "Scenic Newport," bear right at the bottom of the ramp and proceed to the traffic light and straight through. Turn right at the next light onto "America's Cup Avenue." Get in the left lane and at the fifth light proceed up Memorial Boulevard. Take a right at the second light onto Bellevue Avenue. Follow Bellevue Avenue for 1½ miles. Astors' Beechwood is at 580 Bellevue Avenue on your left.

From Boston and points north of Newport: Take I-93 south, Route 128, I-495 East or I-195 to Route 24 south. Follow Route 24 through Fall River into Rhode Island. Take exit 3 (Newport Beaches) to Route 138 south. At the end of the ramp go right and follow through Portsmouth. Travel about eight miles. Turn left onto Route 138A (there is a sign that says Newport Beaches again). Turn left at second traffic light (there is another Newport Beaches sign). Travel past the beach and up the hill. You will see a sign that says Bellevue Avenue Mansions. Turn left at Bellevue Avenue. This is a major intersection with a traffic light and a turn arrow. There is a Talbot's on your near left. Follow Bellevue Avenue for 1½ miles. The Astors' Beechwood Mansion is located at 580 Bellevue Avenue on your left.

From CT, NY, NJ, and points South of

Rhode Island Historic Armories (RIHA) is a consortium of representatives from Rhode Island's 18 historic armories. The group periodically sponsors Rhode Island Historic Armory Week which gives the public access to all 18 armories in the state and their treasures and memories. The mission of RIHA is to draw public awareness to armories and help to preserve these buildings that represent why Americans are free, as well as serve a key role in community bonding.

RIHA's website is www.rhodeislandarmories.org, and e-mail can be directed to toorobert@aol.com. Mailings are to WAR, Inc. (the parent 501(c)(3)) at P.O. Box 614, Westerly, RI 02891. RIHA's director is Roberta Mudge Humble at (401) 738-3844.

Newport: Take I-95 North into RI to exit 3/Route 138. Follow Route 138 over the Jamestown and Newport bridges. Take first exit to "Scenic Newport." Turn right and proceed through the light. Turn right at the next light onto "America's Cup Avenue." Get in the left lane and at the fifth light proceed up Memorial Boulevard. Take a right at the second light onto Bellevue Avenue. Follow Bellevue Avenue for 1½ miles. Astors' Beechwood is located at 580 Bellevue Avenue on your left.

Open Friday, Saturday, and Sunday from February to mid-May. Open daily from mid-May to November. The museum has handicapped access on the first floor only.

Admission and Membership

$10 regular admission, $30 family rate, $8.50 ages 60+, $8.50 ages 6-12. Ages five and under are complimentary. $9 for students (with valid ID). There is a $6/person group rate for groups of 15+ with a reservation. AAA members receive $1 off per person, and AAM members receive one complimentary admission with museum ID

What to See

A visit to the Astor cottage is no ordinary mansion tour. Visitors journey back to 1891 as guests of Mrs. Astor, queen of American society. As Mrs. Astor's family members, society friends, and domestic staff guide visitors through Beechwood, they get a glimpse of the splendid lifestyle the Astor family brought to Newport during the Victorian era.

Visitors are invited to learn the language of the fan, practice the art of flirtation, or perhaps even get caught up in a rousing game of croquet. Gossiping with the housemaids is frowned upon! Whether sneaking into the servants' quarters or ascending the grand staircase, visitors will believe, just for a moment, that they have stepped back to a time gone by.

Don't miss Children's Day June 29, 2001 or Edgar Allan Poe Weekend October 27-28 (call to reserve). Victorian Christmas hours vary from year to year.

There is a very small gift nook at the entrance to the museum, but no food services at the facility.

While You're in the Area

Visitors can tour the other beautiful and opulent mansions operated by the Newport County Preservation Society or walk on the Cliff Walk.

Bell Schoolhouse Museum

Townhouse Square
Wyoming, RI 02898
(401) 364-7075

Overview

The Bell Schoolhouse was a school in use from 1826-1934. It contains books that span the years of educational progress. It also houses part of the bridewell door—as a reminder for behaviour.

Directions and Hours

Take 95 to exit 3A onto Route 138 east. Travel two miles to the junction of Routes 138 and 112. the school is in the point of the triangle.

Or, take Route 1 to Route 2 at the Cross Mills exit in Charlestown to Route 112.

From Newport, take Route 138 west over bridges about 25 miles to the junction with Route 112.

The museum is open May through October, but is not handicap accessible.

Hours: Sunday 1:00-4:00, and by appointment.

Admission and Membership

Admission to the museum is free. Membership to the Richmond Historical Society is $10/year for individuals.

What to See

The museum has a collection of texts used while the school was operational, and original chalkboards still surround the room. The building is still used as an educational facility and community meeting place, making it a living history facility. It's probably the most photographed historical museum in Rhode Island. The last teacher to hold class in the building is still alive and active with the museum in her mid-90s. Some of her former students still drop by as well.

There are annual field trips for fourth graders. There are also special programs worked in conjunction with the current teaching curriculum.

There is a small gift shop. There is no café, but there are sandwich shops in town.

While You're in the Area

The Old Town Clerk's Office, Caroline Mill complex, monument to the Pequot Indians, and the Restored Stagecoach House are also in the area.

Blithewold Mansion, Gardens, and Arboretum

101 Ferry Road (Route 114)
Bristol, RI 02809
(401) 253-2707
www.blithewold.org

Overview

The Blithewold Mansions, Gardens, and Arboretum is a 33-acre estate established as a summer retreat in the 1890s by August Van Wickle, a Pennsylvania coal merchant. The mansion has a wealth of information available as well as most of the original furnishings. The gardens' many trees and shrubs were planted by the family and are maintained as it was when the family lived there. It also features the tallest Giant Sequoia tree east of the Rockies.

Directions and Hours

From I-95: take I-95 east to exit 7. Follow Route 114 for approximately 13½ miles through Barrington, Warren, and Bristol. Blithewold is located on Route 114 on the right.

From Boston: Take Route 24 south. Take Mt. Hope Bridge exit and cross the bridge. Bear left at the fork onto Ferry Road, Route 114. Blithewold is 1/8 miles on the left.

Gardens open daily year-round from 10:00-5:00. The house is open from mid-April to mid-October, Wednesday-Sunday 11:00-4:00 and in the month of December. Please call for December hours.

The house is partially handicap accessible; please call ahead for information.

Admission and Membership

Admission is $10/adults, $8/seniors or full time students, $6/youth (6-17); under 6 is free. Grounds admission is $5 when house is closed. Discounted rates are available for groups but reservations are required. Membership: $30/individual, $50/family and double, $75/Supporting, $100/Contributing, $250/Sponsoring, $500/Patron, and $1,000/Benefactor.

What to See

The Blithewold Mansion has a rich family archives from which special exhibits are prepared to enhance visitors' experiences. Particularly outstanding are the Christmas exhibits. The house remains much as it was when the family was there with most of the original furnishings.

The gardens feature a century-old Chestnut Rose and other original shrubs. From April to early May, there are more than 50,000 blooming daffodils. In the arboretum, visitors can see many specimen trees including Giant Sequoias, Franklinia, Metasequoia, Ginko, Linden, and Beech The horticultural staff are available Sundays, noon-4:00 from mid-April to mid-October.

Special programs include horticultural workshops and programs about the history of the house and its family. Blithewold is also developing more programming for children and offers guided tours for school field trips.

The gift shop offers seasonal Blithewold plants and other exclusive items. There is no café but there are many local restaurants.

While You're in the Area

Bristol is a small, picturesque town steeped in history and still very much the Jewel of the Narraganett Bay. It boasts more than seven museums such as the Cockle Shell Farm Museum, Linden Place (p. 430), Haffenreffer Museum of Anthropology (p. 400), Herreshoff Marine Museum which includes the America's Cup Hall of Fame (p. 402), and the Audubon Society's Environmental Education Center.

The Breakers

Ochre Point Avenue
Newport, RI 02840
(401) 847-1000
www.NewportMansions.org

Overview

The grandest of the Newport summer cottages with 70 rooms, this National Historic Landmark was built for Cornelius Vanderbilt II in 1895. It sits on a 13 acre estate overlooking a spectacular view of the Atlantic Ocean.

Directions and Hours

Visitors can leave their car and purchase an all day pass to ride RIPTA (RI Public Transit Authority 401-781-9400). From Memorial Day through Columbus Day, park at the Newport Visitors Center and ride the Yellow Line trolley to the historic properties of the Preservation Society. Mansion tours with transportation are also available through Viking Tours of Newport (401-847-6921), Gray Line RI (800-934-8687) and Gray Line Boston (800-343-1328).

Directions from Boston Area: Follow 128 south (this is also I-95 South) past the exit where I-95 splits off. At this point, 128 becomes 93 north. Continue to the exit for Route 24 (Fall River). Follow Route 24 to Route 114 south. Follow Route 114 south into town. At the intersection just past Dunkin Donuts and at the corner with Modern Furniture Galleries, turn left at the traffic light onto Route 214, which is Valley Road. Follow 214 to the beach area (passing through three stoplights), bear right past the beach area and continue up to the top of the hill (you are on Memorial Boulevard—a four lane divided road). At the four-way intersection, turn left onto Bellevue Avenue. Proceed south along Bellevue, and follow the signs for the mansions.

Directions from Providence: Follow 195 east to Route 24 (Fall River) to Route 114 south. Follow Route 114 south into town. At the intersection just past Dunkin Donuts and at the corner with Modern Furniture Galleries, turn left onto Route 214, which is Valley Road. Follow 214 to the beach area (passing through three stoplights), bear right past the beach area and continue up to the top of the hill (you are on Memorial Boulevard—a four lane divided road). At the main intersection, turn left onto Bellevue Avenue. Proceed along Bellevue Avenue. Signs for the Newport Mansions are along Bellevue Avenue.

Directions from New York: Follow I-95 north to Rhode Island exit #3. This will bring you to Route 138. Follow signs for the Newport Bridge, (which is a $2 toll bridge) and take the scenic Newport exit off the bridge. At the bottom of the ramp turn right. Proceed through one stoplight. At the second stoplight turn right. This is America's Cup Avenue. On America's Cup Avenue, proceed through six stoplights. At the seventh stoplight bear left up the hill. Continue past one more stoplight. At the next stoplight intersection, at the top of the hill, turn right onto Bellevue Avenue. Proceed along Bellevue Avenue; signs indicating the Newport Mansions are along Bellevue Avenue.

The Breakers is open year-round and is handicap accessible.

Hours: January 2-April 13, 2001: Open weekends, Martin Luther King Day, and Presidents Day, 10:00 A.M. to 6:00 P.M. (last tour is at 5:00 P.M.); April 14-May 20, 2001: Open daily from 10:00 A.M. to 6:00 P.M. (last tour is at 5:00 P.M.); May 21-October 8, 2001: Open daily from 10:00 A.M. to 6:00 P.M. (last tour is at 5:00 P.M.); October 9-October 28: open daily from 10:00 A.M. to 6:00 P.M. (last tour is at 5:00 P.M.); October 29-November 21: open daily open daily from 10:00 A.M. to 6:00 P.M. (last tour is at 5:00 P.M.); November 23-January 1, 2002—Christmas at the Newport Mansions: open daily and decorated for the holidays: open at 10:00 A.M., last tour admission at 5:00 P.M., houses close at 6:00 P.M.; November 24, December 1, 8, 15, and 29—Holiday Evenings 5:00-8:00 P.M.

Admission and Membership

Several admission packages are available for the 11 Newport Mansions administered by the Preservation Society of Newport County. Prices range from $10 for a youth to $29 for an adult. Group discounts for 20 or more visitors are available. Please call for details.

Members enjoy many benefits, including discounts on Newport Mansions Store purchases, free parking, Annual Reports, invitations to special events and programs, and an annual subscription to our journal, the Newport Gazette. Members also receive free and unlimited admission to regular tours at each of the Preservation Society's 11 properties. Membership is Individual $50, Household $75, Steward $250, Patron $500, and Benefactor $1,000, and President's Circle $5,000.

What to See

Hunt directed an international team of craftsmen and artisans to create a 70 room Italian Renaissance-style palazzo inspired by the sixteenth century palaces of Genoa and Turin. Allard and Sons of Paris assisted Hunt with furnishings and fixtures, Austro-American sculptor Karl Bitter designed relief sculpture, and Boston architect Ogden Codman decorated the family quarters. Today, the house is designated a National Historic Landmark.

The house is decorated for the holidays in December.

The Preservation Society of Newport County, Rhode Island's largest cultural organization, preserves and protects the best of Newport County's architectural heritage. Its 11 historic properties and landscapes—five of which are National Historic Landmarks—form a complete essay of American historical development from the Colonial era through the Gilded Age. In keeping with its mission, the Society strives to offer its members and the public a comprehensive view of each property's architecture, interiors, landscapes, and social history.

The Preservation Society was founded in 1945 as a private, nonprofit educational organization. Admission charges, membership dues, fundraising events, and donations help the Society to carry out its mission of protecting Newport's heritage for present and future generations.

The Society also operates seven Newport Mansions Stores located in the largest of its historic properties and in Newport's waterfront shopping district.

The Preservation Society is honored to have ten of its historic properties—The Breakers, Chateau-sur-Mer, The Elms Garden, Green Animals, Hunter House, Isaac Bell House, Marble House, and Rosecliff—designated as Official Projects of Save America's Treasures. The Save America's Treasures initiative is a public-private partnership between the White House Millennium Council and the National Trust for Historic Preservation, dedicated to the preservation of our nation's irreplaceable historic and cultural treasures for future generations.

Contact the Preservation Society at www.NewportMansions.org or (401) 847-1000. The 11 Historic Properties in Newport administered by the Preservation Society of Newport County can be found on pp. 384, 386, 390, 391, 395, 399, 403, 406, 410, 412, and 422.

While You're in the Area

There are 11 Historic Properties in Newport administered by the Preservation Society of Newport County (pp. 384, 386, 390, 391, 395, 399, 403, 406, 410, 412, 422).

The Breakers Stable

Bateman and Coggeshall Avenues
Newport, RI 02840
(401) 847-1000
www.NewportMansions.org

Overview

The Breakers Stable and Carriage House, located a few blocks west of The Breakers, was designed by Richard Morris Hunt and exhibits a collection of Vanderbilt carriages, liveries and harnesses. The stable and carriage complex, together with the adjacent greenhouses for The Breakers, were built in 1895. Before a 1970 fire destroyed an upper story, the brick stables had room for 26 horses, a variety of carriages, and accommodations for at least a dozen grooms.

Directions and Hours

Visitors can leave their car and purchase an all day pass to ride RIPTA (RI Public Transit Authority 401-781-9400). From Memorial Day through Columbus Day, park at the Newport Visitors Center and ride the Yellow Line trolley to the historic properties of the Preservation Society. Mansion tours with transportation are also available through Viking Tours of Newport (401-847-6921), Gray Line RI (800-934-8687) and Gray Line Boston (800-343-1328).

Directions from Boston Area: Follow 128 south (this is also I-95 south) past the exit where I-95 splits off. At this point, 128 becomes 93 north. Continue to the exit for Route 24 (Fall River). Follow Route 24 to Route 114 south. Follow Route 114 south into town. At the intersection just past Dunkin Donuts and at the corner with Modern Furniture Galleries, turn left at the traffic light onto Route 214, which is Valley Road. Follow 214 to the beach area (passing through three stoplights), bear right past the beach area and continue up to the top of the hill (you are on Memorial Boulevard—a four lane divided road). At the four-way intersection, turn left onto Bellevue Avenue. Proceed south along Bellevue, and follow the signs for the mansions.

Directions from Providence: Follow 195 east to Route 24 (Fall River) to Route 114 south. Follow Route 114 south into town. At the intersection just past Dunkin Donuts and at the corner with Modern Furniture Galleries, turn left onto Route 214, which is Valley Road. Follow 214 to the beach area (passing through three stoplights), bear right past the beach area and continue up to the top of the hill (you are on Memorial Boulevard—a four lane divided road). At the main intersection, turn left onto Bellevue Avenue. Proceed along Bellevue Avenue. Signs for the Newport Mansions are along Bellevue Avenue.

Directions from New York: Follow I-95 north to Rhode Island exit #3. This will bring you to Route 138. Follow signs for the Newport Bridge, (which is a $2 toll bridge) and take the scenic Newport exit off the bridge. At the bottom of the ramp turn right. Proceed through one stoplight. At the second stoplight turn right. This is America's Cup Avenue. On America's Cup Avenue, proceed through six stoplights. At the seventh stoplight bear left up the hill. Continue past one more stoplight. At the next stoplight intersection, at the top of the hill, turn right onto Bellevue Avenue. Proceed along Bellevue Avenue; signs indicating the Newport Mansions are along Bellevue Avenue.

The Breakers Stable is open year-round and is handicap accessible.

Hours: January 2-April 13, 2001: Open weekends, Martin Luther King Day, and Presidents Day, 10:00 A.M. to 6:00 P.M. (last tour is at 5:00 P.M.); April 14-May 20, 2001: Open daily from 10:00 A.M. to 6:00 P.M. (last tour is at 5:00 P.M.); May 21-October 8, 2001: Open daily from 10:00 A.M. to 6:00 P.M. (last tour is at 5:00 P.M.); October 9-October 28: open daily from

10:00 A.M. to 6:00 P.M. (last tour is at 5:00 P.M.); October 29-November 21: open daily from 10:00 A.M. to 6:00 P.M. (last tour is at 5:00 P.M.); November 23-January 1, 2002—Christmas at the Newport Mansions: open daily and decorated for the holidays: open at 10:00 A.M., last tour admission at 5:00 P.M., houses close at 6:00 P.M.; November 24, December 1, 8, 15, and 29—Holiday Evenings 5:00 to 8:00.

Admission and Membership

Several admission packages are available for the 11 Newport Mansions administered by the Preservation Society of Newport County. Prices range from $10 for a youth to $29 for an adult. Group discounts for 20 or more visitors are available. Please call for details.

Members enjoy many benefits, including discounts on Newport Mansions Store purchases, free parking, Annual Reports, invitations to special events and programs, and an annual subscription to our journal, the Newport Gazette. Members also receive free and unlimited admission to regular tours at each of the Preservation Society's 11 properties. Membership is Individual $50, Household $75, Steward $250, Patron $500, and Benefactor $1,000, and President's Circle $5,000.

What to See

The Carriage Room contains the renowned road coach *Venture*, driven by Alfred G. Vanderbilt in New York and England. A model train exhibit outlines the history of the New York Central Railroad. The greenhouses and their two-acre summer gardens still provide green and flowering plants and cut flowers for the gardens and interiors of the historic houses of the Preservation Society.

While You're in the Area

There are 11 Historic Properties in Newport administered by the Preservation Society of Newport County (pp. 384, 386, 390, 391, 395, 399, 403, 406, 410, 412, 422).

Bristol Train of Artillery Armory/Museum

135 State Street
Bristol, RI 02809
(401) 521-9136

Overview

Built in 1842, the Armory is a wood-framed clapboard building in the neo-classical style. The Armory is home to the Bristol Train of Artillery, chartered in 1779, which has sent its members to every war in which the country has been engaged since the Revolutionary War. The current headquarters are now a museum containing many rare specimens of military weapons and artifacts, such as field pieces, uniforms, shoulder arms, sabers, documents, and photographs of activities of Artillery members dating back to the American Revolution.

Directions and Hours

From the north: Take I-91 south to Providence. Watch for signs for I-195 east. As you pass the Capitol Building, get into the left lane as the I-

Photo courtesy of the Bristol Train of Artillery Armory/Museum

195 east exit is off to the left. Stay on I-195 until the exit for Route 136. At the end of the ramp turn right and follow Route 136 in Massachusetts into Rhode Island, through Warren, and into Bristol. State Street is off Route 136 to the right. Stay on State Street to the Town Common on the left. Both the armory and the museum are across the street between Our Lady of Mt. Carmel Church and the Lady of Mt. Carmel School.

From the south: Take I-95 north to Providence. Approach the center of Providence and watch for I-195 East. Stay on I-195 East until you see signs for Route 136. Take that exit. At the end of the ramp turn right (south). Then follow the directions above.

The museum is open only by appointment. Call or write Lt. Col. Edward P. Smith at 37 Tyndall Avenue, Providence, RI 02908.

Admission and Membership

There is no admission cost but donations are hoped for. Children must be accompanied by an adult.

What to See

The museum's collection includes some shoulder arms from Colonial flintlocks to World War II rifles. The Armory also has 2 brass muzzle loader cannon and two World War I anti-tank guns. The museum fires them at various holidays and parades.

There is children's programming on request. The museum shows the colonial style uniforms, demonstrates various black powder cannon, and fires rifles and pistols. The museum makes visits to schools when asked. Usual donations to such events are $25 to $50.

On April 28, 2001, the Armory will hold their 225th Anniversary dinner.

The Bristol Fourth of July Parade is one of the oldest and biggest in the nation. Most years there are 200,000 to 300,000 spectators depending on the weather.

There is no gift shop or café but in arranging for a group visit or an appointed tour the museum will provide soda, coffee, milk, cookies and/or crackers and cheese at a reasonable cost. There are also many good restaurants in town.

While You're in the Area

The Herreshoff Yacht Museum (p. 402) is just a few blocks away.

Carpenter's Grist Mill, Moonstone Beach Road, Perryville, Rhode Island.

Carpenter's Grist Mill

364 Moonstone Beach Road
Perryville, RI 02879
(401) 783-5483

Overview

The Carpenter's Grist Mill is a water-powered grist mill grinding only Rhode Island Whitecap Flint Corn. The mill was built by Samuel Perry in 1703 and has been in continuous operation since then.

Directions and Hours

From Route 1 (between Westerly and Wakefield): Turn onto Moonstone Beach Road South. The mill is 400 feet ahead on the left. Parking is on the roadside.

The museum is open by appointment when grinding year round. Please call for grinding dates. The mill is handicap accessible.

Admission and Membership

There is no admission cost.

What to See

Carpenter's Grist Mill is an operating grist mill with water power from Perry's Mill Pond, between granite millstones. Visitors are encouraged to help with the sifting the cornmeal and bagging. Guests receive a sample bag. One of the area's special foods is Jonnycakes made from ground cornmeal. A griddle is always full for visitors' tasting.

The Carpenter's Grist Mill is celebrating their 300th anniversary in 2003.

Groups of school children visit the grist mill to view the grinding operation and learn about flint corn.

The museum does not have a gift shop or a café, but there are many good restaurants nearby in coastal villages.

While You're in the Area

The South County Museum (p. 431) is only 10 miles north, off Route 1 in Narragansett.

Casey Farm (SPNEA)

2325 Boston Neck Rd.
Saunderstown, RI 02874-3820
(401) 295-1030
www.spnea.org

Overview

This 300-acre working farm overlooking Narragansett Bay was a prosperous plantation in the eighteenth century. Five generations of the Casey family made improvements and farmed the land with the help of tenant farmers. Casey Farm is one of the original "Providence Plantations" that gives Rhode Island its name, and one of very few that is nearly the same size that it was in 1702.

Directions and Hours

From I-95 south: Take exit 9 onto Route 4. Follow Route 4 to Route 138 east. Exit onto Route 1A, then turn right at the end of the exit. The farm is a mile away on the right.

From Newport: Take Route 138 west to the Route 1A exit (Narragansett). Go right at the end of the exit. The farm is a mile away on the right.

The museum is open June 1 to October 15.

Hours: Tuesday, Thursday, and Saturday from 1:00-5:00 P.M.

Admission and Membership

$4 for adults, $3.50 senior citizens, ½ off for students and children 6-12. Children five and under, SPNEA members, and residents of Saunderstown are free. AAA members receive a 2 for 1 discount. SPNEA membership is $35/year for individuals and $45/year for a household. Membership includes free admissions to 35 properties and museums across New England.

What to See

Today, resident farm managers operate a organic vegetable farm, with sales to the local community. Tours include the farmyard and family graveyard, and visitors are encouraged to enjoy the farm's hiking trails.

The farm's extensive collection of outbuildings from the eighteenth and nineteenth century are of interest. At the farm, SPNEA is preserving a modern working landscape in a historic context, and the farm animals, productive fields, and ½ acre garden are available for view.

There are extensive school visits in the spring and fall and a summer day camp for ages 5-9 in July and August.

There are several restaurants within two miles of the farm, with food ranging from gourmet sandwiches to pizza to diner fare and ice cream.

While You're in the Area

Attractions nearby include the Gilbert Stuart Museum (p. 430), Smith's Castle (p. 431), the Coastal Resources Institute at the U.R.I. Bay Campus, and the Watson Farm (p. 426)—less than five miles away in Jamestown.

Charles Whipple Greene Museum at George Hail Library

530 Main Street
Warren, RI 02885
(401) 245-7686

Overview

Located on the second floor of the George Hail Free Library, this museum is devoted to the past of Warren, Rhode Island. Collections include Native American artifacts and material relating to Warren's maritime heritage.

Directions and Hours

Take 103 west to 114 south to Warren center. Or take 195 south to 114 south to Warren center.

The museum is open year round, but it is not handicap accessible.

Hours: Wednesday 2:00-4:00.

Admission and Membership

Admission is free; there are no memberships.

What to See

The museum's focus includes the whaling and shipbuilding industry of the nineteenth century. It also contains Charles R. Carr collection of pre-Colombian, Peruvian, and North American Indian artifacts including wampum and glass beads.

There is no gift shop or café.

While You're in the Area

Visitors can also see the Maxwell House on Water Street (p. 430), the Firehouse on Baker Street, and the Warren Artillery (p. 431).

Chateau-sur-Mer

Bellevue Avenue
Newport, RI 02840
(401) 847-1000
www.NewportMansions.org

Overview

Chateau-sur-Mer was built as an Italianate-style villa for China trade merchant William Shepard Wetmore. Mr. Wetmore died in 1862, leaving the bulk of his fortune to his son. During the 1870s, the young couple departed on an extended trip to Europe, leaving architect Richard Morris Hunt to remodel and redecorate the house in the Second Empire French style. As a result, Chateau-sur-Mer displays most of the major design trends of the last half of the nineteenth century. George Peabody Wetmore had a distinguished political career as Governor of Rhode Island and as a United States Senator. The Preservation Society purchased the house in 1969.

Directions and Hours

Visitors can leave their car and purchase an all day pass to ride RIPTA (RI Public Transit Authority 401-781-9400). From Memorial Day through Columbus Day, park at the Newport Visitors Center and ride the Yellow Line trolley to the historic properties of the Preservation Society. Mansion tours with transportation are also available through Viking Tours of Newport (401-847-6921), Gray Line RI (800-934-8687) and Gray Line Boston (800-343-1328).

Directions from Boston Area: Follow 128 south (this is also I-95 south) past the exit where I-95 splits off. At this point, 128 becomes 93 north. Continue to the exit for Route 24 (Fall River). Follow Route 24 to Route 114 south. Follow Route 114 south into town. At the intersection just past Dunkin Donuts and at the corner with Modern Furniture Galleries, turn left at the traffic light onto Route 214, which is Valley Road. Follow 214 to the beach area (passing through three stoplights), bear right past the beach area and continue up to the top of the hill (you are on Memorial Boulevard—a four lane divided road). At the four-way intersection, turn left onto Bellevue Avenue. Proceed south along Bellevue, and follow the signs for the mansions.

Directions from Providence: Follow 195 east to Route 24 (Fall River) to Route 114 south. Follow Route 114 south into town. At the intersection just past Dunkin Donuts and at the corner with Modern Furniture Galleries, turn left onto Route 214, which is Valley Road. Follow 214 to the beach area (passing through three stoplights), bear right past the beach area and continue up to the top of the hill (you are on Memorial Boulevard—a four lane divided road). At the main intersection, turn left onto Bellevue Avenue. Proceed along Bellevue Avenue. Signs for the Newport Mansions are along Bellevue Avenue.

Directions from New York: Follow I-95 north to Rhode Island exit #3. This will bring you to Route 138. Follow signs for the Newport Bridge, (which is a $2 toll bridge) and take the scenic Newport exit off the bridge. At the bottom of the ramp turn right. Proceed through one stoplight. At the second stoplight turn right. This is America's Cup Avenue. On America's Cup Avenue, proceed through six stoplights. At the seventh stoplight bear left up the hill. Continue past one more stoplight. At the next stoplight intersection, at the top of the hill, turn right onto Bellevue Avenue. Proceed along Bellevue Avenue; signs indicating the Newport Mansions are along Bellevue Avenue.

Chateau-sur-Mer is open year-round and is handicap accessible.

Hours: January 2-April 13, 2001: Open weekends, Martin Luther King Day, and Presidents Day, 10:00 A.M. to 6:00 P.M. (last tour is at 5:00 P.M.); April 14-May 20, 2001: Open daily from 10:00 A.M. to 6:00 P.M. (last tour is at 5:00 P.M.); May 21-October 8, 2001: Open daily from 10:00 A.M. to 6:00 P.M. (last tour is at 5:00 P.M.); October 9-October 28: open daily from 10:00 A.M. to 6:00 P.M. (last tour is at 5:00 P.M.); October 29-November 21: open daily from 10:00 A.M. to 6:00 P.M. (last tour is at 5:00 P.M.); November 23-January 1, 2002—Christmas at the Newport Mansions: open daily and decorated for the holidays: open at 10:00 A.M., last tour admission at 5:00 P.M., houses close at 6:00 P.M.; November 24, December 1, 8, 15, and 29—Holiday Evenings 5:00- 8:00 P.M.

Admission and Membership

Several admission packages are available for the 11 Newport Mansions administered by the Preservation Society of Newport County. Prices range from $10 for a youth to $29 for an adult. Group discounts for 20 or more visitors are available. Please call for details.

Members enjoy many benefits, including discounts on Newport Mansions Store purchases, free parking, Annual Reports, invitations to special events and programs, and an annual subscription to our journal, the Newport Gazette. Members also receive free and unlimited admission to regular tours at each of the Preservation Society's 11 properties. Membership is Individual $50, Household $75, Steward $250, Patron $500, and Benefactor $1,000, and President's Circle $5,000.

What to See

Chateau-sur-Mer is a landmark of High Victorian architecture, furniture, wallpapers, ceramics and stenciling. It was the most palatial residence in Newport from its completion in 1852 until the appearance of the Vanderbilt houses in the 1890s. Chateau-sur-Mer was the scene of memorable entertainments, from the "Fete Champetre," an elaborate country picnic for over 2,000 guests held in 1857, to the debutante ball for Miss Edith Wetmore in 1889. Chateau-su-Mer's grand scale and lavish parties ushered in the Gilded Age of Newport.

While You're in the Area

There are 11 Historic Properties in Newport administered by the Preservation Society of Newport County (pp. 384, 386, 390, 391, 395, 399, 403, 406, 410, 412, 422).

Chepstow

Narragansett Avenue
Newport, RI 02840
(401) 847-1000 ext 165
www.NewportMansions.org

Overview

An Italianate-style villa, Chepstow was built in 1860 by resident Newport architect George Champlin Mason as the summer residence of Edmund Schermerhorn. Acquired by Mrs. Emily Morris Gallatin in 1911, the estate continued in the Morris family until bequeathed in 1986 to the Preservation Society with its collections intact and an endowment by Mrs. Alletta Morris McBean.

Directions and Hours

Visitors can leave their car and purchase an all day pass to ride RIPTA (RI Public Transit Authority 401-781-9400). From Memorial Day through Columbus Day, park at the Newport Visitors Center and ride the Yellow Line trolley to the historic properties of the Preservation Society. Mansion tours with transportation are also available through Viking Tours of Newport (401-847-6921), Gray Line RI (800-934-8687) and Gray Line Boston (800-343-1328).

Directions from Boston Area: Follow 128 south (this is also I-95 South) past the exit where I-95 splits off. At this point, 128 becomes 93 north. Continue to the exit for Route 24 (Fall River). Follow Route 24 to Route 114 south. Follow Route 114 south into town. At the intersection just past Dunkin Donuts and at the corner with Modern Furniture Galleries, turn left at the traffic light onto Route 214, which is Valley Road. Follow 214 to the beach area (passing through three stoplights), bear right past the beach area and continue up to the top of the hill (you are on Memorial Boulevard—a four lane divided road). At the four-way intersection, turn left onto Bellevue Avenue. Proceed south along Bellevue, and follow the signs for the mansions.

Directions from Providence: Follow 195 east to Route 24 (Fall River) to Route 114 south. Follow Route 114 south into town. At the intersection just past Dunkin Donuts and at the corner with Modern Furniture Galleries, turn left onto Route 214, which is Valley Road. Follow 214 to the beach area (passing through three stoplights), bear right past the beach area and continue up to the top of the hill (you are on Memorial Boulevard—a four lane divided road). At the main intersection, turn left onto Bellevue Avenue. Proceed along Bellevue Avenue. Signs for the Newport Mansions are along Bellevue Avenue.

Directions from New York: Follow I-95 north to Rhode Island exit #3. This will bring you to Route 138. Follow signs for the Newport Bridge, (which is a $2 toll bridge) and take the scenic Newport exit off the bridge. At the bottom of the ramp turn right. Proceed through one stoplight. At the second stoplight turn right. This is America's Cup Avenue. On America's Cup Avenue, proceed through six stoplights. At the seventh stoplight bear left up the hill. Continue past one more stoplight. At the next stoplight intersection, at the top of the hill, turn right onto Bellevue Avenue. Proceed along Bellevue Avenue; signs indicating the Newport Mansions are along Bellevue Avenue.

Chepstow is open year-round and is handicap accessible.

Hours: January 2-April 13, 2001: Open weekends, Martin Luther King Day, and Presidents Day, 10:00 A.M. to 6:00 P.M. (last tour is at 5:00 P.M.); April 14-May 20, 2001: Open daily from 10:00 A.M. to 6:00 P.M. (last tour is at 5:00 P.M.); May 21-October 8, 2001: Open daily from 10:00 A.M. to 6:00 P.M. (last tour is at 5:00 P.M.); October 9-October 28: open daily from 10:00 A.M. to 6:00 P.M. (last tour is at 5:00 P.M.); October 29-November 21: open dailyfrom 10:00 A.M. to 6:00 P.M. (last tour is at 5:00 P.M.); November 23-January 1, 2002—Christmas at the Newport Mansions: open daily and decorated for the holidays: open at 10:00 A.M., last tour admission at 5:00 P.M., houses close at 6:00 P.M.; November 24, December 1, 8, 15, and 29—Holiday Evenings 5:00-8:00 P.M.

Admission and Membership

Tours are by reservation only. Several admission packages are available for the 11 Newport

Mansions administered by the Preservation Society of Newport County. Prices range from $10 for a youth to $29 for an adult. Group discounts for 20 or more visitors are available. Please call for details.

Members enjoy many benefits, including discounts on Newport Mansions Store purchases, free parking, Annual Reports, invitations to special events and programs, and an annual subscription to our journal, the Newport Gazette. Members also receive free and unlimited admission to regular tours at each of the Preservation Society's 11 properties. Membership is Individual $50, Household $75, Steward $250, Patron $500, and Benefactor $1,000, and President's Circle $5,000.

What to See

Containing the original Morris-Gallatin furnishings together with important nineteenth century American paintings and documents from other former Morris family residences, Chepstow is highly evocative of the taste and collections of a descendant of one of America's founding families, placed in the context of a contemporary Newport summer home. The mansion houses a collection of nineteenth century landscape paintings by Hudson River school artists.

While You're in the Area

There are 11 Historic Properties in Newport administered by the Preservation Society of Newport County (pp. 384, 386, 390, 391, 395, 399, 403, 406, 410, 412, 422).

Coggeshall Farm Museum, Inc.

PO Box 562
Bristol, RI 02809
(401) 253-9062

Overview

Coggeshall Farm Museum portrays the work and lifestyles of a 1790s Rhode Island coastal farm and the communities within which it existed. Its 35 acres of land include a variety of outdoor and indoor exhibits and it hosts a calendar of seasonal farm-related events.

Directions and Hours

Take Interstate 95 to 195 east, exit 7 onto route 114. Pass through Barrington and Warren into Bristol. Continue on 114 one mile after the entrance to Colt State Park. Look for a sign for Coggeshall Farm Museum on the right. Turn right, go 1¼ miles to the stone gateway entrance on the right.

The museum is open from October through February 10:00-5:00 and March through September 10:00-6:00.

Admission and Membership

$1 for adults, $0.50 for children and seniors. Membership is $18/year for individuals, $25/year for families. Admission to scheduled events and workshops varies. Various levels of contributing membership are also available.

What to See

Outdoor exhibits include rare breeds of livestock similar to those found on a farm in the 1790s, heirloom vegetable and herb gardens, and antique and reproduction farming tools and outbuildings, such as the blacksmith shop, stone spring house, and privy.

The museum offers a variety of events throughout the year, such as Maple Sugaring in March, Sheep Shearing in May, Garden Day in July, and a Harvest Fair in September. Admission varies for each event. Workshops and other activities may also be available.

There are three one-week summer camp sessions for children and Children's Days of Merriment, June 11 and 12, featuring eighteenth-century games, music, and family fun. A four-day wool workshop with Norman Kennedy will be held the summer of 2002.

There is no gift shop or café, but Bristol has a variety of restaurants.

While You're in the Area

Herreshoff Marine Museum (p. 402), Blithewold Mansion and gardens (p. 383), and the Heffenreffer Museum of Anthropology (p. 400) are also in the area.

David Winton Bell Gallery

List Art Center, Brown University
64 College Street
Providence, RI 02912
(401) 863-2932

Overview

The Gallery presents six to eight major exhibitions each academic year. Special emphasis is given to the display and elucidation of contemporary art in all media. In addition to its exhibition program, the Gallery maintains a permanent collection of more than 4,000 works of art encompassing the period from the sixteenth century to the present. The collection is particularly rich in contemporary art and works on paper. Included are significant prints and drawings by Rembrandt, Tiepolo, Goya, Daumier, Piccasso, and Matisse, as well as major works by Frank Stella, Lee Bontecou, Anthony Caro, Diego Rivera, Alice Neel, Richard Serra, and Joseph Cornell. The extensive photography collection includes strong holdings by Walker Evans, Aaron Siskind, Harry Callahan, and Larry Clark, among others.

List Art Center exterior, Brown University. Photo Courtesy of the David Winton Bell Gallery.

Directions and Hours

From the North take I-95 south; in Providence take the downtown exit and proceed onto Memorial Boulevard; at College Street turn left; the List Art Center is at the top of the hill on the left.

From the South take I-95 north; in Providence take the downtown exit and proceed onto Memorial Boulevard; at College Street turn left; the List Art Center is at the top of the hill on the left.

From the East take I-195 west; in Providence take the south main street exit and proceed north on Main Street; at College Street turn right; the List Art Center is at the top of the hill on the left.

From the West take Route 6 east; in Providence take the downtown exit and proceed onto Memorial Boulevard; at College Street turn left; the List Art Center is at the top of the hill on the left.

The gallery is open year-round, except for Thanksgiving, Christmas, New Year's Day, July 4, and during the month of August

Hours: Monday-Friday 11:00 to 4:00, Saturday-Sunday, 1:00 to 4:00

The Gallery is handicap accessible. Visitors attending programs located in the List Art Center Auditorium should contact the gallery at (401) 863-2929 for assistance.

Admission and Membership

Admission is free.

What to See

The exhibition program includes an annual student show and a triennial faculty exhibition, as well as an annual New England artists' show. Recent exhibitions include one-person shows by Stephan Balkenhol, Annette Messager, and Ilya Kabakov, and thematic group shows such as "False Witness: Installations by Joan Fontcuberta and Kahn/Selesnick," "Color in Space: Pictorialism in Contemporary Sculpture," and "Film Architecture: Set Designs from *Metropolis* to *Blade Runner*." Smaller, less formal installations, drawing on the permanent collection and loans, are mounted in the foyer adjoining the main gallery. Lectures, symposium and other educational programs accompany each exhibition.

The Bell Gallery does not have a museum shop or a café, but there are many places to eat around the Brown University campus or in downtown Providence.

While You're in the Area

Attractions nearby include the RISD Museum (p. 431), The Rhode Island Foundation Gallery (p. 431), and many small private galleries.

The Doll Museum

520 Thames Street
Newport, RI 02840
(401) 849-0405
www.dollmuseum.com

Overview

Located in a large pink Victorian building in the heart of historic Newport, the Doll Museum has something of interest for everyone. More than 800 dolls dating from the eighteenth century through today are housed in the museum.

Directions and Hours

Located in the heart of historic Newport, the doll museum is accessible from Routes 114 and 24.

The museum is open year round and is not handicap accessible.

Hours: 11:00-5:00 on weekdays, 10:00-5:00 on Saturday; closed Sunday and Tuesday.

Admission and Membership

$2 for adults, $1 for children (to age 11) and $1.50 for seniors. Discounts are offered to groups with advance arrangement.

What to See

When the museum opened in 1987 the lifelong dream of owner Linda Edward was fulfilled. She is dedicated to the preservation, research, and enjoyment of dolls.

There is a gift shop, and many nearby restaurants to enjoy.

While You're in the Area

There are many other attractions nearby, including famous Newport mansions, and museums reflecting the town's maritime history.

The Elms

Bellevue Avenue
Newport, RI 02840
(401) 847-1000
www.NewportMansions.org

Overview

A National Historic Landmark, this French-style chateau built for Philadelphia millionaire Edward Berwind represented the best of gracious living and entertaining when it opened in 1901. The estate includes a 10-acre park and elaborate sunken garden. In 1996, The Elms was designated a National Historic Landmark.

Directions and Hours

Visitors can leave their car and purchase an all day pass to ride RIPTA (RI Public Transit Authority 401-781-9400). From Memorial Day through Columbus Day, park at the Newport Visitors Center and ride the Yellow Line trolley to the historic properties of the Preservation Society. Mansion tours with transportation are also available through Viking Tours of Newport (401-847-6921), Gray Line RI (800-934-8687) and Gray Line Boston (800-343-1328).

Directions from Boston Area: Follow 128 south (this is also I-95 south) past the exit where I-95 splits off. At this point, 128 becomes 93 north. Continue to the exit for Route 24 (Fall River). Follow Route 24 to Route 114 south. Follow Route 114 south into town. At the intersection just past Dunkin Donuts and at the corner with Modern Furniture Galleries, turn left at the traffic light onto Route 214, which is Valley Road. Follow 214 to the beach area (passing through three stoplights), bear right past the beach area and continue up to the top of the hill (you are on Memorial Boulevard—a four lane divided road). At the four-way intersection, turn left onto Bellevue Avenue. Proceed south along Bellevue, and follow the signs for the mansions.

Directions from Providence: Follow 195 east to Route 24 (Fall River) to Route 114 south. Follow Route 114 south into town. At the intersection just past Dunkin Donuts and at the corner with Modern Furniture Galleries, turn left onto Route 214, which is Valley Road. Follow 214 to the beach area (passing through three stoplights), bear right past the beach area and continue up to the top of the hill (you are on Memorial Boulevard—a four lane divided road). At the main intersection, turn left onto Bellevue Avenue. Proceed along Bellevue Avenue. Signs for the Newport Mansions are along Bellevue Avenue.

Directions from New York: Follow I-95 north to Rhode Island exit #3. This will bring you to Route 138. Follow signs for the Newport Bridge, (which is a $2 toll bridge) and take the scenic Newport exit off the bridge. At the bottom of the ramp turn right. Proceed through one stoplight. At the second stoplight turn right. This is America's Cup Avenue. On America's Cup Avenue, proceed through six stoplights. At the seventh stoplight bear left up the hill. Continue past one more stoplight. At the next stoplight intersection, at the top of the hill, turn right onto Bellevue Avenue. Proceed along Bellevue Avenue; signs indicating the Newport Mansions are along Bellevue Avenue.

The Elms is open year-round and is handicap accessible.

Hours: January 2-April 13, 2001: Open weekends, Martin Luther King Day, and Presidents Day, 10:00 A.M. to 6:00 P.M. (last tour is at 5:00 P.M.); April 14-May 20, 2001: Open daily from 10:00 A.M. to 6:00 P.M. (last tour is at 5:00 P.M.); May 21-October 8, 2001: Open daily from 10:00 A.M. to 6:00 P.M. (last tour is at 5:00 P.M.); October 9-October 28: open daily from 10:00 A.M. to 6:00 P.M. (last tour is at 5:00 P.M.); October 29-November 21: open dailyfrom 10:00 A.M. to 6:00 P.M. (last tour is at 5:00 P.M.); November 23-January 1, 2002—Christmas at the Newport Mansions: open daily and decorated for the holidays: open at 10:00 A.M., last tour admission at 5:00 P.M., houses close at 6:00 P.M.; November 24, December 1, 8, 15, and 29—Holiday Evenings 5:00-8:00 P.M.

Admission and Membership

Several admission packages are available for the 11 Newport Mansions administered by the Preservation Society of Newport County. Prices range from $10 for a youth to $29 for an adult. Group discounts for 20 or more visitors are available. Please call for details.

Members enjoy many benefits, including discounts on Newport Mansions Store purchases, free parking, Annual Reports, invitations to special events and programs, and an annual subscription to our journal, the Newport Gazette. Members also receive free and unlimited admission to regular tours at each of the Preservation Society's 11 properties. Membership is Individual $50, Household $75, Steward $250, Patron $500, and Benefactor $1,000, and President's Circle $5,000.

What to See

In 1898, the Berwinds engaged Philadelphia architect Horace Trumbauer to design a house modeled after the French chateau d'Asnieres (ca.1750) outside Paris. Construction of The Elms was completed in 1901 at a cost reported at approximately $1.4 million. The interiors and furnishings were designed by Allard and Sons of Paris and were the setting for the Berwinds' collection of Renaissance ceramics, eighteenth century French and Venetian paintings, and Oriental jades.

The elaborate Classical Revival gardens on the grounds were developed between 1907 and 1914. They include terraces displaying marble and bronze sculpture, a park of fine specimen trees and a lavish lower garden featuring marble pavilions, fountains, a sunken garden and carriage house and garage. These gardens are currently under restoration.

While You're in the Area

There are 11 Historic Properties in Newport administered by the Preservation Society of Newport County (pp. 384, 386, 390, 391, 395, 399, 403, 406, 410, 412, 422).

Fine Arts Center Galleries

University of Rhode Island
105 Upper College Road, Suite 1
Kingston, RI 02881
(401) 874-2627

Overview

The Fine Arts Center Galleries present a changing program of national and international contemporary art. They feature art in all media by established and emerging artists, as well as by New England residents and visiting Department of Art faculty. Recent exhibitions have featured African American, Asian American, Native American, expatriate Chinese, and former Soviet Union artists.

Directions and Hours

Take 95 north to exit 9. Take a right onto Route 138 west and follow it for eight miles to the university.

Or, take 95 south to exit 3A and follow Route 138 east for eight miles to the university.

The galleries are open year round, and is handicap accessible.

Hours: Main Gallery—Tuesday-Friday noon-4:00, 7:30-9:30; Saturday-Sunday 1:00-4:00; Photography Gallery—Tuesday through Friday noon-4:00; Saturday and Sunday 1:00-4:00; Corridor Gallery—daily 9:30-9:00.

Admission and Membership

Admission to all galleries is free (donations are encouraged).

What to See

The Galleries have gained a reputation for mounting multicultural programs in all media, including film, painting, sculpture, and photography.

Appropriate complementary programming accompanies each exhibition. These include visiting artists' talks in galleries, workshops and demonstrations, guest lectures by critics and curators, and experimental films and videos.

There is no gift shop or café. Across the street there is a shopping area with restaurants and a coffee house.

While You're in the Area

Helme House/South County Art Association (p. 401) is also in Kingston.

Governor Henry Lippitt House Museum

199 Hope Street
Providence, RI 02906
(401) 453-0688
www.preserveri.org

Overview

The Governor Henry Lippitt House is a Renaissance Revival mansion that was completed in 1865. It is the finest nineteenth century house open to the public in Providence. The house is a blend of traditional architectural forms and an interior decorative scheme that is quintessentially high style Victorian. Interior craftsmanship includes richly carved woodwork, colorful stenciling, faux marble, and dazzling stained glass windows. The museum was designated as a National Historic Landmark in 1976 and donated by the Lippitt family to the Heritage Trust of Rhode Island in 1981.

Directions and Hours

Take I-95 into Providence to I-95 East. Take I-95 East to exit 3 (Gano Street). Take a right onto Gano Street. At the third traffic light turn left onto Angell Street. Go 5 blocks to Hope Street. The museum is on the corner of Hope Street and Angell Street.

The museum is open year round but from January-March by appointment only.

Hours: Tuesday through Friday 11:00-4:00. Saturday and Sunday 1:00-4:00. Tours are on the hour—the last tour is at 3:00 P.M. Closed Monday and holidays.

Admission and Membership

Adults $5, students and seniors $3. Groups of over 10 people receive a discount of $1 off the ticket price. Membership is $25/year for an individual, $50/year for a family, $100/year for a contributor, $500/year for a sponsor, and $1,000/year for a benefactor.

What to See

The museum sponsors many cultural activities which are open to the public. These include: "Suited for Sundays," a chamber music concert series, Victorian dinner parties, Victorian crafts workshops, historic theatrical performances, and decorative arts lectures and exhibits. A Christmastime museum party takes place every year. The museum is also available for small parties, wedding receptions, and corporate events.

The museum does not have a gift shop or a café but there are many good restaurants within a few blocks.

While You're in the Area

Other museums or interesting attractions nearby include the RISD Museum (p. 431), the John Brown House (p. 408), the Nightingale Brown House (p. 430), the Aldrich House (p. 408), the Stephen Hopkins House (p. 398), and Brown University.

The Governor Stephen Hopkins House

15 Hopkins Street
Providence, RI 02903
(401) 247-4755

Overview

The Govenor Stephen Hopkins House was home of Stephen Hopkins, one of the signers of the Declaration of Independence. He lived in the house from 1742-85. The museum house is filled with period furniture and eighteenth-century artifacts, some belonging to Stephen Hopkins.

Directions and Hours

Take 95 north to 195 east. Take exit 1 and turn right at the second light. Proceed up the hill to the stop sign. The house is on the southwest corner of the second block.

Or, take 195 west to exit 1. Follow as above.

The house is open April 1 to the first week of December, but is not handicap accessible.

Hours: Wednesday and Saturday 1:00-4:00.

Admission and Membership

Admission to the house is free. Membership is not available.

What to See

The museum is one of only a few houses remaining that belonged to the signers of the Declaration of Independence. The house is completely authentic in its furnishings and decorative arts. The sampler collection is of particular interest.

George Washington was also a guest in the house twice, in 1776 and 1781.

There is no gift shop. There is no café, but there are many restaurants in the Providence area.

While You're in the Area

The Rhode Island School of Design Museum (p. 431) and the John Brown House (p. 408) are also nearby.

Green Animals Topiary Garden

Cory's Lane
Portsmouth, RI 02840
(401) 847-1000
www.NewportMansions.org

Overview

This small country estate was purchased in 1872 by Thomas E. Brayton, treasurer of the Union Cotton Manufacturing Company in Fall River, Massachusetts. It consisted of seven acres of land, a white clapboard summer residence, farm outbuildings, a pasture and a vegetable garden. Alice Brayton, his daughter, made the estate her permanent residence in 1940. Gardener Joseph Carreiro, superintendent of the property from 1905 to 1945, and his son-in-law, George Mendonca, superintendent until 1985, were responsible for creating the unique topiaries. It was Miss Brayton who gave the estate its name because of the profusion of "green animals." There are more than 80 sculptured trees and shrubs in the shape of animals and geometric forms, formal flowerbeds, fruit, and vegetable gardens on the estate. The house includes a Victorian toy collection.

Directions and Hours

Green Animals Topiary Garden is located on Cory's Lane in Portsmouth, approximately 30 minutes from Newport's Bellevue Ave.

From Newport: Follow Route 114 north. After passing Raytheon (large industrial complex on your left), continue 1.8 miles. Turn left at light onto Cory's Lane. Green Animals is located ½ mile on left.

From Points North: Follow Route 24 south to Route 114 south. Cory's Lane is first right after Route 24 south ends. At first set of lights, turn right onto Cory's Lane. Green Animals is located one half mile on left.

Green Animals Topiary Garden is open year-round and is handicap accessible.

Hours: January 2-April 13, 2001: Open weekends, Martin Luther King Day, and Presidents Day, 10:00 A.M. to 6:00 P.M. (last tour is at 5:00 P.M.); April 14-May 20, 2001: Open daily from 10:00 A.M. to 6:00 P.M. (last tour is at 5:00 P.M.); May 21-October 8, 2001: Open daily from 10:00 A.M. to 6:00 P.M. (last tour is at 5:00 P.M.); October 9-October 28: open daily from 10:00 A.M. to 6:00 P.M. (last tour is at 5:00 P.M.); October 29-November 21: open daily from 10:00 A.M. to 6:00 P.M. (last tour is at 5:00 P.M.); November 23-January 1, 2002—Christmas at the Newport Mansions: open daily and decorated for the holidays: open at 10:00 A.M., last tour admission at 5:00 P.M., houses close at 6:00 P.M.; November 24, December 1, 8, 15, and 29—Holiday Evenings 5:00-8:00 P.M.

Admission and Membership

Several admission packages are available for the 11 Newport Mansions administered by the Preservation Society of Newport County. Prices range from $10 for a youth to $29 for an adult. Group discounts for 20 or more visitors are available. Please call for details.

Members enjoy many benefits, including discounts on Newport Mansions Store purchases, free parking, Annual Reports, invitations to special events and programs, and an annual subscription to our journal, the Newport Gazette. Members also receive free and unlimited admission to regular tours at each of the Preservation Society's 11 properties. Membership is Individual $50, Household $75, Steward $250,

Patron $500, and Benefactor $1,000, and President's Circle $5,000.

What to See

There are 80 pieces of topiary throughout the gardens, including 21 animals and birds in addition to geometric figures and ornamental designs, sculpted from California privet, yew, and English boxwood. Green Animals is the oldest and most northern topiary garden in the United States. Upon her death in 1972, at the age of 94, Miss Brayton left Green Animals to The Preservation Society of Newport County. Today, Green Animals remains as a rare example of a self-sufficient estate combining formal topiaries, vegetable and herb gardens, orchards, and a Victorian house overlooking Narragansett Bay.

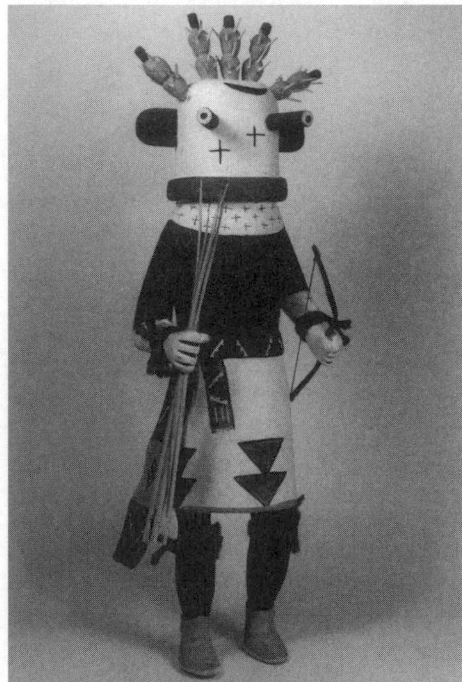

"Hopi Katsina Dolls: Ancestor Spirit Carvings," Haffenreffer Museum of Anthropology. Photo courtesy of Haffenreffer Museum of Anthropology.

While You're in the Area

There are 11 Historic Properties in Newport administered by the Preservation Society of Newport County (pp. 384, 386, 390, 391, 395, 399, 403, 406, 410, 412, 422).

Haffenreffer Museum of Anthropology, Brown University

300 Tower Street
Bristol, RI 02809
(401) 253-8388
www.brown.edu/Facilities/Haffenreffer

Overview

The Haffenreffer Museum of Anthropology, Brown's "university museum," holds collections of more than 100,000 artifacts from the native peoples of the Americas, Africa, Asia, and the Pacific. It is recognized as one of the leading anthropological teaching museums in the Northeast. The museum's four intimate galleries offer a stimulating setting in which to learn about other peoples and their cultures. The museum is located on traditional lands of the Wampanoag peoples.

Directions and Hours

From Providence, take Route 195 East to Massachusetts exit 2 (Route 136 for Newport, RI). Head south on Route 136 for 7.5 miles. Turn left at the Haffenreffer Museum sign onto Tower Street, then go 1.4 miles to the museum. From Newport, take Route 238 North to Route 114 North. After crossing the Mount Hope Bridge, bear right onto Route 136. At the museum sign, turn left onto Tower Street, then go 1.4 miles to the museum.

The museum is open year round. It is not handicap accessible.

Hours: September through May, Saturday and Sunday, 11:00-5:00; June through August, Tuesday through Sunday, 11:00-5:00.

Admission and Membership

Adults $3, Seniors $2, Children $1, Members are free. Brown and Rhode Island School of Design Students are admitted free. American Automobile Association (AAA) members receive a discount; ask the desk guard about other discounts that may be available.

Membership ranges from $10/year for students to $ 1,000+/year (Haffenreffer Society). Members receive, in addition to free admission and a free guest admission, a 10% discount in the Museum Shop; subscriptions to the biannual newsletter *Contexts* and the Calendar of Events; special announcements of exhibitions, films, lectures, tours, and other events; free admission to lectures and other events/activities; and full use of the museum's library by appointment.

What to See

Ongoing exhibits include "Packrats for Posterity? Relevance in the Anthropology Museum," which attempts to answer the question, "What do we do at an anthropology museum and why?" Another exhibit, "Illustrating the Arctic: James Houston and the Inuit," features artworks by James Houston from his years in the Canadian Arctic, as well as works by Inuit artists Houston nurtured and inspired. "Hopi Katsina Dolls: Ancestor Spirit Carvings" includes a variety of katsinas ranging from five inches to 1½ feet. A new student exhibit opening in April 2001 will focus on the museum's extensive collection of weapons from around the world. Educational programming for school groups is also available.

Artifacts at the Haffenreffer Museum include beaded Sioux moccasins, masks from Africa, a Kiowa cradle, arrowheads found in Rhode Island or nearby Massachusetts, a Haida spruce root basket, a Nigerian beaded shirt, a Cashinahua headdress from Peru, a Tlingit frog effigy bowl, or any one of thousands of other objects made and used—recently or many years ago—by people around the world.

Outdoor exhibits feature a tipi (except during the winter months) and a wetu or wigwam. Visitors may also take a short walk to King Philip's Chair, a natural rock outcropping with a "chair" that tradition says King Philip (Metacom) of the Wampanoags sat in when holding councils with his people.

The museum has a small gift shop with a good selection of books about Native Americans and other peoples and cultures. The museum does not have a café, but nearby downtown Bristol offers a number of restaurants and coffee shops.

While You're in the Area

Views of Mount Hope Bay and the city of Fall River, Massachusetts, are excellent from the museum's grounds. In addition, there are several other museums and historic homes in Bristol. Nearby Newport is one of America's top tourist destinations.

Helme House/South County Art Association

2587 Kingstown Road
Kingston, RI 02881
(401) 783-2195

Overview

The South County Art Association was incorporated as a non-profit organization in 1929. Since 1944, it has been located in the historic Helme House (ca. 1802) in Kingston. The Annex building, dating to 1759, is home to the Potter's cooperative as well as to drawing and sculpture studios.

Directions and Hours

From 95 south and north, follow signs for the University of Rhode Island/Kingston and Route 138 west (Kingstown Road). Helme House is on the left just after the main entrance to URI.

The museum is open year round, but it is not handicap accessible.

Hours: Wednesday-Sunday 1:00-5:00.

Admission and Membership

Admission to the museum is free, but donations are accepted. Membership of $50/year includes a bimonthly newsletter, discounts on classes, and exhibition opportunities.

What to See

The South County Art Association has an ongoing education program offering a range of studio art instruction to members and nonmembers. The Helme House gallery exhibits art work by SCAA members as well as outside artists. Members of the Potter's Association ($220/year membership) are entitled to unlimited use of the pottery studio.

There is a gift shop but no café. Restaurants, cafes, and shopping are available in nearby Wakefield or on the URI campus.

While You're in the Area

Pettaquamscutt Historical Society in Kingston, historic Newport, southern Rhode Island beaches, and the town of Narragansett are other attractions worth visiting nearby.

Herreshoff Marine Museum/ America's Cup Hall of Fame

One Burnside Street
Box 450
Bristol, RI 02809
(401) 253-5000
www.herreshoff.org

Overview

The Herreshoff Marine Museum/America's Cup Hall of Fame celebrates the unique accomplishments of the legendary Herreshoff family. Between 1863 and 1945 the Herreshoff Manufacturing Company, site of the museum, produced the world's finest yachts, including eight winning America's Cup defenders—a record in Cup history.

Directions and Hours

The museum is located 0.5 miles south of the center of Bristol and 1.5 miles north of the Mount Hope Bridge on Route 114 and Burnside Street. It is a 25 minute drive from Providence via U. S. 195 and Route 114.

The museum is open April 28-October 31 seven days a week and is handicap accessible.

Hours: 10:00 A.M. to 5:00 P.M.

The Model Room of the Herreshoff Marine Museum, containing more than 500 historic Herreshoff half-models. Photo courtesy of the Herreshoff Marine Museum.

Admission and Membership

$5 adults, $4 children under 12, seniors and students. Groups are by reservation. Membership is $35/year individuals, and $50/year for families. Other options are available as well.

What to See

The museum displays more than 60 classic yachts from the Golden Age of yachting including *Sprite*, the oldest wooden catboat (1860), a rare collection of half-models, photos, historic fittings, a half-size America's Cup replica, *Defiant* (the 1992 America's Cup boat donated by Bill Koch), videos of cup races, and plaques with photos and brief biographies of the Hall of Fame inductees.

The museum waterfront is being restored and will display artifacts from the Herrishoff Manufacturing Company. At the same time the company's Marine Railway is being repaired as well.

The museum does have a gift shop and a café; there are also several good local restaurants.

While You're in the Area

Museums and attractions located nearby include: Blithewold (p. 383), Linden Place (p. 430), the Audubon Education and Environment Center, Coggeshall Farm Museum (p. 393), Bristol Art Museum (p. 429), Bristol Historical Society (p. 429), the Haffenreffer Museum of Anthropology (p. 400), and the Mount Hope Farm.

Hunter House

54 Washington Street
Newport, RI 02840
(401) 847-1000
www.NewportMansions.org

Overview

Hunter House is one of the finest examples of Georgian Colonial architecture from Newport's "golden age" in the mid-eighteenth century. The house was built and decorated when Newport was a cosmopolitan city with a principle of religious tolerance that attracted Quakers, Baptists, Congregationalists, and Sephardic Jews. The great mercantile families lived patrician lives, building harborfront mansions overlooking their trading ships, and entertained in grand style. They bought furniture and silver from local craftsmen and were the patrons of such important early painters as Robert Feke and Gilbert Stuart.

Concerned that the fine interiors of the house would be purchased and removed from the building, a small group of concerned citizens led by Mrs. George Henry Warren initiated a preservation effort, purchasing the house in 1945 and forming The Preservation Society of Newport County. The Preservation Society restored Hunter House to the era of Colonel Wanton (1757 to 1779).

Directions and Hours

Visitors can leave their car and purchase an all day pass to ride RIPTA (RI Public Transit Authority 401-781-9400). From Memorial Day through Columbus Day, park at the Newport Visitors Center and ride the Yellow Line trolley to the historic properties of the Preservation Society. Mansion tours with transportation are also available through Viking Tours of Newport (401-847-6921), Gray Line RI (800-934-8687) and Gray Line Boston (800-343-1328).

Directions from Boston Area: Follow 128 south (this is also I-95 South) past the exit where I-95 splits off. At this point, 128 becomes 93 north. Continue to the exit for Route 24 (Fall River). Follow Route 24 to Route 114 south. Follow Route 114 south into town. At the intersection just past Dunkin Donuts and at the corner with Modern Furniture Galleries, turn left at the traffic light onto Route 214, which is Valley Road. Follow 214 to the beach area (passing through three stoplights), bear right past the beach area and continue up to the top of the hill (you are on Memorial Boulevard—a four lane divided road). At the four-way intersection, turn left onto Bellevue Avenue. Proceed south along Bellevue, and follow the signs for the mansions.

Directions from Providence: Follow 195 east to Route 24 (Fall River) to Route 114 south. Follow Route 114 south into town. At the intersection just past Dunkin Donuts and at the corner with Modern Furniture Galleries, turn left onto Route 214, which is Valley Road. Follow 214 to the beach area (passing through three stoplights), bear right past the beach area and continue up to the top of the hill (you are on Memorial Boulevard—a four lane divided road). At the main intersection, turn left onto Bellevue Avenue. Proceed along Bellevue Avenue. Signs for the Newport Mansions are along Bellevue Avenue.

Directions from New York: Follow I-95 north to Rhode Island exit #3. This will bring you to Route 138. Follow signs for the Newport Bridge, (which is a $2 toll bridge) and take the scenic Newport exit off the bridge. At the bottom of the ramp turn right. Proceed through one stoplight. At the second stoplight turn right. This is America's Cup Avenue. On America's Cup Avenue, proceed through six stoplights. At the seventh stoplight bear left up the hill. Continue past one more stoplight. At the next stoplight intersection, at the top of the hill, turn right onto Bellevue Avenue. Proceed along Bellevue Avenue; signs indicating the Newport Mansions are along Bellevue Avenue.

Hunter House is open year-round and is handicap accessible.

Hours: January 2-April 13, 2001: Open weekends, Martin Luther King Day, and Presidents Day, 10:00 A.M. to 6:00 P.M. (last tour is at 5:00 P.M.); April 14-May 20, 2001: Open daily from 10:00 A.M. to 6:00 P.M. (last tour is at 5:00 P.M.); May 21-October 8, 2001: Open daily from 10:00 A.M. to 6:00 P.M. (last tour is at 5:00 P.M.); October 9-October 28: open daily from 10:00 A.M. to 6:00 P.M. (last tour is at 5:00 P.M.); October 29-November 21: open daily from 10:00 A.M. to 6:00 P.M. (last tour is at 5:00 P.M.); November 23-January 1, 2002—Christmas at the Newport Mansions: open daily and decorated for the holidays: open at 10:00 A.M., last tour admission at 5:00 P.M., houses close at 6:00 P.M.; November 24, December 1, 8, 15, and 29—Holiday Evenings 5:00-8:00 P.M.

Admission and Membership

Several admission packages are available for the 11 Newport Mansions administered by the Preservation Society of Newport County. Prices range from $10 for a youth to $29 for an adult. Group discounts for 20 or more visitors are available. Please call for details.

Members enjoy many benefits, including discounts on Newport Mansions Store purchases, free parking, Annual Reports, invitations to special events and programs, and an annual subscription to our journal, the Newport Gazette. Members also receive free and unlimited admission to regular tours at each of the Preservation Society's 11 properties. Membership is Individual $50, Household $75, Steward $250, Patron $500, and Benefactor $1,000, and President's Circle $5,000.

What to See

Today, the house exhibits examples of the finest achievements in the arts and crafts of eighteenth century Newport. The collections include furniture by the Townsend-Goddard family, premier cabinetmakers of the colonial era who worked in the neighborhood of Hunter House. Newport pewter and paintings by Cosmo Alexander, Gilbert Stuart, and Samuel King are also on display. Hunter House is a National Historic Landmark.

The north half of Hunter House was constructed between 1748 and 1754 by Jonathon Nichols, Jr., a prosperous merchant and colonial deputy. After his death in 1756, the property was sold to Colonel Joseph Wanton, Jr., who was also a deputy governor of the colony and a merchant. He enlarged the house by adding a south wing and a second chimney, transforming the building into a formal Georgian mansion with a large central hall. Colonel Wanton also ordered the graining, or "spreckling," of the pine paneling in several rooms to resemble walnut and rosewood. During the American Revolution, Colonel Wanton fled from Newport due to his Loyalist sympathies. His house was used as the headquarters of Admiral de Ternay, commander of the French fleet, when French forces occupied Newport in 1780. After the war, Colonel Wanton's house was acquired by William

Hunter, a U.S. Senator and President Andrew Jackson's charge d'affaires to Brazil.

While You're in the Area

There are 11 Historic Properties in Newport administered by the Preservation Society of Newport County (pp. 384, 386, 390, 391, 395, 399, 403, 406, 410, 412, 422).

International Tennis Hall of Fame Museum

194 Bellevue Avenue
Newport, RI 02840
(401) 849-3990 or (800) 457-1144
www.tennisfame.com/museum.html

Overview

The Tennis Hall of Fame is located at the Newport Casino, which was the site of the first U.S. National Championship in 1881. The complex of buildings that now houses the Hall of Fame was completed in 1880 as a private club for wealthy summer residents of Newport and was never used as a place for gambling.

Directions and Hours

From Providence and places northwest: Take 95 south to exit 9 (Route 4). Route 4 merges into Route 1. Look for a sign for 138 east and take the first right hand exit. Follow 138 east over the Jamestown Bridge and Newport Bridge (you'll have to pay a $2 toll). Take the first exit off Newport bridge (Scenic Newport) and bear right at the bottom of the ramp. Go straight through the traffic light then turn right at the next light onto America's Cup Avenue, getting into the left lane. At the fifth light go up Memorial Boulevard. Take a right at the second light onto Bellevue Avenue. The Hall of Fame will be on the first block on your left.

From Boston and places north: Take Interstate 93 south, Route 128, Interstate 495 east or Interstate 195 to Route 24 south. Then follow Route 24 through Fall River into Rhode Island. Take exit 1 to Route 138 west. Take a left onto Route 138A. At the second traffic light go left and go to the first major intersection and take a left onto Bellevue Avenue. The Hall of Fame will be the first block on your left.

From the south: Take Interstate 95 North into Rhode Island to exit 3/Route 138. Follow Route 138 over the Jamestown and Newport Bridges (there will be a $2 toll). Take the first exit off the bridge to Scenic Newport. Turn right and go through the light, then turn right at the next light onto America's Cup Avenue. Get in the left lane and at the fifth light drive up Memorial Boulevard and look for the Tennis Hall of Fame on your left.

The International Tennis Hall of Fame and Museum is open year round except for Thanksgiving and Christmas.

Hours: 9:30 A.M. to 5:00 P.M. daily.

Admission and Membership

$8 for adults, $6 for seniors, military, or students with ID, $4 for children under 16, and $20 for a family. Group discount rates are available. Membership is $15/year for a student, $25/year for a Supporter, $50/year for a Friend, and $75/year for a family.

What to See

The Tennis Hall of Fame Museum presents a chronology of tennis's history, from the origins of tennis to today's stars, through interactive exhibits, videos, and memorabilia. The museum's collection has over 7,000 objects and includes a tennis library as well as historic tennis equipment and clothing (both of which have greatly changed over the years). Visitors can view the galleries and learn about the game of tennis. The exhibit galleries showcase tennis players who have been inducted into the Hall of Fame. There is also a Tour Gallery devoted to Billie Jean King.

The Casino's tennis courts are the only competition grass courts open to the public to play on and are the world's oldest continuously used competition grass courts.

The Tennis Hall of Fame hosts the Newport JVC Jazz Festival opening night concert and was the site of the first festival in 1954. The opening of the courts is always an anticipated event. In July the Miller Lite Hall of Fame Tennis Championship is held on the grass courts and the International Tennis Hall of Fame Enshrinement inducts players into the Hall of Fame on Bill Talbert Center Court. For ticket information to either of these events call (401) 849-6053.

The Tennis Hall of Fame Gift Shop is located in the Newport Casino and "The Tennis Store" is open on 192 Bellevue Avenue, where clothing and tennis-related gifts and accessories can be bought.

While You're in the Area

Attractions in the area include the Astor's Beechwood Mansion (p. 381), Touro Synagogue (p. 431), the Newport Art Museum (p. 418), the Museum of Yachting (p. 430), and the Newport Grand Jai-Alai.

Isaac Bell House

Bellevue Avenue
Newport, RI 02840
(401) 847-1000
www.NewportMansions.org

Overview

A restoration work in progress, this National Historic Landmark is one of the finest examples of shingle-style architecture in America. Built in 1883 by McKim, Mead and White for Isaac Bell, a wealthy cotton broker and investor, it combines Old English and European architecture with colonial American and exotic details. The Isaac Bell House is one of the best surviving examples of shingle style architecture in the country. After passing through a succession of owners, the Isaac Bell House was purchased by the Preservation Society in 1996, and is today designated a National Historic Landmark.

Directions and Hours

Visitors can leave their car and purchase an all day pass to ride RIPTA (RI Public Transit Authority 401-781-9400). From Memorial Day through Columbus Day, park at the Newport Visitors Center and ride the Yellow Line trolley to the historic properties of the Preservation Society. Mansion tours with transportation are also available through Viking Tours of Newport (401-847-6921), Gray Line RI (800-934-8687) and Gray Line Boston (800-343-1328).

Directions from Boston Area: Follow 128 south (this is also I-95 South) past the exit where I-95 splits off. At this point, 128 becomes 93 north. Continue to the exit for Route 24 (Fall River). Follow Route 24 to Route 114 south. Follow Route 114 south into town. At the intersection just past Dunkin Donuts and at the corner with Modern Furniture Galleries, turn left at the traffic light onto Route 214, which is Valley Road. Follow 214 to the beach area (passing through three stoplights), bear right past the beach area and continue up to the top of the hill (you are on Memorial Boulevard—a four lane divided road). At the four-way intersection, turn left onto Bellevue Avenue. Proceed south along Bellevue, and follow the signs for the mansions.

Directions from Providence: Follow 195 east to Route 24 (Fall River) to Route 114 south. Follow Route 114 south into town. At the intersection just past Dunkin Donuts and at the corner with Modern Furniture Galleries, turn left onto Route 214, which is Valley Road. Follow 214 to the beach area (passing through three stoplights), bear right past the beach area and continue up to the top of the hill (you are on Memorial Boulevard—a four lane divided road). At the main intersection, turn left onto Bellevue Avenue. Proceed along Bellevue Avenue. Signs for the Newport Mansions are along Bellevue Avenue.

Directions from New York: Follow I-95 north to Rhode Island exit #3. This will bring you to Route 138. Follow signs for the Newport Bridge, (which is a $2 toll bridge) and take the scenic Newport exit off the bridge. At the bottom of the ramp turn right. Proceed through one stoplight. At the second stoplight turn right. This is America's Cup Avenue. On America's Cup Avenue, proceed through six stoplights. At the seventh stoplight bear left up the hill. Continue past one more stoplight. At the next stoplight intersection, at the top of the hill, turn right onto Bellevue Avenue. Proceed along Bellevue Avenue; signs indicating the Newport Mansions are along Bellevue Avenue.

Isaac Bell House is open year-round and is handicap accessible.

Hours: January 2-April 13, 2001: Open weekends, Martin Luther King Day, and Presidents Day, 10:00 A.M. to 6:00 P.M. (last tour is at 5:00 P.M.); April 14-May 20, 2001: Open daily from 10:00 A.M. to 6:00 P.M. (last tour is at 5:00 P.M.); May 21-October 8, 2001: Open daily from 10:00 A.M. to 6:00 P.M. (last tour is at 5:00 P.M.); October 9-October 28: open daily from 10:00 A.M. to 6:00 P.M. (last tour is at 5:00 P.M.); October 29-November 21: open daily from 10:00 A.M. to 6:00 P.M. (last tour is at 5:00 P.M.); November 23-January 1, 2002—Christmas at the Newport Mansions: open daily and decorated for the holidays: open at 10:00 A.M., last tour admission at 5:00 P.M., houses close at 6:00 P.M.; November 24, December 1, 8, 15, and 29—Holiday Evenings 5:00-8:00 P.M.

Admission and Membership

Several admission packages are available for the 11 Newport Mansions administered by the Preservation Society of Newport County. Prices range from $10 for a youth to $29 for an adult. Group discounts for 20 or more visitors are available. Please call for details.

Members enjoy many benefits, including discounts on Newport Mansions Store purchases, free parking, Annual Reports, invitations to special events and programs, and an annual subscription to our journal, the Newport Gazette. Members also receive free and unlimited admission to regular tours at each of the Preservation Society's 11 properties. Membership is Individual $50, Household $75, Steward $250, Patron $500, and Benefactor $1,000, and President's Circle $5,000.

What to See

The Isaac Bell House was remarkably innovative when it appeared in 1883. It is a combination of Old English and European architecture with colonial American and exotic details, such as a Japanese-inspired open floor plan and bamboo-style porch columns. The exterior of the house has been extensively renovated and interior restoration work is continuing. The house is presented for tour as a work in progress.

While You're in the Area

There are 11 Historic Properties in Newport administered by the Preservation Society of Newport County (pp. 384, 386, 390, 391, 395, 399, 403, 406, 410, 412, 422).

Jamestown Museum

92 Narragansett Avenue
Jamestown, RI 02835
(401) 423-0784

Overview

Jamestown is an island community with a rich ferry boat tradition. The permanent exhibit displays this heritage.

Directions and Hours

Take I-95 to Rhode Island Route 4 to Route 138 to Jamestown. Follow signs to the village.

The museum is open July-August. It is not handicap accessible.

Hours: Wednesday-Sunday 1:00-4:00.

Admission and Membership

Admission is free. Membership to the Jamestown Historical Society is $15/year for a family.

What to See

Annual exhibits illustrate some facets of Jamestown history.

There is a no gift shop. Visitors may dine at local restaurants in the village.

While You're in the Area

Nearby attractions include the Jamestown Windmill (p. 430), the Beavertail Lighthouse Museum (p. 429), the Fire Department Memorial Building (p. 429), and the Sydney L. Wright Museum (p. 431).

John Brown House Museum

52 Power Street
Providence, RI 02906
(401) 331-8575
www.rihs.org

Overview

John Brown (1736-1803) began building this brownstone-and-brick house overlooking the Providence waterfront in 1786. John Brown—not the famous abolitionist—is known for his role in the Gaspee affair, which resulted in the first blood of the American Revolution. He had a long and unique career, being an entrepreneur, patiot, privateer, and China trade merchant. His mansion reflects both his position in society and his wealth.

Directions and Hours

From I-95: Take the Gano Street exit. Turn right off the exit. When you come to a blinking light turn left onto Power Street.

The museum is open year round.

Hours: Tuesday-Saturday 10:00 A.M. to 5:00 P.M., Sunday 12:00-4:00 P.M. Closed Tuesday-Thursday in January and February. Open some holidays but contact the museum for more information.

Admission and Membership

$6 adults, $4.50 for seniors and college students, $3 for children 7-17, and $15 for a family. Motor coach, group, and school tours are available by appointment. Rhode Island Historical Society members are free. Membership is $35/year for an individual, $45/year for a family, $25/year for a student or senior, and $35/year for a senior family. Other membership options are available.

What to See

The Rhode Island Historical Society has restored the building, reproducing original colors and french wallpaper. Furnishings include many Brown family pieces, like a nine-shell desk and bookcase, both Rhode Island American colonial furniture products.

Tours are led by guides and last approximately 45 minutes.

While You're in the Area

Attractions nearby include the RISD Museum (p. 431), The Rhode Island Foundation Gallery (p. 431), and many small private galleries.

John Hunt House Museum

Box 4774
East Providence, RI 02916
(401) 438-1750

Overview

The John Hunt House Museum is located in an eighteenth century five-bay Georgian house which has been authentically restored and furnished.

Directions and Hours

From I-195: Take exit 1 in Seekonk, Massachusetts. You are now on Route 114A. Cross Route 44 and after the Rhode Island/Massachusetts border turn on Hunt's Mills Road. Proceed to the end.

From I-95 South: Take exit 2A to Route 1A.

Photo courtesy of the John Hunt House Museum

After about 4 miles veer left off 1A onto 114A to Seekonk (Pleasant Street). Hunts Mills Road is the last street in Rhode Island before the Massachusetts border.

The museum is open from March 1-June 30 and September 1-December 31 and is semi-handicap accessible.

Hours: 9:00 A.M.-12:00 P.M. Tuesday and Thursday. Some Sundays 1:00-4:00 P.M.

Admission and Membership

There is no admission cost, but donations are accepted. Membership is $10/year for an individual, $15/year for a family.

What to See

The museum has restored the eighteenth century gardens and furnished the house in eighteenth century period furniture. The Philip Walker Room is furnished with artifacts from the 1679 Philip Walker House—the oldest house in East Providence. The museum has a varied collection of historical artifacts pertaining to East Providence and the period when the Hunt House was located in Rehoboth, MA and Seekonk, MA, and relocated without moving its foundation. The museum also has an extensive Rumford Baking Powder Company Collection and a reference library.

The museum will hold a garden tour on June 9, 2001, visiting gardens in the Riverside section of the city. The rain date in June 10. Children's programming includes tours to all fifth graders in the city. The children get to play eighteenth century games and walk the Conservation Trail.

The museum has a very small gift shop. There is no café but there is a picnic area outside. Large groups can be served coffee.

While You're in the Area

Interesting attractions nearby include: the East Providence Carousel (p. 429) and the John Brown House (p. 408), which was built at the same time as the Hunt House. The Hunt House is a good example of the restrained country style while the John Brown House is an elegant Georgian mansion.

Kenyon Corn Meal Company

21 Glen Rock Road
Usquepaugh, RI 02892
(401) 783-4054 or 1-800-7-KENYON
www.kenyonsgristmill.com

Overview

Kenyon's Grist Mill is a small family-run operation whose grinding dates back to the 1650s. The original granite millstone is still in full operation. Kenyon's is home to the famous Rhode Island Johnny Cakes.

Directions and Hours

From I 95: Take exit 3A (the Newport and University of Rhode Island exit). This will put you on Route 138 east. Travel 5 miles on Route 138 east. On the right side is a Kenyon's sign. Immediately past this on the left is Old Usquepaugh Road. Take this left (a narrow lane with colonial homes). Continue through the stop sign. The mill will be on your right.

The mill is open year-round. Tours are by

appointment or by chance. The mill is not handicap accessible.

Hours: Monday-Friday 10:00 A.M. to 5:00 P.M., Saturday-Sunday 12:00-5:00 P.M.

Admission and Membership

Admission is free.

What to See

Kenyon Corn Meal Company grinds meals and flours, producing a variety of mixes. All the grinding is done in the age-old tradition. The products are 100% natural grains blended with old-fashioned wholesome mixes with no additives or preservatives.

The mill has a gift shop, which features all of the products produced as well as cooking gifts. The mill has no café, but there is a great pizza place called Sal's pizza located a mile away on Route 138. The University of Rhode Island also offers a variety of café style restaurants which are only three miles east on Route 138.

While You're in the Area

Nearby is Peter Pots Pottery, a pottery and antique store.

Kingscote

Bellevue Avenue
Newport, RI 02840
(401) 847-1000
www.NewportMansions.org

Overview

This Gothic Revival house was built in 1839. Its dining room, added in 1881, includes one of the earliest installations of Tiffany glass. Kingscote (1839-41) is a landmark of the Gothic Revival style in American architecture. Its appearance in Newport marked the beginning of the "cottage boom" that would distinguish the town as a veritable laboratory for the design of picturesque houses throughout the nineteenth century. In 1839 Southern planter George Noble Jones commissioned architect Richard Upjohn to design a summer cottage along a country road, known as Bellevue Avenue, on the outskirts of town. Upjohn created a highly original "cottage orne," or ornamental cottage, in the Gothic Revival style. The general effect was romantic—a fanciful composition of towers, windows, Gothic arches, and porch roofs inspired by medieval tournament tents. The house remained in the King family until 1972, when the last descendant left it to the Preservation Society. Today, Kingscote is a National Historic Landmark. It is a rare example of a Gothic Revival house and landscape setting preserved intact with original family collections.

Directions and Hours

Visitors can leave their car and purchase an all day pass to ride RIPTA (RI Public Transit Authority 401-781-9400). From Memorial Day through Columbus Day, park at the Newport Visitors Center and ride the Yellow Line trolley to the historic properties of the Preservation Society. Mansion tours with transportation are also available through Viking Tours of Newport (401-847-6921), Gray Line RI (800-934-8687) and Gray Line Boston (800-343-1328).

Directions from Boston Area: Follow 128 south (this is also I-95 South) past the exit where I-95 splits off. At this point, 128 becomes 93 north. Continue to the exit for Route 24 (Fall River). Follow Route 24 to Route 114 south. Follow Route 114 south into town. At the intersection just past Dunkin Donuts and at the corner with Modern Furniture Galleries, turn left at the traffic light onto Route 214, which is Valley Road. Follow 214 to the beach area (passing through three stoplights), bear right past the beach area and continue up to the top of the hill (you are on Memorial Boulevard—a four lane divided road). At the four-way intersection, turn left onto Bellevue Avenue. Proceed south along Bellevue, and follow the signs for the mansions.

Directions from Providence: Follow 195 east to Route 24 (Fall River) to Route 114 south.

Follow Route 114 south into town. At the intersection just past Dunkin Donuts and at the corner with Modern Furniture Galleries, turn left onto Route 214, which is Valley Road. Follow 214 to the beach area (passing through three stoplights), bear right past the beach area and continue up to the top of the hill (you are on Memorial Boulevard—a four lane divided road). At the main intersection, turn left onto Bellevue Avenue. Proceed along Bellevue Avenue. Signs for the Newport Mansions are along Bellevue Avenue.

Directions from New York: Follow I-95 north to Rhode Island exit #3. This will bring you to Route 138. Follow signs for the Newport Bridge, (which is a $2 toll bridge) and take the scenic Newport exit off the bridge. At the bottom of the ramp turn right. Proceed through one stoplight. At the second stoplight turn right. This is America's Cup Avenue. On America's Cup Avenue, proceed through six stoplights. At the seventh stoplight bear left up the hill. Continue past one more stoplight. At the next stoplight intersection, at the top of the hill, turn right onto Bellevue Avenue. Proceed along Bellevue Avenue; signs indicating the Newport Mansions are along Bellevue Avenue.

Kingscote is open year-round and is handicap accessible.

Hours: January 2-April 13, 2001: Open weekends, Martin Luther King Day, and Presidents Day, 10:00 A.M. to 6:00 P.M. (last tour is at 5:00 P.M.); April 14-May 20, 2001: Open daily from 10:00 A.M. to 6:00 P.M. (last tour is at 5:00 P.M.); May 21-October 8, 2001: Open daily from 10:00 A.M. to 6:00 P.M. (last tour is at 5:00 P.M.); October 9-October 28: open daily from 10:00 A.M. to 6:00 P.M. (last tour is at 5:00 P.M.); October 29-November 21: open daily from 10:00 A.M. to 6:00 P.M. (last tour is at 5:00 P.M.); November 23-January 1, 2002—Christmas at the Newport Mansions: open daily and decorated for the holidays: open at 10:00 A.M., last tour admission at 5:00 P.M., houses close at 6:00 P.M.; November 24, December 1, 8, 15, and 29—Holiday Evenings 5:00-8:00 P.M.

Admission and Membership

Several admission packages are available for the 11 Newport Mansions administered by the Preservation Society of Newport County. Prices range from $10 for a youth to $29 for an adult. Group discounts for 20 or more visitors are available. Please call for details.

Members enjoy many benefits, including discounts on Newport Mansions Store purchases, free parking, Annual Reports, invitations to special events and programs, and an annual subscription to our journal, the Newport Gazette. Members also receive free and unlimited admission to regular tours at each of the Preservation Society's 11 properties. Membership is Individual $50, Household $75, Steward $250, Patron $500, and Benefactor $1,000, and President's Circle $5,000.

What to See

At the outbreak of the Civil War, the Jones family left Newport never to return, and the house was sold in 1864 to China Trade merchant William Henry King. His nephew David took over the house in 1876, and several years later decided to enlarge Kingscote. He engaged the firm of McKim, Mead and White to make the renovations, including the new dining room. The room combines Colonial American details with exotic ornament—reflecting the architects' interest in combining eastern and western motifs. The innovative use of materials was also important, such as cork tiles as a covering for the wall frieze and ceiling, and an early installation of opalescent glass bricks by Louis Comfort Tiffany.

While You're in the Area

There are 11 Historic Properties in Newport administered by the Preservation Society of Newport County (pp. 384, 386, 390, 391, 395, 399, 403, 406, 410, 412, 422).

Lysander and Susan Flagg Museum and Cultural Center

209 Central Street
Central Falls, RI 02863
(401) 727-7440
www.cflibrary.com

Overview

The Lysander and Susan Flagg Museum and Cultural Center hosts a collection of local history photos and artifacts from the mill town of Central Falls. It is also the home of the Central Falls Veteran's Memorial monument, which holds the names of all those local veterans who died while in the service of their country.

Directions and Hours

From the north: Take 95 south to exit 30. Take a right at the first light onto East Street. Bear left onto Roosevelt Avenue. At the second light, take a right on to Cross Street. Take a right on Clinton after the funeral home. Take a right on Central Street. The museum is on the left.

From the south: Take 95 north to exit 29 Broadway/Cottage Street. Stay left when the off ramp forks. At the first red light take a left onto Central Avenue. Central Avenue becomes Cross Street. Go straight through 4 lights. Take a right on Clinton after the funeral home. Take a right on Central Street. The museum is on the left.

The museum is open year round and it is handicap accessible.

Hours: Wednesday and Thursday 10:00-12:00; group tours available by appointment and additional hours will be added soon.

Admission and Membership

$2 for adults, $1 and students. Group tour discounts are available by appointment.

What to See

The Lysander and Susan Flagg Museum is the home of several exhibits of local history. It hosts an extensive Sullivan Ballou collection. Ballou was made famous in the Ken Burns PBS documentary *The Civil War*. The Central Falls Library, adjacent to the museum, was the meeting place of the Sullivan Ballou Post #3 of the Grand Army of the Republic.

The museum also features Civil War maps, a collection of photos and artifacts documenting the history of the police department, and a room dedicated to the memory of Central Falls veterans.

The museum is also used as a local cultural center and hosts local art exhibitions and music concerts.

There is no gift shop, but the museum sells reproductions of the famous Sullivan Ballou letter. There are several local restaurants in the area and a Dunkin Donuts within one block.

While You're in the Area

Visitors may also want to see the Slater Mill (p. 431), less than a mile away.

Marble House

Bellevue Avenue
Newport, RI 02840
(401) 847-1000
www.NewportMansions.org

Overview

With 500,000 cubic feet of marble, this opulent house was was built between 1888 and 1892 for William and Alva Vanderbilt. It was designed as a summer house, or "cottage," as Newporters called them in remembrance of the modest houses of the early nineteenth century. But Marble House was much more than a cottage; it was a social and architectural landmark that set the pace for Newport's subsequent transformation from a quiet summer colony of wooden houses to the legendary resort of opulent stone palaces. Mrs. Vanderbilt was a leading hostess in Newport society, and envisioned Marble House as her "temple to the arts" in America. Mrs. Belmont sold the house to Frederick H. Prince in 1932. The Preservation Society acquired the house in 1963 from the Prince estate.

Directions and Hours

Visitors can leave their car and purchase an all day pass to ride RIPTA (RI Public Transit Authority 401-781-9400). From Memorial Day through Columbus Day, park at the Newport Visitors Center and ride the Yellow Line trolley to the historic properties of the Preservation Society. Mansion tours with transportation are also available through Viking Tours of Newport (401-847-6921), Gray Line RI (800-934-8687) and Gray Line Boston (800-343-1328).

Directions from Boston Area: Follow 128 south (this is also I-95 South) past the exit where I-95 splits off. At this point, 128 becomes 93 north. Continue to the exit for Route 24 (Fall River). Follow Route 24 to Route 114 south. Follow Route 114 south into town. At the intersection just past Dunkin Donuts and at the corner with Modern Furniture Galleries, turn left at the traffic light onto Route 214, which is Valley Road. Follow 214 to the beach area (passing through three stoplights), bear right past the beach area and continue up to the top of the hill (you are on Memorial Boulevard—a four lane divided road). At the four-way intersection, turn left onto Bellevue Avenue. Proceed south along Bellevue, and follow the signs for the mansions.

Directions from Providence: Follow 195 east to Route 24 (Fall River) to Route 114 south. Follow Route 114 south into town. At the intersection just past Dunkin Donuts and at the corner with Modern Furniture Galleries, turn left onto Route 214, which is Valley Road. Follow 214 to the beach area (passing through three stoplights), bear right past the beach area and continue up to the top of the hill (you are on Memorial Boulevard—a four lane divided road). At the main intersection, turn left onto Bellevue Avenue. Proceed along Bellevue Avenue. Signs for the Newport Mansions are along Bellevue Avenue.

Directions from New York: Follow I-95 north to Rhode Island exit #3. This will bring you to Route 138. Follow signs for the Newport Bridge, (which is a $2 toll bridge) and take the scenic Newport exit off the bridge. At the bottom of the ramp turn right. Proceed through one stoplight. At the second stoplight turn right. This is America's Cup Avenue. On America's Cup Avenue, proceed through six stoplights. At the seventh stoplight bear left up the hill. Continue past one more stoplight. At the next stoplight intersection, at the top of the hill, turn right onto Bellevue Avenue. Proceed along Bellevue Avenue; signs indicating the Newport Mansions are along Bellevue Avenue.

Marble House is open year-round and is handicap accessible.

Hours: January 2-April 13, 2001: Open weekends, Martin Luther King Day, and Presidents Day, 10:00 A.M. to 6:00 P.M. (last tour is at 5:00 P.M.); April 14-May 20, 2001: Open daily from 10:00 A.M. to 6:00 P.M. (last tour is at 5:00 P.M.); May 21-October 8, 2001: Open daily from 10:00 A.M. to 6:00 P.M. (last tour is at 5:00 P.M.); October 9-October 28: open daily from 10:00 A.M. to 6:00 P.M. (last tour is at 5:00 P.M.); October 29-November 21: open daily from 10:00 A.M. to 6:00 P.M. (last tour is at 5:00 P.M.); November 23-January 1, 2002—Christmas at the Newport Mansions: open daily and decorated for the holidays: open at 10:00 A.M., last tour admission at 5:00 P.M., houses close at 6:00 P.M.; November 24, December 1, 8, 15, and 29—Holiday Evenings 5:00-8:00 P.M.

Admission and Membership

Several admission packages are available for the 11 Newport Mansions administered by the Preservation Society of Newport County. Prices range from $10 for a youth to $29 for an adult. Group discounts for 20 or more visitors are available. Please call for details.

Members enjoy many benefits, including discounts on Newport Mansions Store purchases, free parking, Annual Reports, invitations to special events and programs, and an annual subscription to our journal, the Newport Gazette. Members also receive free and unlimited admission to regular tours at each of the Preservation

Society's 11 properties. Membership is Individual $50, Household $75, Steward $250, Patron $500, and Benefactor $1,000, and President's Circle $5,000.

What to See

The house was designed by the architect Richard Morris Hunt, inspired by the Petit Trianon at Versailles. The cost of the house was reported in contemporary press accounts to be $11 million, of which $7 million was spent on the 500,000 cubic feet of marble required for construction. Upon its completion, Mr. Vanderbilt gave the house to his wife as a 39th birthday present. The Vanderbilts had three children: Consuelo, who became the ninth Duchess of Marlborough; William K., Jr., a prominent figure in pioneering the sport of auto racing in America; and Harold, one of the finest yachtsmen of his era who successfully defended the America's Cup three times. After the Vanderbilts divorced in 1895, Alva Vanderbilt married Oliver Hazard Perry Belmont and moved down the street to Belcourt. After Mr. Belmont's death, she reopened Marble House, and had a whimsical Chinese Tea House built on the seaside cliffs, frequently hosting rallies there to promote women's right to vote.

While You're in the Area

There are 11 Historic Properties in Newport administered by the Preservation Society of Newport County (pp. 384, 386, 390, 391, 395, 399, 403, 406, 410, 412, 422).

Museum of Newport History

127 Thames Street
Newport, RI 02840
(401) 841-8770 or (401) 846-0813
www.newporthistorical.org

Overview

The Museum of Newport History provides the whole family with an introduction to the area's rich history and architecture. The Newport Historical Society uses decorative arts, artifacts of everyday life, graphics, hundreds of historic photographs, and audiovisual programs on laserdiscs to tell Newport's story.

Directions and Hours

From points south: Take Interstate 95 North to Route 138 East (exit 3). Follow the signs for the Jamestown and Newport Bridges. Take the first exit off the Newport Bridge, and turn right at the bottom of the ramp onto Farewell Street. Go through a set of traffic lights (you will pass between two cemeteries) and take a left onto Thames Street at the next set of lights. At the first set of lights, the Museum of Newport History at the Brick Market will be on your right.

From points north: Take Route 195 to Route 24 South. The exit appears about a ½ mile beyond a short highway tunnel. Continue on Route 24 South to Route 114 South. This is called West Main Road in the towns of Portsmouth and Middletown and becomes Broadway in Newport. You will be on Route 114 for 20-30 minutes. As you approach the end of Broadway, there will be a small city park (called Washington Square) on your left. Continue straight and you will see the Museum of Newport History directly ahead.

The museum is open year-round. The first floor only is handicap accessible.

Hours: November-March Friday and Saturday 10:00-4:00 P.M., Sunday 1:00-4:00. April-October Wednesday through Saturday 10:00-5:00, Sunday 1:00-5:00, closed Tuesdays.

Admission and Membership

$5 for adults, $4 for senior citizens, $3 for children, and children under 5 are free. Group discounts are available. Membership is $30/year for an individual, $40/year for a family, $50/year for business/professional, $60/year for supporting, $100/year for contributing, $175/year for corporate, $250/year for sponsor, and $1,000 for a life membership.

What to See

The whole museum takes about an hour and a half to go through, and everything in the museum is relevant to the city's history. The museum is an inclusive overview of Newport's diverse history, from its founding to the present. It goes beyond the Gilded Age.

The society will be having a Heritage Fair on September 29-30, 2001 at the Friends Meeting House. The museum offers several programs for children.

The museum does not have a gift shop but there are some Society publications along with other books for sale as well as some cards and souvenirs. There is no café but visitors can eat at nearby Brick Alley Pub on 140 Thames Street or Yesterday's at 28 Washington Square.

While You're in the Area

Other museums or interesting attractions nearby include the Newport Historical House on 82 Touro Street (p. 419), the Colony House on Washington Square, the Wanton-Lyman-Hazard House on 17 Broadway (p. 424), and the Friends Meeting House on the corner of Marlborough and Farewell Streets.

Museum of Rhode Island History at Aldrich House

110 Benevolent Street
Providence, RI 02906
(401) 331-8575
www.rihs.org

Overview

The Museum of Rhode Island at Aldrich House focuses on Rhode Island's history and features changing exhibits.

Directions and Hours

From I-95: Take the Gano Street exit. Turn right off the exit. When you come to a blinking light turn left onto Power Street then take a right onto Cooke Street. The Aldrich House will be on the corner of Cooke Street and Benevolent Street.

The museum is open year round and is handicap accessible.

Hours: Tuesday-Friday 8:30 A.M. to 5:00 P.M.

Admission and Membership

The cost to view exhibits is $1. Membership is $35/year for an individual, $45/year for a family, $25/year for a student or senior, and $35/year for a senior family. Other membership options are available.

What to See

The Aldrich House is currently the interim house for the Rhode Island Heritage Hall of Fame which will one day be part of the Heritage Harbor Museum. Please call ahead to check on exhibits as they change frequently. The Aldrich House is also available for rentals.

The Aldrich House has a bookstore. There are many places to eat in Providence.

While You're in the Area

Attractions nearby include the RISD Museum (p. 431), the Rhode Island Foundation Gallery (p. 431), and many small private galleries.

Museum of Work and Culture

42 South Main Street
Woonsocket, RI 02895
(401) 769-9675
www.rihs.org

Overview

The Museum of Work and Culture is an interactive museum located in the Blackstone River Valley National Heritage Corridor operated by the Rhode Island Historical Society. The museum presents the story of the French Canadians who left the farms of Quebec for the factories of the New England Area. It showcases the remarkable tale of a people's preservation of faith, language, and customs, and their acculturation into the working class of America.

Directions and Hours

From Boston: Take 95 South to 295 South to 146 North. Take the Downtown Woonsocket exit. Then follow direction below.

From Providence: Take 95 North to 146 North to the Downtown Woonsocket exit. Then follow directions below.

From Worcester: Take 146 South to the Downtown Woonsocket exit. Then follow direction below.

Once you take the Downtown Woonsocket exit: Follow the signs for the Visitor's Center and Route 104. Follow 104 (Providence Street) to the end and turn right onto South Main. The Museum is a two-story brick building on the right-hand side.

The museum is open year round and is handicap accessible.

Hours: Weekdays: 9:30 A.M. to 4:00 P.M. Saturdays: 10:00 A.M. to 5:00 P.M. Sunday: 1:00-5:00 P.M.

Admission and Membership

$5 adults, $3 seniors and students. Children under 10 get in free when with an adult. A group of 10 or more can receive a discounted admission price of $4. The museum is free for Rhode Island Historical Society members. Membership is $45/year for a family, $35/year for an individual or a senior family (65 and older), and $25/year for an individual student or senior.

What to See

By viewing the museum's changing exhibit gallery visitors can explore many different topics throughout the year about the history, art, and culture that exists in Woonsocket and the Black River Valley area today. Through the museum's permanent exhibit the visitor journeys through Woonsocket's workday world. Visitors can experience the shop floor of a textile mill and hear people tell their stories on the front porch of a triple decker, listen in a 1920's classroom, and in the 1930s Independent Textile Union Hall.

Special programming includes an annual Fàte du Jour l'An on January 1st from 1:00-5:00 P.M. Tickets are $15 for music, food, and dancing. The museum also offers a Ranger Day program with lectures on several Sunday afternoons throughout the months of January, February, and March. Children's programming is also available, which includes arts and crafts, presentations, and storytellers, all upon request.

The museum does have a gift shop. There are several restaurants nearby.

While You're in the Area

An interesting attraction across the street from the museum is the Blackstone Valley River Boat Excursion, which is open from August through October.

National Museum of American Illustration

492 Bellevue Avenue
Newport, RI 02840
(401) 851-8949
www.americanillustration.org

Overview

The National Museum of American Illustration was founded in 1998 by Judy A.G. Cutler and Laurence S. Cutler to house their art collection from the "Golden Age of American Illustration." The museum is situated on Bellevue Avenue, among the many legendary "Gilded Age" mansions, and showcases the work of masters such as Maxfield Parrish, N. C. Wyeth, and Norman Rockwell.

Directions and Hours

From New York and Connecticut: Take Interstate 95 North to Route 138 East (exit 3A in Rhode Island). Follow Route 138 East for 13 miles. Turn left at the traffic light and continue on Route 138 East. After 2 miles, veer right on 138 East to Newport/Jamestown Bridges. Go over Jamestown Bridge and then Newport Bridge. Take the first exit off Newport Bridge

(Scenic Newport). Turn right off the exit ramp and drive straight through the first set of traffic lights. At the second set of lights, turn right onto America's Cup Avenue, heading South toward the center of town. Then follow directions below.

From Boston and North: Take Interstate 93 South to Route 24 South (exit 4). Follow Route 24 South to Route 114 South (Route 114 South is called West Main Road in Middletown, and Broadway in Newport). Just past the Newport City Hall turn right onto Marlborough Street. Proceed to traffic the light at America's Cup Avenue. Turn right onto America's Cup Avenue, heading South toward the center of town. Then follow the directions below.

From T. F. Green Airport, Providence, RI: Follow signs to Interstate 95 South. Take I-95 South to Route 4 South (exit 9). Follow Route 4 South to the Newport/Jamestown Bridges. Go over the Jamestown Bridge and then Newport Bridge. Take the first exit off Newport Bridge (Scenic Newport). Turn right off the exit ramp and drive straight through the 1st set of traffic lights. At the second set of lights turn right on to America's Cup Avenue, heading South toward the center of town. Follow directions below.

From Newport: Follow America's Cup Avenue past Bowen's and Bannister's Warf on the right, to the traffic light at Thames Street. Go straight through the light—America's Cup Avenue becomes Memorial Boulevard. Follow Memorial Boulevard uphill to the traffic light at Bellevue Avenue. Turn right on Bellevue Avenue, towards the Newport mansions. Continue on Bellevue Avenue for 1 mile. Turn left onto Victoria Avenue. The gate on the left is the main entrance to Vernon Court.

The museum is open by appointment only.

Admission and Membership

Admission is $25. Group discounts are available. Children 12 and under are not allowed admission. Proper casual dress and correct demeanor are required for entry. The museum is committed to accessibility but structural obstacles exist so please call in advance for accommodations required by a disability. The library is open to scholars only by written application to the director. Admission does not include visitation to the gardens at Vernon Court, but will include the Frederick Law Olmsted Park and the Louis I. Kahn Memorial Arch. Membership is available in several categories.

What to See

The museum features masterpieces of American illustrative art, including original paintings and drawings created by Norman Rockwell, Maxfield Parrish, N. C. Wyeth, Howard Pyle, JC Leyendecker, Howard Chandler Christy, James Montgomery Flagg, Charles Dana Gibson, and Jessie Wilcox Smith, as well as other illustrations from the "Golden Age" document moments of American history.

The museum shop features fine art products including books, calendars, notecards, posters, and art prints. There is a café.

While You're in the Area

Interesting attractions nearby include: the Preservation Society of Newport County (p. 385), Astors Beechwood (p. 381), and Rough Point.

Naval War College Museum

686 Cushing Road
Newport, RI 02841
(401) 841-4052
www.visitnewport.com/buspages/navy

Overview

The Naval War College Museum is located in 1820 Founders Hall, a National Historic Landmark on Coasters Harbor Island. Founders Hall is the original site of the Naval War College, the first school of its kind in the world and the senior professional educational institution in the U.S. Navy. It is also where the renowned historian Alfred Thayer Mahan (1840-1914) wrote the epochal book *The Influence of Sea Power Upon History, 1660-1783*, which helped to change the course of history at the beginning of the twentieth century. Museum exhibits focus on the history of naval warfare as studied at the college through the years and on the naval heritage of the Narragansett Bay region. Permanent exhibits deal with the Navy in the region in the eighteenth and nineteenth centuries, and the histories of the three major naval installations established in Newport in the late nineteenth century that continue to the present. Temporary exhibits on naval warfare and naval regional themes occur routinely during the year.

Directions and Hours

Coasters Harbor Island is part of the Newport Naval complex located two miles north of the center of Newport. Museum directional signs are located throughout the city. Public access to the museum is through Gate No. 1 of the Navy Base where visitor passes are available upon request.

The museum is open year round.

Hours: 10:00 A.M. to 4:00 P.M. Monday-Friday and weekends 12:00-4:00 P.M. June-September. The museum is closed on holidays.

Admission and Membership

The Naval War College Museum is a federal, Navy Department activity and admission is free.

What to See

Featured items in the museum's permanent exhibits include the first propeller-driven torpedo made in America (1871), the first torpedo used on U.S. Navy warships (1890s), a collection of models of naval warships associated with the region beginning in the Revolution, and a display of an early naval war game, the unique study method of the College beginning in 1894.

Special exhibits planned for 2001 include a 90th anniversary exhibit of naval aviation that will open on March 19 and will run through September 30; a history of Gould Island (Narragansett Bay); and a torpedo development in World War II exhibit that is scheduled to open June 1 and to run through December 31. A temporary exhibit currently in place is "Posters at War," and consists of U.S. World War II posters. A featured item in a video on home front film industry is propaganda during the war. The museum also has several outdoor displays (Civil War Dahlgren boat howitzer cannon, USS *Constellation* anchor, WWII submarine Mk 14 torpedo, PT boat memorial, 1639 Newport settlement memorial) in the vicinity of the museum.

Visitors to the museum are restricted to the area of the museum and its outdoor displays.

A museum store, operated by the Naval War College Foundation, is located in the building. Adjacent to the area and in close walking distance from the museum is the Naval Station Officers Club which is open to the general public for lunch daily (11:30 A.M. to 1:00 P.M.)

While You're in the Area

There are many museums in the Newport area, along with the town's famed "Gilded Age" mansions.

Newport Art Museum and Art Association

76 Bellevue Avenue
Newport, RI 02840
(401) 848-8200
newportartmuseum.com

Overview

The Newport Art Museum collects and exhibits art with an emphasis on the heritage of Newport and Southeastern New England. Its art school, the Coleman Center for Creative Studies, offers classes in many media to adults and children year round. The museum is housed in Griswold House, Cushing Memorial Building, and the Kahn Building.

Directions and Hours

From Boston and points north: Take Route 24 (onto Aquidneck Island) to Route 138 south (Newport Beaches). Continue on Route 138. Turn left on Route 138A (Newport Beaches), which becomes Memorial Boulevard, to Bellevue Avenue. Turn right on Bellevue. Go two blocks. The museum is at the intersection of Bellevue Avenue and Old Beach Pond and has two small parking areas on its property.

From Providence, New York, and points west: Take Route I-95 to Route 138 east. Cross the Jamestown and Newport bridges ($2 toll). Take the "Scenic Newport" exit. Bear right to America's Cup Avenue; go through several lights. At Perry Mill, the post office, and the wave sculpture bear left onto Memorial Boulevard (Route 138). At the second light turn left onto Bellevue Avenue. Go two blocks. The museum is at the intersection of Bellevue Avenue and Old Beach Road and has two small parking lots on its property.

The museum is open year-round but closed on July 4, Thanksgiving, and New Years Day. Both exhibitions and classrooms are handicap accessible.

Hours: Summer (Memorial Day weekend through Columbus Day weekend): open Mondays through Saturdays from 10:00 A.M. to 5:00 P.M., Sundays noon to 5:00 P.M. Winter (Columbus Day weekend through Memorial Day Weekend): close at 4:00 P.M.

Admission and Membership

Adults $4, $3 age 60 and above, students $2, five and under free. Admission by donation Saturdays until noon. Special discounts: $1 off admission by printing a coupon from the internet; $1 off admission for AAA members. Membership is $40/year for an individual, $50/year for a family, and $30/year for a student or a senior; other categories upon request.

What to See

The Newport Art Museum's collection focuses on the art of the eighteenth, nineteenth, and twentieth centuries. Its 1862 Griswold House, designed by architect Richard Morris Hunt, is a highly regarded example of stick style domestic architecture. Paintings by Howard Gardiner Cushing of his wife are usually on exhibit and are not to be missed.

In the summers the museum presents a series of Wednesday evening Musical Picnics where visitors enjoy a different musical group each week. In the winter the museum presents a series of Saturday afternoon lectures, followed by old fashioned teas, on a wide range of subjects.

In addition to a variety of art classes for children from age three through teens, the Newport Art Museum offers children's art camps during the summer and during school vacations.

The museum has two shops: The Museum Shop, a gift shop, and The Griffon Shop, a volunteer-run consignment shop carrying antiques, collectibles, crafts, and art. There are restaurants within walking distance of the museum.

While You're in the Area

Newport has many other attractions. Within walking distance is the International Tennis Hall of Fame (p. 405), the Newport Historical Society (p. 419), the Redwood Library, and the Touro Synagogue.

The Newport Historical Society

82 Touro Street
Newport, RI 02840
(401) 846-0813
www.newporthistorical.org

Overview

The Newport Historical Society contains a library open for the public for research, a small changing exhibit, and administrative offices. Attached to the back of the Newport Historical Society and available for viewing is the Seventh Day Baptist Meeting House which was built in 1730.

Directions and Hours

From points south: Take Interstate 95 North to Route 138 East (exit 3). Follow the signs for the Jamestown and Newport Bridges. Take the first exit off the Newport Bridge, and turn right at the bottom of the ramp onto Farewell Street. Go through a set of traffic lights (you will pass between two cemeteries) and take a left onto Thames Street at the next set of lights. Take an immediate left onto Touro Street after the lights. Go through one set of lights and you will see our red brick building on the left.

From points north: Take Route 195 to Route 24 South. The exit appears about ½ mile beyond a short highway tunnel. Continue on Route 24 South to Route 114 South. This is called West Main Road in the towns of Portsmouth and Middletown and becomes Broadway in Newport. You will be on Route 114 for 20-30 minutes. As you approach the end of Broadway, there will be a small city park (called Washington Square) on your left. Take the left hand turn that circles around the park onto Touro Street. Go through one set of lights and you will see our red brick building on your left.

The society is open year-round but is not handicap accessible. It is strongly recommended that you call for an appointment to use the library.

Hours: September through mid-June: Tuesday-Friday 9:30-4:30, Saturday 9:30-noon. Mid-June to the end of August: Tuesday-Saturday 9:30-4:30. Closed Sundays and Mondays.

Admission and Membership

Admission is free. Membership is $30/year for an individual, $40/year for a family, $50/year for business/professional, $60/year for supporting, $100/year for contributing, $175/year for corporate, $250/year for sponsor, and $1,000 for a life membership.

What to See

The society's collections include 10,000 objects, paintings (106 portraits listed in the National Gallery's Catalogue of American Portraits), Townsend-Goddard furniture, silver and pewter, tall clocks, historic costumes, other textiles, boat models, and artifacts of everyday life. The society also has over 250,000 historic photographs of all aspects of Newport's past from the 1850's to the present. The library and Archives contain 12,000 volumes of secondary works with the second largest genealogy collection of Rhode Island, 1500 volumes of rare and historical imprints, 1500 shelf feet of archival and manuscript material, church records, land evidence, diaries, atlases, and city records. Other collections include oral histories, architectural drawings and papers of Newport architect J.D. Johnson, Archival film, videotapes, home movies, and slides. The Newport Historical Society properties include: The Wanton-Lyman-Hazard House, The Great Friends Meeting House, The Seventh Day Baptist Meeting House, and The Museum of Newport History at the Brick Market.

The museum does not have a gift shop but here are some Society publications along with other books for sale as well as some cards and souvenirs. There is no café but visitors can eat at nearby Brick Alley Pub on 140 Thames Street or Yesterday's at 28 Washington Square.

While You're in the Area

Other museums or interesting attractions nearby include the Museum of Newport History on 127 Thames Street (p. 414), the Newport Art Museum on 76 Bellevue Avenue (p. 418), the Colony House on Washington Square, the Wanton-Lyman-Hazard House on 17 Broadway (p. 424), and the Friends Meeting House on the corner of Marlborough and Farewell Streets.

Providence Children's Museum

100 South Street
Providence, RI 02903
(401) 273-KIDS
www.childrenmuseum.org

Overview

Providence Children's Museum is Rhode Island's only museum especially for children and their families. Providence Children's Museum is a hands-on place where kids and grown-ups play and learn together. Founded in 1977, the museum moved to Providence's Jewelry district in 1997. Each year, more than 100,000 kids and adults visit the Museum to explore and play.

Directions and Hours

The Museum is located at 100 South Street, close to the junction of Interstates 95 and 195 in Providence, Rhode Island. From I-95 East or West: Take exit 1 (Downtown Providence). Bear left at the first turnaround and continue straight under the highway bridge onto Eddy Street. Take the third right onto South Street and head toward the dragon atop the Museum, at the corner of South and Parsonage Streets.

From I-95 North or South: Take 195 east (exit 20) and follow the directions above. There is free parking available in the Museum's parking lot.

Providence Children's Museum is open Tuesday-Sunday, 9:30-5:00, and Monday holidays in the winter and daily during the summer, Fridays until 8:00 P.M.

Admission and Membership

General admission is $4.50 per person; Museum members are always free. Membership is $55 for two members, $75 for a family of four. The first Sunday of every month, the Museum offers free admission for all. Group discounts are available.

What to See

Providence Children's Museum is fully wheelchair accessible and offers a wide variety of interactive exhibits for kids ages 1-11 and their families. All signs and exhibits are displayed in both English and Spanish and visitors can take a hands-on time travel adventure and even go on a bike ride with a skeleton. In Waterways, kids discover the swirling, whirling ways of water; in TEETH! they brush a giant mouth and, outside, youngsters play in the colorful Children's Garden. Other exhibits give the inside story on recycling, investigate pet ownership, and allow kids to become puppeteers.

The Museum Gift Shop sells sturdy and imaginative toys and souvenirs. The Museum does not have a café, but visitors can dine at nearby restaurants or bring a bag lunch or snack to the Museum.

While You're in the Area

Attractions nearby include the RISD Museum (p. 431), the Rhode Island Foundation Gallery (p. 431), the Governor Henry Lippitt House Museum (p. 397), the Governor Stephen Hopkins House (p. 398), the Continental Sloop *Providence* (p. 429), the Providence Armory (p. 430), the Providence Art Club museum (p. 430), the Providence Athenaeum (p. 430), the Providence Preservation Society Houses (p. 385),

Photo courtesy of the Providence Children's Museum.

the Armory of Mounted Commands (p. 429), and the Museum of Natural History (p. 430).

Providence Marine Corps of Artillery Museum of Military History

176 Benefit Street
Providence, RI 02903
(401) 246-0521

Overview

The Providence Marine Corps of Artillery Museum of Military History houses a collection of military memorabilia donated by members of the Providence Marine Corps of Artillery from 1842-1946.

Directions and Hours

From I-195: Take exit 2.

The museum is open year-round and is handicap accessible.

Hours: By appointment.

Admission and Membership

Admission is by donation.

What to See

The museum's collection includes items from the Dorr Rebellion, the Civil War, the Spanish-American War, the Mexican Border War, World War I, and World War II. The museum also has an extensive military library.

While You're in the Area

The entire Benefit Street area is on the National Registry of Historic Properties. Close by is the eighteenth century State House, the Rhode Island School of Design Museum (p. 431), the John Brown House (p. 408), Brown University's Haffenreffer Museum (p. 400), John Hay Library (p. 430), and the Providence Athenaeum (p. 430).

Rosecliff

Bellevue Avenue
Newport, RI 02840
(401) 847-1000
www.NewportMansions.org

Overview

Commissioned by Nevada silver heiress Theresa Fair Oelrichs in 1889, architect Standard White modeled Rosecliff after the Grand Trianon, the garden retreat of French kings at Versailles. After the house was completed in 1902, at a reported cost of $2.5 million, Mrs. Oelrichs hosted fabulous entertainments here, including a fairy tale dinner and a party featuring famed magician Harry Houdini. "Tessie," as she was known to her friends, was born in Virginia City, Nevada. Her father, James Graham Fair, was an Irish immigrant who made an enormous fortune from Nevada's Comstock silver lode, one of the richest silver finds in history. During a summer in Newport, Theresa met Hermann Oelrichs playing tennis at the Newport Casino. They were married in 1890. A year later, they purchased the property known as Rosecliff from the estate of historian and diplomat George Bancroft.

Directions and Hours

Visitors can leave their car and purchase an all day pass to ride RIPTA (RI Public Transit Authority 401-781-9400). From Memorial Day through Columbus Day, park at the Newport Visitors Center and ride the Yellow Line trolley to the historic properties of the Preservation Society. Mansion tours with transportation are also available through Viking Tours of Newport (401-847-6921), Gray Line RI (800-934-8687) and Gray Line Boston (800-343-1328).

Directions from Boston Area: Follow 128 south (this is also I-95 South) past the exit where I-95 splits off. At this point, 128 becomes 93 north. Continue to the exit for Route 24 (Fall River). Follow Route 24 to Route 114 south. Follow Route 114 south into town. At the intersection just past Dunkin Donuts and at the corner with Modern Furniture Galleries, turn left at the traffic light onto Route 214, which is Valley Road. Follow 214 to the beach area (passing through three stoplights), bear right past the beach area and continue up to the top of the hill (you are on Memorial Boulevard—a four lane divided road). At the four-way intersection, turn left onto Bellevue Avenue. Proceed south along Bellevue, and follow the signs for the mansions.

Directions from Providence: Follow 195 east to Route 24 (Fall River) to Route 114 south. Follow Route 114 south into town. At the intersection just past Dunkin Donuts and at the corner with Modern Furniture Galleries, turn left onto Route 214, which is Valley Road. Follow 214 to the beach area (passing through three stoplights), bear right past the beach area and continue up to the top of the hill (you are on Memorial Boulevard—a four lane divided road). At the main intersection, turn left onto Bellevue Avenue. Proceed along Bellevue Avenue. Signs for the Newport Mansions are along Bellevue Avenue.

Directions from New York: Follow I-95 north to Rhode Island exit #3. This will bring you to Route 138. Follow signs for the Newport Bridge, (which is a $2 toll bridge) and take the scenic Newport exit off the bridge. At the bottom of the ramp turn right. Proceed through one stoplight. At the second stoplight turn right. This is America's Cup Avenue. On America's Cup Avenue, proceed through six stoplights. At the seventh stoplight bear left up the hill. Continue past one more stoplight. At the next stoplight intersection, at the top of the hill, turn right onto Bellevue Avenue. Proceed along Bellevue Avenue; signs indicating the Newport Mansions are along Bellevue Avenue.

Rosecliff is open year-round and is handicap accessible.

Hours: January 2-April 13, 2001: Open weekends, Martin Luther King Day, and Presidents Day, 10:00 A.M. to 6:00 P.M. (last tour is at 5:00 P.M.); April 14-May 20, 2001: Open daily from 10:00 A.M. to 6:00 P.M. (last tour is at 5:00 P.M.); May 21-October 8, 2001: Open daily from 10:00 A.M. to 6:00 P.M. (last tour is at 5:00 P.M.); October 9-October 28: open daily from 10:00 A.M. to 6:00 P.M. (last tour is at 5:00 P.M.); October 29-November 21: open daily from 10:00 A.M. to 6:00 P.M. (last tour is at 5:00 P.M.); November 23-January 1, 2002—Christmas at the Newport Mansions: open daily and decorated for the holidays: open at 10:00 A.M., last tour admission at 5:00 P.M., houses close at 6:00 P.M.; November 24, December 1, 8, 15, and 29—Holiday Evenings 5:00-8:00 P.M.

Admission and Membership

Several admission packages are available for the 11 Newport Mansions administered by the Preservation Society of Newport County. Prices range from $10 for a youth to $29 for an adult. Group discounts for 20 or more visitors are available. Please call for details.

Members enjoy many benefits, including discounts on Newport Mansions Store purchases, free parking, Annual Reports, invitations to special events and programs, and an annual subscription to our journal, the Newport Gazette. Members also receive free and unlimited admission to regular tours at each of the Preservation Society's 11 properties. Membership is Individual $50, Household $75, Steward $250, Patron $500, and Benefactor $1,000, and President's Circle $5,000.

What to See

An amateur horticulturist, it was Bancroft who developed the American Beauty Rose. The Oelrichs later bought additional property along Bellevue Avenue and commissioned Stanford White to replace the original house with the mansion that became the setting for many of Newport's most lavish parties. The mansion is now preserved through the generosity of its last private owners, Mr. and Mrs. J. Edgar Monroe, of New Orleans. They gave the house, its furnishings, and an endowment to the Preservation Society in 1971. Scenes from several films have been shot on location at Rosecliff, including

High Society, The Great Gatsby, True Lies, and *Amistad.*

While You're in the Area

There are 11 Historic Properties in Newport administered by the Preservation Society of Newport County (pp. 384, 386, 390, 391, 395, 399, 403, 406, 410, 412, 422).

Varnum Military and Naval Museum

6 Main Street
East Greenwich, RI 02818
(401) 884-4110
www.varnumcontinentals.org

Overview

The Varnum Military and Naval Museum contains sixteenth through twentieth century military artifacts. The medieval castle style armory was built by the Varnum Continentals in 1913. The building is listed on the National Register of historic places.

Directions and Hours

From I-95: Take exit 8 to Route 401 east to Route 1 (Main Street). Take a left onto Division Street.

The museum is open by appointment and is not handicap accessible.

Admission and Membership

Admission is by donation. Membership is $30/year. Special discounts are available.

What to See

The museum has a World War I and II original poster collection of over 600 different American, French, English, and Canadian posters. It is the official museum for the artifacts collection of the 76th Reserve Division covering its activities from WWI to deactivation in 1994. The museum also has military uniforms of various periods; a collection of military pictures covering various periods of history, including Rhode Island Militia units; a book collection including training manuals, histories, uniforms and equipment; and weapons from the Revolutionary War to the present, as well as historical documents including militia commissions, appointments, and land titles. The museum also has the Rhode Island Train of Artillery leather helmet worn by Captain-Lieutenant Carpenter who was killed at the Battle of Long Island on August 27, 1776.

The museum encourages school and organizational tours.

There is no gift shop or café but on Main Street there are many shops.

While You're in the Area

Nearby is the Varnum House Museum, built in 1773 by Revolutionary War general James Mitchell Varnum.

Wanton-Lyman-Hazard House

Newport Historical Society
17 Broadway
Newport, RI 02840
(401) 846-0813
www.newporthistorical.org

Overview

The Wanton-Lyman-Hazard House was built in 1675 and is the oldest remaining house in Newport (it was also the first to be restored). It is one of the4 finest examples of early colonial architecture in New England.

Directions and Hours

From the south, take I-95 to Route 138 east (exit 3). Follow the signs for the Jamestown and Newport Bridges. Take the first exit off the Newport Bridge, and turn right at the bottom of the ramp onto Farewell Street. Go through a set of traffic lights (you will pass between two cemetaries) and take a left onto Thames Street at the next set of lights. At the next stop sign take a left onto Marlborough Street, then take a right at the next stop sign onto Broadway. The Wanton-Lyman-Hazard House will be on your right.

From the north, take I-95 to Route 24 south. the exit appears about ½ mile beyond a short highway tunnel. Continue on Route 24 south to Route 114 south. This is called West Main Road in the towns of Portsmouth and Middlebury and becomes Broadway in Newport. You will be on Route 114 for 20-30 minutes. As you approach the end of Broadway, you will see the Wanton-Lyman-Hazard House on your left.

The museum has been closed for restoration, but will reopen in summer 2001. Call for days and hours.

Admission and Membership

Admission cost will be determined when the museum reopens. Call for information.

What to See

The house was owned by, among others, a famed Loyalist forced to flee before the American Revolution, a prosperous Quaker merchant, a Revolutionary War veteran, and several prominent Newport lawyers. The house grew with each generation of residents. Throughout its history, the Wanton-Lyman-Hazard House reflected the tastes and aspirations of a thriving seaport town. It is a truly vernacular house, with each modification based upon the background of the owner, the needs of his family, the simplicity of a Quaker dominated town, and the formal architectural influences of a commercial and cosmopolitan entrepot like Newport.

The Wanton-Lyman-Hazard House stood vacant from 1911 until 1927, when it was purchased by the Newport Historical Society. The early steeply pitched roof and plaster cornice still remain, as does the 1720s kitchen. An addition made in 1785 was removed, and the bedroom on the second floor was restored to its seventeenth century appearance. The house is fully furnished with period pieces, many made in Newport, and the colonial garden is currently undergoing restoration.

There is no gift shop or café.

While You're in the Area

Attractions and museums nearby include the Preservation Society of Newport County houses (p. 385), the Abraham Rodrigues Rivera House (p. 429), Belcourt Castle (p. 429), the Hammersmith Farm (p. 430), Kingscote (p. 410), the Artillery Company of Newport Military Museum (p. 380), Astor's Beechwood Mansion (p. 381), the Doll Museum (p. 395), and the International Tennis Hall of Fame Museum (p. 405).

The Warwick Museum of Art

3259 Post Road
Warwick, RI 02886
(401) 737-0010

Overview

The Warwick Museum of Art is a small museum that exhibits local and regional artists. Special programs include a concert series, summer camp, and art classes.

Directions and Hours

From the south, take I-95 north to exit 10. From the north, take I-95 south to exit 10A. The museum is just past Warwick City Hall.

The museum is open from September to June, and summer camp is held June, July, and August. The museum is handicap accessible.

Hours: Wednesday-Friday 4:00-8:00, Saturday-Sunday 1:00-3:00.

Admission and Membership

Admission is free. Membership is $20/year for individuals, $30/year for families, and $15/year for seniors. Discounts are available as well as scholarships for children.

What to See

In October the Warwick Museum of Art features the Rhode Island Open—a juried exhibit of

Rhode Island artists. In June, the museum hosts the Warwick schools art exhibit. The museum sponsors a spring concert series that features in 2001 the Real Jazz Octet on March 3, the New England Brass Guild on April 7, and the Jazz Brothers on May 5. Concerts start at 7:30 pm and admission is $15.

Children's programming includes many visual art classes.

There is a gift shop and visitors can eat at the Crows Nest restaurant on the water.

While You're in the Area

Attractions and museums nearby include Apponaug Village (p. 429), the John Waterman Arnold House (p. 430), and the Kentish Artillery Armory (p. 430).

Watson Farm (SPNEA)

455 North Road
Jamestown, RI 02835
(401) 423-0005
www.spnea.org

Overview

Before European settlement, Native Americans planted their crops of corn and beans on Conanicut Island overlooking Narragansett Bay. In 1789, Job Watson purchased a piece of this rich farmland, and for the next two centuries, five successive generations of the Watson family cultivated the land, changing their crops and practices as needed to adapt to the evolving market.

Directions and Hours

Take Route 138 east across the Jamestown Bridge then take the Helm Street exit. Turn right at the end of the bridge. At the second stop sign turn right onto North Road. The farm is .3 mile on ahead on the right.

From the Newport Bridge: Take the first exit then follow the signs to Jamestown. Turn right onto Narragansett Avenue then turn right again at the blinking light on North Road. The farm is 1.6 miles ahead on the left.

The museum is open June 1-October 15.

Hours: Tuesday, Thursday, and Sunday, 1:00 P.M. to 5:00 P.M. Tours are self-guided.

Admission and Membership

$4 for adults, $3.50 senior citizens, ½ off for students and children 6-12. Children 5 and under, SPNEA members, and residents of Jamestown are free. AAA members receive a 2 for 1 discount. SPNEA membership is $35/year for individuals and $45/year for a household. Membership includes free admissions to 35 properties and museums across New England.

What to See

Today, the property is still a working family farm. The farmers raise cattle and sheep for beef, lamb, and wool markets, grow acres of grass for winter hay supplies, make compost for fertilizer, and cultivate a large vegetable garden. The 1796 house, still used as the farmers' residence, is not open to the public. Visitors are welcome to explore the farmland on their own, following a self-guided walking tour. School programs and group tours are available by appointment.

Watson Farm offers group tours and special programs including tours on the wild plants and herbs in the area and water coloring in a natural setting. Please call or write for details. Also visit SPNEA's Casey Farm in Saunderstown, RI.

While You're in the Area

Nearby attractions include the Jamestown Windmill (p. 430), the Beavertail Lighthouse Museum (p. 429), the Fire Department Memorial Building (p. 429), and the Sydney L. Wright Museum (p. 431).

Westerly Armory

Railroad Avenue and Dixon Street
Westerly, RI 02891
(401) 596-8554
www.geocities.com/Heartland/9717

Overview

The Westerly Armory is one of the eighteen Historic Armories of Rhode Island. It is a proud example of late nineteenth and early twentieth century architecture designed by the well-known firm of William R. Walker & Son. Constructed in 1901-02 it was occupied by the National Guard until 1995. Before the Armory was vacated by the National Guard Westerly Armory Restoration, Inc. (WAR, Inc.) was created for the express purpose of restoring this old, but entirely utilitarian building. Subsequently, through the efforts of WAR, Inc., a substantial sum of money has been raised for this purpose. The Armory is currently rented for private and community events by contacting the Armory at (401) 596-8554. The Armory's drill shed (60' x 100') is a drawing card for community events.

Direction and Hours

From Interstate 95 north or south take exit 1. Follow RI Route 3 toward Westerly for approximately 4 miles to Railroad Avenue. (After bridge over RR tracks.) Turn right on Railroad Avenue for approximately 1/8 mile to Armory on left. A map is available on the website.

The Armory is not open on a regular basis. A tour may be arranged by calling the number above (normally weekday mornings are best). The restoration has allowed extensive use of the Armory by the Community for such affairs as First Night, Christmas parties, antiques shows, militaria shows, dances, and much more.

Admission and Membership

There is no admission charge, but donations are gratefully accepted. Membership criteria are being developed at the present time.

What to See

The Armory contains some memorabilia of local veterans including memorial boards of the 705th AAA and the 243rd Coast Artillery. Antique oil portraits of William R. Walker (architect) and his wife, Eliza hang in the staff room.

Every Wednesday evening, the Westerly Band rehearses at 7:00 upstairs in the Armory which is now their home. The Westerly Band is the oldest continuously playing non-military band in the country.

While You're in the Area

The Armory is close to downtown Westerly. The newly restored historic railroad station is within walking distance of the Armory as well as other quaint and interesting stores, shops, and restaurants in the historic district of Downtown Westerly. Wilcox Park, open to the public, is within walking distance and has lovely acreage including a fish pond and gazebo. Historic Watch Hill, part of Westerly, is 10 minutes away and boasts the earliest flying horse carousel in the nation as well as an assortment of wonderful beaches and boutiques.

Whitehall Museum House

311 Berkeley Avenue
Middletown, RI 02842
(401) 846-3116

Overview

The Whitehall Museum House is a memorial to philosopher Bishop George Berkeley. The museum, an unusual hip-roofed building with a long, sloping lean-to across the back, was Berkeley's residence from 1729-1731.

Directions and Hours

Take 138 south, and take a left onto Turner Road. Take a left onto Wyatt Road, then right onto Berkeley Avenue.

Or, take 114 south, and follow Miantinomi Avenue to Green End, then take a left onto Berkeley Avenue.

The museum is open from July 1-September 1 and by appointment, but only the first floor is handicap accessible.

Hours: Tuesday-Sunday 10:00-5:00.

Admission and Membership

$3 for adults, $1 for children. Membership is $10/year for individuals and $15/year for families.

Groups of ten or more receive a discount rate of $2 per person.

What to See

The main exhibit is furniture from the early part of the 1700s. The house is furnished to show Bishop Berkeley's life in America from 1729-1731. There is also a colonial garden designed and maintained by the Newport Garden Club.

There is no gift shop, but postcards are available. There is no café, but there are many places to eat in nearby Newport and Middletown.

While You're in the Area

Visitors can also see other museums and interesting attractions in Newport.

Wickford Art Association

36 Beach Street
North Kingstown, RI 02852-5745
(401) 294-6840
www.wickfordart.org

Overview

The Wickford Art Association is a 38-year-old association of artists with some 400 members. The Association proudly sponsors the Wickford Art Festival, ranked Number 1 in New England, which features 250 juried exhibitors from around the country. Membership is open to anyone interested in the arts.

WWA owns the Wickford Art Association Gallery, located in Wickford, RI, a quaint historic village. The gallery building has been in operation since 1990, and is host to approximately 24 shows per year, as well as numerous classes and community meetings.

Directions and Hours

From Providence and points north: Take Route 95 south to exit 9, Route 4 south. Follow 5 miles to Route 102 south, toward Wickford Center. Bear right at Center to Route 1A south. Follow 1A approximately ½ mile to the traffic light. Take a left onto Beach Street. The Gallery is on the right at the end of the street.

From Westerly and points south: Take Route 95 north to exit 5, Route 102/Exeter. Follow approximately nine miles to Wickford Center. Bear right at Center to Route 1A South. Follow 1A approximately ½ mile to the traffic light. Take a left onto Beach Street. The Gallery is on the right at the end of the street.

The Gallery is open the year around except from the Christmas holidays to the end of January. It is wheelchair accessible.

Hours: Tuesday through Saturday 11:00-3:00, and Sunday from noon-3:00; closed on Monday.

Admission and Membership

The gallery is free of charge. Membership is $ 35. To achieve artist member status a jurying proceduree is instituted.

What to See

The Gallery presents two-week member and open juried shows of fine art works by contemporary artists in a variety of media—oils, watercolors, pastels, printmaking, etc. Open juried shows are highly competitive.

Most second Tuesdays a lecture or demonstration is offered at a meeting that is open to the public.

The gallery is located next to the town beach and a picnic area is located across the street. Places to eat can be found in downtown Wickford five minutes away.

While You're in the Area

Historic Wickford Village is an interesting place to explore. Wickford Harbor and the adjacent marina are of interest to many visitors.

OTHER MUSEUMS IN RHODE ISLAND

Name	Phone	Town
Abraham Rodrigues Rivera House	401-849-8048	Newport
Apponaug Village	800-4WARWICK	Warwick
Armory of Mounted Commands	401-457-4351	Providence
American Diner Museum	401-331-8575 x102	Providence
Annmary Brown Memorial Library (Brown University)	401-863-1994	Providence
Audubon Society's Environmental Education Center	401-245-7500	Bristol
Babcock-Smith House	401-596-4424	Westerly
Barrington Preservation Museum	401-276-0999	Barrington
Bannister Gallery (RI College)	401-456-9765	Providence
Beavertail Lighthouse Museum	401-423-3270	Jamestown
Belcourt Castle	401-846-0420	Newport
Benefit Street Arsenal	401-246-0521	Barrington
Block Island Historical Society Museum	401-466-2481	Block Island
Bridgeton Car Barn	401-568-0247	Burrillville
Bristol Art Museum	401-254-3617	Bristol
Bristol Historical and Preservation Society Museum	401-253-7223	Bristol
Bristol Naval Reserve Armory	401-253-7000 x53	Bristol
Chase-Cory House	401-624-8881	Tiverton
Clemence-Irons House	617-277-3956	Johnston
Contintental Sloop *Providence*	401-274-7447	Providence
Cranston Historical Society	401-944-9226	Cranston
Cranston Volunteer Firefighters Museum	401-828-4333	Cranston
Crescent Park Carousel	401-435-7518	East Providence
Daggett House	401-333-1268	Pawtucket
Dame Farm	401-949-3657	Johnston
Eleazer Arnold House	617-227-3956	Lincoln
Fire Department Memorial Building	401-423-0062	Jamestown
Fireman's Museum	401-245-7600	Warren
Fort Barton	401-625-6700	Tiverton
General James Mitchess Varnum House Museum	401-884-1776	East Greenwich
General Nathaniel Greene Homestead	401-821-8630	Coventry

Gilbert Stuart Birthplace . . . . .401-294-3001 . . . . .Saunderstown
Glouster Light Infantry Armory . . . . .401-568-6421 . . . . .Chepachet
Greenwood Volunteer Fire Company & Museum . . . . .401-736-8412 . . . . . . .Greenwood
Hammersmith Farm . . . . .401-846-7346 . . . . .Newport
Hannaway Blacksmith Shop . . . . .401-333-1100 . . . . .Lincoln
Heritage Harbor Museum . . . . .401-331-8575 . . . . . . .Providence
Blackstone River State Park . . . . .401-334-7773 . . . . . . .Quinnville
Jamestown Windmill . . . . .401-423-7280 . . . . . . .Jamestown
John Armstrong Store Museum . . . . .401-568-4077 . . . . .Chepachit
John Carter Brown Library . . . . .401-863-2725 . . . . . . .Providence
John Hay Library (Brown University) . . . . .401-863-2414 . . . . . . .Providence
Johnson and Wales Culinary Archives and Museum . . . . . . .401-598-2805 . .South Providence
John Waterman Arnold House . . . . .401-467-7647 . . . . .Warwick
Joy Homestead . . . . .401-463-6168 . . . . .Cranston
Kentish Guards Armory . . . . .401-884-0305 . . . . . . .Greenwich
Library of Rhode Island History . . . . .401-331-8575 . . . . . . .Providence
Linden Place . . . . .401-253-0390 . . . . .Bristol
Lost Manissean Indian Exhibit . . . . .401-466-5060 . . . . . .Block Island
Kentish Artillery Armory . . . . .401-737-0010 . . . . .Warwick
Maxwell House . . . . .401-245-1315 . . . . .Warren
Museum of Natural History . . . . .401-785-9457 . . . . . . .Providence
Museum of Primitive Art and Culture . . . . .401-783-5711 . . .Peacedale Village
Museum of Yachting . . . . .401-847-1018 . . . . .Newport
New England Wireless and Steam Museum . . . . .401-885-0545 . . . .East Greenwich
Newport Armory . . . . .401-848-2398 . . . . .Newport
Newport Artillery Armory . . . . .401-364-6540 . . . . . .Charlestown
Nightingale Brown House . . . . .401-272-0357 . . . . . . .Providence
North Gate Museum . . . . .401-725-2847 . . . . .Lincoln
Old Colony House . . . . .401-846-2980 . . . . .Newport
Old School House . . . . .401-683-9178 . . . . . . .Portsmouth
Old Washington County Jail . . . . .401-783-1328 . . . . .Kingston
Paine House—Museum of the Western RI Civic Society . . . .401-397-5135 . . . . .Coventry
Pawtucket Armory . . . . .401-728-0500 . . . . .Pawtucket
Pawtuxet Rangers' Armory . . . . .401-781-3755 . . . . .Cranston
Portsmouth Historical Society Museum . . . . .401-638-9178 . . . . . . .Portsmouth
Prescott Farm (windmill) . . . . .401-847-6230 . . . . . .Middletown
Preservation Society of Newport County . . . . .401-847-1000 . . . . .Newport
Providence Armory . . . . .401-222-3521 . . . . . . .Providence
Providence Art Club Museum . . . . .401-331-1114 . . . . . . .Providence
Providence Athenaeum . . . . .401-421-6970 . . . . . . .Providence
Providence Preservation Society House . . . . .401-831-8583 . . . . . . .Providence
Quonset Air Museum . . . . .401-294-9540 . .North Kingstown
Redwood Library and Athenaeum .401-847-0292 . . . . .Newport
Rhode Island Black Heritage Society . . . . .401-751-3490 . . . . . . .Providence
Rhode Island Fisherman and Whale Museum . . . . .401-849-1340 . . . . .Newport

Rhode Island Foundation Art Gallery	401-274-4564	Providence
Rhode Island Holocaust Memorial Museum	401-453-7860	Providence
Rhode Island School of Design (RISD) Museum of Art	401-863-2932	Providence
Robbins Museum of Archaelogy	508-947-9005	Middleborough
Rodman Hall Armory, URI	401-874-2242	Kingston
Roger Williams Park Museum of Natural History	401-785-9450	Providence
Samuel Whitehorne House	401-847-2448	Newport
Slater Mill Gallery	401-725-8638	Pawtucket
Smith-Appleby House	401-949-4441	North Providence
Smith's Castle	401-294-3521	North Kingston
South County Museum	401-783-5400	Narragansett
Sydney L. Wright Museum	401-423-7280	Jamestown
Thames Science Center Museum	401-849-6966	Newport
Tomaquag Indian Memorial Museum	401-539-2786	Hope Valley
Touro Synagogue	401-849-7385	Newport
USS *Saratoga* Museum	401-831-8696	Providence
Warren Artillery Armory	401-245-1704	Warren
Warren Federal Blues' Armory	401-245-4376	Warren
Warren Fire Museum	401-245-3790	Warren
Watch Hill Lighthouse Museum and Coast Guard Station	401-789-4422	Watch Hill
Watson House	401-792-8296	Kingston
Western Hotel	401-568-6253	Burrillville
White Mill Park	401-568-4300	Pascoag
Wickford Historic Village	401-295-5566	South Kingston
Woods-Gerry Mansion	401-454-6141	Providence

VERMONT

American Museum of Fly Fishing

PO Box 42
Manchester, VT 05254
(802) 362-3300
www.amff.com

Overview

Founded in 1968, the American Museum of Fly Fishing has assembled the world's largest collection of fly fishing art and artifacts available to the public. The museum celebrates fly fishing in all of its dimensions: sport, history, ethics, philosophy, biology, art, craft, and literature.

Directions and Hours

From Albany, New York, and points south: Take NY7 (which becomes VT 9) to US7 in Bennington, Vermont. Take a left onto US7 in Bennington to historic US7A north. It is 16 miles to Manchester. The museum is 3 buildings north of the Equinox Hotel (on the left) at the intersection of US7A and Seminary Avenue.

The museum is open year round. It is handicap accessible.

Hours: Daily 10:00-4:00, except holidays.

Admission and Membership

Admission is $3 for adults; children under 12 and members are free. Membership starts at $35.

What to See

The American Museum of Fly Fishing maintains a program of permanent and traveling exhibits that present the fly fishing items of the famous and not-so-famous. These exhibits include a selection of the finest rods, reels, flies, and other equipment from the sport's master craftsmen and women, as well as the oldest documented flies known to exist.

A traveling exhibit, "Anglers All," will be touring the country for the next two to three years.

There is a gift shop. Visitors can eat at several Manchester-area restaurants. The Village Fare, Mulligan's, and the Marsh Tavern are all within walking distance of the museum.

While You're in the Area

The renowned Orvis Fly Fishing School is a half-mile from the museum, and the Southern Vermont Art Center is located nearby. In addition, Manchester has long been a mecca for outlet shoppers.

The Arlington Gallery Norman Rockwell Exhibition

Route 7A
Arlington, VT 05250
(802) 375-6423

Overview

Arlington, Vermont, was the hometown of Norman Rockwell from 1939 to 1953. The gallery features hundreds of examples of Rockwell's printed works. Some of the models for his work are gallery hosts.

Directions and Hours

The gallery is 15 minutes from Manchester and Bennington. It is located on historic route 7A.

The museum is open year round.

Hours: May to October, daily, 9:00-5:00; November to April, weekdays 10:00-4:00, weekends and holidays 10:00-5:00.

Admission and Membership

$2 per person.

What to See

The exhibition is housed in an historic 1875 church, which is listed on the National Register of Historic Places. A 15-minute film is shown continuously. Visitors can meet some of Rockwell's models, whom he described in his autobiography as "the sincere, honest, homespun types that I love to paint."

The gallery's gift shop offers prints, figurines, plates, and books. There is no café.

While You're in the Area

Visitors may also wish to see the nearby covered bridge green, with Rockwell's house in the background.

Barnet Historical Society

PO Box 26
Barnet, VT 05821
(802) 633-2310
www.barnetvermont.net

Overview

The Barnet Historical Society offers exhibits at two sites: the Goodwillie House, which is open several times each year, and at the Barnet Village School, open year-round as part of the town library. Barnet's daily life of the nineteenth and twentieth centuries is housed in the Goodwillie House, which probably sheltered African Americans headed north via the Underground Railroad.

Directions and Hours

To the Barnet Village School: From I-91 take exit 18. Turn east and then take the first left onto Church Street. The schoolhouse is on the right, one-tenth of a mile down the hill. Goodwillie House is 2.5 miles away in Barnet Center. Ask for directions when making appointments.

The Goodwillie house is open by appointment during warm weather only. The Barnet Village School is open year-round Wednesday, Thursday, and Saturday and is handicap accessible.

Admission and Membership

Admission is by donation. Membership is $5/year.

What to See

Barnet's history is tied to its river mills and its free-thinking residents. Visitors can view a croquet set produced by the Roy Brothers in East Barnet. Guests are encouraged to ask about Rogers's Rangers, who got lost in Barnet before Vermont was a state. You can also get directions to Ben Thresher's Mill, which is now undergoing restoration.

The Junior Historical Society brings a lively sense of local history alive in their work at the annual Vermont History Expo each June in Tunbridge.

The museum does not have a gift shop or café.

While You're in the Area

A museum nearby is the Fairbanks Museum and Planetarium (p. 445) in St. Johnsbury.

The Bennington Museum

West Main Street
Bennington, VT 05201
(802) 447-1571
www.benningtonmuseum.com

Overview

The Bennington Museum is a regional history

and art museum that traces its roots back to 1854, opening at its present location in 1928. Through objects and works of art made and used by early settlers visitors can experience the history of Vermont. Pottery, glass, and a furniture collection are among a few of the displays. The museum also has the largest collection of Grandma Moses paintings with her worktable, painting equipment, and awards.

Directions and Hours

The museum is located on West Main Street (Route 9), one mile west of the intersection of Route 7 and Route 9 in downtown Bennington, Vermont.

The museum is open daily from November 1 through May 31, 9:00 A.M.-5:00 P.M. and June 1-October 31, 9:00 A.M. to 6:00 P.M. Closed Thanksgiving Day, Christmas, and New Year's Day. It is handicap accessible. Tour programs operate year-round for bus groups and schools; special rates are available.

Admission and Membership

Admission $6 adults, $5 students/seniors, under 12 free. Special rates for families, seniors, groups, and buses. The museum is entirely handicapped accessible. Membership is $5/year for students, $30/year for individuals, $50/year for a family, $75/year for a contributing, and $150/year for a sustaining. Please contact the museum for other membership options.

What to See

The museum has the Grandma Moses Schoolhouse that she attended as a child (moved from East Bridge, NY), which displays her personal belongings, photographs, and other family memorabilia. Visitors can hear the story of the famous Battle of Bennington as well as view historical artifacts including the Bennington Battle flag, thought to be the oldest American flag in existence, along with uniforms, firearms, early tools, lighting devices, dolls, and toys. The museum also has a collection of American glass with over 5,000 samples of pressed and free-blown glass from the nineteenth and early twentieth century. There is a special exhibition gallery with changing exhibits. Also on display is the "wasp," a 1925 luxury touring car, American paintings and sculpture, American furniture, and a genealogy and local history library.

Photograph by Nicholas Whitman, courtesy of the Bennington Museum.

In May 2000 the museum opened a Bennington Pottery Gallery and Study Center which showcases a collection of ceramics produced in Bennington over the last two centuries.

The museum offerss the Hadwen Woods Nature Trail and the Pavilion, a covered outdoor picnic area.

Children's programming includes vacation fun shops for students with a variety of craft and hobby activities offered for students 4 and older and Summer History Camps with fun and educational children's programs on a variety of topics.

There is a gift shop.

While You're in the Area

Other museums and interesting attractions nearby include the Park McCullough House (p. 464), Hemmings Motor News, and Hildene (p. 452).

Bethel Historical Museum

Church Street
Bethel, VT 05032
(802) 234-5039

Overview

The Bethel Historical Museum is located on the upper floor of the 1816 Brick Church on the town green in the Bethel Historic District. The village developed around the mills along the Third Branch of the White River and was a prosperous nineteenth-century industrial and railroad center. Other significant buildings are an 1803 former inn, an 1805 brick meetinghouse, an 1846 Gothic Revival Christ Church, railroad buildings, late nineteenth-century commercial blocks and a 1906 beaux arts bank.

Directions and Hours

Take exit 3 from I-89 north or south. Go 3.2 miles from the exit on Route 12 north to Bethel Brick Church.

The museum is open July, August, and September. It is not handicap accessible.

Hours: second and fourth Sundays, 2:00-5:00.

Admission and Membership

Admission is free; donations are welcome. There are no memberships.

What to See

The museum features eighteenth- and nineteenth-century room vignettes in a keeping room and parlor; a collection of agricultural tools; children's toys; a small quilt collection; local documents, photographs, and paintings; and domestic artifacts, needlework and children's clothing.

Regular programs are offered throughout the year. Free fall foliage historic walks are available.

There is no gift shop, but the museum sells publications regarding Bethel history. Visitors can eat at Wilson's Diner and Eatons Sugar House in Bethel or Lupine's, Village Pizza, and the Three Stallion Inn in Randolph.

While You're in the Area

The Billings Farm and Museum (p. 435), Woodstock Historic Museum and District, Vermont Institute of Natural Science (p. 481), Rochester Historical Museum (p. 487), Royalton Historical Museum (p. 487), Randolph Historical Museum (p. 467), Joseph Smith Memorial in South Royalton, and the Plymouth Notch Historic District are some of the many attractions nearby.

Billings Farm & Museum

Route 12 & River Road
PO Box 489
Woodstock, VT 05091
(802) 457-2355
www.billingsfarm.org

Overview

The Billings Farm was established in 1871 by Frederick Billings, a native Vermonter who became known for his work as a lawyer, conservationist, pioneer in reforestation, scientific farm management, and as a railroad builder. Billings Farm & Museum is a premiere Jersey dairy farm that continues a century-long tradition of agricultural excellence. The farm offers active programs and historical exhibits that explore Vermont's rural heritage, engaging visitors in interactive learning that encourages an appreciation for agriculture and sustainable land use.

Directions and Hours

From Interstate 89: Take exit 1 (Woodstock/Quechee). Turn left onto Route 4 and follow for approximately 10 miles into Woodstock. Then follow Route 12 north ½ mile out of town.

The Billings Farm & Museum is open May 1 through October 31 10:00 A.M. to 5:00 P.M.; Thanksgiving weekend, December weekends, and December 26-31 10:00 A.M. to 4:00 P.M.; with Sleigh Ride Weekends on January 13-14 and February 17-19, 2002 10:00 A.M. to 3:00 P.M. The museum is handicap accessible.

Admission and Membership

Adults $8, Seniors $7, children 13-17 $6, children 5-12 $4, and kids 3-4 $1. Group tours (consisting of 10 or more people) are available with a reservation. The charge is $5 per person. Membership is $25/year for individuals, $45/year for families, $65/year to be a Friend, and $100/year to be a Supporter. Business memberships are also available.

What to See

The farm house examines the beginnings of the Billings Farm. The 1890 Farm House at Billings Farm was built as a multi-purpose addition to Frederick Billing's expanding farm operation and exemplifies the farm's role as a model dairy operation in Vermont and Frederick Billing's determination to apply progressive solutions to practical agricultural problems. Fully restored to its nineteenth century form, the house contains a business office for the farm manager, an apartment for the manager and his family, a creamery, and an adjoining ice house.

The museum's farm life exhibits depict the values and lives of Vermont farm families during a time when their way of life was threatened by shifts in the agricultural economy. Through self-guided tours of the horse barn, milk room, calf nursery, and dairy barn visitors and students to the farm are educated about daily life on this farm a century ago. A series of educational programs and activities featuring the livestock and farming operation are offered each day. Visitors can even stop in for the afternoon milking of the herd which begins at 3:00 P.M. and hear an explanation of the process of milk production.

Each season features an extensive schedule of special events—from the Plowing match in May to a monthlong Quilt Exhibition in August to Christmas at Billings Farm.

Many of the Billings Farm & Museum programs are geared toward a family audience of all ages. Special events always feature activities for children. Children's Day and Family Halloween are designed especially for children.

There is a museum shop that features an array of gifts and books relating to the themes of farming, rural life, and land stewardship. A Dairy Bar offers sandwiches, ice cream, drinks, and light snacks. There are also a number of restaurants in the Woodstock area.

While You're in the Area

Museums and attractions nearby include the March-Billings-Rockefeller National Historic Park, the Woodstock Historical Society, the Vermont Institute of Natural Science (p. 481), the President Coolidge Birthplace, Plymouth (p. 466), and the Montshire Museum of Science (p. 459).

Birds of Vermont Museum

900 Sherman Hollow Road
Huntington, VT 05462-9420
(802) 434-2167
www.ejhs.k12.vt.us/homepages/birds/index.html

Overview

The Birds of Vermont Museum offers a unique opportunity to observe birds that will not fly away! It is dedicated to promoting knowledge and appreciation of birds through the art of woodcarving.

Directions and Hours

The museum is eight miles from the Richmond exit (exit 11) off I-89, in the town of Huntington. At the stoplight in Richmond Village turn right (south) towards Huntington and follow the signs. Driving through Richmond, pass the Old Round Church, a historic landmark and unique 16-sided 1813 church. Cross the Huntington town line and turn right onto Sherman Hollow Road. Go one mile to the museum, ½ mile past the Audubon Nature Center.

The museum is open May 1- October 31. It is open November 1-April 30 by appointment only. The museum is handicap accessible.

Hours: Daily 10:00 4:00.

Admission and Membership

Adults $4, seniors $3, children 3-11 $2. Group Rates: adult $3.50, senior $2.50, children $1.50. AAA sanctioned and reduced rates. Memberships are $15/year for individuals and $25/year for families.

What to See

The museum features more than 440 life-size, biologically accurate carvings of over 200 species, including most of Vermont's nesting birds in natural habitat displays with actual nests and wooden eggs. There is a gallery of extinct and endangered birds of North America, tropical birds, a display of raptors, and Winter Birds and Wetland Dioramas, all done by Bob Spear, one of Vermont's leading naturalists. Live birds at the many feeders in the garden can be viewed through a one-way window. There are several nature trails to the pond and butterfly garden, as well as in the woods. Binoculars are available.

There is an annual celebration on Migratory Bird Day, the second Saturday in May, from 10:00 to 4:00. Activities include guided bird walks, bird banding, lectures, a live bird program with rehabilitated birds, binoculars and scopes for sale, bird feed and feeders on display, and woodcarving demonstrations.

The museum has a gift shop with bird related items (books, t-shirts, binoculars). There are four eating places in nearby Richmond, and there are outdoor tables at the museum for picnics.

While You're in the Area

The museum is half a mile from the Green Mountain Audobon Nature Center.

Brattleboro Historical Society, Inc.

PO Box 6392
Brattleboro, VT 05302
(802) 258-4957

Overview

The Brattleboro Historical Society, Inc., owns a collection of Estey organs, the manufacturer of which was a major local employer at the turn of the century. The society is a repository for all local artifacts and information for the town of Brattleboro.

Directions and Hours

From I-91 north from Massachusetts, take exit 2 and turn left onto Western Avenue. Proceed east approximately one mile and bear left at the fork. Proceed approximately 1.5 miles; turn left onto Oak Street. Take the next right onto Grove Street and look for the police sign. The museum is on the third floor of the municipal building.

The museum is open year round. It is handicap accessible.

Hours: Thursday 1:00-4:00, Saturday 9:00-12:00.

Admission and Membership

Admission to the museum is free. Membership is $5/year.

What to See

There are more than 40 Estey organs in the Historical Society's collection.

There is no gift shop but gift items are available. There are several restaurants in the area.

While You're in the Area

The Windham County Historical Society in Newfane, Vermont (p. 453), is nearby.

Brattleboro Museum and Art Center

10 Vernon Street
Brattleboro, VT 05301-3390
(802) 257-0124
www.brattleboromuseum.org

Overview

The Brattleboro Museum and Art Center (BMAC) is housed in Union Station, a renovated former railroad station which is a landmark building on the National Register of Historic Places. BMAC is a non-collecting institution, producing frequently changing contemporary and historic art and humanities exhibitions, as well as extensive educational activities and programs. An annual theme links together all of the museum activities providing innovative and timely parameters for interdisciplinary discourse.

Directions and Hours

From Interstate 91, take exit 1 in Brattleboro. Travel north on Route 5. The museum is located at the intersection of Routes 5, 142, and 119.

BMAC is open from mid-May until early November. The galleries are wheelchair accessible.

Hours: Tuesday through Sunday, 12:00-6:00, closed major holidays.

Admission and Membership

Admission for adults is $3, seniors $2, college students $2, and children 18 and under are free. Members receive free admission during normal gallery hours, and reduced or free admission to museum programs. Individual membership is $30/year, Family $50/year, and Senior $20/year. Members of Consortium of New England Community Art Museums member museums receive free admission.

What to See

Each season, the Museum offers 10 to 12 exhibits based on an annual theme. The museum houses a permanent exhibit (maintained by the Brattleboro Historical Society) of Estey Organs, reed organs manufactured in Brattleboro. BMAC presents many evening lectures and programs related to the annual exhibit theme, as well as weekend family festivals and special events, throughout the season.

While You're in the Area

The Museum is located in lively downtown Brattleboro, Vermont, rich in natural and cultural sites of interest. Restaurants, cafes, coffee shops, art galleries, and boutiques abound in the downtown area.

Bread & Puppet Museum

753 Heights Road (Route 122)
Glover, VT 05839
(802) 525-3031/(802) 525-6972

Overview

The Bread & Puppet Museum is housed in a 150-year-old, 100-foot-long dairy barn. It features one of the biggest collections of some of the largest puppets in the world. Puppets range in size from tiny cardboard cutouts to towering 18-foot giants. Masks, graphics, and paintings also recreate scenes from Bread & Puppet Theater shows from the early 1960s to present day.

Directions and Hours

The museum is near I-91 exits 24 and 25. Follow Route 16 to Route 122, just south of Glover.

The museum is open from June 1-November 1 and by appointment. It is not handicap accessible.

Hours: Daily, 10:00-6:00.

Admission and Membership

Admission is free; donations are appreciated. Tours can be arranged for a moderate fee.

What to See

Entrance level exhibits include the "Kitchen of the Washerwomen," featuring life-size puppets hard at work in a cluttered, old-fashioned kitchen; a scene from "Ah! Or the First Washerwoman Cantata," with larger-than-life royal family and demon; and a scene from "The White Horse Butcher," with a crowd of white-masked suited men and dogs capturing the White Horse.

Upstairs, visitors can view the flaming red "Birdcatcher in Hell" exhibit, with huge demons, birds, and a gigantic head of Yama, the King of Hell; a crowd of 15-foot-tall Garbagemen and Washerwomen; The Last Supper scene, with over-lifesize puppets that were used in many political demonstrations; and the 18-foot papier mache head of Mother Earth.

"The Last Supper," Puppets made 1964-66, Bread & Puppet Museum. Photo by Alex Williams.

Starting in mid-July and running through August, the museum hosts outdoor and indoor shows with puppets and masked performers every Sunday afternoon. A Sunday afternoon puppet circus for children also runs from mid-July to August.

A gift shop sells posters, handprinted banners and graphics, postcards, and many publications. There is no café, but visitors can eat in Barton, Hardwick, Newport, and Lydonville, all 20-30 minutes drive away.

While You're in the Area

The Old Stone House in Brownington (near Orleans), the Fairbanks Museum (p. 445), and the St. Johnsbury Athenaeum (p. 471) are other local attractions.

Cabot Creamery

Visitors Center
Main Street
Cabot, VT 05647
(800) 837-4261
www.cabotcheese.com

Overview

Cabot Creamery began in 1919, when a few farm families started the Cabot Creamery for $5 per cow. Cabot Creamery has been dairy farmer owned since 1919. Visitors can see where the taste of Cabot begins as they view a video and tour the creamery plant and see the process of cheese making.

Directions and Hours

From I-89: Take exit 8 at Montpelier (Route 2 east). At Marshfield go left on Route 215. It is then five miles to Cabot Village.

From I-91: Take exit 21 at St. Johnsbury to Route 2 west. At Marshfield go right on Route 215. It is then five miles to Cabot Village.

The museum is open from February through December. Closed in January. It is handicap accessible.

Hours: June-October: 9:00 A.M. to 5:00 P.M. Open daily. November-May: Monday-Saturday 9:00 A.M. to 4:00 P.M.

Admission and Membership

$1 per person, children under 12 free.

What to See

Free tours are offered for educational groups. Free yogurt is given to school groups. Cabot Creamery offers a sample table where visitors can taste all Cabot's cheeses, dips, and other Vermont specialty foods.

Guests can nibble their way through the gift shop. Visitors can eat at Rainbow Sweets in Marshfield or restaurants in Montpelier or St. Johnsbury.

While You're in the Area

Other museums and interesting attractions nearby include the Fairbanks Museum and Planetarium (p. 445), Maple Grove, and the Vermont Historical Society in Montpelier Pavilion (p. 478).

Camp Meade

961 U.S. Route 2
Middlesex, VT 05602
(802) 223-5537
www.campmeade.com

Overview

This former CCC Camp allows visitors to step back in time to the 1930s and 1940s. Camp Meade offers more than 25 professional indoor and outdoor exhibits that present an extensive collection of artifacts, photographs, videos, audio recordings, and lifelike displays. All generations can learn how this country struggled through the breadlines of the Great Depression to the assembly lines, ration lines, and the frontlines of World War II.

Directions and Hours

From I-89: The museum is immediately off exit 9 from I-89 on Route 2. It is five miles west of Montpelier.

The museum is open from May through mid-October and is handicap accessible.

Hours: 9:00 A.M.-4:30 P.M. Monday-Saturday.

Admission and Membership

$5 per person. $4.50 for senior citizens. $12 for a family of 4. Special discounts are available for groups. Camp Meade offers overnight lodging with 19 cabins. Cabin rates begin at $48 a night.

What to See

Camp Meade offers a variety of historical objects: World War II vehicles, a 1942 Stuart Tank, jeeps, a 1942 Ambulance, a halftrack, a weasel, an ATII Airplane from 1942, a Korean F-86 airplane, and a Vietnam helicopter. Camp Meade also has a research library.

There is a museum store and a Camp PX. Visitors can eat in nearby Montpelier and Waterbury.

While You're in the Area

Other museums and interesting attractions nearby include Ben and Jerry's factory, Green Mountain Coffee Roasters, a chocolate factory, and Cold Hollow Cider Mill (p. 486).

Cavendish Historical Society Museum

Main Street, Route 131
Cavendish, VT 05142

Overview

The Cavendish Historical Society collects items related to the town of Cavendish. There are photographs, ephemera, news articles, and other artifacts.

Directions and Hours

Take 91 to Route 8, then take Route 131 to Cavendish.

Or, take 103 to Proctorsville and onto 131. Continue to Cavendish.

The museum is open from the last Sunday in June to the second Sunday in October.

Hours: Sunday 2:00-4:00.

Admission and Membership

Admission to the museum is free. Membership is $5/year for individuals and $8/year for families.

What to See

In addition the artifacts of the town, the museum holds an annual flea market on the Saturday before the Fourth of July. The Historical Society meets on the fourth Monday from May through October.

There is no gift shop. There is no café, but there are sandwich shops nearby.

While You're in the Area

Black River Academy Museum and President Calvin Coolidge's Homestead (p. 466) are also in the area.

Chaffee Center for the Visual Arts

61 South Main Street (Rt. 7)
Rutland, VT 05701
(802) 775-0356

Overview

The Chaffee Center for the Visual Arts is located in a stately Queen Anne Victorian, which is listed on the National and State Registers of Historic Places. It features regular exhibitions and the work of over 200 Vermont artists

Directions and Hours

The Chaffee Center is located on Route 7 in Rutland.

The center is open year round, and is partially handicap accessible.

Hours: Monday-Saturday 10:00-5:00, Sunday 12:00-4:00.

Admission and Membership

Suggested donation is $2 per person. Membership is $30/year for individuals and $45/year for families.

What to See

The Chaffee Center presents 10 featured exhibitions annually. It also features a juried artist membership of over 200 Vermont artists whose work can be viewed year round in the upstairs members galleries. Art classes are available for children.

There is no gift shop or café. Visitors can eat nearby in downtown Rutland.

While You're in the Area

Killington Ski Resort is a nearby local attraction.

Charleston Historical

Museum Drive
West Charleston, VT 05872
(802) 723-4833

Overview

Charleston Historical is housed in an old village schoolhouse built in the 1850s.

Directions and Hours

Charleston Historical is located off Route 105 in West Charleston Village.

It is open June-October and is not handicap accessible.

Hours: Wednesdays 2:00-4:00 P.M. or by appointment. Call (802) 895-4329 or the number listed above.

Admission and Membership

There is no cost for admission. Membership is $3/year for an individual, $7/year for a family, anything over $7 for a contributing membership,

Charleston Academy circa 1857. Photo courtesy of the late Mable Bowen Davis.

and $100 for a life membership.

What to See

Charleston Historical contains a lot of Charleston history going back to its founding in 1803.

Children's programming includes school tours.

There is no gift shop or café but a nearby store has a deli.

While You're in the Area

Other places of interest nearby include Newport and Brownington.

Chimney Point State Historic Site

7305 Vermont Route 125
Addison, VT 05491
(802) 759-2412
www.HistoricVermont.org

Overview

The museum at Chimney Point State Historic Site interprets both the Native American heritage and the French heritage of present-day Vermont. Native Americans camped at the site on Lake Champlain long before the French started a settlement there in 1731.

Directions and Hours

From northern and eastern Vermont: Take Route 7 south to Route 22A. In Addison turn onto Route 17 west. The museum is located on the left immediately before the Lake Champlain Bridge.

From southern Vermont: Take Route 30 or Route 22A north to Route 125 west. Take the left turn immediately before the Lake Champlain Bridge.

From New York State: Cross the Lake Champlain Bridge, which is 4 miles east of Route 9 north and 22. Take the first right immediately after crossing the bridge.

The museum is open from late May through mid-October. The museum is handicap accessible for the downstairs galleries and the restrooms. The upstairs gallery, however, is not handicap accessible.

Hours: 9:30 A.M. to 5:00 P.M. Wednesday through Sunday.

Admission and Membership

Adults $2, children under 15 free. School groups are free. Tour/bus groups are $1.50 per person.

What to See

The museum building dates from the 1780s and contains a period taproom, a post office, a collection of Native American stone tools, and galleries containing Native American and French exhibits. Today the eighteenth century tavern houses an interpretive exhibit of 8,000 years of Native American history. To provide an overview of the Native American and French settlement of the Champlain Valley the museum uses artifacts and an audio-visual component. The exhibit begins with the earliest archaeological evidence and concludes with a look at contemporary issues and cultural traditions. There is also a restored nineteenth century tavern, once visited by Thomas Jefferson and James Madison, and a 1920s Post Office.

Every summer there is a temporary exhibit which alternates between French and Native American topics. Each September the museum hosts an Atlatl Championship. (The atlatl is a Native American spear-throwing tool.) The public is welcome to watch or participate in the event.

The museum offers school programs based on archaeology and Native American stone tools.

There is a gift shop. Visitors can eat at the Bridge Restaurant, located across the street.

While You're in the Area

Other interesting places to visit while you are in the area are: the Lake Champlain Maritime Museum (p. 486), DAR State Park and Campground, and Crown Point State Park.

Corinth Historical Society Museum at the Corinth Academy

Cookeville
Corinth, VT 05039
(802) 685-3812

Overview

The Corinth Historical Society Museum focuses on the history of the town of Corinth.

Directions and Hours

Take I-91 to Route 25. Head west to the bridge and follow the sign to Cookeville (Cookeville Road). Continue on that road into Cookeville. Turn right at the village green.

The museum is open in July and August. It is handicap accessible.

Hours: Saturday 10:00-12:00.

Admission and Membership

Admission to the museum is free. Membership is $3/year for individuals and $5/year for families.

What to See

The Corinth Historical Society Museum features relics from Corinth's past, such as artifacts from the Corinth bobbin mills, Walt Colby glass plate negatives, and material by Eleanor Porter, author of *Pollyanna* and other beloved children's books.

There is a gift shop, and visitors can eat at local establishments nearby.

While You're in the Area

Nearby attractions include the Porter Music Box

Museums in the Champlain Valley

For centuries, Lake Champlain was an important highway for Native Americans, and later, for European settlers. During the Revolutionary War, Continental Soldiers used the old forts at Crown Point and Ticonderoga, and a new fortress at Mount Independence, to defend against a British Invasion from Canada. In the summer of 1777, the Continental Army retreated from the forts, but faced the British at the Battle of Hubbardton and the Battle of Bennington. Today, visitors can trace the movement of the armies through the Champlain Valley. There are museums at Crown Point and Fort Ticonderoga in New York. In Vermont, a visit to Mount Independence (p. 459), the Hubbardton Battlefield (p. 454), and the Bennington Battle Monument help tell the story of the Burgoyne's Campaign before the defeat of the British Army at the Battle of Saratoga. In addition to the war sites, the Lake Champlain Maritime Museum also interprets the Revolutionary War in the Champlain Valley.

Museum (p. 466) and the Randolph Historical Museum (p. 467).

Cousteau Museum

Harveys Lake Cabins and Campground
190 Campers Lane
West Barnet, VT 05821
(802) 633-2213
www.harveyslakecabins.com

Overview

Jacques Cousteau, as a young boy, first learned how to dive in Harveys Lake while attending summer camp. The Cousteau Museum is still evolving and is currently a collection of pictures, stories, and memorabilia located in a scenic environment along the lake.

Directions and Hours

From I-91: take exit 18 (Barnet/Peacham). Go west for five miles to the village of West Barnet. Go over the bridge next to a white church. Take the first dirt road on the right. Go to the end of the road and to the large gray house.

The campground is open May 15-October 15. The Cousteau Museum will be open in the Spring of 2004.

Admission and Membership

The museum is not fully up and running at present; please call for admission costs and membership information.

What to See

Harvey's Lake Cabins and Campground is the oldest private campground in Vermont. There are 11 lakefront cabins fully furnished with antiques, along with campsites with W/E/S for RV, popups, and tents.

There is a gift shop. Visitors can eat local take out, and general stores and restaurants are located 9-12 miles away.

While You're in the Area

Other museums and interesting attractions nearby are the Barnet Historical Society (p. 433) and the Fairbanks Museum (p. 445).

East Poultney Green

Poultney , VT 05764
(802) 287-5268
www.rootsweb.com/~vtphs

Overview

Union Academy (ca. 1791), the Melodeon Factory (ca. 1830), and the East Poultney Schoolhouse (ca. 1896) is a cluster of three buildings on the East Poultney Green. Other historic structures, such as an 1806 church, pre-1830 houses, the Horace Greeley print shop, and the Eagle Tavern (a haunt of Ethan Allen and his brothers) are within walking distance.

Directions and Hours

Take Route 30 to Poultney and Route 140 to East Poultney and the town green. From Route 4, head south on 30. From Route 7, head north on 30.

The museum is open June through August, daily 1:00-4:00 or by appointment. The museum is not handicap accessible

Admission and Membership

Admission is free. Membership is $5 a year.

What to See

Union Academy and the 1791 schoolhouse are restored structures. Restored melodeons are demonstrated as well as exhibited in the Melodeon Factory. A large collection of period clothing as well as Poultney artifacts including agricultural and industrial exhibits are featured as well.

Every August the buildings are opened as part of the East Poultney Day celebration. Exhibits, antiques, and collectible vendors are featured on the green.

There is no gift shop. Visitors can eat at the East Poultney store or in downtown Poultney.

While You're in the Area

Other local attractions are the Slate Museum in Granville, New York and the Hubbarton Battlefield (p. 454), which is the only Revolutionary War battlefield in Vermont.

Enosburgh Museum

55 Railroad Street
Enosburgh Falls, VT 05450
(802) 933-2102 or (802) 933-4403

Overview

The Enosburgh Museum is located in the old Freight Depot in the center of Enosburgh Falls, which was a center of activity in the late 1800s and early 1900s. The museum is located near the Opera House, Quincy Hotel (now the Somerset Inn), and passenger depot. The museum has a nice collection of Enosburgh-related items. Nearby is an old caboose from the Central Vermont Railway that houses area railroad memorabilia. Both are located on the Missisquoi Valley Rail Trail .

Directions and Hours

From Route 105 in Enosburg Falls, take a right onto Depot Street then a right onto Archambault Street and an immediate left onto Railroad Street.

Coming from the east on Route 105 take a left onto Pleasant Street and a right onto Railroad Street. The museum is a green building with yellow trim.

The museum is open from the first Saturday in June through the first Saturday in October. It is handicap accessible.

Hours: Saturdays 1:00-4:00.

Admission and Membership

Admission is free. Membership is $20 for five years or $5/year.

What to See

The museum features a bottle collection and other items from the several medicine manufacturers located here at the turn of the twentieth century, the most famous being the Dr. B. J. Kendall Company and Kimball Bros. The museum also has a large collection of doctor's instruments from early doctors in the area. The countryside surrounding Enosburgh is famous for its beautiful farms.

The Enosburgh Historical Society and the Enosburgh Business Association sponsor Enosburgh History Alive Day and Applefest on the first Saturday in October. This day features Enosburgh's historic past, old time ways and games, an outdoor farmer's market, and music. On the first Saturday in June, Enosburgh hosts the Annual Vermont Dairy Festival featuring almost anything dairy.

Abe's Cabin, a log cabin with period furnishings, is located near Lincoln Park and is part of the Enosburgh Museum. It is open Wednesday evenings from 8:00-9:00 during the summer on band concert nights in the park. It is also open on special occasions, such as for the Dairy Festival and History Alive Day.

There is no gift shop, but the museum does sell Enosburgh-related gifts. Visitors can dine at several eateries nearby.

While You're in the Area

The Bridge of Flowers and Light is an arch cement bridge recently restored for pedestrian use. It spans the Missisquoi River near the falls.

Fairbanks Museum and Planetarium

1302 Main Street
St. Johnsbury, VT 05819-2248
(802) 748-2372
www.fairbanksmuseum.org

Overview

The Fairbanks Museum and Planetarium is

northern New England's premiere museum of natural history. St. Johnsbury industrialist Franklin Fairbanks, a lifelong amateur naturalist who collected examples of nature's artistry and diversity throughout the world, founded the museum in 1889. When his collection grew too large for his home, Fairbanks commissioned architect Lambert Packard to design the museum in which to make his collections available for display and study. Today, the museum's mission remains to "stimulate understanding of the natural and human environments and their interrelationships, through programs, exhibits, services, and collections."

Directions and Hours

From Boston, Concord, New Hampshire, and the White Mountains: Take I-93 to its end point at I-91. Take I-91 north to exit 20. Bear right onto US 5 north. Take the first left turn and proceed up the hill to St. Johnsbury Academy. Proceed two blocks. The museum is on the right.

Photo courtesy of the Fairbanks Museum and Planetarium.

From Hartford, Springfield, and southern Vermont: Take I-89 south from Burlington to the Montpelier exit. Take US 2 east for 40 miles to St. Johnsbury. Bear left at St. Johnsbury Academy. Proceed two blocks. The museum is on the right.

From the north (Newport, Vermont, and Quebec): Take I-91 south to Exit 21. Turn right at the end of the exit ramp onto US 2 east. Take US 2 one mile into St. Johnsbury. Bear left at St. Johnsbury Academy. Proceed two blocks. The museum is on the right.

From the east (Lancaster, New Hampshire, and Maine): Take US 2 west into St. Johnsbury. Turn right at Dunkin Donuts. Take the first left (Maple Street) up the hill to Main Street. Turn left and proceed one block. The museum is on the left.

The museum is open year-round. Planetarium shows are presented from January through June and September through December. The museum's main floor exhibits, gift shop, and lecture room are all wheelchair accessible. Handicapped parking spaces are available directly behind the museum.

Hours: Museum: Monday-Saturday (9:00 A.M. to 5:00 P.M.) and Sunday 1:00-5:00 P.M. Planetarium: Saturdays and Sundays at 1:30 P.M. During July and August planetarium shows are presented at 11:00 A.M. Monday through Friday and every day at 1:30 P.M.

Admission and Membership

Adults $5, ages 5-17 $3, seniors $4, families $12 for up to 3 adults and any number of children in the immediate family. Planetarium shows are $3. Membership is $30/year for individuals and $40/year for families.

What to See

Visitors can explore 18,000 square feet of exhibits and collections including: natural science, rural history, astronomy, cultures from Vermont and around the world, collections of northern New England's bird and wildlife, and a array of large mounted animals. The museum also features a Northern New England Weather Center, a children's nature center with live animals and themed exhibits in July and August, and an exhibition hall that blends the flavor of the nineteenth century with twenty-first century programs and services.

There is a small museum gift shop. There are several restaurants nearby as well as a park for picnics.

While You're in the Area

Barnet Historical Society (p. 433), Cabot Creamery (p. 439), the Old Stone House Museum (463), and Peacham Historical House (465) are all nearby.

Fairfax Historical Society Museum

1181 Main St.
PO Box 145
Farifax, VT 05454
(802) 849-6638
www.geocities.com/Heartland/farm/9445/index.html

Overview

The Fairfax Historical Society Museum building, built in 1807, is one of the oldest in Fairfax. It was once the town hall, a one-room schoolhouse, and most recently, a casket showroom for the Hayes-Rich Funeral Home.

Directions and Hours

From I-89, get off at exit 18. Go south on Route 7 for 100-200 yards then take a left onto Route 104A. Take 104A all the way to Route 104 and then take a right and go east on 104. The museum is located in Fairfax Village on the left across the street from Ross's Auto Repair.

From Stowe/Smugglers Notch: take Route 15 to Route 104 then go into Fairfax Village. The museum is located on the right.

Open July and August on Sundays, 2:00-4:00 and by appointment. The museum also has opening hours on the last two Sundays in September and the first two Sundays in October, 2:00-4:00. Handicap accessible.

Admission and Membership

There is no admission but donations are accepted. Annual membership: $2/single, $5/family, and $100/lifetime.

What to See

The Fairfax Historical Society has the front counter woodwork from the old Fairfax post office and a lot of yearbooks from Bellows Free Academy in Fairfax, and the former New Hampton Institute. The collection includes old scrapbooks, photos, and everyday household items used throughout the years as well as items from former businesses and some military objects.

The historical society also gives presentations for students of all grades. The quarterly meetings have a program dealing with Fairfax and Vermont history. There are also some items for purchase at the museum.

There is no café but there are several nearby restaurants including the Foothills Bakery in

Fairfax Historical Society Museum. Photo by Michael Cain.

Fairfax Village and the Country Pantry outside the village. Local stores also have deli counters.

While You're in the Area

Local sites include the St. Albans Historical Museum (p. 469) and the birthplace of Chester A. Arthur (p. 486) in Fairfield.

The Garipay House

Hartford Historical Society
1461 Maple Street
PO Box 547
Hartford, VT 05047-0547
(802) 296-3132

Overview

The Hartford Historical Society's museum consists of an expanding collection of memorabilia from the town's past displayed in the former home of a local doctor, whose office is also open as an exhibit.

Directions and Hours

From I-91 north take the White River Junction exit 11 and head north on Route 5. The second light turn left, crossing the White River. Turn left at the next light onto Route 14 west. Proceed 1 mile. The Garipay House is on the right immediately before the Foodstop and across from the bridge.

From I-91 south, take the Wilder exit 12. Turn right onto Route 5. Turn right onto Route 5 south. At the stoplight turn right. Proceed 1 mile. The Garipay House is on the right immediately before the Foodstop and across from the bridge.

The museum is open year round except for the month of January. It is not currently handicap accessible.

Hours: The first Sunday of each month, 1:30-4:00; the first Tuesday, 6:00-8:00; or by appointment.

Admission and Membership

Admission to the museum is by donation. Membership ranges from $10/year for seniors to $25/year for commercial/institutional.

What to See

At one time the Town of Hartford had the largest railroad station in New England. The town was chartered in 1761 and has been an important transportation link since that time, including river travel, railroads, and now the junction of two major interstate highways. The museum reflects the town's nature as a historic crossroads.

There is a small gift shop. There are many eating establishments in the area, ranging from fast food to fine dining.

While You're in the Area

Quechee Gorge, the Grand Canyon of Vermont, is surrounded by a state park. Nearby White River Junction has an active railroad depot and a historic engine, coal car, and caboose on display.

Grafton Historical Society

PO Box 202
Grafton, VT 05146
(802) 843-2584

Overview

The Grafton Historical Society Museum exhibits a wide variety of local artifacts, memorabilia, and photographs presented in thematic displays changed annually.

Directions and Hours

Take Route 91 north or south to the Bellows Falls, Vermont exit. Follow Route 21 west to Grafton. The museum is in the center of town on Main Street.

The museum is open from Memorial Day to Columbus Day or by appointment by calling (802) 843-1010. It is not handicap accessible.

Hours: Saturday, Sunday, and holidays, 10:00-12:00 and 2:00-4:00.

Admission and Membership

$3 per person; children under 12 are free. Membership is $5/year for singles, $10/year for families, and $25/year for contributing.

What to See

The museum's collection of soapstone artifacts is considered one of the finest in the state. Other artifacts include writing implements, pens, inkwells, blotters, and slates as well as farm tools and household implements. Textiles such as quilts, samplers, lace, embroidery, and costumes are also displayed. The museum also features the town's new history: "Five Dollars and a Jug of Rum, a History of Grafton, Vermont, 1754-2000."

There is no gift shop or café. The Daniels Café is right around the corner from the museum and the Old Tavern, a 200-year-old inn, serves lunch.

While You're in the Area

The Nature Museum at Grafton (p. 486) is a small museum of natural history that visitors can also see in the area.

Green Mountain Perkins Academy and Historical Association

PO Box 147
South Woodstock, VT 05071
(802) 457-1481

Overview

The Green Mountain Perkins Academy is a well preserved three-story, eleven-room school building built in 1848 for educating scholars after grammar school. The building features original wooden desks in the study hall as well as literature, maps, and local artifacts of the period.

Directions and Hours

Take I-89 or 91 to White River Junction. Follow Route 4 for 14 miles to Woodstock, Vermont, then head south on Rt. 106. Go 5 miles to the small village of South Woodstock. Look for the sign in view of the post office by the old brick

Historic Grafton Village

In Grafton, visitors won't find factory outlets, big souvenir stores, or even a lot of paved roads. What they will find is a lovingly restored nineteenth century village, along with miles of woodland trails for walking, biking, and skiing. The village is composed of about 40 buildings, most of them constructed in the early 1800s. Of note are the two churches, one clapboard and one brick with outstanding examples of steeples and windows. The purity of the village architecture has been preserved with great care.

Settled in 1780, Grafton grew quickly and its inhabitants prospered through the nineteenth century. By 1850, over 10,000 sheep drifted through its meadows while farming, milling, and soapstone quarrying occupied the locals. The unspoiled homes in this tiny village include some of the finest examples of eighteenth and nineteenth century architecture in Vermont. The Windham Foundation (a private, nonprofit foundation) is committed to preserving rural Vermont, particularly the restoration and maintenance of many of the historic buildings of Grafton—including the Old Tavern, an inn which has been providing gracious hospitality for 200 years.

Today, visitors may learn about the plant and wild life of the area by visiting The Nature Museum (p. 486) or stop by the Grafton History Museum (p. 448) to enjoy an intimate glimpse of life in Grafton during the last 200 years. Walking tours are available through the Information Center or the Historical Society. Call 802-843-2489 or 802-843-1010.

Green Mountain Perkins Academy. Photo by Fred C. Clark Jr.

Grange Hall. The Academy is across the brook on the hill edge of the school yard.

The Academy is open July and August. It is not handicap accessible.

Hours: Saturday 2:00-5:00; Saturday-Monday on Labor Day Weekend.

Admission and Membership

Admission is by donation of $2 per person.

What to See

The Academy building and furniture were built by local craftsmen. The collection includes many maps of the period, and the history of some of the students. The historical association hosts tours for local fourth grade classes and other school groups by appointment.

There is no gift shop or café. Visitors can eat across the street in South Woodstock Village's Country Store and Deli by the post office.

While You're in the Area

The Woodstock Historical Society and the Dana House on Elm Street in Woodstock are other local attractions.

Greensboro Historical Society

Breezy Avenue
Greensboro, VT 05841

Overview

Each summer the Greensboro Historical Society prepares a different exhibit on some aspect of local history.

Directions and Hours

Take exit 21 off I-91 in St. Johnsbury. Follow Route 2W to W. Danville. Take Route 15 to Route 16N. Follow for about a mile. Take a left at the sign to Greensboro (Caspian Lake). At intersection, take a right toward the village. The historical society is at the center of town on the right.

The museum is open July 1-Labor Day. It is handicap accessible.

Hours: Tuesday through Thursday 10:00-1:00, Saturday 10:00-12:00.

Admission and Membership

Admission to the museum is free. Membership is $5/year.

What to See

The historical society has special programs, but they are not museum-focused. Children's programming is available.

There is no gift shop. Visitors can eat at Lakeview Inn or Highland Lodge.

While You're in the Area

Nearby attractions and museums include the Bread & Puppet Museum (p. 438), the Old Stone House in Brownington (p. 463), the Fairbanks Museum (p. 445), and the St. Johnsbury Athenaeum (p. 471).

Henry Sheldon Museum of Vermont History

1 Park Street
Middlebury, VT 05753
(802) 388-0773
www.middlebury.edu/~shel-mus

Overview

The Henry Sheldon Museum is the oldest community history museum in the United States. Founded by Henry Sheldon, a single-minded collector and tireless preserver of the past, it opened in 1884 in an elegant 1829 Federal-style house. The museum collection feature one of Vermont's premier collections of furniture, paintings, documents, and artifacts.

Directions and Hours

The museum is located in the center of Middlebury, just off Route 7.

The museum is open year round and is handicap accessible.

Hours: Monday-Saturday 10:00-5:00. The Research Center is open Tuesday-Friday from 1:00-5:00.

Admission and Membership

$4 for adults, $2 for children 6-18, $10 per family, and $3.50 for seniors. Membership is $20/year for individuals, $35/year for dual/families, and various levels of contributing memberships. Group discounts and discounts for VGMA and AAA members are available.

What to See

In the 1829 Judd-Harris House, 10 rooms highlight the collection in the context of the region's early settlers. Early Vermont furniture is found in the collection, along with paintings, tools, household objects, clothing and textiles, musical instruments and one-of-a-kind oddities. The Research Center contains thousands of manuscripts, photographs, newspapers and ephemera.

The museum offers public programs such as craft workshops lectures related to special exhibitions year round for both adults and children. Temporary history and art exhibits are on view throughout the year. The museum also hosts annual events: Antique Appraisal Day in May, Henry Sheldon Museum Pops Concert in June, Traditional Crafts Day and Twilight History Cruise in July, and A Glimpse of Christmas Past exhibit and open house in December.

The Henry Sheldon Museum shop offers gifts, home accessories, jewelry, toysand games, and books on antiques, Vermont history, and Americana. There is no café, however, there are several restaurants within walking distance.

While You're in the Area

The Vermont State Craft Center, Frog Hollow (p. 487) is within walking distance of the museum. Also nearby are the Vermont Folklife Center and Middlebury College Museum of Art (p. 456).

Herrmann's Royal Lipizzan Stallions

Route 2
North Hero, VT 05474
(802) 372-8400
www.champlainislands.com/visitor/lipizz.html

Overview

Each summer the Herrmann family works with the Champlain Islands Chamber of Commerce to develop a summer home on North Hero Island for the Herrmann family, riders, and stallions.When not performing, the barn is open to the public. The Herrmann family has had Lipizzans since Austrian Emperor Ferdinand II gave them to Knight Ritter von Schoevel as a gift to ride into battle. Descendents have been training and riding the horses for nearly 300 years.

Directions and Hours

Lipizzan Park is located on Route 2 in North Hero, 1½ miles north of the North Hero Drawbridge. North Hero is easily accessible from Canada, New York, and Vermont. If coming from Canada take 15 to Rouses Point, New York or take 225 to Alburg, Vermont. From Vermont take I-89 exit 17 to Route 2 west. From New York take the Lake Champlain Ferry from Plattsburgh.

Hermann's Royal Lipizzan Stallions will be in residence from July 12 through August 29, 2001.

Hours: Performances are every Thursday and Friday at 6:00 P.M. and every Saturday and Sunday at 2:30 P.M. There is a free open barn at other times.

Admission and Membership

Tickets range from $8 to $15. Children are free on Friday evenings (2 children per adult). No reservations are necessary; performances are in a large open arena.

What to See

The program consists of classical equitation set to music. The Lipizzan program has some of the last horses in the world capable of executing moves like Airs Above the Ground. The finale of the program is the Military Quadrille, where 4 to 8 stallions perform the movements of ancient military drills once used as battle preambles.

Refreshments are available on site.

While You're in the Area

Nearby is St. Anne's Shrine on Isle La Motte (p. 470).

Higley House Museum

Castleton Historical Society
407 Main Street
Castleton, VT 05735-0219
(802) 468-5523 or (802) 265-3208

Overview

The Castleton Historical Society collects and preserves artifacts and information about people and places in Castleton for the future generations, collects oral history, and presents programs of local historical interest. The exhibit on display this year is Vintage Clothing, which is presented by the Woman's Club.

Directions and Hours

From Route 4: Take exit 5. Turn toward Castleton. At Route 4A turn west. About half a mile on the left is a 1811 brick house with a sign in front. Park along Main Street in front.

The museum is open year-round and is handicap accessible.

Hours: Saturday morning 10:00-11:00 A.M. all year-round. Summer hours (from May 30-October): 10:00-11:00 A.M. Saturday, 1:00-3:00 P.M. Sunday, or by appointment.

Admission and Membership

Donations are accepted. Membership is $5/year for an individual. Children must be accompanied by an adult. Groups of 10 or more are asked to divide and view areas separately.

What to See

The Higley Homestead is an 1811 brick Federal style home. On the grounds is a display of old carriages. The museum features stenciled walls, Castleton artifacts, Higley memorabilia, and exhibits.

The museum does not have a gift shop or a café. A deli and a pizza place are only a short walk away. Birdseye Diner (a restored 1950 diner) is ¼ away on Main Street.

While You're in the Area

Other interesting places to visit while you are in the area include Castleton State College campus, the Slate Valley Museum in Granville, NY, and the Revolutionary War battle site at Hubbardton Battleground (p. 454).

Hildene

Historic Route 7A South
Manchester, VT 05254
(802) 362-1788
www.hildene.org

Overview

Abraham Lincoln's descendents lived until 1975 in this 24-room Georgian Revival mansion built by Robert Todd Lincoln. The interior of the home has been preserved intact with original furnishings and personal family effects.

Directions and Hours

From Route 7 take exit 4 (Manchester). Travel south about two miles from the center of town. The entrance to Hildene is on the left.

The museum is open from mid-May through October. It is partially handicap accessible.

Hours: Daily 9:30-4:00.

Admission and Membership

$8 for adults, $4 for youths. Group discounts are available. Call or visit the web site for membership details.

What to See

Some features not to miss at Hildene are President Lincoln's stovepipe hat (one of three in existence), the formal gardens in June, and a 1908 Aeolian organ that is played for every tour.

Special events are scheduled throughout the year, and children's programming is available. Visitors can enjoy cross-country skiing in winter.

There is a gift shop and a snack bar on the premises.

While You're in the Area

Visitors may also wish to see the Bennington Museum (p. 433) and the Park McCullough House (p. 464) in Bennington, and the Southern Vermont Arts Center (p. 476) in Manchester.

Historical Society of Windham County

PO Box 246
Route 30
Newfane, VT 05345
(802) 365-4148

Overview

The museum houses a collection that illustrates the history of Windham County, first settled in the 1760s. Highlights include early Vermont furniture, portraits, textiles, Civil War battlefield souvenirs, and West River Railroad artifacts.

Rear facade of Hildene with garden view. Photo courtesy of Hildene.

Directions and Hours

The museum is located on Route 30, 10 miles north of Brattleboro in the center of Newfane village, just south of the village green. Take I-91, exit 2.

The museum is open late May through late October, but is not handicap accessible.

Hours: Wednesday through Sunday 12:00-5:00.

Admission and Membership

Admission is free but donations are accepted. Memberships vary from $10 to $50.

What to See

Special exhibits change annually and are taken from the museum collection. An illustration of life in Newfane in the mid-nineteenth century is scheduled for 2001. The program is drawn from the diaries written and furniture made by Universalist preacher Otis Warren.

There is no gift shop or café, but a deli and fine dining are located in Newfane.

While You're in the Area

Newfane village green is a renowned local attraction, with a Greek revival courthouse and two churches. The site of the first settlement is nearby on Newfane Hill. Three covered bridges are within easy driving distance.

Holland Historical Society

Gore Road
Holland, VT 05830

Overview

The Holland Historical Society is located in a 150-year-old church that became property of the historical society in 1972.

Directions and Hours

From Derby Line take Holland Road to Valley Road to Gore Road.

The historical society is open by appointment during the summer, but is not handicap accessible.

Admission and Membership

Admission to the museum is free. Membership is $3/year for individuals, $5/year for families, and $100 for a lifetime membership.

What to See

The historical society displays church artifacts, photographs, and farm tools. The facility is also available for rental. Old Home Sunday is held the first Sunday in August.

There is no gift shop. There is no café, but there are restaurants in the area.

While You're in the Area

The Haskel Opera House and Library, Orleans County Historical Society's "Old Stone House" (p. 463), and the Stanstead Historical Society Museum are also in the area.

Hubbardton State Historic Site

Monument Hill Road
East Hubbardton, Vermont
c/o Vermont Division for Historic Preservation
7305 Vermont Route 125
Addison, VT 05491
(802) 273-2282 or (802) 759-2412
www.HistoricVermont.org

Overview

This is the only Revolutionary War battlefield located entirely in Vermont. As the Continental Army retreated from Mount Independence, the British Army caught up with the rear guard at Hubbardton. The battle lasted for only a few hours on July 7, 1777, but helped to delay the British invasion that ended in defeat at Saratoga. The visitor center has exhibits about the Revolutionary War and a fiber optic map detailing the progress of the battle.

Directions and Hours

In central Vermont: Take U.S. Route 4 to the Castleton exit. From that exit go north on Monument Hill Road for seven miles. The Battlefield is on the left in East Hubbardton.

The museum is open from late May through mid-October. It is handicap accessible.

Hours: 9:30 A.M. to 5:00 P.M. Wednesday-Sunday.

Admission and Membership

Adults $1, children under 15 free. School groups are free.

What to See

Every summer, at the beginning of July, reenactors camp at Hubbardton to commemorate the battle. The public is welcome to visit the encampment and watch the mock military engagements.

Special events will take place in 2002 for the 225th anniversary of the Battle of Hubbardton.

Programming for students involves archaeology and artifact activities.

There is a gift shop. Food is available in nearby in Castleton and Rutland. There are also picnic tables near the visitor's center.

While You're in the Area

Other interesting places to visit while you are in the area are Castleton Historical Society (p. 452), Vermont Marble Museum (p. 480), Wilson's Castle (p. 485), Bomoseen State Park, and Halfmoon State Park.

Hutchinson/Taylor House

37 Church Street
PO Box 1680
Norwich, VT 05055
(802) 649-0124
www.bachelderinn.com

Overview

The Hutchinson/Taylor House includes exhibits on maple sugaring, old grist mills, war uniforms, a local old chair factory and much local information.

Directions and Hours

Take I-91 either north or south to exit 13. If heading north, turn left. If heading south, turn right. Take route 5 north to Norwich Congregational Church on Church Street. The Hutchinson/Taylor House is the fourth house on the right. There is a sign in front of the house. It is approximately one-half mile from I-91.

The house is open year round. It is partially handicap accessible.

Hours: Wednesday 2:30-4:30 or by appointment.

Admission and Membership

Donations are accepted. Membership is $6/year for seniors and students, $10/year for individuals, $15/year for families, $110 for lifetime individual, and $150 for lifetime family.

What to See

The Hutchinson/Taylor House (ca. 1773) is the oldest house in town and the former location of Norwich University, which is now located in Northfield Vermont. The museum features a lot of local information and pictures, some of which are for sale. It also displays many old tools, two early kerosene cooking stoves, and paintings by local artists.

A limited supply of books, note cards, and local pictures are for sale. Visitors can eat at the Norwich Inn Dining Room or three take-out restaurants within walking distance or travel two miles to Hanover for more dining opportunities.

While You're in the Area

The Montshire Museum of Science (p. 459), the Hood Museum (p. 377), and Dartmouth College Campus are all within two miles and easy to locate.

Hyde Log Cabin

U.S. Route 2
Grand Isle, VT 05458
(802) 372-5440

Overview

The Hyde Log Cabin was built in 1783. It was lived in by members of the family into the 1940s.

Directions and Hours

Take Route 89 to exit 17, then proceed onto Route 2 for approximately 15 miles.

The cabin is open from the Fourth of July until Labor Day, but is not handicap accessible.

Hours: Thursday-Monday 11:00-5:00.

Admission and Membership

$1 for adults, children under 14 are free. Membership to the Grand Isle Historical Society is $5/year for individuals.

What to See

The cabin is furnished as it was when it was built. There are many items belonging to the Hyde family, including the manuscript of a novel written by a Hyde son-in-law in 1839. There are also items from the Battle of Plattsburg, which occurred during the War of 1812.

The Grand Isle Historical Society sponsors periodic events and speakers.

There is no gift shop. There is no café, but there are sandwich shops nearby.

While You're in the Area

The Grand Isle Fish Hatchery is also in the area.

Manchester Historical Society

Mark Skinner Library
Manchester, VT 05254
(802) 362-2607

Overview

Since 1897 the Manchester Historical Society has collected memorabilia, photographs, and artifacts relating to the settlement and growth of Manchester.

Directions and Hours

The museum is located at the intersection of Route 7A and West Road, just north of the Equinox Hotel.

The museum is open year round by appointment, but is not handicap accessible.

Admission and Membership

Admission is free.

What to See

The society will feature a railroad exhibit as part of the Vermont Historical Society's Expo 2001 to be held June 23-24 in Tunbridge, Vermont.

There is no gift shop or café, but visitors can eat at area restaurants.

While You're in the Area

Other nearby attractions are historic Hildene (p. 452) and the Southern Vermont Arts Center (p. 476).

Middlebury College Museum of Art

Center for the Arts
Route 30
Middlebury, Vermont 05753
(802) 443-5007
www.middlebury.edu/~museum

Overview

Through its permanent collection and special exhibitions, the Middlebury College Museum of Art displays and interprets works of art from ancient times to the present. The Museum is an integral part of the cultural and educational mission of Middlebury College, offering a variety of teaching opportunities, lectures, and forums. In addition, the museum serves the surrounding communities in New England and New York with programs for local schools and the public.

Directions and Hours

The town of Middlebury is located midway between Rutland and Burlington, Vermont on Route 7. The Museum is located in the Middlebury College Center for the Arts on Route 30, approximately one-half mile from Route 7. From Route 7, follow signs through downtown Middlebury to Route 30. Free parking is available.

The museum is open year round, with the exception of Mondays, all College holidays, August 13-27, 2001, and December 24-January 2, 2002. The museum is handicap accessible.

Hours: Tuesday-Friday 10:00-5:00, Saturday and Sunday noon-5:00.

Admission and Membership

Admission is free. Friends of the Art Museum support both the education and acquisitions programs of the Middlebury College Museum of Art. Membership Fees: Student, $15; Individual, $30; Family, $50; Contributor, $100; Sponsor, $250; Patron, $500.

What to See

The Museum's collection of several thousand objects ranges from antiquities through contemporary art, with an emphasis on photography, nineteenth-century European and American sculpture, and contemporary prints. A survey of objects from the permanent collection is always on view, with separate galleries devoted exclusively to the nineteenth and twentieth centuries.

The Christian A. Johnson Memorial Gallery, located in the Museum, shows changing exhibitions throughout the year. Organized by the Museum and other institutions, these exhibitions highlight the artistic achievements of cultures and artists not represented in the Museum collection. In conjunction with special exhibitions and the College curriculum the Museum sponsors programs and events including lectures, gallery talks, and films. All events and programs are open to the public, though reservations are sometimes required.

Upcoming exhibitions include "Confrontational Clay: The Artist as Social Critic"

(June 26-August 5, 2001), "Young America: Treasures from the Smithsonian American Art Museum" (September 11- November 25, 2001), "Teenie Harris: A Legacy in Black and White, 1939-1975" (January-April, 2002), "Stories in Art" (January-May 2002), "David Bumbeck Prints and Sculpture" (May-August, 2002), and "Sabra Field" (May-August, 2002).

The education program, run by the museum with student and community volunteers, serves primary and secondary schools in the museum's vicinity. In addition, the museum sponsors several family art events throughout the year. The education program also offers teacher workshops, school tours, and family workshops.

The Museum sells selected catalogs, posters, and note cards at the reception desk. Rehearsals Café is adjacent to the Museum and offers light lunch fare.

While You're in the Area

Also in Middlebury are the Henry Sheldon Museum (p. 451), the Vermont State Craft Center at Frog Hollow (p. 487), and the Vermont Folklife Center (p. 487). Other nearby points of interest include the Shelburne Museum (p. 474), the Rokeby Museum (p. 468), the Robert Hull Fleming Museum (p. 487), and Fort Ticonderoga.

The Miller Art Center

9 Elm Hill
PO Box 313
Springfield, VT 05156
(802) 885-2415

Overview

The MAC is home to the Springfield Art and Historical Society. The 1861, white pillared, brick mansion is on the National Historic Register, and overlooks downtown Springfield.

The center houses a large collection of Primitive paintings by distinguished artists such as Fletcher, Powers, and Brown. A large collection of toys and dolls by the Joel Ellis, Vermont Novelty Works is on permanent exhibit. Springfield is known worldwide for its Machine Tool Businesses. The Center has available an extensive archival collection of the town once known as the heart of "Precision Valley". We also offer monthly changing art exhibits featuring local artists.

Directions and Hours

From Interstate 91 take exit 7. Follow signs to center of town. The museum overlooks Main Street.

The museum is open April 15 to November 1, and is partially handicap accessible.

Hours: Tuesday-Friday 10:00-4:00, Saturday 2:00-5:00, winter hours by appointment.

Admission and Membership

Admission is free, but donations are accepted. Memberships range from $15/ year to $50/year.

What to See

The center is part of the Machine Tool Heritage Trail and is located on The Connecticut River Byway. The view from the museum of the Black River Falls is amazing!

Museum collections include Richard Lee Pewter, Bennington Pottery, nineteenth/twentieth century paintings, Vermont Novelty Works toy collection, and Machine Tool Companies archives/photos. There is also a Genealogy Room

The center offers a Living History group based on the United States Sanitary Commission (which became the Red Cross) of the Civil War period. This group is involved in Civil War Encampments statewide and is available for community, school, and organization presentations year-round.

The museum also offers an award winning Middle/High School Intern program—Comtu Falls USSC, a Civil War living history reenacting group, and several children's art classes each year.

There is no gift shop, but books and art are for sale. Visitors can eat at several great restaurants a two minute walk away.

While You're in the Area

Fort at #4 Living History Museum (p. 377) is located across the Connecticut River in New Hampshire, five miles away.

Milton Historical Museum

PO Box 2
13 School Street
Milton, VT 05468
(802) 893-2267

Overview

The Milton Historical Museum is located in the former Episcopal Church which was built in 1891. It is located in the historic district of Milton, Vermont, which for over 100 years was a small town of about 2,000 people. Milton has grown in the past fifty years to a population of over 10,000. The museum remains a link to Milton's past.

Directions and Hours

Take Interstate 89 to exit 17. Take Route 7 north to Milton. Turn right at Main Street and right onto School Street.

The museum plans to be open year round; currently hours are by appointment. The museum is handicap accessible.

Admission and Membership

The museum is free, but donations are accepted.

What to See

Permanent exhibits include a historic church bell originally hung in the West Milton Church, and a bicentennial quilt made by members of the historical society in 1982 to commemorate the arrival of the first five settlers in 1782. There are also exhibits highlighting local doctors and businesses and a large collection of Milton photographs from 1890-1918. The museum also features a Victorian living room, vintage wedding gowns, farming and carpentry tools, and historical books, documents, and maps.

There is no gift shop, but there are several local restaurants.

While You're in the Area

The Shelburne Museum (p. 474) and the Robert Hull Fleming Museum (p. 487) are similar nearby small-town museums. The Lake Champlain Basin Science Center (p. 486) in Burlington is 16 miles from Milton.

Montshire Museum of Science

One Montshire Road
Norwich, VT 05055
(802) 649-2200

Overview

The Montshire Museum of Science is a hands-on science museum with dozens of exhibits on natural history, space, technology, and physical science. The museum has 110 acres of property bordering the Connecticut River, which includes easy-to-moderate nature trails, some of which are handicap accessible.

Directions and Hours

Heading north on I-9, take exit 13. Turn right immediately onto Montshire Road.

Heading south on I-91, take exit 13. Turn left at the light. Take the first right onto Montshire Road.

The museum is open year round. It is handicap accessible, as are some of the trails.

Hours: Daily 10:00-5:00.

Admission and Membership

$5.50 for adults, $4.50 for children 3-17, free for children under three.

What to See

The museum features many outstanding natural history exhibits, including aquariums with aquatic life found in Vermont and New Hampshire. Visitors can learn about their natural heritage and see the "real thing" on the nature trails. During the summer, the museum offers daily hands-on activities, including a snake show that features one of the museum's resident boa constrictors.

Programming for children and families is offered throughout the year, and the museum presents school programs to 20,000 students annually. Summer camp programs are available for children ages 4-15.

The new Silvio O. Conte Wildlife Refuge Education Center, with 20,000 square feet of exhibit space, will open in the spring of 2002. Science Park, a collection of outdoor exhibits, is scheduled to open in the summer of 2002.

There is a gift shop but no café. Many local restaurants are located within one

mile of the museum in Hanover, New Hampshire.

While You're in the Area

Visitors may also wish to see the Billings Farm Museum (p. 435), the Hood Museum (p. 377), and the American Precision Museum (p. 486).

Mount Independence State Historic Site

Mount Independence Road
Orwell, Vermont
c/o Vermont Division for Historic Preservation
7305 Vermont Route 125
Addison, VT 05491
(802) 948-2000 or (802) 759-2412
www.HistoricVermont.org

Overview

Mount Independence State Historic Site has a museum and a series of hiking trails that inter-

"Voices of the Revolution" multimedia statue at Mount Independence State Historical Site in Orwell, Vermont. Photo courtesy of the Vermont Division for Historic Preservation.

pret the site of a Revolutionary War fortress. Directly across Lake Champlain from Fort Ticonderoga, this peninsula was fortified by Continental Soldiers in 1776. As a part of Burgoyne's invasion from Canada, British troops captured the fort in 1777, but abandoned it later that year after their defeat in Saratoga. Exhibits about the Revolutionary War are located in the new museum building. There are over six miles of hiking and walking trails that take visitors past ruins of a hospital, soldier's huts, and earthworks.

Directions and Hours

The site is located six miles west of State Route 22A and the village of Orwell in western Vermont. To reach the site take Route 73 west from Orwell, then take the first left hand turn and leave Route 73. This is a paved town road that forks; take the right fork. The road will turn to gravel and go parallel to Lake Champlain. Once again the road will fork; take a sharp left-hand turn that curves up a hill. The parking lot for Mount Independence is on the left at the top of the hill.

The museum is open from late May through mid-October. The museum is handicap accessible, but the walking trails are not yet.

Hours: 9:30 A.M. to 5:00 P.M., seven days a week.

Admission and Membership

Adults $2, children under 15 free. Bus/tour groups are $1.50 per person; school groups are free. Call the site for information about the Mount Independence Coalition.

What to See

The museum at Mount Independence houses a collection of Revolutionary War artifacts, many of which were recovered from the site or from Lake Champlain. A new, multimedia statue of soldiers comes to life and tells the stories of the men who endured many hardships while building and guarding the fortress.

Every summer, during the last weekend in July, Revolutionary War reenactors camp on the mount. The public is welcome to attend *Soldiers Atop the Mount*. Special events are planned for the summer of 2002, the 225th anniversary of the British capture of Mount Independence.

Programming for students involves archaeology and artifact activities.

There is a gift shop. Food is available in nearby Orwell and Benson.

While You're in the Area

Other interesting places to visit while you are in the area are Fort Ticonderoga, Hubbardton Battlefield (p. 454), and the Henry Sheldon Museum (p. 451).

National Museum of the Morgan Horse

122 Bostwick Road
Shelburne, VT 05482
(802) 985-8665
htt://members.tripod.com/nmmh

Overview

The National Museum of the Morgan Horse is based on the history of the Morgan horse breed. This breed can be traced back to one horse, known by its owner's name, Justin Morgan. Operated under the American Morgan Horse Institute, the museum features an exhibit area and research center.

Directions and Hours

Take Route 7 south through Shelburne. Turn right at the first light after the Shelburne Museum onto Bostwick Road.

The museum is open year round, and is handicap accessible.

Hours: Monday-Friday 9:00-4:00; Memorial Day-Columbus Day, Saturday 10:00-2:00.

Admission and Membership

$1 for adults, children are admitted for free. Membership is $25/year for individuals.

What to See

In addition to exhibits on the history of the Morgan Horse and its founding horse, there is regular educational programming and scheduled Morgan Horse demonstrations. The museum also offers annual agricultural showcases called "Morgan Field Days."

There is a gift shop, and there are several restaurants and cafés in the area.

While You're in the Area

The Shelburne Museum (p. 474), Shelburne Farms (p. 473), and the Vermont Teddy Bear Company (p. 487) are also in the area.

New England Maple Museum

US Route 7 in Pittsford
PO Box 1615
Rutland, VT 03748
(802) 483-9414

Overview

The New England Maple Museum features the complete history of Vermont's famous maple sugaring industry from its early beginning to present day refinement. In addition to audiovisuals and a syrup sampling area, the museum houses the largest collection of maple sugaring artifacts in existence.

Directions and Hours

The museum is located in the village of Pittsford, 8 miles north of Rutland on US Route 7.

The museum is open seasonally and closed from January to mid-March.

It is handicap accessible.

Hours: Daily, May 20 to October 31, 8:30-5:30; mid-March to May 19 and November 1 to December 23, 10:00-4:00.

Admission and Membership

$2.50 for adults, $2 for seniors, and 75¢ for children over 6 years. Discounted rates are $2.25 for AAA members and $1.25 per person for groups of more than 12.

What to See

The New England Maple Museum features the Shorty Danforth collection of maple sugaring artifacts, over 80 feet of hand-painted murals of maple sugaring scenes by Vermont artist Grace Brigham, and a collection of mid-twentieth-cen-

New England Maple Museum. Photo by Alois Mayer.

tury artist Paul Winters's depictions of the history of maple sugaring.

Visitors who cannot make it to the museum during the six weeks in spring when the sap runs can still experience a full-scale maple sugaring simulation, which demonstrates the process from sap to syrup. Interactive displays and lively exhibits will interest children.

There is a gift shop, featuring specialty foods, crafts, and gifts as well as a complete line of maple products. Visitors can dine at JR's Café on Route 7, Patricia's Restaurant in Brantion, or Sewards Family Restaurant in Rutland.

While You're in the Area

Visitors may also wish to see the Wilson Castle (p. 485) and the Vermont Marble Exhibit (p. 480). There are four covered bridges within two miles of the museum.

Noyes House Museum

122 Main Street
Morrisville, VT 05661
(802) 888-7617

Overview

The Noyes House Museum is a local history museum located in a ca. 1820 18-room federal house. It displays a collection of clothing, photos, furnishings, toys, medical equipment, and tools relating to nineteenth-century domestic life.

Directions and Hours

The museum is located on Route 100 (Main Street) in downtown Morrisville, 20 miles north of Interstate 89.

The museum is open mid-June to Labor Day, but only the main floor is handicap accessible.

Hours: Wednesday-Saturday 1:00-5:00, and by appointment.

Admission and Membership

Admission to the museum is free. Membership is $10/year for individuals, $20/year for families, and $25/year for businesses.

What to See

The Noyes House Museum's collection includes the Cheney pitcher collection, comprised of 2,000 items. There is Civil War memorabilia including an Andersonville prison engraving. Firefighting equipment is on display, as well as Victorian toys, clothing, and furniture.

There is an annual Open House with a free concert, quilt show, and rug show. Several programs of historical nature, arranged through the Vermont Council on the Humanities, are given each year.

There is no gift shop, but some historical books are for sale. There is no café, but there are four restaurants within walking distance.

While You're in the Area

Stowe ski area, Smuggler's Notch, the Trapp Family Lodge complex, and Green River State Park are also in the area.

Old Constitution House State Historic Site

Main Street
Windsor, VT 05089
(802) 672-3773
www.historicvermont.org

Overview

The Old Constitution House was originally a tavern owned by Elijah West, where the first constitution of the "Free and Independent State of Vermont" was adopted on July 8, 1777. This constitution was the first in America to prohibit slavery and the first to establish universal voting rights for all adult men.

Directions and Hours

The museum is located on Main Street at the northern end of the village of Windsor on US 5, between exits 8 and 9 on I-91.

The museum is open from late May to mid-October. It is partially handicap accessible.

Hours: Wednesday-Sunday, 11:00-5:00.

Admission and Membership

$2/adults, children 14 and under are free.

What to See

The Old Constitution House features late-eighteenth- and early-nineteenth-century artifacts displayed in several period rooms that reflect its early use as a tavern. A permanent exhibition, "A Free & Independent State" examines Vermont's formative years, from the struggle for political independence to statehood in 1791. Revolutionary War period artifacts are also on display, including the only extant copy of the sermon delivered at the Windsor "constitutional convention" in 1777.

There is a small gift shop with books and postcards. Visitors can find refreshment at several eateries in Windsor village.

While You're in the Area

Visitors may also wish to see the American Precision Museum (p. 486) in Windsor; Saint Gaudens National Historical Park in Cornish, New Hampshire; President Calvin Coolidge State Historic Site (p. 466) in Plymouth, Vermont; and Billings Farm and Museum (p. 435) in Woodstock, Vermont.

Old Round Church

Richmond Historical Society
Round Church Road
PO Box 453
Richmond, VT 05477
(802) 434-3654

Overview

Old Round Church is an 1813 16-sided church built by five denominations and used for community meetings until 1973. It has since been restored and reopened for visitors.

Directions and Hours

Take I-89 to Richmond (exit 11). Follow Route 2 east for two miles to a traffic light. Take a right at the light onto Bridge Street. The Round Church is about ¼ down Bridge Street on the left.

The Old Round Church is open from May-Columbus Day, 10:00 A.M. to 4:00 P.M. The church is open only on weekends in September, daily the first week of October. The church is not handicap accessible.

Admission and Membership

Admission is free but donations are encouraged. Membership is $10/year for a family, $5/year for an individual, and $100 for a life member.

What to See

An Annual Pilgrimage usually occurs on the last Sunday in July.

The church does not have a gift shop but postcards are available. There are three nearby restaurants.

While You're in the Area

Attractions nearby include the Green Mountain Audubon Nature Center (p. 486), and the Birds of Vermont Museum (p. 436).

Old Stone House Museum

28 Old Stone House Road
Browington, VT 05860
(802) 754-2022
www.oldstonehousemuseum.org

Overview

The Old Stone House was built in the 1830s by Alexander Twilight, the country's first African-American college graduate. Originally a school dormitory, it is now part of a museum complex that includes four other historic structures and 55 acres of land. The Old Stone House also contains the collections of the Orleans County Historical Society.

The Old Stone House Museum. Photo courtesy of Orleans County Historical Society.

Directions and Hours

Take exit 26 off I-91. Proceed east on route 58 through the village of Orleans. Follow signs to Brownington and the museum.

The museum is open May 15-October 15. It is partially handicap accessible.

May 15-June 30, Friday-Tuesday 11:00-5:00; July-August, daily 11:00-5:00; September 1-October 15, Friday-Tuesday 11:00-5:00.

Admission and Membership

$5 adults and $2 students. Membership is $15/year for individuals and $25/year for families. AAA members receive a 20% discount and NEMA and VMGA members are free.

What to See

The historical society collections include decorative art and folk art, household tools, agricultural tools, textiles, toys, and ephemera relating to the history of the region. Special exhibits focus on school life, children's toys, and individual towns in Orleans County. An 1840s barn features the exhibit "A Hard Row to Hoe: Two Centuries of Farming in Orleans County."

The largest annual public event is Old Stone House Day, held in August on the Sunday closest to Bennington Battle Day. In 2001, it will be held on August 19. The event includes a museum open house, musical entertainment, a farmer's market, craft demonstrations, children's activities, and a picnic lunch.

The museum works extensively with area schools and hosts a week-long history day camp in July.

There is a gift shop. There is no café, but there are restaurants in surrounding villages.

While You're in the Area

The Fairbanks Museum and Planetarium (p. 445) and St. Johnsbury Athenaeum (p. 471) are both a half hour away in St. Johnsbury.

Park-McCullough House

PO Box 388
Park and West Street
North Bennington, VT 05257
(802) 442-5441
www.parkmccullough.org

Overview

The Park-McCullough House is a 35-room 1865 Victorian mansion built for Trenor and Laura Hall Park. Built in the French Empire style, it was home to two of Vermont's governors. The interior is an unspoiled representation of Victorian life: all the interior fittings, decorations, furniture, and paintings have been preserved intact, affording an opportunity to step back into the period just after the Civil War.

Directions and Hours

From Route 7 take 7A to 67A into the center of North Bennington. Take a left and proceed one block.

The museum is open from late May to late October, and is handicap accessible.

Hours: Daily 10:00-4:00.

Admission and Membership

Admission is $6 for adults, $5 for seniors, $4 for teens age 12-17, children under 12 are free. Membership is $15/year for seniors and students, $25/year for individuals and $45/year for families or dual membership.

Children must be supervised.

What to See

The Park-McCullough House is a recently designated official project of the Save America's Treasures program. It is treasured for its avant garde design as well as for the two governors who lived there, the four presidents who visited, and the contributions of the family to the growth of the nation in the post-Civil War period. Collections include furniture, china, paintings, drawings, costumes, textiles, silver, and historic documents, including Abraham Lincoln memorabilia.

Visitors can take a guided tour, stroll the grounds, take a nature walk through the Mile Round Woods, and explore the Carriage Barn, gardens, and children's Playhouse, a miniature version of the "Big House." The museum also hosts a concert series and special Victorian Christmas tours, among other scheduled events. Tea with Lizzie on the Veranda can also be requested.

The museum is creating an Education Center in the Carriage Barn. It will host changing exhibitions and a video presentation that was created as part of a HGTV series. Children's programming is also in the works.

There is a gift shop, and the nearby Powers Market will create box lunches for bus tours as well as for individuals and families.

While You're in the Area

The Bennington Museum (p. 433) and the Bennington Battle Monument are local attractions.

Photo courtesy of the Park-McCullough House.

Peacham Historical House/Ashbel Goodenough Blacksmith Shop

104 Thadeus Stevens Road
Peacham, VT 05862
(802) 592-3571/(802) 592-3989

Overview

The Peacham Historical House is a former schoolhouse built in 1820. It houses annual rotating displays and features an old store and industries room. The Ashbel Goodenough Blacksmith Shop is a brick blacksmith shop with a working wooden forge.

Directions and Hours

On Route 2 head south from Danville Green 7 miles to Peacham Corner. Turn right on Church Street.

From I-91, take exit 18 (Peacham/Barnet). Turn right and travel 7 miles to South Peacham. Take a right to the corner, about one mile.

The center is open from June to October. It is partially handicap accessible.

Hours: Sunday and Monday, 2:00-4:00; July 4 and October 4, 9:00-4:00.

Admission and Membership

Admission is free. Membership is $5 for individuals and $10 for families.

What to See

The Peacham Historical House features an old-fashioned telephone exchange, with two phones and a switchboard, as well as a nineteenth-century store with period furnishings. Displays show sugaring and buttermaking techniques. The Industries Room has a lumbering exhibit.

The Ashbel Goodenough Blacksmith Shop features many facets of the blacksmithing trade, including farrier's and wheelwright's displays as well as a quarrying exhibit.

Special programs include "World War I," "George Harvey, Maker of a President" (Wilson), and "Peacham Butter Print Makers." A Peacham Ghosts Walk will be held on July 4 and October 4.

There is a small area in the Store room where souvenirs and other items are sold. There is no café, but restaurants are nearby. Joe's Pond is a 15-minute drive, and light lunches are served at Bayley-Hazen Store in South Peacham.

While You're in the Area

The Saint Johnsbury Athenaeum, featuring Bierstadt's "Domes of the Yosemite," (p. 471) and the Fairbanks Museum and Planetarium (p. 445) are other area attractions.

Porter Music Box Museum

Route 66
Randolph, VT 05060
www.portermusicbox.com

Overview

The Porter Music Box Company, Inc., is the world's only manufacturer of the largest disc music box. Visitors can see how they are made and hear the collection of antique music boxes.

Directions and Hours

Take 89 to exit 4, then take Route 66 west.

The museum is open year round for group tours, is open seasonally for the general public, and is handicap accessible.

Hours: May-December, Monday-Saturday 9:30-5:00; January-April by reservation.

Admission and Membership

$5 for adults, $3 for children three to twelve. There is a group rate of $3 per person (10 or more people).

Memberships are not available.

What to See

The museum features large antique cylinder and disc music boxes that were popular in the 1800s. There are also dolls and dome pieces, as well as a rare Steinway, Duo-Art reproducing piano from 1926.

There is a gift shop that sells CDs and tapes of music box music, music boxes, and gift items. Visitors can eat in downtown Randolph, ¾ mile from the museum.

While You're in the Area

The Porter Music Box Museum is located near the Neighborly Farms of Vermont. They produce maple syrup and cheese, and are family owned and operated.

President Calvin Coolidge State Historic Site

Plymouth Notch Historic District
Plymouth, VT 05056
(802) 672-3773
www.historicvermont.org

Overview

The village of Plymouth Notch remains much as it was on August 3, 1923. It was then that Calvin Coolidge, visiting his own family home, received the presidential oath of office upon news of President Warren Harding's death. Eleven buildings are open to the public, many with the original contents.

Directions and Hours

Take Route 4 to VT 100A, and travel for six miles.

The site is open from late May to mid-October, and is handicap accessible.

Hours: daily 9:30-5:00.

Admission and Membership

$6 for adults, children 14 and under are admitted free. A family pass is $20.

What to See

The site contains the largest collection of artifacts related to Calvin Coolidge, including presidential gifts of state. There is also the Coolidge Birthplace, Coolidge Homestead, general store, cheese factory, and community dance hall (that served as the 1924 summer White House office). The President is buried at the steep hillside cemetery which is a short walk from the village green.

There is a modern visitor's center and two walking trails. Also on the site is one of the nation's best collections of nineteenth-century farm equipment.

There are three museum shops. Visitors can eat the on-site Wilder House, which was formerly the home of the President's mother.

While You're in the Area

The Billings Farm and Museum (p. 435), the Marsh-Billings-Rockefeller National Historical Park (p. 486), Mount Independence State Historic Site (p. 459), and the Justin Morrill Homestead (p. 486) are also in the area.

Randolph Historical Museum

Salisbury Street
Randolph, VT 05060

Overview

The Randolph Historical Museum is located on the second floor of the police building. The museum's centerpiece is Leonard's Drug Store and soda fountain, which served the town from 1893-1958.

Directions and Hours

The museum is located 3 miles west of exit 4 off I-89 or 8 miles west of Vermont Route 14. It is a short distance from the railroad depot in Randolph village, opposite the post office.

The museum is open from June to October. It is handicap accessible.

Hours: 1:00-5:00 on the first Sunday of the month and by appointment.

Admission and Membership

Admission is free. Donations are welcome. Contributing memberships range from $5 to $100.

What to See

The museum's Leonard's Drug Store exhibit includes original medicines, a soda fountain, and a working wall telephone. Other exhibits include a turn-of-the-century kitchen and period furnished parlor and bedroom as well as a recreated barber shop. Artifacts such as farm tools, a locally made pipe organ, an antique camera collection, Randolph-made stoves, bicycles, and band instruments are also on display.

School groups often tour the museum and a speaker is available for schools.

There is no gift shop but the museum does sell history books. Visitors can eat at local establishments within sight of the museum.

While You're in the Area

Randolph is also home to the Music Box Museum (p. 466).

Rockingham Meeting House

Meeting House Road, off Vermont Route 103
Rockingham, VT
(802) 403-3941

Overview

The Rockingham Meeting House is a 1787 New England meeting house preserved in essentially its original state.

Directions and Hours

The museum is located off Route 103, about one mile north of the intersection with Route 5.

The museum is open from May to October. It is partially handicap accessible.

Hours: Daily 10:00-5:00 pm.

Admission and Membership

Admission is $0.50.

What to See

The Rockingham Meeting House building is an attraction in its own right. There is also a historic cemetery adjacent to the meeting house. There are no real displays; the historic building (and attached cemetery) which is its own display. A few small building related items are shown quite informally.

An annual pilgrimage, including a speaker and music, is held at the meeting house the first Sunday in August.

There is no gift shop, but a few items are for sale. There is no café, but visitors can eat at nearby restaurants.

While You're in the Area

There are historical museums in Bellows Falls and Saxtons River (p. 472).

Rokeby Museum

4334 Route 7
Ferrisburgh, VT 05456
(802) 774-7728
www.rokeby.org

Overview

Rokeby Museum is a 90-acre historical site and National Historic Landmark that was home to a remarkable Quaker family from 1793 to 1961. From early settlers to nationally active abolitionists to distinguished artists and writers, each generation of Robinsons left its mark on their home, their state, and their country. The site was designated a National Historic Landmark in 1997 for its unsurpassed underground railroad history. Numerous letters in the collection (of about 15,000) describe fugitive slaves by name and in some detail.

Photo courtesy of The Rokeby Museum.

Directions and Hours

Rokeby is located on Route 7 in Ferrisburgh, midway between Burlington and Middlebury, three miles north of Vergennes and two miles south of North Ferrisburgh village center. Look for the historic site marker and front entrance sign.

Rokeby Museum is open from mid-May to mid-October. It is handicap accessible.

Guided house tours are available Thursday through Sunday at 11:00, 12:30, and 2:00. Grounds and outbuildings are open Tuesday through

Sunday from 10:00 to 4:00. The hiking trails are open daylight hours year round.

Admission and Membership

$6 for adults, $4 for seniors/students, $2 for children under 12. Membership is $20/year for individuals, $10/year for seniors, and $30/year for families.

What to See

Rokeby Museum includes an intact cultural landscape of 90 acres, showing 200 years of land stewardship. Landscape features include stone walls, wells, ponds, and foundations. The intact nineteenth-century farmstead includes eight authentic outbuildings in their original locations and near original condition. The Federal style house is filled with 200 years of the family's personal belongings and domestic furniture.

Visitors may experience the site in several ways. Guided house tours feature the most significant building on the site—a fully furnished historic house (ca. 1790, 1814, 1893). The house presents the Robinsons' domestic life and taste, social and religious beliefs and attitudes, and literary and artistic interests and talents through four generations. It is seen by guided tour only, with tours limited to twelve people.

Surrounding the house is an intact nineteenth-century farmstead, with eight viewable outbuildings as well as several foundations, wells, and other features. The outbuildings are remarkable examples of vernacular architecture still in mostly original condition and location. This part of the site and is seen by self-guided tour with or without and an audiotape.

The approximately 75 acres of former farmland is crossed by two main and several interconnecting hiking and walking trails. A half-mile section of one trail is marked with interpretive stops corresponding to a brochure and constitutes a self-guided tour.

The museum hosts the annual Rokeby Wool Festival in July and Pie and Ice Cream Social in August. Children's programming is available.

There is no gift shop, but items are for sale in the house. Visitors may picnic on the grounds or travel to Shelburne Village (15 minutes) or Middlebury (30 minutes) for numerous restaurants.

While You're in the Area

The Shelburne Museum (p. 474) in Shelburne is 10 miles north on Route 7. The Lake Champlain Maritime Museum (p. 486) is located nearby in Ferrisburgh. The Henry Sheldon Museum of Vermont History (p. 451) is in Middlebury, Vermont.

St. Albans Historical Museum

PO Box 722
Corner of Church Street and Bishop Street
St. Albans, VT 05478
(802) 527-7933

Overview

The museum is an 1861 three-story brick Renaissance Revival schoolhouse that houses memorabilia. Displays include the Central Vermont Railway Room, the Military Room, the Margaret Armstrong Room (featuring collections from the homes of two Vermont governors), the Sterling Weed Room (with the life and times of the this patriarch of Vermont music), a French Heritage exhibit, an Abenaki Exhibit, a Home & Hearth Room, and a Children's Room.

Directions and Hours

Come in to St. Albans on Highway 7. Turn east on Fairfield Street. Go one block and then turn onto Church Street. The museum is a three story brick building. The museum name is over the front door. Park at the rear of the building.

The museum is open mid-June to the end of the first week in October. It is handicap accessible.

Hours: 1:00-4:00 P.M. Monday-Friday. Other times by appointment.

Admission and Membership

$3 per person. Children 14 and under and school groups are free. Young children should be accompanied by an adult. The museum is owned by the St. Albans Historical Society. Membership in the historical society is $15/year for an individual. A family membership is $25/year.

What to See

A newly installed diorama equipped with lights and sound present the history of the northwest corner of Vermont and St. Albans. The Lake Champlain Basin Diorama looks at Lake Champlain as it appeared in 1864, the year of the St. Albans Raid. The raid is the feature story and there are maps and archival photographs. Also on display are the following exhibits: the October 19, 1864 raid by confederate soldiers, the Central Vermont Railway (featuring a recording of a dispatcher at work, a model of the 1923 roundhouse, railroad lanterns, photographs, and bells), a military display ranging from the Revolutionary War to Desert Storm (including uniforms that go back to the War of 1812, weapons, medals, ribbons, journals, scrapbooks and photographs), a Children's Room (with displays of antique toys, dolls, furniture, winter sports equipment, and a barber shop) a Doctors, Nurses, and Dentists exhibit (with a doctor's black bag, surgical tools, and other turn of the century medical equipment), a Sterling Weed music room (big band era), early toys, Abenaki Indian artifacts, and items from home and hearth, including two spinning wheels, vintage sewing machines, a nineteenth century dress form, reticules, bags, fans, baby clothes, a "Fisk" loom, and a quilt collection.

Meetings take place on the second Monday of the month April through November from 7:00 P.M. with guest speakers on local and Vermont history. The public is welcome. at no charge. Please contact the museum for details and/or a schedule.

Children's programming includes school group tours.

The museum does have a gift shop. Visitors can eat at Jeff's Maine Seafood, the Foundry, The Rock, Simple Pleasures, and numerous other restaurants.

While You're in the Area

Museums and attractions nearby include the Shelburne Museum (p. 474), the Robert Hull Fleming Museum (p. 487), Shelburne Farm (p. 473), and the University of Vermont Horticultural Research Farm.

St. Anne's Shrine

92 St. Anne's Road
Isle La Motte, VT 05463
(802) 928-3362 or (802) 928-3385
www.sse.org

The Way of the Cross. Photo courtesy of St. Anne's Shrine.

Overview

St. Anne's Shrine is situated on 13 acres overlooking the Adirondack Mountains on the site of Fort St. Anne, Vermont's oldest settlement (constructed in 1666), where the first Mass in Vermont was celebrated. Though the fort itself was shortlived, the site continued to be a favorite stopping place for Lake Champlain travelers in the succeeding years of war and peace. Interesting relics of those historic days are on display at the Shrine.

Directions and Hours

Easily accessible from Canada, New York, Interstate 87, and Vermont Interstate 89. Take Route 2 through the Champlain Islands to Route 129 on Isle La Motte.

St. Anne's Shrine is open from mid-May through Mid-October. The Shrine is handicap accessible.

Hours: Open daily from 9:00-6:00.

Admission and Membership

There is no cost for admission.

What to See

A 15 inch gold leafed statue of Our Lady of Lourdes is but one of many grottos and statues on the Shrine grounds. The Shrine has a display that houses artifacts from the original Fort dating back to 1666. Located on the site where it is claimed that Samuel de Champlain landed in 1609 at Isle La Motte is a majestic granite statue, sculptured at Expo '67 in Montreal.

Eucharistic celebrations are offered daily and on Sunday.

A sandy beach is available for families and groups who want to take advantage of a nice day. A dock is also available for tourists and pilgrims who want to visit the Shrine by boat.

There is a gift shop as well as a café. Picnic facilities are also available.

While You're in the Area

Other museums and interesting attractions nearby by are: the Isle La Motte Historical Society, Fisk Quarry, and Hyde Log Cabin, the oldest dated cabin in the United States (p. 456).

St. Johnsbury Athenaeum & Art Gallery

1171 Main Street
St. Johnsbury, VT
(802) 748-8291
www.stjathenaeum.org

Overview

The St. Johnsbury Athenaeum and Art Gallery is a private, nonprofit public library and art gallery. The Athenaeum serves the people of St. Johnsbury as a center of culture and learning and stands as a monument to the nineteenth-century belief in learning—a true "athenaeum." Because of its remarkable architecture and first-class collection of American paintings, the Athenaeum is one of only 10 libraries in the nation to be declared a National Historic Landmark.

Directions and Hours

The St. Johnsbury Athenaeum is located at the top of Main Street. From I-91 take exit 21. Turn right at the end of the ramp onto US2 East. Proceed one mile into St. Johnsbury, then bear left at St. Johnsbury Academy. The Athenaeum is on the left at the top of the intersection with Eastern Avenue.

The Athenaeum is open from 10:00 to 5:30 every weekday and until 8:00 in the evening on Monday and Wednesday. Saturday hours are 9:30 to 4:00.

Admission and Membership

Donations are welcome. There are fees for special tours and school groups.

What to See

The Athenaeum is a legacy of the Fairbanks family of St. Johnsbury, inventors and manufacturers of the world's first platform scale. With his wealth Horace Fairbanks assembled works of art—copies of the old masters, nineteenth-century European and American paintings, and an exquisite group of landscapes in the Hudson River style. Dominating the gallery from its inception has been the magnificent 10-by-15-foot canvas of the *Domes of the Yosemite*, by Albert Bierstadt. Docents greet visitors each day and provide information and special tours can be arranged.

Gifts from the Gallery are available. There is no café.

While You're in the Area

The Fairbanks Museum and Planetarium (p. 445) is also in St. Johnsbury.

Saxtons River Historical Society Museum

PO Box 18 Main Street
Saxtons River, VT 05154
(802) 869-2566

Overview

This 1836 former Congregational Church at the head of Main Street is now home to a rich repository of artifacts that tell the story of the people of this small village, which has been declared a National Historic District. The village's manufacturing past, social fabric, and family connections are recalled through photographs, collections, and the printed word.

Directions and Hours

The museum is located on Route 121, 5 miles west of Bellows Falls. From I-91, take exit 5 to Route 5 north to Bellows Falls. Then take Route 121 west from Bellows Falls at the traffic light. The museum is located in the center of Saxtons River.

The museum is open during the summer. It is partially handicap accessible.

Hours: Sunday 2:00-4:30 and by appointment.

Admission and Membership

Admission is free; donations are accepted. Membership is $5 for individuals and $10 for families.

What to See

The museum collection includes nineteenth-century tinware items crafted locally, photographs printed from glass plate negatives, children's toys and hand-carved models, a furnished Victorian parlor and kitchen, Civil War memorabilia, the story of the local street railway, and samples of eighteenth- and nineteenth-century local art.

The second story is also open to visitors and contains the former church sanctuary, a beautiful tracker organ, and stained glass windows.

The society also maintains the Hearse House and its nineteenth-century horse-drawn hearse and the former Burial Vault, which features a collection of farm implements, blacksmith tools, and other devices used in workshops and mills once powered by the Saxtons River. Both are located at the nearby cemetery and are open during museum hours.

Brief histories of the village, prints, maps, postcards and note cards are available for purchase. Fine dining is available at the Inn at Saxtons River and Averill's Restaurant. Lighter fare is served at The Golden Egg diner.

While You're in the Area

Nearby attractions include the eighteenth-century Rockingham Meeting House (p. 468), the oldest public meeting space in Vermont, five miles away in Rockingham; the former Adams Grist Mill (p. 486), now a museum, and the Green Mountain Flyer old-time train ride, 5 miles away in Bellows Falls; and the Grafton Historical Society Museum (p. 448) and the Nature Center at Grafton, eight miles away in Grafton.

Shaftsbury Historical Society

Route 7A
Shaftsbury, VT 05262

Overview

The Shaftsbury Historical Society maintains and operates a local history museum in the oldest Baptist church in Vermont. It features 6,000 catalogued artifacts, books, and documents.

Directions and Hours

Route 7A is a major highway.

The museum is open from June 15 to

October 15, but it is not handicap accessible.

Hours: Tuesday-Sunday 2:00-4:00.

Admission and Membership

Admission is free, but donations are accepted. Membership in the historical society is $2/year for students, $5/year for individuals, and $10/year for families. Various levels of contributing membership are also available.

What to See

The Shaftsbury Historical Society's headquarters is a restored 1846 Greek-revival Baptist church. The church's adjoining cemetery dates back to 1769. Exhibits are explained by volunteer hosts. The museum has an extensive collection of historic documents, pictures, records, costumes, and artifacts. Numerous free publications about local history are available. The museum contains tools, clothing, railroad memorabilia, old gravestones, and items pertaining to Baptist Church doctrine and history. Exhibits include a one-room schoolhouse and an exhibit on Religious and Scientific Views of Creation.

The society sells a variety of books on local history as well as historic maps and postcards. The museum has no café, but Wade's Café is two miles south of the museum.

While You're in the Area

The Bennington Museum (p. 433), the Park-McCullough House in North Bennington (p. 464), and the Norman Rockwell Museum in Arlington (p. 432) are also in the area.

Shelburne Farms

1611 Harbor Road
Shelburne, VT 05482
(802) 985-8686
www.shelburnefarms.org

Overview

Shelburne Farms is a 1,400-acre working farm, national historic site, and nonprofit environmental education organization that welcomes visitors to tour its landscape and gardens or explore the magnificent farm barn.

Directions and Hours

Take Route 7 south to Shelburne. Head west on Harbor Road. The museum is located at the junction of Harbor Road and May Road.

The museum is open mid-May to mid-October. It is partially handicap accessible.

Hours: 10:00-4:00; property tours daily at 9:30, 11:00, 12:30, 2:00 and 3:30; breeding barn tours daily at 1:00; tea tours Tuesday and Thursday at 2:30.

Admission and Membership

$5 for adults, $4 for seniors and children 3-14, free to members. Guided property tours are $10 for adults, $9 for seniors and children 3-14, and free to members. Breeding barn tours are $5 per person. Tea tour at the Inn is $15 per person. Group tours are $6 per person. Membership is $50/year for families.

What to See

Shelburne Farms was established in 1886 as the model agricultural estate of William Seward and Lila Vanderbilt Webb. The design of the farm was guided by Frederick Law Olmstead. Visitors can enjoy the property in a variety of ways. Miles of walking trails wind through woodlands and meadows. The Welcome Center features a 15-minute educational slide show every half hour. A 0.75 mile walking trail or tractor-drawn shuttle leads to the historic Farm Barn, which features a children's farmyard and cheesemaking exhibit. Guided tours of the property are available daily and last 1.5 hours. Tours of the breeding barn and a tea tour at the Inn are also available for an additional fee. The breeding barn was built in 1891 and was once the country's largest open-span structure. The 24-room inn was built in 1887-1900.

There is a gift shop. There is no café, but visitors can eat nearby in Shelburne.

While You're in the Area

Visitors can also see the Shelburne Museum (p. 474) in Shelburne.

Shelburne Museum

U.S. Route 7
PO Box 10
Shelburne, VT 05482
(802) 985-3346
www.shelburnemuseum.org

Overview

Founded in 1947, the Shelburne Museum is one of the largest and most distinctive museums of folk art, Americana, decorative arts, historic houses, and paintings—including Impressionist masterpieces. The village-like setting of 38 structures consists of period homes and galleries, a covered bridge, a lighthouse, and the 220-foot paddlewheel steamboat *Ticonderoga*. Each year new exhibitions highlight significant aspects of American art, history, and culture.

Photo courtesy of the Shelburne Museum.

Directions and Hours

From I-89: Take exit 13. Proceed south on Route 7 for seven miles. The museum is on the right. If traveling from the south and west the museum is on Route 7, 35 miles north of Middlebury, Vermont.

The museum is open April through mid-December. Hours vary with the season so please contact the museum before visiting. The museum is handicap accessible for most museum buildings and galleries.

Admission and Membership

Early spring and late fall: adults $8.75, children $3.50. Summer: adults $17.50, children $7. Group discounts for 15 or more people are available as well as discounts through area hotels. Membership is $35/year for individuals, $55/year for a dual membership, and $70/year for a family.

What to See

Exhibitions include American paintings, quilts, and hooked rugs. In 2002 the museum will present an RV show.

A family center, Owl Cottage, is open daily in the summer offering hands-on craft workshops and games for kids. The museum also has a vintage 1920s carousel open for rides throughout the summer, and a nineteenth century playground.

There is a gift shop and a café, open daily.

While You're in the Area

Other museums and interesting attractions nearby by are: the Vermont Teddy Bear factory tours, Shelburne Farms (p. 473), Rokeby Museum (p. 468), Ethan Allen Homestead (p. 486), the Robert Hull Fleming Museum (p. 487), and Spirit of Ethan Allen cruises on Lake Champlain.

Sherburne Historians

1879 River Road
Killington, VT 05751
(802) 422-3783

Overview

The Sherburne Historians features an informal history of the Sherburne/Killington area.

Directions and Hours

The museum is located one mile off Route 4.

The museum is open year round. It is handicap accessible.

Hours: Monday, Wednesday, and Friday 10:00-5:00, Tuesday and Thursday 1:00-5:00, Saturday 9:00-12:00.

Admission and Membership

There is no admission to the museum. A family membership is $10 and a single membership is $5.

What to See

The museum's collection includes rural Vermont items and depicts the history of the town, including schools, village mills, Killington Ski Area development, and local resident history.

There is no café or gift shop.

While You're in the Area

Visitors may wish to take advantage of the landscape and experience scenic chairlift rides offered locally.

Shores Memorial Museum

202 Center Street, PO Box 85
Lyndon Center, VT 05850
www.lyndonvermont.com

Overview

The Shores Memorial Museum is owned by the town of Lyndon and operated by the Lyndon Historical Society. The museum features a working man's Victorian home built in 1896 by James Shores. Room exhibits include a formal dining room, kitchen, parlor, and bedroom. The attached barn displays a working hobby printing press.

Directions and Hours

Take I-91 to exit 23. Proceed north on Route 5 for one mile. Turn left onto Route 122. Follow one mile to Lyndon center. The museum is on the left; a sign is posted.

The museum is open Memorial Day to Labor Day and is not handicap accessible.

Hours are scheduled by group reservation.

Admission and Membership

Admission is free. Membership to the historical society is $5/year.

What to See

The Shores Memorial Museum offers seasonal special exhibits and special events, such as a Victorian Tea and limited performing arts affairs. Children's programming includes a Living Classroom Partnership and the Lyndon Institute.

There is a gift shop but no café.

While You're in the Area

A local attraction is the town of Lyndon's five covered bridges.

Shrewsbury Historical Society and Museum

5419 Route 103
Cuttingsville, VT 05738

Overview

The Shrewsbury Historical Society and Museum is an historic church building, renovated and dedicated in 1891, nestled in Cuttingsville, which is in a valley of the Green Mountains.

Directions and Hours

From Rutland, Vermont, take Route 7 south to Route 103. Follow 103 about 11 miles to Cuttingsville.

From Ludlow, Vermont, take Route 103 about 11 miles to Cuttingsville.

The museum is located in a white church building next to Laurel Glen Cemetery.

The museum is open from July to October. It is not yet handicap accessible.

Hours: Saturday and Sunday 1:00-3:00.

Admission and Membership

The museum is free. Memberships are $10/year for individuals, $15/year for families, $30/year for contributing members and $125 for life (individual or couple).

What to See

The museum displays nineteenth-century household items and furniture, costumes, photographs, books, diaries, toys, and other memorabilia. There are also video and audio tapes of townspeople and special events as well as current Shrewsbury history in scrapbook form.

The museum will participate in the Vermont History Expo 2001, which will be held in June in Turnbridge, Vermont. This event features about 80 historical societies and their collections.

The museum sells picture notecards and postcards. Visitors can eat across the street at Over Easy's.

While You're in the Area

The Bowman Mausoleum, a renowned sculpture built in 1881, is located next door to the museum. Visitors can also access the Long Trail and the Appalachian Trail about three miles north on Route 103.

The Southern Vermont Arts Center

930 West Road
PO Box 617
Manchester Village, VT 05254
(802) 362-1405
www.svac.org

Overview

Located on 407 acres at the base of Mount Equinox, the Southern Vermont Arts Center is Vermont's oldest cultural institution and considered one of the most beautiful sites in New England. The Center recently opened the Elizabeth de C. Wilson Museum designed by Hugh Newell Jackobsen that features shows from museums around the country. The Arkell Pavilion features concerts, films, and lectures throughout the season.

Directions and Hours

Take Route 7A south through the Center of Manchester. Turn left onto Ways Lane. Turn right onto West Road and go ¼ mile—on the left is the entrance of the Arts Center.

The museum is open year-round and is handicap accessible.

Hours: Summer: Tuesday-Saturday 10:00-5:00, Sunday 12:00-5:00 P.M. Winter: Monday-Saturday 10:00-5:00.

Admission and Membership

Adults $6, students $3, children under 13 free. A group tour of 15 or more is $4 per person. Membership is $55/year for an individual and $10/year for a student (21 and under). Other membership options are available but please call the center for details.

What to See

The center features artwork by the region's leading artists displayed in 10 newly renovated galleries. In addition to artwork for sale, the center has an impressive permanent collection featuring Reginald Marsh, Grandma Moses, and Luigi Lucioni.

In July and August of 2002 a special exhibition of photographs by Linda McCartney will take place.

There are many children's programs throughout the year.

The museum does have a gift shop and a café. The café is open for the summer session only.

While You're In the Area

Other interesting places to visit while you are in the area are the Bennington Museum (p. 433), Hildene (p. 452), and shops in Manchester Center.

Sugarbush Farm

591 Sugarbush Farm Road
Woodstock, VT 05091
(802) 281-1757 or (802) 457-1757
www.sugarbushfarm.com

Overview

Sugarbush Farm is a 500-acre working maple, cheese, and beef farm with lots of effort put into educating both children and adults about how maple sap is collected and boiled into maple syrup, as well as information and displays on beef, dairy, and packaging of cheese. The sugar house is open year-round for looking and learning, but is operation in the springtime, and shows visitors how maple sap is collected and boiled down into syrup

Directions and Hours

From Route 4: Turn off U.S. Route 4 at Taftsville (located 10 miles west of White River Junction, 3 miles east of Woodstock). Cross the red covered bridge and go to the top of the hill and turn left onto Hillside Road. Follow the yellow directional signs to Sugarbush Farm, 3 miles from the covered bridge.

The farm is open year-round except on Thanksgiving and Christmas. It is not handicap accessible.

Hours: Weekday hours 7:30 A.M. to 5:00 P.M. Weekends and holidays 9:00 A.M. to 5:00 P.M. Call ahead for visits after 4:30 P.M. or during the winter and early spring for road conditions, as the farm is lived in and is often open later than the posted times.

Admission and Membership

Admission is free.

What to See

Visitors can tour the maple sugar house and see how trees are tapped in the spring, how sap is collected with horses and a sled, and then boiled in a wood-fired evaporator. Guests can also take a nature walk in to the woods to see the actual maple trees and how they are not planted in rows, but grow where the actual seeds takes them. The farm consists of a house, a farm store and packing area built around 1850, a sugarhouse, a smoke house, aging coolers, and various barns.

Visitors enjoy a sampling table of 55 jams, as well as 10 kinds of cheese, 4 grades of syrup for tasting, and mustards.

There is a gift shop selling cheese, maple syrup, Vermont made jams, mustards, crackers, postcards, and cookbooks. Cold drinks and snacks are sold on the farm. The nearest town is five miles away with lots of eating places.

Photo courtesy of Sugarbush Farm.

While You're in the Area

Other museums and interesting attractions nearby are: Billings Farm and Museum (p. 435), Marsh-Billings Rockefeller National Historic Park, Montshire Museum of Science (p. 459), and the Vermont Institute of Natural Science (p. 481).

UVM Morgan Horse Farm

74 Battell Drive
Weybridge, VT 05753
(802) 388-2011
www.ctr.uvm.edu/cals/farms/mhfarm.htm

Overview

The University of Vermont Morgan Horse Farm is a National Historic Site that features a Victorian barn housing 60 to 80 Morgan horses. It is a working farm and breeding facility and receives 40,000 to 50,000 visitors annually.

Directions and Hours

Take Route 7 to Main Street in Middlebury. Follow Main Street to Route 125 East to Weybridge Street to Pulp Mill Bridge Road to Morgan House Farm Road. Turn left at the stop sign. Look for a sign for the farm a half mile down the road. The farm is on the right side.

The farm is open from May 1-October 31. It is handicap accessible.

Hours: Daily 9:00-4:00.

Admission and Membership

$4 for adults, $3 for teens, $1 for children 5-12. Group rates of $3.50 per person for 20 or more adults are available.

What to See

Colonel Joseph Battell began breeding Morgans on his farm in the 1870s. He deeded his farm to the U.S. government in 1907, thereby helping to save the breed from extinction. Highlights of the farm are the beautiful landscape, the historic Victorian barn, and, of course, the Morgan horses. Visitors can take a 20-minute guided tour and watch a 15-minute informational video, both are offered hourly.

The farm sponsors an annual foal raffle. Vermont Day Open House will be held August 15, 2001, from 10:00-3:00. This event includes free admission. The farm also features an apprentice program.

There is a gift shop filled with hundreds of horse- and farm-related items and snacks are available, but there is no café. Visitors can eat in Middlebury or picnic on the grounds.

While You're in the Area

The Henry Sheldon Museum of Vermont History (p. 451) is nearby in Middlebury.

Vermont Historical Society

109 State Street, Pavilion Building
Montpelier, VT 05609-0901
(802) 828-2291
www.state.vt.us/vhs

Overview

The Vermont Historical Society museum is housed in the Pavilion Building and currently has changing exhibitions on the state's history. In November 2001, the Historical Society will close for renovations. The final exhibition open to the public until the end of October 2001 will be, "Baseball in Vermont: An Enduring Love of the Game," which traces the history of baseball in the state for the past 100 years. The Vermont Historical Society plans to reopen with a totally renovated space and new exhibits in the fall of 2002.

Directions and Hours

Take exit 8 off I-89 (north or south) to Montpelier.

Due to upcoming renovations and expansion, the museum may be closed at times. Call to confirm hours. Normal hours for the museum are Tuesday-Frday 9:00-4:30, Saturday 9:00-

4:00, Sunday noon-4:00. Library hours are Tuesday-Friday 9:00-4:30, and the second Saturday of each month 9:00-4:00. From Independence Day through Columbus Day the

Vermont History Expo

In Vermont's 251 towns and cities, local history is kept alive by small bands of organized volunteers - the membership of Vermont's 170 plus local historical societies. Many of the societies house their collections in museums located in the community center or, as often, in a historic building slightly off the beaten path. Once a year, their collective efforts are showcased in a statewide exposition dedicated to the celebration of Vermont's rich heritage.

The Vermont History Expo 2001, presented by the Vermont Historical Society, will be held the weekend of June 23-24, from 10 A.M.-5:00 P.M., on the grounds of the Tunbridge World's Fair, a Vermont treasure in its own right. Located close to the geographic center of the state, the fair grounds are included in the Tunbridge Village Historic District. They have been home to the celebrated "(little) World's Fair" for the past 129 years.

Nearly 100 local historical societies, from every corner of the state, participate in the Vermont History Expo. They will be joined by 26 of Vermont's major museums and heritage attractions.

All aspects of the expo, from entertainment to food, have a Vermont heritage connection. Performers will entertain the crowd on one of two stages throughout the weekend. Ten presenters will offer diverse programs related to Vermont history. Expo visitors may also participate in the 16 Hands-on-History workshops for adults and children presented by the participating museums.

Museum and heritage attraction staff will also direct the Children's Entertainment Area where historical productions, such as a puppet show starring Presidents Jefferson and Madison and the first-person performance of Roxanna Watts, an 1850 farmwife in Peacham, Vermont, will take place.

Civil and Revolutionary War buffs will not want to miss the fully replicated encampments set up on the grounds, complete with tents, flags, cook fires, equipment, and uniformed soldiers engaged in the daily activities of the time.

For those interested in tracing their family's history, genealogists from the Genealogical Society of Vermont, the Vermont Historical Society, and the Joseph Smith Birthplace Memorial will staff a Genealogy Resource Center, complete with computers.

Some of Vermont's outstanding traditional crafts people will exhibit, demonstrate, and sell their Vermont-only, hand-crafted products in a juried show with a Silent Auction. Vermont authors will be on hand to sign their latest books.

Also on the fair grounds, a working blacksmith shop, a nineteenth century one-room schoolhouse, and a barn housing vintage equipment will be open for expo visitors. Vermont Heirloom Animals will take up residence in the agricultural fair's stables.

Daily admission costs are adults $5, children and students (6-18 yrs.) $3. Children age 5 and under are admitted free. There is a 20% discount for groups of 20 or more.

For information call the Vermont Historical Society at (802) 828-2291.

museum is also open Mondays 9:00-4:30.

The museum is handicap accessible.

Admission and Membership

$3 for adults, $2 for students and seniors, children under six free. Group tours are $1.50/person, with the driver complimentary. Regular/family membership is $30/year ($25/year for seniors 62 and over) and includes free admission to Vermont Historical Society Museum and Library, a subscription to the *InContext* quarterly newsletter, a 10% discount on purchases in the museum store, a subscription to *Vermont History*, the Society's scholarly journal, and reduced rates for lectures, tours, workshops, and other special programs.

What to See

The Vermont Historical Society is the only museum in the state that interprets and collects for all periods of the state's history. The museum of the Vermont Historical Society will reopen after renovations in the fall of 2002 with a new exhibition that will give an extensive overview of the state's history.

The society has an Education Department staffed with a full-time educator, two part-time museum teachers, and volunteer docents, who lead many school tours through the museum. There is a lending library through which teachers may borrow a selection of Vermont history books for a period of six weeks, and the society also loans history kits to school for two- and three-week rentals. Kits contain books, reproduction artifacts, maps, and classroom activity suggestions. Also available to schools is a slide packet entitled, "In an Era of Great Change: A Teaching Packet Exploring Vermont 1820-1850." Other children's programming includes sponsoring the annual Vermont History Day competitions and hosting events at the museum such as the Winter Holiday Festival.

The gift shop carries books on agriculture and industry, architecture, art and antiques, baseball in Vermont, biographies, genealogy, government, Native American Abenaki, oral and social history, teaching resources, town histories, and travel. Also carried are a wide range of children's books, as well as cassettes, compact discs, calendars, maps, videos, and an assortment of gifts for adults and children. All items have a Vermont theme. There are 27 restaurants within walking distance of the Historical Society, with all types of foods and a wide range of pricing. The society has a listing and map available for visitors at the museum desk.

While You're in the Area

The State House is right next door to the Pavilion. Nearby in Montpelier is the T. W. Wood Art Gallery (p. 487). The Rock of Ages Granite Quarry (p. 487) is located in Barre, several miles from Montpelier.

Vermont Marble Exhibit

52 Main Street
Box 607
Proctor, VT 05765
(800) 427-1396
www.vermont-marble.com

Overview

The Vermont Marble Exhibit, established in 1933, is the world's largest marble museum. The museum features historic displays, a movie, a hall of presidents display, a marble chapel, resident sculptors, and a new world geology room.

Directions and Hours

From U.S. Route 4 in West Rutland: Take exit 6. Turn east on Route 4A and then go north on Vermont Route 3 to Proctor. Go left over the marble bridge and bear right to the Exhibit.

From the north: Bear right on Vermont Route 3 from U.S. Route 7 in Pittsford, to Proctor. Turn right over the marble bridge and bear right to the exhibit.

The museum is open from mid May to the end of October and is handicap accessible.

Hours: 9:00 A.M. to 5:00 P.M., seven days a week.

Admission and Membership

Adults $6, seniors $4, teens 15-18 $3, and children under 15 free. Groups of 20 or more receive a discounted price of $2.50 per person.

What to See

A new exhibit, "Earth Alive," lets visitors experience the Earth's geological history and ongoing evolution with an 160 foot mural depicting the Earth's composition, its planetary relationships, volcanic eruptions, cave environments, and more. Guests can view over 100 different displays, including classical sculpture galleries, a full size triceratops fossil, a historical photography and immigrant exhibit that traces the life of the Vermont Marble Company, and an 11 minute film about the history of Vermont Marble Company, its immigrant work force, and the present status of the marble industry. Resident sculptors can also be viewed bringing blocks of marble to life.

The museum provides hands-on activities for children and welcomes school groups for geology and mineralogy field trips.

The museum does have a gift shop and offers coffee and snacks. There are two delis located close by.

Photo courtesy of the Vermont Marble Exhibit.

While You're in the Area

Other museums and interesting attractions nearby are Wilson Castle (p. 485), Vermont Maple Museum, and the Rockwell Museum (p. 432).

Vermont Raptor Center

Vermont Institute of Natural Science
27023 Church Hill Road
Woodstock, VT 05091-9642
(802) 457-2779
www.vinsweb.org

Overview

Visitors to VINS can witness up close the grace and power of owls, hawks, falcons, and eagles. The Vermont Raptor Center is an educational center and clinic devoted to birds of prey. Visitors can see and learn more about Bald Eagles, Peregrine Falcons, Snowy Owls, and more than 20 other raptor species. Self-guided nature trails allow people to walk through the 78-acre nature preserve.

Directions and Hours

Take Route 4 into Woodstock, Vermont. Turn onto Church Hill Road. (When facing stone church on the west end of the Woodstock green, Church Hill Road is the road heading uphill to the left of the church.) VINS is the light green barn on your right after approximately 1.5 miles

The institute is open Monday through Saturday, 10:00-4:00, year round, and is handicap accessible. Closed Sundays. Guided tours are offered Monday through Saturday, June through October.

Admission and Membership

Adults $6, Students (age 12-18) $3, Children (ages 5-11) $2, VINS members and children under five free. Membership is $25/year for individuals, $45/year for families, and $15/year for seniors.

What to See

The Vermont Raptor Center is an attraction as a fully operational rehabilitation center as well as a living museum. The museum gives visitors rare insight into these high-flying hunters and treat injured raptors so they can return to the wild. During the summer months into fall, daily raptor encounters, guided tours, and raptor in-flight demonstrations allow visitors an up-close look at birds of prey usually only seen through binoculars.

VINS has outreach programs bringing raptors and other teaching animals to schools, as well as summer day camps and nature education programs for children preschool to teens.

There is a Nature Gift Shop, which offers a 10 % discount to VINS members and AAA members. There is no café, but Woodstock is one of the top 10 most visited towns in Vermont, with a number of restaurants and cafes.

While You're in the Area

The Billings Farm Museum (p. 435) is also in in Woodstock.

Vermont Ski Museum

PO Box 1511
Stowe, VT 05672
(802) 253-9911
www.vermontskimuseum.org

Overview

The Vermont Ski Museum is dedicated to the sport of skiing in Vermont.

Directions and Hours

Take Route 89 to exit 10. Travel north on Route 100 for ten miles. The museum is on the right at the traffic light in Stowe Village.

The museum is open year round, and is handicap accessible.

Hours: daily 10:00-8:00 during the summer; daily 10:00-6:00 during the winter.

Admission and Membership

Admission to the museum is free. Membership is $50/year for families.

What to See

At the museum, skiing is seen through the presentation and promotion of its history, artifacts, memories, and accomplishments of its people.

There is a gift shop. There is no café, but there are restaurants within walking distance.

While You're in the Area

The Shelburne Museum (p. 474) and the Fairbanks Museum (p. 445) are both about an hour away.

Weathered Barn Doll Museum

452 George Road
PO Box 332
Williamstown, VT 05679
(802) 433-6077

Overview

The museum is housed in a barn built in 1952. The main farmhouse was built in the 1800s, and was a stop on the Underground Railroad during the Civil War. The dolls number in the thousands and many are arranged in scenes, both inside and outside.

Directions and Hours

From Route 89, take exit 5. Go to the bottom of the hill where the school signs are, and turn left. Proceed to the four corners, and turn left onto Flint Road. Go right at the second house onto

George Road. The museum is at the end of George Road. (There is a big yellow house and barn; the museum is in the barn.)

From Route 14 south, turn right onto exit 64. Go to the bottom of the hill where the school signs are, and turn right. Proceed to the four corners, and turn left onto Flint Road. Go right at the second house onto George Road. The museum is at the end of George Road. (There is a yellow house and barn; the museum is in the barn.)

The museum open from Memorial Day weekend to Labor Day weekend. It is handicap accessible.

Hours: Tuesday-Sunday 9:00-2:00; Monday and after hours by appointment.

Admission and Membership

$7 for adults, $4 for children, free for children under 4. Discounts are available for senior citizens, Scouts, and school groups.

What to See

Some attractions at the doll museum are a troll village, an Indian village, an old fashioned country store, and an underwater scene with mermaids. A Barbie and Ken wedding, complete with attendants, minister, and guests is another scene not to miss. Exhibits change yearly, featuring new scenes and new dolls.

The museum plans to add a gift shop in 2002. Visitors can eat two miles away at the Autumn Harvest Inn or at the Behind the Scenes Café in downtown Williamstown.

While You're in the Area

The Spider Web Farm and the Limehurst Lake Campgrounds are other local attractions.

Weathered Barn Doll Museum. Photo compliments of Peggy Coolidge.

White School Museum

c/o Burke Mountain Club
East Burke, VT 05832
(802) 626-9823

Overview

The White School Museum is maintained and operated by the Burke Mountain Club, which merged with the local historical society in 1922. The White School building became a place to preserve the relics of the early days of the town of Burke.

Directions and Hours

Take 91 north to Lyndonville. Proceed through the village on Route 5. After the village, take 114 north to East Burke Village. The museum is at the village entrance.

The museum is open from late spring to fall foliage season. It is not handicap accessible.

Contact the caretaker at the Burke Mountain Clubhouse (see phone above) for hours.

Admission and Membership

Admission is by donation.

What to See

The White House Museum, built in 1817, is an early

schoolhouse named for several families who lived in the area. The building was the largest schoolhouse in town and at one time housed 80 scholars for winter session. The seats in the schoolhouse are said to be original. The building was moved from its original site to where it now stands in 1923. It is filled with early Burke artifacts.

There is no gift shop or café.

While You're in the Area

Visitors may also want to see the Burke Meeting House, built in 1825, in Burke Hollow and the Burke Mountain Club building (ca. 1920), which houses the Community Library.

Williamstown Historical Society Museum

PO Box 338
Vermont Route 14 (Main Street)
Williamstown, VT 05679-0338
(802) 433-1283
www.pages.prodigy.com

Overview

The museum houses a fine collection of local artifacts from 1790 to the present, showing the agricultural, social, and industrial past of Williamstown. The museum building itself is a historic structure, built in 1836 as a Universalist Church, later an Odd Fellows hall.

Directions and Hours

From Interstate 89, take exit 5 (Northfield-Williamstown). Follow VT Route 64 east to Williamstown village, approximately 4 miles. Turn right on Route 14 (Main Street) south. The Historical Society building is on the right side, between the Congregational Church and the town office building.

The museum is open by appointment or by chance from May to October, and is not handicap accessible.

Admission and Membership

Admission is free. Memberships range from $5/year to $100/year.

What to See

The museum features a collection of Modern Woodmen of America ritualistic pieces; odd fellows ritualistic pieces and furniture; a fine collection of agricultural implements and tools; Universalist Church items; the gravestone of Eunice martin (died in 1810) with the chair built for her; the Walker family chair, brought to town on horseback in 1796; the Jeffords kettle, brought to town in 1791; and an extensive postcard display, with over 130 views of Williamstown.

Photo courtesy of the Williamstown Historical Society

The society has programs of historic interest, preceded by a potluck supper at 6:00 P.M. on the first Tuesday of each month, May through October.

There is no gift shop or café, but visitors can eat at the Pump & Pantry or Behind the Scenes Café in Williamstown.

While You're in the Area

The Weathered Barn Doll Museum (p. 482), also in Williamsburg, has over 7,000 dolls on display.

Wilson Castle

PO Box 290
Center Rutland, VT 05736
(802) 773-3284

Overview

Wilson Castle, a real castle built in the 1800s in the heart of the Green Mountains, is a monument to the heritage of the past. The castle has been the home of five generations of the Wilson family.

Directions and Hours

The castle is located in Proctor, Vermont, on the West Proctor Road.

From Business Route 4—Traveling west of Rutland: Turn right ½ mile beyond Route 3. Traveling east of Rutland: Turn left 2½ miles from West Rutland. If you are using the Rutland Bypass Route 4: Take exit 6 and then follow the direction for traveling east.

The museum is open from late May through mid- to late-October. The castle is handicap accessible.

Hours: 9:00 A.M. to 6:00 P.M., 7 days a week.

Admission and Membership

Adults $7, seniors $6.50, children ages 6-12 $3. Age 6 and under free.

What to See

The castle's design is a mixture of European styles. English brick forms the façade of the castle, and is complemented by 19 open proscenium arches, along with a turret, a parapet, and a balcony. The castle consists of 32 rooms, 84 stained glass windows, and 13 fireplaces finished with imported tiles and bronze.

Furnishings in the castle include far Eastern and European antiques, Chinese scrolls, and Oriental rugs. The art gallery, with walls stenciled in gold lead with a 34-foot ceiling and a skylight, is used to exhibit sculpture, paintings, and photographs. Also on the grounds are cattle barns, stables, a carriage house, and a gas house. The castle has a 45 minute guided tour. Visitors can also walk the 115 acre estate grounds and can feel free to bring a picnic lunch.

There is a gift shop. Picnic tables are available or visitors can eat in Rutland, five miles away

While You're In the Area

Other interesting places to visit while you are in the area include the Vermont Marble Exhibit and the New England Maple Museum (p. 461).

Some other museum associations in New England:

Connecticut League of History Organization
Fairfield Historical Society
636 Old Post Road
Fairfield, CT 06430
(860) 535-1492

Bay State Historical League
Lyman Estate/The Vale
185 Lyman Street
Waltham, MA 02154
(781) 899-3920

Maine Archives and Museums
60 Community Drive
Augusta, ME 04330
(207) 897-2236
www.mainemuseums.org

New England Museum Association
Boston National Historic Park
Charlestown Navy Yard
Boston, MA 02129
(617) 242-2283
www.nemanet.org

Vermont Museum and Gallery Alliance
c/o Billings Farm and Museum
P.O. Box 489
Woodstock, VT 05091
(802) 457-2671
www.uvm.edu/~vhnet/hpres/org/VMGA/vmga.html

Other Museums in Vermont

Name	Phone	Town
Abenaki Tribal Museum and Cultural Center	802-868-2559	Swanton
Adams Old Stone Grist Mill Musuem	802-463-3706	Bellows Falls
American Precision Museum	802-674-5781	Windsor
Artist's Loft and Gallery	802-257-5181	Brattleboro
Bennington Center for the Arts	802-442-7158	Bennington
Black River Academy Museum	802-228-5050	Ludlow
Boyden Valley Winery	802-644-8151	Cambridge
Brick Schoolhouse Historical Society Museum	802-524-3318	Georgia
Brookfield Historical Society	802-728-5320	Brookfield
Chester A. Arthur Birthplace	802-828-3051	Fairfield
Chittenden Mill	802-899-3225	Jericho
Cold Hollow Cider Mill	802-244-8771	Waterbury Center
Dakin Farm	800-993-2546	Ferrisburg
Derby Historical Society	802-766-5324	Derby
Discovery Museum and Planetarium	802-878-8687	Essex Junction
Ethan Allen Homestead	802-865-4556	Burlington
Green Mountain Audubon Nature Center	802-434-3068	Huntington
Helen Day Art Center	802-253-8358	Stowe
Historical Society Museum (Royalton)	802-763-8830	Royalton
Justin Morrill Homestead	802-765-4003	Strafford
Lake Champlain Basin Science Center	802-864-1848	Burlington
Lake Champlain Chocolates	802-864-1807	Burlington
Lake Champlain Maritime Museum	802-475-2022	Vergennes
Maple Grove	800-273-3334	St. Johnsbury
Marsh-Billings-Rockefeller Natural Historical Park	802-457-3368 x22	Woodstock
Mary Bryan Memorial Gallery	802-644-5100	Jeffersonville
Middletown Springs Historical Society Museum	802-235-2144	Middlebury
Morse Farm Sugarhouse and Museum	802-223-2740	Montpelier
Nature Museum at Grafton	802-843-2111	Grafton
Norman Rockwell Museum of Vermont	802-773-6095	Rutland Town
Norwich University Museum	802-485-2360	Northfield

Original Maple Grove Maple Museum and Factory	802-748-5141	St. Johnsbury
Poultney Historical Society Museum	802-287-4042	East Poultney
Putney Historical Society	802-387-5962	Putney
Return Home Farm Museum	802-754-2043	Coventry
Robert Hull Fleming Museum	802-656-0750	Burlington
Rochester Historical Society	802-767-4453	Rochester
Royalton Historical Society Museum	802-763-8567	Royalton
Rock of Ages Granite Quarry	802-476-3119	Graniteville
Russell Collection of Vermontiana	802-375-6153	Arlington
Rutland Historical Society	802-775-2006	Rutland
Simon Pearce Glass	802-674-6280	Quechee
Southern VT Natural History Museum	802-464-0048	Jacksonville
Sugarmill Farm and Museum	800-688-7978	Barton
T. W. Wood Gallery and Arts Center	802-828-8743	Montpeller
Vermont Arts Exchange	802-442-5549	North Bennington
Vermont Folklife Center Archives	802-388-4964	Middlebury
Vermont State House	802-828-2228	Montpelier
Vermont State Craft Center at Windsor	802-674-6729	Windsor
Vermont Teddy Bear Company	802-985-3001	Shelburne
Vermont Veterans' Militia Museum	802-338-3360	Colchester
Vermont Wildflower Farm	802-985-9455	Shelburne
Wallingford Historical Society	802-446-2336	Wallingford
West Windsor Historical Society	802-484-7474	Brownsville
Francis Colburn Gallery (University of Vermont)	802-656-2014	Burlington
Windham County Historical Society	802-365-4148	Newfane

Index by Subject

African-American/African/Underground Railroad

Aircraft

Aquariums

Art Museums and Galleries

Cars, Carriages, and Motorcycles

Children's Museums

Food

Gardens and Arboretums

Literary/Theatrical Figures/Books and Libraries

Medical and Pharmaceutical

Military Museums/Memorials/Important Sites

Music

Outdoor/Agricultural/Living History/Villages/House Clusters/Farm Museums/Nature Museums

Photography, Film, and Visual Arts

Police/Firefighting/Law Enforcement/Postal

Political and Historical Figures/History Museums/Historical Sites

Railroad and Mass Transit Museums

Religious Museums/Churches

School and Children's Programs

Sculpture, Ceramics, Furniture, and Decorative Arts

Sewing/Quilting/Costume

Toy/Doll Museums

Science/Technology/Inventions/Tools

Ship/Nautical/Lighthouse/Maritime Museums

Sports and Recreation

Textile Museums/Mills/Industry/Working Museums

INDEX BY NEARBY ROADS

Note that roads with the same number may not be the same road from state to state (if they're state roads). all roads with two or more museums in the same state on or near them have been listed. Exit numbers are listed where available on major highways.

Route 1A

Route 2A

Route 3

Route 4

Route 4A

Route 5

Route 6

Route 7A

Route 8

Route 9

Route 66

Route 72

Route 73

Route 74

Route 77

Route 83

Route 84

Route 87

Route 89

Route 90/Mass Pike

Route 91

Route 95/Connecticut Turnpike (see 495 for Maine Turnpike)

Route 100

Route 101

Route 102

Route 103

Route 105

Route 106

Route 113

Route 114

Route 116

Route 118

Hopkins Vineyard		CT	35
Lourdes in Litchfield		CT	44

Route 119

Amos J. Blake Museum		NH	337
Barrett House		NH	340
Brattleboro Museum and Art Center		VT	438

Route 122

Fisher Museum of Forestry		MA	242
Bread & Puppet Museum		VT	438
Shores Memorial Museum		VT	475

Route 125

Stevens-Coolidge Place		MA	321
Old Sandown Meeting House		NH	366
Chimney Point State Historic Site		VT	442
UVM Morgan Horse Farm		VT	478

Route 126

Codman House "The Grange"		MA	230
Danforth Museum of Art		MA	238
DeCordova Museum and Sculpture Park		MA	239
Gropius House		MA	254

Route 127

Paper House		MA	300
Sandy Bay Historical Society and Museums		MA	311

Route 128

Pownalborough Court House		ME	178
Adams National Historical Park	7	MA	212
Arnold Arboretum of Harvard University	Rte. 9	MA	215
Arthur Griffin Center for Photographic Art	36, 37A	MA	215
Beauport	end	MA	220
Beverly Historical Society and Museum	Beverly	MA	221
Cape Anne Historical Museum		MA	225
Cogswell's Grant	15	MA	231
Codman House "The Grange"	28	MA	230
Concord Museum	28	MA	234
DeCordova Museum and Sculpture Park	28	MA	239
Discovery Museums		MA	241
Frederick Law Olmsted National Historic Site	20	MA	245
Gore Place	26	MA	251

Route 190

Route 195

Route 196

Route 198

Route 201

Index by State

Connecticut

Massachusetts

New Hampshire

Rhode Island

Vermont

Index by Town

Connecticut

Maine

Massachusetts

New Hampshire

Rhode Island

Vermont